Mobile Broadcasting with WiMAX:
Principles, Technology, and Applications

Mobile Broadcasting with WiMAX: Principles, Technology, and Applications

Amitabh Kumar

AMSTERDAM • BOSTON • HEIDELBERG • LONDON • NEW YORK
• OXFORD PARIS • SAN DIEGO • SAN FRANCISCO • SINGAPORE
• SYDNEY • TOKYO

Focal Press is an imprint of Elsevier

Acquistions Editor: Angelina Ward
Assistant Editor: Katy Spencer
Marketing Manager: Amande Guest
Developmental Editor: Beth Millett
Publishing Services Manager: George Morrison
Project Manager: Paul Gottehrer
Cover Designer: Alisa Andreola
Focal Press is an imprint of Elsevier
30 Corporate Drive, Suite 400, Burlington, MA 01803, USA
Linacre House, Jordan Hill, Oxford OX2 8DP, UK

Library of Congress Cataloging-in-Publication Data
Application submitted

British Library Cataloguing-in-Publication Data
A catalogue record for this book is available from the British Library.

ISBN: 978-0-240-81040-9

For information on all Focal Press publications
visit our website at www.books.elsevier.com

08 09 10 11 5 4 3 2 1

Printed in the United States of America

Working together to grow
libraries in developing countries

www.elsevier.com | www.bookaid.org | www.sabre.org

ELSEVIER   BOOK AID
            International   Sabre Foundation

DEDICATION

This book is dedicated to my mother.

God must be very great to have created a world that leaves a mystery as to whether he created it.

—*Richard Wurmbrand*

TABLE OF CONTENTS

PROLOGUE

MOBILE BROADCASTING WITH WIMAX

There are so many applications on the Web that are just pent up, waiting to come to mobile devices.

—Sean Malony, Intel Corporation

WiMAX is still in its early days of technology. Some believe perhaps too early to make any predictions about how widely the technology will be used and what its effects would be on existing applications. But mobile and wireless technologies have demonstrated a facet which appears a matter of fact today, but astonishing when viewed in hindsight. This is about adding 25 million mobile users in a month, a number which exceeded the total number of phone lines installed in many countries a couple of decades back. Mobile devices are now the workhorse of the new generation of "knowledge workers," accompanied by their new lifestyles and the new "knowledge economy age," as painstakingly explained by Stephen Covey in *The 8th Habit*.

Mobile WiMAX is today in a similar setting. When the standards for Mobile WiMAX were released in 2005, the world was looking at a new, potentially disruptive technology. The offerings were amply clear: high realistic data rates of over 1 Mbps per user, an IPv6 core network, mobile IP, voice and multimedia applications guaranteed by quality of service, mobility, handoffs and roaming, open architecture etc. This was followed shortly thereafter by the industry coming together under the auspices of the WiMAX Forum to have initial profiles announced and certified, and by the end of 2007, over 300 commercial trials had been conducted and many commercial networks commissioned across the globe.

Now is the time when the potential of WiMAX to develop an entirely new generation of applications is at its prime. WiMAX brings in not only application-specific sustained connections in a wireless environment but also brings with it new technologies and an open architecture. WiMAX, which is based on IEEE802.16 standards, has been conceived as a completely "open" technology with IP as its core and ready applicability of a multitude of applications ubiquitous on the net. The fact that Mobile WiMAX networks will be used for an entirely new generation of applications is evident from the M-Taiwan initiative, which focuses on a universal broadband connectivity platform and an initiative to develop new applications. (M-Taiwan program is described in Chapter 21).

What exactly is implied by *Mobile Broadcasting with WiMAX*, the title of this book? In a literal sense, it would imply using WiMAX networks to offer broadcasting services to mobiles. This, indeed, is one of the intended uses of the new technology, and in this manifestation would perhaps be simply called "Mobile TV using WiMAX." However, the potential use of WiMAX networks goes far beyond using it for broadcast purposes alone, which is well accomplished by other networks as well.

WiMAX is a wireless architecture, defined up to the MAC layer, which can interface to many networks, including IP-based networks and the internet. It therefore provides an interactive two-way environment for applications similar to mobile networks. However, this is where the similarity ends with mobile networks at their present stage of implementation. Mobile networks, in most cases, provide a very restricted environment for access to the internet. They have applications which are defined by 3GPP such as video calling or 3GPP streaming, but do not provide an open environment for generic applications. The handsets may support some additional applications, which may be based on specific middleware implemented.

The connectivity speeds in Mobile WiMAX are good enough to download or upload video in real time, with each user using only a small fraction of the cell resources. This means that the services can be made available to a large number of users in a given area. Collaborative video services, user originated broadcasting, peer to peer services are some of the manifestations of the environment which WiMAX networks can provide. As a technology designed with multiple levels of QoS, each suited for a different type of service means that the network is not designed for a specific service. It can carry multimedia as well as voice in any of the manifestations including VoIP. As we shall see later in the book, the technology is designed to be able to cater individually to users suffering from poor transmission conditions or near cell edges. It can direct very high effective isotropic radiated power to ensure uninterrupted reception by the use of advanced antenna systems or beam forming. The beam forming can also suppress interference, thus enabling a user to operate with highest data rates and from greatest distances. Mobile WiMAX also has a multicasting and broadcasting service, designed to serve a large number of users.

WiMAX therefore creates a unique usage environment which support video as well as web services such as multimedia instant messaging, presence or video push to talk as just random examples of its potential usage. The new services can be two-way or multi-way and truly interactive. The end user devices can be fixed or nomadic, mobile or wireless. These can be dedicated or multifunctional such as a mobile handset. The book is intended to address the new ecosystem of services, technologies and applications which can flourish in the new space created by WiMAX technologies.

Do users need such an environment or ecosystem? The answer to this is simple. The users want as much to watch a video clip on the mobile as much as they want to upload their own video when on a holiday. Or upload pictures to a studio for printing. Or update multimedia wall displays across the nation!

The usage of this new ecosystem requires users and operators to delve into the details of a number of factors, which range from considerations of spectrum, user devices, end-user software and clients, content protection, etc. Some of these issues are common with traditional broadcast services, while others are entirely new. Also new are the network architectures in which the services are expected to operate.

At the same time, there is a need to recognize that the existing networks for broadcasting, internet and cellular mobile need to coexist for a long time. Terms such as "disruptive technology" do not mean that is the end of digital TV or HDTV. In fact, the screen size is of no critical importance. What it means is that the days of linear programming in its present manifestation may be limited. It is more than likely to undergo a metamorphosis into interactive, on demand and push broadcasting methodologies. WiMAX networks will, therefore, continue to operate in a multi-technology environment. This requires network architectures that facilitate multiple networks to operate together.

Mobile Broadcasting using WiMAX has been written to describe an overall framework, which can be used to generate new applications in mobile web access and broadcasting. It is as much about a future journey as it is about what WiMAX and existing technologies provide today.

PREFACE

The best time to plant a tree is 20 years ago. The second best time to plant a tree is today.

—African Proverb

ABOUT THIS BOOK

This book is exclusively dedicated to WiMAX. The focus of the book is on the applications of WiMAX networks, with delivery of multimedia content to wireless and mobile devices being the area of greatest attention. WiMAX has crossed a number of major milestones in the recent past. These include setting standards, adopting implementation profiles to be used in base stations and user devices, developing chipsets, certifying devices by the WiMAX Forum, trials in over 300 networks and finally successful commercial operating networks in many countries. With the adoption by the ITU of OFDMA-TDD technologies as one of the air interfaces under the IMT-2000 (third-generation networks), the WiMAX has passed from being a sophomore to graduation. It is now a mature technology, ready for implementation with an entire ecosystem of equipment devices and interfaces. Its applications will not be merely providing new interfaces to existing technologies but generate a new a paradigm of mobile devices which will integrate wireless access, multimedia content and web information architectures. This book is about this new paradigm.

Both broadcasting and mobile web access are at very important crossroads today. The sector is rife with many developments which are of relatively recent origin. In the field of broadcasting, these include the transition to digital broadcasting, HDTV, IPTV, and mobile

TV as being some of the more visible facets. However, much larger forces are work in transforming the network architectures and consumer behavior which incessantly modify the manner in which broadcasting will need to be handled in the immediate future. The emergence of IPTV as a result of IP networks becoming capable of carrying video services with desired quality is just one example. Mobile web access is at the same time undergoing a metamorphosis of its own. It is seeking out technologies, which take it to the next level of connected applications with multimedia, collaborative group interactions, secure and structured transactions, 3D and location-based information being the prime denominators of new applications. It so happens that the new technologies ushered in by Mobile WiMAX with its open architecture, high-speed wireless connectivity with QoS, IPv6 and mobile IP in the core networks meet just these requirements of the new generation of mobile web applications. If this was not enough, the targets of both broadcasting and mobile web services are increasingly the very same device: a mobile handset connected to wireless and mobile networks.

The technologies of mobile WiMAX are an ideal vehicle for a new generation of mobile web applications that are being supplemented by a simultaneous shift in consumer behavior. The major change in the consumer behavior can be very briefly summarized as a strong move towards mobility. The mobility is of devices as well as applications. The 3 billion mobile phones, increasing wireless access (over 100,000 WiFi hotspots) and media becoming mobile by virtue of large memories which can be incorporated in the smallest of devices (80GB iPods™ and iPhone™) is a manifestation of mobility. This coupled with the availability of Web 2.0 services including online commerce, connectivity services such as RSS feeds, blog lines, and online communities such as MySpace™ are paradigms which tend to make more and more people use media-related services from mobile devices, in addition to fixed or wireline devices at home.

Until now the integration of Web 2.0, VoIP, and broadcasting has been very limited—these have operated as virtually independent networks. The trend towards a unified offering is getting accelerated as the core networks begin to move to all IP and be reorganized as next-generation networks (NGN). WiMAX networks present an important facet of making this transition. It is now becoming increasingly clear that the NGNs will not be focused towards wireline devices, as previously envisaged. Wireless devices and applications, including transmission of multimedia content in various forms, will be important requirements of these networks. It also will help take broadcasting wireless. The networks (both fixed and mobile WiMAX) provide features to guarantee QoS even in wireless environments, a feature which has been missing in the WiFi or streaming mobile TV. They can provide for high user densities with mobile broadcasting and multicasting services (MBS) and high data rates with special techniques of advanced antenna systems and beamforming. They can provide spectral densities close to 4 bits/Hz and in urban and rural environments can be used to provide data rates ranging from 16 Mbps to over 75 Mbps.

WiMAX networks are now providing an element for the seamless extension of broadband wireless or mobile Web 2.0 services to marry the traditional broadcast and on-demand media which has been missing so far. This element is the quality of service and service flows per application, which is a basic feature of WiMAX networks. WiMAX networks provide city-wide roaming and high data rates to support media and internet applications, each with guaranteed QoS. However, QoS can only be achieved if the end to end configurations support the same. It is lost if the media under transmission traverses unprotected internet without parameters to guarantee the QoS. It requires a planned integration of the IP networks with the WiMAX including the mobile stations or client devices. How do we achieve it? How do we integrate cellular systems and WiFi hot spots which are already interoperable with each other in many mobile networks? How do we integrate IPTV and DSL systems to provide a complete network with WiMAX as access medium?

WiMAX as a new technology will be very disruptive to traditional broadcast or mobile web applications and, therefore, there needs to be early recognition and use of it to advantage. It can shift business models, technologies, and processes. There can be no excuse for not using it to advantage. The spectrum allotted for mobile WiMAX has just begun to fall in place in most countries and WiMAX forum certified Mobile WiMAX devices are beginning to roll off the assembly lines. The adoption by the ITU of ODDMA-TDD as one of the air interfaces for IMT-2000 can only help to accelerate the process.

In this environment there are many questions which need to be solved, and on high priority. Which technology (fixed or mobile WiMAX) to use and in which spectrum band to minimize cost and ensure availability of client devices or mobile Stations? Can I use unlicensed spectrum? In which bands? Which devices will be available which will work in this band? What type of dimensioning can I do for my network in urban and rural areas? How many users can be accommodated in each sector or cell area? How much bandwidth can they use? What services can be provided over this bandwidth? How do I provide an integration of Web 2.0 services? How do the traditional IPTV network or DTH network acquire WiMAX extensions? What type of network architectures are needed to achieve this integration?

The answering of all these questions requires an insight into the WiMAX networks, their network architectures, spectrum bands, client devices, handsets and economics; which is the object of this book. It also seeks to provide an applications oriented view of how WiMAX technology can be used in existing broadcast networks (irrespective of their Web 2.0 ambitions).

The discussion of WiMAX principles, technologies and applications in the book in no way a reflection on the potential growth of mobile networks as they exist today using GSM, CDMA or 3G technologies. Indeed, any manifestations of WiMAX implementations will need to coexist with the existing networks for the foreseeable future. The book therefore focuses on network architectures and applications which will enable this to happen.

This book is not about bits and bytes of WiMAX or details of its standards. There are many excellent books which cover this topic. Hence these topics are presented very briefly. Excellent network planning software packages are also available which help plan cells, base stations, frequencies and backhauls. The book also does not contain any programming. It is more oriented towards network architectures, applications and enablers for deployment of networks such as chipsets, handsets and software architectures. It is focused on how operators, service providers and users can benefit from the new technology. The technology presented may appear in somewhat detailed at places, but only to the extent of gaining a full insight from a user point of view. The book also provides an important insight into the enabling processes happening in the WiMAX forum and other bodies, how their efforts are focusing on mobile devices, and how it is expected to bring forth new opportunities in the future.

ORGANIZATION OF THE BOOK

The book is organized into four sections. The sections are designed to be read independently based on the background of the reader.

Section I provides an introduction to wireless networks and mobile multimedia. It is comprised of three chapters. Chapter 1 (Why WiMAX for Broadcasting?) provides an insight into the new opportunity presented by the WiMAX technologies for delivery of multimedia content. Chapter 2 provides an introduction to broadband wireless technologies including those represented by WiFi , Wireless LANs (based on 801.11 a, b, g, or n) and the Wireless MAN technologies (represented by

802.16) including WiMAX networks. Chapter 2 helps appreciate how a new broadband wireless medium has emerged in a world today dominated by WiFi or cellular mobile networks and its implications. Chapter 3 provides an introduction to mobile multimedia. This chapter helps understand the requirements which mobile and wireless networks must fulfill to efficiently carry mobile media.

Section II (Broadband wireless technologies) lays the foundation for designing applications or network architectures using the technology of WiMAX. Towards this end, this section covers fixed and mobile WiMAX characteristics (Chapter 4) and design of Wimax transmission networks (Chapter 5). Leaning on a more practical side, the deployment status of wireless and WiMAX networks is presented (Chapter 6) together with standards convergence in mobile multimedia broadcasting (Chapter 7). The enabling framework for running applications over WiMAX networks is then completed by the next four chapters which focus on Chipsets for WiMAX devices (Chapter 8), Client devices for WiMAX (Chapter 9), Software architectures to support mobile multimedia (Chapter 10) and Spectrum for WiMAX Networks (Chapter 11). The section concludes with a discussion of network architectures for mobile WiMAX in Chapter 12.

Section III (Mobile broadcasting technologies) goes straight into the architectures required for the broadcasting of mobile multimedia. The section begins with Chapter 13 (broadcasting mobile multimedia with WiMAX–network architectures). This chapter provides an insight of how a network designed to serve both broadcast and multicast applications, as well as integration with mobile web services would be structured. This is followed by a discussion on the two existing facets of mobile and IP broadcasting i.e. Mobile TV technologies (Chapter 14) and IPTV with WiMAX networks (Chapter 15).

Section IV (Converged architecture, design and applications) brings together the threads of mobile WiMAX technologies, network architectures, network enablers (chipsets, CPEs, software for client devices) and broadcasting, developed independently in the book, to look at converged applications and networks from a practical perspective. Towards this end, this section has chapters on broadcast applications of mobile WiMAX networks (Chapter 17), interactive applications with WiMAX (Chapter 18) and content security (Chapter 19). These chapters are preceded with Chapter 16, which provides a technology overview of broadcast networks using WIMAX. A business case for mobile WiMAX (Chapter 20) and case studies for WiMAX networks are also included (Chapter 21). The section includes Chapter 22, which seeks to analyze the factors which will have potential impact on development of WiMAX applications in future.

INTENDED AUDIENCE

The book brings together two facets that exist today as independent streams, that is, broadcasting and web applications. These have existed virtually as independent streams in the past but are now finding common ground. Network operators, service providers, application designers, and users will benefit from the book by the insight it provides with the emerging common platforms and how they might use it to deliver applications in the new mobile medium. To this end, it is useful for technology and management professionals in the fields of broadcasting, communications, wireless networks, IPTV, WiMAX and mobile services to understand the WiMAX technology and the new application environment. It is also useful for existing broadcasters and service providers, application designers to understand the power of the new wireless media represented by WiMAX and how it can be harnessed. It is useful for strategists and consultants looking at new projects worldwide. This book is also intended to be useful to students by relating practical applications and networks to the WiMAX technology in its holistic form.

ACKNOWLEDGMENTS

A work of this nature is dependent on information from many sources. I thankfully acknowledge the use of information based on the work of the WiMAX forum, IEEE, Digital Video Broadcasting forum (DVB) and 3rd Generation Partnership Project (3GPP) among other organizations. The use of information from vendors and operators on their products and services is thankfully acknowledged.

The encouragement to take up this work came from Angelina Ward, senior acquisitions editor at Focal Press, who also was instrumental in framing the flow of content in the book and at various stages in the process of conceptualizing, writing and presenting the work in its final form. I am also thankful to Katherine Spencer, assistant editor at Focal Press in guiding me in preparing content and for submission of material among the host of activities which go into publishing a book of this nature. My sincere thanks go to Paul Gottehrer, Senior Project Manager, Focal Press, for interactively taking me through the production process.

I am indebted to Mr. Merill Weiss, the Series Editor of "Focal Press Media Technology Professional Series" for his review of the book.

I am also thankful to Puja K. Gupta at T-Mobile and Ronil Dhruva at Microsoft for helping me with many facets of the book.

Amitabh Kumar
Kumar.amitabh@gmail.com

SECTION

I

INTRODUCTION TO WIRELESS NETWORKS AND MOBILE MULTIMEDIA

1

WHY WiMAX FOR BROADCASTING?

Current 3G mobile networks, which were designed to primarily manage low bandwidth services like voice and data, would suffer if only six percent of wireless subscribers were to simultaneously view unique/personalized, streaming video during peak hours. To prevent this scenario, mobile providers need to begin planning now to find a way to deliver and backhaul the traffic being driven by video applications.

—John Roese
Chief Technology Officer, Nortel, in The Future Made Simple

We have witnessed some major trends in the past decade. These trends are not subtle, as is the case with some older technologies. Instead, they are bold and obvious. They present a goldmine to those willing to flow with them, and they are completely disruptive to others who stand in their way. The disruptions come about not merely because delivery technology has changed, such as the move to digital or high definition (HD), or a better medium of delivery has become available, such as satellite, wireless, or Internet Protocol Television (IPTV). Rather, these trends have their origin in a complete change in lifestyles, entertainment, and information flows, which have been impacted by a series of definitive events to the extent that the entire landscape now stands changed completely. Therefore, they leave no opportunity to continue to operate in the traditional ways to either aggregate content for entertainment or to deliver it to the customers. What are these definitive events?

The beginning of the trend was the heralded great performance being unveiled in the mobile arena. The three-dimensional effect of the growth of the number of users from a few hundred million to over three billion in a decade—each connection becoming capable to handle hundreds of kbps of data rates, and each device becoming capable of handling multimedia content, pictures, and videos—has had the effect of making lifestyles and workflows go mobile. Live content started appearing on TVs, which originated from mobile users, and TV services appeared on mobiles as mobile TV. Internet via mobile networks was a different game—the small screens and limited applications made web access of limited use except on PDA phones or "pocket" PCs.

The development of a WiFi chip in 2003 heralded a new dimension to the move toward wireless services. The number of WiFi users rose to 120 million by 2005, 200 million by 2006, and is slated to top a billion in 2008. With the embedding of WiFi in virtually all mobile devices from smartphones, PCs, PDAs, and media players, to gaming devices, hotspots of WiFi which could connect at tens of megabits per second emerged in hundreds of thousands of hotspots. Wireless also offered mobility of a different kind. It unleashed the world of internet in the mobile domain with its applications such as Skype, instant messaging, browsing, and blogging, and effectively mobile communities. Where available, users preferred the wireless use of internet rather than traditional mobile voice or data services. Wireless also made it possible to have home gateways connecting to PCs, media players, or mobile phones with storage everywhere. On-demand content or web-based content, such as from YouTube™ or user-generated TV stations on the internet started to be as important as traditional linear broadcasting, and the differences between the two is beginning to blur.

Wireless mobility with WiFi was, however, not everywhere, and this was compensated to an extent by availability of content on the go. Large memory sizes (such as 80 GB in iPods), availability of wireless data hotspots, IP-based broadcasts, and download services led to media going completely mobile. An 80-GB device can hold thousands of hours of video or movies (recorded at 256 KBps, for example). Multimedia transmissions now take place in formats that are suited for mobile screens in addition to traditional screens.

While all the transformation was happening in the mobile field, the internet was not static. The internet first gave way to user communities with users numbering hundreds of millions and an environment of usage which linked to everyday lives such as those for:

Online content: YouTube™, Google Video, Wikipedia, websites offering thousands of TV channels (www.itv.com, beetv.com)
Online communities: Myspace, Blogger, Linkedin, Del.icio.us
Online commerce: amazon.com, B&N, eBay
Online business internet: Virtual desktop and office (Google Writely, MS Office Live, Numbler, Groovy)

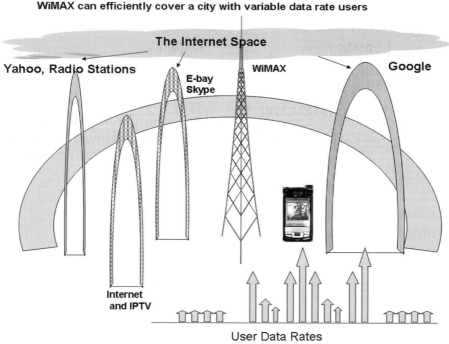

FIGURE 1-1 Broadcasting and data in WiMAX environment

Online collaboration: MS Live collaboration, Rallypoint, Writeboard
Web services: salesforce.com, Ta-da lists, Netsuite, Amazon web services
Search enabled business: Google, collective intellect, edgeio
Connectivity services: RSS feeds, blog lines, mobile Google, Yahoo mobile

At the same time the use of the internet also evolved to a new structured formulation, deriving information from millions of unstructured sources and databases. The new move led to the emergence of a new way of using the internet, which revolved around the use of the web as a core, rather than using it as a linkage platform. This was Web 2.0, based on structured data flows, with applications based on merging of information across the internet, assimilation of communities, and syndication of data as podcasts and RSS feeds.

The new environment, however, requires constant high-speed connectivity. The environment, which was created by the expanding use of wireless, with users and communities being mobile, now needed the final thrust toward a universal use by combining the diverse mobile and internet worlds of cellular and wireless with high-speed, low-cost, and reliable performance available across large areas without having to hop between hot spots. WiMAX, when it entered the scene at the beginning of 2005, represented much more than a medium of city-wide connectivity. It was designed to maintain quality of services with guaranteed service flows and an architecture that was completely open and integrated with the IP world.

1.1 BEING A FOURTH-GENERATION BROADCASTER

With mobility being the most common attribute, users now overwhelmingly prefer those operators that can offer services that can be used while on the move. This means that an IP-based wireless service provider that can offer all of the Web 2.0 services, offer media broadcasting, and also bundle in "on-demand" and "traditional TV" broadcasts, has an obvious advantage over a pure broadcaster. Until recently, this was not possible because of the difficulty of offering live media over the internet with any degree of reliability or availability on the one hand, and getting interactivity with users in broadcast networks on the other hand.

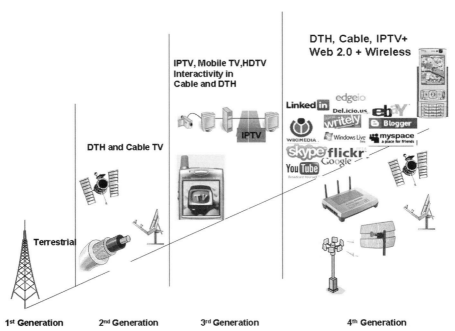

FIGURE 1-2 Fourth-generation broadcasting

The availability of Mobile WiMAX coupled with interoperability with WiFi hotspots and cellular networks is changing all that very rapidly. WiMAX offers guaranteed quality of service (QoS) and service flows, which coupled with end-to-end QoS offered by IPv6 networks can deliver as flawless a quality as can be delivered over traditional cable or DSL networks. So much so that purely traditional broadcasting, including HD, will suffer severe disadvantages if not coupled with the availability of Web 2.0 services and business internet community services.

The traditional broadcasting business has not been left untouched with the changes that have been in the offing. Even traditional direct-to-home (DTH) and cable TV operators are now building wireless connectivity networks to enhance the traditional services by including broadband wireless internet. Mobile operators, offering broadband internet and mobile TV, which were generally offered as "walled garden," i.e., closed to internet services such as Skype (or VoIP), are now collaborating with WiFi operators to offer IP multimedia system (IMS)-based roaming between wireless and cellular mobile services.

With a steady growth of IPv6 in wireless networks and the conversion of traditional networks to IP-based networks and next-generation networks (NGN) architecture beginning in 2008, the stage is set for integration of the mobile internet and broadcasting seamlessly into network architectures. Broadcasting to mobiles with traditional transmissions and on-demand media will be just an extension of the new networks fully integrated with Web 2.0 and community internet services such as Presence and instant messaging, among others.

The WiMAX networks form a very important part of the wireless rollout of the next-generation networks. They also provide a replacement for major wired extensions of broadcast services, broadcast content feeder networks, and news-gathering networks available today by enriching them with the new broadband features.

1.2 WIRELESS AND MOBILE NETWORKS

Wireless access has been available to us for many years now. Its most visible manifestation has been in the form of wireless LANS and the WiFi hotspots. These allow internet access using universally available WiFi cards or embedded chips in laptops, PDAs, and other devices from airports, hotels, and cybercafés to university campuses and yachts. The users can browse the net, make VoIP calls using software such as Skype, access mail, or upload pictures and videos from digital cameras. They can also watch video by streaming from any of the video sources or downloading video files. This type of use of the net

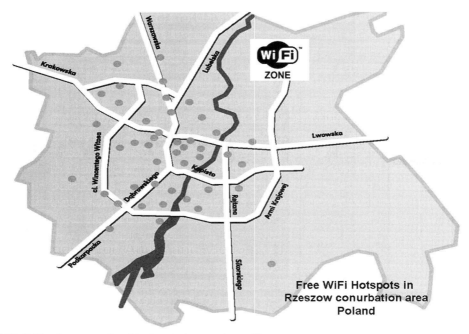

FIGURE 1-3   An example of hotspots in a metropolitan area

has been commonplace and uses wireless broadband technologies characterized by the use of 802.11 (a, b, or g) standards.

WiFi hotspots have witnessed a sharp growth, and thousands of such spots are now commonplace in every major city. Each such spot, however, covers a small area, and the services can be used only while the user is still in this area, even though there may be another WiFi spot adjoining it. Essentially, the WiFi provides a fixed wireless broadband access.

The WiFi hotspots can cover up to 300 meters, and while in a hotspot the user can use data rates of 10 to 20 Mbps based on shared usage, actual distance from antenna, and visibility.

Interactive maps of hotspots are available on sites such as Flickr™ or gWiFi.net.

The alternative to the users for data connectivity has been, for example, to use a mobile network data card (e.g., a CDMA2000, HSDPA, or an EV-DO card) in the laptop. The cellular networks provide nationwide coverage with full mobility and seamless roaming. In fact, some carriers have been promoting the EV-DO as a "universally available hotspot," including in areas such as airports where WiFi connectivity may also exist. In case of 3G networks, it is possible to connect at data

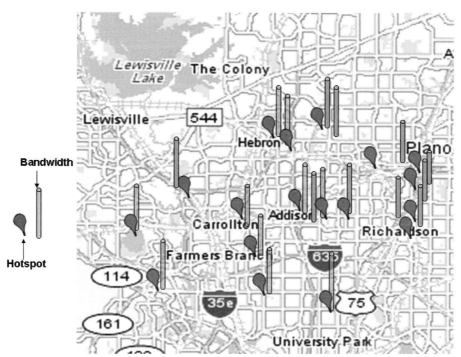

FIGURE 1-4 A conceptual depiction of WiFi hotspots with typical characteristics—high bandwidth, small coverage area

rates reaching 2 Mbps, which suffices for most mobile applications. This includes a streaming mobile TV service or a video download from a music store. Technically the mobile data connectivity provided by mobile networks is flawless.

This cellular data connectivity comes at a price however. The mobile 3G spectrum has been one of the most highly priced resources in the telecommunications space, as has been the cost of infrastructure in rolling out the 3G networks by the carriers with an eye on higher multimedia broadcasting and data revenues. In India, for example, a mobile operator with over 1.3 million users in Delhi has a 2G spectrum of just 8.8 MHz. Hence using 5 MHz 3G data carriers (e.g., in HSDPA) for data connectivity is nothing short of a dream. On the other hand, WiMAX spectrum of 7 + 7 MHz each has been given out to over a dozen operators and is used in WiMAX data and voice networks.

Viewed in another context, the total spectrum available to a 3G carrier can start from 10 + 10 MHz and may be limited to 15 + 15 MHz in typical implementations. Any multimedia data service operates at the cost of resources which can be alternatively utilized for highly paying voice

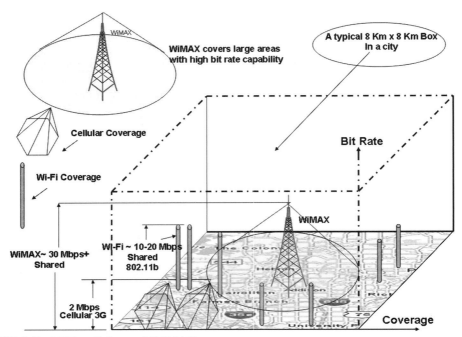

FIGURE 1-5 WiFi, cellular, and WiMAX coverage

conversations typically termed as "airtime." The cost of data services in mobile networks has therefore not dropped sufficiently to encourage the widespread, unlimited, and/or ubiquitous use.

The spectrum available for wireless LANs and WiFi ranges in the hundreds of MHz if both the licensed and unlicensed bands are considered. The WiFi networks are essentially an extension of the internet wirelessly to the user, bringing with it all the protocols and applications of the internet including the VoIP services , streaming and download of video, real-time audio streaming off internet radio stations, etc. The usage may be free at public places or prices are determined by the conventional internet unlimited usage pricing (e.g., $20 to $40 per month unlimited wireless broadband) and low-cost services such as Skype rather than high costs associated with mobile networks (charged as per kbyte).

The introduction of WiFi in mobile phones did not take much time to materialize. With the availability of Bluetooth, for example, a mobile phone can be used to make a Skype call using a laptop connected by WiFi to the net or receive a streaming video feed using the net. This possibility did not go unnoticed by the cellular mobile industry, which responded to the challenge with the introduction of WiFi-capable phones.

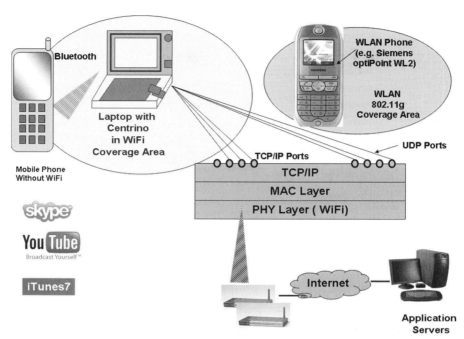

FIGURE 1-6 Accessing internet applications using WiFi

There are many examples of such phones, such as Samsung i600, Nokia E61, N80i, Motorola CN620, A910, Siemens optiPoint WL2, etc. among others.

Cellular phone networks have begun incorporating the use of "multiple network access" as a part of the their overall architecture. This is best evidenced in the launch of unlicensed mobile access (UMA) (now called the generic network access or GNA). This permits the users to switch automatically to WiFi for VoIP calls or broadband internet whenever in the area of coverage of such hotspots. It is particularly convenient to use in the home if WiFi connectivity is available. The calls meant for the cell phones are automatically diverted to the WiFi network saving on more expensive usage of network or better reception in many areas where the cellular signals are weaker. GNA is discussed in greater detail later in the book.

1.3 WiMAX: A NEW OPPORTUNITY FOR MULTIMEDIA BROADCASTING

In the meantime, the metropolitan area wireless networks (MANs) development work was progressing under the IEEE 802.16 committee which evolved standards for wireless MANs. The WiMAX Forum, an industry body founded in 2001 to promote conformance to standards and interoperability among wireless MAN networks, then brought forth the WiMAX as it is commonly known today. WiMAX is a standards-based technology for wireless MANs conforming to parameters which enable interoperability.

WiMAX developments have been moving forward at a rapid pace since the initial standardization efforts in IEEE 802.16. Standards for Fixed WiMAX (IEEE 802.16-2004) were announced as final in 2004, followed by Mobile WiMAX (IEEE 802.16e) in 2005. In Europe, the standards for wireless MANs were formalized under the ETSI as HiperMANs. These were also based on IEEE 802.16 standards but did not initially use the same parameters (such as frequency or number of subcarriers). These were later harmonized with the WiMAX standards.

The IEEE 802.16d standards provide for fixed and nomadic access, while the 802.16e standards also provide mobility up to speeds of 120 kilometers per hour. The WiMAX network technology is an evolutionary one as it uses orthogonal frequency-division multiplexing (OFDM), which makes the transmissions resistant to fades and multipath effects. Moreover it also permits location-independent usage (nomadic), as well as usage at vehicular mobile speeds in Mobile WiMAX. The wireless MAN technologies are designed to cover much larger areas compared to the WiFi technologies, which create hotspots of a few hundred meters at the most. The range of WiMAX transmissions can extend 20 km even in semi-urban environments. The WiMAX mobile standards have been designed to provide broadband wireless access connections with seamless handover as well as roaming capability.

Initially WiMAX was seen as being able to primarily provide connectivity between WiFi hotspots. However the rapid developments now happening in both WiMAX as well Mobile WiMAX are positioning it as a mainstream customer access service rather than just a backhaul service.

WiMAX has seen widespread growth since the standards were adapted, and operators worldwide have either already started providing WiMAX-based networks or are gearing up to launch these in the near future. The availability of WiMAX networks entirely changes the manner in which multimedia applications can be handled over the wireless networks. The large spectrum, for example, 20-MHz blocks with each operator, coverage with a single tower of 20 to 30 km (or

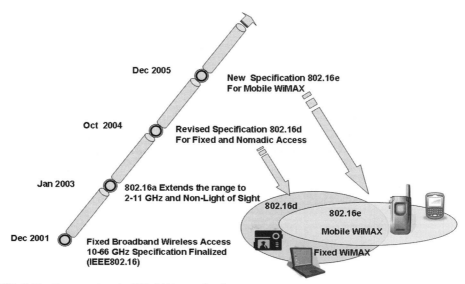

FIGURE 1-7 Progression in WiMAX standards

more), and the high data rates achievable make the networks very attractive for multimedia broadcasting.

Multicast content over WiMAX networks can be delivered to hundreds of thousands of users enabling a new era of interactive broadcasting with the usage of the return path. It is the capability of WiMAX networks in providing high bandwidth with QoS deployable over large areas, which is seen as a key advantage of WiMAX.

Figure 1.8 shows a typical WiMAX network architecture. The applications such as IPTV and iTunes multimedia download operate as normal internet applications and can be accessed by users on fixed wireline networks such as DSL. In addition, they can be also delivered over Fixed WiMAX networks (IEEE 802.16-2004) and Mobile WiMAX networks (IEEE 802.16e). In case of deliveries to Mobile WiMAX, the call set-up may be routed via the IP multimedia service (IMS) described in later chapters in the book. Other 3GPP services, such as video calling, instant messaging, or Presence, would require the use of the IMS.

Handsets for WiMAX have been available since 2006, signifying early interest in the use of this technology, which has the potential to deliver multimedia services to mobile handsets.

Samsung, which introduced the SPH-M8000 WiMAX phone in 2006, had launched it based on a client-server–based architecture, with the WiMAX server being available within a range of 1 km. The phone was based on WiBro, the Korean version of Mobile WiMAX

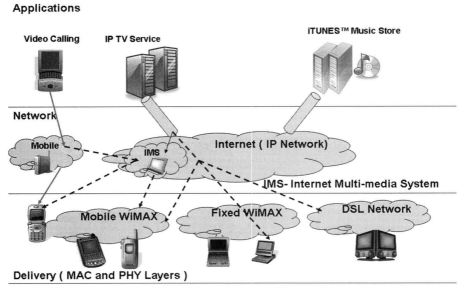

FIGURE 1-8   Delivering multimedia services via WiMAX

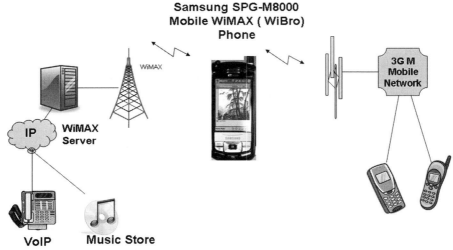

FIGURE 1-9   Samsung WiBro phone in multinetwork environment

operating in the 2.3-GHz band and can be used at vehicular speeds up to 120 kmph.

The introduction of alternative architectures, such as Mobile WiMAX, has the potential of bringing the internet and services such as mobile IPTV directly to handsets in a manner similar to the FM radio.

1.4 WiMAX: FASTEST-GROWING WIRELESS TECHNOLOGY

The growth of WiMAX ever since the standards were adopted in 2005 has been multi-fronted with simultaneous developments in the client devices (or customer premises equipment, CPEs), base stations, chipsets, and other transmission equipment. As spectrum gets assigned, rollout of the networks is following very quickly, and each network commissioned has a potential of enabling hundreds of thousands of client devices. Certification by the WiMAX forum for interoperability and conformance to specifications has been a very proactive step in the process of developing the market with devices that can be used anywhere in any network. The experience of mobile networks (2G and 3G) has shown that growth rates of 100 percent per year have been possible. The benefits of high-speed broadband access, commonality with IP technology and applications, seamless mobility and roaming, and the availability of spectrum surpassing 3G networks has already placed WiMAX on the watch list as a potentially disruptive technology for cellular mobile networks. Global economies of scale have not yet arrived for WiMAX, but cannot be far behind. A unique advantage WiMAX is enjoying is the extremely rapid introduction in developing countries where the cellular penetrations are still low and the demand of broadband wireless access is seen as vital for the development of the country.

1.4.1 Universal Client Devices

The WiMAX technology has long been seen to be on the horizon, but practical implementations were few largely owing to the lack of universal availability of WiMAX receiving devices (CPEs) either as attachments or as embedded chipsets. However the long wait is now over, with the commencement of deliveries of Fixed WiMAX (IEEE 802.16-2004) and Mobile WiMAX chipsets by over a dozen vendors.

Past experience has shown the role of industry associations in ushering in interoperable devices is extremely valuable in successful large-scale use of these devices. We have seen that in the case of the WiFi alliance for WiFi networks, and 3GPP in the case of 3G networks, this plays a major role in this regard. As mentioned earlier, in the case of WiMAX networks the WiMAX Forum is playing this role.

Mobile handsets have already appeared with support of Mobile WiMAX. These include devices such as Samsung SPH-P9000, which operates in the WiBro networks, the Korean version of Mobile WiMAX. PC card adapters, USB adapters, and indoor CPEs are now available from many vendors conforming to the WiMAX-Forum-specified implementation profiles.

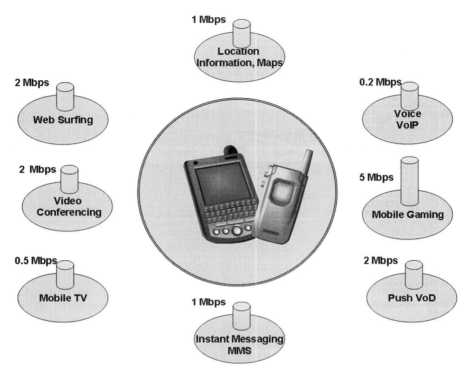

FIGURE 1-10   Examples of mobility applications

1.4.2 Trend towards High Data Rate Applications and Mobility

There are two distinct trends: one toward mobility, and another toward high data connectivity applications typically characterized by Web 2.0 applications. The use of Web 2.0 relates to applications that use the internet as a core and are based on collaborative communities and structured information architectures. The use of websites such as YouTube™, Amazon, Flickr™, Google, etc. creates communities of users for daily activities with increasing use of images and voluminous data. The data connectivity requirements for these activities can easily exceed 1 Mbps per user.

The Law of Mobility propounded by Russ McGuire, Director of Strategy at Sprint Nextel, states that the "Value of a product or services increases exponentially with mobility." This law indeed explains why customers are willing to pay more for a smartphone than a PC with larger memory, screen size, and processing power. The fact that a smartphone or a mobile TV phone is with the user 100 percent of the time and can be used while on the move makes it equally, if not more, valuable for the service providers as well as the user than a home TV or a home computer.

The new paradigm of usage requires high bandwidth available at low cost, which is the prime strength of wireless networks, even compared to cellular 2G or 3G networks.

1.4.3 Trend towards all IP Networks

The trend toward the use of WiMAX for IPTV applications and delivery of interactive mobile TV is in no measure fueled by the pervasive nature of the IP networks. The technologies and applications have a large installed base with architectures defined by the internet engineering task force (IETF) RFCs. The wireless networks are seen as an extension of the IP networks beyond the physical wire.

The IPTV, for example, uses IP protocols and delivers TV channels with Quality of Service (QoS) safeguards. This helps provide streamed services such as broadcast television, which is not possible on the internet owing to it being a "best effort" delivery network. In fact, the technologies of mobile multimedia broadcasting such as DVB-H are based on IP datacasting and use an all-IP infrastructure with only the delivery being affected using the DVB-T framing structure and air interfaces.

1.4.4 Quality of Service in Mobile WiMAX Networks

WiMAX is an alternative mechanism for providing an IP network with QoS guarantees, which can permit the delivery of multimedia content with desired QoS over a wireless medium and in a mobile environment.

Mobile multimedia technologies such as DVB-H, DAB-IP, and DMB are different from the traditional broadcast technologies for stationary receivers (ATSC, DVB-T) primarily because of the following criteria:

- Additional layer of forward error correction (FEC)
- Robust modulation such as COFDM to overcome Doppler shifts and multipath propagation
- Power-saving techniques that permit the receiver to be active only for a fraction of the time.

Mobile WiMAX networks tend to achieve a similar level of functionality but with the additional feature of two-way connectivity. This is, however, limited to vehicular speeds in the range of 120 kmph reflecting city driving conditions. The OFDM modulation used in the PHY layer is physically robust against multipath interference, permits incremental resource allocation, and ensures that subcarriers assigned to a service or user are able to deliver the data streams at the rates required by the application. The parameters can be changed dynamically in adverse conditions to maintain the quality of service (for example, in streaming video). Mobile WiMAX also uses FEC and interleaving to overcome frequency selective fading effects, not unlike the mobile TV transmission technologies. The "Adaptive Burst profile" permits the parameters to be adjusted on a frame-by-frame basis, including the modulation (QPSK to 64 QAM), FEC coding rate, and overhead features (preamble and guard times).

Moreover a QoS can be assigned to each service flow, and this parameter is used by the MAC layer to guarantee the required QoS by exchange of MAC-layer messages. The messages ensure that additional packages are assigned for each identified service for which a QoS has been set to meet the desired goals. This approach contrasts with priority queuing, which is still in a manner, a best-effort delivery.

Mobile WiMAX thus comes very close to the mobile multimedia delivery networks in terms of robustness of transmission and the QoS features, which can ensure reliable service in a mobile environment. At the same time, the potential costs can be much lower because of the high-cost 3G spectrum used in cellular networks, which can be overburdened for resources in dense usage environments. WiMAX is also based on open network architecture and integrates well with IP networks or the internet.

1.4.5 Multimedia Broadcast Requirement in Dense User Areas

Metro usage is characterized by very high-density usage. Even though 3G cellular networks are designed to give a theoretical peak maximum of 2 Mbps, the vendor-rated average speeds fall in the range of 200–400 kbps with limited users being able to use the service simultaneously. 3G-HSDPA and long-term evolution technologies have been designed to take the data usage to higher levels, but the limited spectrum available remains a constraint. WiMAX provides for a greater data usage per Hz of spectrum (with efficiencies reaching 3.74 bps/Hz of spectrum or 3.74 Mbps per MHz). These are 50 to 60 percent higher than those achieved in 3G networks based on an HSDPA data rate of 14 Mbps in 5 MHz or 2.8 bps/Hz).

However, a key advantage of Mobile WiMAX is that it can be used with multiple input and multiple output antennas (MIMO). Use of MIMO along with special techniques that are native to the WiMAX standards such as spatial multiplexing (SM) or space time coding (STC) mean that in non-line-of-sight environments (NLOS), such as cities with tall buildings or interior areas, MIMO provides a much higher data rate than that possible with single antennas. Using MIMO in line-of-sight environments can nearly double the data rates available and spectrum efficiencies soaring to 7 bits/Hz. Another feature available in Mobile WiMAX, as we will see in later chapters, is the use of advanced antenna systems (AAS), which can point the beam at each user by electronic steering. This helps increase the signal-to-noise ratio and eliminate interference.

WiMAX systems cater to much higher user density by virtue of the ability to have a frequency reuse of one (i.e., all cells have the same frequency), and sectorization or dividing the cell into three or six sectors, effectively multiplying the capacity by almost the same factor.

1.4.6 Security Architectures

WiMAX systems have been designed with a view toward a high-security environment, which is supported by both encryption (i.e., AES) and authentication schemes (such as extensible authentication protocol, EAP). These are covered in later chapters.

1.5 SERVICES OVER WiMAX NETWORKS

WiMAX networks are designed to be able to interface with different types of networks (including IP, TDM voice, ATM, or others). A provision has also been kept for service-specific support by providing quality-of-service classes based on characteristics of different services. WiMAX networks can support VoIP, video, voice, or data using the same architecture by merely defining appropriate classes of service. They can also carry multicasts as well as web syndication feeds such as RSS simultaneously with other services, providing a rich user experience.

All the advantages of WiMAX, however, do not mean that these networks will immediately start replacing the mobile networks. In fact, quite to the contrary, these will continue to work side by side providing voice data and multimedia options to users in the foreseeable future.

2

INTRODUCTION TO BROADBAND WIRELESS NETWORKS

The world of wires has already begun its long descent into oblivion as wireless technology improves to the point where wires become obsolete.

—Thomas Frey
Executive Director; DaVinci Institute

2.1 INTRODUCTION

Broadband wireless networks are forming an increasingly important medium of connectivity. Virtually every device, from an MP3 player such as Sansa™ or Zune™, or a gaming device such as Nintendo DS or Sony PSP, is now being designed to work with wireless broadband networks or wireless LANS. Wireless connectivity became virtually universal because of the efforts of the Wireless Fidelity Alliance (now called WiFi), which went beyond the standards underlying the wireless networks (IEEE 802.11) to start a certification program to test interoperability of wireless devices. Devices that conformed to the interoperability in WiFi implementation were given the stamp of "WiFi," signifying that they were interoperable as per the industry alliance. The WiFi certification program, which went beyond the standards to pin down operational modes and specific parameters for full interoperability and, as we see later, backward compatibility, became a part of history and has been the single most important factor for being able to use wireless adapters or embedded chips (now generically called WiFi) universally. Today, personal computers and laptops, almost without exception, support WiFi-embedded chipsets. PDAs and smartphones support WiFi connectivity for access to the wireless LAN and use of the phone for internet connectivity when in WiFi zones.

We lay so much stress on the wireless certification program by the WiFi Alliance because the process is now being repeated for wireless metropolitan area networks (wireless MANs or ETSI HiperMAN represented by IEEE 802.16 standards) with the WiMAX Forum now playing the role played earlier by WiFi Alliance, in other words, profiles of implementation of standards and providing a certification program for interoperability testing. This has led to interoperable WiMAX devices entering the market and beginning to be deployed in personal devices, such as mobile phones or PCs and WiMAX networks springing up in every country in the world. We use the term WiMAX for wireless MAN devices that follow the profiles and certification of the WiMAX Forum™ throughout this book.

2.1.1 Why Are Wireless Devices Important?

Why are wireless devices important? There are many reasons. The first one is quite obvious—both freedom from wires and mobility. Most such devices, particularly mobile devices, are comprised of small mobile terminals or ultra-mobile PCs. Wireless devices are better suited for video sharing (such as via YouTube™), media download-ing, gaming, or transferring photographs to processing labs than get-ting tied to a wired internet point. An example is the BluOynx, which is a mobile server that can store media information and, through its WiFi connectivity, can serve as a gateway to the external world. Users do not need a PC to use the server; it connects using a mobile phone.

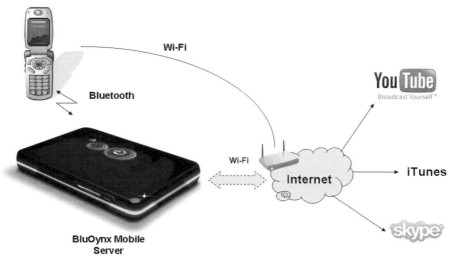

FIGURE 2-1 Example of a wireless device, BluOynx™

The new paradigm of universal wireless connectivity is set to be enhanced further with the devices adding support for Metropolitan Area Networks (MANs) most commonly represented by WiMAX. These broadband wireless networks take the connectivity beyond the realm of the local wireless hotspot (or wireless LAN) and provide connectivity in an environment in which the user is moving from place to place. This connectivity can range from the use of wireless-enabled devices at any location in the coverage area (referred to as nomadic) and may include use in a mobile environment such as in a moving car. The use of wireless devices designed for WiFi is possible in a wide range of locations by using global roaming services (such as those provided by a global roaming company called FON). The connectivities outside the hotspots can be provided either by cellular mobile networks or by wide area broadband wireless networks.

The wireless networks do provide a significant advantage in terms of speed and the cost of usage, hence their increasing proliferation. As the rollout of WiMAX networks gains momentum, the availability of devices such as media players, cameras, and gaming devices is expected to rise dramatically enabling a totally new range of applications.

In this chapter, we give an overview of the wireless LAN networks commonly denoted as WiFi as a prelude to an introduction to WiMAX networks. Why do we want to begin with wireless local area networks and WiFi? The reason is that the WiMAX networks took off, in a way,

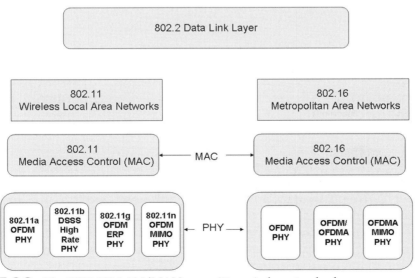

FIGURE 2-2 The IEEE 802 LAN/MAN committee wireless standards

from where the wireless LANs left off. Wireless MANs have the same logical structure comprised of PHY and MAC layers. The WiMAX networks have features enhanced for extending the range through a different technology in the PHY layer (in other words, OFDM) and providing added features in the MAC layer to support quality of service (QoS), etc.

Both the standards originate from the IEEE 802 LAN/MAN committee of the IEEE, the standards body responsible for both the networks. Both the "wireless networks" are organized under the IEEE 802.2 data link layer of the IEEE. While the MAC layer of WiFi is based on contention-based access, the MAC layer of wireless MANs is designed using a scheduling algorithm. Both the "networks" provide wireless access, albeit in slightly different ways, and it is logical to begin with 802.11 networks. However, the real reason why we must briefly discuss WiFi is that most devices are not only likely to support both WiMAX and WiFi, a fact already proven by devices which have entered the market, but also provide inter-working between the two networks. Hence, WiFi and WiMAX are interlinked, inseparably, and we begin with wireless local networks.

2.2 WIRELESS LOCAL AREA NETWORKS

The task of providing wireless extensions to Local Area Networks (LANs) was entrusted to a committee of the IEEE called the 802.11. The standards generated by the group are today universally used and are commonly called the WiFi standards even though they encompass a range of technologies. We provide a brief overview of these standards.

2.2.1 IEEE 802.11

The first LAN standard released by the IEEE in 1997 was the 802.11 standard. The standard claimed a modest speed of 2 Mbps of capacity, but was important as it provided for the first time the capability to connect to the LANs without the accompanying cable. The 802.11 standard made use of the 2.4 GHz unlicensed band. The low bandwidth standard has been superseded by the later versions and is currently no longer used.

The 802.11 standards continued to use the same mechanism for distribution of traffic, in other words, Carrier Sense Multiple Access (CSMA), with the exception that instead of collision detection as on a physical LAN, the wireless protocols use "collision avoidance," wherein the transmission begins only if no carrier is sensed. The access mechanism is sometimes called CSMA/CA and is used in conjunction with

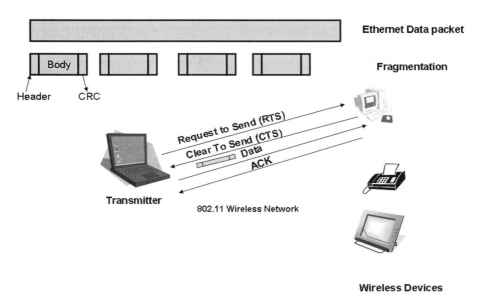

FIGURE 2-3 An IEEE 802.11 wireless network

a positive acknowledgment from a receiving device, called ACK. The mechanism of access (called virtual carrier sense) is comprised of of a request-to-send packet sent by the transmitting devices and then immediately listening for its acknowledgment [called clear-to-send (CTS)]. The transmission continues for a certain fixed time after the receipt of a positive ACK, after which the process of RTS/ACK needs to be repeated. The protocol is only suitable for thin traffic as there is a time lag before transmission begins and probability of collision cannot be ruled out from other devices.

Being an extension of the Ethernet LAN, the 802.11 retained the same packet length as the Ethernet (1518 bytes). However, as such long packets would have high probability of collision or errors on a wireless medium, a fragmentation of the Ethernet packet is carried out in the MAC layer and the fragments are transmitted sequentially using the RTS/CTS and the ACK mechanism. The modulation scheme employed was binary phase shift keying (BPSK).

While it is convenient to use unlicensed bands such as 2.4 GHz (a band of 83.5 MHz between 2.4000 to 2.4835 GHz), these bands are also associated with an unknown number of other operating devices and possibility of interference. For this reason, the wireless LAN physical layer implementations provide for features such as frequency hopping, spread spectrum techniques called direct sequence spread spectrum

(DSSS) or orthogonal frequency-division multiplexing (OFDM).These terms will be discussed briefly later in the book. However, in later implementations, the use of DSSS or OFDM is more common in comparison to frequency hopping.

Frequency Hopping

For the purpose of use of frequency hopping technology, the ISM band under IEEE 802.11 is divided into 1 MHz channels in the range of 2.402 to 2.479, which provides 78 channels (the United States, Canada, Europe, and Asia with variations in some countries). Frequency hopping systems have a predetermined sequence of hopping and hop size (26 frequencies in most cases). Both the transmitter and receiver hop every 0.4 second in frequency, which helps avoid interference and collisions.

Direct Sequence Spread Spectrum (DSSS)

Spread spectrum systems avoid interference by spreading the spectrum of the signal over a wider band. These also use a spreading code, which is used to recover the stream at the receiver and also distinguish it from other carriers or noise. As spreading requires a wider bandwidth, 5 MHz channels are used for spread spectrum systems in the 2.4 GHz band.

The 85 MHz wide 2.4 GHz band is usable with 11 identified center frequencies placed at a gap of 5 MHz each. The channels allowed to be used are:

United States and Canada: Channels 1 to 11 (2.412 to 2.462 GHz)
Europe: Channels 1 to 13 (2.412 to 2.472 GHz)

However, as only three frequencies are non-overlapping and based on the bandwidth, only some of the center frequencies are usable in a typical implementation.

The 802.11 standard had two implementations at the physical layer. These were the direct sequence spread spectrum (DSSS) and the frequency hopping spread spectrum (FHSS) variants. Because of its frequency hopping nature, it is possible to use the 802.11 on 15 access points or 15 simultaneously transmitting devices in the same area.

The later versions of IEEE 802.11x, which were introduced to overcome the low-bandwidth availability in the original 802.11 specifications, were based on using new modulation techniques and different frequency bands offering higher bandwidth.

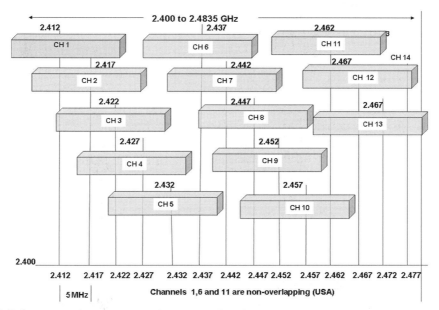

FIGURE 2-4 Center frequencies in the 2.4 GHz band

2.2.2 IEEE 802.11b

In September 1999, the IEEE released the specifications of the 802.11b standard, which operated in the same band of 2.4 GHz but could operate up to 11 Mbps. This placed its use in the same range of speeds that could be handled on the Ethernet at that time (10 Mbps). This standard is the most widely used standard for wireless LAN access and is used in a majority of WiFi-enabled devices.

The 802.11b standard at the physical layer uses DSSS modulation with a bandwidth of 11 MHz (shared as in the case of LANs). It can be used to form a maximum of three simultaneously transmitting devices in a given area. (In other words, three active channels can be supported at any given instant.)

The modulation scheme used is called complementary code keying (CCK), which is a variant of M-ary orthogonal keying with a variant of CDMA being used for the modulation. The operations permitted are at 5.5 Mbps or 11 Mbps. The newer versions of IEEE, when needing to provide backward compatibility to IEEE 802.11b, operate in the 2.4 GHz band with CCK modulation.

In indoor environments, 802.11b provides for operation up to 30 m at 11 Mbps or 100 m (typical) at 1 Mbps. The rates can scale up or down by using a feature known as adaptive rate selection based on signal quality.

2.2.3 IEEE 802.11a

In the same time frame, that is, October 1999, the IEEE also released another variant of the 802.11 standard. The 802.11a standard is designed to operate in the 5 GHz band (typically 5.15 to 5.35 and 5.725 to 5.825 GHz). This band also forms a part of the National Information Infrastructure (NII) in the United States. The band is not unlicensed, although the devices operating in a majority of countries may not require a license. The devices operating with 802.11a are sometimes called WiFi5 to denote the frequency band of operation.

In 802.11a, operation is possible up to a maximum of 54 Mbps (turbo mode) as shared bandwidth making possible its use in high-bandwidth applications such as video. The devices can also operate at lower bandwidths of 6, 9, 18, 24, 36, or 48 Mbps.

The band of 5 GHz is characterized by high loss with distance from the transmitter and the inability of signals to pass through obstructions such as walls. In order to overcome these, the 802.11a standard made a major improvement in the physical layer by using the OFDM modulation. In OFDM, the data to be transmitted is divided into a large number of orthogonal subcarriers. Each subcarrier now carries only a few kbps of data as against tens of megabits if a single carrier was to be used. Because of this, the symbol time of each subcarrier is very large and the subcarriers are not individually affected by frequency selective fading common in NLOS environments. The OFDM systems are very resistant to frequency selective fading and propagation path delay variations when the number of subcarriers is large. In the case of 802.11a, the number of subcarriers used is 52, of which 48 are for data and 4 are for pilots. In this regard, it differs considerably from broadband wireless MANs discussed later in this chapter where the number of subcarriers

Nokia N80i

WiFi
IEEE 802.11b/g

FIGURE 2-5   Nokia N80i with WiFi access (picture courtesy Nokia)

used is 256 (that is, for Fixed WiMAX) or higher (for example, 512 to 2048 for Mobile WiMAX based on bandwidth).

The 802.11a devices can operate from 100 to 250 feet (35 to 80 meters) in indoor and outdoor environments, respectively. The 802.11a standard was also approved for use in the European Union (EU) in late 2002, a delay caused by spectrum use considerations. The EU use is based on an amended frequency scheme.

2.2.4 IEEE 802.11g

The third standard to be ratified by the IEEE was 802.11g. This standard is also based on the use of OFDM modulation as in 802.11a, but in the 2.4 GHz band, which is universally available. The 802.11g standard was designed for backward compatibility with 802.11b and hence used complementary code keying (CCK) with 5.5 Mbps and 11 Mbps rates similar to 802.11b. This provides backward compatibility with other 802.11b devices. However, it also maintains the data rates of 6, 9, 18, 24, 48, and 54 Mbps using OFDM modulation. With the dual advantage of high speed (up to 54 Mbps) and use of unlicensed bands (2.4 GHz), the client devices for 802.11g became universally available. It is common to find the support of all three standards (802.11a/b/g) in many products.

The OFDM in 802.11b/g is based on a 64-point Fast Fourier Transform (FFT). This is equivalent to having 64 subcarriers in the allotted bandwidth. Of these subcarriers, 48 are for carriage of data, 4 are pilot subchannels, and the remaining are used as null carriers. The PHY layer uses a rate of 250 K symbols per second. Table 2-1 depicts the gross data rates, which are achievable using various modulation schemes.

TABLE 2-1

Data rates achievable using 802.11g

Modulation	FEC Code Rate	Coded Bits per Subcarrier	Coded Bits per OFDM Symbol	Data bits per OFDM Symbol	Data Rate (20 MHz Channel) Mbps (250 K Symbols/ Sec)	Required S/N dB
BPSK	½	1	48	24	6 Mbps	4
BPSK	¾	1	48	36	9 Mbps	5
QPSK	½	2	96	48	12 Mbps	7
QPSK	¾	2	96	72	18 Mbps	9
16 QAM	½	4	192	96	24 Mbps	12
16 QAM	¾	4	192	144	36 Mbps	16
64 QAM	½	6	288	192	48 Mbps	20
64 QAM	¾	6	288	216	54 Mbps	21

The table also shows the relationship of data rate with the S/N, which is available as per the transmission conditions. It is evident that as the S/N falls, the modulation of each subcarrier must revert to the lower densities. This directly impacts the bit rates available over the wireless link.

2.2.5 IEEE 802.11n

While the 802.11b/g standards operated in the 2.4 GHz band and permitted maximum data rates (shared) of up to 54 Mbps, the need for higher-speed connectivity remained, particularly in view of the physical LANs moving up in speeds of up to 1 Gbps. For this purpose, the IEEE has set up a task force with the objective of development of 802.11n standards operable in 2.4 or 5 GHz bands and able to support maximum bit rates of up to 700 Mbps (typical in shared environments of above 100 Mbps). The new standard is now close to formal approval (expected in late 2008). However, devices based on 802.11n, which operate in the 5-GHz band, are available.

IEEE 802.11n is based on the enhancement of existing standards by adding on to the MIMO technologies. The use of MIMO essentially involves the use of two or more transmitting and receiving antennas, thus implementing spatial multiplexing for increased data throughput. The path diversity available via multiple antennas also helps increase the range of coverage.

In summary, the most commonly used standard for wireless LANs is the 802.11b, which has the highest number of compatible devices in use, while the use of 802.11b/g is increasing because of higher-speed applications needing to be supported.

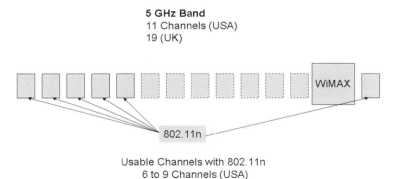

FIGURE 2-6   5 GHz spectrum band provides 6 to 9 non-overlapping channels for 802.11n

2.2.6 Application Example of 802.11a/b/g/n: Apple TV

Even though the 802.11n standards are in a draft stage, Apple has announced Mac platforms that support the 802.11a/b/g and n (draft) wireless local access technologies.

The Apple TV™ is a base device that connects using an HDMI connector to the TV set. It obtains content to be displayed by connecting via WiFi to the MAC or PC in the home. Live applications permit the downloading of songs, Podcasts, or video clips, which can then be played on the TV.

Apple TV uses streaming over 802.11g/n wireless interfaces from up to three PCs or laptops in the wireless coverage area. The PCs can use iTunes7™ for live streaming over wireless. It also has other interfaces such as component video, optical, and analog RCA. Apple TV can handle enhanced-definition or high-definition widescreen (1080 i 60/50 Hz, 720 p 60/50 Hz), or standard definition 576 p 50 Hz (PAL format), or 480p 60 Hz (NTSC).

It is essentially a wireless extension of all TV channels, as well as other media content present in the PC or the net, that makes it possible to view IPTV, downloaded content, or broadcast channels on the TV. YouTube™, for example, can be streamed on AppleTV.

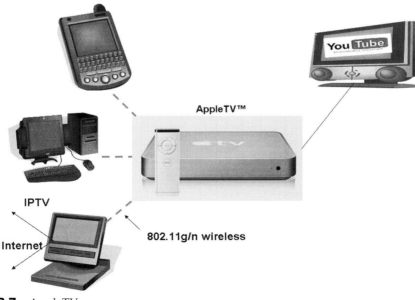

FIGURE 2-7 AppleTV

2.2.7 Long-Distance WiFi

WiFi is quite correctly recognized as a short-distance hotspot technology because of the sharp degradation of signal quality, particularly that caused by the echoes and NLOS conditions common in indoor operating environments. However, where clear line of sight is available, it is possible to extend the range of received signals, particularly if antennas are used, which can provide some directional gain. Such point-to-point links using wireless LAN technologies have been, in fact, fairly common in providing connectivity in unlicensed bands with quick set-up times.

The effective isotropic radiated power (EIRP), E, is given by:

$$E = P * AT$$

And the received power by:

$$R = E * A_R * P_L$$

where P = transmitted power, P_L = Path Loss, and A_T and A_R are the transmitting and receiving antenna gains respectively. In dB terms:

$$E(dBm) = P(dBm) + A_T(dB)$$

A parabolic antenna, for example, having a gain of 24 dBi at each end can boost the link margins by up to 48 dB. An omni-directional rod antenna (e.g., from Radiolabs) can provide a gain of 8 dBi.

FREE SPACE PATH LOSS

The path loss is easily calculated by Friis formula:

$$PL = 92.45 + 20 \log F + 20 \log D$$

where F is frequency in GHz and D is the distance in Km.
The formula gives the following results for 2.45 GHz:

Distance	Path Loss
1 Km	100 dB
3 Km	110 dB
5 Km	114 dB
10 Km	120 dB

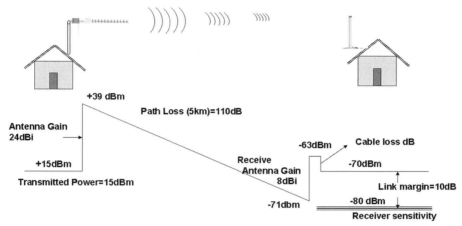

FIGURE 2-8 Typical link analysis of a wireless link

There are limitations on the effective isotropic radiated power in most countries in urban environments that limit the distances over which the links can be established. (In Europe, the limit is +20 dBm.) The typical power of a WiFi transmitter is 330 mW or 15 dBm. The receiver is also important in long-distance WiFi links. The typical receiver sensitivity is −75 to −85 dBm. The link distance can be estimated by keeping a link margin of 6 dB to 10 dB. In rural areas where the transmitted powers can be 30 dBm (1 watt) with parabolic antennas, it is possible to have links ranging from 5 to 10 Kms. Over greater distances, factors such as interference also become significant apart from path loss.

$$Link\ Margin(dB) = EIRP(dBm) - PL(dB) + A_R(dB) \\ + Receiver\ Sensitivity(dBm)$$

The second obstacle to establishing long-distance links is the access contention issue. Where long distances are involved, the standard protocols are inadequate to prevent simultaneous transmissions or sustain reasonable data rates because of the RTS/CTS mechanism. Many proprietary variations have been made to the access protocols, which provide an orderly way to access the wireless medium specifically for long-distance links. The handshaking and collision detection requirements are eliminated with an orderly transmission mechanism leading to higher rates of data transfer. Intel has recently demonstrated software operating on laptops which makes this possible.

The 802.11a-2007 standards also add 5 MHz and 10 MHz OFDM modes to the standard. In order to reduce the intersymbol interference, the guard time (800 ns) is quadrupled to 3.2 μs by clocking at one-fourth rate. This gives additional protection against intersymbol interference.

2.2.8 Wireless Mesh Technologies

The limitations of the WiFi networks to span long distances in the absence of clear LOS had led to some vendors developing networks with nodes that could operate in a mesh configuration. The nodes have transmitters with multiple radios and are designed to be self-configuring. In this type of network configuration, the objective is that every node should be able to see one or more other nodes, all of which work in a mesh configuration. The links to the internet are provided by one or two nodes in a mesh. Mesh networks, because of their self-configuring nature, are also self-healing in case any one node stops operation for any reason, as an alternative path can be established via alternative nodes. For this reason, it is also robust against interference happening erratically in different areas, a common feature in unlicensed and even licensed bands. A mesh network also effectively works around uneven terrain and LOS obstacles that would otherwise make link establishment between two points impractical. There are many examples of cities or communities that have been wired with mesh networks provided by companies such as Tropos® networks or Strix® wireless.

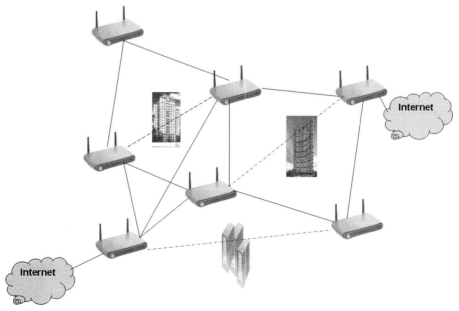

FIGURE 2-9   A wireless mesh network

Because of the definite advantages of a mesh technology, the IEEE 802.11s task group has been working on the "Mesh WiFi standards" finalization as an initiative from industry leaders including Intel. Today most of the mesh networks use proprietary protocols, which may not directly interface with existing hotspots based on 802.11a, b, or g standards. The objective is to have a mesh technology with backward compatibility and capability to connect to hundreds of millions of clients (WiFi receiving devices) that exist today. For this purpose, the enhancements in 802.11 focus on the MAC layer without disturbing the physical layer as in 802.11a, b, g, or n standards.

2.3 BROADBAND METROPOLITAN AREA NETWORKS

As we have seen, the wireless LAN technologies are based on the use of CSMA/CA where each remote station needs to hear and make sure that there are no transmissions before commencing its own transmission after a randomly generated delay. Further it can only transmit after it receives a positive acknowledgment of its request to transmit. These factors mean the wireless radios can at best provide only around half the data rates as those that would be possible in an equivalent bandwidth in a transmission without contention with other devices. Further, the range of wireless LANs is generally limited to around 30 m for an indoor environment and around 100 m for outdoor coverage with line of sight. The sustainable data rates also decline sharply with distance as error rates and retransmissions rise.

At the same time, there is a distinct area of requirement for wide area connectivity where the following features are important:

1. IP-based core network with end-to-end IP connectivity with wireless extensions being an integral part of the IP network architecture.
2. Support of high-burst bit rates typical in a LAN environment (say 20 Mbps to 100 Mbps).
3. QoS parameters to configure circuit emulation or real-time polling services to support voice and MPEG video type of services in addition to best-effort services.
4. Provide support for power saving, mobility, and handover for use in nomadic or mobile environments.
5. Use universal client devices (or customer premises equipment, CPEs) such as those for WiFi (802.11b/g), which are widely deployed and can enable reception in all devices universally.
6. Provide Quality of Service (QoS)-based usage.

7. Provide security of access and content, essential in a wireless city-wide or rural environment.
8. Be able to use different frequency bands and channel bandwidths, licensed and unlicensed, which may be available to different operators.

Because metropolitan area wireless networks could not use access technologies such as CSMA/CA because of the long distances and consequent delays involved, an access scheme was needed to meet these objectives. The quest for broadband wireless technologies was addressed by the IEEE 802 committee, which laid the foundation of Wireless MANs later formalized under the WiMAX standards.

It is noteworthy that the 801.16 standards that were finalized by the IEEE were not meant to compete in any way with the WiFi, which are the standards for wireless LANs and will continue to be used in LANs, albeit with improving technologies such as OFDM and MIMO as in 802.11n. In fact, the wireless MAN standards serve to complement the "hotspots" offered by the WiFi technologies by taking wide area connectivity beyond such hotspots.

Before the advent of wireless MANs based on IEEE technologies, MANs on optical fibers or other physical media were quite common. Similarly MMDS distribution systems (mostly analog) have been used in the past in a line-of-sight environment to provide wireless extensions of the internet or cable TV. Broadband wireless MANs, on the other hand, needed an evolution of technology to meet the objectives of city-wide connectivity at high enough data rates to meet the objectives of real-time video, audio, and data services. This evolution was provided by the feasibility of practical implementations of OFDM systems with a large number of subcarriers, a technology made feasible by chipsets, which provide implementation of algorithms that are needed to generate and handle these subcarriers.

Fixed, Nomadic, and Mobile Access

Another aspect of the use of wireless services is mobility. At present, the wireless access networks represented by technologies of IEEE 802.11 do not provide for any mobility. ITU has recognized three types of wireless access (F.1399 recommendations).

- Fixed access: Wireless access application in which the location of the end-user termination and the network access point to be connected to the end user are fixed.

- Nomadic wireless access: Wireless access application in which the location of the end-user termination may be in different places but it must be stationary while in use.
- Mobile wireless access: Wireless access application in which the location of the end-user termination is mobile.

Mobile wireless access requires dealing with mobility, as well as hand-offs. In the absence of other wireless broadband services in the past, the demand has traditionally been met by using the data services provided by the cellular mobile networks such as GPRS or EDGE in GSM-based networks or data services available in CDMA2000 networks. The introduction of 3G technologies (both CDMA and GSM networks) have raised the data rates that can be used over the networks. 3G evolution technologies such as HSDPA for 3G-GSM-evolved networks and 1xEV-DO for CDMA2000-evolved networks are oriented toward providing data capabilities in a wide area and mobile environment. In a 5 MHz slot, HSDPA can provide peak downlink speeds of up to 14.4 Mbps while 1xEV-DO operating with a 1.25 MHz carrier can support link rates of up to 2.4 Mbps (1xEV-DO rev A).

3G cellular systems are certainly a medium for providing high-speed connectivity for a range of applications including voice, video, and multimedia, and the wide range of applications deployed are testimonies to their success. The 3G connectivity, however, comes at a price premium because of the limited spectrum and large number of users needing access for voice and data services.

2.3.1 IEEE 802.16

The Institution of Electrical and Electronics Engineers (IEEE) established a group in 1998 (termed 802.16) to look at the wide area broadband wireless access issues and to recommend air interfaces and modulation techniques. The group gave its first recommendation in June 2001 specifying the 802.16 standard. The recommended standard could be used in various frequency bands from 10 to 66 GHz; the transmission recommended was by using a single carrier with modulation ranging from QPSK to 64 QAM. Based on the modulation scheme selected and the bandwidth, the system was envisaged to support data rates from 32 Mbps to 134 Mbps. The multiplexing was based on time division multiplexing (TDM/TDMA). The air interface of 802.16 was accordingly designated as wireless MAN-SC with SC standing for single carrier. The single-carrier modulation used by the system was expected to be used in line-of-sight (LOS) environments with directional antennas at both ends to limit multipath propagation effects

TABLE 2-2

Migrating from LAN environment to MANs

Feature	Wireless Local Area Networks (802.11)	Wireless Metropolitan Area Networks (802.16)
Area of Operation	Area of operation is small (10–50 M).	Area of operation is much larger, can extend to 20 Kms or more.
Frequency of Operation	Due to local area of operation, unlicensed bands are used. 2.4 GHz and 5.6 Ghz (NII band) are common.	Due to large area of operation where many systems may be populated, licensed band use is more common.
		Licensed 2.3, licensed 3.5 and unlicensed 5 GHz bands are most common.
Bandwidths	Due to local area of operation large bandwidths are used (e.g., 20 MHz in 802.11b).	Bandwidths used depend on spectrum allocated. Channel bandwidths of 1.75 MHz, 3.5 MHz, 5 MHz, 6 MHz, 7 MHz, 14 MHz, 10 MHz, and 15 MHz are most common.
Access Contention	The access is based on CSMA/CA and is similar to Ethernet.	The access is based on defined protocols for TDD, FDD, and TDMA.
Quality of Service (QoS)	There is no defined QoS or guarantee against delays.	QoS is built in the MAC layer with predefined service classes and delay profiles. Scheduling mechanisms are implemented at the MAC layer to maintain QoS.
PHY Layer	WLANs have either a single carrier or a small number of subcarriers based OFDM (e.g., 64 point). NLOS performance at high bandwidths is limited.	MANs use predominantly OFDM with 256 point OFDM (extending to 2048 point in Mobile WiMAX). These are highly resilient against frequency selective fading and multiple path interference.
Resource Allocation to Users	The users contend for available spectrum. A single high-bandwidth user can reduce availability to others significantly.	Users are allocated resources by the base station based on TDMA or OFDMA schemes.
Modulation Schemes	Modulation schemes are fixed, e.g., direct sequence spread spectrum (DSSS) or complementary code keying (CCK)	Modulation schemes can be adaptive based on a per user and per frame basis.

which would otherwise cause high intersymbol interference. The channel widths proposed in 802.16 were 20 MHz, 25 MHz, and 28 MHz.

The specification of the 802.16 was not limited to the specification of the physical layer (PHY), as has been described above, but included the specifications of the MAC layer, which provides the TDD and FDD functions.

Even though the IEEE 802.16 standard in its original form was not used widely, it laid the foundation for wireless MANs and the IEEE 802.16 committee became the focal point of all developments involving broadband wireless access.

2.3.2 IEEE 802.16a

There was a recognition that it was essential to target the use of Wireless MANs to NLOS environments including its use within buildings. The frequencies selected were in the 2 to 11 GHz band so as to make NLOS operations feasible. It was also considered essential that the feature set of modulation and multiple access schemes should be limited to predefined combinations so as to ensure that the receivers could be designed around a common standard with full interoperability.

OFDM was introduced as one of the transmission schemes (along with single carrier as in 802.16) to address the NLOS issues. OFDM, by virtue of its multiple subcarriers, assigns only a low bit rate to be carried by a single carrier thereby increasing its symbol time. The carriers are thus not severely impacted as multipath delays still cause the reflected signals to fall with the symbol duration. More details of OFDM technologies are provided later in the book.

The IEEE 802.16a standard was published on April 1, 2003, and was based on use of OFDMA wherein individual subcarriers (or groups) were assigned to different users for the uplink path. The standard also envisaged the use of transmit diversity using the Alamouti Space time code.

PHY Layer in 802.16a

The model of physical layers (PHY) selected in 802.11a included three variants:

1. A single-carrier physical layer
2. A 256-subcarrier OFDM PHY
3. A 2048-subcarrier OFDM PHY

Even though three PHY layers are possible as per the standards, for interoperability considerations it was considered desirable that only the 256-subcarrier OFDM PHY be used.

Other features that were adopted in the PHY were "flexible channel widths" and "dynamic frequency selection." The PHY also included forward error correction (FEC) concatenated with the Reel Solomon (RS) convolution coding for robust performance in NLOS environments.

MAC Layer in 802.16a

The MAC layer in 802.16a is designed to provide a guaranteed QoS through well-defined QoS classes, as well as provide error-free data to the upper layers. It is also designed to support a large number of users through access protocols to allocate bandwidths to users. QoS classes, such as T1/E1 emulation, guaranteed delay, etc., are possible on a request/grant basis.

The MAC layer of 802.16a supports slotted TDMA protocol on the uplink and TDM on the downlink. The allocation of slots to be used is given by the base station, and the topology is a point-to-multipoint topology. OFDMA was also a protocol supported in 802.16a as a multiple access protocol on the uplink.

The following are the key features of the 802.16a standard:

- Recommended frequency range 2 to 11 GHz.
- Omni-directional antennas.
- NLOS usage and usage in indoor areas.
- OFDM and OFDMA modulation for downlink and uplink transmissions.

IEEE 802.16d Project

In 2003, the IEEE 802 committee started a project entitled 802.16d with an objective of harmonizing the European Telecommunications Standards Institute (ETSI) HiperMAN with the IEEE wireless MAN standards. The report of this group, which became available in 2004, set the foundation of fixed wireless MANs or ETSI HiperMAN as they are used today. In order to stimulate developments, the standards were frozen and institutionalized under the IEEE 802.16-2004. Further initiatives in promoting the use of a predefined, limited set of profiles to promote wider usage go to the credit of the WiMAX Forum.

2.3.3 Fixed WiMAX IEEE 802.16-2004

The IEEE 802.16 group served to establish the basis of MANs and validated the technologies in many implementations, some with proprietary variations. The MANs could be used in both the licensed and unlicensed bands and support NLOS operations using OFDM technologies. High-bit rates of up to 75 Mbps could be achieved depending on the distance and the urban or rural environment. The IEEE 802.16d standards were frozen after modifications under the auspices of the WiMAX Forum and were named as "IEEE 802.16-2004 Fixed WiMAX" standards.

IEEE 802.16 STANDARDS

Frequency Band: 2–11 GHz
Channel Bandwidths: 1.25 MHz, 1.75 MHz, 3 MHz, 5 MHz, 7 MHz, 8.75 MHz (WiBro), 10 MHz, 14 MHZ and 15 MHz
OFDM Subcarriers: 256 or 2048
Multiplexing Schemes: TDM/TDMA and Burst TDM
Modulation Schemes: QPSK,16 QAM, or 64 QAM (adaptive)
Duplexing Schemes: TDD and FDD

The IEEE 802.16 physical layer (PHY) provides the following options:

- Wireless MAN-SCa is a single-carrier option and is intended for use in LOS environments.
- Wireless MAN-OFDM with 256 subcarriers, which is mandatory in the unlicensed bands. This mode features TDM in the downlink direction and TDMA in the uplink direction.
- Wireless MAN-OFDMA with 2048 carriers. This mode provides OFDMA access by separating the users using FDD in the uplink direction in addition to TDMA.

2.3.4 WiMAX Forum Certification Profiles

In the meantime, the WiMAX Forum (established in 2001) wanted to have a common standard for access profiles to facilitate interoperability and make the use of broadband wireless access universal across a large series of devices. For this reason, it initiated a certification program in 2005 to freeze the many permutations of parameters that are possible, such as number of OFDM subcarriers, frequency, bandwidths, and modulation technologies. The objective of the certification program was to prescribe specific tests for both the PHY and the MAC layers to ensure:

- Conformance to the WiMAX Forum specifications.
- Interoperability testing to ensure that the equipment from multiple vendors is interoperable in the same network or application.

The WiMAX Forum selected certain "Initial Certification Profiles" by selecting a subset which could be implemented widely and tested for conformance to prescribed air interfaces and interoperability with

TABLE 2-3

Fixed WiMAX certification profiles

S.No	Bandwidth	Frequency	Technology	OFDM SC
1	3.5 MHz	3.4–3.6 GHz	FDD	256
2	3.5 MHz	3.4–3.6 GHz	TDD	256
3	7 MHz	3.4–3.6 GHz	TDD	256
4	7 MHz	3.4–3.6 GHz	FDD	256
5	10 MHz	5.725–5.850 GHz	TDD	256

multiple vendors. The initial certification profiles have considerable importance as these are likely to be available widely in implementations of WiMAX.

The WiMAX Forum has defined two system profiles:

- Fixed WiMAX (based on IEEE 802.16-2004)
- Mobile WiMAX (based on IEEE 802.16e-2005)

Fixed WiMAX Certification Profiles

Under the Fixed WiMAX system profile, five certification profiles had been announced until the end of 2007 as "Release 1" (see Table 2-3).

Release 1 of Fixed WiMAX Certification Profiles

Figure 2-10 demonstrates how the WiMAX Forum took a multidimensional approach to fix the parameters from among many values available under the IEEE 802.16 and created a "funnel" to fuel the growth of Fixed WiMAX services, rather than letting the vendors and users get lost in the maze of combinations available. The IEEE and the WiMAX Forum in the specifications, which were frozen for implementation in June 2004, selected the OFDM subcarrier size as 256 with QPSK, 16 QAM, and 64 QAM being the only options for modulation. Only the 3.5 and 5.8 GHz bands were considered for initial implementations. The bandwidths were specified in a range that would facilitate individual operators to set up systems as per their spectrum holdings. This set of parameters was specified as "Certification profile Release 1" for Fixed WiMAX, with the implication that further releases in the future would take care of other parameters that were permissible as per IEEE 802.16-2004 standards but not yet included in initial profiles. The certification has two aspects: compliance with specifications and actual interoperability tests.

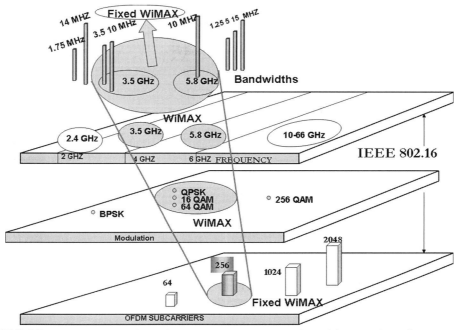

FIGURE 2-10   IEEE 802.16 and Fixed WiMAX parameter set selected for initial certification profiles

Certification Process: Waves

With the initial certification profiles having been issued as Release 1, the next job was to conduct interoperability tests between base station manufacturers, handset makers, chipsets makers, etc. and to certify the devices as interoperable. The interoperability for Fixed WiMAX (IEEE802.16-2004) and Mobile WiMAX was carried out by the WiMAX Forum® in "waves," with each wave representing certain features, which were certified in interoperability tests (called plugfests). Users of WiMAX devices then had complete clarity on the level of conformance based on the "release" and "wave" for which the conformance was cited. For Fixed WiMAX, the certification was designated to be in two waves:

- **Fixed WiMAX Release 1 Wave 1:** Basic functionality including air interface, network entry, dynamic services, and bandwidth allocation
- **Fixed WiMAX Release 1 Wave 2:** Optional modules: Quality of Service (QoS) and advanced encryption standard (AES).

In each release and profile, new products can be included provided there are at least three vendors who submit their products with this

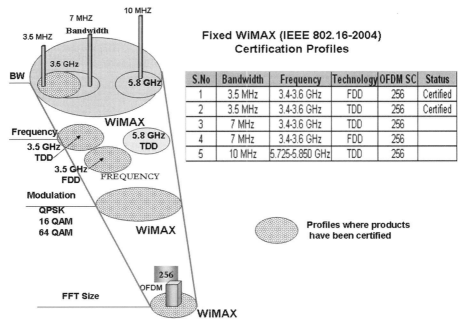

FIGURE 2-11   Fixed WiMAX (IEEE802.16-2004) certified products

profile. At the same time, all future releases are expected to be compatible with the previous releases. For example, Release 2 for Wave 1 will be compatible with Release 1 of Wave 1 and Wave 2. The certification of Wave 1 has been completed for Fixed WiMAX with over 25 products having been certified by early 2007.

As may be seen from Figure 2-11, for Fixed WiMAX bandwidths of 3.5 MHz and 7 MHz in the 3.5 GHz band, and 10 MHz in the 5.8 MHz band, are the only ones selected for initial certification by the WiMAX Forum. The frequency bands selected for certification are the 3.5 GHz and 5.8 GHz bands. The band of 3.5 GHz is the preferred band for Fixed WiMAX deployments as per the CEPT/CRC recommendation 13-04. The above selection of certification profiles is based on harmonization with ETSI also (where these are termed as ETSI HiperMAN) for WiMAX deployments in Europe. The frequency 5.8 GHz falling in the unlicensed band is available in some countries only and is subject to EIRP restrictions.

The selection of 256-point OFDM as being the sole subcarrier profile for Fixed WiMAX indicates the desire to standardize the OFDM chipsets and inter-vendor working. The frequency bands selected and the bandwidths of 3.5 and 7 MHz for 3.5 GHz, and 10 MHz for 5.8 GHz operation are consistent with assignments in many countries (e.g., 7 MHz was used for analog MMDS systems for one TV channel).

Future profiles likely to be open for certification in the next round will include the 2.5–2.69 GHz band and bandwidths of 5 MHz and 5.5 MHZ.

2.3.5 Quality of Service in Fixed WiMAX

The WiMAX protocol design is based on a connection-oriented approach and each connection is identified with a connection identifier (CID). The identification of each connection together with its service flow requirements provides the MAC layer with the basic QoS, which needs to be maintained for a specific connection.

Applications that run over IP networks can be of different types with widely varying requirements. File transfer applications are insensitive to delays in contrast to VoIP calls where the sensitivity of time delays is the highest. Similarly, services like video have the requirements of the delivery of a certain number of frames per second. The connection must therefore provide a sustained guaranteed throughput. In real-time transactions, the packet lengths may be small but these need to be delivered without any errors and minimum delay.

We have seen the service classes defined in asynchronous transmission mode (ATM), which undoubtedly led to its success as an effective transmission protocol. ATM defines the following service classes:

- Constant bit rate services (CBR): The concept of constant bit rate services over an underlying IP connection was designed to achieve the capabilities of TDM-type networks, which provide switched voice and data services such as 64 Kbps voice. The CBR class of service is designed for traffic with low bit rates, which are highly sensitive to delays.
- Variable bit rate services (VBR) are designed to interface with applications, such as compressed video, which provide bit rates that vary from frame to frame. In order to address real-time video or audio, the services are further classified as real-time-VBR services (RT-VBR) and non-real-time-VBR services (NRT-VBR).
- Best effort services, where there are no guarantees of delay or throughput, which may depend upon the overall traffic on the links at a particular time.

In order to effectively address various applications, Fixed WiMAX has defined four scheduling services, each with its own characteristics of data transfer and designed to fit one or specific applications. The QoS classes are used by the MAC layer data scheduler to manage the data flows over the connection. The following are the scheduling services defined in WiMAX:

1. **Unsolicited grant service (UGS)** is designed to parallel the CBR services of the ATM. The UGS service is associated with very stringent scheduling and control for throughput, delay, and jitter of the connections associated with UGS. The UGS is designed to support TDM emulation such as T1/E1 emulation.
2. **Real-time polling service (rtPS)** is designed to parallel the real-time VBR services of ATM. rtPS provides guarantees on throughput and delays (latency) but with a larger tolerance margin as suitable for video services characterized by buffered frame delivery. The service class is meant to be used for MPEG-2 or MPEG-4 video, where the support of fixed frame rates but variable bit rates are the normal characteristics.
3. **Non-real-time polling service (nrtPS)** is designed for applications that are not real-time such as e-mail and file transfer. The nrtPS provides fixed throughputs but without any guaranteed latencies. These are similar to the non-real-time variable rate services of ATM (NRT-VBR).
4. **Best effort (BE)** services, as the name suggests, provide no guarantees on throughput or latency. The service flow parameters in this case provide for maximum sustained bit rate and request/retransmission policy.

Each of the scheduling services defined above is characterized by a QoS "parameter set," which includes maximum latency, maximum jitter, maximum sustained rate (MSR), minimum reserved rate (MRR), and priority.

The QoS parameters are maintained by the services flow requirements established at the MAC layer, ARQ mechanism, as well as the PHY layer with its resource assignment (subchannels assigned) and different physical-layer parameters, such as adaptive modulation. Service flows are applicable to both uplink and downlink direction and are carried by a 32-bit service flow identifier (SFID), which is associated with a 16-bit connection identifier.

While the QoS requirements are set in 802.16, it does not provide any guidelines as to how such QoS requirements should be provided. Practical WiMAX systems implement QoS by maintaining per service flow queuing, per service flow behavior monitoring and assigning various levels of priority.

2.4 PERFORMANCE COMPARISON OF WiMAX AND WiFi SYSTEMS

While WiMAX and WiFi systems are designed for entirely different environments, the discussion on the QoS for WiMAX brings out the major differences in performance of applications when using the two different media.

The WLAN systems (802.11x) are intended for communications over short distances. This is reflected in the symbol times and guard times for these systems. For example, in 802.11a, the symbol duration is $3.2\,\mu s$ and the guard interval is $0.8\,\mu s$. These values tailor well with the indoor environment and short delays. On the other hand, in Fixed WiMAX the same are $64\,\mu s$ symbol time and $8\,\mu s$ guard band. This gives the WiMAX system the capability to operate over large distances and still be able to manage the reflected signals within the guard band so that it does not interfere with the next symbol.

As we have seen in the case of broadband wireless systems represented by 802.11x (WiFi, WLAN), the access to the medium is always based on contention and collision avoidance. This requires each packet to seek access to the wireless medium and can be a serious problem for traffic based on short packets such as VoIP or voice. The requirements of different classes of traffic are well addressed in WiMAX as it allocates the resources (e.g., subchannels) based on the QoS. The WLAN is well-suited for enterprise traffic comprising of data, particularly when it is relatively insensitive to delays or jitter.

2.5 IEEE 802.16E MOBILE WiMAX

As the products for Fixed WiMAX (IEEE 802.16d-2004) were getting ready for certification after the freezing of the certification profiles in 2004, there was considerable interest in technologies that could support nomadic or mobile environments.

The following types of mobile environments were considered:

- Nomadic: Where the subscriber station may periodically connect from different points in the network and may involve different base stations. Handover support for a live connection is not required in this case.
- Portable: The subscriber station is a portable device, and handover support is required as it moves across base stations.

- Simple mobility: This is a mode expected to support mobile stations with speeds up to 60 kmph and a hard handover with possible brief interruption
- Full mobility: Support of mobility at vehicular speeds (up to 120 kmph) and a seamless handover.

The IEEE completed the specifications of the Mobile WiMAX through its release of IEEE 802.16e specifications in December of 2005. The WiMAX Forum also finalized the certification profiles that were used to certify the initial products.

2.5.1 Challenges of the Mobile Wireless Environment

The mobile environment presents many challenges, which need to be addressed in any technology that enables mobility. The following are the typical requirements in a mobile environment:

- Signals received at mobile devices can vary greatly over short distances and can contain severe errors. Hence the protocols need to be robust enough to deal with the transmission conditions. In the case of Mobile WiMAX, this is dealt with by keeping the OFDM/OFDMA mode of transmission with a scalable physical layer and a maximum FFT size of 2048. The large number of carriers reduce the data carried per carrier proportionately, thus increasing the symbol time and possibility of intersymbol interference. Mobile WiMAX also uses other technologies such as beamforming and MIMO to have spatial diversity, better link margins, and reduction of interference.
- Mobile devices are constrained by battery power and processing capabilities. Hence the physical layer design needs to keep in mind features for power saving. In particular, features such as a common TDM downlink frame for all active devices as used in Fixed WiMAX was changed to a TDMA mode with downlink bursts meant for individual mobile devices or device groups.
- In Fixed WiMAX, the subscriber devices are assigned a fixed time slot for uplink transmission, at which time they must transmit on all subcarriers (i.e., 200 data subcarriers in a 256 OFDM system) simultaneously. In Mobile WiMAX, the mobile device needs to transmit only on the assigned subcarriers, reducing the peak power requirements.
- The mobile devices by their very nature can move in and out of various areas which may be operating fixed services in unlicensed bands. The Mobile WiMAX has been specified only in specific licensed bands. The actual bands of allocation will be country-specific.

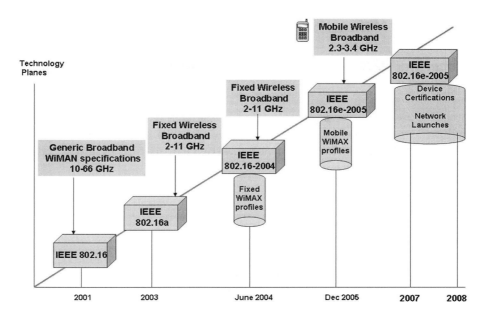

FIGURE 2-12 Technology rollout for wireless MAN services

Mobile WiMAX has been designed to cater to vehicular speeds of up to 120 km per hour. Hence the physical layer needs to deal with the Doppler shifts in frequency. Currently, Mobile WiMAX systems have been defined only for the 2.4 GHz and 3.4 GHz bands, leaving out the higher frequency bands above 3.8 GHz. Doppler shift in these bands and at the licensed frequencies is very small at vehicular speeds of up to 120 kmph. Even the effects of this Doppler shift can be overcome by being able to increase the guard band interval.

These varying requirements have been reflected in the Mobile WiMAX standards (IEEE 802.16e-2005). In fact, the industry has started veering around to the view that Mobile WiMAX as point-to-multipoint broadband wireless technology could be used for fixed, nomadic as well as mobile applications at vehicular speeds. In a sense, this means that it is not necessary to segregate fixed applications from mobile ones by using different technologies and profiles. This continues to be the current approach. However, it should be recognized that the frequency bands of operation are different for the Fixed and Mobile WiMAX technologies as are the profiles. Hence implementations would depend on the available spectral resources. Mobile WiMAX profiles, for example, are defined only for the frequency bands of 2.3 to 2.4, 2.5 to 2.7, and 3.3 to 3.4 GHz, while Fixed WiMAX systems as per IEEE 802.16-2004 are possible in the 2 to 11 GHz frequency band.

2.5.2 Mobile WiMAX Technology

Mobile WiMAX is based on the use of OFDMA (orthogonal frequency division multiple access). OFDMA involves the assignment of subchannels in both the uplink and downlink direction to various subscribers as a multiple access arrangement. This is in contrast to having multiple transmissions only in the uplink direction in case of fixed WiMAX.

This method of allocation of subcarriers leads to an increase in range over which the subscriber stations (in the case of Mobile WiMAX, the mobile stations) can be connected. For example, in the downlink direction, lower power is transmitted for the stations that are close to the base and correspondingly higher power is available for the stations that are located far from base station. This helps increase the range of coverage. Similarly in the uplink direction, in the case of Fixed WiMAX, each subscriber station transmits on all the subcarriers simultaneously though for a short allotted time). In the case of OFDMA, the uplink carriers (N) are divided among M different groups. Each of the groups is thus assigned N/M OFDM carriers. If B is the channel bandwidth occupied by N OFDM carriers, the bandwidth used by each group is only 1/M of the total bandwidth. This is equivalent to an S/N increase of 10 log(M). The increase of S/N translates to an equivalent increase in the range of each station.

The OFDMA by virtue of division of carriers also potentially protects the transmissions from intersymbol interference. For example, in a 10 MHz bandwidth with 35 subchannels, the bandwidth available to each subchannel is only 10/35 = 3.2 MHz versus 10 MHz if all subcarriers are used.

2.5.3 Mobile WiMAX Certification Profiles—Release 1

The IEEE 802.16e-2005 had prescribed the frequency band of 2 to 6 GHz for Mobile WiMAX and various options for bandwidths as well as multiplexing. The WiMAX Forum has, however, selected a subset of these parameters for mobile WiMAX certification profiles in Release 1 (Figure 2-13).

Mobile WiMAX uses 512 OFDM carriers for a bandwidth of 5 MHz and 1024 subcarriers for bandwidths of 7 and 10 MHz. This is in contrast to Fixed WiMAX where the number of carriers is 256 (fixed). For initial certification profiles, the WiMAX Forum has selected an FFT size of 512 carriers and a guard band of 1/8. The frame size selected is 5 ms.

The WiMAX Forum has assigned codes to certification profiles which are given in Table 2-4.

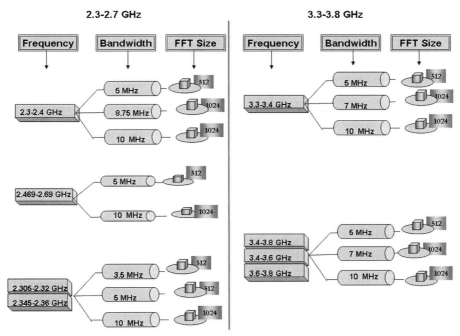

FIGURE 2-13   Release 1 certification profiles in Mobile WiMAX

IEEE 802.16e-2005 STANDARDS

Frequency Band: 2–6 GHz
Channel Bandwidths: 1.75 MHz, 3.5 MHz, 5 MHz, 7 MHz, 8.75 MHz (WiBro), 10 MHz and 15 MHZ
OFDM Subcarriers: 128, 256, 1024, or 2048
Multiplexing Schemes: TDM/TDMA and OFDMA
Modulation Schemes: QPSK, 16 QAM or 64 QAM (adaptive)
Duplexing Schemes: TDD and FDD

Following are the Mobile WiMAX certification profiles together with the identity assigned to each profile.

Waves in Mobile WiMAX Certification
The certification of WiMAX products and interoperability testing (known as plugfests) are handled by the certification working group under the WiMAX Forum. The forum has declared the profiles selected

TABLE 2-4

Mobile WiMAX certification profiles

Profile ID	Certification profile
1A	2.3–2.4 GHz, 8.75 MHz, TDD
1B	2.3–2.4 GHz, 5/10 MHz, TDD
2B	2.305–2.320 GHz, 2.345–2.360 GHz, TDD
3A	2.496–2.690 GHz, 5/10 MHz, TDD
4B	3.3–3.4 GHz, 7 MHz, TDD (subject to regulatory clearances)
5AL	3.4–3.6 GHz, 5 MHz, TDD
5BL	3.4–3.6 GHZ, 7 MHz, TDD

as certification profiles as well as the time frame for the testing of these profiles in different waves.

- Wave 1 air protocol interoperability.
- Wave 2 outdoor CPEs, MIMO, quality of service, and security features.
- Wave 3 indoor CPEs, PC cards, nomadic services (handoffs).
- Wave 4 full mobility.

In order to speed up the process of use of Mobile WiMAX in NLOS environments and using indoor CPEs, the WiMAX Forum has accelerated the inclusion of MIMO in Wave 2 certifications and the 3A profile (2.496–2.690 GHz) has also been directly introduced as Wave 2. This was no doubt influenced by the need for early introduction of the Mobile WiMAX standards with features such as MIMO and advanced antenna systems and the need for systems entering the market to conform to the wave 2 certification profiles. Wave 2 requires the devices to support two antennas so that the advantages of MIMO and beamforming can be derived.

Some of the WiMAX equipment manufacturers, as well as operators, are planning to develop and deploy the Wave 2 products only in view of the better efficiencies in utilization of available spectrum. For example, many PC cards for Mobile WiMAX are today available as MIMO Wave 2 compliant, but awaiting certification, which indicates to the users the features that the device is expected to support. In the WiMAX certification process a minimum of three vendors are required for certification testing. While many tests are done in quarterly plugfests, these do not replace the formal approval process.

3

INTRODUCTION TO MOBILE MULTIMEDIA

One ought, every day at least, to hear a little song, read a good poem, see a fine picture, and if it were possible, to speak a few reasonable words.

—Johann Wolfgang Von Goethe

The advent of new devices such as iPods™ with 80 GB of capacity, Sansa™, and mobile phones with mega pixel cameras and MMS capabilities makes it unmistakable that the media has now gone truly mobile. It is created on devices that are mobile, transmitted on mobile medium, and viewed on sites accessible from mobile devices such as iTunes or YouTube.

For a traditional broadcaster looking at new markets, it presents a new opportunity as well as a challenge. How to address new mobile devices? What are the media formats best suited for this purpose? What type of broadcasting works well with devices that have only a four-inch screen but a huge storage? Is "one way" encrypted broadcasting with no content protection the best way to deliver multimedia? Or is it better to operate as a "media store," supplying content with digital rights management (DRM) for viewing? How to directly integrate collaborative web applications and mobile commerce (sometimes referred to as Web 2.0 and Mobile 2.0) with broadcasting?

Fortunately WiMAX as a medium for interactive and mobile broadcasting presents excellent approaches to address the new markets. The new mobile ecosystem is now not only limited to cellular mobile networks but is a new space created by the fusion of technologies from many once-diverse worlds.

Till very recently, the mobile ecosystem consisted almost entirely of devices that became mobile by virtue of the cellular networks. These

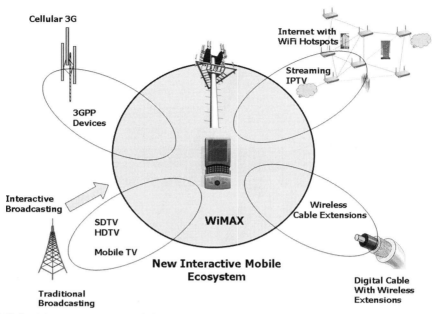

FIGURE 3-1 New interactive mobile ecosystem

networks, designed primarily to handle voice, later evolved to handle high-speed data using 3G networks. The procedure for call connection, file formats, and encoder types have been fully defined for these devices by the third-generation partnership projects (3GPP and 3GPP2). For these reasons, these devices are sometimes referred to as 3GPP devices.

At the same time the internet, which still remains the largest interconnected network in the world, has been acquiring wireless extensions, initially by virtue of 802.11x networks (WiFi) and now with 802.16x (wireless MANs) and WiMAX networks. In the case of WiFi, the WiFi Alliance has ensured interoperability and roaming among the devices and networks. Most mobile devices today contain a WiFi interface. The IP world has also been characterized by the use of transmission of multimedia using IPTV or media streaming.

The cable and broadcasting worlds, which have been competing as well as complementing each other, have traditionally been comprised of transmission of standard-definition TV (SDTV) and high-definition TV (HDTV). Their entry in the mobile world has been quite recent and is based on the use of mobile TV technologies such as DVB-H, DMB, or MediaFLO. We will be reviewing these technologies as well in the later chapters. For the present, it would suffice to say that the mobile TV technologies have aligned themselves closely to the 3GPP for media formats, but this is now changing as these gear up to address stand-alone devices as well.

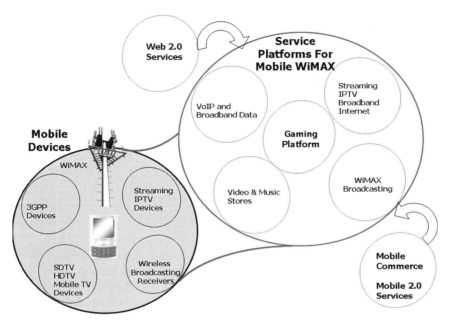

FIGURE 3-2 Service platforms for Mobile WiMAX

3.1 MOBILE WiMAX: THE NEW MOBILE ECOSYSTEM

WiMAX networks now present a new mobile ecosystem. With WiMAX having been defined only up to the MAC layer, it represents a wireless extension to any of the networks, with the appropriate convergence sublayer. The new mobile space created by Mobile WiMAX can therefore address not only the existing 3GPP devices (that is, mobile phones) but also a range of new devices that build on any of the many technologies of broadcasting, cable TV, internet, IPTV, and gaming by providing them with a wireless dimension.

A number of services can use the platform provided by Mobile WiMAX to provide multicast streaming IPTV, VoIP and broadband data, media downloads, and gaming amongst others.

3.2 WHAT IS MOBILE MULTIMEDIA?

When mobile devices began to be targeted for the delivery of multimedia (video, music, pictures, animations, flash movies, and voice), a number of issues needed to be settled. These include:

- Technologies used for multimedia in the mobile domain
- File formats used for multimedia
- Transport protocols to be used on mobile networks
- Procedures for call set-up, release, and transfer of multimedia content

Many of these characteristics depend on the mobile devices themselves. How large are the screen sizes? What are the capabilities they possess to handle multimedia files, e.g., in MPEG-2, MPEG-4, or Windows Media? Can they handle multiple services at one time?

In this chapter, we will discuss some of these characteristics that set mobile devices apart from fixed desktop devices or home TVs. The mobile world is today dominated by mobile networks using the GSM, CDMA, or 3G technologies. Devices that can handle multimedia on these networks number in the hundreds of millions. Hence many of the media formats that exist in industry today are those defined by the 3GPP or 3GPP2. We will be discussing these media formats with the understanding that the Mobile WiMAX networks are not really bound by these formats.

3.2.1 Encoding for Audio and Video

Mobile devices are characterized by small screens, limited processing power, and limited memory.* This implies that complex encoding and decoding tasks for video and pictures, graphics, and animations, etc. need to be defined as subsets of the full-resolution, full-powered desktop applications.

The implication of the limited capabilities of mobile devices has been in the definition of encoding standards and encoder profiles (such as MPEG-4 simple profile level 1) to ensure that these can be safely used in a wide range of devices. Specific formats for video, voice, and audio encoding have been prescribed for use in GSM and 3G (UMTS or CDMA) networks.

3.2.2 Screen Sizes, Frame Rates, and Resolutions

Mobile devices are characterized by the use of small screen sizes, e.g., CIF (352×288), QVGA (320×240), or QCIF (176×144). These correspondingly have a lower resolution than the SDTV or a desktop (SVGA or XGA). The frame rates of video offered on mobile devices may be at the prescribed NTSC or PAL rate (30 or 25 frames per second, respectively) or may be at lower rates (e.g., 15 frames per second). The service providers make a selection of the screen sizes and frame rates over which certain services (e.g., Mobile TV) may be offered.

---

* It should be recognized that the capabilities of mobile devices have been growing exponentially. With advanced graphics and multimedia processors, 2GB micro SD cards, 8M pixel cameras, and full VGA resolution screens already available, it is expected that there will be essentially no major limitations on these devices except power consumption in the next two years.

3.2.3 File Formats

A number of file formats for video, music, and voice are prevalent in the industry.*

These can range from completely uncompressed video and audio to compressed and commonly used formats such as MPEG-4 video and MP3 or AAC audio. The file formats are also standardized by bodies such as 3GPP and 3GPP2, in order that the files can be delivered and played by universally used players.

When video is used in a broadcast environment, it is not sufficient to merely have raw or encoded data. It needs to be associated with metadata that describes the file and media properties. It is common to use ISO-based file format containers for storage and transmission of multimedia information. 3GPP files, for example, are based on an ISO file container format.

3.2.4 Transmission Media

The transmission of content to mobile devices implies the use of wireless media. The media can be a cellular network such as GSM, GPRS, CDMA-1X, CDMA-2000, or 3G evolutions, such as EV-DO and HSPA. Wireless is a very challenging environment for the delivery of multimedia. This is because the signal strengths and, consequently, the error rates can vary sharply as the user moves in the coverage area. The protocols used are expected to recover the data to deliver error-free files. However, for real-time services, such as video or music streaming, the maintenance of a basic transmission rate is critical. There are various mechanisms to deal with sustained rates of data transfer such as buffering, service flows in WiMAX, and automatic reassignment of resources. The operators need to make a selection of these parameters for service planning.

3.2.5 Service Definitions and Transfer Protocols

The transfer of multimedia information can involve a number of steps. These can include setting up a connection, selecting services (voice call, video call, browsing, etc), negotiation of parameters (e.g., data rates for streaming), and tearing down connections after successful data transfer. Some services may involve point-to-multipoint data transfer, such as a video conferencing service. The 3GPP, for example, defines certain predefined services such as MMS messaging, 64 Kbps

---

* For a comprehensive overview of digital multimedia refer to *Mobile TV: DVB-H DMB, 3G Systems and Rich Media Applications* by Amitabh Kumar published by Focal Press, Boston, 2007.

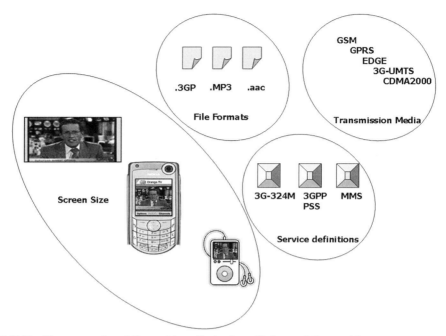

FIGURE 3-3   Elements of mobile multimedia in the cellular mobile world

circuit switched data call (3G-324M), packet switched streaming (3GPP-PSS), multimedia broadcast and multicast service (MBMS), etc. The services may be associated with specific transfer protocols such as Flute for file transfers.

To summarize, mobile multimedia has a number of elements:

- Multimedia files
- Handling graphics and animation
- Call set-up and release procedures to deliver multimedia
- Multimedia transfer protocols
- Multimedia players or receive end clients

3.3 MOBILE MEDIA IN 3GPP

3.3.1 3GPP Standardization Areas

3GPP
The 3GPP is a partnership project of a number of standards bodies, which are setting standards for third-generation cellular mobile services and long-term evolution technologies (LTE). 3GPP specifically refers to the third-generation partnership project of GSM-evolved 3G

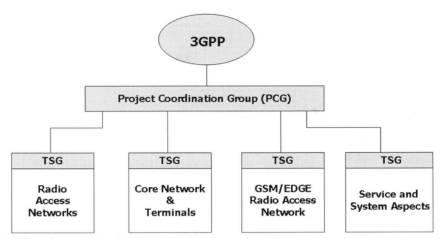

FIGURE 3-4 3GPP standardization areas

networks, i.e., 3G-UMTS. Evolution technologies such as HSDPA and HSUPA for higher-speed data transfer are a result of a coordinated effort by the 3GPP. The 3GPP releases include standards for encoding, decoding of audio, video graphics, and data, as well as call control procedures and cell phones and user devices.

The 3GPP operates via a project coordination group, which oversees the activities of four TSGs. Coordination with external organizations is the responsibility of the TSGs. To ensure compatibility and interoperability between broadband wireless access networks (802.16) and 3GPP systems, the WiMAX Forum has been accepted as an external organization with which the 3GPP TSGs are authorized to liaise.

3GPP2

The 3GPP2 partnership was created to provide specifications and an evolution path for technologies for the cellular networks based on the ANSI-41 (CDMA-1x RTT) and its evolutions. Its members included organizational partners such as the Telecommunications Industries Association (TIA) USA, ARIB and TTC Japan, TTA Korea, and CCSA China, among others.

Evolution to Packet-Switched Architecture

One of the major areas of standardization of both the partnership projects has been the migration from circuit-switched domains used in the GSM and ANSI-41 CDMA networks to packet-switched domains. In case of 3GPP the new architecture for migration to packet-switched domains is the IP multimedia system (IMS), while under the 3GPP2 it is envisioned under the multimedia domain (MMD).

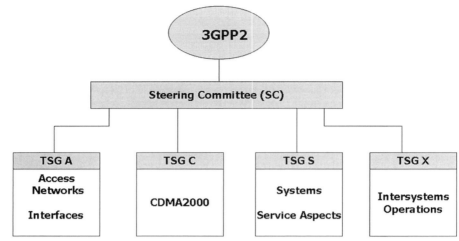

FIGURE 3-5   3GPP2 standardization structure

3.3.2 3GPP Mobile Media Formats

In the following sections, we will be reviewing progressive evolutions to the data transmission speeds and delivery mechanisms with new releases of the 3GPP. Instead of considering these releases in an abstract manner, it is also important to understand the forces that have been driving these changes.

The simplest way to demonstrate this is the use of megapixel cameras. A 2-Mp camera has a picture file size of approximately 6 MB with 24 bits per pixel. Transmission of such pictures via MMS became practical when HSDPA handsets were introduced in 2006 (e.g., by Cingular, now part of AT&T), which could provide a data rate of 1.8 Mbps. This made it possible to download a picture in less than 30 seconds using such a service. HSDPA was unveiled in 3GPP Release 5 and was a result of forecasting impending higher connectivity requirements.

Streaming video (MP4) or MP3 music as well as RSS feeds are some of the most commonly used services on cellular networks needing high-speed packet-based connectivity and support of streaming services. The 3GPP IP multimedia system (IMS) was unveiled in Release 5 of the 3GPP and the packet streaming services were defined in Release 6 of 3GPP. These have become the basis of packet IP connectivity of mobile devices and video on 3G and HSDPA networks. The new enhancements in 3GPP permit mobile blogging, video sharing (YouTube™), or picture sharing (Flickr™) types of services with portals, IP-based connectivity, and large file transfer capability.

The IP multimedia system (IMS), which was unveiled in Release 5 of the 3GPP, was destined to become one of the most important developments toward the migration to IP-based core networks. Today it provides the only widely implemented mechanism for fixed-mobile convergence by virtue of its core network and SIP-based call initiation and media gateways to all types of networks. We will be discussing the IMS system in detail as a core feature in networks in Chapter 13.

The mobile environment today requires users to be continuously connected to networks, even though there may be little activity. At the same time, on becoming active, the users expect the minimum latency in restarting the applications. With the increasing base of UMTS and HSDPA users, this has meant that mechanisms to keep thousands of users continuously connected per cell needed to evolve. This very feature, a result of lifestyle evolution, is being introduced in Release 7 of the 3GPP as continuous packet connectivity (CPC).

Large storage is now a common feature of all smartphones and mobile devices, demonstrated in no better manner than the iPhone™ or iPods™ with 80 GB of storage. Release 7 of the 3GPP provides for a new approach in dealing with multimedia and large files by providing for a high-speed protocol based on USB technology. The new enhancements permit the UICC to be considered as a large and secure storage, including use of flash memory technology, an OMA smartcard web server, and enabling remote file management technologies.

The following sections discuss the evolution of networks to handle multimedia capabilities of mobile devices.

3.3.3 3GPP Media Formats and WiMAX

Mobile media specifications as finalized by the third-generation partnership projects (3GPP and 3GPP2), though applicable only to the cellular networks, form an extremely important set of guidelines for all mobile devices in general. 3GPP defines the entire protocol stack up to the application level in order that the applications (such as MMS or Push to Talk) work in an identical manner across thousands of operators or service providers. The IEEE approach has been to define the 801.16 specifications only up to the MAC level with the specific objective that these can be integrated in various networks via the convergence layer. As evident from Figure 3-1, the Mobile WiMAX device ecosystem includes a range of devices including the 3GPP devices. In the initial years, the WiMAX-enabled cellphones will constitute a large share of the mobile devices used in WiMAX networks. Even mobile stations designed specifically for WiMAX will need to interwork with 3G networks while roaming. The 3GPP mobile media specifications are therefore important design elements for applications in WiMAX networks.

3.3.4 File Formats for Mobile Multimedia in 3GPP

What are the file formats for 3GPP? The third-generation partnership project (3GPP) for third-generation cellular telephony has defined a standard file format to contain audio/visual sequences that may be downloaded to cellular phones.

The 3GPP2 has also adapted the use of file formats that are similar. The files are based on the ISO file format and within the file, as with all files in the ISO family, there is an intrinsic file-type box, which identifies the specifications to which the file complies, and which players are permitted by the content author to play the file. This identification is through a four-letter parameter, called *brands*.

The media files are generated by the encoders and are based on MPEG-4 and H.263 coding standards for the initial releases of 3GPP. The files that are used in GSM, 2.5G, and 3G WCDMA networks are denoted by .3gp and are based on MPEG-4 video and AAC, AMR audio. The files used in CDMA and evolved networks CDMA-2000, CDMA-1x, and 3X are denoted by .3g2 and are also based on the same codecs, i.e., MPEG-4 for video and AAC, AMR for audio with additional support for QCELP.

MPEG-4 is an objects-based encoding standard and constitutes a layered structure with separation between the coding layers and the network abstraction layers, making it ideal for delivery over a variety of media. MPEG-4 also has a large number of profiles that can enable its application to either very low bit-rate applications, while at the same time maintaining the flexibility to go up to higher bit rates through enhancement layers, or to broadcast quality transmissions right up to high definition (HD). MPEG-4 is also ideally suited for handling of computer-generated and animation objects, such as synchronized graphics and text, face and body animation, and many other applications. The MPEG-4 Part 10 is also standardized as the ITU standard H.264 and fits into the MPEG-4 framework.

3GPP File Formats for Circuit-Switched 3G-324M Services

As the MPEG-4 has many profiles and levels, the 3GPP has standardized the following as the baseline specifications for use over 3G networks with 3G-324M encoders/decoders (see Table 3-1).

The standards in Table 3-1 were considered necessary to limit the complexity of the encoders and decoders used in mobile devices which could be used over circuit-switched 3G-324 M services. The MPEG-4 Simple Visual Profile Level 1 has support for H.263 baseline profile codec. The MPEG-4 Simple Visual Profile Level 1 has adequate error resilience for use on wireless networks while at the same time having low complexity. It also meets the need for low delay in multimedia

TABLE 3-1

3GPP file format for 3G-324M networks

Codec Feature	Specification
Video Codec	MPEG4 simple profile level 1, recommended support of MPEG-4 simple visual profile level 1 (ISO/IEC 14496-2)
Frame Rate	Up to 15 FPS
Resolution	176 × 144
Audio Coding	AMR coding and decoding is mandatory, G723.1 is recommended

communications. The encoding mechanism recommends the enabling of all error resilience tools in the simple visual profile.

Conversational calls using 3G-324M are largely based on the H.263 protocols. The 3GPP recommends the features and parameters that should be supported by such codecs, and such extensions are covered in the Mobile Extension Annex of the H.263.

The support for the MPEG-4/AVC (H.264) codec with full baseline profile has been recommended as optional in Release 6 of the 3GPP. Today the support of H.264 in many networks is quite common.

ISO File Formats

3GPP files (.3gp) are "structurally" based on the ISO file formats, which are the primary standards for MPEG-4-based files. The ISO/IEC formats have been standardized by the ISO Moving Picture Expert Group and have been earlier derived from Quick Time™ formats. The 3GPP file format described in Table 3-1 is a simpler version of the ISO file format (ISO-14496-1 media format) supporting only video in H.263 or MPEG-4 (visual simple profile) and audio in AMR or AAC-LC formats.

The .3gp and .3gp2 formats, both of which are based on the ISO file format, have structures to incorporate inclusion of non-ISO codecs such as H.263, AMR, AMR-WB (for 3GPP), and EVRC and QCELP (for 3GPP2).

The ISO File Container

The ISO file format essentially provides a "container" in which the media metadata and information is carried based on a universally accepted format (Figure 3-6). For this purpose, the ISO base media file format defines a *file type* box called *ftyp*. This field precedes any variable-length

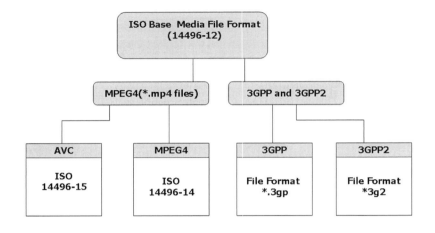

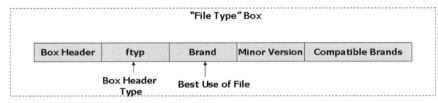

FIGURE 3-6   MPEG file format definitions in ISO

fields such as media data. The file type box also contains fields called "brand" and "compatible brands." The field "brand" describes the best use of the file while "compatible brands" gives a list of compatible formats, e.g., players where the playback may be possible. The values which can be used are defined by the 3GPP and 3GPP2 .

Brand
The field "brand" can be used to indicate the 3GPP release version, thus indicating to the receiver the file capabilities. In general, higher releases such as Release 7 will be compatible with the lower releases and these will fall in the "compatible brands field." An ISO-compatible file in 3GPP (Release 5 and beyond) would also have the value "isom" as a "compatible brand" to indicate compatibility of the file with the ISO base line format.

3GPP2 has its own specific values for these fields.

MPEG-4 Content in ISO Containers
MPEG-4 format (.mp4) (ISO 14496-14) allows multiplexing of multiple audio and video streams in one file (which can be delivered over any

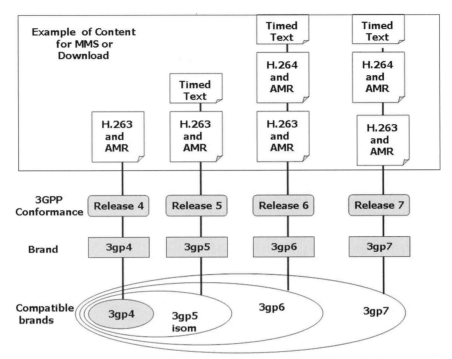

FIGURE 3-7   Examples of brand usage in 3GPP files for MMS and download

type of network using the Network Abstraction Layer). It also permits variable frame rates, subtitles, and still images.

The MPEG-4 file structure has two parts: Wrapper and Media.

Wrapper (Container)

The Wrapper or Container file supports:

- MPEG-4, H.263
- AAC and AMR audio
- Timed Text tracks

Media

The media consists of a hierarchy of atoms containing metadata and media data, and the tracks consist of a single independent media data stream. Each media stream should have its own hint track.

3.3.5 3GPP Releases, New Services, and Multiple Content Types

The 3GPP has been adding new features, higher data rates, IP-based multimedia system (IMS), provisions for broadcast and multicast services (MBMS), and accommodation for different media types in its successive releases beginning with the 3GPP release in 1999. The latest specification of media file formats is given in 3GPP TS 26.244 V7.0.0 (2006-06)—3GPP file format (3GP) (Release 7). We will be reviewing briefly the developments in the 3GPP releases as they relate to media formats and services on mobile networks.

The first release of the industry-coordinated specifications for the mobile networks was in 1999. Since then there have been progressive developments, which have been reflected in further releases and upgrades. The 3GPP release in 1999 resulted in the adoption of a Universal Terrestrial Radio Access (UTRA) and also standardized a new codec-narrowband AMR.

3GPP Release 4 (March 2001)

The 3GPP Release 4 marked the migration to IP-based infrastructure from the legacy circuit-switched services. It also introduced packet-switched streaming services, which had been common on the IP-based networks (e.g., the internet). The 3GPP Release 4 embraced an all-IP core network-based on IPv6. It provided for the following main features:

- **New Messaging Systems**: Provided for enhanced messaging systems including Rich Text Formatting (RTF) and still image and Multimedia Messaging (MMS).
- **Circuit-Switched Network Architecture**: The release in 1999 provided for bearer independent network architecture.
- **IP Streaming**: The release provided for a protocol stack which provided for streaming of real-time video over the network.
- **GERAN—GPRS/EDGE interface**: The release 4 provided for the EDGE/GPRS interface.

3GPP Release 5 (March 2002)

Reflecting the rapid pace of standardization in 3G systems, the 3GPP release in 2002 unveiled the IP-based Multimedia System (IMS) as the core of the 3G mobile networks. The entire network is based on IP, which is packet-based, and bearer services are derived from the IP-based network. It provides for conversational calls based on SIP (Session Initiation Protocol). 3GPP Release 5 for the first time introduced the concept of HSDPA (High-Speed Downlink Packet Access). It also provided for a wideband AMR (AMR WB) codec and end-to-end QoS. HSDPA is a major step toward the services such as Unicast Mobile TV on 3G networks.

The framework provided by the IMS of Release 5 sets the stage for end-to-end IP-based multimedia services breaking away from the circuit-switched architecture of the previous generations. It also

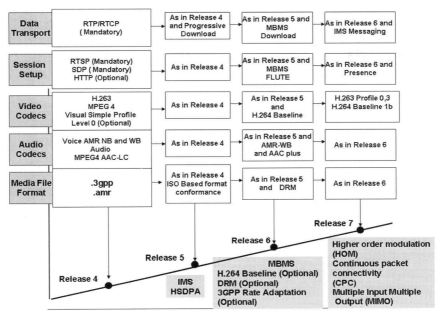

FIGURE 3-8   3 GPP releases for mobile multimedia

provides for an easier integration of instant messaging and real-time conversational services. The messaging enhancements include enhanced messaging and multimedia messaging.

It is important to note that the IMS is access-independent. Hence it can support IP-to-IP sessions over packet data GPRS/EDGE or 3G, packet data CDMA, IP wireless LANS 802.11 and 802.15, as well as wire-line IP networks. The IMS consists of session control, connection control, and application services framework. Security interfaces were also introduced in Release 5, which included the access security, access domain security, and lawful interception interface.

3GPP Release 6

A major feature of Release 6 was the introduction of the Multimedia Broadcast and Multicast Services (MBMS). The following were the major new features of Release 6 of 3GPP:

- Wide-band Codec: Release 6 introduced an enhancement of the AMR wide-band codec (AMR-WB+) for better sound quality and coding.
- Packet-Streaming Services (3GPP-PSS protocols).
- Wireless LAN to UMTS interworking, whereby a mobile subscriber can connect to a wireless LAN using the IP services via the W-LAN.
- Digital rights management.

- Push services for pushing of content to mobile devices (Flute).
- Multimedia Broadcast and Multicast Services (MBMS).

The 3GPP packet-streaming services, which were introduced in Release 6, also brought in new media types for streaming. New "brands" were introduced for the description of these services in the ISO basic media file formats in order that the content could be identified and directed to the appropriate players in receiving devices. Examples of new brands introduced are:

Streaming servers: 3gs6
Progressive download: 3gr6
MBMS: 3ge6

3GPP Release 7

HSDPA, which was a high-speed data service unveiled in the 3GPP-Release 5, has been very successfully deployed with over 150 commercial networks operational by 2007. 3GPP Release 7 (the work on which is almost complete in 2007) provides for further enhancements in the HSPA services (combination of HSDPA and HSUPA services) to HSPA+. Many of the enhancements in Release 7 are designed to provide better support for interactive services such as picture and video sharing. It also aims to improve the real-time conversational services by providing for advanced features for voice and video over IP. The enhancements include, among others:

- Higher-order modulations (HOM), e.g., 64 QAM vs. 16 QAM in Release 6
- Continuous packet connectivity (CPC)
- Multiple Input Multiple Output (MIMO)
- Evolved EDGE interfaces
- Enhanced receivers

The enhancements provided by Release 7 are backward compatible with previous releases (Rel-99/Rel-5/Rel-6).

The continuous packet connectivity feature is designed to increase the number of users who can be accommodated in a cell in active and inactive states. This is done by reducing the overheads for HSPA users and also introducing the concept of discontinuous uplink transmissions and downlink receptions (termed as DTX/DRX). A channel quality indicator has also been introduced (along the lines of WiMAX) for optimizing transmissions.

3.4 GRAPHICS IN A MOBILE ENVIRONMENT

Graphics is an important part of any multimedia content. We are quite familiar with vector graphics, which is preferred over "raster graphics." In raster graphics, images are represented as bitmaps leading to larger file sizes whereas in vector graphics, the images are represented by mathematical relations, which are computed prior to display. Consequently vector graphics is comprised of files, which are not only much smaller in size, but are also scalable to any screen size without loss of resolution.

The industry standard for vector graphics is the scalable vector graphics (SVG), which is a world wide web consortium (W3C) standard. In the mobile environment, a subset of the SVG called the SVG-Tiny (or SVG-T) has been defined. SVG-T is a rich XML-based language and by the very nature of scalable vector graphics has the attribute to automatically resize and fit any size of mobile display. It can provide a time-based (rather than frame-based) animation for accurate presentation and provides support for various commonly used video and audio formats and graphics files (JPEG, PNG, etc.). One of the powerful features supported is the "mouse-style pointer" and "pointer click" for providing users the control to steer the application through rich graphics.

The Mobile SVG profile also called SVG-T was adapted by the 3GPP and is now recommended for use in mobile phones conforming to the standards. The first formal adaptation of the SVG 1.1 profile for mobiles (SVG-T) was in 2003 by the W3C, after which these were adapted by the 3GPP as 2D graphics standards for applications such as MMS. In 2005, the SVG 1.2 version was adopted. SVG 1.2 remains the standard adopted for use even in Release 7 of the 3GPP.

3.5 MEDIA SYNCHRONIZATION AND PRESENTATION FORMAT IN 3GPP

Synchronized Multimedia Integration Language (SMIL) is the industry standard for presentation of multimedia content in a time-synchronized manner and scene description. It provides for presentation to be generated from multiple content elements comprised of video, audio, timed text, graphics, and voice (which are represented by different clips and MIME types) to be integrated and presented in a predefined manner.

The 3GPP has adopted the use of a subset of SMIL 2.0 for use in mobile applications. The SMIL elements, which are supported, are

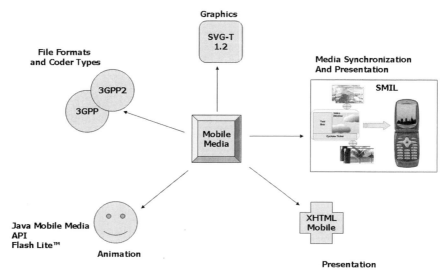

FIGURE 3-9   Mobile media constituents

given in 3GPP TS 26.234. SMIL is the prescribed language for services such as MMS, Presence, and IMS messaging (3GPP Release 7). In addition, XHTML mobile profile is also required to be supported for scene description. The XHTML mobile profile is defined by the WAP forum.

SECTION

BROADBAND WIRELESS TECHNOLOGIES

4

UNDERSTANDING WiMAX

The fundamental core of WiMAX technology is its flexibility. Companies have lost so much money by implementing different technologies that they are not going to make those mistakes again.
—Dr. Mo Shakouri
Chairman of marketing for the WiMAX Forum

Section II of this book is devoted to understanding the standards of WiMAX (IEEE 802.16-2004 and IEEE 802.16e-2005) and gain an understanding into the principles involved in planning a transmission network.

This chapter focuses on the standards of WiMAX and how the PHY and MAC layers support features that are unique to WiMAX such as understanding of:

- Propagation characteristics of WiMAX networks and indicative capacities of WiMAX-based systems
- WiMAX Forum® certification profiles and their importance
- Support of multiple output multiple input (MIMO), advanced antenna systems (AAS), and beamforming for enhancing system capacities.
- Nomadicity and roaming in Mobile WiMAX systems.

Chapter 5, which follows, is devoted to the design of WiMAX-based network planning and deployment.

4.1 BASICS OF OFDM

As OFDM is the primary technology used in the WiMAX systems in the physical layer, it is essential to understand the basics of this technology and how it enables high bit rates to be sustained in a wireless environment with NLOS operation.

In real-life transmission environments, multipath propagation and echoes from objects lead to the received signals arriving at the destination in a time-delayed fashion. These signals suffer frequency selective fading as a result of the multipath propagation effects. When a carrier is used to carry high data rates (i.e., a short symbol time), the received signals have enough delay spread to fall into the slots of other symbols thereby causing intersymbol interference. In the case of a single-carrier modulation, this type of propagation limits the data rates that can be used in non-line-of-sight (NLOS) environments.

The technology of OFDM is based on the use of a large number of carriers spread in the allocated bandwidth, with each carrier being modulated by a proportionately lower data rate than would be the case in a single-carrier scenario.

EXAMPLE OF USING MULTIPLE CARRIERS FOR DATA TRANSMISSION

As an example, a bandwidth of 10 MHz may be used with 1024 (1 K) carriers, each carrying only one-thousandth of the data rate carried by the single carrier.

The lower data rate per carrier increases the symbol time proportionately. In the case of 1 K carriers, for example, it increases by 1000 times. Using a data rate of 10 Mbps with QPSK coding (2 bits per symbol) gives a symbol rate of 5 M symbols/sec or a time per symbol of 0.2μ seconds. At the speed of light, an object in an urban environment (typically 1 Km away) generates a round-trip delay of 6.6μ seconds. This reflected signal would be completely out of sync with the direct signal. However, if 1 K carriers are used, each carrier carries only 5 K symbols/sec and the symbol time is 200μ seconds. The delay of 6.6μ seconds is thus less than 1/30th of the symbol duration.

The technology of increasing the number of carriers evidently helps in making the signals robust against multipath propagation. However, implementing multiple carriers in real-life implementation scenarios (where perfect band-pass filters for each carrier cannot be expected), requires that the carriers have a special relationship with each other. This relationship is called "orthogonality." A carrier is orthogonal with respect to another carrier if its sideband nulls (in frequency) fall at the main lobe frequency of the next carrier so that the next carrier is unaffected by the

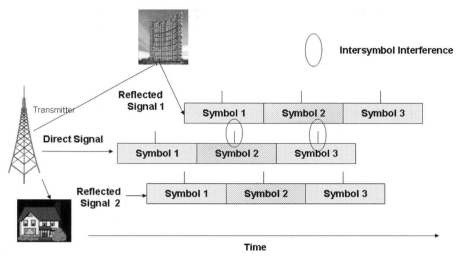

FIGURE 4-1 Intersymbol interference in single-carrier operations

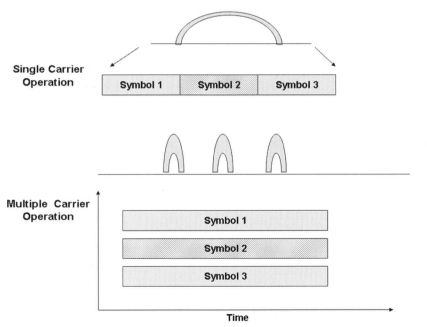

FIGURE 4-2 Symbol times increase in multicarrier operation

presence of the first carrier. In OFDM systems, each carrier is orthogonal
with respect to the other carriers, so that the sidebands of the carrier
cancel out rather than interfering with the next carrier. The principle of
using orthogonal carriers has given the name OFDM to the technology

of using multiple carriers. OFDM is a common technology used in achieving high bit rates in all wireless and wireline systems, which may be subject to frequency selective fading or intersymbol interference from reflected signals. OFDM systems provide a very robust transmission technique for NLOS environments.

OFDM is also used in wireless systems (such as 802.11n), wireline systems such as DSL, and WiMAX systems (both fixed and mobile), and will be used in the next generation of the long-term evolution of cellular technologies (3G-LTE).

Implementation of OFDM systems is not done in the frequency domain (i.e., generating 1000 subcarriers and modulating them) but rather in the "time domain" by generating the symbols that carry the entire information and then performing an inverse fast fourier transform (IFFT) to generate the frequency domain signals. Such processing requires millions of computations per second and is only possible by virtue of today's high MIPS processors, which can be embedded in the WiMAX chipsets. Even though the principles of orthogonal frequency division were known since the late fifties, such implementations would have been impracticable even ten years back.

While in theory implementations of multiple carriers in OFDM can be completely orthogonal by using perfect filters (or infinite number of iterations in IFFT), in practice there is a need for a "guard band" to be provided between two symbols, which takes care that the intersymbol interference is limited to within the guard bands leaving the next symbol unaffected.

4.1.1 Orthogonality in Frequency

Pure carriers are represented by sine waves. In order that a number of carriers be orthogonal, the nulls (or zero crossings) of all other carriers should fall at the peak of one particular carrier. If T_S is the symbol time during which one particular carrier is present, then it is evident that for orthognality the next carrier frequency should be separated from the first by $1/T_S$. Hence if the first carrier is at frequency f_0, the next carrier should be at $f_0 + 1/T_S$. The following carrier will be at $f_0 + 2/T_S$ and so on, the expression for the carrier frequencies being given by $f = f_0 + n/T_S$ where $n =$ the number of subcarriers. The gap between carriers is given by $\Delta f = 1/T_s$.

The process of placing subcarriers such that they are orthogonal to each other applies for any number of subcarriers, i.e., 256, 1024, or 2048, etc. As long as the principle of orthogonality is followed, the symbols are non-interfering.

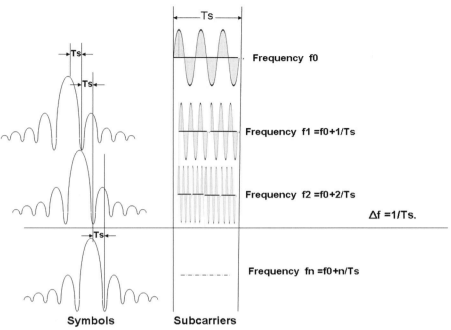

FIGURE 4-3 In OFDM subcarrier frequencies are separated by $1/T_s$, where T_s is the time between the OFDM symbols

Figure 4-4 depicts the transmission of a single OFDM symbol of a time duration, say T_s. In frequency domain, it is mapped to all 256 subcarriers in frequency, which are spaced $\Delta f = 1/T_s$ apart from each other. All the subcarriers persist for a duration of only T_s. Hence, one OFDM symbol generates all the 256 subcarriers simultaneously after which the next symbol, which follows after the guard band, generates its own 256 subcarriers again for a duration of T_s. As the subcarriers are orthogonal, they are non-interfering with each other and can be converted back to the OFDM symbol at the receiver.

The amount of data which is carried by each subcarrier will depend on the considerations of intersymbol interference. For example, if the delay spread due to multipath signals is 10 μ seconds, then the symbol time needs to be much larger than the delay spread. If we take a factor of 10 to be a reasonable factor to overcome intersymbol interference, then the symbol time will be 100 μ seconds. This permits the subcarriers to be spaced 1/100 MHz apart or 10 KHz apart. A 5-MHz channel can thus accommodate 512 subcarriers.

The bandwidth represented by the time delay spread is called the coherence bandwidth of the channel.

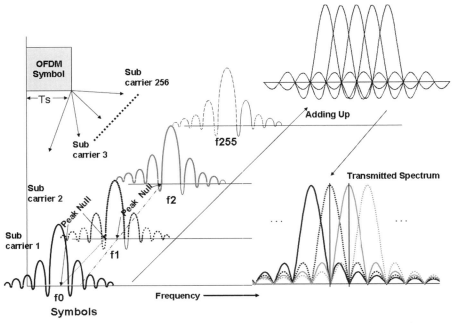

FIGURE 4-4   Subcarriers in OFDM are spaced in frequency to maintain orthogonality

CALCULATING THE NUMBER OF SUBCARRIERS BASED ON DELAY SPREAD

The number of subcarriers can be calculated for a given bandwidth based on the delay spread and bandwidth. As an example, if the delay spread is 20μ seconds, in order that the subcarriers have flat fading, the symbol duration should be at least 10 times the delay spread or 200μ seconds. The symbol duration is then 200μ seconds (including the guard band) and the bandwidth of each subcarrier is $1/200 = 5\,\text{KHz}$. If the channel bandwidth is $1\,\text{MHz}$, 200 subcarriers are required for OFDM operation.

4.1.2 Time Domain Representation of OFDM Signals

As all processing of the signals happens in the time domain, it is useful to view the process of OFDM in the time domain. Representation of signals in the time domain from frequency domain can be done by using a Discrete Fourier Transform (DFT). While in the frequency domain the signals are represented by subcarriers spaced in frequency, in the time domain the same signal is represented by "symbols," which are separated in time. The Fourier Transform is called discrete as it is

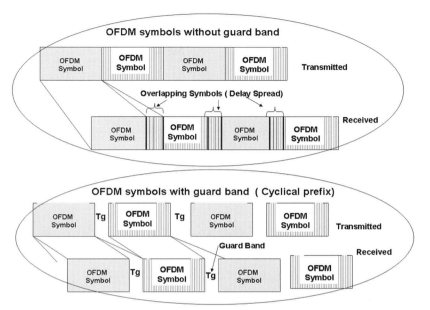

FIGURE 4-5   Guard band is necessary for avoiding interference between OFDM symbols

applied on sampled values of the signal over the sampling time intervals. In common implementation, this process is called the Fast Fourier Transform (FFT).

The representation of signals in the time domain and the frequency domain is interchangeable. If all subcarriers in the frequency domain are adjacent to each other without any guard band, the OFDM symbols in the time domain would appear adjacent to each other. In practice, there needs to be a gap between the symbols (called guard band), which allows the OFDM symbol delay spread.

In the absence of any guard band, the delay spreads of the transmission medium will fall within the OFDM symbols. On the other hand, if the guard band is kept larger than the delay spread of the channel, the delayed signals will fall in the guard band before the next symbol begins and will not cause intersymbol interference or interference within the same symbol (Figure 4-5).

The transmission in the guard band can be a null or it can be an extension of the transmitted signals. In practice, the implementation of the Discrete Fourier Transform (DFT) is done by using a periodic version of the input signal and the process is called circular convolution. The periodic version of the input signal has M finite values, where M is the number of samples in the symbol duration and is periodic beyond this. In order to create a guard band, a cyclical extension of the

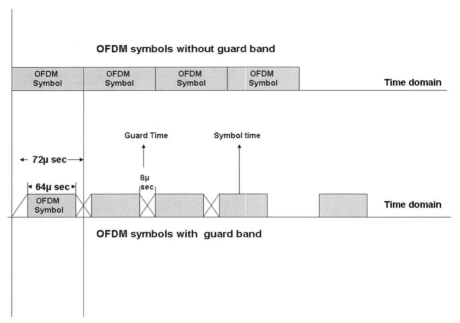

FIGURE 4-6 An example of OFDM symbols in time domain showing guard bands

transmitted symbol is introduced in the guard band period. The cyclical extension essentially converts a linear convolutional channel into a circular convolutional channel. Delayed signals fall within the period of the cyclical extension, which does not carry any information.

A simplified representation of the process of OFDM modulation is given in Figure 4-7. The input to the modulator is a bit stream of B bits/sec. The signals after the QAM modulation (a QAM symbol mapper) are in the form of symbols, which are represented by matrices of vectors. The symbol stream is divided into N substreams each with bit rate of B/N bits/second where N = number of carriers used in OFDM.

The N streams that are generated are presented for Inverse Fast Fourier Transform. The cyclical prefixes are added to the symbols to achieve the guard bands. The IFFT generates the OFDM carriers in the baseband, which are modulated with the RF carrier of desired frequency. In practice, a number of additional functions are needed. For example, the process of IDFFT gives rise to carriers with a high peak to average power ratio (PAPR). This is reduced by using a limiter.

The process of demodulation of OFDM is similar except that the DFT is used to convert the frequency domain signals to time domain for processing (Figure 4-8).

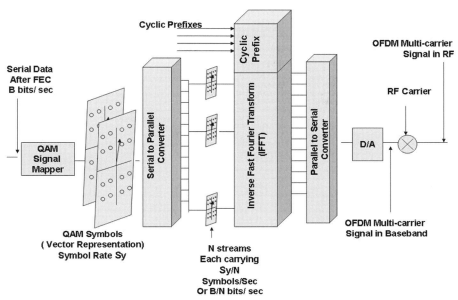

FIGURE 4-7   A simplified representation of OFDM modulation systems with *N* carriers

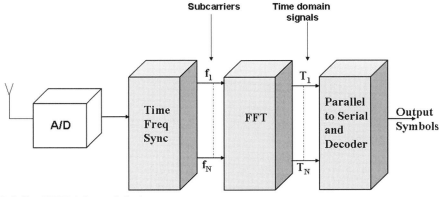

FIGURE 4-8   OFDM demodulation

4.2 PROTOCOL LAYERING IN WiMAX

The protocol structure of WiMAX is designed to support all IP-layer protocols. WiMAX is defined over the PHY and MAC layers, which have features to deliver QoS and security to applications that use the services. For this purpose, the MAC layer has been specially designed wherein QoS parameters can be set for each connection established using WiMAX. The QoS parameters can include delay, jitter, and bit rates, which are required to be delivered over each connection. The MAC layer then assigns resources in the form of OFDM symbols or subchannels to each application to ensure that the services are delivered reliably with the preset parameters.

In order to support various functions, the MAC layer is logically defined in the form of three sublayers under IEEE802.16-2004. These sublayers and their functions are:

- **The Convergence Sublayer (CS)** is responsible for interfacing with a range of different types of higher layers, each represented, for example, by a different network type. Examples of higher layers that can use IEEE 802.16 as an underlying network include ATM networks, Internet, TDM-based voice networks, etc. The CS layer interfaces with different networks by accepting MAC service Data Units (MSDUs) from these networks and converting them to MAC Protocol Data Units (MPDUs) for transmission over the air. The CS layer therefore accepts ATM cells or IP packets or TDM frames from the higher layers, each of which is identified with a connection identifier (CID). Each connection identifier is associated with certain bit rates and QoS.
- **MAC Core Part Sublayer** (CPS) provides the main functions of connection control, access to physical layer, and bandwidth allocation.
- **The Privacy Sublayer** provides authentication and key management.

The WiMAX Forum has initiated the process of integration of WiMAX PHY and MAC layers in other networks by prescribing support for only Ethernet and IP at the convergence sublayer in the initial stage. The WiMAX MAC layer should therefore be considered a subset of the IEEE 802.16-2004, wherein only the IP network and Ethernet connectivity have been retained in order to make the protocols more efficient (Figure 4-9). This, however, does not preclude their support in the future. In fact, by using the convergence sublayer, the MAC can support any future protocol.

The WiMAX MAC layer also supports automatic retransmission request (ARQ), which enables an error correction mechanism. This mechanism operates in MAC and PHY layers by requesting retransmissions of packets that are received in error. This helps maintain a high throughput as the errors need not be corrected at higher layers, which would have otherwise lowered the efficiency.

The common part sublayer (CPS) of WiMAX provides, apart from other functionalities, the functions of allocation of bandwidth for the users. The access to time slots of the TDMA frame is thus fully managed by the MAC layer. The subscriber stations can only gain access to the

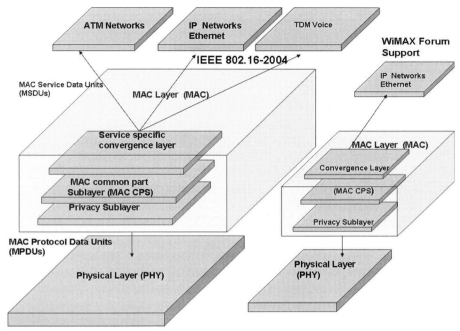

FIGURE 4-9   Protocol layering in IEEE 802.16-2004 and WiMAX

time slots when a specific allocation is conveyed to them in the MAP messages for both uplink and downlink. All the bandwidth control is thus maintained at the base station.

The subscriber stations can, however, draw the attention of the base station by making a request for bandwidth in the contention time slot, which follows the downlink subframe of the PHY.

4.2.1 Protocol Layering in Mobile WiMAX

Figure 4-10 shows the structure of protocols in Mobile WiMAX. In addition to the convergence sublayer, the Mobile WiMAX protocols need to support mobility and handover. This part is handled by the "mobility agent," which is a part of the protocol structure used for Mobile WiMAX networks. The higher layers of the applications are thus isolated from the issues arising from the mobility of the user devices.

4.2.2 Fixed WiMAX PHY

The physical layer in Fixed WiMAX is based on the use of 256 subcarriers. As these subcarriers are generated by the use of 256-point IFFT (Inverse Fast Fourier transform), the PHY layer of WiMAX is said to consist of 256-point FFT.

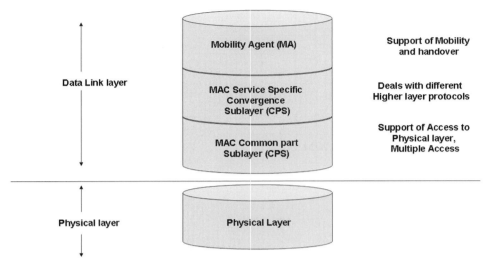

FIGURE 4-10   Mobile WiMAX protocol layers

The amount of data that can be carried by each subcarrier depends on the bandwidth of the channel. Of the 256 subcarriers, 192 are assigned for carriage of data, 56 subcarriers are guard band subcarriers, and 8 are assigned as pilot subcarriers. In actual implementations, 28 lower guard band, 27 upper guard band, and one DC subcarrier are not activated, leaving only 200 "activated" carriers. The suppression of guard band carriers helps in spectrum shaping. Of these 200 activated subcarriers, 8 subcarriers are used as pilot subcarriers and 192 are used for data.

The subcarriers are separated by a guard time in order to reduce intersymbol interference. The guard time in the case of Fixed WiMAX can be $\frac{1}{32}$, $\frac{1}{16}$, $\frac{1}{8}$, or $\frac{1}{4}$, and is specified based on the bandwidth. For initial certification profiles at 3.5 MHz a value of $\frac{1}{8}$ is commonly used.

Using this value of the guard band, the subcarrier frequency spacing for a channel bandwidth of 3.5 MHz for 256 subcarriers and a guard band of $\frac{1}{8}$ is given by:

$$\text{Fixed WiMAX subcarrier frequency}$$
$$\text{spacing} = 3500\,\text{KHz}/(256)*8/7 = 15.625\,\text{KHz}$$

This corresponds to a symbol time of 64 μ sec. The corresponding guard time will be $\frac{1}{8}$ * 64 = 8 μ sec. The total OFDM symbol duration comprised of the guard band and the subcarrier will thus be 72 μ sec.

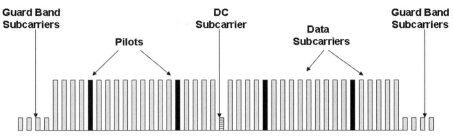

FIGURE 4-11 Subcarriers in WiMAX

RELEVANCE OF SUBCARRIER SPACING IN MOBILE ENVIRONMENTS

At the prescribed maximum limit of speed in WiMAX standards, i.e., 125 Km/hour (35 m/sec) and at a frequency of 3.4 GHz (0.085 m wavelength), the Doppler shift works out to

$$F_D = 35/0.085 = 400 \, Hz$$

At a subcarrier frequency of 15.625 KHz, the intersymbol interference caused by the Doppler shifts can be shown to be below -30 dB.

It is necessary to "over sample" the signals by an equivalent factor in order to generate the guard bands. For bandwidths in multiples of 1.75 MHz (i.e., 3.5 MHz and 7 MHz) the oversampling factor is 8/7.

In practice, the guard time is not vacant but is used to carry a cyclical prefix where a fraction of the beginning and end of symbol are appended to the symbol.

OFDM is a "block transmission system," i.e., a group of symbols are grouped and sent after application of forward error correction codes. In the frequency domain, these are represented by N subcarriers, which are orthogonal. There is thus no interference within the symbols sent in a block. Block coding is explained later in this chapter.

4.2.3 Estimating Data Rates in Fixed WiMAX

Data rates in Fixed WiMAX depend on a number of parameters. The raw data rate achievable depends on the type of modulation used, coding rate deployed, and bandwidth. The selection of parameters, such as modulation and error coding rate, is adaptive, therefore the data rates can change with transmission conditions as well. The FFT size for IEEE 802.16-2004 WiMAX systems is fixed at 256, of which data

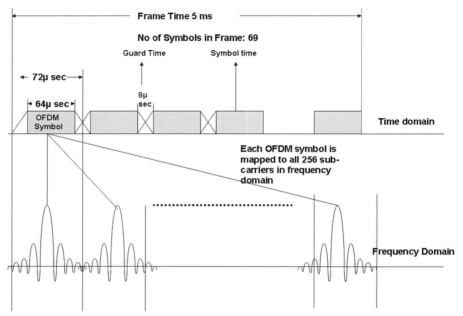

FIGURE 4-12   OFDM symbol and guard times in WiMAX (example for 3.5 MHz bandwidth)

subcarriers are 192, with 8 pilot subcarriers and 56 null/guard band subcarriers.

Estimating Raw Data Rates

For illustrative purposes and to show how various factors affect the data rates of the Fixed WiMAX systems, we undertake a brief exercise of estimation of raw data rates based on parameters of the WiMAX system.

1. Modulation

The data-carrying capacity of the system depends on the type of modulation used. Modulation in WiMAX systems is adaptive (QPSK, 16 QAM, and 64 QAM are mandatory in Fixed WiMAX for downlink. For uplink only support of QPSK and 16 QAM is required).

The bits per subcarrier are given by:

$$B = \log_2(M)$$

where B = bits/symbol for the subcarrier modulation and M denotes the level of modulation (416 or 64 etc.). For an OFDM system with 192 subcarriers, the number of bits carried by an OFDM symbol are $192 \times B$ where B = bits/subcarrier symbol.

TABLE 4-1

Modulation type and bits per OFDM symbol

Modulation	Coded Bits per Subcarrier	Coded Bits per OFDM Symbol
BPSK	1	192
QPSK	2	384
16 QAM	4	768
64 QAM	6	1152

This is demonstrated in Table 4-1.

2. Error Coding

FEC (forward error correction) coding is used in WiMAX (both convolutional coding and RS coding), which has a bearing on the physical data rates on the channel versus the actual delivered channel data rates. The support of ½, ⅔, ¾, and ⅚ convolution code rates is mandatory in Fixed WiMAX. The effect of applying a code rate of ½, for example, is to reduce the channel data rates to one half of the raw data rates.

3. Bandwidth

Increasing the bandwidth of the WiMAX system has the impact of increasing the subcarrier spacing as the FFT size is fixed in Fixed WiMAX at 256. The subcarrier spacing is given by:

$$\text{Subcarrier spacing, } \Delta f = (\text{BW}/256)* OS$$

where OS = oversampling rate (e.g., $\frac{8}{7}$ for guard band of ⅛).

As an example, for a bandwidth of 3.5 MHz the subcarrier spacing is 15.625 KHz, while for a bandwidth of 7 MHz the subcarrier spacing is 31.25 KHz. Increasing the subcarrier spacing has the impact of reducing the symbol time as $T_s = 1/\Delta f$.

In the above example, at 3.5 MHz, the OFDM symbol time is 64 μ seconds, while for 7 MHz it is 32 μ seconds (total symbol durations are 72 and 36 μ seconds, respectively, after accounting for guard bands). A decrease of OFDM symbol time has a direct impact on the number of symbols carried per second and thus the total bit rate.

Putting all the three factors, i.e., the number of OFDM symbols carried per second, the number of bits per symbol, and the coding rate (CR), gives an approximation of the total raw data rate, as well as the payload data rate available for the channel.

Symbols per Frame and Frame Rate

It would have been a simple matter to calculate the raw bit rates using the above information by using

$$\text{Raw Bit Rate} = (\text{OFDM symbols/sec}) * (\text{Bits/Symbol})$$

$$\text{Data Rate for Channel} = \text{Raw bit Rate} * \text{Error Coding Rate}$$

However, it needs a minor correction, i.e., the organization of OFDM symbols in frames and consequently the slightly reduced symbol rate caused by frame overheads. As per the specification of OFDM PHY, the OFDM symbols are transmitted in TDMA frames. The frames can be 2.5, 4, 5, 8, 10, 12.5, or 20 ms. Smaller frame sizes can provide lower latency for high-bandwidth applications.

As an example with a 3.5 MHz channel bandwidth with a 5 ms frame time, the symbols per frame are 69 (each symbol is 72 μ seconds) and the symbol transmission rate is 13,800 symbols/sec. If the OFDM symbols are carried using 64 QAM (1152 bits/symbol), this gives a data rate of 15.9 Mbps. The data rate available to the MAC layer will be lower; for example, if a coding rate of 5/6 is used, the data rate is 13.2 Mbps.

Table 4-2 shows the data rates based on these derivations for 3.5-, 7-, and 10-MHz bandwidths, which are part of initial certification profiles for Fixed WiMAX.

The data rates given in the above table should be considered indicative only. The achievable data rate given in the table shows a gross rate of 13.2 Mbps for a 3.5 MHz bandwidth channel. This gives it a spectral density of 13.2/3.5 = 3.74 bits per sec per Hz. The high spectrum efficiency along with the capability of operations in NLOS environment are the strong points of WiMAX. It should be noted that the data rates in the table have been derived as raw data based on usage of 192 subcarriers, but without consideration of other overheads, changes in guard time with bandwidth, and uplink to downlink traffic divisions. The gross data rate will need to include the uplink overhead symbols, such as the preamble and allocation of slots for different users, and in practice, only 188 of the 192 subcarriers may be devoted to data.

To summarize the formulae used in the above table, these can be derived from

$$\text{Raw Bit Rate} = (\text{OFDM symbols/frame}) * (\text{Frames/sec}) * (\text{Coded Bits/Symbol})$$

$$\text{Data Rate for Channel} = \text{Raw Bit Rate} * \text{Error Coding Rate}$$

TABLE 4-2

Fixed WiMAX OFDM parameters

Parameter	3.5-MHz Bandwidth	7-MHz Bandwidth	10-MHz Bandwidth
No. of subcarriers	256	256	256
No. of used subcarriers	192	192	192
Guard interval	1/8	1/8	1/8
Over-sampling factor	8/7	8/7	8/7
Sampling rate (BW × over-sampling actor) million/sec	4	8	11.4
Subcarrier spacing (KHz)	15.625	31.25	43.75
Useful OFDM symbol width (μ) Second	64	32	22.86
Guard interval	8	4	2.74
Total OFDM symbol width	72	36	25.6
Frame length (typical)	5 ms	5 ms	5 ms
Symbols per frame	69	138	195
Symbol rate	13,800	27,600	39,062.5
Coded bits symbol 64 QAM (before FEC)	1152	1152	1152
Data bits per symbol with 5/6 FEC	960	960	960
Maximum data rate with 64 QAM and 5/6 FEC (Mbps)	13.2	26.5	37.5

Uplink and Downlink Traffic

WiMAX systems can be based on either FDD or TDD. In the case of FDD, the uplink and downlink are separate frequencies while the same frequency is shared in the case of TDD by time division duplexing. The WiMAX frame is thus divided into time slots for downlinks and uplinks. The total data rate available via the WiMAX channel is divided between the downlink and uplink based on usage requirements. For example in Table 4-2, the maximum data rate for 3.5 MHz bandwidth based on use of 192 subcarriers and 5/6 FEC is shown as 13.2 Mbps. If, for example, the downlink to uplink traffic ratio is 3:1, the available data rates are 9.9 and 3.3 Mbps, respectively. This will be achieved in TDD systems by allocating an appropriate number of subchannels or OFDM symbols for transmission in the uplink and downlink directions.

Data Rates and Distance from Base Station

In the previous derivations, we have seen the maximum data rate for different bandwidths for Fixed WiMAX with 192 subcarriers being used for data (Table 4-2). The error coding rates taken are also the lowest, i.e., a rate of 5/6. Such data rates will be achieved only in ideal transmission conditions with a high SNR and perhaps in the vicinity of the base stations. These are linked to the sustainability of the highest modulation scheme, e.g., 64 QAM. It is quite obvious that such high modulation cannot be maintained over the entire length of the link or in an NLOS environment. In such cases, the error rates will rise and the adaptive modulation feature will drop the modulation to lower-density modulation, i.e., QPSK or BPSK. This will mean that the data rates will drop. Hence frequently quoted figures such as WiMAX being able to provide up to 38 Mbps over 25 Km for 10 MHz bandwidth would not be factually correct for all distances. The data rates will change through the entire coverage area and will depend on whether the reception is LOS (which might attain these bit rates at 1 Km) or NLOS. In the case of NLOS reception, the data rates may drop significantly because of the change of modulation and ARQs and the link might operate at lower rates.

As an example, it is instructive to consider a bandwidth of 3.5 MHz and consider the impact of different modulation schemes. Table 4-3 provides these figures.

Figure 4-13 exhibits the typical scenario in a MAN environment. As the distance from the base station increases, the signal-to-noise ratios fall and the adaptive modulation feature adjusts the modulation scheme used. This leads to the typical bell-shaped curve of available bit rates falling. Hence, in a MAN environment as the distance from the transmitter increases, the users in different zones would be able to use different modulation schemes and get a lower data rate in fringe areas or areas that are not in line-of-sight. These observations are applicable for an omnidirectional antenna and free space propagation as shown here. WiMAX has features such as beamforming which can improve SNR significantly even for receivers in fringe areas and maintain high-modulation densities as shown later in this chapter.

Application of FEC-Data Blocks

In the foregoing analysis, we have made some simplistic assumptions about the application of FEC. In WiMAX, FEC is applied on certain fixed-block lengths of data, which have been defined based on the modulation type. The block sizes are used so that the data generated after FEC can be carried by one OFDM symbol if all the subcarriers are used. Table 4-4 gives the block lengths on which the data rate can be applied and the coded block lengths.

For example, using 64 QAM the block of data generated after FEC is 144 bytes = 1152 bits. With each subcarrier in 64 QAM supporting 6 bits, the 1152 bytes require 192 subcarriers. The case is similar with

TABLE 4-3

Raw data rates in fixed WiMAX PHY with 3.5-MHz bandwidth with various modulation schemes

Modulation	Coded Bits per Subcarrier	Coded Bits per OFDM Symbol	Raw Data Rate, Mbps (3.5-MHz Channel) Mbps at Symbol Rate of 13.80 K Symbols/Sec)
BPSK	1	192	2.65
QPSK	2	384	5.30
16 QAM	4	768	10.60
64 QAM	6	1152	15.90

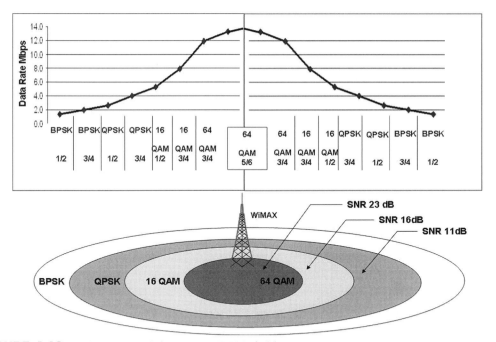

FIGURE 4-13 Adaptive modulation in WiMAX field environment

16 QAM, where the 96 bytes (736 bits) generated after application of FEC are carried by 192 subcarriers using 4 bits per subcarrier.

If these block codes are applied to the Fixed WiMAX raw data rates indicated earlier in Table 4-3, the usable data rates are correspondingly reduced in the same ratios while increasing the error resilience. These data rates for Fixed WiMAX are given in Table 4-5.

TABLE 4-4

Block sizes for coding in Fixed WiMAX

Modulation	Uncoded Block Size (Bytes)	Convolutional Code Rate	RS Code Rate	Overall Coding Rate	Coded Block Size (Bytes)
BPSK	12	1/2	(12,12,0)	½	24
QPSK	24	2/3	(32,24,4)	½	48
QPSK	36	5/6	(40,36,2)	¾	48
16 QAM	48	2/3	(64.48,8)	½	96
16 QAM	72	5/6	(80,72,4)	¾	96
64 QAM	96	3/4	(108,96,6)	⅔	144
64 QAM	108	5/6	(120,108,6)	¾	144

TABLE 4-5

Usable data rates in Fixed WiMAX (example of a 3.5 MHz bandwidth system)

Modulation	FEC Code Rate	Coded Bits per Subcarrier	Coded Bits Per OFDM Symbol	Raw Data Rate (3.5 MHz Channel) Mbps (at Symbol Rate of 13.80 K Symbols/Sec)	Data Rate (3.5 MHz Channel) Mbps (at Symbol Rate of 13.80 K Symbols/Sec)
BPSK	½	1	192	2.65	1.3
BPSK	¾	1	192	2.65	2.0
QPSK	½	2	384	5.30	2.6
QPSK	¾	2	384	5.30	4.0
16 QAM	½	4	768	10.60	5.3
16 QAM	¾	4	768	10.60	7.9
64 QAM	¾	6	1152	15.90	11.9
64 QAM	⅚	6	1152	15.90	13.2

4.2.4 Subchannels and Framing in Fixed WiMAX (IEEE 802.16-2004) PHY

WiMAX systems are used in a point-to-multipoint configuration with one base station transmitting in the downlink direction to a number of subscriber stations (SS). Transmissions by different SS happen in time slots allotted to them in a TDD system or on fixed subcarriers in an FDD system.

In addition to the framing structure, one of the salient features of WiMAX is the subchannelization which allows each subscriber station to use only a part of the bandwidth assigned to it leading to a very highly efficient utilization of the spectrum. As discussed earlier, OFDM systems are characterized by the transmission of one OFDM symbol on all the available subcarriers simultaneously. For example, in Fixed WiMAX, one OFDM is transmitted over all the available 192 data subcarriers (360 data subcarriers in the case of Mobile WiMAX). One OFDM symbol, using 64 QAM (6 bits/symbol) modulation thus can have $192 \times 6 = 1152$ bits in Mobile WiMAX ($360 \times 6 = 2160$ bits in Mobile WiMAX).

If there was no way to further subdivide this capacity, a CPE, each time it needed to transmit, it would need to transmit a large block of data. In order to make the process more granular, a scheme of subchannelization is followed.

4.2.5 Subchannels

Subchannelization in Fixed WiMAX is done in the uplink direction only (subscriber station to base station). In the downlink direction, all the subcarriers (i.e., 192) are assigned to the base station.

In the uplink direction, 16 subchannels are defined, of which any number (1, 2, 4, 8, or 16) can be assigned to a subscriber station. Only one subscriber station can transmit on a particular subchannel at one time. As there are 192 data subcarriers, one subchannel implies $192/16 = 12$ subcarriers in the frequency domain. This implies that a subscriber station can transmit at bit rates which represent 1/16 of the bits carried in an OFDM symbol or its multiples. For Fixed WiMAX, it works out to 12 subcarriers $\times$ 6 bits/subcarrier = 72 bits with 64 QAM modulation. (Because of the block allocation scheme shown in Table 4-4, i.e., 96 uncoded bytes for 64 QAM, this gives $96/16 = 6$ as the bytes per subchannel, or 48 bits/subchannel.) This feature of WiMAX makes it possible for CPEs to transmit even small blocks of data, maintaining low latency without impacting on the system capacity in the form of partially used symbols. Put another way, in the time duration of an OFDM symbol (T_s) which has 16 subchannels, 16 subscriber stations can transmit simultaneously if one subchannel each is allocated to them.

Subchannelization and Link Budget

The subchannels help efficient utilization of bandwidth by subdivision of an OFDM symbol to 16 subchannels and thus permit a terminal (also base station in the case of Mobile WiMAX) to transmit only a few (i.e., 23 data subcarriers for Mobile WiMAX instead of 360 for a 512 subcarrier OFDM system). This helps concentrate the available power and increase the link budget. In the case of Mobile WiMAX, transmitting on only one subchannel gives a power advantage of 16 times

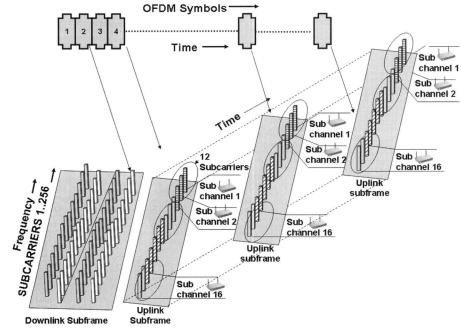

FIGURE 4-14 A conceptual depiction of subchannelization in WiMAX; each OFDM symbol in uplink frame can have up to 16 subchannels, each subchannel is a group of 12 data subcarriers

(i.e., simultaneously transmitting on 1/16th of the available subcarriers). This is equivalent to a link budget enhancement of 12 dB.

Subchannelization and Minimum Allocable Data Units (MAU)

Subchannelization also helps in reducing the minimum amount of data which the CPE or base station may transmit and thus reduces the data granularity. This is directly reflected in an increase in the system capacity. For example, in Fixed WiMAX used for VoIP, if a subscriber station has only 64 bits of data to transmit in a particular frame, it is not bound to transmit a frame with 1152 bits. Instead it can transmit as few as 72 bits representing a subchannel. In practice, as given in Table 4-4, the coding is applied in blocks of data. For 64 QAM the block size is 96 bytes, and MAU is 96/16 = 6 bytes.

System capacity for WiMAX is discussed in Section 4.5.

4.2.6 Frame Structure

In TDD-based OFDM systems, which form by far the most common form of implementation, the downlink is in the TDM mode while the uplinks from various base stations are in the TDMA mode.

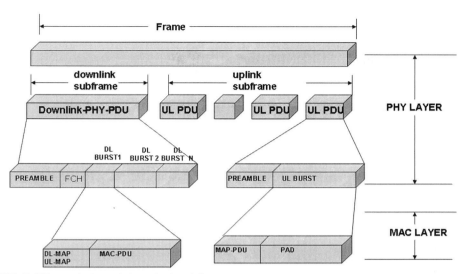

FIGURE 4-15   Uplink and downlink subframes in a TDD WiMAX system

A frame is divided into two parts (subframes):

1. A downlink subframe, which contains the time slot allocation information and the downlink bursts for various subscriber stations (SS).
2. An uplink subframe containing a variable number of uplink protocol data units (PDUs) originating from various active subscriber stations. The subscriber stations get specified time slots and subcarriers (i.e., subchannels) to send their data during the uplink subframe.

The durations of the uplink subframe and the downlink subframe can be adjusted during the transmission, giving great flexibility in allowing specific terminals to change data rates based on requirement.

As shown in Figure 4-15 the frame structure involves both the MAC layers and the PHY layer. In the downlink direction the downlink subframe carries the data of all the subscriber stations. It begins with a preamble, which helps synchronize all the terminals and mark the beginning of a new frame. The preamble is followed by the frame control header (FCH), which carries the frame configuration information including the MAC access protocol (MAP) message length and the subchannel information. This is followed by the DL bursts for all active devices. Each MAP message provides information on the downlink and uplink maps for the specific subscriber station and the usable subcarriers.

It also contains information on the available subcarriers and their modulation.

The burst structure of Fixed WiMAX can be more clearly seen as depicted in Figure 4-16, in which the bursts are mapped against the available subcarriers. It may be seen that in Fixed WiMAX, in both uplink as well as downlink directions, all the subcarriers (i.e., 256) are used by the base station or the subscriber stations for their allotted specific times, the details of which are carried in the PDUs. There is no allocation of different subcarriers for different subscriber stations in base station transmissions. The following is the sequence of events which takes place:

- The downlink frame begins with a preamble for synchronization and initial channel estimation. This is followed by the frame control header (FCH), which contains the information pertaining to the frame such as the modulation, usable subcarriers, and the length of MAP messages and the location of the DL bursts.
- The next OFDM symbol is a downlink burst, which is broadcast to all users. This contains the UL-MAP and DL-MAP messages (coded in error-resistant modulation such as BPSK).

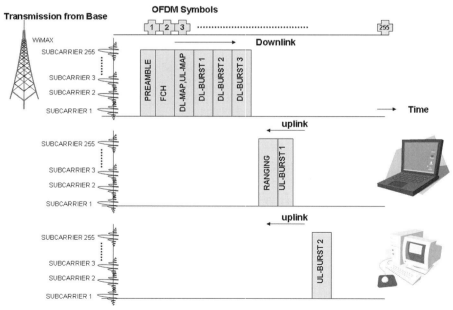

FIGURE 4-16 TDD frame structure for Fixed WiMAX

- The subscriber stations receive the DL and UL MAC layer packets and are aware of the burst times allocated within a frame. The SS also become aware of the parameters to be used, such as modulation schemes. The base station also identifies an uplink "ranging period," wherein any subscriber stations which are not in the network can indicate their request for access.
- In the uplink subframe, after the ranging period the various subscriber stations that are active send their data in the assigned time slots.

4.2.7 Authentication Services

Any new subscriber station seeking access from a base station needs to authenticate itself. Authentication in IEEE 802.16 is based on the use of CCIR X.509 certificates. The certificates are embedded in all the hardware for WiMAX. Whenever a subscriber station needs initialization or needs to change its service flow QoS parameters such a request needs to be authenticated by the authorization module. The authorization is done by exchange of messages for authentication between the MAC layers. Authentication and security are dealt with in more detail in Chapter 19.

4.2.8 Propagation Models

In the foregoing analysis, the propagation has been assumed to be under ideal free space conditions. More realistic analysis is possible by modeling the landscape as dense urban (city center), urban, semi-urban, and rural. A number of statistical schemes are available for this purpose. Some of these include COST231, Okamura-Hata, ITM 122, and ITU-R P.1225. Modeling using these schemes can be done using any of the network planning packages for WiMAX.

4.3 MOBILE WiMAX (IEEE 802.16e-2005)

Mobile WiMAX has been designed to bring in many features which place the new wireless MAN services on a completely new footing. The IEEE 802.16e standard brings in features such as scalable OFDMA, support of mobility and handover, advanced antenna systems, beamforming, multiple input multiple output antenna systems (MIMO), spatial multiplexing, encryption, and authentication, etc. Most new developments in base station technologies, CPEs, and service architectures are now taking place in the area of Mobile WiMAX.

4.3.1 Mobile WiMAX PHY Layer

The PHY layer of Mobile WiMAX is based on the use of scalable OFDMA. The FFT size can vary from 128 (for 1.25 MHz bandwidth) to 2048 (for 20 MHz bandwidth). The parameters selected by Mobile WiMAX for initial certification profiles maintain the carrier spacing as 10.94 KHz as the number of subcarriers varies with bandwidth. This means that the useful symbol time duration as well as the guard time remains fixed. The number of OFDM symbols per 5 ms frame, therefore, also remains fixed at 48 symbols per frame of 5 ms (applicable only for WiMAX initial certification profiles; as per IEEE 802.16e-2005, other frame sizes are possible as described later in the chapter).

As exhibited in Figure 4-17, the channel bandwidth determines the number of OFDM subcarriers that are used in the scheme of scalable OFDMA. In all cases, the subcarrier spacing in the frequency domain remains fixed at 10.94 KHz. This implies a fixed OFDM symbol duration of 102.9 μ seconds and a symbol count of 48 per 5 ms per frame. With a guard band of ⅛ (11.4 μ seconds), the useful symbol time is 91.4 μ seconds.

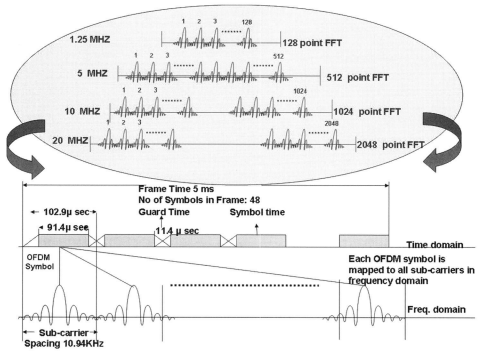

FIGURE 4-17 Mobile WiMAX OFDM parameters

4.3.2 Subchannelization in Mobile WiMAX

Unlike Fixed WiMAX where the subchannels are allowed only in the uplink, Mobile WiMAX has provisions for subchannels to be allocated both in the uplink and downlink. As there are 16 subchannels available, the minimum allocable unit to a mobile station is one subchannel. This is equivalent to 1/16 of the available subcarriers.

Apart from the number of subchannels allotted for a mobile station, the manner in which the carriers are assigned to the subchannels is also important. The carriers allotted to a subchannel are not generally adjacent. Allocating adjacent subcarriers reduces the frequency diversity, as any frequency selective fading would impact the bulk of adjacent carriers. Instead, it is more common to have the subchannels constituted with subcarriers distributed randomly over the entire group of carriers. This provides greater resilience to frequency selective fading.

Band Adaptive Modulation and Coding (AMC)

This is a scheme where the subcarriers in WiMAX are allotted as contiguous or adjacent subcarriers. In this scheme, the frequency diversity to a particular station is reduced owing to the adjacent location of subcarriers. However the allocation of the subcarrier frequencies to a particular substation is possible based on the frequency response the station is experiencing. This helps the station to maximize its signal-to-noise ratio (or carrier-to-interference ratio, C/I). This type of diversity is called the multi-user diversity.

Pseudo-Random Allocation of Subcarriers

This is a scheme where the subchannels are formed by distributing the subcarriers randomly across the frequency spectrum. The support of this mode is mandatory in WiMAX implementation.

The scheme of allocation of subcarriers to subchannels may result in partial utilization of subcarriers (PUSC) or full utilization of subcarriers (FUSC).

In accordance with the WiMAX profiles for initial certification the support of 15/17 subchannels is required for 5 MHz bandwidth for uplink/downlink, respectively. This figure is 30/35 subchannels for 10 MHz bandwidth.

The implication of sub-channelization is that the base station and mobile station may transmit data in a given frame, which is equivalent to just 1/16th of an OFDM symbol (or 1/35th of an OFDM symbol in the case of Mobile WiMAX). This can help in increasing the system capacity by allocating the unused time to other mobile stations and

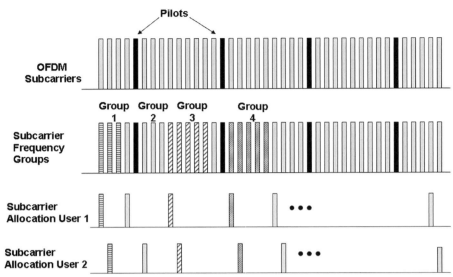

FIGURE 4-18   Subscriber allocation using pseudo-random techniques

improve link budget for the mobile stations by up to 15 dB in the case of mobile WiMAX.

4.3.3 Frame Structure in Mobile WiMAX

Mobile WiMAX frame structure has been designed to be truly flexible in regard to the bit rates which can be made available to each terminal in both uplink as well as downlink directions. While Mobile WiMAX can operate using both FDD and TDD modes, only the TDD mode has been selected for initial implementation profiles. The frame structure of Mobile WiMAX, consists of TDD frames each comprised of a downlink subframe and an uplink subframe. The subframes are separated by a transmit receive transition gap (TTG) or a receive transmit transition gap (RTG), in order that there is no overlap in transmissions. The downlink subframe begins with a preamble (used for synchronization). The preamble is followed by the frame control information (FCH), which provides information on the length of MAP messages, coding scheme, and the subchannel information. This is followed by the downlink map and uplink map. The MAPs carry information on the subframe structure which will be used and the time slots as well as subchannels allotted to the terminals. A subchannel is made available to all mobile terminals to perform ranging. The terminals can use this channel to perform closed loop power adjustment and also new mobile terminals can make a request for subchannel allocation.

The uplink subframe in the case of Mobile WiMAX thus consists of bursts originating from individual mobile devices. The downlink

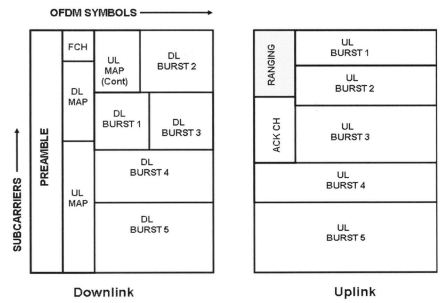

FIGURE 4-19 Downlink and uplink frames in Mobile WiMAX

subframe is transmitted entirely by the base station but contains sub-channels assigned for individual mobile stations.

The assignment of subchannels and time slots for individual subscribers is very flexible and can vary on a frame-by-frame basis. A typical representation of time slot and subcarrier allocation is given in Figure 4-19.

It is evident that the MAP messages which authorize the mobile terminals to transmit and receive in certain time slots using assigned subchannels are quite critical. These are therefore transmitted with the highest reliability such as BPSK with half-rate coding.

A portion of the uplink subframe is assigned for being used as a "ranging channel" where new stations can make requests to the base station for time slot assignment. The use of this channel is for network entry, connection maintenance, bandwidth request, and efficient handover (HO).

The access to this slot is on a contention basis by using a signaling scheme based on code division multiple access (CDMA). Up to 256 sets of ranging codes (each 144 bits) can be generated. These are divided into four groups: handover ranging, bandwidth requests, initial requests, and periodic requests.

As shown in Figure 4-20, the downlink as well as uplink subframes consist of bursts, which are pre-identified in a particular frame for all mobile devices that have registered for access to the network. Thus a particular mobile terminal assigned burst 2 may receive only the data

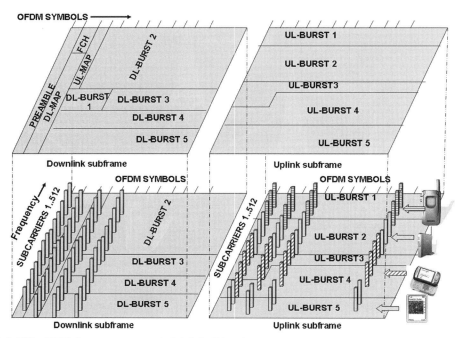

FIGURE 4-20   TDD frame structure in Mobile WiMAX

pertaining to the downlink burst 2 and transmit only on the subchannel (and subcarriers) assigned for burst 2. This helps the mobile terminal to be able to transmit with relatively lower power than would be the case if it had to transmit on all the 512 or more subcarriers.

4.3.4 Other Physical Layer Features of Mobile WiMAX

Adaptive Modulation

Mobile WiMAX provides for the use of adaptive modulation and coding schemes. The support of QPSK, 16 QAM, and 64 QAM is mandatory for the base stations. The mobile stations need to support QPSK and 16 QAM and may optionally support 64 QAM. The adaptive modulation scheme is rightly called so, as the modulation scheme can change from frame to frame. Thus a mobile operating at 64 QAM may suddenly find itself with an error rate above a threshold and switch to 16 QAM or finally to QPSK. The higher-density modulation schemes support a higher data rate but a lower tolerance to intersymbol interference or noise. The support of the different modulation schemes is a powerful feature to maximize the bit rates in actual usage environments.

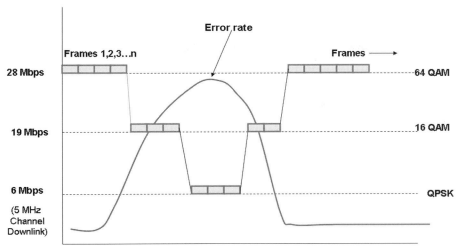

FIGURE 4-21 Adaptive modulation schemes maximize bit rate in low error rate environments

TABLE 4-6

Mobile WiMAX-supported code and modulation schemes

Modulation/Coding	Downlink	Uplink
Modulation	QPSK,16 QAM, 64 QAM	QPSK,16 QAM, 64 QAM (Optional)
Convolutional Code (CC) rate	½, ⅔, ¾, ⅚	½, ⅔, ⅚ (optional)
Convolutional Turbo Code (CTC) rate	½, ⅔, ¾, ⅚	½, ⅔, ⅚ (optional)
Repetition rate	X2,X4,X6	X2,X4,X6

Forward Error Correction (FEC)

Forward error correction (FEC) is a common feature of all digital transmission and broadcast applications, wherein the errors can be corrected by redundancy information carried in the transmitted signal itself. This avoids the need to repeat frames and maintain throughput. The redundant bits can be carried through different schemes ranging from parity bits to simple repetition of the transmitted signal. However, for maximum efficiency the FEC bits need to be tailored to the characteristics of the transmission system. Convolutional coding with Reed Solomon (RS) error correcting codes are the prescribed coding schemes for WiMAX.

The FEC coding applied can also change to optimize the data transfer rates. The coding is determined by the base station based on the data quality as conveyed in the channel quality indicator (CQI) channel. Table 4-6 provides the types of modulation and coding rates that are supported by Mobile WiMAX.

Bit Interleaving and Hybrid Auto Repeat Request (HARQ)

Transmission errors can be caused due to a variety of reasons. The errors caused by thermal noise occur randomly without any pattern in the bit stream and can be characterized by a bit rate (say 1×10^{-11}). More common are the errors due to interference which occur in bursts. When burst errors occur, they can impair all adjacent bits (say 100 bits for one burst error). This may impair both the data as well as the error correction bits, unless due precautions are taken.

Bit interleaving is a process where the order of transmission of bits is changed so that a burst error will not affect bits which are spaced out in the scheme. The bits impacted then fall in the area of several error correction zones and the original data can be more easily recovered. In the case of OFDM, a burst frequency interference may affect a few adjacent subcarriers. However, if these subcarriers are carrying bits that have been interleaved, the impact can be reduced by the error correcting codes with better probability of recovery.

The physical layer in Mobile WiMAX also supports hybrid auto repeat request (HARQ), wherein a dedicated acknowledgment channel is provided in the uplink direction (ACK channel). The mobile station can signal a positive and negative acknowledgment to trigger retransmission at the physical layer itself, thereby improving the throughput.

4.3.5 Data Rates in the Mobile WiMAX Environment

As in the case of Fixed WiMAX, Mobile WiMAX is based on the use of adaptive modulation, which can vary from QPSK, 16 QAM to 64 QAM. The type of modulation applied, as well as the FEC, is based on the channel quality parameter received by the base station and the mobile terminal.

The second parameter that determines the data rates that can be supported is the bandwidth. Channelization schemes are possible for various bandwidths ranging from 1.25 MHZ to 20 MHz. The number of OFDM carriers is scalable from 256 to 2048 depending on the bandwidth used. As the bandwidth is increased, the number of subcarriers is also increased in order to maintain the same subcarrier spacing, i.e., 10.94 KHz. The fixed subcarrier spacing gives a total symbol time of 102.9 μ second. With a guard band of 12.5 percent, this translates into a useful OFDM symbol duration of 91.4 μ seconds and a guard time of 11.4 μ seconds.

The calculation of total data rates is quite straightforward in Mobile WiMAX as it has a fixed subcarrier spacing and symbol time. For example, for a bandwidth of 5 MHz, there are 512 subcarriers of which

TABLE 4-7

Data rates in Mobile WiMAX environment

Parameter	1.25 MHz Bandwidth	5 MHz Bandwidth	10 MHz Bandwidth	20 MHZ Bandwidth
No of subcarriers	128	512	1024	2048
No of data subcarriers	72	360	720	1440
Cyclical prefix	1/8	1/8	1/8	1/8
Guard interval	3/25	3/25	3/25	3/25
Oversampling factor	8/7	8/7	8/7	8/7
Sampling rate (BW × oversampling factor) Million per second	1.43	5.71	11.43	22.86
Subcarrier spacing (KHz)	10.94	10.94	10.94	10.94
Useful OFDM symbol width (μ) per second	91.4	91.4	91.40	91.4
Guard interval	11.4	11.4	11.4	11.4
Total symbol width (μ) per second	102.825	102.825	102.825	102.825
Frame length (typical)	5 ms	5 ms	5 ms	5 ms
Symbols per frame	48	48	48	48
Data symbols per frame	44	44	44	44
Symbol rate per second	9600	9600	9600	9600
Bits per symbol with 64QAM (before FEC)	432	2160	4320	8640
Data Bits per symbol with 5/6 FEC	360	1800	3600	7200
Maximum data rate with 64QAM and 5/6 FEC (Mbps)	3.2	15.8	31.7	63.4

360 are data subcarriers. If 64 QAM modulation is used (6 bits per symbol), the number of bits that can be coded per OFDM symbol is $360 \times 6 = 2160$ bits. In Mobile WiMAX, the frames are 5 ms (200 frames per second) and each frame has 48 symbols of which 44 are usable for data. Hence, the symbol transmission rate is $200 \times 44 = 8800$ usable symbols per second. With each symbol carrying 2160 bits, this gives a data rate of $8800 \times 2160 = 19$ Mbps. If an FEC of 5/6 is applied, the data rate is $19 * 5/6 = 15.4$ Mbps.

Table 4-7 lists the data rates for different bandwidths, as well as other operating parameters. It should be noted that these rates are based on the usage of 44 OFDM symbols per frame for traffic and are indicative and do not take into account downlink/uplink TTG gaps or traffic ratios.

Table 4–7 provides the overall data rates possible without detailed consideration to uplink and downlink traffic divisions. The data rates in uplink and downlink direction depend on the time slots allocated.

TABLE 4-8

Mobile WiMAX data rates with PUSC subchannel (courtesy WiMAX Forum)

System parameter	Downlink	Uplink	Downlink	Uplink
System bandwidth	5 MHz		10 MHz	
FFT size	512		1024	
Null subcarriers	92	104	184	184
Pilot subcarriers	60	136	120	280
Data subcarriers	360	272	720	560
Sub-channels	**15**	**17**	**30**	**35**
Symbol period		102.9 μ seconds		
Frame duration		5 msec		
OFDM symbols per frame		48		
Data OFDM symbols per frame		44		

Modulation & code rate	5 MHz Channel		10 MHz Channel	
	Downlink, Mbps	Uplink, Mbps	Downlink, Mbps	Uplink, Mbps
QPSK,1/2	3.17	2.28	6.34	4.7
16 QAM 3/4	9.5	6.85	19	14.11
64 QAM 3/4	14.26	10.28	28.51	21.17

Considering the most common implementations for these parameters and bandwidths of 5 MHZ and 10 MHZ, Table 4-8 provides the bit rates which can be expected.

Allocation of Subcarriers in Mobile WiMAX: PUSC and FUSC

The allocation of subcarriers in WiMAX can be based on two schemes, i.e., Partial Utilization of Subcarriers (PUSC) or Full Usage of Subcarriers (FUSC). In the PUSC scheme (which was described briefly above and is mandatory in WiMAX implementations as per the initial certification profiles), not all subcarriers are allocated for uplink and downlink transmissions. This implies that subcarriers assigned near the cell edges can be limited and different from adjoining cells in order to avoid interference. This effectively increases the frequency reuse to 3 or higher at the cell edges based on the manner of allocation. In FUSC, all subcarriers are allocated for traffic.

4.3.6 Framing in WiMAX

The WiMAX specifications (IEEE 802.16e-2005) permit certain fixed frame sizes. Frame sizes of 2.5 ms, 4 ms, 5 ms, 8 ms, 10 ms, 12.5 ms, and 20 ms can be used. The number of symbols that are included in a frame can be worked out from the symbol time. For example, if the frame time selected is 5 ms and the symbol time is 103 μ seconds, the number of symbols in a frame is $5000/103 = 48$ symbols. For initial certification profiles by the WiMAX Forum, a frame size of 5 ms has been selected.

4.3.7 MAC Layer in Mobile WiMAX

The MAC layer of Mobile WiMAX follows the basic functions of establishing connections, resource allocation, and ensuring quality of services as in IEEE 802.16. Mobile WiMAX is based on the use of OFDMA/TDD and hence involves additional functions for the allocation of subchannels to mobile stations in a flexible and scalable manner to meet the QoS committed for the service. The MAC layer is the service interface of a WiMAX system. The services delivered using Mobile WiMAX (as in the case of Fixed WiMAX) are connection oriented.

Mobile WiMAX Classes of Service

Mobile WiMAX supports the following five classes of service:

- **Unsolicited grant service (UGS):** Designed for support for fixed bit rate circuit emulation services (T1/E1). In UGS, the base station schedules the capacity in the frames without any explicit request for each packet of data. Automatic scheduling also helps in reducing overheads involved in requesting the resource and their allocation. The parameters of UGS are defined by the bit rate and the maximum latency and jitter tolerated.

- **Real-Time Polling Service (rtPS):** Designed to support services, such as video, which periodically generate variable-size data packets. An example can be a video-streaming service requiring the transmission of a field (one half of frame) every 20 ms. In this case, the subscriber station needs to make a request for each packet to be transmitted. Resources for the rtPS are reserved based on connection type and service flow parameters, but unlike the UGS, are made available only on request. In the absence of a request by an rtPS class device, lower-priority services such as "best effort" may get to use the available capacity. rtPS with resources being allocable in real-time can provide low latency real-time transmissions possible which are needed for video or VoIP services. Parameters for services using rtPS are defined as the minimum sustained rate, maximum latency, and jitter.

- **Non-Real-Time Polling Service (nrtPS):** Designed to support applications where the delays generated by the system are not critical such as FTP. In nrtPS, requests for bandwidth need to be made, and it is allocated based on meeting requirements of higher-priority services.
- **Best-Effort Services (BE):** Designed to support services without any minimal-level guarantees such as web browsing. The performance achieved in BE services depends on the service flows committed for other services and can vary sharply based on locality (city center, urban, or rural) and time of day.
- **Extended Real-Time Variable-Rate Services (ERT-VR):** Is a combination of UGS and rtPS. Unsolicited periodic grants of bandwidth are provided but with flexibility in having dynamic data rates. The service is designed for support of applications such as VoIP with silence suppression. The support of ERT-VR is a new feature supported in Mobile WiMAX only.

Bandwidth Grants in Mobile WiMAX
The bandwidth is granted based on two criteria:

- **Grant per connection (GPC):** Where the bandwidth is allocated to a connection identified by a connection identifier (CID). In this case, the subscriber station uses the allotted bandwidth only for this connection. For example, if a subscriber station has two connections, each of which needs an E1 (2 mbps) emulation UGS service, then bandwidth is allocated to each connection, adequate to support an E1 service. In this case, the subscriber station may request more bandwidth for additional applications, but the same will not influence the bandwidth granted to the two E1 connections.
- **Grant per subscriber station (GPSS):** The allotted bandwidth is for a subscriber station and is divided by the station to the various connections using the service. An example can be a mobile station which is being used for browsing and file download simultaneously receiving streaming music and thus requesting bandwidth based on average usage requirements. It may request for incrementing or decrementing the aggregate bandwidth based on the actual usage of individual applications.

IEEE 802.16 MAC layer has been designed to have a self-correcting mechanism to grant bandwidth and recover from errors rather than using a request-acknowledgment mechanism which would have been too slow and inefficient. There are primarily four mechanisms by which a subscriber station may request bandwidth from the base station:

- Unsolicited grants: The bandwidth parameters are negotiated at connection time and there are no subsequent requests for bandwidth. Fixed bits of data in each frame are reserved for this application. However considering the possibility of errored frames and loss of bandwidth due to adaptive modulation, a provision has been kept in grant management sub-header. The sub-header has a "slip indicator flag" which indicates to the base station that the transmission is building a backlog for the particular service and the BS can allocate additional bandwidth for the same. The sub-header also has a "poll me" bit request field, which leads the BS to send a poll message to the subscriber station to see if it needs additional bandwidth.
- Bandwidth request via MAC packet: A subscriber station needing bandwidth can send a bandwidth request via a MAC layer packet, (with no data).
- Bandwidth request sent with MAC data packet (piggyback request): Bandwidth request can also be sent by a grant-per-application application along with a data packet (MAC PDU).
- Bandwidth requests via polling: Inactive stations which are not sending PDUs to the BS can respond to polls by the BS to indicate their bandwidth requests. The polling messages can be of unicast type (i.e., addressed to each station) or multicast type (addressed to all stations or stations in a group, which may respond if they have a bandwidth requirement). In addition, station polling messages are sent by the BS when it receives a message from an existing terminal with a bit set for additional bandwidth.

Quality of Service in Mobile WiMAX

WiMAX is connection oriented and the QoS is ensured via the mechanism of "Service Flows." Providing a QoS associated with each connection is what differentiates WiMAX from other wireless technologies as it can ensure that a particular service (such as voice or streaming video) can be delivered with agreed parameters over the WiMAX connection. As many of the QoS types require dynamic allocation of resources, these are managed by MAC messages which convey the dynamic service demand requirements.

When an initial connection is made to a device, the connection is identified by a connection ID (CID). All the protocol data units which flow to the device contain the connection identifier as well as

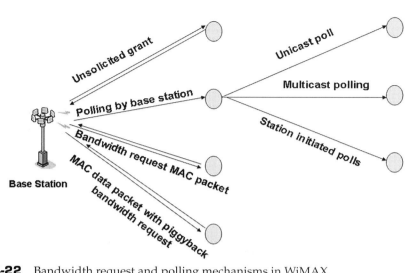

FIGURE 4-22   Bandwidth request and polling mechanisms in WiMAX

the service flow ID (SFID) which has been established for this connection. The key functional block of MAC layer which ensures the service flows and ensures quality of service is the MAC scheduler. The scheduler functions by determining which packets would flow over the air interface from among many applications, each with its class of service. The scheduling is done for both the uplink and the downlink based on the quality of the channel as conveyed by the mobile terminal in the uplink quality channel. The allocations, which are done by the scheduler, are conveyed as MAP messages and the resource allocation can be changed on a per frame basis. As per the Mobile WiMAX standards, the schedulers have the capability to operate on different types of subchannels in the physical layer. For example, the schedulers can use PUSC in subcarrier allocation for frequency diversity or can provide frequency selective scheduling based on the type of frequency response being experienced by the mobile station.

4.3.8 Mobility Management in Mobile WiMAX

One of the features that distinguishes the Mobile WiMAX from Fixed WiMAX is the mobility management as a mobile device traverses the region between adjacent cells. Mobility management function needs to accomplish the following:

- The base stations need to keep track of all mobile stations within their range, whether active or idle. This ensures that when there

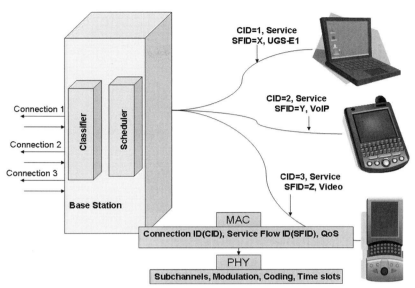

FIGURE 4-23 QoS support in Mobile WiMAX

is a need to transmit data packets to a mobile station, its location is known. This function is called location management.

• The base station and mobile station must be able to seamlessly perform authentication with new base stations as they come into range and perform handover from one base station to the other. This function is called handover management.

• The mobile stations need to conserve power to have an extended battery life. For this purpose two modes are defined in Mobile WiMAX. In the first mode called the "sleep mode," the mobile station remains without any communications with the base station for predefined periods of time. In sleep mode, the resources of both the base station as well as the mobile station are saved from unnecessary traffic load. To the base station the station will appear to be unavailable when in sleep mode. The second mode is called the idle mode in which the mobile station is available to the base station for receiving incoming traffic as conveyed on the downlink bursts. Registration with a particular base station is therefore not necessary. In an idle mode, the mobile station can move across the network without the need for handoff at every base station.

As at any given time, a number of base stations may receive the signals from a mobile station, it is appropriate to refer to them collectively as the "network." In Mobile WiMAX, the concept of being able to register a mobile station location within a relatively large area, comprised of several base stations, is used. Hence when a mobile station reports its position, its position is registered in a centralized database as a location update, over a relatively large area comprised of many base stations. The location updates are then not needed for every change of base station. This helps in high-density user environments represented by very small cell sizes (e.g., Pico cells).

However, the mobile station can transmit or receive data from one base station (BS) at a time. The process of location management happens in the following manner:

- The mobile station reports its position periodically, and the network authenticates the user and maintains its position in a database. The location update is done by all networks that might form the roaming operator group.
- In the case of an incoming call (or data request) the network sends a paging message to all base stations in the area where the location of the mobile station has been registered. The mobile station will respond to the base station where it had last executed the handover.

Mobile WiMAX addresses the mobility issues at vehicular speeds, i.e., up to around 125 kmph.

4.3.9 Handoffs in Mobile WiMAX

Handoffs are required as a mobile terminal moves out of the range of one base station and into the range of the next base station. Mobile WiMAX is designed to carry various types of traffic including voice, data, multimedia and video. Some of the traffic types are delay sensitive (such as voice) while others (such as file transfer) can be tolerant of significant delays. Handoffs are handled in Mobile WiMAX by use of MAC messages.

There are three mechanisms which have been prescribed for handoff in IEEE 802.16e.

- **Hard Handoff (HHO):** This is a handoff method in which, based on the signal strength, the mobile station breaks contact with a base station first and then makes contact with the new base station. The result is a break, with potential loss of some packets for data. This approach is the break-before-make approach. However, the Mobile WiMAX network protocols are engineered to keep delay less than 50 ms. Hard handoff support is mandatory in Mobile WiMAX.
- **Fast Base Station Switching (FBSS):** This is a soft handover method in which the mobile station is in contact with all active

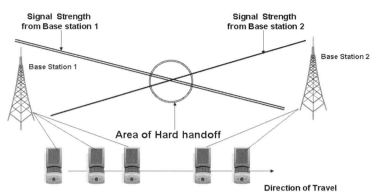

FIGURE 4-24 Hard handover in Mobile WiMAX

base stations in the coverage area. The handover occurs by sending a message on the channel quality indicator (CQI) channel.

- In FBSS, while the mobile station communicates with only one base station (called the anchor base station), it maintains contact via the ranging channel with all other base stations in the "active set" and a database of all base stations in range. The base stations also maintain the data on mobile stations which are in the location. The data is called the active set data. The data from the mobile station is monitored by all the base stations in the active set.

- The mobile station makes a decision on the base station changeover after measuring the signal strength and the channel quality received from all base stations in the active set. The decision to change the anchor base station is conveyed by the mobile station in the CQI channel. The next frame transmission and reception then happen with the new anchor station. A requirement of the FBSS is that the base stations be perfectly synchronized.

- **Macro Diversity Handover (MHDO):** In macro diversity handover, the process of handover is made even more seamless by having the mobile station be in simultaneous communication with all the base stations in the active set. The base stations are expected to operate in frame synchronous manner and the downlink signals from all base stations add to the received signal at the mobile station. In the uplink the signals are also received by all base stations and the best uplink signals are selected. The stations which operate simultaneously with the mobile station are called the diversity set.

4.4 ADVANCED ANTENNA SYSTEMS AND MIMO IN WiMAX

One of the strong features of Mobile WiMAX is the support of smart antenna technologies and multiple antennas which help to increase

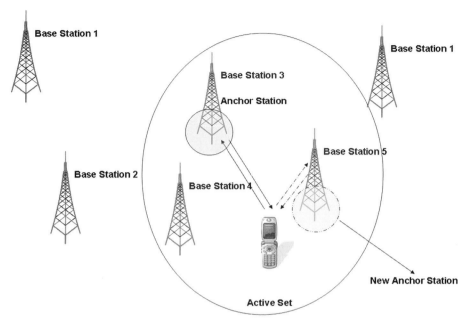

FIGURE 4-25   Fast base station switching

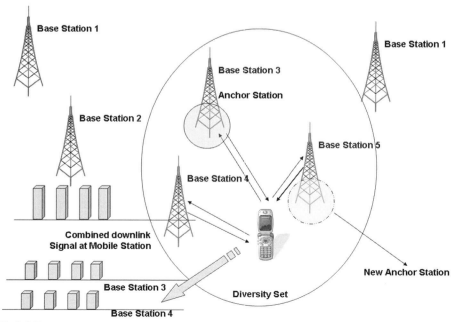

FIGURE 4-26   Macro diversity handover

the throughput which can be attained in a given transmission environment. As we have seen, by virtue of the use of OFDMA, the data rates are divided among subcarriers, with each data carrier carrying only a relatively low data rate (large symbol time). Hence the probability of intersymbol interference is quite limited. Equalization of carriers normally needed in single-carrier environments is therefore not needed in OFDM/OFDMA systems.

These features characterizing WiMAX make possible the use of smart antenna technologies. Multiple antennas, beamforming, or spatial diversity are therefore easily handled without complex operations. Advanced antenna systems, use of multiple antennas, and spatial diversity are now supported by most chipsets and customer premises equipment for Mobile WiMAX. The Release 1 certification profiles in Mobile WiMAX require the support of space time coding (STC), spatial multiplexing (SM), and adaptive beamforming. Release 1 Wave 2 certification profiles also require the support of 2 × 2 MIMO systems. As per the certification requirements, the mobile stations are required to support all the features as per Wave 1 or Wave 2 profiles (as applicable) so that they are interoperable with any base station operating as per these profiles. However, the support of individual features in base stations or the number of transmit and receive antenna elements is optional.

Release 1 Wave 1 Certification:
The Release 1 Wave 1 was primarily aimed at ensuring the key functionality as per the IEEE 802.16e recommendations and WiMAX Forum-specified parameters. This included OFDMA, QoS Support, handoff support, H-ARQ, encryption and authentication (AES and PKMv2), power control, idle and sleep modes, and header compression.

Release 1 Wave 2 Certification:
The Wave 2 certification profiles needed backward compatibility as a necessary feature. The additional functionalities required for Wave 2 included:

Base Stations: MIMO, beamforming, Ethernet IO, multicast and broadcast service (MBS).
Mobile Stations: MIMO, beamforming, MBS (all mandatory); Ethernet IO (Optional).

4.4.1 SIMO

The simplest operating configuration at a base station can be a single input and single output (SISO), i.e., one transmit and one receive antenna. This does not take advantage of any spatial diversity possible.

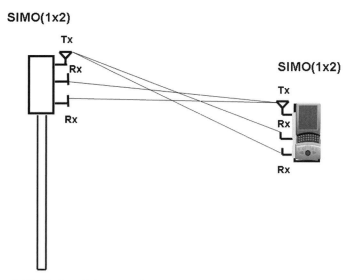

FIGURE 4-27   A SIMO (1 × 2) base station

The first step toward using diversity is to use a single input multiple output configuration, e.g., one transmit and two receive antennas. This configuration is called single input multiple output (SIMO). For example, a base station with one transmit and two receive antennas would be SIMO (1 × 2). By using SIMO, the received signal quality gets enhanced by receiving two spatially separated streams.

4.4.2 Multiple Output Multiple Input (MIMO)

MIMO involves the transmission of two streams using two spatially separated antennas. The streams are received at the receiver by using spatially separated antennas. The streams are then separated by using the space time processing, which forms the core of the MIMO technology. A base station using two transmit antennas and two receive antennas is referred to as MIMO (2 × 2).

MIMO Matrix A

One technique to use 2 × 2 MIMO is to send identical data streams on both the transmit antennas and use space time coding techniques (STC) to take advantage of the space and time diversity achieved. Using STC with 2 × 2 MIMO improves the effective SNR seen by the receiver and thus permits the use of the highest modulation coding with relatively low FEC. This effectively increases the data transmission rate close to the theoretical maximum rates of the system. This mode of operation where the two transmit antennas carry two identical data streams using space time coding is called MIMO Matrix A.

MIMO Matrix B

In a high SINR environment, i.e., when the transmission conditions are good or when the transmission involves LOS links, the two transmit antennas can carry independent data streams by using a technique called spatial multiplexing (SM). This provides multipath diversity for each of the two streams and the peak data rate handled over the physical layer can go up to nearly double of a single stream in ideal transmission conditions. The transmission rate is significantly higher than a single transmit antenna even in characteristic field conditions (typically 50 percent higher). This technique of using MIMO (i.e., by using spatial multiplexing) is called MIMO Matrix B.

MIMO systems have the capability to advantageously use both SM and STC by switching between MIMO Matrix A and Matrix B based on transmission conditions. This is called adaptive MIMO switching. In a high SNR environment, Matrix B is used to enhance link capacity. As SNR declines (say by the user moving to a shadow zone or going to the edge of the base station), the MIMO mode is switched to Matrix A and spatially separated antennas provide space diversity in reception and provide improved error rate performance of the link.

MIMO 2×2 base stations require additional antennas, as well as additional transmit and receive chains. But the increased cost is justified in urban environments characterized by NLOS. The improvements achieved by space and time diversity make the systems more efficient and provide for reliable link operations.

$N \times M$ MIMO

In general, three can be 1 to N transmitting antennas and 1 to M receiving antennas, and the system can operate in $N \times M$ MIMO mode. The Mobile WiMAX standard covers up to four antennas on transmit and receive sites, i.e., modes of up to 4×4 MIMO. Mobile WiMAX also supports adaptive MIMO switching (AMS) between the various MIMO modes based on transmission conditions, distance of user from base, etc.

Transmit Diversity

Transmit diversity makes use of space-time block coding schemes to provide transmit diversity in the downlink. This essentially requires at least two transmit antennas and at least one receive antenna. One of the choices of codes used is the Alamouti codes which are a part of the Mobile WiMAX standard. The transmit diversity technique does not require any prior knowledge of the location or path of the mobile subscriber.

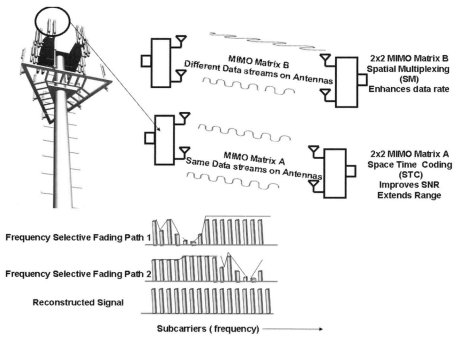

FIGURE 4-28   Multiple input multiple output antennas (MIMO, 2 × 2)

4.4.3 Beam-Forming Technologies

Omni-directional antennas, such as a dipole, provide radiation in all directions (360 degrees) in the horizontal plane whereas have lobes in the elevation or the vertical plane. Typically such antennas can provide a gain of 9 dB. However the transmission of energy in all directions in the azimuth is wasteful, leading to a lower power received by a mobile station for the same transmitted power. Sectorized antennas (i.e., which radiate in sectors of 120 degrees or 60 degrees) are better in enabling the directivity of the transmissions, as well as enabling frequency reuse as shown in Chapter 5. However, the ideal situation is to be able to direct the beam toward the receiver, thus funneling the highest power for the transmitter as well as the receiver.

Mobile WiMAX supports beam forming in both the uplink and the downlink directions. The beam forming is done by using the feature of WiMAX to supply appropriately phased signals to different antennas resulting in the transmitted signals forming a beam in the desired direction. This type of beamforming is called "adaptive beamforming" and is a part of advanced antenna system (AAS) technologies supported by Mobile WiMAX. Beam forming provides higher gain in both transmit and receive directions and improves link budget by higher

Base station antenna Array

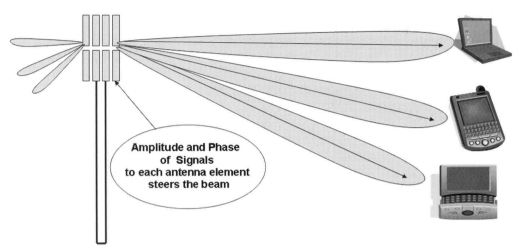

FIGURE 4-29   Antenna beam forming in Mobile WiMAX

received signals, as well as elimination of interference originating from different directions. Beam forming can deliver gains of around 9 dB in typical operating environments.

How is Beam Forming Accomplished?

Adaptive antenna systems use a matrix of antenna elements the input phase and amplitude of each is controlled to achieve the maximization of radiation in one direction while suppressing it in other directions. With a sufficient number of elements, highly directed electronically steered beams can be achieved. Beam forming not only directs and collects maximum energy from the direction of the user, but also helps suppress multipath signals emanating from other directions as well as sources of interference very effectively. The direction of the beam is determined dynamically by signal and interference conditions.

A variant of this approach is to use dynamically phased antennas to determine the direction of arrival from a "direction of arrival algorithm" (DoA) and to direct the energy in the same direction. There is also a third technique wherein there are a number of antennas each with a fixed beam in a particular direction which is preset. The antennas are merely switched to the user in the appropriate direction. However, this technique, called antenna switching, does not fall under the category of adaptive antenna systems.

Antenna beam forming, in general, is based on the knowledge of the location of the user and is effective for pedestrian or low vehicular speeds.

4.4.4 MIMO and Mobile WiMAX Certification Profiles

The incorporation of 2×2 MIMO technologies in the WiMAX Forum certification profiles for Wave 2 has led to a number of base equipment as well as CPE manufacturers to work toward early certifications. A large number of devices are now available as Wave 2 certified. The WiMAX Forum is continuing to work toward interoperability and certification of Wave 2 products comprising of smart antenna and MIMO technologies.

The previous WiMAX standards and certification had involved only single antenna techniques. The use of 2×2 MIMO can extend the bit rates for a bandwidth of 10 MHz to 40 Mbps downlink and 12 Mbps uplink based on the space time coding as against 22 Mbps and 6 Mbps, respectively, when a single antenna is used. The Wave 2 products are expected to speed up the development of the Mobile WiMAX adoption.

4.5 SUBSCRIBER DENSITIES IN WiMAX

One of the important parameters for network planners and service providers is: how many subscribers can be served in the area of a base station? The question can also be put in a different manner: how many users can be supported in a km^2 of area? This question is critical for any operator or service provider as they dimension their systems and estimate potential revenues. The answer depends on many variables such as the data rates and types of services per subscriber and the transmission environment. However the number of subscribers can be estimated for planning purposes based on certain parameters. These are listed below in Sections 4.5.1 through 4.5.5.

4.5.1 Minimum Allocable Data Unit (MAU) per CPE

The minimum number of subchannels which can be allocated to one active subscriber is one. It may be recalled that the WiMAX initial certification profiles already specify the number of subchannels in the uplink and downlink. (For 5 MHz systems it is 17 uplink and 15 downlink subchannels; for 10 MHz systems it is 35 downlink and 30 uplink subchannels using the PUSC scheme). This can be used to calculate the minimum allocable data units.

Example of Calculating Minimum Allocable Data Units (MAUs) in Mobile WiMAX

As an example of illustrating the minimum allocable data units, will consider the case of a 10 MHZ bandwidth Mobile WiMAX system. The characteristics of such a system are given in Tables 4-7 and 4-8. For 64 QAM 10 MHz bandwidth, the raw channel capacity per symbol, with an OFDM symbol duration of 102.9 microseconds (48 symbols in 5 ms frame or 9600 symbols per second) is

$$\text{Raw data rate per symbol} = 6 \text{ bits/subcarrier} * \text{number of data}$$
$$\text{subcarriers} = 6 * 720 = 4320 \text{ bits (Table 4-7)}$$

Considering the number of subchannels as 30 (downlink) for a 10 MHz system (FFT size of 1024), this gives a minimum allocable bandwidth of 4320/30 = 144 bits per subchannel per OFDM symbol. If FEC is considered to be at $^3/_4$ rate, the MAU, representing the data that can be carried by one subchannel is 144 * $^3/_4$ = 108 bits. This means that a device generating 108 bits every 5 ms needs one subchannel in a frame. If a device is allotted one subchannel in every frame (200 frames per second, 44 data OFDM symbols per frame, i.e., 8800 data symbols per second), it would have a capacity of 1.2672 Mbps after FEC (0.95 Mbps usable data rate before FEC of ¾).

Alternatively, the same figure can be derived from Table 4-8, which gives the data rates obtainable using a 10 MHz bandwidth system with FEC of $^3/_4$ and 64 QAM as 28.512 Mbps in the downlink direction. This data rate is derived based on 44 OFDM symbols per frame of 5 ms or 8800 OFDM symbols per second. The data rate per symbol is therefore 28.512/8800 = 3.24 kilobits. For 30 subchannels, it gives a capacity of 108 bits per subchannel per symbol.

The figure is the same in a 5 MHz system with 15 subchannels and FFT size of 512 because the number of data subcarriers and subchannels are both halved. The MAU determines the "granularity of data." The low bit rates from CPEs which can be supported have a direct bearing on increasing the subscriber count.

A device generating bit rates of less than 108 bits/frame will lead to unused capacity in a particular frame unless it can tolerate higher latencies. Devices that can tolerate higher latencies can be scheduled in frames spaced out in time. Such devices may be able to stack up the requests subject to latency requirements.

Video Carriage

As another example, we can consider the carriage of a unicast video generating a frame every 20 ms (50 frames per second). If one subchannel is allocated in 1 out of 4 frames (frame rate of WiMAX is 200 frames per second), it can operate at a bit rate of 0.95 Mbps/4 = 238 Kbps, adequate for a mobile device using H.264 or any of the commonly used formats. Moreover, if such a WiMAX system is used only for video, it can handle over 120 such streams in the downlink direction based on 30 subchannels.

VoIP
As another example, consider a VoIP service running at 16 Kbps. Due to low latency requirements, its transmission can be scheduled in every frame (i.e., every 5 ms) or every alternate frame (10 ms). The VoIP service requires only 80 bits per 5 ms, which can be handled with one subchannel.

MAUs in Fixed WiMAX
Fixed WiMAX does not support subchannels in the downlink direction. Hence, all the subcarriers for an OFDM symbol need to be allocated to a subscriber station in the downlink direction. These values are given in Table 4-4. For example, using 64 QAM, the MAU is 144 bytes after FEC or 108 bytes before FEC of ¾. This is equal to 864 bits per OFDM symbol.

The base stations support features of fragmentation of MAC data units, as well as packing multiple MAC data units in order to match to OFDM symbols and achieve better link efficiencies.

4.5.2 Frequency Plan and MIMO
In our analysis above, we have already dwelled on other factors that control the subchannels available. Some of these are:

- The number of sectors operated per base station. Operating three sectors, for example, is equivalent to operating three radio channels and can increase the available data rates in the area of a base station to nearly threefold.
- The number of frequencies available (each frequency provides an additional set of OFDM symbols).
- The scheme of allocation of subcarriers. In practice, i.e., using PUSC, not all subcarriers will be allocated near cell edges. Hence to any cluster of customers near a cell edge, a lower number of subchannels may be available.
- Use of MIMO with spatial multiplexing (SM) can also increase the available subchannels by 80 to 100 percent in good transmission conditions as the SM transmits an independent data stream.

4.5.3 Service Types and Data Rate per Customer
The second determinant to dimensioning the number of customers is the types of services used by the subscribers and the "activity factor." If a subscriber is using a circuit emulation service, for example (using UGS), it has a fixed number of subchannels allocated to it. The number of such

customers which can be catered to would be fixed based on the bandwidth. For example, with reference to Table 4-8, at 10 MHz, and using the modulation scheme of 64 QAM $^3/_4$, an uplink data rate of 21 Mbps can be supported as a peak value. Hence, if circuit emulation guaranteed bit rate services are provided at 256 Kbps uplink rate, a maximum of about 80 customers can be supported per sector. If 2×2 MIMO is used with spatial multiplexing, the number can rise to about 150. In practice, this number will be lower, to cater to, fall back of modulation to 16 QAM for example.

A similar situation exists for variable rate services such as video, which need a sustained average bit rate despite frame-to-frame variations. A multicast video service at 6 Mbps, for example, uses up 25 percent of the capacity of a 10 MHz system which is 28 Mbps for downlink.

To arrive at the maximum number of subscribers that can be served in general, we need to consider the mix of services and consequent data rates. The number of subscribers can then be calculated subject to their data rate being above the MAU. In the case of low data rate CPEs, if higher latency is possible, a subchannel can be allotted every alternate frame to double the subscribers with half the data rate each, but latency of 10 ms.

Fast scheduling, i.e., on a per-frame basis, is one of the advantages of Mobile WiMAX. The scheduling can change from one subchannel in a frame to the full capacity available, i.e., up to 30 or 35 subchannels giving a leeway for data to have burst rates of up to 30 times based on traffic conditions subject to the usage by other subscriber stations for higher-priority services.

It needs to be kept in mind that while we are discussing the maximum number of subscribers based on available subchannels, the data rate available per channel may change sharply with change in carrier-to-interference ratio (C/I). In WiMAX, the signal levels received at the mobile and base station terminals are important since users that see better C/I ratios can use higher-order modulation schemes therefore consuming less of available subchannels in a given sector.

Because of these considerations, operators use 25 to 60 percent of the theoretical maximum capacities for dimensioning of services.

4.5.4 Contention Factor

The third factor that determines the number of customers that can be served is the contention factor. The contention factor is commonly used in designing access to services such as the internet and refers to the number of passive subscribers to active subscribers. In a residential area, for example, those users who are actively using the services may be much smaller than the registered number of users with a particular service provider. The contention may range from 1:5 for business areas to 1:30 for residential areas.

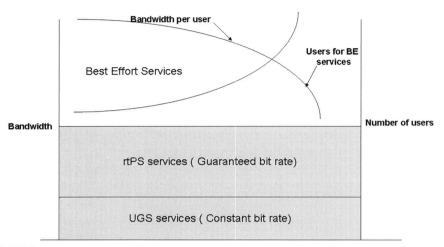

FIGURE 4-30 Users per sector in WiMAX

Putting the three factors together, the number of subscribers can be estimated as

$$\text{Subscribers} = (\text{total data rate}/\text{data rate per subscriber}) \times \text{contention factor}$$

The data rate that these customers see will depend on the transmission conditions and consequently the modulation type that can be maintained. The data rates per OFDM symbol or subchannel can be improved with use of techniques such as MIMO or antenna beamforming. As the transmission conditions deteriorate due to any reason, the data rates will fall and the activity factors will also fall as the users schedule more requests for the subchannels, each of which is now bearing a lower data rate.

4.5.5 Base Station Capacities, Service Flows

Base stations have a limit on the number of active connections, e.g., 512 active connections per sector for base stations such as WMX 3000 or Flexwave™ base station. However, these base stations can cater to 7168 service flows per sector, i.e., 14 service flows per connection. These service flows denote different applications arising from the same connected host or subscriber station. The number of active connected subscribers can grow with the number of sectors. For example, a Packetwave PM 3000™ base station from Aperto Networks can handle one sector and 512 active connections, while the PM 5000 base station can handle 12 sectors (6144 active connections).

4.5.6 Statistical Performance Estimation

Precise estimation of the number of users and data rates is, therefore, an empirical process and can be done based on statistical profiling. The parameters that the statistical models use include the user demographics, location of users relative to base station, and transmission environment (dense urban, urban, suburban, or rural and LOS or NLOS transmission, CPE types, and services mix). The WiMAX Forum has prepared hypothetical models for WiMAX systems in a metropolitan area for the purpose of analysis and performance comparison of different systems under the same model. The model also includes a mix of user profiles, which are classified as "professional," "high-end consumer," or "casual users," and a consumer mix which defines percentages of different types of users. For performance comparison purposes, ITU channel multipath models that include 1 to 3 multiple paths and different pedestrian speeds are often used.

In general, most WiMAX network design software packages provide various modeling environments.

The actual sizing of applications supported will not depend on the maximum data rates that the channel bandwidth can support or the MAU size alone. In fact, it will be determined by a mix of all factors, the physical environment in which the systems operate, and the characteristics of the CPEs such as antenna gain and receiver sensitivities.

4.6 SUMMARY: FEATURES OF MOBILE WiMAX

In this chapter, we have reviewed the technology of Fixed WiMAX and Mobile WiMAX, including their physical (PHY) and Media Access Control layers (MAC) and principles of OFDM, the core technology used in WiMAX systems. The detailed discussion on the MIMO and beam forming has been included primarily for awareness in selection of base station technologies in an urban environment characterized by high user densities and NLOS environment.

Mobile WiMAX provides robust transmission in NLOS and mobile environments with speeds up to 125 Kmph. Its key features can be summarized as below:

- Mobile WiMAX is very flexible in allocating resources for both uplink and downlink traffic. It provides QoS guaranteed classes in which quality is maintained by controlling access to the wireless medium.
- The scheduling is available on a per-frame basis for both the uplink and downlink by using MAP messages at the beginning

of every frame. Hence the system is ideally suited for rapidly changing transmission conditions.

- Mobile WiMAX provides for very robust channel coding for forward error correction. The convolutional coding (CC) and CTC provide high resilience against errors.
- The transmission can be tailored to the channel conditions by using the schemes of Partial Utilization of Subcarriers (PUSC) and Full Usage of Subcarriers (FUSC).The subcarriers can be allotted to a subchannel by being adjacent in frequency or based on random allocation.
- The use of smart antenna techniques (space time coding, beamforming) can provide diversity reception or increase in peak data rates. The use of 4×4 MIMO is inbuilt in the Mobile WiMAX standards.
- Mobile WiMAX assigns only a few subcarriers to each mobile station on which they are expected to transmit. This reduces the peak power requirements very significantly.
- The handover in Mobile WiMAX can be very flexible, with each mobile station being in contact with an active set of base stations. In both the fast base station switching and macro-diversity handover, the handover happens without loss of data or latency. At the same time the mobile stations can go in sleep mode and need not be active for every ranging message.

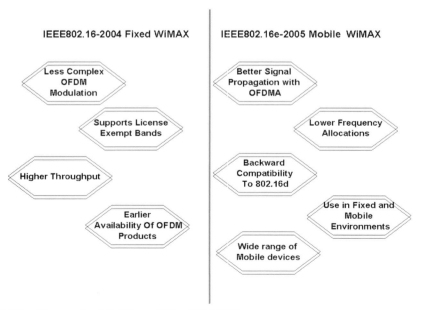

FIGURE 4-31 Comparing Mobile and Fixed WiMAX

5

DESIGN OF WiMAX TRANSMISSION NETWORKS

Reality is that which, when you stop believing in it, doesn't go away.
—Philip K. Dick
How to Build a Universe that Doesn't Fall Apart
Two Days Later (1978)

5.1 INTRODUCTION

WiMAX is a flexible and innovative technology with high-spectral efficiency. We have seen the main features of the WiMAX physical and MAC layers and how they function in tandem to provide a connection oriented service with guaranteed QoS and security features. In this chapter, we go beyond the technology specifications and PHY and MAC layer functions to look at:

- The link budgets
- Impact of interference
- Network design considerations
- Multiple antenna techniques in network design

The individual components of a WiMAX system, conforming to the standards and WiMAX Forum certification profiles such as base stations, backhaul networks, receiver terminals, etc., are available from many vendors. These components can be put together to create a complete system based on WiMAX characteristics and design principles that follow from them.

This chapter is devoted to the design of the WiMAX networks and a study of the principles that are involved in determining the capacity of the systems. WiMAX systems can be engineered with high reliability across varied terrain because of the robustness of the technology, provided certain basic guidelines are followed. We look at the requirements for successfully engineering the networks.

As the requirements placed on WiMAX networks in city, semi-urban, and rural environments are different, the principles to be followed in estimating capacity depend on many factors, many of which are empirical in nature. These factors include density of users in a given area, nature of transmission environment presented by buildings, indoor areas, mobile and nomadic behavior arising from travel between city centers and residences, and the nature of applications. Exact determination of the bit rates is therefore an empirical exercise which needs to draw upon the principles of WiMAX network design as well as the local demographics and user behavior. Statistical modeling of user densities and application types can help arrive at usage patterns which may closely correlate with the actual performance. Fortunately, WiMAX systems are easily scalable and inaccuracies in arriving at the exact figures can be made good by adding an additional "blade" in a base station, for example.

In this chapter, we confine our discussions to the principles involved in WiMAX network planning.

5.2 LINK ANALYSIS OF WiMAX SYSTEMS

Estimating the performance of the WiMAX system in line-of-sight (LOS) and non-line-of-sight (NLOS) environments is the first step in the process of creating a transmission network for WiMAX. Link analysis involves selecting the frequency band used and determining the signal strengths based on propagation characteristics in the frequency band selected. However, while this would have completed the process for an ordinary radio system, WiMAX has many weapons in its armory to improve the SNR or increase data rates even in adverse transmission conditions. We have seen some of these tools including adaptive modulation, use of diversity techniques, and advanced antenna systems to provide improved link performance even in an NLOS urban environment. Finally, it has the capability to sustain QoS for various service flows established, which override any data rate variations that still persist after the tools of transmission have done their jobs. We take a journey through the entire process now. Estimating what the overall system performance will be, considering all the tools available, is the job of link analysis, and we do that now.

5.2.1 Spectrum Bands Used in WiMAX

Mobile WiMAX is based on the use of scalable OFDMA and can operate in different frequency bands (e.g., 2.3, 2.5, 3.3, or 5.8 GHz) and

TABLE 5-1

Fixed WiMAX certification profiles

Frequency band (MHz)	Channelization (MHz)	Duplexing
3400–3600	3.5	TDD
3400–3600	7.0	TDD
3400–3600	3.5	FDD
3400–3600	7.0	FDD
5725–5850	1	TDD

TABLE 5-2

Release 1 Mobile WiMAX initial certification profiles (Source: WiMAX Forum)

Channelization	FFT Size	Data Carriers	Carrier Spacing	2.3 to 2.4 GHZ	2.305 to 2.32 GHZ	2.345 to 2.36 GHz	2.496 to 2.69 GHz	3.3 to 3.4 GHz	3.4 to 3.8 GHz
5 MHz	512	408	11 KHz	TDD	TDD	TDD	TDD	TDD	TDD
7 MHz	1024	840						TDD	TDD
8.75 MHz	1024	840	9.765 KHz	TDD					
10 MHz	1024	840	11 KHz	TDD	TDD	TDD	TDD	TDD	TDD

system bandwidths from 1.5 MHz–20 MHz. The number of subcarriers increases based on the available bandwidth, and hence there is no degradation caused by multipath interference even as bandwidth gets scaled up to 20 MHz. As we reviewed earlier, the WIMAX forum has selected certain frequency bands and profiles in which certification of equipment for interoperability is being done. While there is no bar on deploying systems which may not have been approved for inclusion in WiMAX certification profiles, it is advantageous for operators as well as vendors to utilize equipment that has been WiMAX-forum certified and is interoperable. In the future, these profiles will be extended to include new frequency bands and bandwidths.

For Fixed WiMAX, Table 5-1 gives the approved certification profiles.

For Mobile WiMAX, the WiMAX Forum has indicated that the Release 1 certification profiles will encompass the frequency bands of 2.3, 2.5, 3.3, and 3.5 GHz and bandwidths of 5, 7, 8.75, and 10 MHz. The WiMAX Forum has specified parameters for each of these profiles, which include the FFT size, number of data carriers, and guard interval. The other parameters such as OFDM symbol time and subcarrier bandwidth can easily be easily derived. Table 5-2 lists the Release 1 Mobile WiMAX certification profiles.

5.2.2 Path Loss and Link Budgets

The path losses are given by:

Free Space Loss $(FSL) = (C/(4 \pi DF))^2$ where F = frequency of operation, C = speed of light, and D = distance.

In log terms this can be represented as $FSL = 92.45 + 20 \log F + 20 \log D$ where F = frequency in GHz and D = distance in Km.

The receive power can be derived as $Pr = (Pt * Gt * Gr) * FSL$ where Pr = received power, Pt = transmitted Power, Gt = Gain of transmitting antenna, and Gr = Gain of receiving antenna.

In log terms this can be written as $Pr(dBm) = Pt(dBm) + 10 \log Gt + 10 \log Gr - FSL(dB)$.

As an example, if the power transmitted is 1 watt (30 dBm) with 15 dBi antennas for transmission and reception, the power received at 10 Km at 2.5 GHz will be

$$Pr = 30 + 15 + 15 - 92.45 - 40 - 7.96 = -60.4\,dBm$$

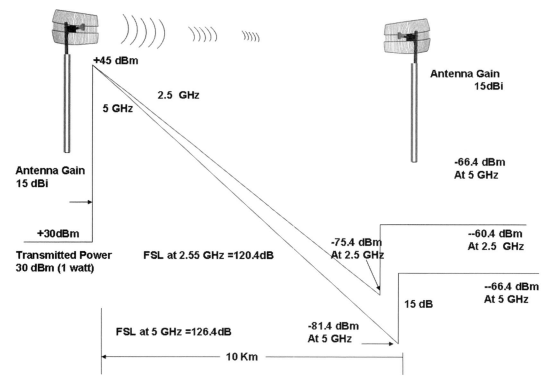

FIGURE 5-1   Link analysis of a WiMAX system operating at 2.5 and 5 GHz

At 5 GHz the power at the same distance will be

$$Pr = 30 + 15 + 15 - 92.45 - 40 - 13.98 = -66.4\,dBm$$

The received power at 5 GHz is thus 4 times less than that received at 2.5 GHz and 9 times less than at 800 MHz. However, to an extent these will be covered by a higher antenna gain in actual practice.

Because of the power received reducing with the square of the frequency, the frequency of operation of WiMAX systems inherently places it at some disadvantage over cellular systems operating at 800 MHz, for example, in terms of base station spacing and distances covered.

In actual transmission conditions, the height of transmitting and receiving antennas is not sufficiently high to achieve LOS transmission. The received waves are then the sum of direct and reflected waves, and the received power needs to be calculated based on empirical formulas which factor in the type of terrain and the type of antenna systems used to take advantage of diversity.

5.2.3 Link Analysis for Mobile WiMAX Receiver

In order to understand the mobile WiMAX transmission environment, we consider an example of 10 MHz bandwidth (1024 FFT size) transmission using a WiMAX base station with 10 watts power output and using an antenna with antenna gain of 15 dBi. Table 5-3 provides the parameters which are used for the transmission example.

As indicated earlier, the transmission in a suburban environment needs to take into account shadowing losses due to NLOS transmission conditions. In order to model the transmissions it is common to use empirical transmission models such as COST 231- Hata propagation model or other models. In our analysis, we take a loss of penetration as 10 dB and a shadow fade margin of 5.56 dB.

1. Downlink Link Analysis

For a given receiver (PCMCIA WiMAX Card) for a transmitter configuration with dual 15 dBi antennas each transmitting 40 dBm in diversity mode, the maximum allowable path loss is given by (Table 5-4):

The table clearly shows the difference in maximum path loss allowed for 64QAM vis-à-vis QPSK, which has a bearing on the distance.

TABLE 5-3

Operating parameters and transmission characteristics

Operating Setup	
System Parameters	Values
Bandwidth	10 MHz
FFT size	1024
Subcarrier spacing	10.94 kHz
Symbol duration	102.9 microseconds
Guard duration	11.4 microseconds
Useful symbol time	91.4 microseconds
Subchannels	30
Data Subcarriers	720
Pilot Subcarriers	120
Transmitter Characteristics	
Power output per antenna	40 dBm
Antenna gain	15 dBi
No. of antennas	2
Antenna diversity gain	3 dB
Effective EIRP	58
No. of subcarriers	840
Power per subcarrier	28.5 dBm
Propagation Characteristics	
Propagation model	Suburban (COST 231)
Penetration loss	10 dB
Log normal shadowing loss	5.56 dB
Fast fading margin (traffic)	2 dB
Interference margin	2 dB
Total margin	19.56 dB

2. Uplink Link Analysis

A similar analysis can be done for the uplink, where the mobile is the transmitting device and the base station is the receiver. Considering the example of the PCMCIA card with 23 dBm power output and 0 dBi antenna gain, and the base station receiver sensitivity of −103 dBm

TABLE 5-4

Link analysis in Mobile WiMAX environment

Link Analysis Base Station to Mobile			
Parameter	QPSK	16 QAM	64 QAM
Receiver sensitivity	−100 dBm	−90 dBm	−80 dBm
Total margin to be maintained	19.56 dB	19.56 dB	19.56 dB
Receive antenna gain	2 dBi	2 dBi	2 dBi
RX diversity gain	3 dB	3 dB	3 dB
Signal required at receiver	−85.4 dBm	−75.4	−65.4 dBm
Transmitted power (dBm)	58	58	58
Maximum path loss	−143.4 dB	−133.4 dB	−122.4 dB

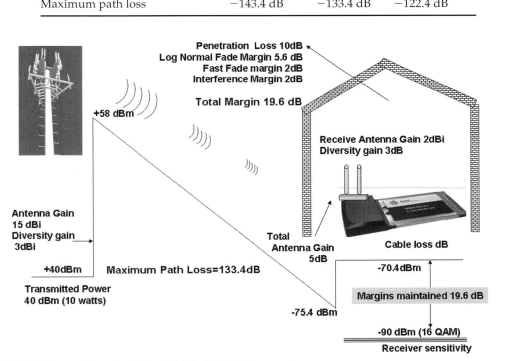

FIGURE 5-2   Link analysis in a Mobile WiMAX network

(all subcarriers used), the maximum path loss works out to −123 dBm (Table 5-5).

It is worth noting that if a lower number of subcarriers are transmitted, the power transmitted is divided into a smaller number of subcarriers and the allowable path loss will be higher.

TABLE 5-5

Uplink analysis in Mobile WiMAX

Uplink Analysis (Traffic Channels)	
Mobile Transmission	Traffic Mode
Transmitted rated power	23 dBm
Transmit antenna gain	0 dBi
EIRP	23 dBm
Propagation Margins	
Penetration loss	10 dB
Interference margin	3 dB
Log normal fade margin	5.6 dB
Fast fading margin	2 dB
Total margin	20.6 dB
Available subcarriers	840
Reception at base station	
Rx antenna gain	15 dBi
Rx diversity gain	3 dB
Base station reciever sensitivity	−103 dBm
Composite (64 QAM)	
Maximum path loss	−123.4dB

PATH LOSS PERMISSIBLE WITH PARTIAL UTILIZATION OF SUBCARRIERS

As an example, if in the uplink direction, the 840 subcarriers are divided in 35 subchannels and 3 subchannels are allocated to the mobile unit (72 subcarriers), the power transmitted per subcarrier will be $23 - 10 \log(72) = 4.42$ dBm per subcarrier. The receiver sensitivity per subcarrier at this subchannelization is $-103 -10\log(840) = -132.24$ dBm (where -103 dBm is the composite receiver sensitivity). Hence, this gives the maximum allowable path loss as -133.9 dB.

The above link analyses are oversimplified, as these are based on the receiver sensitivities provided in the data sheets of receivers and base stations. Certain values are assumed for the fade margin, interference, penetration loss, etc., which depend on the empirical model used for evaluation. In practice, the difference in margins in using different models can exceed 70 percent.

5.2.4 Antenna Techniques in WiMAX

The WiMAX standards specify the antenna techniques that can be used to enhance transmission quality and data rates. The specification of antenna systems in the standards helps the equipment manufacturers supply baseband and RF equipment that will support the specified antenna systems. Antenna techniques have been briefly covered in Chapter 4. We review their features with some practical examples.

Multiple Antenna Technologies and Beam Forming

Multiple antenna technologies are generically referred to as MIMO, signifying the use of multiple inputs and multiple outputs. The MIMO techniques fall in the category of closed loop and open loop MIMO systems. Closed loop MIMO systems are user-location-aware systems and lead to transmissions based on beam forming (called transmitter adaptive antenna technologies). Open loop MIMO systems, on the other hand, are characterized by predetermined sector and antenna element configurations. Therefore time-dependent information on transmission conditions is not used to alter the transmission pattern.

The WiMAX standards specify two types of open loop MIMO systems.

1. MIMO Matrix A, which Uses Space-Time Block Coding (STBC)

In STBC the same stream of data is replicated and transmitted over two or more antennas. The data streams are encoded using space-time codes, which make the transmitted streams mathematically orthogonal. The receiver can select the signal that is least affected by the transmission errors or use maximum ratio combining (MRC) to reconstruct the transmitted signal. The MIMO Matrix A, as is evident, primarily provides space diversity without increasing bit rates.

2. MIMO Matrix B, which Uses Spatial Multiplexing (MIMO-SM)

The MIMO Matrix B is designed to enhance the capacity by splitting the transmitted stream into two (or more) parts and transmitting them on the same frequency but using a different base station antenna. The received signals can be distinguished at the receiver by using multiple antenna elements which can pick up the spatial signatures of the streams so that they can be decoded separately.

It is evident that MIMO Matrix A is meant for use in low signal-to-interference environments (low SINR) and MIMO Matrix B can be used in high SINR environments to increase cell capacity. Two

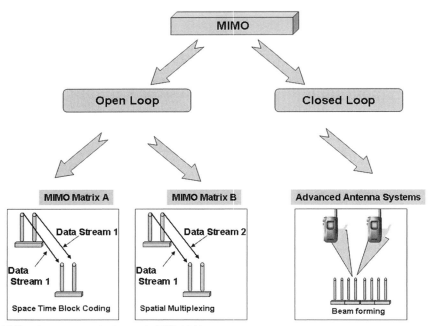

FIGURE 5-3   Antenna techniques in WiMAX

antenna systems have been mandated by the WiMAX Forum for the Wave 2 certification profiles.

The closed loop MIMO systems (advanced antenna systems and beam forming) is an optional feature in the Mobile WiMAX IEEE 802.16e standards. The beam forming techniques use an antenna array at the transmitter and receiver along with advanced signal processing. The amplitude and phase of the signals supplied to the antennas are so phased as to change the direction of the beam toward the location of the receiver (software for beam forming antennas is supplied by vendors such as Arraycom®).The higher antenna gains achieved with beam forming together with reduction of interference at the receiver lead to significantly improved link performance. The beamforming needs to be operative within the selected frame intervals (e.g., 5 ms to 20 ms). The advanced processing capabilities available today in the chipsets make the implementation of closed loop MIMO systems and advanced antenna techniques, including beam forming, practical.

An Example of a Base Station Supporting MIMO and Advanced Antenna Systems

An example of a base station that supports MIMO as well as beam-forming is the Airspan® HiperMAX™ base station. The base station

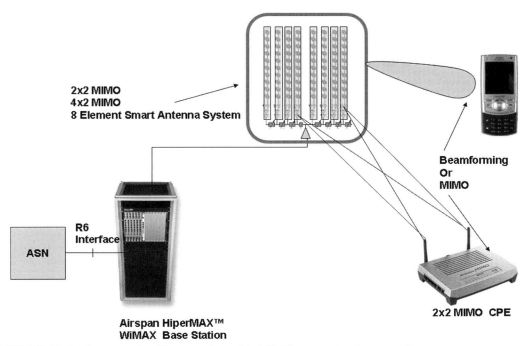

FIGURE 5-4   An example of base station with MIMO or smart antenna system

connects to the Access Service Network (ASN) via the standard designated WiMAX interface between base stations and ASN (called R6) and
provides support for either MIMO or beamforming. It can support:

- Fixed WiMAX (OFDM) and Mobile WiMAX (scalable OFDMA)
- FDD profiles or TDD profiles
- 2×2 MIMO or 4×2 MIMO
- 4- or 8-channel smart antenna system

5.2.5 Comparison of MIMO and Advanced Antenna System (AAS) Usage

The closed loop MIMO systems represented by AAS are at present an
optional feature in IEEE 802.16e. The AAS systems work on the principle of beamforming designed to target an individual user located anywhere in a cell area. Technically this provides a beam whose maximum
power is directed to the user and improves the signal-to-interference
ratios at the receiver, while keeping the transmit powers to an optimum.

AAS systems are comprised of a set of antennas that act as a phased
array. The generation of phased array signals based on user location
increases additional complexity in the system as compared to open loop

MIMO systems with space-time diversity and sectorization. It also requires the phased array antennas to be precisely calibrated and aligned. In urban environments, the beamforming antennas need to be able to operate in an environment where the signals are reflected from buildings and other objects. This effectively reduces the beam angle and the gain of the beamforming antenna reducing some of the benefits which would otherwise arise from the precision beamforming technology. The open loop MIMO systems such as 2×2 MIMO, which are designed to operate in NLOS environments, can give a robust performance in such a usage scenario. MIMO antennas with sectored beams can have higher gain than beams generated from phased array antennas. MIMO systems can also be switched to operate either as diversity systems or to give higher data rates based on user transmission quality indication.

Based on the application of the COST 231-Hata suburban propagation model, a simulation comparison in the 2.5 GHz mobile WiMAX range gives the following relative channel capacity indicators with 1×2 SIMO being taken as the base case:

1×2 SIMO	1.0
2×2 MIMO	1.55
Beamforming	1.65
Beamforming and MIMO	1.85

5.3 FREQUENCY PLANNING IN WiMAX

What are the key factors of frequency planning in a WiMAX network? (a) **Frequency Band**: The frequency band would be either a licensed band or an unlicensed one. The propagation losses increase in proportion to the square of the frequency. Hence, the higher frequency bands present a challenging environment in providing transmissions over large cell areas.

The WiMAX has designed profiles to work in both licensed and unlicensed frequency bands. However, the availability of various bands (whether unlicensed or otherwise) is country-specific. A detailed analysis of the bands and their characteristics is presented in Chapter 11.

In general, license-exempt bands, such as 5 GHz (5.25–5.85 GHz) in United States, give an option of fast rollout without awaiting spectral resources. The cost of such systems can also be lower because of the standard frequency band being used rather than a customized country-specific band. On the other hand, the unlicensed bands can present higher levels of interference due to other unlicensed systems in use.

Moreover, such interference can appear anytime, even though the initial installation was done after testing a sigh signal-to-interference ratio. However such problems may be minimal in rural areas where a fast rollout is a priority.

The licensed bands are the only ones currently recommended for use for Mobile WiMAX as per details in Table 5-2. In Europe and many other countries, the 3.5 GHz band is being licensed for Mobile WiMAX applications. The band of 2.495 to 2.690, which was earlier earmarked for wireless MMDS systems, is used in the United States and is called the Broadband Radio Service (BRS).

The type of spectrum required also depends on the technology selected (i.e., FDD or TDD). In the frequency division duplex mode a paired spectrum is needed for the uplink and the downlinks. This is not possible in the unlicensed frequency bands. Again, most of the initial implementation profiles of WiMAX are based on the use of the time-division duplexing (TDD).

We should recognize that many of the WiMAX systems in quest for a common set of bands of operation in various countries have been placed in the 2.5 GHz, 3.5 GHz, and 5 GHz bands.

(b) **Network Antenna Types**: The use of sectorization, and advanced antenna systems such as beamforming can enhance the usable capacity of a cell, as discussed in the previous section. Likewise, the use of MIMO or space diversity antennas has a bearing on the cell capacities.

5.3.1 Cellular Deployment and Frequency Reuse

Frequency Reuse in Cellular (GSM or CDMA Systems)

The traditional model of cellular planning in networks such as GSM is to have adjacent cells operate on different frequencies. For complete frequency separation between adjacent cells, a set of 7 frequencies is required. This is represented by a reuse factor of 1/7, i.e., the same frequency can be reused in 1 of every 7 cells (each group of 7 cells is a cluster). As the number of users per cell rises, the cells can be made smaller. This leads to a possibility that even with a low reuse factor, the signals will interfere in other cells.

As per common notation, the frequency reuse factor can be written as:

Frequency reuse factor = Number of clusters covered/Number of frequencies

For one cluster (of 7 cells) where 7 frequencies are used, the frequency reuse factor is 1/7. The frequency reuse factor indicates how efficiently the frequencies are being used.

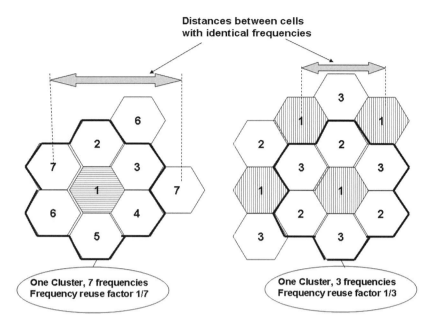

GSM Network Cellular frequencies

FIGURE 5-5   Frequency reuse in GSM cellular systems

The number of frequency reuse schemes (FRS) in this case is 7 as there are 7 different ways in which the frequencies can be arranged in the cluster. A higher FRS indicates superior quality of service due to lower interference.

It is possible to have an implementation with 3 frequencies covering one cluster. This gives a frequency reuse factor of 1/3. The frequency reuse schemes are 3, being the three different ways in which frequencies in cluster can be organized. In cellular GSM systems, a frequency reuse such as 1/3 has a larger possibility of interference from adjacent cells (Figure 5-5).

It is evident that in case of a frequency reuse factor of 1/3, the given set of frequencies (for example, 9 frequencies) can provide services to a greater number of users, if the co-channel interference can be contained. (Co-channels are the channels that operate on the same frequency.)

In the case of CDMA, the modulation scheme is based on the use of codes for deciphering signals and the channels can operate on the same frequency. In a CDMA system, therefore, the adjacent cells can operate on the same frequency. This implies a frequency reuse factor of 1.

5.3.2 Frequency Reuse in WiMAX Systems

WiMAX is also characterized by a very high degree of resilience to co-channel interference, i.e., the capability of decoding the signals in the presence of signals at the same frequency from adjacent cells or base stations. Mobile WiMAX has been designed with the capability of being used with a frequency reuse factor of one, i.e., all the adjacent cells in a cluster can use the same frequency. A frequency reuse of 1, however, results in areas near the cell edge having signals at the same frequency from adjacent cells, which appear as interference.

The feature of WiMAX of being able to assign subchannels with frequency segmentation can be used to assign users near the cell edge with a set of subcarriers which are separated in frequency. This provides better protection against co-channel interference as within the same channel the subcarriers fall in a different frequency. Interference near cell edges can be reduced and the capacity increased if a sectorization scheme is used, which directs energy away from cell edges.

Single Frequency per Sector with Sectorization

In order to better represent sectorization, which is also a feature of WiMAX, it is typical to denote the frequency reuse schemes as (c,s,f) where c is the cluster number, s is the number of sectors per cell, and f is the number of frequencies per cluster. Using this nomenclature, a frequency reuse of 1 without sectorization will be represented as (c,1,1). If three sectors are used per cell, then the frequency reuse is still 1 (one frequency per cluster), but it has higher capacity and lower interference. This can be represented as (c,3,1)

The maximum interference is at the cell edges if sectorization is not used, but this is reduced considerably with sectorization. It should be noted that OFDM works best only with a high signal-to-interference ratio, and performance near the edges can be very poor without sectorization or without PUSC frequency reuse schemes. The additional advanced antenna features such as beamforming can further improve the signal-to-interference ratio (SINR) in a single frequency environment by directing the transmitted energy in a narrow cone. This can give a signal-to-interference ratio improvement of 6 dB per sector. Use of MIMO also provides improvement in signal-to-interference ratios with the use of spatial multiplexing. In the case of a single frequency, the number of frequency reuse schemes (FRS) is one. However, it is possible to create additional frequency reuse schemes by using only part of the subcarriers available.

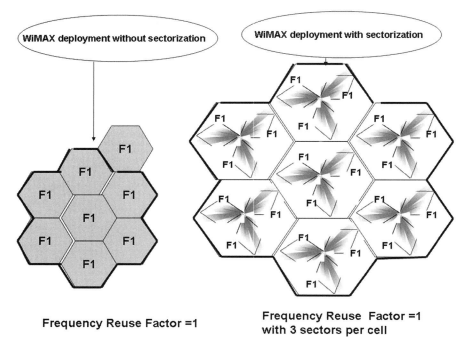

FIGURE 5-6   Frequency allocation of adjacent cells in WiMAX with frequency reuse of 1

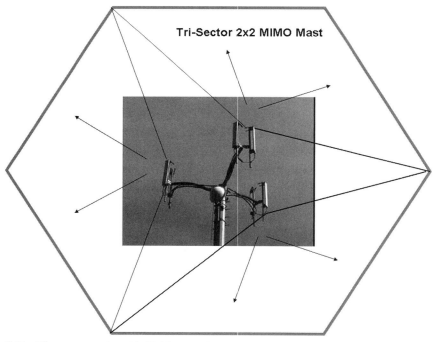

FIGURE 5-7   Three-sector 2 × 2 MIMO mast (image courtesy Nortel)

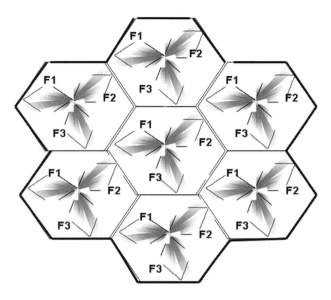

**Frequency Reuse Schemes =3
(1,3,3)**

FIGURE 5-8 Using different frequencies per sector in WiMAX

Using Multiple Frequencies per Cell

In most WiMAX applications, having a single frequency in all the cells and all sectors may not suffice. To increase the system capacities and to reduce interference, additional frequencies are used, based on the availability with an operator. There are different ways in which the additional frequencies can be used.

The first technique is to use different frequencies for each sector in a cell. If the cells are divided into three sectors each, and the three frequencies are used in an identical fixed manner in each sector (Figure 5-8) the number of frequency reuse schemes is 3.

Using different frequencies per sector (3 frequencies) implies a frequency reuse factor of $1/3$, an indicator of efficiency of spectrum utilization over a given area. This is only 33 percent of what can be achieved with a frequency reuse factor of 1. As spectrum is a constrained resource and highly priced, it is preferable to use better sectorization and use schemes for getting a better reuse specifically at cell edges by using only part of the subcarriers (e.g., $1/3$) to effectively get a frequency reuse of 3 at the edges alone. The users nearer to the cell center continue to make use of all the subcarriers as required.

If three frequencies are available to an operator, it might still like to operate with sectorization schemes by using all the frequencies, but as independent radio channels (Figure 5-9).

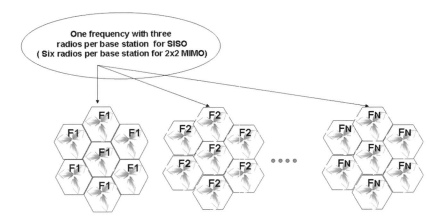

Frequency reuse factor =1

Frequency reuse schemes= N where N= number of Frequencies

FIGURE 5-9   Operating different frequencies as independent channels

For example, if an operator has access to 15 MHz of spectrum with 5 MHz channelization, it would prefer to operate three independent channels of 5 MHz at different frequencies, each with 3 sectors or 6 sectors to multiply the capacity rather than use 15 MHz divided into three sectors in each cell. Using up all three channels in a cell still gives the operator a capacity equivalent to 3 times the data rate for a 5 MHz channel (~16 Mbps), i.e., a total of ~48 Mbps (combined uplink and downlink) as against operating 3 radios (9 sectors) with a data rate approaching about 75 percent of 3 × 48 Mbps or ~108 Mbps. (The loss of 25 percent can be factored in because of lower data rates caused by higher interference and is an estimated figure only.)

Using Subcarrier Groups for Higher Frequency Reuse Schemes

The third approach is to use frequency-separated subcarriers in each of the sectors to give additional frequency reuse schemes (FRS). In general if there are N frequencies (F_1 to F_N), S is the number of sectors per cell and if the available bandwidth is divided among M groups of subcarriers in a manner so that the subcarriers are separated by frequency, the number of frequency reuse schemes (FRS) is:

$$FRS = N \times S \times M$$

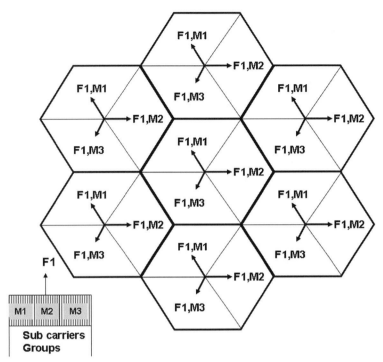

FIGURE 5-10 Frequency reuse schemes with subcarriers

Figure 5-10 demonstrates the frequency in each cell being divided into three groups (M1, M2, and M3) with only one group being used in each sector of the cell. Effectively, therefore, each cell in fact operates on a different frequency because the subcarriers are on non-overlapping frequencies. This is categorized as a $1 \times 3 \times 3$ FRS with 1 frequency, 3 sectors, and 3 groups of subcarriers separated in the frequency being used. Effectively three dimensions—frequency, subcarriers, and beam forming—are used to create frequency reuse schemes in the above implementation.

Zone Switching

There is also a fourth dimension, which is the distance from the transmitter, termed as the zone of usage, which can be further used to enhance the frequency reuse schemes. This is done by zone switching, wherein a different set of subcarriers is allocated within the same cell based on the zone. The allocation of subcarriers based on zone is done by the implementation of the fractional frequency reuse scheme (FFRS).

The FFRS is implemented by using the first half of the downlink frame to address receive terminals in Zone 1 (near to transmitters) and the second half of downlink frame to address the receive terminals in

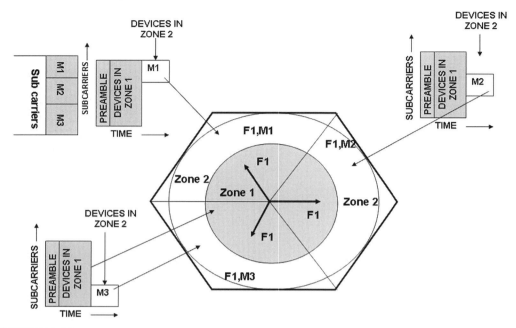

FIGURE 5-11   Zone-wise use of subcarriers in Mobile WiMAX

Zone 2 (near the cell edge). In Zone 1, for example, in the first half of the downlink frame, all the subcarriers are used, while in the second half of the frame only a part of the subcarriers separated in frequency are used. Hence, near the cell edges, where the co-channel interference would otherwise be the highest, the subcarriers are, in fact, separated in frequency. In the near zone, where the signals are strong, all the subcarriers are used for higher-cell capacity realization.

5.3.3 Examples of Support of Sectorization and Frequency Reuse in WiMAX Base Stations

Flexwave WMX5000

An example of how base stations permit sectorization with increased capacity for users can be had from the specifications of the Flexwave™ base station. The base station (WMX5000) can operate in any of the bands. A single base station chassis can cater to 12 sectors, which can be operated in 1:1 or 1:N redundancy. With 512 users per sector, the base station can cater to 6144 subscribers in each cell area (based on 12 sectors/cell). It can support up to 7168 managed unidirectional service flows. The QoS, which can be guaranteed by the base

Service/ User Support Features	
Maximum no of sectors	12 (Non-redundant),6 with 1:1 redundancy
Active connected Subscriber units	Upto 6144 (512 per sector)
Unidirectional service flows	Upto 7168 managed
QoS	UGS,rtPS,nrtPS,BE,CIR

**FlexWave™ Carrier Grade
WiMAX Base Station**

FIGURE 5-12 Sector, user support in a typical WiMAX base station (picture courtesy ADC Telecommunications Inc.)

station, is as per the WiMAX standards and includes UGS, rtPS, nrtPS, BE, CIR, etc.

It is interesting to understand the specifications of a WiMAX base station and how the different schemes for frequency reuse can be implemented in practice. For this purpose, we look at the specifications of HiperMAX™ base station (a product of Airspan Networks Inc.).

The HiperMAX base station can be used for Fixed WiMAX, or with a software upgradation, for Mobile WiMAX. The base station consists of the indoor unit and the outdoor RF sections which are connected using a fiber optic cable. The RF section, which gets its input from the indoor unit baseband "Blades," can be connected to the antenna system of choice including elements to form advanced antenna systems.

The following antenna types are supported by the HiperMAX™;

- MIMO Matrix A
- Tx and Rx diversity
- 2 × 2 MIMO Matrix B
- 4 × 2 MIMO Matrix B
- Smart Antenna System. HiperMAX™ can support 8 element arrays for 2.5 G and 3.5 G systems.

Each base station baseband blade can be configured to support up to 6 active channels with full redundancy or 12 active channels without redundancy. A GPS timing source provides accurate timing necessary in a set of base stations. Antennas containing up to 8 elements each are connected to the blade through the RF unit.

TABLE 5-6

HyperMAX WiMAX base station features (courtesy Airspan Networks)

Base Station Features	Support	Remarks
Physical layer	OFDM, OFDMA	
Frequency bands	3.3–3.8, 2.3–2.4, 2.5–2.7, 4.9–5 GHZ	
Transmit power	Up to +40 dBm per antenna element	
Receiver sensitivity	Upto −115 dBm with 1/16 subchannelization	
Standards compliance	IEEE 802.16e-2005	
Uplink subchannelization support	1/2,1/4,1/8,1/16,1/32 (Mobile WiMAX)	
MIMO support	Yes	Open MIMO features
Space division multiple access (SDMA) support	Yes	
Sector angles	60, 90, 120, 180, omni	
Multi-channel transmit diversity	Yes	
N order receive diversity	Yes	
Adaptive antenna support	Yes	Advanced antenna features
Spatial frequency interference rejection support (SFIR)	Yes	
Configurable frame durations	2.5, 4, 5, 8, 10, 12.5, 20 ms	

There is also a smaller version of the base station available (MicroMAX), which can support up to 12 base station radios. Each base station radio can connect to an antenna, which is configured for 60, 90, 120, 180 degree or omni-directional radiation.

5.3.4 Building WiMAX Networks: Pico, Micro, and Macro Base Stations

WiMAX systems are implemented in a wide range of environments. These can range from sparsely populated rural areas, where a town may be covered by a single base station, to high-density user areas, e.g., in a city center. Both these have different requirements. Base stations in sparsely populated areas need to be self-contained with maximum functionality built in to the base station itself. These may have a single sector, used perhaps with an omni antenna. In high-density areas, in order to support maximum active connected users, multiple sector base stations are needed with beam forming and MIMO to maximize data rates and cater to multipath effects.

In industry terminology, the base stations can be classified as micro, pico, or macro based on the need they fulfil. The network working group of WiMAX Forum has also defined "Profiles" of base stations based on the functionality contained in a base station. These profiles, called ASN profiles, are covered in Chapter 12. At this point, it would suffice to mention that Profile B base stations have the gateway capability built in the base station to connect to external networks (such as IP networks). Such base stations are termed ASN Profile B. These are well suited for areas where a single base station needs to be installed to initiate coverage.

Micro and pico base stations are needed in high-density areas with short cell radii. Many such cells will exist in small area, and thus the architecture needs to support connectivity to a separately located gateway (called access service network gateway or ASN-GW) instead of replicating the functionality in each base station. Such base stations conform to Profile C of the ASN if they have their own radio resource management functionality but no gateway functionality. Many pico stations then operate under a common ASN with a single gateway connecting to external networks. A pico base station conforming to Profile C would typically cover one sector and support wave two profile features such as AAS and MIMO.

Micro and pico base stations are available from all the major equipment vendors. An example of pico base stations is the Telsima StarMAX 5200 base station, conforming to ASN profile C. Other examples from Aperto® Networks are the PacketMAX™ 3000 and PacketMAX 2000 base stations. All are single-sector base stations. PacketMAX2000 is an outdoor mountable base station. PacketMAX3000 is an indoor unit stackable for higher capacities.

Macro base stations are multi-sector base stations (e.g., capable of supporting 12 or more sectors each with 2×2 MIMO or AAS). An example of such a base station (Flexwave® WMX 5000) has already been given in Figure 5-12. A carrier-grade base station with similar capabilities available from Aperto networks is PacketMAX5000, which can support 12 sectors.

5.3.5 Transmission Environment in WiMAX

The WiMAX networks present a complex operating environment. This is because many variables come into effect when trying to estimate the optimal network design. For example, the following factors may be important:

- The base stations as well as subscriber stations can be considered to be operating in a matrix in which the mobile station receives

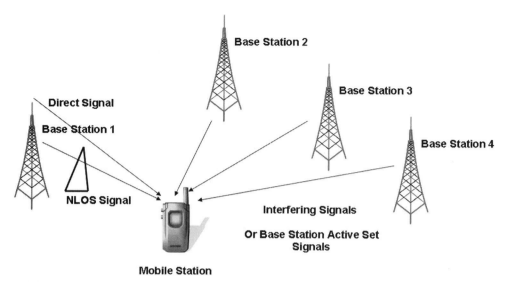

FIGURE 5-13   Operating environment in WiMAX networks

signals from one base station and interference from other stations.

- The path loss is based on the terrain needs to be estimated by the
  ground propagation loss rather than a free space loss (FSL).
- The reception environment is NLOS, hence the shadowing effects
  need to be considered.
- WiMAX offers a range of space-time diversity technologies (such
  as MIMO) in which multiple carriers may be radiated at the same
  frequency from one base station using different antennas.
- The use of smart antenna technologies gives an opportunity of
  beam forming and increasing sector capacity significantly.
- The mobile terminal needs to be in contact with more than one
  base station for handover and ranging.

The environment of operations can be represented by Figure 5-13.

At the same time, the designers of WiMAX have given powerful
tools which can be used to improve the peak data rates which can be
achieved on individual links. We have seen some of these technologies
in earlier discussions:

- Antenna beam forming technologies can be used to improve signal-to-interference performance
- Multiple input-multiple output (MIMO) systems can be used to
  enhance path diversity or increase data rates

FIGURE 5-14   Accton™ 802.16e PCMCIA card

- Peak to average power control (PAPR) is used to limit very high transmitted powers caused by the statistical addition of subcarriers
- The carriers can be allotted to subchannels based on random allocation or frequency contiguous allocation of subcarriers to tailor transmission to the site multipath effects

Before we proceed to consider a typical transmission network design, it is instructive to look at a typical receiver terminal and a base station to appreciate the type of environment which is presented.

For this purpose, we look at the characteristics of a WiMAX PCMCIA card (Accton™), which is based on IEEE802.16e mobile WiMAX and designed to work with Windows XP laptops.

Table 5-7 gives the characteristics of the PCMCIA WiMAX receiver.

It is instructive to note that the PCMCIA receiver has a receiver sensitivity of −100 dbm for QPSK, while it is only −80 dbm for 64 QAM. This shows that such a receiver would operate with 64 QAM only in proximity of the base station and fall back on 16 QAM (−90 dbm sensitivity) and QPSK(−100 dbm sensitivity) as the distance from base station increases.

Even though it is an indoor device (plug-in card), it supports two antennas for receive diversity. The antenna gains are quite small (2 dbi), reflecting the challenging environment in which the receiver needs to work.

5.4 TOOLS FOR DESIGN OF WiMAX TRANSMISSION NETWORKS

WiMAX transmission network design is based on fundamental practices similar to those involved in the design of cellular networks. This includes:

- Identification of appropriate cell sites in urban and rural environments

TABLE 5-7

Characteristics of a Mobile WiMAX receiver (Accton PCMCIA)

WiMAX Receiver (Accton™ PCMCIA Card)	Specifications
Physical Layer	Scalable OFDMA
Frequency Bands	2.3–2.4 GHz, 2.5–2.7 GHz, 3.4–3.6 GHz
Transmit Power	Upto 23 dBm with 16 QAM 3/4
Receiver Sensitivity	−100 dBm QPSK, −90 dBm 64 QAM, −80 dBm 64 QAM
Antennas	1 TX, 2Rx with MRC, Internal omni antenna, Antenna gain 2 dBi
Antenna Gain	2 dBi
Standards Compliance	IEEE 802.16e-2005 (D12)
Cyclical Prefix	1/8, 1/16
Duplexing Mode	TDD
Coding Rate	1/2, 2/3 and 3/4
Channel Bandwidths	3.5, 4.375, 5, 7, 8.75, 10 MHz
Data Transfer Rates	Downlink 5 Mbps and higher, Uplink 384 Kbps and higher

- Estimate area of coverage based on tower height, nearby buildings and user density
- Check local interference at site
- Obtain regulatory permissions

The network growth of WiMAX can be quite rapid after initial installations because of the increasing availability of lower-priced CPEs, and the network may need to be dynamically enhanced.

A number of software tools are available to more realistically estimate the transmission losses based on different propagation models, work out configuration parameters, and maintain network models. These can be quite helpful in planning and maintenance process in multi-operator WiMAX, broadband, and cellular environments.

An example of a software package is from ICS telecom from ATDI Inc. The software is dedicated to network design in OFDM environment. The package helps by:

- Estimating more accurately the available data throughputs by specifying the uplink to downlink duration ratios, symbols in TTG, number of overhead symbols in downlink and uplink, etc.
- Simulating multipath reflections
- Selecting sub-channelization schemes for improving cell edge performance

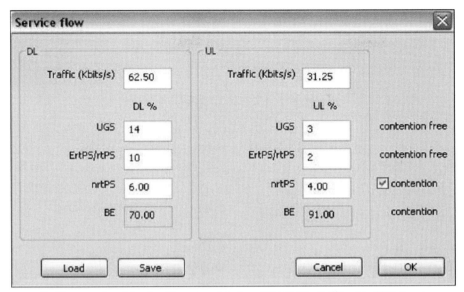

Traffic request and Service Flows provisioning at the Mobile Unit level in ICS telecom

(Image courtesy ATDI Inc.)

FIGURE 5-15   Screenshot of software package ICS Telecom from ATDI, Inc. for provisioning service flows

- Performing link analysis for uplink and downlink
- Estimating bit rates based on distance and modulation
- Estimating performance of multiple element arrays
- Radio network planning
- Service flows, QoS, and resource estimation
- Handoff estimations in an active set of base stations with map based displays
- Impact of interference

An example of a screen view for computing service flows in ICS Telecom is given in Figure 5-15.

5.5 EXAMPLES OF WiMAX NETWORKS FOR SPECIFIC APPLICATIONS

A WiMAX network, in general, consists of a number of base stations, which are interconnected with each other either directly or via backhaul paths. The backhaul can be via optical fiber or a wireless link with the latter being the more popular technology because of the high cost of wired links.

Going beyond generalized network architecture, there are a number of specific WiMAX network architectures which are of interest. The type of architecture to be implemented will also depend on the applications that are planned to be supported on the network apart from broadband wireless access (BWA). We discuss these here.

5.5.1 WiMAX Deployments with WiFi as Last Mile

One of the early applications of WiMAX has been the support of WiFi hotspots. It is estimated that 90 percent of computing and entertainment devices now being shipped (such as laptops, PDAs, UMPCs, music players) are now WiFi-enabled. The number of hotspots has also been growing exponentially. The primary providers of such hotspots are Wireless ISPs (WISPs), with the major service being SIP/H.323 based VoIP communications apart from internet access. The VoIP SIP clients are available (or can be downloaded) in almost all such devices which make use of WiFi.

WiMAX networks are seen as ideal methods of interconnecting the thousands of hot spots which exist in a city. This strategy is undoubtedly due to the universal availability of WiFi clients in various devices till the time the WiMAX clients (CPEs) become more common over the years and attain price equivalence with the WiFi products.

WiMAX in early deployments is therefore seen as an optimum technology to provide backhaul to the hotspots and enable wireless connectivity for the entire city, albeit with a combination of WiMAX and WiFi.

An architecture model of interest, therefore, is of WiMAX being a connecting point for WiFi hotspots (WiFi in the last mile). (A mesh model of connectivity is also possible using IEEE 802.16 Mesh MAC option but is not at present a WiMAX standard.) In this model of implementation, the WiFi hotspots can be embedded anywhere in the coverage area of a WiMAX base station.

The design considerations in this type of network can be different from a network that is a pure WiMAX network expected to serve mobile WiMAX devices even in an indoor NLOS environment. In this case, the WiFi hotspots can have external high-gain antennas, which would enable them to use the most dense modulation schemes and high data rates. In such cases, the data rates will be limited by the capacity of the WiMAX system.

The WiMAX base stations can be either all connected with wireless backhauls to a central POP or may be connected as a mesh network with one or two backhauls. Mesh networks are more practical with micro WiMAX -cells of 1 to 2 km, where individual backhauls would be impractical. Sectorization is also possible to increase the capacity.

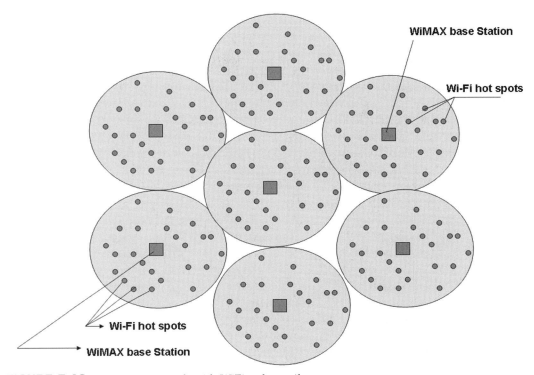

FIGURE 5-16   WiMAX network with WiFi as last mile

For example, with 60-degree beam widths, each frequency gives six sectors with the capacity getting enhanced by six times.

WiMAX networks with WiFi as the last mile primarily find their application in BWA and VoIP-type applications enabling a WISP to offer VoIP across an entire city bypassing the cellular or fixed-line networks.

5.5.2 WiMAX Networks for Fixed, Nomadic, or Mobile Access

While a WiFi last mile network provides an attractive way to connect hot spots, it should be remembered that the QoS attributes of WiMAX do not reach the end-user devices. Such a network needs to be considered as an IP network with WiFi extensions with the attributes of guaranteed support of video or circuit emulation services missing. Hence, the objective of all operators is ultimately to move to a network where the last mile is WiMAX with QoS assurance for the wireless link. Such a network would provide native support to all WiMAX certified devices. As the availability of WiMAX CPEs or client devices rises, such networks are likely to be more common.

Design considerations of this type of network would need to factor in WiMAX client devices, receiver sensitivities, and indoor NLOS operations. Advanced antenna techniques are important in such architectures which deal with mobile or nomadic devices. The availability of indoor CPEs with MIMO support supports such applications.

The size of the cells would depend upon the data rates and user densities. To support a large number of users in a small area, the cells need to be very small (pico cells or micro cells) while the cells in rural areas or lower densities can be based on the range of coverage of a base station.

In a typical operating environment, there will be a number of cells in a given area cluster all of which need to be connected to the POP via backhauls. The backhauls can be to a local POP in the cluster or be managed via a mesh network of WiMAX cells with the base stations in the mesh providing routing functions for data traffic.

The need for backhaul using wireless implies that the frequency planning is needed for the WiMAX network, as well as the backhaul network. IEEE 802.16 technology provides for both types of linkages: a PMP NLOS network operating in the 2 to 13 GHz range, as well as a backhaul network which is point-to-point and can operate at frequencies falling in the range of 13 to 80 GHz.

As in the case of cellular networks, it is possible to plan the backhaul in the 13 GHz+ frequency range for backhauls as these are point-to-point connections. The FCC in the United States has made available 70/80 GHz bands for point-to-point connectivity. At this frequency, 10 GHz bandwidth is available, which translates into a usable data rate from 1 to 10 Gbps. The backhaul in WiMAX networks has a major impact on the applications, such as unicast and multicast video in aggregation of traffic as we will see in the later chapters.

Some of the parameters that go into design of the network are as follows:

- Frequencies for the PMP cells (2.4, 3, 4, or 5.6 GHz or unlicensed bands)
- Bandwidth of channels and number of bandwidth slots for the operator
- Sectorization with multiple beams per frequency
- User density and the number of service flows to be supported
- Data rates and user densities needed per cell
- Cell location based on data rates needed to be supported
- Distance Vs data rate trade off
- Frequencies for backhaul networks
- Calculation of tower heights based on site surveys and fresnal zones

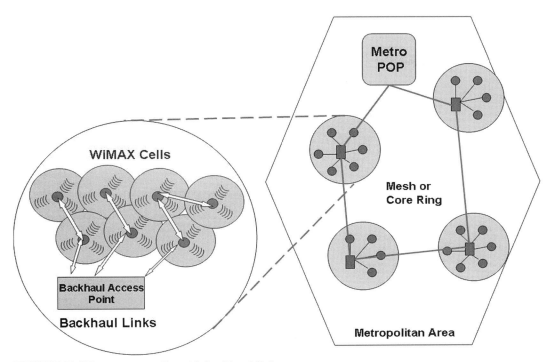

FIGURE 5-17   WiMAX cells with backhaul links

5.6 TIMING AND SYNCHRONIZATION IN WiMAX NETWORKS

By the very nature of the network, i.e., multiple base stations operating at the same frequency and Time Division Duplex operations (TDD), it is evident that the network needs to be precisely synchronized. The IEEE 802.16 protocol provides for guard bands as small as 5 microseconds between the transmit and receive subframes, which require a time accuracy of 1 microsecond in the frame transmissions. The WiMAX standards prescribe the use of GPS at the base stations in order to achieve this timing. The necessity of the use of a GPS receiver at every site (including base stations) and clear satellite look from each location has made it imperative to also consider alternative technologies. In addition to the timing of the wireless portion of the network, it is also necessary to synchronize the entire network including the transmission network, broadband wireless backbone, and content servers to follow the same timing source.

An alternative is to use the IEEE 1588 Precision Timing Protocol (PTP). To give a brief background, the use of IEEE 1588 has been necessitated because of the use of the networks to carry native IP traffic rather than IP being carried over TDM frames such as T1 or E1. The

Next Generation Networks (NGN) do not necessarily have a TDM or frame-based connected links that could be used to get the timing of stations in a slave mode.

The IEEE 1588 envisages the use of a client in each base station. Sync timing is distributed using IEEE 1588 clocks in the network. The master clocks establish two-way connections with each base station (or any other slave device) to distribute accurate timing. The IEEE 1588 would be caesium-based sources with 1×10^{-11} timings and also use the GPS timing source.

6

BROADBAND WIRELESS NETWORKS: DEPLOYMENT STATUS WORLDWIDE

The horse is out of the stable, it's running around the track and there isn't another one in sight.
—Barry West, President of Xohm and CTO of Sprint Nextel Corp., on the status of Mobile WiMAX networks in the United States. Keynote at WiMAX World USA, 2007

The word *broadband,* when mentioned, usually gets associated with ADSL, FTTH, or cable-delivered internet. It is only recently that broadband has begun to imply a wireless mode of connectivity as well, and that, too, in relation to WiFi networks. Today's broadband wireless networks have three manifestations:

- WLANs, mesh networks, or WiFi at home or public places based on 802.11a, b/g
- Wireless MANs based on 802.16 including WiMAX systems
- Broadband via cellular wireless networks, such as EV-DO or HSPA

All the networks achieve the objective of providing broadband wireless connectivity. However, WiMAX deployments that are based on OFDM multi-carrier technologies and support advanced antenna systems (AAS) are providing today a new tier of connectivity with high-spectral efficiency.

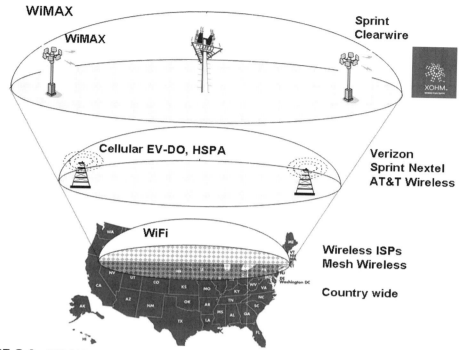

FIGURE 6-1   WiMAX networks provide a third dimension to wireless broadband

6.1 BRIEF HISTORY OF WIRELESS BROADBAND DEPLOYMENTS

Broadband wireless access has always been the dream of every service provider and user on the move. Being able to connect wirelessly, teams of salesmen, technicians, or delivery fleets, has been on the agenda of every business. No less important has been the potential availability of wireless access for leisure seekers who need to be able to surf and make travel plans while travelling in far-flung areas or remote cities. Admittedly, the cellular networks have been quick to fill this void. Beginning with limited surfing and broadband connectivity, their capabilities have expanded to cover the existing void. The connectivity offered by EV-DO or HSDPA data cards, for example, provides a full-fledged broadband experience, even away from the public WiFi hotspots.

However, if the objective is to deliver broadband internet to everyone, as stated by most countries, we begin to need to look beyond the cellular-delivered broadband. The cellular networks as they are configured today are predominantly designed for voice traffic, and the data networks are just overlays. These need extra spectrum in the cellular or

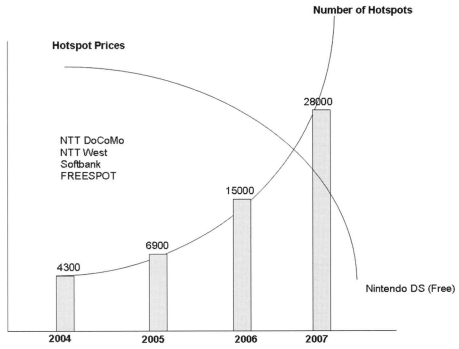

FIGURE 6-2   Hotspots (WiFi) in Japan

3G bands, and this extra spectrum tends to be scarce. Moreover, attempting to deliver broadband to a large number of users or large number of mobile devices is quite onerous in 3G mobile networks because of the limited resources available and the network architecture.

The public hotspots where WiFi is available free or for a nominal fee have been growing exponentially, largely reflecting the latent need for ubiquitous connectivity. This need has no doubt been accentuated by the number of consumer devices that can use of WiFi when available, such as PSPs, cell phones, or music players. Across various countries, there is now a trend to have the WiFi connectivity in hotels, airports, gaming parlors, malls, and public places. The free public access is prompting more and more public agencies such as healthcare, utilities, libraries, municipalities, railways, etc. to have their services and portals online as well, fully enabled for free broadband usage.

The number of WiFi hotspots was expected to have exceeded 200,000 in 2007.

On the other hand, the broadband wireless networks or Wireless MANs carry with them their own fascination. These technologies, as we have discussed in detail, are designed bottom up for carriage of broadband data unlike the slotted TDM networks at the core of cellular networks. WiMAX networks provide capabilities to operate in a number of frequency bands, licensed or unlicensed, with bandwidths going upto 20 MHz, allow for multisector operation and MIMO-based data rate scaling thus providing very high spectral efficiencies. The goal of wireless broadband for a much larger user base thus becomes practical with WiMAX implementations. It is no surprise therefore that many hundreds of trials of the new technologies have taken place and now given way to commercial implementations.

Many of the WiMAX implementations today are based on the IEEE 802.16-2004 fixed WiMAX technologies, though the newer implementations are largely of Mobile WiMAX (IEEE 802.16e-2005). We now take a look at some of these implementations.

6.2 REGION- AND COUNTRY-SPECIFIC IMPLEMENTATIONS

6.2.1 Asia

Many countries in Asia have well-developed cellular networks but are characterized by lack of broadband connectivity. The use of WiMAX is seen as a quick and efficient way to serve well-dispersed populations with broadband wireless connectivity. Providing universal broadband connectivity has been adapted as a goal by many countries, and WiMAX networks are seen as the best way forward towards attaining this goal.

India

India has been an early adapter to the use of WiMAX networks. Despite the country having a cellular subscriber base of over 200 million (by the third quarter of 2007), the number of fixed line connections remained below 50 million. Broadband connectivity, despite many initiatives by the Telecommunications Regulatory Authority of India (TRAI), has remained below 10 million. The 3G spectrum for cellular operators could not be allocated to the users because of procedural factors. This has resulted in the cellular network data offerings being limited to GPRS and CDMA 2000 (1x). The growth of ADSL-based broadband networks has been limited because of the bulk (over 90 percent) of the fixed lines being held by the state-owned public sector companies. IPTV services over ADSL have been launched, but lack of regulatory clarity has not made it possible for the operators to get pay TV content on the networks in a significant way.

With an objective of extending the broadband connectivity to even rural areas, WiMAX spectrum in India had been allocated to a number of operators in 2005 in the 3.3 to 3.4 GHz band. The allocations were on the basis of circles (there are at present 22 circles in India). Some operators such as Sify, VSNL, and Bharti have obtained licenses in all circles resulting in countrywide footprint. Other major operators who are investing heavily in WiMAX networks include Idea, Aircel, Reliance, BSNL, and MTNL.

Bharti Airtel was one of the early deployers of the WiMAX technology (IEEE 802.16-2004) with presence in eight cities in India as early as 2006. The deployment was based on technology from Alvarion Ltd. and used Breezemax™ 3300 base stations. The services were targeted for broadband connectivity to corporate customers in addition to providing backhauls for cellular broadband. The deployment of WiMAX by BSNL is targeted at rural connectivity, voice, and broadband.

Sify, which is one of the largest wireless ISPs, has also rolled out its network based on Fixed WiMAX technology from Proxim wireless in the 5.8 GHz license-free band in over 200 cities of India. The network claims to provide mobility features even though the 5.8 GHz band does not yet fall in the domain of WiMAX forum-certified bands for mobile WiMAX.

Aircel and VSNL are also using WiMAX to provide broadband wireless connectivity to business customers. The VSNL network based on Aperto network's PacketMAX technology covers six cities in the first phase: Kolkata, Bangalore, Chennai, Ahmadabad, Hyderabad, and Pune. Aircel network is based on IEEE 802.16-2004 technology from Alvarion and covered over forty cities by the end of 2007.

BSNL, India's state-owned operator, also began its roll out of WiMAX networks in 2006 beginning with the major cities. Its initial network is based on Aperto network's 5000 base stations and PM 300 subscriber units.

All installations in India have been based on the use of the Fixed WiMAX technology or pre-WiMAX networks in the 5.8 GHz unlicensed band because of the spectrum allocations. Trials of mobile WiMAX based on IEEE 802.16e technology have been carried out by some operators such as C-DOT Alcatel. Spectrum in the 2.5 to 2.69 GHz for Mobile WiMAX is yet to be allocated and Mobile WiMAX networks are expected to be operational in 2008.

Philippines
Pacific Internet, a major ISP in Asia Pacific has been assigned spectrum in the 2.5 to 2.7 GHz band for mobile WiMAX and is building out a mobile WiMAX network. It has 15 MHz of spectrum.

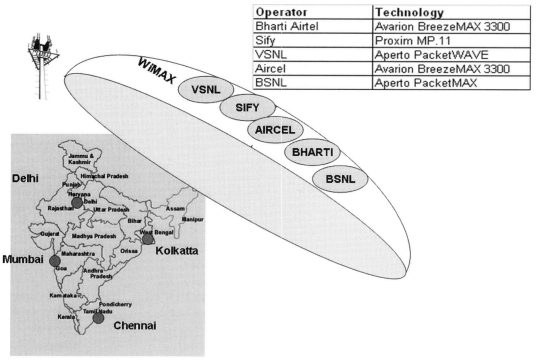

Operator	Technology
Bharti Airtel	Avarion BreezeMAX 3300
Sify	Proxim MP.11
VSNL	Aperto PacketWAVE
Aircel	Avarion BreezeMAX 3300
BSNL	Aperto PacketMAX

FIGURE 6-3   WiMAX in India

Japan

Yozan Japan WiMAX + WiFi deployments
Yozan in Japan heralded the replacement of optical fiber connecting WiFi hotspots with WiMAX links. Its service was commercialized in December 2005 in the 4.9 GHz band. Using the IEEE 802.16-2004 technology, it implemented the connectivity of up to 100 WiFi hotspots with each WiMAX base station. These WiFi base stations were interestingly called "Bitstand WiFi" stations.

The WiMAX network of Yozan is being upgraded to Mobile WiMAX technology in the 2.5 GHz band.

Mobile WiMAX in Japan
Almost all the major players in the broadband market in Japan have done trials with mobile WiMAX IEEE 802.16e-2005 and are ready to provide commercial services. These include NTT DoCoMo, KDDI, Softbank/Vodaphone, Yozan, eMobile, etc. Yozan, for example, had installed over one hundred WiMAX base stations by September 2006

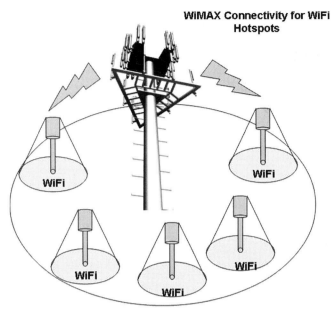

FIGURE 6-4   Yozan (Japan) 4.9 GHz WiMAX network for WiFi connectivity

in the Tokyo metropolitan area. The network was built out by Airspan networks. Yozan has since expanded services to other areas. The Network of Softbank, rolled out by Motorola, is a parallel network for WiMAX-based IP connectivity.

The Japanese government has, however, decided that the 2.5 GHz spectrum will not be allotted to the existing 3 mobile operators but rather would be given to new entrants. NTT DoCoMo (40 million 3G subscribers), KDDI (28 million), and SoftBank (17 million) were the major operators when this decision was announced in 2007. This is leading to a realignment of operators in providing the Mobile WiMAX services.

Australia
There is no better example of a WiMAX network coverage than the one unveiled by Unwired Australia. The network is based on technology from Navini networks, which currently is proprietary and is based on multi-carrier synchronous CDMA (MC-SCDMA). Unwired holds licenses in the 3.4 and 2.3 GHz bands. In 2007, the 512/128 Kbps broadband service from Unwired was being offered at A$50 per month with 600 MB of data transfer and additional usage at A$15 per GB. The plans extend up to 1024/256 Kbps with 12 GB of data at A$110 per month.

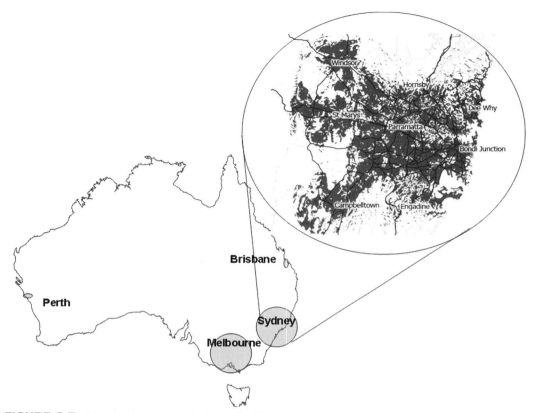

FIGURE 6-5   Unwired coverage in Australia (2007, Picture Courtesy Unwired.com)

Licenses in Australia in the "unlicensed bands" are issued under the wireless access services (WAS).The WAS licenses in the 2.4 and 5.8 GHz band and are technology neutral. This has led to a number of operators offering services based on other technologies as well, which add to the broadband wireless availability in Australia. Examples are the MobileFi services based on IEEE 802.20 and Personal Broadband Australia services based on iBurst technology.

Austar is another WiMAX operator with licenses in the 3.5 and 2.3 GHz bands.

Pakistan

Pakistan Mobile Communications, a mobile operator providing services under Mobilink is rolling out an IEEE 802.16e network in the major cities of Pakistan. The network is based on technology provided by Alcatel-Lucent. Another group, Wateen Telecom, is deploying a

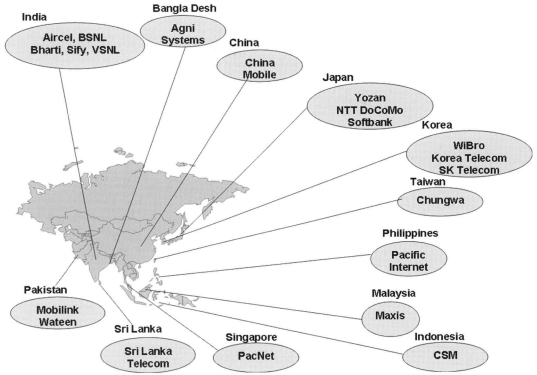

FIGURE 6-6 WiMAX spreads out across Asia Pacific

mobile WiMAX network in Pakistan covering 22 cities based on Motorola WiMAX technology.

Indonesia

Citra Sari Makmur (CSM), one of Indonesia's largest telecommunications operators, has rolled out a WiMAX network countrywide. The equipment is provided by Aperto networks. The network supports a complete mix of services including data, voice, and multimedia.

China

China has always been keenly watched by the industry observers because of its selection of its own versions of technologies for mobile as well as broadband. In case of WiMAX, however, it has opted for the use of IEEE standards and WiMAX forum profiles. China Mobile been providing WiMAX services in Bejing and Qingdao and is also providing these services for the 2008 Olympics. Its service has received the WiMAX forum certification. The operations are in the 3.5 GHz band.

Vietnam

The implementation of WiMAX in Vietnam is very innovative in the use of the IPSTAR connectivity for the backhauls, while using WiMAX networks for terrestrial connectivity. The typical coverage is a village of a few km² which is covered by a single omnidirectional antenna in the 3.3 GHz WiMAX band. The equipment for the network is provided by Airspan networks. This type of implementation ensures that only one IPSTAR terminal is needed in a typical coverage area, with hundreds of possible customers connected.

Another implementation is based on the use of an Alvarion BreezeMAX station.

6.2.2 Middle East

The Middle East has been characterized by fast-growing telecom networks with the latest technologies. WiMAX networks have been envisioned to bridge the gap in broadband wireless connectivity. A number of networks have been installed for trials and commercial services at a rapid pace in the Middle East.

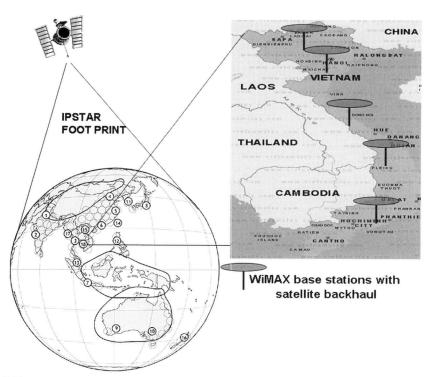

FIGURE 6-7   WiMAX in Vietnam

Bahrain

A nationwide WiMAX service is now available in Bahrain. The service is provided by Zain (formerly mobile telecommunications company, MTC). It provides broadband access and fixed line (nomadic) services. Zain™ is offering the services under Zain@home branding which bundles broadband, mobile, and fixed line services.

Saudi Arabia

A number of WiMAX deployments have taken place in Saudi Arabia. The Saudi Telecommunications Company (STC) has rolled out a nationwide WiMAX network with technology from Redline communications and WiMAX forum-certified products. This network is operational in Riyadh, Jeddah, and Dammam. In Riyadh, a city-wide network has been commissioned in cooperation with Intel and Communications and Information Technology Commission (CITC). Bayanat Al-Oula, a telecommunications company, is also rolling out its WiMAX network based on technology from Samsung.

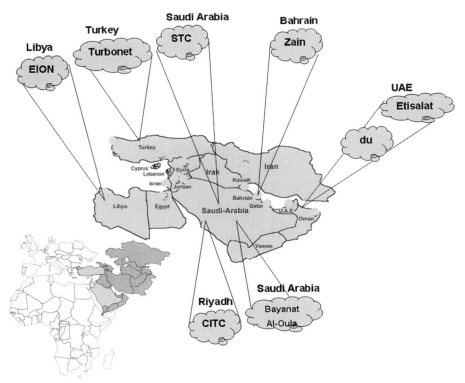

FIGURE 6-8 WiMAX in the Middle East

Libya

WiMAX services in Libya are provided by EION wireless and are based on Libra MAX technology. The platform operates in the 3.5 GHz band. Prior to this, the primary source of broadband connectivity has been the BGAN network of Inmarsat. The BGAN network is satellite based.

UAE

In UAE, two operators, Etisalat and du (a mobile operator) have been issued licenses in the 3.5 GHz band for mobile WiMAX and the networks of the two operators have been rolled out.

Egypt

The National Telecommunications Regulatory Authority (NTRA) in Egypt has opened up the band of 3.4 to 3.6 GHz for WiMAX services. It is possible for WiMAX systems to operate in the 5.725 to 5.85 GHz bands on an uncoordinated and unprotected basis. A number of customers are using pre-WiMAX products in this band for wireless-based connectivity. This includes some novel applications such as connectivity to ships in coastal waters.

Turkey

WiMAX services are available in Turkey via a wireless Internet service provider, Turbonet. The WiMAX systems have been supplied by Aperto Networks. In addition, Turk Telecom has also started rollout of a WiMAX network.

6.2.3 Europe

The European Union has 27 member states, and its telecommunications are governed by the EU 2003 regulatory framework. In Europe, the 2.5 to 2.69 GHz band, which is the primary band for mobile WiMAX certification profiles, had been earmarked for 3G evolution (IMT-2000) or UMTS technologies, as per the WRC 2000 recommendations. Some allocations are being done in the 2.3 GHz mobile WiMAX band, where these frequencies are available. This leaves the 3.5 GHz band for fixed WiMAX deployments or the unlicensed bands (5.150 to 5.350 GHz and 5.470 to 5.725 GHz). The unlicensed bands can only be used with transmit power control (TPC) and dynamic frequency selection (DFS) to prevent interference to other installations. These restrictions have led to a range of systems in these bands claiming certification either for fixed WiMAX or offering "pre-WiMAX" systems in these bands. Some operators have moved to 10.5 GHz (such as MAC telecom

Belgium, in addition to its operations in the 3.5 GHz). With the WRC 2007 now having approved the use of OFDMA-TDD (used in mobile WiMAX) as one of the approved technologies for 3G terrestrial interfaces under the IMT, it is expected that service providers will be able to deploy mobile WiMAX systems in this band in the near future.

Auctions of the 3.5 GHz spectrum are being processed in Portugal and Italy in 2007, which should see emergence of new WiMAX networks.

Greece

Greece has licensed 2×28 MHz and 2×21 MHz slots in the 3.4 to 3.6 GHz spectral band. There are four licensed operators in Greece: OTE, Q-Telecom, Craig Wireless, and COSMOLINE. Craig wireless has launched a WiMAX network in the 3.5 GHz band, along with Nortel in major cities of Greece. OTE Athens, the major telecommunications carrier, has also rolled out its network based on technology from Aperto networks.

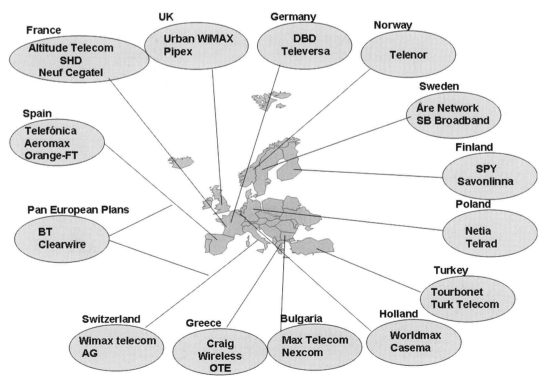

FIGURE 6-9 WiMAX in Europe

Poland

Four operators have been licensed for WiMAX in Poland, in the 3.6 to 3.8 GHz bands as nationwide licensees. These licenses are held by PTC, Netia, NASK, and Clearwire. In addition, there are also regional licenses in this band. Netia has already commenced WiMAX operations based on technology from Alcatel. Telrad networks with technology from Alvarion has also launched WiMAX services in two regions with VoIP being the primary offering. Multimedia Polska, the Polish cable operator, is rolling out a WiMAX network based on technology from Airspan networks to add voice and data to its existing services.

United Kingdom

WiMAX services have been operational in United Kingdom, primarily in the unlicensed 5.8 GHz band (e.g., by Urban WiMAX). Operators holding broadband wireless licenses in the 3.6 GHz band are now looking at WiMAX service launches in the licensed bands based on the principle of technology neutrality. UK Broadband and Pipex are now rolling out WiMAX networks in the 3.6 GHz licensed bands.

Germany

Six operators have been granted nationwide licenses for WiMAX in Germany in 2006 in the 3.5 GHz band. DBD, one of the licensed operators has commenced offering WiMAX services (broadband internet and VoIP) based on technology from Airspan networks. Networks of other licensees are expected to go on line in 2008.

Norway

WiMAX services are being provided in Norway based on the IEEE 802.16-2004 fixed WiMAX technology by Telenor. Auction for the 2.5–2.69 GHz band has been held in Norway in November 2007 and the licensees are expected to roll out the networks during 2008.

Sweden

Åre Network has launched WiMAX services in Sweden based on technology from Redline (RedMAX™). SB Broadband has also launched a network in the 3.5 GHz based on technology from Navini Networks. The network is based on pre-WiMAX 802.16e.

Finland

Over 45 companies hold WiMAX licenses in Finland, primarily in the 3.5 GHz band. These licenses were awarded based on a "beauty contest."A number of operators are providing WiMAX based services including SPY, Savonlinna, Mikkelin Puhelin (MPY), etc.

6.2.4 Latin America

Latin America is characterized by well-urbanized conglomerations and yet a low telecom penetration (20 percent for fixed line telephony and 35 percent for mobile phones). This makes WiMAX an optimum technology for coverage in countries including Brazil, Mexico, Argentina, etc. It is therefore no surprise that Latin America is at the forefront of WiMAX deployments. There are many trials and commercial implementations that have taken place in Latin America.

Argentina

WiMAX had an early start in Argentina, with Millcom (now Ertach) launching its 802.16-2004 network based on Alvarion technology in 2004. The services were launched with 50 MHz of spectrum in the 3.4 to 3.7 GHz band. The network was targeted largely to serve business customers with data and VPN connectivity with QoS. The WiMAX market in Argentina has been characterized by a lot of M&A activity resulting in a consolidation of operators. Ertach was acquired by Telmex in 2006.

Brazil

Brazil is well covered by mobile networks. It had over 110 million mobile subscribers by middle of 2007. Mobile operators have also upgraded their networks to offer high speed data services. WiMAX services can be provided in Brazil in the 3.5 GHz band.

In Sao Paulo, Brazil, TVA has built a mobile WiMAX network with MIMO. The network has been built by Nortel on behalf of TVA and has the capabilities to provide mobile TV, Video, VoIP and mobile e-commerce. This gives TVA, a pay TV operator, a chance to offer triple play services over mobile WiMAX including broadband in its portfolio. The technology is specifically aimed at providing web services, blogging, etc. in addition to pay TV channels delivered over WiMAX. TVA's product portfolio today includes TVA Digital channels, DVR, HDTV, Portable TVA (Slingbox), Ajato, and TVA Voz.

Columbia

Orbitel along with Siemens, for example has launched a mobile WiMAX network in the city of Cali, Columbia. The network is based on Siemens's WayMax@dvantage technology and has data rate packages

FIGURE 6-10 WiMAX in Latin America

from $40 to $300 per month. In 2006, a Colombian company Telecom launched a pre-WiMAX network in select cities of Colombia.

Puerto Rico

Islanet Inc, an ISP has launched WiMAX services ("Volare") in the 2.5 Ghz band based on technology from Navini networks. The services are targeted at the residential as well as business customers. The technology is based on 802.16e but is a pre-WiMAX implementation.

6.2.5 Africa

Africa, with its sparse data connectivity and broadband services, has been an ideal implementation ground for WiMAX services. WiMAX networks are either operational or under trial in almost every country in the continent.

Algeria

A WiMAX-based multiservices network was launched in Algeria in July 2005, making it the first country in north Africa to offer such a service. The services are provided by SLC (Smart Link Communications) and provide VoIP, broadband wireless access, and data connectivity (VPNs) over the WiMAX network. The WiMAX network has proved especially advantageous in this case owing to an effective coverage of large areas in mountainous terrain. The ARPT has granted WiMAX authorizations to the fixed telephony operators (Algerie Telecom and CAT) and the VoIP operators (Smart link communications, LastNet, EEPAD, Icosnet, Wataniya, Anouar Net, and Vocalone).

South Africa

Telkom SA has been granted spectrum in the 3.5 MHz band (2 × 28 MHz) for rolling out a WiMAX-based nationwide network. Other operators have also been given spectrum in the 3.5 GHz band. After initial trials in Pretoria and Durban, Telkom has rolled out a nationwide network. Neotel, South Africa's second national operator, is also going ahead with WiMAX in cooperation with Motorola. Other major ISPs and wireless operators such as iBurst, Sentech, and Internet Solutions have also rolled out WiMAX-based services.

Nigeria

In West Africa (Nigeria), Direct on PC Ltd (DOPC) has been moving ahead with its 802.16e Mobile WiMAX deployments in the 2.3 GHz band. These have been based on technology from Navini networks (Smart WiMAX). The services are being rolled out to cover the principal cities of Nigeria, i.e., Abuja, Lagos, and Port Harcourt. The services offered are primarily broadband for both the home segment and the SMEs. The network is state of the art with advanced antenna systems, MIMO, and beamforming.

Mauritius

Mauritius has well-developed telecom networks. It had its first WiMAX network operational in 2005. The WiMAX infrastructure was installed by ADB networks with technology from Navini networks. Being an island nation, the network is used for data voice as well as IPTV. Another operator, Emtel, has been awarded a license and is sourcing the equipment from Alvarion.

Zambia

WiMAX services in Zambia are being provided by an ISP Zamnet. It uses technology from Navini networks and is pre-WiMAX mobile based on IEEE 802.16e. The service is now available in the major cities of Zambia.

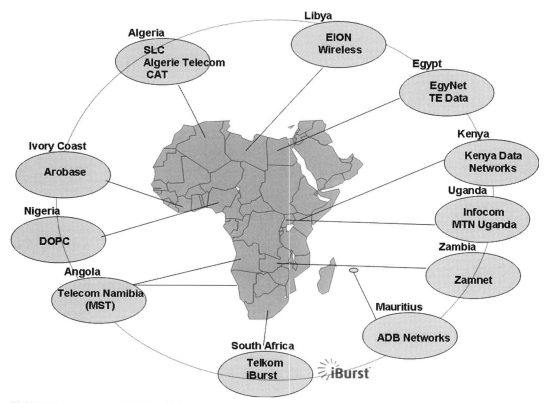

FIGURE 6-11 WiMAX in Africa

SUMMARY

In summary, we see that WiMAX networks have been introduced globally. The initial deployments have been based on fixed WiMAX because of the need to provide an overlay network of wireless connectivity. The services introduced have been a mix of data, VoIP, and video streaming services. The new deployments now happening are focusing on the use of mobile WiMAX technology. Increasing availability of WiMAX PC cards, chipsets for mobile phones, and PDAs is expected to accelerate this trend.

7

STANDARDS CONVERGENCE IN MOBILE MULTIMEDIA BROADCASTING

The reason why the Ten Commandments are short and clear is that they were handed down direct, not through several committees.
—*Dan Bennett*

7.1 INTRODUCTION: A VIEW OF THE STANDARDS WORLD

Why do we need to go into various standards when we look at mobile multimedia or broadcasting using WiMAX networks? After all, are the WiMAX networks not going to be wireless extensions of other networks? This is a common question and quite natural. There are, of course, very good reasons. First of all, it is not completely true that WiMAX will be only an extension of existing networks. The development in mobile WiMAX network architectures, as well as the trend in deployments of applications, indicates that a very major move is underway. This will ultimately lead to open architecture networks including migration to NGN, and WiMAX networks are a very important part of this move. Secondly, we are now moving toward integrating multiple applications and services, which have developed separately in their own environments of broadcasting, communications, and internet, to work in the same mobile device. Hence standards from many different domains, which existed virtually independently in their specific areas, now need to converge by developing extensions to each standard as it moves into a converged environment.

A simple example is the use of internet over mobile networks. IP applications (including IP streaming) have developed as internet applications under the aegis of the Internet Engineering Task Force (IETF) as RFCs. For example, the real-time streaming protocol used over the internet (RTSP) is governed by RFC 2326. When the use of this application, in this case the "streaming application," moves to a different environment, e.g., a mobile network, the same standard cannot be used. Mobile devices are limited in terms of resources, such as processing and memory, and have their own standards and architecture for voice and data connectivity. "Streaming" has therefore been adapted as a different standard called 3GPP-PSS (3GPP packet-switched streaming) under the third-generation partnership project, which incorporates the signalling as well as the data streaming protocols for implementation on mobile networks.

The mobile world has evolved under the umbrella of standards developed by the 3rd Generation Partnership for a 3GPP for GSM evolved 3G networks, and 3GPP2 for CDMA-evolved 3G networks. IETF has liaisoned with the relevant standards bodies to modify standards where there are dependencies. Similarly the digital video broadcasting standards have developed under the aegis of the Digital Video Broadcasting Forum (DVB). The standards as they apply to broadcasting for digital handhelds are given by the DVB-H under the DVB umbrella of standards. There are also other standards bodies which have developed their own standards for mobile TV. The DMB standard for mobile TV, which has been modified from the DAB standards, is another example.

As all the services, which have developed independently for their own networks such as for television broadcasting, radio, internet, voice, streaming via internet, mobile services, etc., now attempt to target the same or similar mobile devices for final delivery of their services, the standards world is also witnessing considerable convergence and requirements of cooperation between different standards bodies.

Figure 7-1 demonstrates the case of a commercially available WiMAX mobile phone, which can operate using WiFi and GSM or CDMA networks. The WiMAX services are based on IEEE 802.16e standards, while the system parameters are used as profiles of the WiMAX Forum. In order to operate with the GSM, 3G-UMTS, or CDMA2000 networks, the handset needs to be able to implement the GSM forum 3GPP(2) standards and comply with OMA guidelines for encryption in order to operate in a multi-operator environment. For voice calls to legacy networks, it would use the 3GPP and ITU based standards H.324 (3G-324M) while WiFi services would be governed by the IEEE standards with parameters selected by the WiFi alliance. Reception of broadcast video is possible by a DMB-T or a DVB-H receiver implemented in the mobile device.

The device, therefore, needs to implement software stacks or support middleware for many different standards and originating from the requirements of many standards organizations.

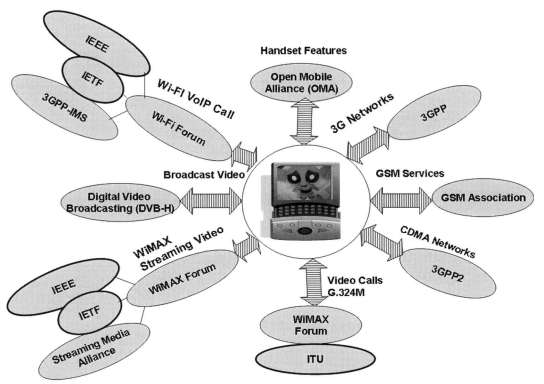

FIGURE 7-1 A mobile device operating with multiple services is governed by interdependent standards setting from multiple organizations

As new WiMAX devices enter the world, they do not therefore operate in a standalone environment governed only by the IEEE 802.16e or WiMAX Forum guidelines. In real life, they will need to interface with a multiple standards world for different services, many of which are proprietary.

A complete treatise of the standards bodies would be beyond the scope of the book and be of little utility in the context of WiMAX networks. Hence, we will discuss in brief the standards organizations that have dependencies with WiMAX or services provided over these networks.

It will not be out of place to mention that such a high level of dependencies of standards is of relatively recent origin because of different types of services now targeting the same devices. It is also because of the need of new mobile devices to deal with legacy networks or to operate services which remain dependent on proprietary implementations.

7.2 STANDARDS BODIES AND INDUSTRY ASSOCIATIONS

Setting of standards is a holistic process. It is based on developing a wide range of protocols, interfaces, and architectures under which a service can operate. Examples of bodies involved in the standards-setting process include the IEEE, IETF, ITU, DVB, ETSI, EIA, etc. These apex standards bodies work in liaison with standards organizations based in different countries as well as independent organizations and associations of manufacturers or users.

At the next stage are industry associations which adopt specific ways of implementing the standards so that they can work in an interoperable way in a given industry, e.g., within cellular mobile networks or in WiMAX-based networks. The GSM alliance, 3GPP, or the DVB for video broadcasting are examples of such associations. These associations may define services and protocols, which will be used in specific networks based on the standards available for the industry. There are many vendor and operator alliances as well. The Open Mobile Alliance (OMA) for standardizing mobile applications and handsets, ISMA for IPTV and streaming applications, etc., are some examples.

In this chapter, we will first look at the diverse standards bodies that have generated standards in their own fields. We then look at the various services in a converged environment and seek to observe how the convergence is coming about. As the convergence is a continuous process, the devices and products that make it to the market need to freeze on standards and service definitions periodically. Products and services become available based on these standards until a next upgrade is announced. Hence, we need to be aware of the constantly moving standards processes. This is particularly so in the field of WiMAX, where even though the services are available in a number of networks, the process towards convergence is an ongoing one.

7.3 AN OVERVIEW OF INTERNATIONAL STANDARDS ORGANIZATIONS

7.3.1 IETF

The Internet Engineering Task Force (IETF), an open international community, has been largely responsible for the way the internet works today. Each aspect of internet core architecture and how its protocols or services work is defined by the request for comments (RFCs) approved as standards (STDs) by the IETF. It has a number of working groups (over 130), each dealing with a different area such as transport, architecture, or security of the internet. Initially, all proposals are

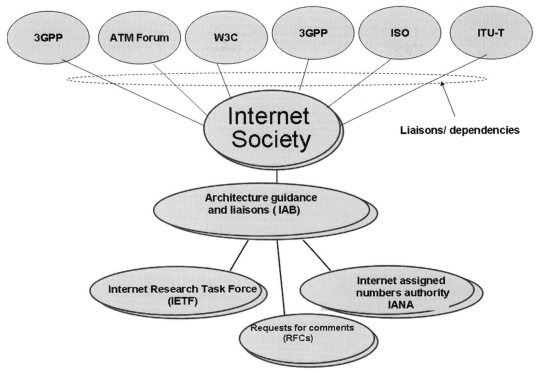

FIGURE 7-2 An architectural overview of IETF

submitted as RFCs for review by the committee and later adopted as standards if found acceptable. All the standards for internet applications such as file transfer protocol (FTP), Telnet, internet relay chat (IRC), real-time streaming protocols, etc. exist as RFCs. Any host computer that follows the requisite RFCs can work on the internet. New RFCs with additional features are continuously added, outdating the old RFCs. The IETF work is now being coordinated by the Internet Society (ISOC, formed in 1995), which is the organizational face of the task force.

The IETF liaises with 3GPP, ATM forum, IEEE, ISO, ITU-T, and World Wide Web Consortium (W3C) in order that the IETF standards reflect the multidisciplinary uses the internet is being put to and its extensions beyond the traditional "Net." An example of this multidisciplinary work is over fifty related dependencies of 3GPP in IETF, which has made modifications to the standards in liaison with the 3GPP project. The IETF standards, once formulated, do not undergo any changes in other standards bodies such as 3GPP.

7.3.2 DVB

The Digital Video Broadcasting (DVB) project is a consortium (formed in 1993) and has been engaged in delivering global standards for delivery of video, audio, and data services. Its standards are well known and used in over 60 percent of digital TV transmissions globally. The DVB forum has a membership from broadcasters, equipment manufacturers, regulatory bodies, and consumer products vendors among others. DVB has also formulated standards for mobile TV (DVB-H) and multimedia home platforms (MHP).

The DVB standards cover all aspects of video and audio handling from compression, transmission, and broadcasting, to decoding etc. The standards cover the entire spectrum of services that are a part of customer interaction, such as electronic program guide (EPG), interactive TV (MHP), and data transmissions over DVB network. The DVB streams can be transported over IP, ATM, or satellite systems. DVB has a standard for IP datacasting, including encryption of elementary streams (service protection and purchase) and transmission of EPG under DVB-CBMS, which has been used by many broadcasters.

The DVB-H however does not provide terminal specifications. This has resulted in a highly varied implementation of DVB-H on the terminal devices. This has led to terminals being non-interoperable in different networks. This shortcoming of DVB-H under the CBMS profile has been challenged by the OMA, which is a key body in directing developments towards interoperable handsets and applications. The OMA-BCAST standard for transmission of mobile TV is an example of the initiatives of OMA.

7.3.3 IEEE

The Institution of Electrical and Electronics Engineers (IEEE), a nonprofit international organization, has been involved in formulating standards for a wide range of technologies relating to electrical engineering, wireless, and networking. However, the most notable standards of IEEE have been in the fields of WAN, MAN, and networking under the IEEE 802 committee. Other notable standards from IEEE have been POSIX (IEEE 1003), very high speed integrated circuit hardware description language (VHDL, IEEE 1076), Public Key Cryptography (IEEE 1363), and Firewire (IEEE 1394) amongst others. The IEEE 802.16 standards (IEEE 802.16-2004 and IEEE 802.16e-2005) form the leading edge of standardization work being done in IEEE.

IEEE has been coordinating with a number of external organizations including 3GPP for air interfaces, interference issues, and long-term evolution technologies. The inclusion of OFDMA-TDD as one of the IMT2000 interfaces is a result of coordination efforts between the WiMAX Forum, 3GPP, WRC, and ITU.

7.3.4 ITU

The standards for telecommunications networks, transmission, and signalling were formulated by the erstwhile Consultative Committee on International Telephone and Telegraph (CCITT), which is now ITU-T. The ITU-T standards are very well known in the telecommunications domain. The ITU is a part of the United Nations and has membership from all member governments ("administrations"). As the telecommunications networks were largely circuit switch-based, the development of standards has been oriented towards circuit-switched networks. Data communications standards have been based on X.25 packet-switched networks, ISDN, and seven layer OSI model. Video communications standards have followed the same pattern with H.263 being the standard for video coding and H.323 for video conferencing. Signalling (e.g., to set up a call) is based on a separate bearer working between exchanges where calls are set up (Q.931). With the development of the internet and the new protocols and technologies it has brought in, the traditional telecommunications were paralleled by VoIP (call set-up based on SIP), video and audio streaming (RTP and RTSP, Real™, Windows media,™ etc.), and there have been efforts to converge the standards. The new standards under the ITU are known by the collective name next-generation networks (NGN). The basic difference between the present networks and the NGNs is that the NGNs are packet (i.e., internet protocol-based) networks with multiple access networks. This sets the future directions for the entire telecommunications industry to move to IP-based networks and signifies a convergence of all technologies, fixed and mobile.

In order to have integration with mobile networks, the ITU has agreed to adopt the model of the fixed-mobile convergence which was agreed on by the 3GPP. This model of the fixed-mobile convergence makes use of the IP multimedia subsystem (IMS) as defined by the 3GPP, or the Internet Multimedia Domain (IMD) defined by 3GPP2.

The convergence of standards between the ITU, ETSI, and the DVB is also an ongoing process. Adoption of J.202 recommendations on content formats for interactive TV applications reflects its alignment with the most current version of the ETSI GEM (globally executable MHP). ITU has also recently announced the recommendations for IPTV under its J.700 series of recommendations.

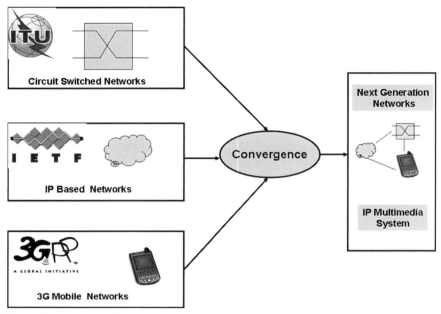

FIGURE 7-3 Convergence in networks

7.3.5 MPEG

The Moving Pictures Experts Group (MPEG) is a part of the International Standards Organisation (ISO). Compression standards formulated under MPEG have been widely used and adapted as international standards. Standards for encoding of motion video (video and audio) were initially standardized by the MPEG as MPEG-1 standard (ISO 11172), which is still used in VCDs today. The MPEG-1 format was based on a resolution of SIF (352 × 288 pixels for PAL, 352 × 240 for NTSC) against the broadcast TV resolution of 720 × 480 for NTSC. The next standard of MPEG, i.e., MPEG-2, supported various resolutions and profiles from QCIF to HDTV. For standard definition TV it offered bit rates from 1.5 to 15 Mbps based on parameters selected. The MPEG-2 was unique in a way, as it was not only a compression standard but also provided the specifications of a transport stream called the MPEG-2 transport stream. The MPEG-2 transport stream carries a number of streams of audio, video, and data, which can be separately identified by their individual program IDs (PIDs) or grouped as programs. MPEG-2 transport streams can be carried over different media including internet or ATM.

The need for lower bit rates through more efficient compression techniques was needed for technologies, such as video streaming,

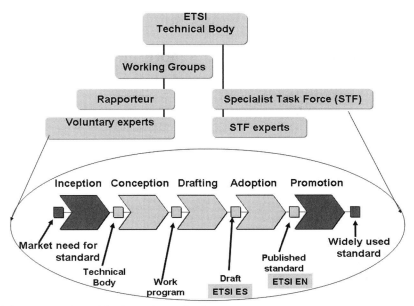

FIGURE 7-4 ETSI technical body and standards process

where sustained bit rates of 1.5Mbps for MPEG-2 video were not practical. The MPEG-4 family of compression standards presented a quantum jump in technology by using the techniques of object-based coding. A version of MPEG-4 (MPEG-4 part 10 or advanced video coding) has been adapted by the ITU as H.264 and is becoming the most widely used standard in commercial TV broadcasting after MPEG-2, which still forms the largest installed base. Satellite HDTV deliveries are now being based on the use of H.264 standards. The H.264 standards provide freedom in the selection of the network layer and thus can be used on any type of permanently connected or switched networks, which may be fixed line or mobile.

7.3.6 ETSI

The European Telecommunications Standards Institute (ETSI), despite its name suggesting being limited to Europe, is a very important standards organization as its recommendations and standards are followed in Europe and large parts of Asia as well as the rest of the world. ETSI is involved in standardizing telecommunications IT and broadcasting.

ETSI standards are conceptualized and presented through the ETSI technical body which, in turn, works through specialist task forces and working groups. ETSI standards can have different status, i.e., as reports (prefixed by ETSI TR), as draft standards (ETSI ES), and ETSI-adopted standards (ETSI EN). ETSI also has a wide-ranging liaison with other standards bodies such as DVB, IETF, ITU, etc. Some of the ETSI standards such as those for DVB-H are now approved European standards. ETSI has been responsible for liasioning with the WiMAX Forum to harmonize the IEEE 802.16 standards as ETSI HiperMAN standards.

7.4 OTHER STANDARDS BODIES AND OPERATOR ASSOCIATIONS

7.4.1 The WiMAX Forum®

The WiMAX Forum is a nonprofit corporation. It has been formed by the participants in the WiMAX industry for WiMAX standardization and certification of interoperability among various products, among other objectives. The goal of the WiMAX Forum is to accelerate the global deployments of standards-based WiMAX networks. While the standards of both Fixed WiMAX and Mobile WiMAX have been formulated by the IEEE, the WiMAX Forum needs to fix spectrum bands, bandwidths, modulation types, error coding rates, etc. which will be used in order to have compatible products. The work of the WiMAX Forum, therefore, represents an important facet of the actual deployment of WiMAX services worldwide.

The WiMAX Forum consists of a number of working groups, each of which deals with a specific area such as networking, applications, regulatory, marketing, global roaming, etc. It is evident that there are dependencies in the work of the various groups and also with other organizations such as IETF, DVB, 3GPP-2, and ITU-T.

The regulatory working group in WiMAX is responsible for worldwide spectrum policy and selection of bands to be selected for WiMAX devices. The network working group (NWG) is responsible for finalizing the network specifications, which represent the WiMAX operating environment The March 2007 report of the NWG details the network architecture and principles of interworking with other networks connected to WiMAX. The certification working group (CWG) is responsible for certification testing of WiMAX devices and organizing Plugfests where the interoperability of various vendor products can be tested in each other's networks directly. (The certification process still needs to go through the WiMAX certification labs). The service provider working group is responsible for mobile system and air interface requirements. The desire of the WiMAX Forum for an accelerated move toward global interoperability is reflected by the formation of the

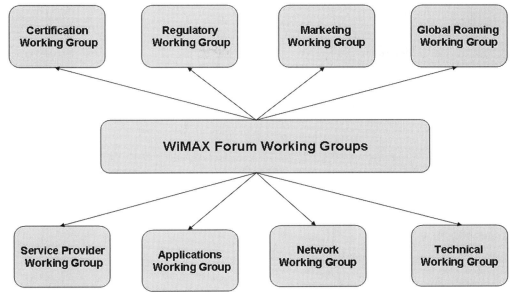

FIGURE 7-5 WiMAX Forum working groups

global roaming working group which is working towards accelerating the global roaming process. The WiMAX Forum has specified the use of Mobile IP (MIPv6) in the Mobile WiMAX as a part of its Network Working Group recommendations.

7.4.2 Third-Generation Partnership Projects: 3GPP and 3GPP2

We have briefly reviewed the role of 3GPPs in Chapter 3. In the cellular mobile domain, the 3GPPs provide the complete framework of protocols, file formats, and services that operate in these networks. The 3GPP is a partnership project of a number of standards bodies which are setting standards for third-generation cellular mobile services. In fact, there are two fora which are involved in these efforts. The 3GPP which has its origin in the GSM-based and GSM-evolved network operators (GSM, GPRS, EDGE, and 3G-WCDMA) is the first such forum and the 3GPP2 focused on providing a roadmap for CDMA-based evolved networks (CDMA 2000, CDMA 1X, CDMA 3X, etc.) is the second forum. The 3GPP constituted in 1998 had as its objective to provide globally applicable technical specifications for a third-generation system as it evolves from the 2G and 2.5 G technologies. The latest releases from the 3GPP and the 3GPP2 now present a harmonized and coordinated picture of the radio interfaces, file formats, protocols, and call set-up procedures, as well as the user equipment capabilities. It is

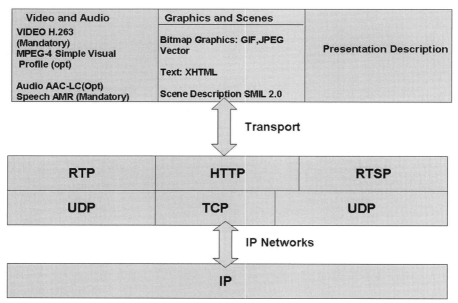

FIGURE 7-6   The streaming protocol stack specified by the 3GPP

to the credit of these bodies that mobile devices can work in any network with common services. The recommendations of the 3GPP2 are issued as releases with each release adding additional features, support of new services, or codec types.

The framework provided by the IP Multimedia system of the Release 5 of 3GPP sets the stage for end-to-end IP-based multimedia services breaking away from the circuit-switched architecture of the previous generations. It also provides for an easier integration of the instant messaging and real-time conversational services.

Streaming, an important application, has been standardized for 3G networks under the 3GPP-packet-switched streaming. The 3GPP-PSS defines the complete protocol stack for call establishment and the transfer of data using the IP layer. The audio and video file formats and formats for graphics, scene description, and presentation of information are also described. Complete protocol stacks such as, 3GPP-PSS lend a uniformity to call set up and multimedia data transfers across various networks even though they may be based on different air interfaces.

7.4.3 ISMA

IPTV is now a key delivery technology for providing TV and VoD services over fixed line, cable, wireless, and mobile networks. It has evolved in different countries and operator networks that are based on vendor- or operator-specific implementations. The Internet Streaming Media Alliance (ISMA) is an alliance of industry players interested in open international standards in the media streaming industry. The streaming industry today is based on either proprietary protocols such as Microsoft TV, Real, Windows Media, or protocols that have been issued by different standards organizations such as DVB (IP TV based on MPEG-2 transport stream or DVB-IPI), ITU, 3GPP, etc., in addition to the IETF standards based on RTP and RTSP. The goal of the alliance is to accelerate the adoption of open standards for streaming of media content including video, audio, and data. ISMA specifications for streaming have been issued as ISMA 1.0 and ISMA 2.0 and are used in Apple QuickTime™. ISMA also has a working group for IPTV where ISMA is driving the integration of multimedia IPTV standards. The issues involved in open standards include common encryption, definition of network interfaces which permit diverse networks to be connected, and call initiation and termination across diverse networks requiring the integration of IMS and SIP in the standards. ISMA has already issued ISMAcrypt 1.1 specification which is used in DVB-H. It has also issued ISMA 2.0 specification which is capable of providing end-to-end video encryption independent of the codec types used and flexibility in "key" management systems used for authentication and encryption.

Apart from the open standards for IPTV, ISMA offers its own "Plugfest" and interoperability testing for IPTV.

7.4.4 ATIS

The Alliance for Telecom Industry Solutions (ATIS) is a body involved in IPTV standardization. It is a U.S.-focused organization and its IPTV interoperability forum (IIF) is engaged in the development of ATIS standards, which will facilitate interoperability and interconnection among IPTV networks. The members of ATIS include major telecom operators and manufacturers, and their unified approach to IPTV is likely to set a definitive direction for the industry, which is beset with multiple standards. For this purpose, ATIS is preparing a reference architecture for IPTV, digital rights management (DRM), quality of experience (QoE) parameters for IPTV, and IPTV QoS metrics framework. The services which are covered include, among others, video on demand and interactive TV. ATIS has already finalized the IPTV architecture requirements (ATIS-0800002) and IPTV DRM interoperability requirements (ATIS-0800001). ATIS has also formed an IPV6 task force to comply with the U.S. government directive on use of IPV6 by June 2008.

FOCUS GROUPS IN ATIS

- Next-generation networks (NGN)
- Network security
- Voice over IP
- Data interchange
- Wide area ethernet
- Mobile wireless services

7.4.5 Digital Living Network Alliance (DLNA)

The Digital Living Network Alliance (DLNA) is an industry alliance of consumer electronics, personal computers, and mobile devices companies. DLNA is engaged in harmonizing standards for IP-networked platforms and digital homes. The objective is to work with the standards bodies such as IEEE, W3C, universal plug and play (UPnP), and IETF, among others, to realize an environment where devices can connect on the IP-based networks, get automatically configured through UPnP, and share media content. Initially, it is targeting devices such as personal computers, storage devices, set-top boxes, PVRs, and media players. The UPnP specification specifies two types of devices: audio video media servers and media-rendering devices.

DLNA has released its first specification DLNA 1.0, which deals with the UPnP media servers. Future releases will serve media-rendering devices. The carriage of DVB services is also planned to be supported in the DLNA future releases.

7.4.6 Open Mobile Alliance (OMA)

OMA is an association of over 300 companies representing mobile operators, handset and device suppliers, IT companies, etc. with a mission to "facilitate global user adoption of mobile data services by specifying market driven mobile service enablers that ensure service interoperability across devices, geographies, service providers, operators, and networks." OMA has been working toward creating an interoperable environment by laying guidelines for implementation of technologies. The standards in many cases do not specify either the parameters which should be used for implementation or the characteristics of handsets. This gap is filled by the OMA. It also organizes "Techfests" on the lines of "Plugfests" by the WiMAX Forum to test the interoperability between various products and technologies.

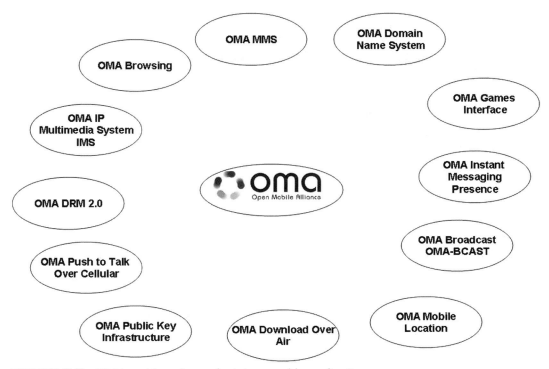

FIGURE 7-7 OMA enabler releases for interoperable applications

A large number of mobile applications today follow the OMA guidelines including those for digital rights management (DRM), OMA MMS, OMA browsing, e-mail notification, instant messaging and presence service (IMPS), OMA game services client server interface, OMA push-to-talk over cellular, OMA downloads over the air, etc.

OMA interoperability specifications are essentially "enabler releases," which are used in implementing interoperable specifications.

It is quite evident that OMA today plays a key role along with 3GPP(2) in the design and specifications of services which operate over mobile networks. These range from client server services such as game clients to browsing, MMS, and location-based services.

The status of OMA by virtue of its partnerships has implications on new devices which may enter the markets, e.g., based on new technologies such as mobile WiMAX (IEEE 802.16e). While these devices may be based on open standards aligned with IETF, IEEE 802.16e is defined only up to the MAC level. The design of new applications is entirely possible, but the considerations of interworking with over 3 billion existing mobile devices will imply being able to create interfaces to interwork with applications designed with OMA enablers. Alternatively, it is possible to use IMS for protocols and media conversion. IMS is discussed in Chapter 12 (Mobile WiMAX Network Architectures).

In this chapter, we wish to draw attention towards the key role played by the OMA as an association in determining the use of standards.

7.4.7 Open Handset Alliance

Any discussion on the OMA must also mention the role of the Open Handset Alliance, which is a recently created association of industry players committed towards developing applications, services, and handsets which are based on open standards. One of the initiatives of the alliance is the release of *Android*, which is the first complete, open, and free mobile platform. The new platform being released in mid-2008 is complete, and it covers the operating system, middleware, and mobile applications. The open platform helps go beyond "walled gardens" created by applications that need to work on proprietary platforms or restrict users in installing open applications. The Open Handset Alliance is backed by Google and has Sprint as one of the members. The nationwide rollout of WiMAX by Sprint, the biggest WiMAX event of 2008, makes the developments in this arena especially interesting.

7.5 HOW FAR ARE WE FROM TRULY CONVERGED STANDARDS?

The new paradigm in the industry providing multimedia broadcasting is the delivery across multiple networks and devices which include mobile phones, PDAs, or wireless devices. The delivery needs to be end-to-end secure and with a high QoE.

The implementations at present in various networks, both fixed and mobile, remain quite independent of each other. Not only that, even in different segments, such as fixed networks, the IPTV is implemented through a multiplicity of protocols which depend on the operator or vendor implementing them (i.e., proprietary) or based on a major organizational standard (DVB, 3GPP). Open standard-based implementations are not yet common.

For true convergence, apart from the technical compatibility across networks, there is a need for a common security, operations support, and business support architecture. Open networks have the advantage of having a much larger base of developers who can be involved in developing much richer applications. However, the existing devices create a large overhang and continue to provide their own engines of growth.

8

CHIPSETS FOR WiMAX DEVICES

Computers are composed of nothing more than logic gates stretched out to the horizon in a vast numerical irrigation system.

—Stan Augarten
State of the Art: A Photographic History of
the Integrated Circuit (1985)

We have seen that the WiMAX technologies take a quantum leap from the existing wireless and MMDS technologies for delivery of broadband content with quality of service (QoS). The technologies are not only based on OFDM, which provides high resilience against intersymbol interference common in NLOS transmission, but are implemented with very flexible features such as setting up of service flows at connection time, and are maintained despite adverse conditions through scalable OFDMA, subchannelling schemes, adaptive modulation, partial utilization of subcarriers, or beam forming which overcome the vagaries of wireless medium to deliver a QoS guaranteed performance. The networks are designed for mobility and handover as well as nomadic and stationary applications, are open in architecture and merge well with IP-based networks or legacy networks using IP Multimedia subsystem (IMS).

8.1 REALIZING WiMAX FUNCTIONS IN PHYSICAL DEVICES

The technologies of WiMAX which are specified in the PHY and MAC layers need to be implemented in physical circuits in order that the functional elements of WiMAX (and Mobile WiMAX) can be available to higher-order layers and applications. These physical components function by carrying out discrete fast Fourier transform (FFT) and inverse discrete fast Fourier transform (IFFT) for demodulation and modulation of data signals, thereby requiring an efficient implementation of digital signal processing (DSP) to realize the desired functions. The

WiMAX chipsets represent a realization of the protocols and architectures, which have been developed by the IEEE 802.16 and standardized by the WiMAX forum. As the developments of the standards for Mobile WiMAX are of relatively recent origin, many of the chipsets are pre-WiMAX standard chipsets, followed by those meeting the requirements of Wave 1 and Wave 2 certifications and finally those that have been used in devices that have received certification.

8.1.1 Defining the Environment

Apart from the requirements of efficient running of the WiMAX protocols, the mobile handsets require many additional functionalities. The communications functions may include support of cellular networks (GSM or CDMA) in the same handset, and support for WiFi wireless access and Bluetooth. In addition, support of the mobile device peripherals and a wide range of applications is required (Figure 8-1). These functions are implemented by using one or more chipsets.

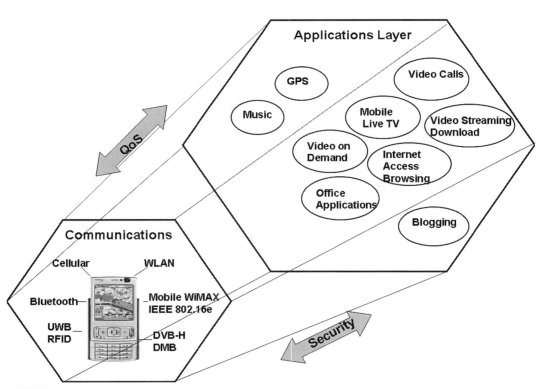

FIGURE 8-1   Functional environment of a WiMAX mobile station

The various functions indicated as well as the applications will typically be achieved by

- Chipsets implementing the basic functionalities, such as radio reception, WiMAX base band functions of PHY layer, such as OFDM processing and MAC-layer functions such as connections, scheduling, service flows, and network interfaces.
- Application processors running the various applications and peripheral control.
- Specialized chipsets for applications such as GPS, mobile TV, and cellular network access.

Figure 8-2 depicts a schematic of a WiMAX mobile station with various functional blocks.

The WiMAX chipset consists of a group of chips (or systems on a chip) which address the distinctive functions of RF, OFDM processing, and the MAC layer processing, including network interfaces, respectively. The first group is the RF, which carries out the functions of

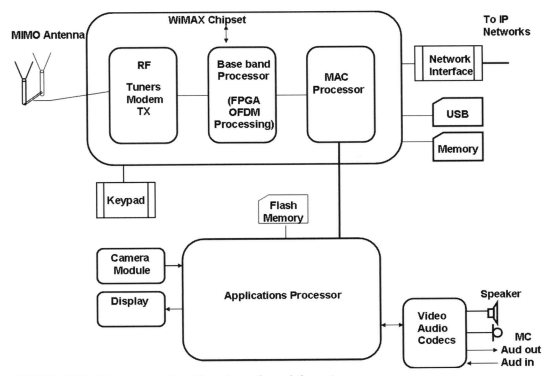

FIGURE 8-2   Block schematic of functions of a mobile station

RF tuning, reception, and transmission (including those from MIMO antennas). This is followed by the OFDM processors, which are usually realized by field programmable gate arrays (FPGAs) and perform the matrix-based functions such as IFFT and FFT. The MAC-layer functions of managing connections and service flows from external networks are managed by the functional group of MAC-layer processing.

The mobile station will, in all probability, need additional applications functions, such as handset-based camera, video calling, and multimedia services. Such specialized functions are handled by using an applications processor. However, every handset may not support an applications processor. Finally, the handset may also contain chips for cellular network functionality for dual operation on cellular and WiFi or CDMA networks.

It should be recognized that it is not necessary to perform all the functions such as OFDM processing, MAC layer scheduling, and MAC packet generation by using separate chips for each function. These can be also implemented in software that runs on an appropriate processor. For example the Samsung SPH M8000 phone which supports WiMAX is based on Intel PXA272 520 MHz CPU and implements the protocols in software.

In general, the software and hardware functions go hand in hand, i.e., for each functional block there would be a set of functions that are implemented in hardware and others that are handled in software. A number of different reference designs can be achieved ranging from use of hardware implementations for every function, to a largely software-based implementation.

8.2 REQUIREMENTS OF CHIPSETS FOR MOBILE WiMAX

A mobile WiMAX chipset needs to compliant with IEEE 802.16e scalable OFDMA with FFT sizes from 256 to 1024. In addition, a mobile WiMAX chipset would support the following features:

- Compliance with the wave 2 or the later current certification profiles under the WiMAX forum to support interoperability in base stations or mobile stations. This implies support of specific parameters such as number of OFDM symbols, FFT size, number of subchannels, bandwidth, and frequency of operation.
- "On chip" features to support use in various bands, current and future. Typically this would require that the chipset not contain frequency-sensitive components, such as SAW filters and rather use direct frequency conversion radios.

- Support low chip count and low space footprint, in order that it is usable in the small-sized mobile devices, as well as embedded systems.
- Use low power in active and sleep modes, to conserve battery life.
- Be available with complete firmware, reference design, and system design kits for easy integration.

8.3 SYSTEMS ON CHIP (SOC) FOR WiMAX

A SoC is an application-specific integrated circuit, where often one "piece of silicon" or chip can contain all the functions required for a specific application. Functions such as implementation of mobile WiMAX is one such application where the functions including RF, PHY-layer processing, MAC-layer processing, network interface, etc. can be ideally implemented by using a single piece of silicon as SoC.

The development costs of such a chip may be higher, but in volume productions there is considerable advantage of simplicity in the end design realization. SoC are designed using the VHSIC HDL (Very

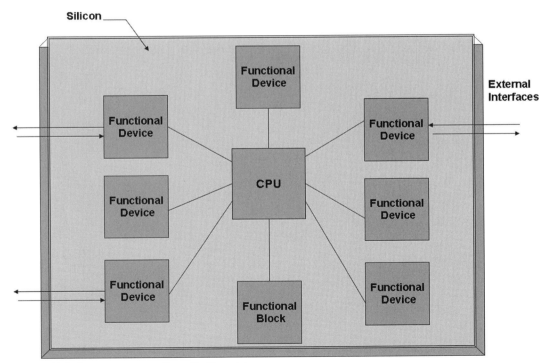

FIGURE 8-3 Systems on Chip (SoC) architecture

High-Speed Integrated Circuit Hardware Description Language) and VHDL (a structural language describing the description of the device). The high-level languages are used to develop the functional blocks needed on the SoC. Some functional blocks that are widely used in the industry, such as processor cores, are standard and available against payment of royalty for the intellectual property while others are open source and available for free use.

The SoCs are usually supplied with reference designs and system design kits (SDK), which help quick development of applications.

8.4 FIXED WiMAX SOCs

Fixed WiMAX SoCs are designed for implementing WiMAX systems as per IEEE 802.16-2004 standards. Most of the SOCs available are designed to conform to the Release 1 specifications, waves 1 to 3 of Fixed WiMAX. Conformance to initial certification profiles ensures that CPEs and base stations designed with these devices fully conform to the initial release profiles for fixed WiMAX and are interoperable.

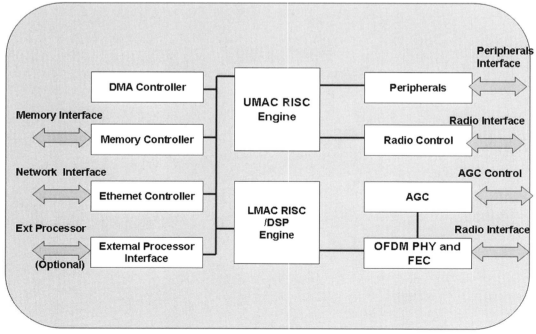

FIGURE 8-4   Fujitsu WiMAX 802.16-2004 SoC-MB87M3550 block schematic

8.4.1 Fujitsu IEEE 802.16-2004 Fixed WiMAX SoC

Fujitsu had introduced an IEEE 802.16-2004 compliant SoC (MB87M3550), which became quite popular and was used in a number of installations of WiMAX. The SoC was designed for the entire range of frequencies from 2 to11 GHz and bandwidths of 1.75 to 20 MHz. (The RF unit is external to the SoC.) The SoC was designed to support the base station, as well as the subscriber station and supports subchannelization in the uplink as per IEEE 802.16-2004 standards. It is based on dual RISC processors for MAC-layer functions (upper layer and lower layer).

The SOC is designed to operate in the license-exempt frequency bands at 2.4, 5.8, and 11 GHz as well as licensed bands at 2.5, 3.5, 3.6, and 5.8 GHz. It should be noted however that the RF components are external to the SoC. It supports half FDD, full FDD, or TDD operations. The FFT size is fixed at 256 (256 OFDM PHY) with adaptive modulation as per QPSK, 16 QAM, and 64 QAM. The network interface is provided through an Ethernet engine. The SoC can handle data rates of 75 Mbps when using all 192 subcarriers in a 20-MHz bandwidth system.

8.5 MOBILE WiMAX CHIPSETS

Mobile WiMAX chipsets are designed to support the IEEE 802.16e-2005 specifications for mobile WiMAX. With the WiMAX Forum having issued wave 2 certification guidelines, which involve the use of MIMO, there has been a move toward introducing chipsets or design architectures, which can help realize 2×2 MIMO in customer premises equipment(CPEs) in order that these can be used in high data rate or extended range NLOS WiMAX environments.

Most of the chipsets available fully support the Release 1 wave 1 requirements, and the newer chipsets entering the market all comply with wave 2 requirements as well, which includes MIMO.

8.5.1 Fujitsu IEEE 802.16e-2005 Mobile WiMAX SoC

MB86K21 is a SoC from Fujitsu that is compliant with mobile WiMAX IEEE 802.16e-2005 specifications. The SoC has been designed for use in mobile stations and terminals, as well as in PC cards and to meet wave 2 certification requirements. It provides a scalable 512/1024 FFT size and bandwidths of 5 and 10 MHz for mobile applications. It supports adaptive modulation schemes with QPSK, 16 QAM, and 64 QAM and has been tested to over 18 Mbps of throughput in lab environments.

The SoC has a USB interface and a PCI bus interface for interface in PC or mobile station environments. It provides support for antenna diversity and 2×2 MIMO or Space Time Coding (STC). The SoC has been designed to optimize power consumption. The chip is rated at

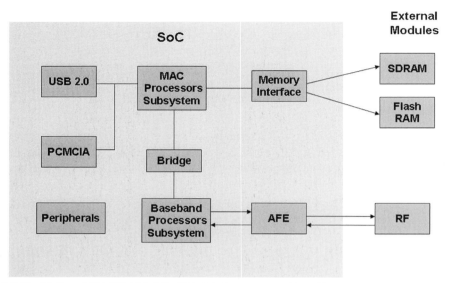

FIGURE 8-5   Fujitsu MB86K21 Mobile WiMAX Systems on Chip (SoC) block diagram (Picture Courtesy Fujitsu)

500 mW for 45 Mbps data download and 10 mW in sleep mode. The SoC does not include the RF part for which an external RF module needs to be connected. Memory (Flash RAM, SDRAM) are also not built in the SoC and need to be connected externally.

System Design Kit for Fujitsu MB86K21 SoC

A system design kit (SDK) and PC card reference design platform for type II PC card is available from Fujitsu for integration of SoC in mobile devices and PCs. The reference design is based on the use of 2.4 to 2.469 GHz frequency RF, which is as per the certification profile for 2×2 MIMO systems. The software available for the reference design includes the MAC-level drivers and APIs, which can be used to interface to application software programs.

The reference design software provided by Fujitsu also includes maintenance functions such as measurement of online performance and MAC management messages.

8.5.2 Beceem® BCS200

Beceem, which is known for having launched the world's first mobile WiMAX chipset, MS100, in September 2005 and the MS 120 chipset in 2006, has now unveiled the BCS200 chipset for mobile WiMAX as per IEEE 802.16e standards. Beceem chipsets are based on two tightly coupled products—the baseband IC for PHY and MAC layer, and the RFIC for providing the RF functions. The MS120 chipsets is comprised

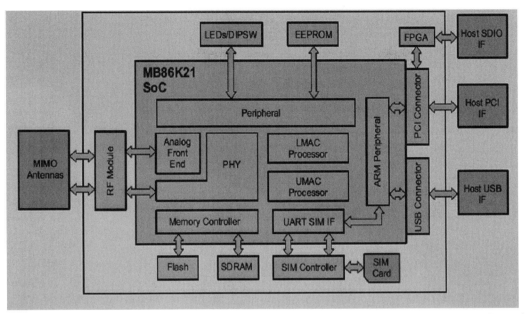

FIGURE 8-6 Fujitsu system design kit block diagram for SoC MB86K21 (Picture courtesy Fujitsu)

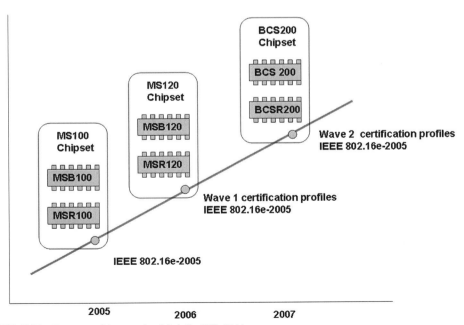

FIGURE 8-7 Beceem chipsets for Mobile WiMAX

of MSB120 baseband IC and MSR120 radio IC. While the MSB 120 is fully compliant with the IEEE 802.16e-2005 standards for baseband, the MSR120 transceiver provides operations in the 2.x and 3.x GHz bands. The MS120 chipset is designed to meet the WiMAX wave 1 certification profile requirements.

The BCS200 chipset also is comprised of a baseband IC supporting the realization of PHY and MAC layers (BCS B200) and an RFIC (BCSR200) for supporting a fully integrated base station or mobile station realization as per wave 2 certification profiles. The RF chip has two receive chains and one transmit chain. It can be used with two receive antennas and two transmit antennas with single output common to the antennas realizing a single input multiple output (SIMO) configuration.

The RFIC has a direct conversion transceiver and can be used for 2.x GHZ and 3.x GHZ bands as per wave 2 certification profiles. The chipset is designed for use in both base stations (realizing a SISO or MIMO configuration) or a mobile station with SIMO configuration.

BCS200 is designed for use in wave 2 certification profiles of IEEE 802.16e, which includes the use of MIMO and beam forming in mobile environment. The BCS200 has many features that are designed to comply with the certification profiles and provide highest data throughputs. These include, for example, the use of multiband multi-channel direct conversion radio (DCR). This not only improves the signal quality by eliminating the surface acoustic wave (SAW) filters but also makes the use of the BCSB200/BCSR200 chipset assembly possible in different markets with spectrum bands of 2.3, 2.5, 3.5, and 3.3 GHz. The elimination of the SAW filter, which has different space footprints for different bands, places the chipset in a new domain with complete flexibility in use in various networks. The reduction of component count by elimination of the filter also makes it better suited for

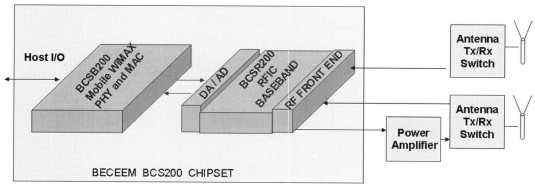

FIGURE 8-8 Beceem BCS200 chipset

use in mobile devices, such as handsets or PDAs, which are the primary devices where the wave 2 WiMAX will be used.

Beceem BCS200 comes with a reference design kit which enables quick development of prototypes and WiMAX modem products. The reference design kit comes with all the firmware and the host driver software for easy integration.

Beceem chipsets have been used in Samsung WiMAX phones and plug-in modules. Sprint's U.S. network of mobile WiMAX is based on Samsung devices in the Washington, D.C. area. The roll-out features PC cards, UMPCs, and plug-ins, followed by mobile devices and handsets. The BCS200 chipset is also being used by Sanyo to offer dual-mode handsets for various markets.

8.5.3 Intel WiMAX Connection 2300

Intel has brought out a chipset (WiMAX connection 2300) that is designed to engineer dual mode handsets operable with both mobile WiMAX and WiFi (802.11n) networks. The chip needs to be interfaced with the radio section of the mobile handset to complete the functions of baseband and the RF. Intel's multiband WiMAX/WiFi radio is one such RFIC which can be used. Intel connection 2300, apart from supporting the IEEE 802.16e functionality, also supports the 802.11n wireless connectivity. As both technologies are based on the use of MIMO, this combination provides an optimal use of the radio transceivers and antennas.

The connection Intel WiMAX 2300 is an important development as it is likely to be used in Intel's next-generation Centrino mobile platforms.

Intel also has a dual-mode (IEEE 802.16-2004 fixed WiMAX and 802.16e mobile WiMAX) chipset (WiMAX connection 2250). The upgrade from 802.16-2004 to 802.16e can be done over the air.

8.5.4 Runcom® RNA200

The Runcom RNA200, along with the Fujitsu and Beecam, has been one of the early movers in the mobile WiMAX SoC arena. RNA200 is, however, unique in some ways as the SoC not only includes the implementation of the PHY and the MAC layer functions but also includes an embedded CPU (ARM 1136) and analog modules to reduce the chip count and space footprint. The RNA200 baseband modem (called "Tornado") needs only an RFIC, SDRAM, and serial Flash memory to complete all the functionalities. The RFIC in use would depend on the frequency band. The baseband modem RNA200 can be used in all applicable mobile WiMAX frequency bands as it supports FFT sizes of

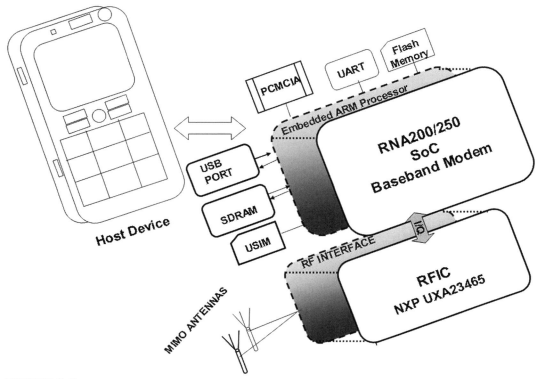

FIGURE 8-9   RUNCOM RNA200 Mobile WiMAX SoC

512, 1024, and 2048. The modem supports space time coding (STC) as well as MIMO technologies, and with a 20 MHz bandwidth data rates of 80 Mbps can be achieved. Using 14 Mbps bandwidth, 56 Mbps data rates are achievable.

The baseband modem can be used with a range of RFICs. An example is the NXA23465 from NXP semiconductors. The interface to the RFIC is an analogue baseband I/Q interface. It includes 10 bit A/D and D/A converters with PLL for this purpose. The host interface functions include USB, compact flash (CF), card bus, UART, host port, SDIO, and USIM interfaces. The RNA250(ASIC version of SoC) and the NXA23465 WiMAX MIMO transceiver were among the first products to have been certified under the wave 2 (MIMO) Mobile WiMAX profiles. RNA200, ASIC version, is designed for use in handsets, PDAs, PCMCIA cards, USB dongles, or as part of the chipset of laptops.

The MAC layer supports both IPv4 and IPv6 over Ethernet and bandwidth requests, and allocations can be made based on channel quality indicator (CQI). It can provide multiple secondary connections and service flows as per network layer requirements.

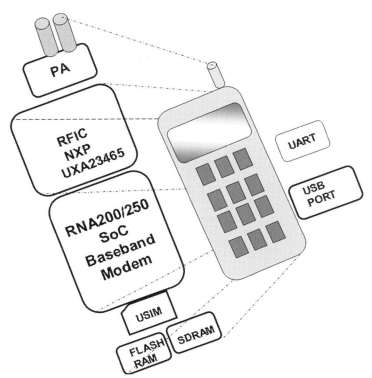

FIGURE 8-10 Conceptual WiMAX implementation on a mobile device

The SoC also provides a high level of applications support. It has been designed for "triple play" applications involving the use of voice, video, and data in both mobile and fixed environments. For this purpose the installed firmware includes a VoIP core and functions for supporting videoconferencing, video calling, and e-learning. Both legacy telephony and VoIP are supported. The data functions include virtual private networks and turbo internet.

Runcom SoCs have been used to power various PC cards and USB products. These include Kyocera which demonstrated Mobi TV™ streaming television over WiMAX. The highly integrated architecture of RNA200 SoC is primarily responsible for its being able to provide miniature devices such as Flash cards, WiMAX PC cards, and USB adopters.

Some of the features of RNA200 are:

- IEEE 802.16e air interface physical layer specifications compliant.
- High throughput: 56 Mbps for 14 MHz channel.
- On-chip modulation and demodulation, for substantial cost savings, and short time to market.

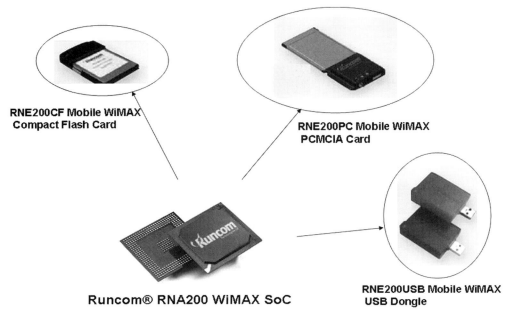

FIGURE 8-11 The integrated architecture of RUNCOM RNA200 SoC can be used in miniature devices (Images courtesy Runcom)

- IEEE 802.16e air interface MAC layer specifications compliant.
- High-spectral efficiency up to 4 Bps/Hz.
- Uses 2 K, 1 K, and 512 FFT sizes for broadband downstream/ upstream transmission.
- Automatic power adjustment to meet variable transmission conditions.
- Adaptive modulation for upstream and downstream: QPSK, 16 QAM, and 64 QAM.
- Uses advanced turbo coding FEC to achieve low BER.
- Includes analogue base-band I/Q as direct interface to RFIC module.
- Includes 10-bit A/D, 10-bit D/A, and PLL cores.
- Includes USB, CF, card bus, UART, host port, SDIO, and USIM interfaces.
- Includes VoIP core.
- Includes STC and open loop MIMO (future releases) capabilities.
- High throughput: 80 Mbps for 20 MHz channel.
- Increases coverage and immunity in adverse multipath environment.
- Supports dynamic bandwidth allocation techniques.

- Complete design kit enables fast evaluation, development, and compliance testing.
- Supports antenna diversity and smart antenna techniques (optional).
- Supports space time coding (optional).

Base Station Solutions

Runcom also provides base station solutions based on the RNA200 family of SoCs. The RNU2000N is a single-sector base station that is fully self-contained and includes a radio transceiver. Base station reference design channel cards (RNE2000B) are also available.

8.5.5 TelSIS® Wireless 2 × 2 MIMO SoC

TCW 1620 is a WiMAX SoC from TeleCIS Wireless that is designed for implementing 2 × 2 MIMO in CPEs. The TCW 1620 ASIC has dual transmit and dual receive support built in the chip to directly implement wave 2 compliant 2 × 2 MIMO. The SoC has a power consumption of only 300 mW for complete support of MAC and PHY functions making it suitable for portable devices such as WiMAX USB adapters and PC cards.

As most CPEs are self-installed and meant for use in NLOS environment (i.e. indoors), these need to have diversity-based transmit receive antennas for satisfactory wireless connectivity. The use of 2 × 2 MIMO is claimed to increase the range to 2.5 times or to deliver up to 15 dB of additional performance.

WiMAX SoC for PDAs and Mobile Phones with 2 × 2 MIMO

TeleCIS Wireless is also introducing TCW 2720, which is also 2 × 2 compliant and supports space time coding (STC), spatial multiplexing, and adaptive MIMO switching meeting WiMAX Forum wave 2 certification requirements. TCW 2720, with power consumption of below 250 mW, is designed for mobile devices, media players, mobile phones, PDAs, etc. as a 2 × 2 MIMO WiMAX modem.

8.5.6 Wavesat UMobile™

Wavesat, which is well known in the WiMAX arena for its earliest certified products in the Fixed WiMAX (IEEE 802.16-2004) based on the DM256 chip, has also announced a IEEE 802.16e-compliant chipset (called the UMobile™). The Mobile WiMAX chipset and reference designs provide full mobility against fixed or nomadic applications for the previous chips. UMobile™ is also compliant with the WiBro network.

UMobile implements the full MAC and PHY layers in a single chipset. It is wave 2 compliant with 2×2 MIMO compatibility and smart antenna features. The chipset has some features which are unique. Firstly, it has on-chip DRAM. Hence, external DRAM is not required as in some other chipsets. This helps reduce the chip count and the space footprint. Second, it is based on ultra-low-power DSP cores, which help achieve a power consumption of only 150 mW, which is one of the lowest in the industry (average 250 mW). It has a fully programmable architecture with the chip being able to support multi-mode operations including wireless LANs and OFDM/OFDMA. In a multimode use, the chip can support legacy networks of 802.11 a/g or IEEE 802.16 fixed or mobile implementations.

8.5.7 Intel Montevina®

With a view to usher in new mobile devices with low power and higher performance, Intel is now moving towards a new processor platform ("Penryn"). Montevina will be Intel's first Centrino processor technology for notebooks to offer the option of integrated WiFi and WiMAX wireless technologies for greater wireless broadband access. This will also be based on the Penryn processor technology. The release is happening in 2008. Intel's roadmap also includes ultra-low-power UMPCs and other devices codenamed "Menlow," which will consume just 10 percent of the power today consumed by the first generation of UMPCs.

8.6 BASE STATIONS

The requirements of chipsets for base stations, despite the common technology of IEEE 802.16e, are not identical to the chipsets for handsets where space, power consumption, and uplink requirements are different from a base station. Base stations also have additional functions of downlink and uplink resource management and backhaul links to the access service network (ASN) and connectivity service networks (CSNs) (network definitions are given in detail in Chapter 13).

The base stations may vary from one single channel self-contained micro base station to multichannel, multi-sector base stations and at the apex level the ASN. Base station designs also differ from rural areas to metros. In metros, the frequency reuse of 1×3 with sectorization would typically be used to increase the serviceable user density.

Figure 8-13 shows the block diagram of a channel card in a WiMAX base station. The channel card is comprised of an RF section, which has the RF power amplifier and does an up-conversion of frequency for transmission and down conversion for reception. One channel card is

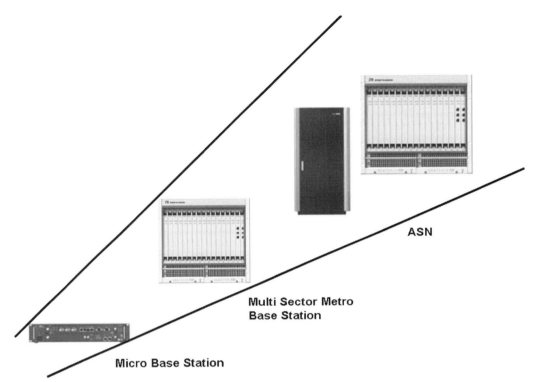

ASN

Multi Sector Metro
Base Station

Micro Base Station

FIGURE 8-12   Base stations in a WiMAX network

needed for each frequency (and each sector). The channel cards (called "blades") are connected in a common base station chassis having a motherboard.

The network interface is provided by the MAC convergence sublayer, which establishes network connection over an IP interface.

8.6.1 Freescale™ WiMAX implementation

For a typical implementation for a mobile WiMAX base station, the scalable WiMAX solution from Freescale™ semiconductors provides a good example. A single channel card implements the functionality required for the radio transmission and reception and the PHY and MAC layer implementations. The PHY layer is implemented by two quad core 500 MHz digital signal processors (DSPs, MCS8126). An FPGA is used for time domain processing. The MAC layer processing is done by a communications processor (MPC8555), which is based on "PowerPC™" technology.

Network termination (Gigabit Ethernet, Serial I/O, and Rapid I/O interconnect) is supported by the network interface section running a

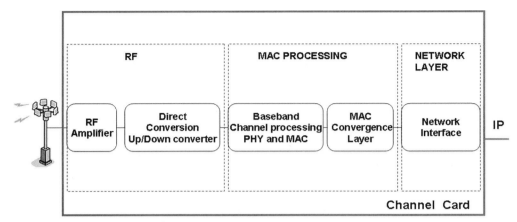

FIGURE 8-13   Block diagram of a channel card in a WiMAX base station

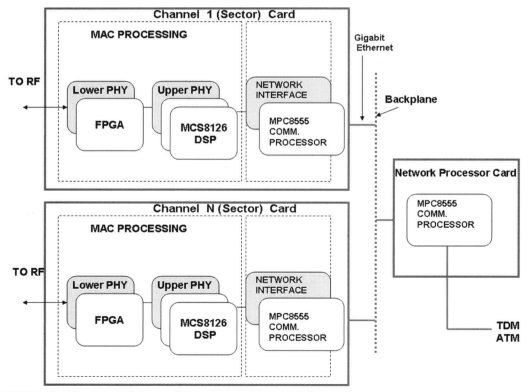

FIGURE 8-14   Freescale™ implementation of a WiMAX base station

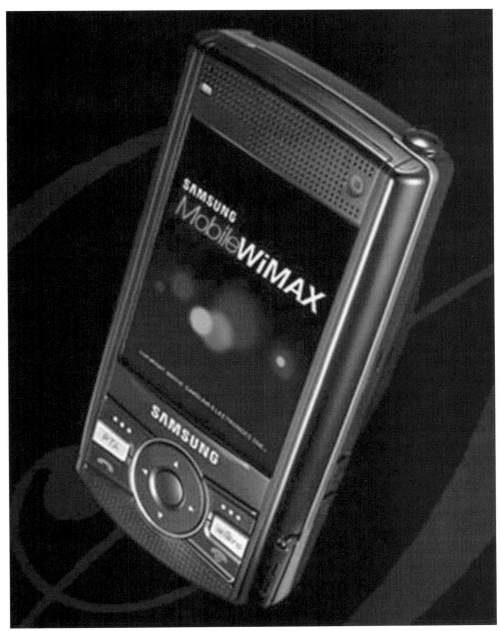

FIGURE 8-15 Samsung SPH M8100 Mobile WiMAX, CDMA, and T-DMB phone

communications processor (MPC8555) and Freescale's QUICC™ engine technology.

The base station can be used for both Fixed WiMAX (IEEE 802.16-2004) and Mobile WiMAX (IEEE 802.15e-2005) applications.

8.7 HANDSETS

WiMAX CPEs and handsets are covered in the next chapter, which explores different types of Fixed WiMAX and Mobile WiMAX CPEs designed using the WiMAX SoCs. In this chapter, it would suffice to say that all progress in the development of CPEs is primarily governed by the WiMAX SoCs and their certification under the WiMAX forum.

8.7.1 Mobile WiMAX PDA Phone Samsung SPH M-8100

The Samsung SPH M-8100 is the first mobile phone which made its advent as an IEEE 802.16e (WiBro and Mobile WiMAX)-compliant device. The phone is CDMA2000, 1xEV-DO/IEEE 802.16e compatible and also has T-DMB-compatible mobile TV interface. It also has a "TV out" port. The phone can also be used for video conferencing by a VGA camera. There is also a second 2-megapixel camera available on the phone. It also has wireless internet and its applications include voice calls, video calls, and internet browsing. The phone is based on Windows mobile 5.0 PPC PE operating system and has 64 MB RAM.

The phone is being used in Korea's WiBro network. It is also being demonstrated for use in the Sprint 4G network for broadband wireless in the U.S. (IEEE 802.16e mobile WiMAX and CDMA2000 1900 MHz).

Its other features are:

- Multi-format music and video support
- Bluetooth stereo music profile (A2DP)
- Bluetooth/USB
- Digital power amp
- MS Office view and edit
- External memory: MMC micro

8.7.2 Developments in WiMAX SOCs

WiMAX SoCs are undergoing a greater and greater integration with the prime considerations being minimum component count, lowest space footprint, and lowest power consumption. These considerations themselves arise from the need to embed the WiMAX SoCs in media players, PDAs, cellphones, and other miniature devices. The mass production of these devices with associated lower costs is slated to happen in 2008 onwards, driving the prices down.

9

CUSTOMER PREMISES EQUIPMENT (CPES) FOR WiMAX

We think WiMAX is a big-screen technology; ask someone else about using it in handsets.

—Ron Peck, Intel Corp.

In 2003, WiFi (802.11) can be said to have made its true debut, when WiFi chips became widely available. Earlier, the computers could only be enabled for WiFi by using PC cards inserted in PCMCIA slots. Within two years, every laptop shipped was WiFi-enabled. However, enabling PDAs with WiFi was still a step away. At this time, WiFi was being embedded in all PCs and laptops using mini-PCI cards or mounting the WiFi-enabling modules. The modules, however, were still too large for the PDAs and cellphones. After the availability of tiny footprint chipsets, WiFi entered the domain of PDAs, cellphones, and portable music players. In 2005, 120 million WiFi chipsets were sold, and this figure rose to 200 million in 2006; 1 billion are expected to be sold in 2010. The number of WiFi hotspots has risen to over 500,000 in 2008. The prices of WiFi modules fell from over $50 when introduced in 2003 to under $5 today.

WiMAX is said to be at a similar stage today. The chipsets such as UMobile™ from Wavesat implement the WiMAX solution in one chip. The products are being certified by the WiMAX Forum, which makes them interoperable with WiMAX networks universally. It would therefore be no surprise if the WiMAX products which provide high-speed connectivity with QoS across the city should become ubiquitous by 2009.

The availability of the receiving devices for WiMAX has depended on three major factors:

- Finalization of the standards and release of certification profiles by the WiMAX Forum.

- Availability of chipsets based on the profiles released.
- WiMAX certification after interoperability testing in "Plugfests" and WiMAX-authorized labs.

The use of CPEs is further subject to spectrum available in individual countries to network operators. It is no surprise, therefore, that the initial WiMAX CPEs that made their debut were Fixed WiMAX (IEEE 802.16-2004) devices. The WiMAX Forum has completed Release 1 testing for all parameters and over a hundred WiMAX-certified products are available for fixed WiMAX. So far as the Mobile WiMAX is concerned, the certification process has already been under way, and a number of devices have been certified. The release of wave 2 devices, which support MIMO, has been accelerated, and products are being released every quarter as "WiMAX certified." New devices such as chipsets, USB attachments, PC cards, etc. are being announced almost every week and comply with IEEE 802.16e-2005 mobile WiMAX standards. In many cases, certification follows later. With the products being software up-gradable in most cases, and the new technologies being backward compatible, it is expected that once introduced in networks, they will continue to function for their useful life.

9.1 IMPORTANCE OF WiMAX CERTIFICATION PROFILES

WiMAX certification profiles have been discussed earlier in Chapter 2. The certification profiles that are announced by the WiMAX Forum become a lead for the vendors to develop and test interoperable products. The interoperability and the conformance to the agreed profiles is generally done at Plugfests, where a number of vendors participate (for both the base station and the mobile stations) and the parameters of interoperability are tested in a multi-vendor environment. The Plugfests are managed by the Certification Working Group (CWG) of the WiMAX Forum.

The WiMAX Forum has completed the Release 1 certification of Fixed WiMAX (IEEE 802.16-2004) devices. All certified profiles for Fixed WiMAX are presently based on a fixed FFT size of 256 and frequencies of 3.5 and 5.8 GHz as follows:

- 3.5 GHz band—bandwidths of 3.5 and 7 MHz
- 5.8 GHz band—bandwidth of 10 MHz

For Mobile WiMAX, the second Plugfest was held in February 2007 at Malaga, Spain, and had more than twenty-five equipment vendors participating in the event. The third event was held in May 2007 in France. The fourth Plugfest was held in Taipei in October 2007. A number of vendors demonstrated complete ecosystems for WiMAX, including base stations, CPEs, and network components as per Wave 2 requirements. Many new multimode handsets were announced, such as Qisda (an EDGE/WiMAX dual mode phone) and Motorola (a CDMA/WiMAX dual-mode phone). These indicate the directions of developments of CPEs.

The profiles which have been included for certification for the Wave 2 (MIMO) are given in Table 9-1.

It should be recognized that the IEEE 802.16 standards permit many profiles outside the WiMAX specified parameters, with additional frequency bands, FFT sizes, and bandwidths. Many of these would get included in the later releases or waves of the WiMAX Forum, and equipment that is WiMAX Forum certified will be available. In particular it is expected that profiles in the 700 MHz band may become available owing to the potential availability of this band in many countries as a result of "digital dividend."

The certified profiles at any give point of time represent the equipment that has already undergone interoperability testing and therefore would be freely available and usable without interoperability risks. It also does not prohibit any operator from using a different frequency band, particularly if it has been allocated in any country together with equipment compliant with the IEEE 802.16e-2005. However, it would be best done after ascertaining the availability of mobile stations, which would be operable in that particular band as these would be considered proprietary.

TABLE 9-1

Mobile WiMAX Profiles for which devices have been certified in Wave 2 (Mobile WiMAX with MIMO)

Class Index	Band	Channel Bandwidth	FFT Size
1A	2.3–2.4 GHz	8.75 MHz	1024
1B	2.3–2.4 GHz	5/10 MHz	512/1024
3A	2.496–2.69 GHz	5/10 MHz	512/1024
5A	3.4–3.8 GHz	5 MHz	512
5B	3.4–3.8 GHz	7 MHz	1024
5AL	3.4–3.6 GHz	5 MHz	512
5BL	3.4–3.6 GHz	7 MHz	1024

TABLE 9-2

Mobile WiMAX Release 1 profiles (notified in February 2006)

Channel bandwidth	FFT Size	2.3–2.4 GHz	2.305–2.32 GHz 2.345 –2.36 GHz	2.496–2.69 GHz	3.3–3.4 GHz	3.4–3.8 GHz	Other bands
1.25 MHz	128	▨	▨	▨	▨	▨	▨
5 MHz	512	▨	Release 1	Release 1	Release 1	Release 1	▨
7 MHz	1024	▨	▨	▨	Release 1	Release 1	▨
8.75 Mhz		Release 1	▨	▨	▨	▨	▨
10 MHz	1024	▨	Release 1	Release 1	Release 1	Release 1	▨
20 MHz	2048	▨	▨	▨	▨	▨	▨

▨   Possible Future Release

Release 1   Mobile WiMAX Release 1 profiles notified in February 2006

Table 9-2 provides a full listing of Release 1 system profiles for mobile WiMAX. Release 2 may add new bands or additional FFT sizes or bandwidth profiles based on industry feedback.

In summary, the present focus is on three bands for mobile WiMAX: the 2.3, 2.5 GHz bands, and the 3.4 GHz band, where the initial certifications have taken place. For new operators planning for quick deployment of services with mass adoption using universal clients, these bands present the best bets.

9.2 WiMAX CPES

Based on the two distinct technology lines of fixed WiMAX (IEEE 802.16-2004) and IEEE 802.16e, it would appear that the WiMAX receivers could simply be classified in one of the above two categories. However, the WiMAX receiver ecosystem comprises a wide range of devices for fixed, nomadic, and mobile use.

- First of all, there were receivers that were introduced in the early phase of standards development. These devices adopted certain proprietary features which were claimed by the manufacturers to provide superior performance but could not claim compliance with IEEE 802.16 standards.
- Also at the early stages of development devices came in that were based on the selection of operating parameters which do not yet fall in the WiMAX certifications. These conform to the IEEE 801.16 standards, but do not fall in the category of "WiMAX-certified products"

by virtue of the frequency band used or parameters, such as band-width, number of OFDM carriers, etc. As the WiMAX Forum is conducting certification Plugfests only for specified profiles, these devices currently cannot get the certification stamp. (Examples are IEEE 802.16e devices operating in the 5.8 GHz band.) WiMAX profiles may be defined for such devices in the future and hence these devices are proprietary but can be classified as pre-WiMAX.

- The third category are devices that are WiMAX Forum-certified. These devices follow the parameters that are specified by the WiMAX Forum for certification. Not all these devices are standalone receivers, however, even though they do use a chipset which is WiMAX compliant. Many of the devices are intended to add on WiMAX to an existing list of networks already available such as WiFi and Cellular mobile. In the same category are devices, such as USB cards or adapters, which enable broadband connectivity using WiMAX for laptops or ultra-light PCS, which already have WiFi and perhaps HSDPA or EVDO connectivity.

At the same time, there is a new category of devices emerging which fall in the category of standalone devices for broadband or WiMAX

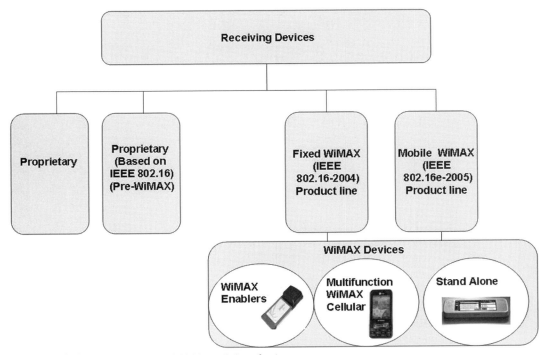

FIGURE 9-1 Classifying WiMAX receiving devices

connectivity alone. The approach is similar to the release of the WiFi Nokia N810 internet tablet. The device is essentially a media player and broadband access device which connects to a WiFi network and has GPS location-based services. Many standalone devices, designed to be standalone WiMAX devices, are under testing for certification.

9.3 FIXED WiMAX (IEEE 802.14-2004) SUBSCRIBER STATIONS

Fixed WiMAX networks based on IEEE 802.16-2004 standards are primarily designed to provide high-speed data links or broadband internet to enterprise or SOHO customers. A typical installation would be comprised of a rooftop antenna and a WiMAX receiver configured for connectivity to a number of devices. Indoor CPEs are also available. Fixed WiMAX has the advantage that it can be set up in the unlicensed bands providing immediate connectivity to rural or semi-urban communities. Figure 9-2 demonstrates the essential elements of a fixed WiMAX installation. It will not be out of place to mention that most of the new installations today are being based on the 802.16e technology in view of its other advantages in regard to configuring clients and services. Some of the devices available follow the fixed WiMAX standard IEEE 802.16-2004 but are upgradable to 802.16e.

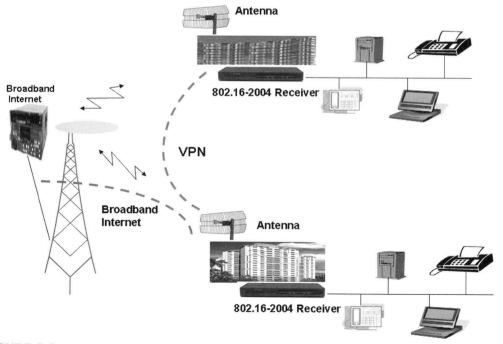

FIGURE 9-2   Fixed WiMAX usage environment

9.3.1 Example of Indoor CPE: Airspan EasyST™

An example* of indoor CPEs is the EasyST indoor CPE from Airspan Networks, Inc. The CPE is available as a modular unit which can be used as a standalone unit alongside a PC or be stacked with a WiFi router (802.11b/g) to connect all WiFi devices.

Another optional add-on stackable unit is a VoIP unit, which supports two standard telephone lines and an Ethernet port. The voice calls support is provided by the QoS features of the 802.16 link. The indoor antenna provides a gain of up to 8.5 dBi and indicates the optimum position without the need for connecting to a PC for signal strength. Once registered on the network, the parameters are automatically downloaded by remote configuration on the WiMAX network. The unit is based on Intel WiMAX connection 2250 connection device. EasyST™ is designed for self-installation. It has a built-in web server, which allows configuration parameters to be seen or set.

In addition to the self-install version of the CPE with NLOS transmission and internal use, i.e., EasyST, it is also possible to mount an

FIGURE 9-3 EasyST™ CPE from Airspan Networks (Images courtesy Airspan Networks)

---

* Examples of WiMAX customer premises equipment (CPEs) have been randomly chosen from a very large range of available products with comparable performance.

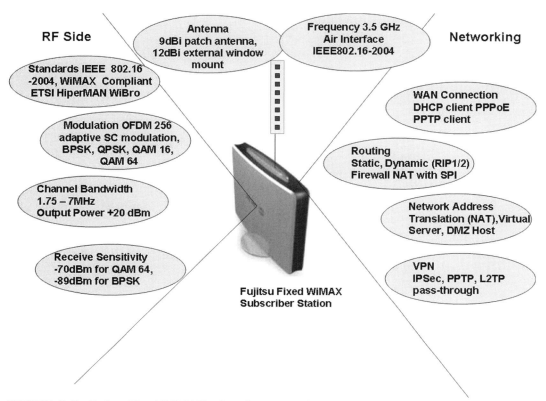

FIGURE 9-4   Fujitsu Fixed WiMAX subscriber station (Image courtesy Fujitsu)

external antenna for higher gain. This option, available under ProST, is meant for higher data rates or SOHO applications. Both the devices work with all base stations which are IEEE 802.16-2004 compliant.

9.3.2 Fujitsu Fixed WiMAX Indoor Subscriber Station

Another example of a CPE for IEEE 802.16-2004 and ETSI HiperMAN fixed WiMAX applications is the Fujitsu WiMAX indoor subscriber station. The station has a 9 dBi inbuilt antenna, as well as an option for an external antenna (12 dBi). The unit is designed to operate in the frequency band of 3.5 GHz and operates in the TDD mode. Channel bandwidths supported are from 1.75 MHz to 7 MHz. The unit provides a LAN interface RJ-45. It can be used in conjunction with WiFi adaptors or VoIP add-on modules to provide the full range of services.

Designed to facilitate networking at the customer premises, the Fujitsu subscriber station can be fitted with an optional networking add-on module. The module handles the WAN connection, static or dynamic routing, network address translation (NAT), virtual server, firewall, and VPN functions.

9.4 MOBILE WiMAX (IEEEE 802.16E) CPES

9.4.1 WiMAX Enabling Devices: PC Cards

PC cards that can enable personal computers and laptops have been the first to appear on the scene in the category of enablers for Mobile WiMAX. The first products were for WiBro in Korea following the launch of services in 2005. Subsequently these have become available progressively for Mobile WiMAX.

What Do the PC Cards Contain?

The PC cards, which act as enablers of WiMAX connectivity, need to provide full support of the physical and MAC layer functions. The cards contain:

Integrated antennas have 2 segment MIMO for Wave 2 devices. Multiple antennas may be installed based on the band supported.

- WiMAX Chipset (SoC) for providing PHY/MAC functions for IEEE 802.16e support, including scalable OFDMA, support of security functions (PKMv2, AES, DES, 3DES), support of authentication functions (EAP) etc.
- RF transceiver for WiMAX transmissions/receptions in different bands.
- Support of IEEE 802.16e air interface and mobile station (MS) functions such as user authorization, IP network access via IP convergence layer, support of QoS requests, service grants, and support of mobility profiles.
- A utility program that runs on the host computer with a graphical user interface (GUI) to provide support for setting up the configuration, viewing link status, and providing software upgrades.

Features to Seek When Buying a PCMCIA Card for WiMAX

As the WiMAX rollouts are in early stages and many networks are based on pre-WiMAX standards, it is useful to carefully check the features of the card to determine if whether it will meet all the requirements. Some of the features to check for would be:

- Form factor of the card and the laptop or PDA slot: The cards are available in physical form factors of a PCMCIA card

(12.5 cm × 5.8 cm) and an Express form factor card (10 cm × 3.3 cm).

- The operating system supported by the PCMCIA card client: Most WiMAX cards available today are for Windows XP and Windows Vista.
- Support of frequency bands: The cards may support some or all of the certification profiles. For ease of use in various WiMAX networks, support of all the bands, i.e., 2.5, 3.3, and 3.5 GHz, is desirable.
- WiMAX certification and regulatory approvals: The device should preferably have passed the WiMAX certification tests and have regulatory approvals (such as from FCC for use in the United States).
- Support of mobility: Most devices will support mobility, but it is an important item to check, specifically for pre-WiMAX devices or proprietary devices. Some of the cards available in the market may be network-specific because of country-based policies on spectrum allocation.

Telsima StarMAX™ PC Cards

Telsima Corp., in the United States, is one of the manufacturers of WiMAX PC cards based on IEEE 802.16e standards. Its cards are available in both PCMCIA (StarMAX 3210) and Express form (StarMAX 3220) formats. The cards come with Windows Vista or Windows XP-based clients, which can be used to set the operating parameters, such as band of operation and bandwidth, etc.

Telsima StarMAX cards comply with wave 2 MIMO 2 × 2 specifications and can be used in mobile, nomadic, or fixed environments. They support EAP authentication of clients with AES or DES encryption. Typical applications of the WiMAX card are broadband internet connectivity, streaming video and audio, and VPNs. Table 9-3 lists the specifications of StarMAX 3210.

Accton™ WiMAX PCMCIA Cards

Accton, Taiwan, has a range of PCMCIA Mobile WiMAX 802.16e-compliant PC cards for different frequency bands. Accton PCMCIA cards have a new twofold external antenna for a higher gain, polarization support, and a higher transmitted power of 23 dBm. It has a 1TX, 2 receive antennas, and is Mobile WiMAX wave 1 compliant. The PCMCIA card is based on the use of BC-MSB120 MAC/baseband chipset and MSR120 RF transceiver. Designed to support adaptive modulation schemes with downlink modulation up to 64 QAM and uplink

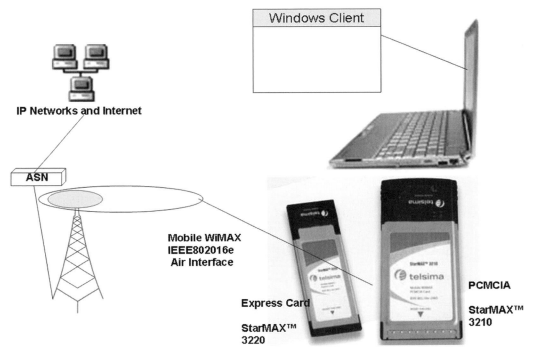

FIGURE 9-5 Mobile WiMAX connectivity using Telsima StarMAX™ PC cards (Picture courtesy Telsima)

TABLE 9-3

WiMAX PC card specifications from Telsima

	Telsima StarMAX™ 3210 WiMAX Card Specifications
Air Interface	IEEE 802.16e-2005, SOFDMA, MIMO, TDD, 2.5/3.3/3.5 GHz, Two integrated antennas
Transmit Power (Typical)	+20 dBm
Antenna	2 Segment MIMO
Security	PKM v2, DES, AES, 3DES
Authentication	EAP-PKMv2
Power Consumption	Below 2.5 W
LED Indicators	WiMAX Link Status, Power Status
Mechanical Dimensions	PCMCIA form factor, Dimensions: 58 × 125 mm (StarMAX 3210)
	Express Card Form Factor, Dimensions 33 × 100 mm (StarMAX 3220)
Regulatory Approvals	EMI/EMC: FCC Class B, FCC Part 15C, CE, RoHS Compliant

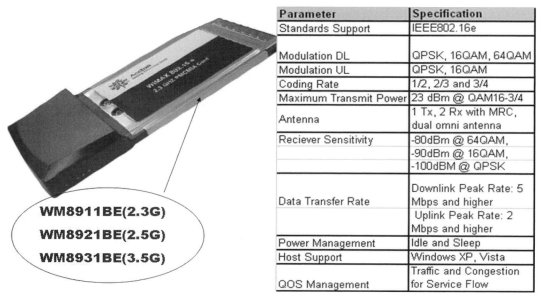

Parameter	Specification
Standards Support	IEEE802.16e
Modulation DL	QPSK, 16QAM, 64QAM
Modulation UL	QPSK, 16QAM
Coding Rate	1/2, 2/3 and 3/4
Maximum Transmit Power	23 dBm @ QAM16-3/4
Antenna	1 Tx, 2 Rx with MRC, dual omni antenna
Reciever Sensitivity	-80dBm @ 64QAM,
	-90dBm @ 16QAM,
	-100dBM @ QPSK
Data Transfer Rate	Downlink Peak Rate: 5 Mbps and higher
	Uplink Peak Rate: 2 Mbps and higher
Power Management	Idle and Sleep
Host Support	Windows XP, Vista
QOS Management	Traffic and Congestion for Service Flow

FIGURE 9-6   Accton™ WiMAX PCMCIA cards (Picture courtesy Accton)

modulation up to 16 QAM, the PC card claims speeds of 5 Mbps (peak) downlink and 2 Mbps uplink. The RF receiver has a high sensitivity of −80 dBm for 64 QAM and −100 dBm for QPSK. Standard features such as security/encryption (PKMv2-AES), QoS, and service flow management, etc., are supported.

The cards are available in three versions:

- WM8911BE- 2.3 to 2.4 GHz (WiBro) with 8.75 MHz bandwidth
- WM8921BE- 2.496 to 2.696 GHz with 5 or 10 MHz bandwidth
- WM8931BE- 3.3 to 3.6 GHz with 5,7 or 10 MHz bandwidth

ZTE 802.16e PC Card

ZTE, a wireless multi-technology company from China, has a PC card compliant with 802.16e and WiMAX standards. The card, designed to be used with PCs, has 24 dBm power output with built-in antennas. It can be used in the configurations:

- One transmit and two receive
- Two transmit and two receive (future release)

It operates with scalable OFDMA with bandwidths of 5 MHz, 10 MHZ, and 20 MHz. With 10 MHz bandwidth, a throughput of

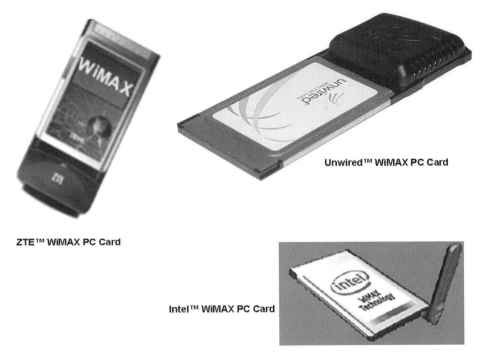

FIGURE 9-7   Mobile WiMAX PC cards (images courtesy ZTE, Intel and Unwired)

>2 Mbps on the downlink and 1 Mbps on the uplink can be supported. It supports a frequency reuse of 1×1 or 1×3. For mobility, all the three modes of handover, i.e., hard handoff, FBSS, and macro-diversity handover are supported.

GEMTEK WIXS PC Cards
GEMTEK offers a Mobile WiMAX-compliant PCMCIA card (WIXS-140) with IEEE 802.16e and ETSI-HiperMAN standards. It is available for the 2.5 to 2.7 GHz band and supports channel bandwidths of 5 and 10 MHz. The PC card is specified for fixed or nomadic use. The device is also meant for Windows platforms.

Clearwire WiMAX PC Card (Pre WiMAX)
Clearwire, in the United States, which has been actively engaged in rolling out WiMAX networks in the recent past is providing its customers a PC card for WiMAX, after approval by the FCC. It claims the support of an average speed of 1.5 Mbps on the card. The card, which is manufactured by Motorola (Expedience™ from Motorola MOTOwi4

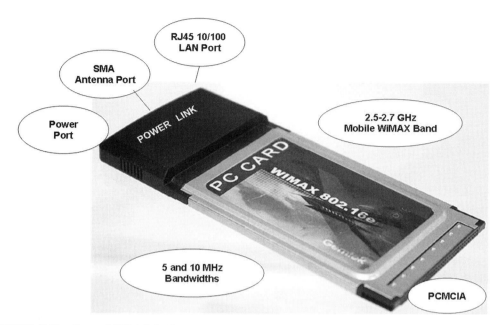

FIGURE 9-8 Gemtek™ Mobile WiMAX PC Card for 2.5 GHz band (Picture courtesy Gemtek)

FIGURE 9-9 WiMAX PC cards from Motorola, U.S. (Picture courtesy Motorola and Clearwire)

series) is operable in the mobile WiMAX band of 2.496 to 2.690 GHz and can operate in bandwidths of 3.5/5/5.5/6 MHz in TDD mode.

9.4.2 USB Adapters

An alternative way to enable a device with WiMAX connectivity is to use a mobile WiMAX USB adapter. This type of usage covers a large universe of devices such as cameras, cellphones, PDAs, video and audio players, etc., which may not have a PCMCIA slot. USB adapters have the advantage that they avoid RF interference, which may be caused with devices that need to be inserted, such as PC cards. It also has the advantage that it can be connected at will, e.g., to download music and mail, or to send pictures without the attachment making the device bulky for daily use. The adapters can also be used to make VoIP calls with appropriate software in the host. The WiMAX USB adapters are similar to the WiFi USB 2.0 adapters, which are in use at hotspots to enable connectivity, except that these can be used citywide.

Airspan™ USB Adaptor

A Mobile WiMAX USB adapter from Airspan networks was the first to be available among the products of this category. The device called MiMAX™ USB adapter is WiMAX wave 2-compliant and is designed for full support of 802.16e air interfaces and specifications and support of MIMO. When used with external antennas which support beam forming, it can deliver performance equivalent to a normal CPE. It can operate in all the mobile WiMAX frequency bands including 2.3–2.4 GHz, 2.5–2.7 GHz, and 3.3–3.7 GHz. It also has a SIM card slot for SIM card-based authentication schemes.

MiMAX offers plug and play features typical of USB 2.0 devices. It can be used with any device with a USB port including PCs or UMPCs with Windows or MAC operating systems. An optional accessory, WiMAX finder, is available which helps in detecting WiMAX coverage availability.

Samsung SPH H1200 USB Dongle

The SPH H1200 USB dongle is a dual network (WiBro/HSDPA) device and extends mobile voice, data, and video capabilities to devices when connected to the USB port. Dual network feature ensures a high data rate connectivity (13 Mbps) in WiBro coverage areas at low cost and wireless connectivity in other areas. It has additional built-in security to limit usage to authorized users.

9.4.3 Mobile WiMAX Home Gateways and Indoor CPEs

PC cards are not the best way to connect to WiMAX in a home environment or where multiple CPEs may be needed to be connected in a SOHO office. Many homes now have home gateways, which are connected using DSL broadband. It is possible to enable home devices with WiMAX-based broadband connectivity by using indoor CPEs.

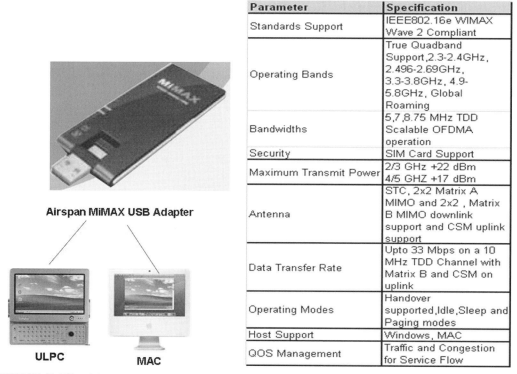

Parameter	Specification
Standards Support	IEEE802.16e WIMAX Wave 2 Compliant
Operating Bands	True Quadband Support,2.3-2.4GHz, 2.496-2.69GHz, 3.3-3.8GHz, 4.9-5.8GHz, Global Roaming
Bandwidths	5,7,8.75 MHz TDD Scalable OFDMA operation
Security	SIM Card Support
Maximum Transmit Power	2/3 GHz +22 dBm 4/5 GHZ +17 dBm
Antenna	STC, 2x2 Matrix A MIMO and 2x2 , Matrix B MIMO downlink support and CSM uplink support
Data Transfer Rate	Upto 33 Mbps on a 10 MHz TDD Channel with Matrix B and CSM on uplink
Operating Modes	Handover supported,Idle,Sleep and Paging modes
Host Support	Windows, MAC
QOS Management	Traffic and Congestion for Service Flow

Airspan MiMAX USB Adapter

ULPC   MAC

FIGURE 9-10   Airspan MiMAX USB Adapter (Image courtesy Airspan Networks)

(These CPEs can also be used with an external antenna mounting giving a much superior data link performance.) Indoor CPEs have a LAN port which can be used in a SOHO LAN, connecting to a home gateway or used with a WiFi router to interconnect home devices. An indoor CPE may thus enable game consoles, VoIP phones, streaming or VoD TV programs, PCs, and music players to connect using the same gateway to the net or other users on P2P networks. If home gateways are not available, WiFi add-ons can be used to make the home WiFi-enabled using WiMAX as the connectivity link.

When connections are needed to many devices requiring a sustained high bit rate for data transmissions, the signal in indoor areas needs to be strong enough to support 64 QAM downlink modulation. This can be achieved by using external antennas or by using special indoor antennas. Typically CPEs with indoor antennas are for self-installation by the user, whereas any outdoor antennas require professional installation.

FIGURE 9-11   Samsung SPH H1200 USB dongle (Picture courtesy Samsung)

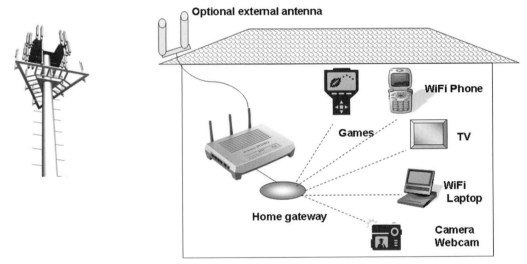

FIGURE 9-12   Indoor WiMAX CPE in a networked environment

GEMTEK WIXS-141

An example of an indoor CPE is the Gemtek™ WIXS-141 mobile WiMAX (IEEE802.16e compatible) device from Gemtek. The indoor unit is designed for 2.5–2.7 GHz band and bandwidths of 5 or 10 MHz as is the case for PC cards. It has a RJ-45 LAN port for connection to a home gateway or a SOHO LAN. The device is designed for fixed/ nomadic use. The WIXS-141 supports a single antenna. The CPE has SMA connector for external antenna and a port for supplying power to a booster if required.

Motorola CPEi 300

Motorola provides a complete WiMAX ecosystem for WiMAX including IMS-based core network, base stations, ASNs, and CPEs. Motorola's

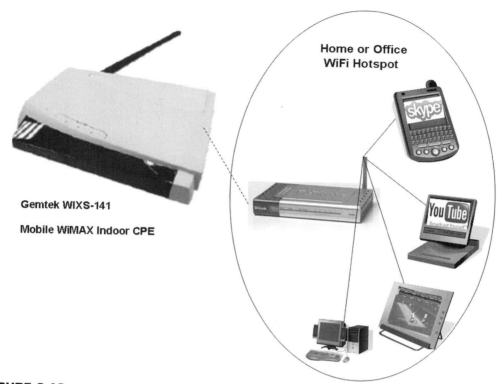

FIGURE 9-13   Gemtek WIXS-141 Indoor CPE (Image courtesy Gemtek)

CPEi 300 is designed for indoor use on IEEE 802.16e Mobile WiMAX networks. It is a desktop device based on Intel WiMAX Connection 2250™ chipset. The device has a low form factor, features Plug and Play installation and self-configuration on the network. It is fully featured in terms of being able to support multiple antenna operations.

9.5 WiMAX WITH CELLULAR PHONES

The idea of having a cellular phone as a repository of movies or updating them using a live data connection has already been demonstrated by phones such as LG KU990 ("Viewty"). Equipped with EV-DO, the phone can be used to access YouTube. It is also DiVX-certified and can be used to view DiVX movies. It has a 5 Mp camera and 120 fps video recording. This brings into focus the need to have high-resolution video devices connected by high-speed data links. WiMAX provides a more efficient way to achieve this connectivity.

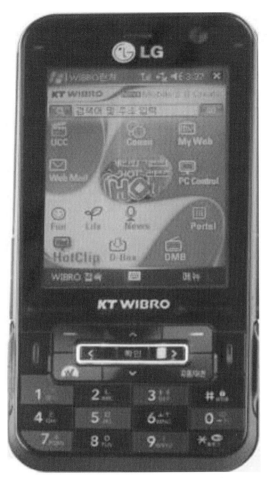

FIGURE 9.14   LG WiBro KC1 Smartphone (Picture courtesy LG)

9.5.1 LG WiMAX KC1 Smartphone

LG has released a smartphone, which is compatible with the Korean implementation of the IEEE 802.16e mobile WiMAX network. The phone (KC1) is a multifunction device which supports a DMB receiver for mobile TV in addition to the WiMAX functionalities. The phone is based on Windows mobile 5 and has a 2 Mp camera. It has a 2.4 inch touch VGA screen.

9.5.2 Samsung SPH-M8100 WiMAX Handset

Samsung has launched a series of handsets for the Korean WiBro market and also demonstrated products for mobile WiMAX based on IEEE 802.16e. The SPH-M8100 is a PDA smartphone which is aimed at

Connectivity
1X EV-DO
WiBRO
Bluetooth A2DP
T-DMB

2.8 inch color screen display

2MP and VGA Camera
Qwerty Keyboard

FIGURE 9-15   Samsung SPH M8100 WiBro phone (Image courtesy 3g. co. uk and Samsung)

high connectivity options and multimedia services. It comes with 1xEV-DO connectivity in addition to WiBro which gives it an ability to operate in WiMAX environment (where available) or switch to EV-DO for 3G high speed connectivity. It also has a T-DMB receiver built in for mobile TV and music on the go. It also has Bluetooth with A2DP for hands-free voice and music applications. Other features supported include a 2 Mp camera and a VGA camera for video calling, an MMC card slot, and a TV out port.

9.6 STANDALONE DEVICES FOR MOBILE WiMAX

9.6.1 Ultra Light PCs

Samsung SPH-9000 and SPH-9200 Ultra Mobile PCs (UMPC)

Samsung has unveiled a Mobile WiMAX compatible UMPC which is based on Intel's Rosedale WiMAX chip. The PC has 256 MB RAM and 30 GB hard disk drive and operates on the Windows XP operating system.

A follow up device is the SPH-9200, which features 512 MB of RAM, 30 GB HDD, and 800 × 489 touch screen. It also has a 1.3 Mp camera.

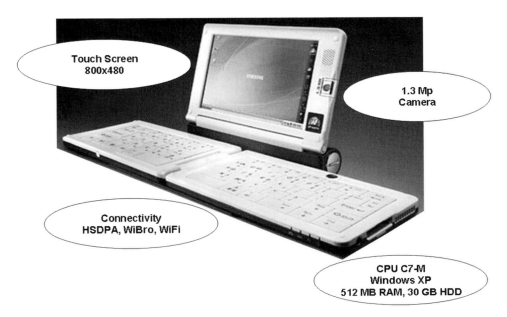

FIGURE 9-16 Samsung Mobile WiMAX UMPC SPH-9200 (Image courtesy Samsung)

In terms of connectivity, it supports WiFi, HSDPA, and Mobile WiMAX (WiBRO).

9.6.2 Gaming Devices

POSDATA

POSDATA Korea has brought out a mobile WiMAX gaming device that can be used in the 2.3 and 2.5 GHz bands. The company is involved in the entire ecosystem of the Mobile WiMAX products from base stations to user terminals. The gaming device (G100) can be used to connect to the internet, and to download and play games using WiMAX networks.

The gaming device features a four-inch TFT–LCD screen for a wide view and better gaming experience. The gaming controls are revealed by the sliding mechanism of the device.

POSDATA also provides a USB WiMAX receiver (U100) for enabling other WiMAX devices, such as ULPCs and music players.

9.6.3 Will WiMAX CPEs Be as Ubiquitous as the WiFi?

Most of the newly developed chipsets are designed to support multi-mode operations. For example, the wave set UMobile™ supports OFDM/OFDMA, as well as WiFi (IEEE 802.11 b/g).

FIGURE 9-17   G100 gaming terminal and USB WiMAX receiver from POSDATA, Korea

With use of direct conversion radio technology in chips, the support of multiple bands is possible. Already USB adapters, such as those from Airspan, provide global roaming with quad band support.

It is expected that the PC cards, USB adapters, etc., when introduced will comply with the Mobile WiMAX band of 2.5–2.69 GHz in addition to some other bands where certification profiles have been announced by the WiMAX Forum. Going ahead, it is also expected that the WiMAX enablers, instead of being available as separate attachments, will be available as embedded devices in music players, cameras, and cell-phones. This will ensure virtually universal usage possibilities in various networks and countries.

9.7 TRENDS IN MOBILE WiMAX CPES

Mobile WiMAX CPEs are now ready for heralding in the next stage where they are set to enter virtually all mobile devices ranging from handsets, media players, gaming devices, etc. The new evolution requires new-generation chipsets with lower form factor, as well as power consumption. The devices need to be self-contained and not depend on host processors. The new initiatives of companies such as Intel and picoChip™ towards new embedded processor lines based on Mobile WiMAX are expected to change the user devices landscape completely in the coming two years. Operators need to be ready to use the media opportunities available with the new-generation devices.

10

SOFTWARE ARCHITECTURES FOR MOBILE MULTIMEDIA WIRELESS DEVICES

I wish to God these calculations had been executed by steam.
—Charles Babbage (1821); A mechanical engineer
who originated the idea of a programmable computer

Why does a service provider need to take into account the software and operating systems for mobile devices? The answer lies in the fact that providing staple services such as voice or internet no longer provide any competitive advantages which can be sustained against competition. The emergence of mobile virtual network operators (MVNOs) or application integrators, such as mobiTV®, are testimonies to this market reality. In order to be able to provide an integrated operating interface for mobile media applications, as well as Web 2.0 services or mobile web access, it is necessary to delve into how the applications and user interfaces will interwork with the underlying operating system and software. In effect, the operators need to envisage the end-to-end ecosystem, including the CPE and the software components that will complete the application delivery. With more and more interactive applications, games and two-way information flows coming into the domain of multimedia services, just broadcasting content has become an oversimplistic view of the new environment.

10.1 EVOLUTION OF MOBILE OPERATING SYSTEMS

The area of software for the mobile phones has undergone a complete transformation within a short span of about a decade. The change in

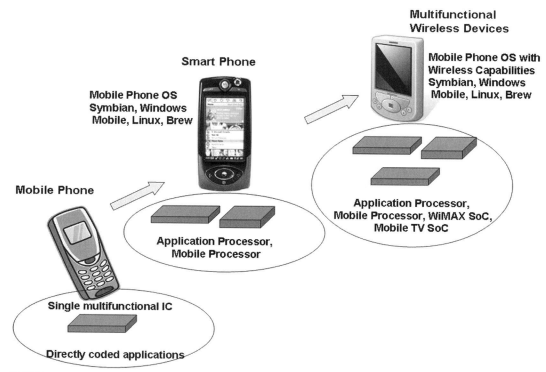

FIGURE 10-1   Mobile devices evolution

the software architectures has undoubtedly followed the evolution of chipsets, processors, and other devices installed in the phones. The initial implementations were completely based on the limited processing power, memory, and power consumption of the mobile devices. This continues to be true today, as well, but the environment in which the mobile wireless devices operate has changed. Smartphones have advanced to the use of application processors for multimedia, SoCs for WiMAX, mobile TV, or WiFi-based communications and multiple cellular standard support such as 3G or CDMA. This has resulted in the use of multiple devices in the handsets to handle these functions, placing additional requirements on the software of the phones. The mobile phones also need to connect to the internet and gaming servers and perform tasks such as music downloads or make VoIP calls.

10.1.1 Application Environment Definition
The wireless application environment with mobile devices is given in Figure 10-2.

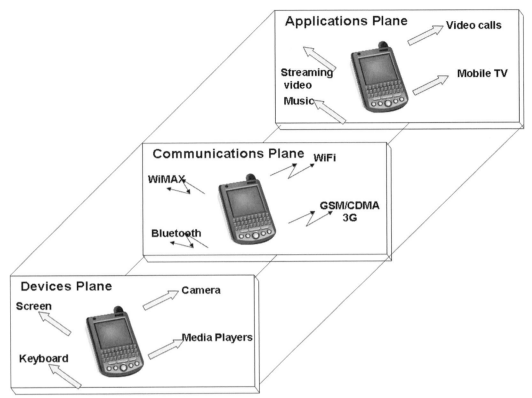

FIGURE 10-2   Applications environment for wireless mobile devices

The mobile devices consist of a number of hardware elements such as keyboard and screen, camera, Bluetooth, media players, joysticks, mouse, etc. The types of hardware elements can change from device to device and need to have short evolutionary cycles, including the capability to add new devices or modify existing devices. These devices form the hardware plane of the device. The communications plane forms the next logical grouping of functions on the phone. The mobile phone hardware is usually controlled by a processor (sometimes called a mobile processor owing to the mobile specific design and low power requirements). Mobile phone operating systems need to provide support for the mobile processor as well as the hardware elements. The mobile OS, together with the phone firmware, controls the local devices such as the camera, media players, keyboard, and touch screen display.

The communications plane has its own hardware (such as SoCs for WiMAX, Mobile TV or GSM, CDMA, or 3G modems). As a base requirement, a smartphone, ULPC, or PDA would have a WiFi and Bluetooth capability. Even if it is operating on a Mobile WiMAX network, it would also need a WiFi connectivity, Bluetooth for local devices, and cellular network connectivity for voice calls. The communications plane is characterized by the use of a number of communications "stacks," which are modules of programs that enable different types of connectivity and, in general, implement protocols needed to run a particular type of service.

Finally the applications plane is the group of programs which provide the user applications making use of the underlying hardware and communications capabilities as necessary. The applications environment is also dynamic. The type of applications can change very fast, and the software structure on the phone needs to enable this to happen. The applications programmers cannot be burdened with the need to seek the details of the hardware devices or the communications stacks. In fact, they need ready-made modules even for parts of applications as APIs. The need for a complete abstraction of handset functions as viewed from the applications plane is therefore a necessity.

10.1.2 Software Structure Definition

The application environment definition, in fact, gives clear pointers to the requirement of software structure in mobile phones. These are as follows:

- The mobile device needs an OS which performs the basic tasks of device and media control. In addition, it needs to support many of the basic communications stacks which are fundamental to any type of networking such as TCP/IP. These are performed by the operating system.
- The software programmers need to be able to view all functions as APIs or function calls and cannot be involved in any specific programming for a particular task, such as connecting to a network and downloading a media file. This implies the use of a middleware, such as Java or Brew or third-party middleware, which provides all the functions as APIs. Java, for example, supports APIs for mobile media (MMAPI), wireless, gaming, etc.
- Applications programming forms the apex level of programs and typically would entirely depend on the APIs available and middleware modules for different functions.

As we have briefly explained in the chapter on chipsets (Chapter 8), many of the functions such as WiMAX connectivity and WiFi, are jointly performed by a set of chips, which go into forming the hardware of the mobile wireless device. The SoCs and chipsets come with their reference design kits and have all the requisite drivers and APIs for common mobile OS and middleware platforms. These are useful for integration with the middleware and the overall applications framework. This is usually carried out in four stages.

- The operating system for the mobile wireless devices. The operating systems for mobile devices have evolved to meet the specific needs of the mobile operating environment with limited resources. The examples of such operating systems are Symbian, Windows Mobile, Brew, Palm OS, and Linux.
- A middleware layer, which implements basic functionalities in a common manner across multiple hardware sets and operating systems. Examples of middleware can include EPG presenters, media players, media streamers, VoIP software cores, Codec implementations, etc. Middleware can be based on J2ME or other software implementations.
- A user interface layer, which provides a common interface to the users for a particular carrier.
- A series of applications, which operate using the mobile handset resources and the networks available. These can include instant messaging (IM), mail, IPTV service, and mobile TV service, office applications, PDF readers, etc.

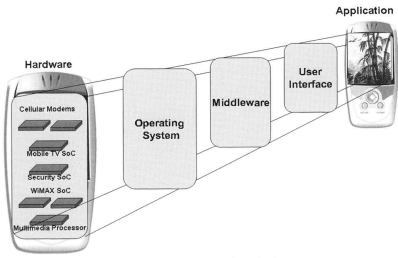

FIGURE 10-3 Software architecture in a mobile wireless device

In this chapter, the software architecture features for the four layers, i.e., operating system, middleware, user interface, and application software, are discussed.

In the area of applications, the implementation of collaborative activities, interactivity, community building, blogging, etc. are based on service elements such as instant messaging (IM) and Presence. In this chapter, we also examine the client software needed for IM and Presence services. Integration of IM and Presence with broadcast and multicast applications provides for highly integrated and interactive broadcast applications.

10.1.3 What Is Special about the Mobile Wireless Devices?

The combination of multimedia devices such as MP3 players, hi-resolution camera, video players, etc., and the need to be able to connect to multiple networks including WiFi, WiMAX, cellular take the requirements placed on the operating system to a new level of functionality. Handling multiple tasks simultaneously requires a multitasking capability in the software. In addition, handling functions such as 3D animations, graphics, and video conferencing require powerful chipsets such as multimedia processors, WiMAX modems, 3D animation chipsets, mobile TV chipsets etc., to work in a closely knit and integrated environment. Mobile wireless devices, unlike the cellphones, may have a higher resolution screen, e.g., with VGA resolution as the use of multimedia applications or office applications need not be limited by cellular network data rates. However, the limitation on battery usage remains the same, which makes the job of software development quite challenging.

10.2 OPERATING SYSTEMS FOR MOBILE DEVICES

10.2.1 What Are Important Features of Operating Systems for Mobile Wireless Devices?

In order to meet the performance requirements of mobile wireless devices, the OS assumes critical importance. The following are some of the important attributes of an OS for mobile wireless environment:

- Native support of important communications protocols such as TCP/IP, IPv4, IPv6, WLAN, and WiFi. The protocol stacks which are not natively supported will need to be implemented as middleware or application packages making the portability of applications more difficult.

- Capability of operating in a multiple chipset environment. The OS needs to support hardware for WiMAX, Encryption, 3D gaming and graphics, multimedia processor, cellular modem chipsets, mobile TV chipsets, and audio/video codecs based on the phone design.
- Provide fast context switching for multiple applications to be supported simultaneously on the mobile phone (such as making a voice call, watching video, and uploading a mail message simultaneously).
- Provide flexibility in user interface design. The design of a user interface is important for operators in order to distinguish products and offer specialized services. Users do not select the handsets based on the OS but on the user interface, applications, and branding. Mobile virtual network operators (MVNOs) and wireless operators need a lot of flexibility in offering innovative features, animations, and graphics as a part of user interface. The success of companies such as UIQ has been solely in providing attractive user interfaces.
- Provide high degree of hardware portability. Mobile and wireless industries today operate in an environment where the number of mobile devices released in different markets and varying capabilities can be quite high in a year. It is important for the operating system to have a hardware abstraction layer to have high portability of the entire software set up to new devices.
- Provide native support for Java, Flash, or similar software for development of applications in a device-independent environment. Java for example provides wireless messaging API, Mobile Media APIs (MMAPI), which make it possible to port a number of programs written for the mobile environment. Some users, however, consider Java to be burdensome and slow down the speed of applications and prefer other development environments.
- Provide a robust development environment. The richness of applications in any given area depends on how many developers are able to work on new products and the software development environment. Skill sets in proprietary systems are hard to come by and in any event have a longer lead time or higher cost. Open source operating systems such as Linux are potentially advantageous in these scenarios. However, in the case of Linux, the native support of devices, communications, and networking protocols has been limited.

10.2.2 Operating System-based Support of 3GPP and Wireless Features

The mobile phone operating systems have been evolving to support new requirements, such as wireless access, operation on new processors, and incorporating more advanced protocols and features. The prominent operating systems are Symbian, Brew, Windows mobile, Palm OS, and Linux. Support of wireless is now a part of the communication stacks in the major operating systems. Application clients, such as those for supporting IM and Presence, are not yet part of operating systems and need to be provided as plug-ins at the application layer. It is quite common today to have handsets that support either an XMPP (Jabber) client or an IMS client for interfacing with the IM and Presence applications.

10.2.3 Symbian™

Symbian is one of the prominent operating systems for mobile phones and is known for coming out with new releases for support of new features. Symbian is supported by major mobile manufacturers and claimed over 85 percent of the smartphone world market in 2006.

Symbian was formed by Motorola, Nokia, Ericsson, and Psion in 1998 for developing operating systems for mobile devices. The first mobile phone based on Symbian was released in 2000 (Ericsson R380).

The Symbian operating system had been designed specifically for mobile phones as compared to some operating systems which are derived from desktop systems. The Symbian OS, therefore, had APIs for messaging, browsing, communications, Bluetooth, IrDA, keyboard, and touchscreen management and supports Java Virtual Machine (JVM). This enables the applications to be written in Java for better portability.

Symbian platforms quickly began to be associated with providing rich interworking applications and interfaces for mobile phones after their launch. Features such as full HTML browser, video telephony, streaming, messaging, presence, "Push-to-Talk," Java Support, branded keys, default wallpapers, operator menus, etc. were well appreciated. The Symbian platforms also provided support to Java, 3GPP, 3GPP2, OMA, and BREW®. The Symbian 9.2, which was released in 2006, had introduced native support of USB 2.0 and support of WiFi as well as unlicensed mobile access (UMA) services for VoIP type applications.

Japan's FOMA network has been the biggest user of the Symbian OS, which it had used exclusively until recently when it began support of Linux as well. Symbian OS is used extensively in Nokia phones. It is also used widely in Europe and Asia. Some of the latest phones announced based on Symbian include Nokia N95 (S60 3rd Edition Feature pack 1; Symbian 9.2), LG KS 10, Sony Ericsson P1i, FOMA F704i.

Symbian has recently come out with the OS version 9.5 which provides native support for multi-standard mobile TV, support of camera features and multimedia applications. The key features of Symbian OS 9.5 are given in Table 10-1. The feature-rich support by the OS to the applications is evident.

TABLE 10-1

Symbian 9.5 Operating System Features

	Symbian OS 9.5	Supported Features
1	Wireless Capabilities	Support of WiFi, UMA (WiFi to 3G Roaming), Bluetooth V2.0, IrDA
2	Multimedia Capabilities	Multimedia Transfer Protocol over USB (MTP) RTP/RTCP, audio and video support for recording, playback and streaming, multi-mega pixel cameras, advanced features, audio and video codec interfaces
3	Support for TV	Support for multi-standard digital TV including DVB-H and DVB-T, Digital TV hardware abstraction
4	Network Support	3G-WCDMA (3GPP R4 and R5 IMS support), CDMA2000-1x, HSDPA, HSUPA, GSM, GPRS (classes A, B, and C); and EDGE (Circuit and packet switched)
5	Communications Protocols Supported	TCP/IP Stack (IPv4 and IPv6), SIP, RTP, and RTCP WAP 2.0, WAP Push, Infrared, Bluetooth, USB 2.0
6	Java Support	Latest release Java standards support for MIDP 2.0, CLDC 1.1 (JSR 139), Wireless Messaging (JSR 120), Bluetooth (JSR 082), Mobile 3D Graphics API (JSR 184), Personal Information management API etc., JSR 248
7	Messaging Capabilities	Internet e-mail with SMTP, POP3, IMAP-4 SMS, and EMS
8	Graphics Support	Graphics Accelerator API, 2D and 3G graphics support, UI Flexibility (e.g., display sizes, orientation, and multiple displays)
9	Developer Options	C++, J2ME MIDP 2.0, WAP Reference Telephony abstraction layer, high-level multimedia service abstraction Eclipse and CodeWarrior-based development environments
10	Security	Cryptographic algorithms AES, DES, 3DES, RC2, RC4, RC5 Encryption and certificate management, Secure Protocols (SSL, HTTPS, TLS) DRM framework and reference implementation IPSec and VPN client support
11	Data Synchronization	Over the Air (OTA) data synchronization, PC-based synchronization through Bluetooth, Infrared and USB, etc.
12	Telephony	Multimode Enhanced Telephony (2.5/3 G), IMS, SIP/SDP support

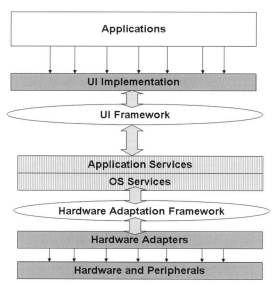

FIGURE 10-4 Symbian OS architecture

The Symbian 9.5 supports the latest CPU architectures with real-time capabilities and provides support for single-chip hardware platforms. The support of new processors such as ARM Cortex A8 implies that applications that need PC-class performance can now be implemented on mobile devices. This is important for the new generation of devices which implement full VGA (720 × 480) resolutions on PDAs, UMPCs, etc.

Symbian OS Architecture

The Symbian OS architecture is given in Figure 10-4. The architecture of Symbian is somewhat unique as it has a user interface layer, which is separate from the operating system and hence needs to be selected individually by the phone manufacturer. The user interfaces (UIs) are developed by Nokia, UIQ, and network operators such as NTT DoCoMo for its FOMA network. The applications access the OS services via the UI framework. The abstraction of hardware adaptation makes it suitable for faster implementation on various chipsets and processor cores.

Symbian Mobile Phone Series

Symbian OS-based phone designs vary considerably depending on the screen size and nature of use, i.e., a multimedia phone or a PDA

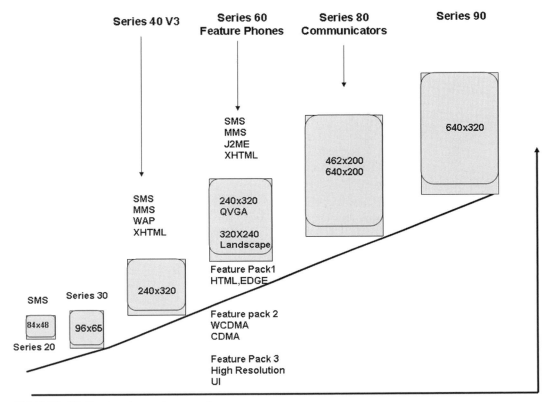

FIGURE 10-5 Symbian phone series

device, etc. Symbian has come out with a functional set of series for its phones, which are characterized by the screen size and the support of various features. These range from S20, which were introduced for the initial release of phones to S60 used for smartphones. There are additional releases, e.g., S80 for mobile communicators and S90 with varying size of displays and feature support. Figure 10-5 depicts the progression of Symbian operating systems.

Among the Symbian phones, S60 from Nokia was the first OS to implement a major enhancement in processor capacities and it has proved to be very popular. It also heralded the release of the first multitasking phone OS. The S60 series phones support more powerful phone processors and multimedia application processors, which gives them an edge in terms of performance in multimedia applications, internet browsing, and a host of other applications. The Nokia N95 provides an example of the advanced series of the S60 phones. The N95 is based on the OMAP2420 chipset including an ARM 11 processor.

More than 50 phones based on the S60 series have been released. The S40 series of phones is designed to be a "normal" phone, but the differences are narrowing with respect to S60 with advances in processor capabilities. An example of this is the Nokia 5300 (S40 series) and the Nokia 5700 (S60 series), which provide similar features and user interface.

The Symbian phones are also available under the UIQ series, primarily from Sony Ericsson and Motorola. The UIQ series of phones is based on the user interface technology from UIQ Technologies AB (now acquired by Sony Ericsson). The UIQ user interfaces provide more advanced animations, transition effects, and themes and reinforce the importance of having the OS separate from the user interfaces.

The Symbian operating system, with its high representation in the smartphones category, also has the highest number of downloadable software applications. Examples of applications include RSS feed readers, Bloglines, IPTV streaming programs, and mobile multimedia-related programs.

10.2.4 Symbian 9.5 FreeWay™

Symbian has further enhanced its operating system to support high-end smartphones, very high speed data connectivities, and support of new wireless technologies such as mobile WiMAX. The enhancement of the Symbian 9.5 platform, which happened under the FreeWay communications infrastructure, has added a number of new features which include:

- An improved SIP stack
- Ability of the handset to switch between 3G and WiFi networks
- Support of location based technologies and GPS navigation
- Support of networks such as WiMAX
- Switching between bearers with application continuity
- Support of higher-speed connections, better context switching
- Integration of "ActiveSync" for over the air connectivity with Microsoft Exchange servers
- Compatibility with existing applications such as web browsers

10.2.5 Linux-Based Operating Systems

Linux-based operating systems have a niche space in the mobile devices operating systems owing to their open source nature. However, in percentage terms, their use is less than 10 percent.

Linux is distributed under GPL (General Public License) implying that its source code must be made publicly available whenever a compiled version is distributed. The kernel has been adapted by phone manufacturers because of its open source software and future availability of open source software and applications. China, for example, has adapted the use of Linux as OS (Linux embedded version "mLinux") for use in its 3G mobile networks, a fact which will influence the mobile market considerably. Linux had over 30 percent share of the smartphone market in China in 2006. Also major manufacturers and operators including NTT DoCoMo, Vodafone, NEC, Panasonic, Motorola, and Samsung have announced support of a global platform for open Linux adoption. Most phone vendors are now working on Linux because of the availability of third-party software, which is especially important at the high end, such as multimedia applications.

The Linux core is, however, limited in functionality and a majority of mobile phone functions such as multimedia support, communication functions, connectivity services, and platform management services need to be supported by middleware. Figure 10-6 depicts how the Linux OS kernel is located vis-à-vis the applications. A large part of

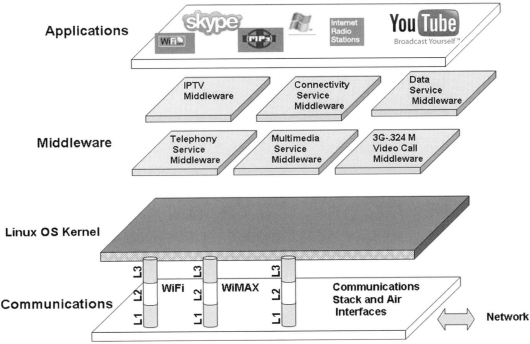

FIGURE 10-6 Typical Linux environment in mobile multimedia devices

the functions of the phone needs to be supported by software modules, which are beyond the OS. This has, however, not deterred many vendors in giving preference to Linux as it is an open source. Uniform and bug-free implementation of the software modules has, however, raised concern as to the stability of the phone as its operation now depends on external modules. To alleviate these concerns, the CE Linux Forum is now working on a global reference architecture and common API for various components of software and middleware. The common architecture will include the videophone framework, telephony framework, and multimedia framework.

Linux Mobile Foundation (LiMo)

The Linux Mobile Foundation (LiMo) was formed in December 2006 with an objective of providing a complete ecosystem for mobile software. The LiMO intends to provide a complete open source mobile phone architecture with APIs and certification processes to facilitate the development of Linux-based phones and other mobile devices.

The LiMo foundation focuses on the middleware and enabling software for the UI and application layers. There are other Linux phone working groups, as well, and the major manufacturers have released their APIs used in Linux-based mobile phones.

Many vendors have opted for commercial versions of Linux to have better functionality, which is natively supported by the OS while retaining its open source nature. An example is NTT DoCoMo which has selected Monta Vista® Linux to be an OS for the FOMA phones in addition to Symbian™. Monta Vista Linux™ provides for easy integration of advanced multimedia applications and a standard development platform for wireless handset designs. NEC Corporation has

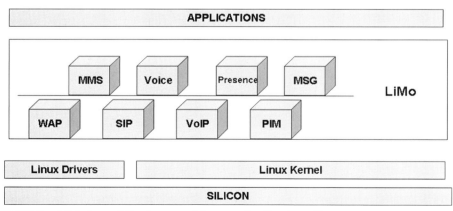

FIGURE 10-7   LiMo in mobile phone architecture finalization effort

developed phones based on Monta Vista Linux for FOMA (N900iL and N901iC).

mLinux is an embedded version of Linux adapted for use in 3G networks in China. Embedded Linux implies a Linux kernel which has been ported to a particular CPU and is available as code in memory on the SoC (System On Chip) or board of the CPU. mLinux supports all major CPUs such as: ARM9, Intel Xscale, MIPS, Motorola Dragonball i.Mx, and Texas Instrument OMAP processors (710, 730, 1510, and 1610), among others. mLinux features an enhanced bootloader and short boot times of less than 2 seconds. It has multiprocessing and multithreading capability, memory management, and provides support for pipelining. It also supports many protocols and network cards.

Example of a Linux-based Mobile Wireless Device

An example of a mobile wireless device based on Linux is the Nokia Internet tablet N800. It supports multiple networks including the mobile WiMAX . The software architecture of the N800 is based on the Linux desktop from GNOME (GNU Object Model Environment). GNOME provides a stable and reliable development platform, which is user friendly and open source. This is supplemented with MAEMO application development environment (open source developments for internet tablets). For multimedia applications, software components from Gstreamer have been embedded in the N800 (also available under GNU). Gstreamer provides a multimedia framework for streaming media players and handling of video and audio. The Linux Xwindows system is provided by "Matchbox windows manager," which is an open source environment for Xwindows on handheld devices. The GUIs are provided by GTK (a multiplatform kit for preparing user interfaces). It uses the official Linux Bluetooth protocol stack (Bluez). It also uses open source digital media players from Helix community. The access to local phone resources (keyboard, mouse, joysticks, multimedia hardware) is provided by SDL (Simple Direct Media layer cross platform multimedia library). Interprocess communications are handled by Dbus, a freedesktop.org tool.

10.2.6 Garnet™ OS

The Palm OS has recently been renamed and introduced with enhancements as the Garnet™.

Palm has virtually been the symbol for PDAs since the days of the Palm Pilot. It is only recently that the market has diversified through other PDAs based on Linux and Pocket PCs based on Windows Mobile.

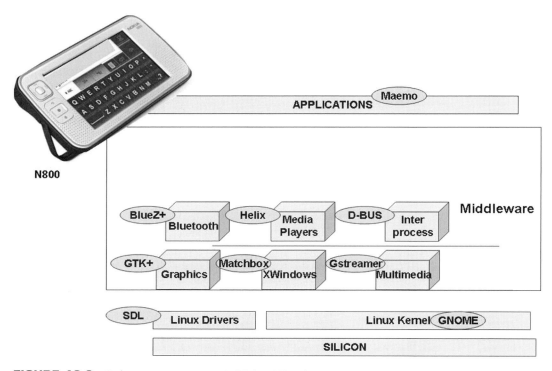

FIGURE 10-8 Software components in Nokia N800 (Picture courtesy Nokia)

The Palm OS is a multitasking OS, which provides protective memory management and Hot Sync capabilities. Palm supports the ARM and Motorola 68000 processors. The Palm OS has two versions: Palm OS® Cobalt (OS 6) and Palm OS® Garnet OS 5. The current release of Palm OS Cobalt® supports Bluetooth® and WiFi. The Palm OS Garnet® is based on the Palm 5.2 and 5.3 operating systems.

System development kits (SDKs) are available for the Palm OS. Applications can be developed using C, Visual Basic, C++, and Java among other programming languages. A number of commercial development suites are also available, which provide processor-specific applications and development tools.

A lot of third-party software is available for the Garnet OS such as music players, video players, and utilities. Palmsource has also announced support of a Palm OS platform on Linux.

10.2.7 Windows Mobile

Windows Mobile is based on the Windows CE™ operating system. This is a 32-bit operating system with 4 GB of directly addressable memory space. Many users and developers have a clear preference for Windows mobile because of its commonality with the desktop Windows system and its support for desktop applications and file formats as mobile extension to the office applications. In particular, smartphones and PDAs, which are used as "mobile offices," are prime candidates for the Windows Mobile operating system as they can use the Windows Mobile Office application, which integrates seamlessly with the desktop and office applications (including Microsoft Exchange Server and SQL server). Typically, these have a QWERTY keyboard (or a touch-screen input) and a large display of QVGA or sometimes VGA resolution. The phones support e-mail and Microsoft Office applications among others. Windows Mobile comes in two versions: Windows Mobile for Pocket PC and Windows Mobile for smartphones. Windows Mobile Pocket PC version is designed for devices with QWERTY keyboards or touch-screen for input, while the smartphone version is for phones with numeric keypads.

Microsoft has also released Windows Mobile 6.0 for the smartphones. The new OS does away with the distinction between pocket PCs and smartphones. Apart from Microsoft Office Mobile™ there are many third-party applications that are available for Windows Mobile-based devices.

Windows Mobile 6.0

The Windows Mobile 6.0 aligns the user look and feel of the mobile devices to the Windows Vista™ operating system. Editing of Office documents is possible and Windows Live mail can operate on mobile devices with the use of the new version. The support of Exchange 2007 has been one of the main objectives of the release of Windows Mobile 6.0 along with the alignment with Vista™ and Windows Live™ Online services. It also supports WiFi and VoIP over wireless. A number of devices based on the Windows Mobile 6.0 have emerged. Some examples are the devices from HP (iPAQ514), RIM, HTC (HTC710), T-Mobile, Wing, etc. The development of new devices and downloadable applications based on the new OS is expected to be a continuous feature.

Windows Mobile Phones for WiMAX

Windows Mobile OS is of considerable importance for application developers because of the large-scale deployment of the Sprint WiMAX network in the United States, which will lead to the surge in UMPCs and smartphones for a host of new internet and multimedia-based services. This is likely to be followed in short order with releases in multiple markets worldwide. We are therefore looking at a migration of PC applications to UMPCs and mobile devices. A number of mobile devices have been available for WiMAX and WiBro based on the Windows Mobile OS and more are emerging to meet the requirements of the entire range—from smartphones with small screens and QVGA resolution to UMPCs with full VGA resolution.

In the range of smartphones for WiMAX, the handsets for these are available from Samsung and LG, primarily owing to their early use in the Korean WiBro network. LG KC1 is a phone (based on Windows Mobile 5 Pocket PC premium). The phone supports Mobile WiMAX, WiFi, and mobile TV based on T-DMB. It works on the CDMA EV-DO network as well. A similar device from Samsung is the Samsung SPH-M8100 (based on Windows Mobile 6) being used in WiBro in Korea. Both the devices support the CDMA EV-DO network in addition to the Mobile WiMAX (WiBro in Korea) and WiFi networks.

10.2.8 BREW

BREW™ (Binary Runtime Environment for Wireless) is an open-source development platform promoted by Qualcom for use on CDMA-based devices. Being open source implies that the source code is made available to developers for use and further developments. In addition BREW also provides a SDK free of charge to developers. The software developers can use a windows development environment such as Microsoft visual studio 6 for application development and an ARM compiler for code generation. It has powerful user interface tools (UiOne™) which enable developers and phone manufacturers to modify or personalize the interfaces. The applications developed can be viewed in the "open marketplace" and downloaded over air using the application delivery management.

The applications can be categorized into various categories:

- BREW applications, which have been developed and are available to any manufacturer as fully developed mobile phone services
- User applications, which can be developed by using the BREW environment and development tools
- Third-party applications, which can be downloaded

Brew® applications include Push to Chat, e-mail, photo sharing, wireless broadband, location-based services (LBS), multimedia players, etc.

Examples of BREW's predeveloped application program interfaces, which were available with BREW 2.1 to operate over the ARM9 processor or MSM 6100 chipset, included the camera module (enabling applications to access the camera), 3D graphics engine, MPEG 4 video module (enabling MPEG 4 video-based applications in the mobile device), position location, encryption (HTTPS, SSL), and multimedia modules. APIs for real-time streaming, USB support, and removable storage media were introduced with BREW 3.1 release.

The UiOne user interface development tools make it possible for operators or service providers to customize user interfaces. It also enables the users to personalize the interface and services over the air.

There are some limitations of BREW, however, as only BREW-authenticated developers can test applications in BREW handsets.

While the BREW platform was initially oriented solely to the CDMA networks and mobile station modem (MSM) chipsets from Qualcom, it now includes products for the 3GSM and the mobile multimedia transmission networks. The universal baseband modem (UBM), for example, is intended to serve the mediaFLO-, DVB-H-, and DMB-based services.

Multimedia Capabilities of BREW

BREW is known for efficient development of multimedia applications because of the direct porting of the BREW components on hardware and chip-based firmware. 3D graphics and gaming applications needing high interactivity operate more efficiently because of this architecture. In addition, scalable vector graphics (SVG) can be directly integrated with BREW. SVG is scalable over multiple display sizes, has smaller file sizes than rasterized or bit mapped formats, such as JPEG or BMP, has rich text options, interactivity, and can be created by powerful tools, such as Adobe Go Live CS2, or Ikivo® Animator. BREW supports SVG animation and playback including play, pause, and rewind of content. It has APIs for key presses, rotate, pan, zoom focus, pointers, and key presses.

The multimedia applications of BREW are also supported by its multimedia components which include:

- Support of MPEG-4 encoding and playback
- Camera interface, JPEG compression, and recording of video
- 3D graphics engine
- Mobile-assisted position location
- Connection and content security through HTTPS, SSL, and encryption
- Media support for various video and audio formats

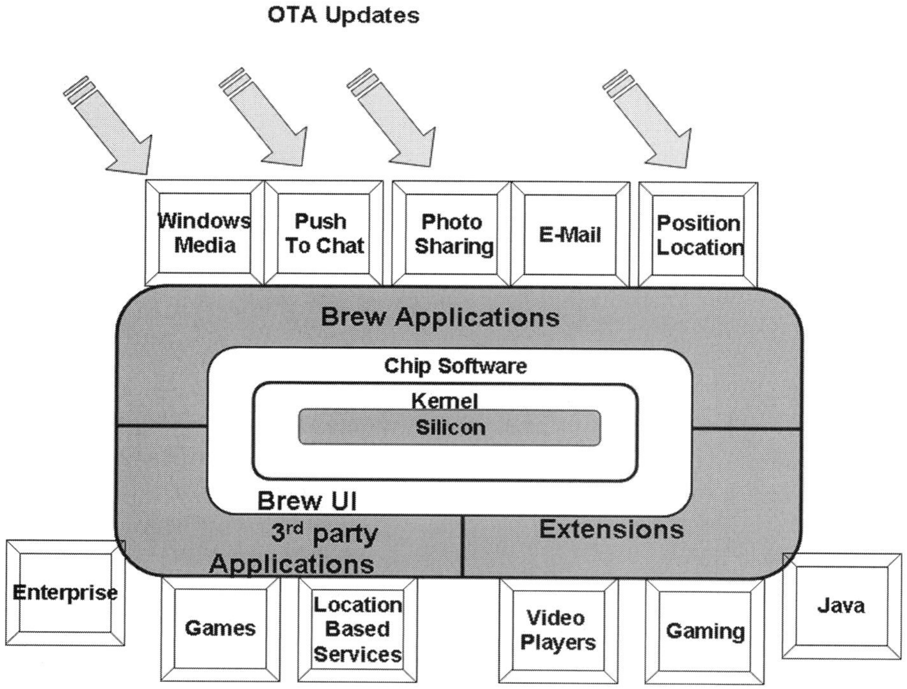

OTA Updates

FIGURE 10-9   BREW software architecture

- Streaming and playback of PCM and QCP media formats
- Serial, USB interface, and removable storage
- Battery management
- Messaging services

A number of extensions to the BREW operating platform are available, for example, Microsoft Games (MSN games) on the BREW platform, J2ME on BREW, Microsoft "Live Anywhere," Microsoft MSN messenger, and Microsoft Office Mobile.

BREW Support of Broadband Wireless

BREW platforms provide support of broadband delivered over wireless (802.11x) or via CDMA-based networks using the MSM or UBM chipsets from Qualcomm. The support of Mobile WiMAX or WiMAX chipsets had not been announced till late 2007. However, because of the widespread use of CDMA in the United States, Korea, India, and some other countries, which are also the strongest movers into WiMAX networks, it may be expected to be available with full APIs.

10.2.9 Android

A new mobile software platform system based on "open standards" has been announced by the Open Handset Alliance. While there are more than thirty companies backing the Android OS, the major ones are Google, Motorola, Sprint, T-Mobile, Qualcom, and HTC. Android is a complete framework for the mobile handset consisting of the OS, middleware, open internet applications, and a development environment. The OS core is based on Linux.

10.3 MIDDLEWARE IN MOBILE WIRELESS DEVICES

In real-life operating scenarios, it is important to be able to implement various applications and user interfaces uniformly across many platforms, operator networks, or multiple handsets types. It may be recalled that most applications such as IPTV, streaming, or handling of audio or video using MPEG4, etc., have many implementation profiles or standards. In such cases, it becomes essential to ensure that the applications execute in an identical manner and have easy portability. Middleware plays this role. Commonly used functions provided by middleware include implementing various types of codecs, communications and protocols, streaming , video calling, etc., used in 3G and broadcast networks. The services modules, which middleware provides, can be used by the application software to develop full-fledged applications.

Another example of middleware can be had from the middleware for NTT DoCoMo's FOMA network. FOMA is a 3G network in Japan and provides services such as i-Mode™ (Internet Access), i-appli™ (Internet Applications), Deco-Mail™ (HTML E-mail), Chara-Den™ (videophone with cartoon-type characters), and Chaku-motion™ (combining video and AAC audio to signal incoming calls). The services are network specific. The operators are naturally interested in the service operating in an identical manner on all the phones irrespective of the operating system or the software structure.

There are two methods to achieve this. The first is that the applications be written in a language such as Java (Java MIDP 2.0 and J2MEE), which is independent of the operating platform. The second is to have specific middleware to support all the services which are network specific (e.g., all FOMA services). Initially the FOMA phones were released with Java-based applications and having Symbian OS, which provides very strong native support towards realizing application stacks such as those for H.264 coding, H.263 video calls, AAC audio coding, various players and display drivers, and Java-based applications and games.

10.3.1 Trends in Mobile Devices Firmware: Support of Web 2.0 Services

All the launches of new features on mobile devices are clear pointers toward simpler and intuitive access to internet and Web 2.0, including collaborative and structured application services, and keeping the user connected to the bloglines, RSS feeds, etc. This contrasts from the first generation of smartphones, where setting up internet access, making the browser work, or viewing streaming video were quite elaborate tasks in themselves. The networks such as Mobile WiMAX bring mobile internet to the phones at much lower prices than the cellular networks, and enabling of Web 2.0 services is the key to higher revenues, as well as the popularity of the network services.

The examples of such inclination on the part of the network operators are manifold. The SPH M8100 smartphone for mobile WiMAX has a RSS button for one-key enabling of RSS 2.0 feeds from the WiMAX network. Mail or internet can be launched with screen icons of directly supported keys. Moreover, the phone uses the WiMAX and the WiFi networks as the primary access media for VoIP and video calls, video conferencing, etc. The office applications are directly usable by use of a dedicated key and are well supported by the Windows Mobile 6.0 system.

Similar features are observed in the Linux-based Nokia N800 Tablet, which is designed for the U.S. Mobile WiMAX market. The device supports internet radio and RSS feeds, email and instant messaging, internet calling with video or voice, browsing, music and video players, connectivity to Web 2.0 services, and other internet-related features. Nokia N800 provides an alignment of a desktop PC, with its full range of applications with the features of mobility and wireless access via WiFi and WiMAX.

IPTV Middleware: An Example

An example of IPTV middleware is from Thin Multimedia, Inc., which is known for its mobile middleware platforms. Its middleware is used for encoding and delivering multimedia content across many operator platforms in a uniform manner. It also provides a platform for delivery of IPTV services using a turnkey software called thinIPTV™.

thinIPTV™ is platform neutral and can operate on Java, Symbian, BREW, or Linux platforms and supports all current IPTV standards. It provides a very efficient real-time broadcast for mobile handsets. The mobile handsets receive the multicast services over the broadband network using a thin IPTV client middleware.

Thin multimedia also provides thinHardware IP™, which is a set of reference designs that can be used with SoCs to optimize performance

FIGURE 10-10 Samsung SPH M8100 based on Windows Mobile 6.0 with web-enabled services (Picture courtesy Samsung)

and obtain uniform implementation profiles. It has been commercialized with some SoCs.

Another example is Impulsesoft™ Bluetooth audio solution for Windows mobile platform. This middleware uses the Windows mobile OS Bluetooth stacks to build an A2DP compliant audio system. The middleware permits streaming audio to be delivered over the Bluetooth headsets, a function not available in the OS.

10.3.2 Java-based Mobile Device Architectures

Java Virtual Machines (JVM), which implement the Java micro edition (J2ME) based on the MIDP 2.0 profile, are very common in the mobile handset architectures. By 2007, there were an estimated one billion mobile devices based on Java in use. Java 2 Microedition (J2ME) is a powerful environment for development of applications for mobile devices, such as cellphones or PDAs. Applications written with J2ME are portable and provide quick development cycles for new products such as games, animated clips, etc.

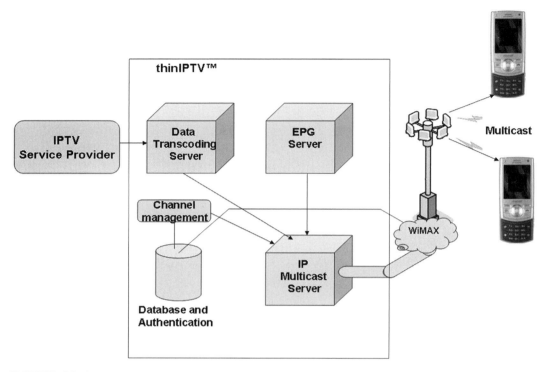

FIGURE 10-11   Thin IPTV platform

Java used on mobile phones is described by the Mobile Information Device Profile (MIDP) for the Connected Limited Device Configuration version 1.1 (CLDC 1.1). The MIDP device profiles provide for the limited environment of mobile phones or PDAs, with small memory footprints; and the programs are leaner, needing lower resources. The CLDC 1.1 configuration is defined under the Java Community Process (JCP) and defines the types of devices on which such applications can run uniformly. The CLDC target devices are mobile phones with limited memory of 160KB to 512 KB. Further mobile phones operate in an environment where the signals may be lost from time to time because of transmission conditions. Applications which are based on protocols such as WAP require constant connectivity between the server and the application. On the other hand, the Java applications can run on devices which can be disconnected from the network. The CLDC configuration is indeed defined for such devices.

One reason for the wide use of the Java architecture is the availability of APIs, which are approved under the Java community process and implemented by the device manufacturers (e.g., handset manufacturers) as a part of the JVM. We would like to discuss some important APIs which are relevant to multimedia and wireless applications.

Mobile Media API (MMAPI)

MMAPI was designed to be used as an optional API and is defined under JSR 135 (with extensions under JSR 234). The API is designed to seek multimedia data and render it on devices available on the platform. By creating an abstraction for data sources and players, and being able to seek capabilities of devices, it becomes a development medium, which is independent of the device platform. All manufacturers, such as Motorola, Sony, Erickson, and Nokia, provide their implementation of the MMAPI, which can be used with developmental tools to develop or port existing applications in a short time frame and with predictable performance. The memory requirement for MMAPI for CLDC devices can vary from 128 KB to 512 KB (runtime).

Limitations of Present Releases of Java Micro Edition for New Generation of Mobile Devices

The J2ME specifications with profile MIDP 2.0 were initially targeted at devices that were highly limited in resources such as screen size and memory. This is no longer the case with the new generation of devices where PC-like capabilities are needed in a mobile wireless environment. Also the existing connection framework for establishing data connections does not prescribe the bandwidth needed for a session or modify it midway. New APIs are being defined such as Network Mobility and Mobile Data API (JSR 307), which address these limitations. The mobile data API is designed to be able to select the session resources such as bandwidth, choose a medium from many available ones (such as WiFi, 3G or WiMAX), prescribe latency limits, and select a traffic class (conversational, streaming, interactive, or background). The network mobility API provides features for mobility management such as monitoring of features of available WiFi, WiMAX, or cellular networks and permit applications to set device and network preferences.

The need for applications to be able to prescribe devices and networks, define session attributes, and prescribe QoS parameters is also leading to the definition of a new upgraded profile MIDP 3.0. In order to evolve to a multitransport network with roaming such as with IMS, new APIs are being defined such as IMS API (JSR 281), which will permit QoS parameters to be set for IMS sessions.

Of special interest is the mobile broadcast service API for handheld terminals (JSR 272). This optional API provides for Java clients

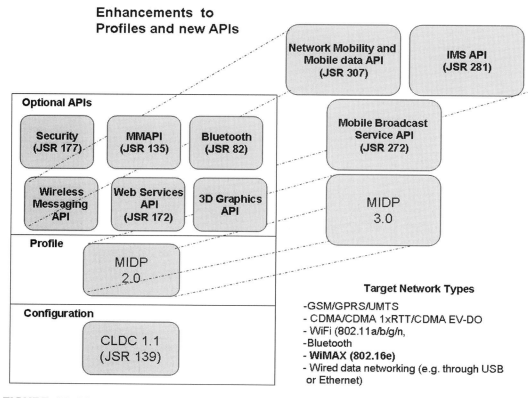

FIGURE 10-12 Enhancements to profiles and new APIs in Java Micro Edition

interface to interface for interactive broadcasting. The API provides for access to:

- Service guides
- AV broadcasting stream to allow viewing of the program by using MMAPI (JSR-135)
- Subtitles, tickers, and image and hypertext data, which can be delivered via broadcast
- Plan consumption of a service (such as recording)
- Receiving and running applications over the air
- Managing service subscription and payments

In addition there are other APIs, such as DRM API (JSR 300) and Java TV (JSR 927), which are needed for a full implementation of the desired features via the JVM. These APIs will be available in the future.

10.4 APPLICATION CLIENTS

Mobile devices used in a multimedia environment are likely to have a wide range of application software. This will include various types of multimedia players, video and picture sharing software and clients for Instant Messaging and Presence, and mail and office applications.

10.4.1 Jabber-based Mobile Clients

One of the methodologies of providing IM and Presence services is based on the use of streaming XML protocols and is defined by the XMPP protocols (previously called Jabber) (RFC 3920 and 3921). Jabber services are comprised of a server network (e.g., OPN from Adobe systems or Jabber XCP from Jabber Inc.) and a mobile client running in the handsets. XMPP services are defined in greater detail in Chapter 13.

The clients that can be used include iChat, GAIM, (a multiprotocol IM client), Exodus (a Jabber Client), Trillion (multi-protocol multimedia chat client), etc.

10.4.2 SIP or IMS Mobile Clients

SIP-based phone clients can interact with any communication server which uses SIP signaling protocols including IP multimedia (IMS)-based networks. SIP clients can provide services such as VoIP, instant messaging, and Presence, in addition, to any other services which may be defined in the IMS system. As Push to talk over Cellular, IM, and Presence services have been in use in a number of mobile networks over many years, there are a large number of clients available that can be used based on the underlying operating system (such as Symbian or Windows Mobile, Linux, BREW, etc.) and the middleware structure (e.g., JVM).

10.4.3 Application Clients for Other Services

Mobile devices used in today's environment need to have access to office applications, media players, games and entertainment applications, and applications for mobile commerce. A number of application clients are available for use in different operating systems and middleware used.

Example of J2ME Application Clients: Zesium™, Germany

Picking an example at random, Zesium is a suite of application clients which can be used in a mobile device which supports a JVM implementation based on J2ME.

- Blog2Go: mobile blogging services application
- mobileDoc: read Word and Excel documents
- Fussball Mobil: soccer on mobile
- mBid24: provides access to major eBay services
- MobileZip: file compression/decompression on a mobile
- News2Mobile: retrieve RSS on mobile phone
- mobilePdf: PDF files support on mobile devices
- Picture enhancement software: photo quality improvement
- mobileSafe: mobile application that stores password
- Mahjong: China puzzle game

(All the application names are copyrights of Zesium.)

Zesium mobile clients can be used in any mobile device with Java support.

10.5 SUMMARY

The software for mobile devices, including the user interfaces, is one of the most important aspects of providing a new service. The capability of installing new software applications depends on the support of the OS and its features, such as Java support. In most cases, owing to the rapid pace of development of new applications, use of middleware for new applications is the best way to proceed forward as it gives a device independent implementation of various features.

It is also important to be able to select a user interface independent of the underlying OS and middleware as it helps distinguish the services of a new operator and makes user-configurable changes possible, giving the service a distinct edge.

11

SPECTRUM FOR WiMAX NETWORKS

In theory, WiMAX can achieve speeds of 100 Mbps: all an operator needs is 30 MHz of spectrum to play around with. The problem is there aren't that many operators around with such a large block of spectrum.
—Rupert Baines, VP Marketing, picoChip

Spectrum is one of the key requirements for the deployment of WiMAX services. Many of the technologies being developed for WiMAX depend on the frequency band in which the systems can be deployed (i.e., 2.4 GHz, 3.5 GHZ, or 5 GHz). This is because all the parameters, such as usable bandwidths, transmitted power, FFT size, and propagation characteristics, depend on the frequency band. Access to the spectrum and its cost holds the key for commencing deployment of WiMAX in many countries despite the technologies having been available for a while now.

11.1 AN OVERVIEW OF FREQUENCY ALLOCATION PROCESS BY THE ITU-R

The allocation of spectrum for various applications and technologies is an internationally coordinated process. The International Telecommunications Union (ITU), which is an international organization with representations from telecommunications administrations of all countries, coordinates the internationally accepted usage of spectrum for various applications. This function was previously handled by a committee of the ITU called the CCIR (International Radio Consultative Committee), which was subsequently renamed the ITU-R. Major frequency-related decisions are taken under the fora of World Radio Conference (WRC), which is a global conference held once every four years, and issued as Radio Regulations. The last WRC meeting was held in November 2007. The WRC is assisted in its work by Regional Radio Committees (RRCs), which provide regionally coordinated inputs on frequency allocations.

Regional bodies also provide their inputs to the ITU. The agreements reached at WRC, after approval by the ITU-R, are issued as international recommendations on frequency spectrum allocations, applications, and channelling plans. Individual countries have the option to adopt the recommendations in their original form or with amendments as the situation of spectrum usage in the country demands. However, where the usage of spectrum is for applications that are international in nature, such as satellite communications, or that have a cross-border impact, following internationally agreed allocation plans is mandatory. The modality of spectrum allocation, i.e., unlicensed or licensed, free or paid, allocated or auctioned, is left to the individual governments. As individual governments are a part of the overall coordination process in the ITU, the acceptability of the recommendations is very high, and these are usually treated as standards rather than recommendations.

The allocation of spectrum has been a process steeped in history beginning with the allocation of frequencies for wireless radio and telegraph communications. Since then, technologies have advanced through many generations involving satellite communications, broadcasting, broadband wireless, navigation, and many other applications. The CCIR (now ITU-R) have periodically considered new applications, revised existing allocations and recommended the use of additional bands for new applications. Global adaptation of frequency bands and specific allocations such as C and Ku bands for satellite communications,

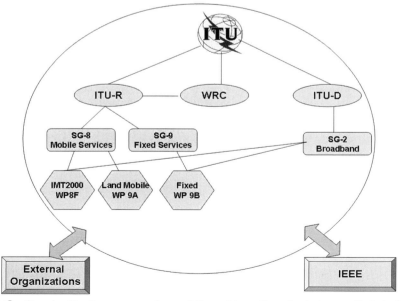

FIGURE 11-1 Standardization process for mobile and broadband wireless radio interfaces in ITU

L-band for maritime mobile, and frequencies in 800, 1800, and 1900 MHz for cellular mobile and 3G have made international use of these bands and global roaming possible.

While the WRC makes periodical revisions in its global framework of allocations, because of legacy systems, such as satellite systems, terrestrial microwave links, and other uses including defense, the allocation of bands for new services has always lagged well behind the development of technologies. There is also a scarcity of spectrum as the bands that are ideally suited for certain technologies already stand allocated for various services. New services such as mobile TV, Mobile WiMAX, and 3G long-term evolution are the latest contenders for a harmonized allocation of spectrum for growth.

11.1.1 Spectrum Allocation Considerations

Allocation of spectrum for new applications is limited by the considerations of use of existing systems. An example is the satellite communications in the C-band, which operate at a very low power in the C-band and extended C-bands (3.5–4.2 GHz and 5.8–6.5 GHz). Satellite systems with life of up to 18 years and a planning cycle of 5 years thus straddle the spectrum bands with long projected usage patterns. Over 600 satellite networks are in operation today with nearly 50,000 frequency assignments relating to over 3000 earth stations, the network having been built assiduously over the last 30 years. However, the development cycle of new technologies, such as WiMAX or 3G (IMT 2000), is an order of magnitude shorter than the 23-year life of satellite systems. Such systems need to coexist with the new technologies that emerge and are allowed access in adjacent bands (i.e., WiMAX in the 3.5 GHz and 5.6 GHz bands).

Because of legacy usage and potential interference issues, the allocation of spectrum cannot be viewed as merely the allocation of frequencies for certain applications. Additional dimensions to the frequency include the maximum power that can be transmitted, out-of-band interference caused by such transmission, and the tolerance of the licensed system to interference from other systems. Moreover, such spectrum allocations may be subject to channeling plans that prescribe bandwidths and associated center frequencies. In addition, the use of spectrum would be subject to regulatory provisions that are country-specific. Moreover, the spectrum may be allotted for terrestrial or satellite usage, and interchange of usage would be inadmissible or subject to specific licensing.

The spectrum can also be reused based on the transmission characteristics. For example, base stations in cellular systems may reuse frequencies in adjacent cells in case of CDMA or in COFDM SFN networks (such as DVB-H). In other cases (i.e., GSM), the frequencies may be reused only in alternate cells where the transmission has weakened sufficiently so as not to cause any interference. In mobile WiMAX, the frequency reuse factor can be still higher by converting each cell into three or more sectors with frequency reuse.

It should also be recognized that many of the spectrum allocations are country specific such as those of cellular mobile services, digital radio, or the NII bands in the U.S.

11.2 AN OVERVIEW OF SPECTRUM BANDS

It is interesting to take an overview of commonly used services and associated spectrum bands in major regions of the world. One might be tempted to take a simplistic view of the spectrum allocation processes and consider only the band specific to the service being planned such as WiMAX and ignore the spectrum allocations for other services such as 3G. However it needs to be remembered that most mobile devices are likely to be multimode devices with WiFi, WiMAX and 3G cellular networks being available on the same devices. Further the mobile devices are likely to roam in and out of the coverage areas of individual services while maintaining call connectivity. Mobile devices in order to interwork in different networks need to be equipped with sets of antennas which can work in different bands as well as chipsets which handle the multimodal operations. Moreover services such as multimedia broadcasting (i.e., Mobile TV) are likely to be received over one of the many available media- 3G, WiFi, WiMAX, or broadcast technologies such as DVB-H or MediaFLO. Hence an integrated view of frequency allocations is important. Above all an integrated view of allocations also helps in understanding the constraints under which the frequency bands for WiMAX have been created and the likely operating scenario in these bands. Figure 11-2 shows these allocations.

Spectrum for Broadcast Services

It is evident that the legacy broadcast services, i.e., terrestrial analog broadcasts in the VHF and UHF bands III, IV, and V (174–854 MHz) and satellite communications and broadcasting in C and Ku bands (3.4–4.2, 5.9–6.5, and 10–14 GHz), take up a large portion of the available spectrum. Cellular mobile services (GSM) occupy the 860–900 and 940–980 MHz bands, and 3G UMTS or MSS services occupy the 1800–2100 MHz bands. In addition, the L-Band at 1600 MHz is also used to host the maritime mobile and aeronautical services.

Digitalization of TV services, which is a major activity in most countries, is placing considerable pressure on the VHF and UHF terrestrial

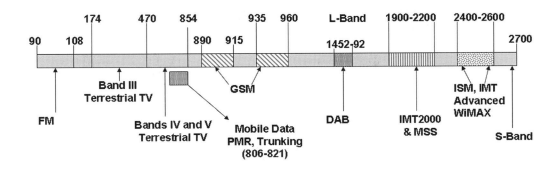

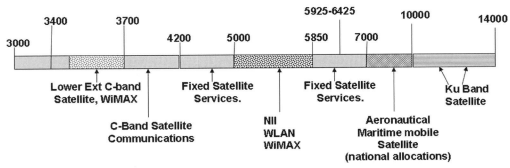

FIGURE 11-2   A macro view of frequency allocations

frequencies because of the requirements of dual analog-digital transmissions. With the phase out of analog transmissions, some spectrum will be freed (digital dividend), which will be allocated to new services. The U.S. spectrum auctions in the 700 MHz of 2008 band by the FCC are indicators of this trend. These bands are also contenders for future use of IEEE 802.16 services as WiMAX once they are adopted by the WiMAX Forum.

The C-band and Ku band fixed satellite services are currently used in over 300 fixed satellite systems globally for broadcasting and communications, both direct to home (DTH) and to cable headends. This is leading to a very critical situation as the WiMAX services are considered for allocation of spectrum in the 3.4–3.7 GHz and 5 GHz bands. The 5 GHz band has been reserved for National Information Infrastructure (NII) in the United States and is being used for WLANs and WiMAX services.

Spectrum for Cellular Mobile Services

Mobile services operate based on multiple standards with GSM and CDMA being the major technology lines. Table 11-1 indicates the

TABLE 11-1

International allocations for 2/2.5G mobile services

	International Allocations ITU R. M.1073-1	Usage
800 MHz band	824–849 MHz paired with 869–894 MHz	CDMA-based mobile services
900 MHz band	890–915 MHZ paired with 935–960 MHz	GSM band
	880–890 paired with 925–935 MHz	E-GSM band
1800 MHz	1710–1785 MHZ paired with 1805–1880 MHz	GSM band
1900 MHz	1850–1910 MHZ paired with 1930–1990 MHz	Part of IMT-2000 But also used as American PCS and other systems

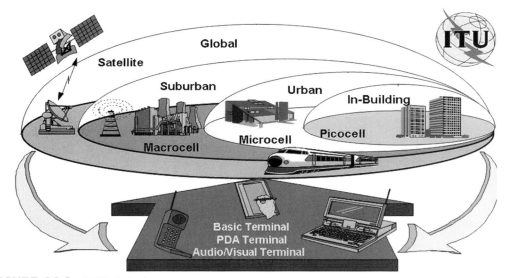

FIGURE 11-3   IMT 2000 vision

frequencies that were allocated for GSM- and CDMA-based services in order to facilitate global roaming (see Table 11-1).

ITU had initiated the planning for the radio interfaces and the spectrum requirements for the next generation of mobile services in its IMT 2000 working group. The IMT 2000 envisages the use of macro cells, micro cells, and pico cells with predicted data rates possible. IMT

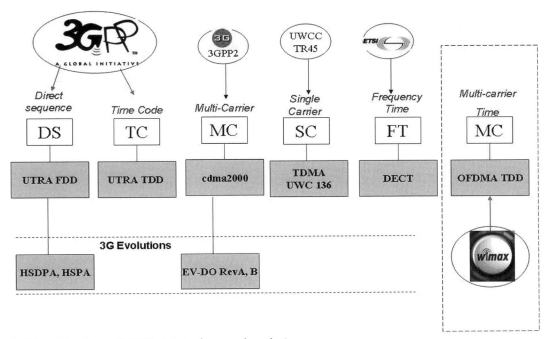

FIGURE 11-4   IMT 2000 air interfaces and evolutions

2000 defines data speeds of 144 Kbps at driving speeds, 384 Kbps for outside stationary use or walking speeds, and 2 Mbps indoors. The IMT 2000 initiative had started in the early 1990s, and the data rate projections were quite modest. New services such as mobile TV had not been envisioned.

The spectrum recommended by IMT 2000 for the third-generation services included five types of air interfaces and the provision for both the terrestrial mobile as well as the mobile satellite services (MSS).

These air interfaces were as follows (Figure 11-4):

- UMTS Terrestrial Radio Access-Frequency Division Duplexing (UTRA-FDD), a 3GPP standard
- UMTS Terrestrial Radio Access-Time Division Duplexing (UTRA-TDD), a 3GPP standard
- CDMA2000, a 3GPP2 standard
- Single-Carrier Time Division Multiple Access (SC-TDMA)
- Digital Enhanced Cordless Telecommunications (DECT)

In October 2007, OFDMA-TDD, used in Mobile WiMAX, has been added as the sixth air interface. Details of this are discussed later in the chapter.

The first two of these standards fall under the UMTS forum and are based on uplinks and downlinks being based on TDD and FDD,

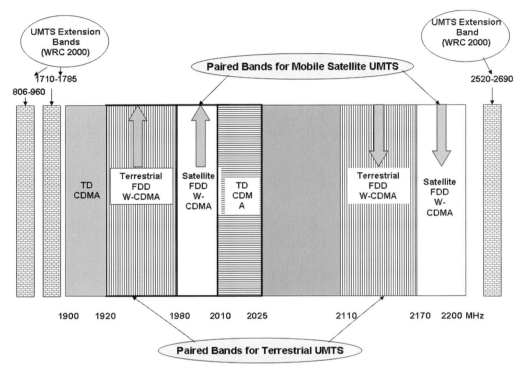

FIGURE 11-5   Spectrum for IMT 2000 services showing terrestrial and MSS bands (European allocations)

respectively. FDD systems require a paired spectrum, whereas TDD systems can operate in the same 5 MHz slot.

IMT 2000 was based on the WARC 1992 and included the frequency bands of 1885–2025 MHz paired with 2110–2170 MHz (i.e., 140 MHz). These bands included:

- Terrestrial/UMTS
    ⇒   FDD: 1920–1980 MHz/2110–2170 MHz
    ⇒   TDD: 1900–1920 MHz and 2010–2025 MHz

The ITU recommendations for IMT 2000 have been implemented in various countries and regions according to their selection of technologies, air interfaces, and setting aside of spectrum. In the European Union, for example, the spectrum band of 1900–2200 has been earmarked for different technologies, both terrestrial and satellite based (MSS). UMTS extension bands, as approved by WRC 2000, will become available in CEPT (Europe) in 2008, i.e., a portion of 806–960 MHz, 1710–1785 MHz, and 2520–2690 MHz (Figure 11-5). The extended bands may also be

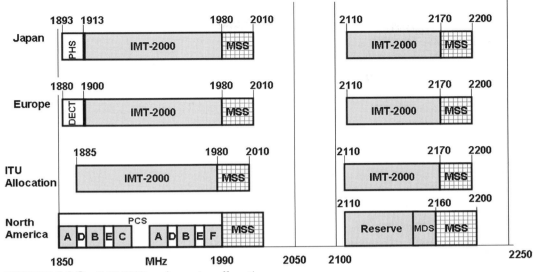

FIGURE 11-6 IMT 2000 and country allocations

usable for OFDMA-TDD systems based on IEEE 802.16e technologies as the ITU has adopted this as a standard air interface.

China has opted to use SC-TDMA as the preferred option for 3G rollout in the 2300–2400 GHz band.

The satellite-based mobile services (MSS) have had scant interest after the commercial failure of low earth orbit (LEO) global mobile systems, such as Iridium and ICO, but mobile multimedia satellites with MSS bands are expected to be in service during 2008.

The IMT 2000 spectrum was, however, already occupied in the United States by PCS (personal communication systems), i.e., CDMA- and TDMA-based systems in the 1900 MHZ band. For cellular services, the 1850–1990 MHz spectrum was divided in 5 bands named A to E and auctioned to different operators. FCC allowed technology neutrality in the use of frequency bands, which has led to introduction of GSM-based systems in the 1900 MHz band, and 3G-UMTS systems are emerging in other bands being allocated.

The divergence of the American allocations has been because of historical reasons (i.e., existing operating cellular systems); but this has created a difficult situation as far as roaming in these bands is concerned.

Digital Audio Broadcasting (DAB)

Digital audio broadcasting (DAB) is possible via two technologies S-DAB (satellite DAB) and T-DAB (terrestrial DAB). Digital audio

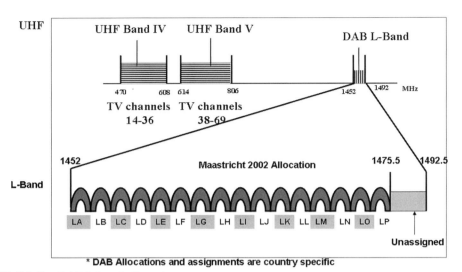

FIGURE 11-7 DAB L-band allocations

broadcasting services were allotted spectrum in the L-band (1452–1492 MHz) by WARC '92. In Europe, the channel allocations in the band were done as per the Maastricht 2002, which permitted common handsets to be used across Europe. The upper 25 MHz of the 40 MHz band was permitted for use by satellite-based DAB services.

In the United States, the FCC has allocated the S-Band (2320–2345 MHz) for satellite radio services, which are being provided by Sirius and XM Radio (DARS). This allocation of 25 MHz permits 12.5 MHz to be used by each operator. The United States has also developed the IBOC (In Band On Channel) standard for DAB. The standard has an ITU approval for DAB services. It uses the existing FM band of 88–108 MHz by using the sidebands of the existing FM carriers for additional digital carriers.

Mobile TV Services

Spectrum for mobile TV services based on terrestrial broadcasting has been a contentious issue in most countries. In fact, one of the reasons for the adoption of multiple standards for mobile TV can be attributed to the availability or the lack of spectrum for different technologies. DVB-H technologies use the DVB-T infrastructure, which is being rolled out in Europe, Asia, and some other regions to piggyback mobile services and hence has found greater acceptance. In some cases (such as the UK), the allocations for DVB-H have been difficult because of the ongoing digitalization. DAB-IP technology for mobile

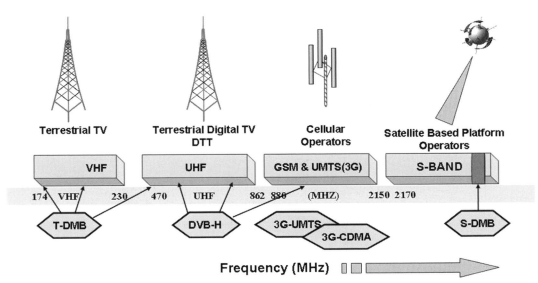

FIGURE 11-8 Overview of spectrum for mobile TV services

TV made its debut in the United Kingdom as the DAB allocations made the service feasible. In the United States and Korea, where ATSC systems are used, DVB-H requires new networks. These are being rolled out by new companies rather than existing broadcasters, such as HiWire. At the same time, MediaFLO services have been launched by Verizon by using the 700 MHz band, which was held by it as a result of spectrum auction.

MediaFLO services from AT&T are being launched in 2008. The allocations of spectrum for mobile TV using terrestrial broadcast technologies are now being treated as a high priority in most countries and allocations using the VHF or UHF bands are the most common.

11.3 CONSIDERATIONS IN THE USE OF SPECTRUM FOR WiMAX

The natural question before WiMAX operators and regulators has been that of allocation of suitable spectrum for WiMAX and IEEE 802.16 services. The WiMAX standards are of relatively recent origin and hence are late entrants for the race for spectrum amongst various competing technologies. However, the WiMAX systems do have a legacy. This legacy is that of the wireless systems belonging to the IEEE 801.11 a/b/g standards, which mostly operate in the 2.4 GHz ISM bands. The new technology of WiMAX, therefore, became a contender for the use of the wireless spectrum in the license-free ISM bands. The second legacy pertains to the use of MMDS systems, which operate in a point-to-multipoint fashion, albeit with analog transmissions. Fixed WiMAX systems are seen as a replacement of the last mile by MMDS or cable systems and thus became a contender for the spectrum owned previously by these technologies. The license-free bands, however, are not ideally suited for wide bandwidth and sustained data rate services because of the multiplicity of users and uncertainties on the availability of resources; hence licensed bands came into vogue for these services, in addition to the license-free bands. The WiMAX services, therefore, operate in both licensed and unlicensed bands.

It may be mentioned that the IEEE 802.16 standards envisage the use of a wide range of frequencies from 2–66 GHz. However, the WiMAX Forum has focused on the use of 2–10 GHz as the operating frequencies. In addition the WiMAX Forum initial certification profiles have parameters (such as FFT size, modulation types) defined only up to 6 GHz and specifically for mobile WiMAX, below 3.8 GHz.

11.3.1 Which Bands Are Best Suited for Mobile WiMAX?

Standing aside for a moment from which bands are available or adopted by the WiMAX Forum for initial profiles, it is important to recognize certain factors that make some frequencies more suitable for use in WiMAX systems, both fixed and mobile.

Path Loss

The first factor of importance is the operating frequency and the path loss. Path losses in WiMAX transmission may arise because of three basic factors:

- **The free space path loss (FSL)**, which is given by the equation:

$$FSL = 10 \, Log \, (4 \, \pi \, D \, F/C)^2$$

  Where D = distance from transmitter, F = frequency and C = Speed of light
  - The path losses increase with the square of the frequency. Hence the path loss at 2 GHz (IMT2000 frequency band) is about 12 dB higher than the UHF band at 0.5 GHz. This is compensated somewhat with the antenna size.
  - The increase in FSL with the square of the frequency requires the cell sizes at higher frequencies to be smaller in order to maintain link margins. Also, the higher frequencies such as

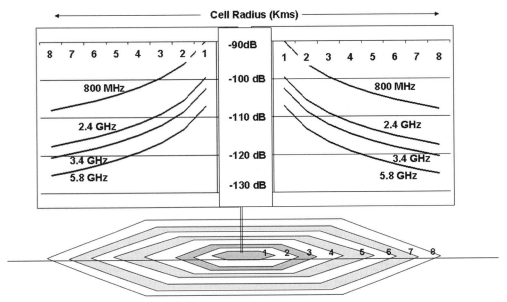

FIGURE 11-9 Free space loss at various operating frequencies

5.8 GHz and above are best suited for line of sight environment. In NLOS conditions, a link at 5.8 GHz would support NLOS customer premises equipment at distances less than a Km.

- **Loss due to non-line of sight operations (NLOS)**: As WiMAX systems in urban environments operate in a NLOS manner, there is a loss in received signals which depends on the reflected signal strengths. Frequencies above 10 GHz cannot be received in NLOS conditions and hence are treated separately. (These are not in the WiMAX Forum consideration of 2–10 GHz.) In general lower frequencies such as 800–2000 MHz have better performance for NLOS conditions than the higher bands. The signal strength in most NLOS conditions varies sharply with the location of the receiver due to reception of waves reflected from many objects. Ground propagation models are required for path loss analysis rather than free space loss. Hence, an additional margin needs to be given for the loss expected. Multiple antenna techniques with spatial diversity are used in WiMAX to improve margins in NLOS conditions.
- **Loss caused by in-building penetration**: Losses caused by in-building penetration depend largely on the type of wall and whether the indoor location has windows. They are not very frequency dependent, at least in the zone of consideration of 2 GHz

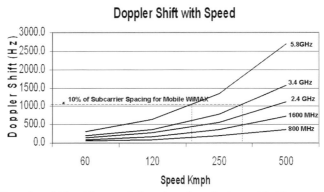

FIGURE 11-10   Doppler shift with speed showing the relation with 10 percent of subcarrier spacing of 10.94 KHz (as per WiMAX Forum initial certification profiles)

to 4 GHz. In buildings, losses can range from 2 dB (for a room with windows) to 6 dB (for a brick wall). The losses can go up to the 10–12 dB range for indoor areas that have enclosures built with metal.

Doppler Shift and Coherence Time

For systems meant for mobile use, the Doppler shift is an important consideration in system design. In the case of mobile WiMAX systems, which are meant to cater to vehicular speeds of up to 120 kmph, the effects of Doppler shift are relevant only at higher frequencies.

The Doppler shift is given by the following formula:

$$Ds = (VF/C) \cos(A)$$

Where Ds = Doppler shift, V = velocity of user, C = speed of light and A = angle between the incoming signal and direction of motion. Figure 11-10 shows the relationship of Doppler shift with operating frequency and speed. Frequency shifts need to be less than 10 percent of the subcarrier spacing in order to maintain correct timing between different mobile stations, which may be operating with a base station.

WiMAX is a multicarrier transmission system based on OFDM. The uplinks in WiMAX (both FDD systems and TDD systems) operate in a TDMA mode. Each subscriber station (which may be a mobile device) is assigned its own time slot and the transmissions must take place within this slot. Other devices have the right to transmit in the other slots as allotted in the frame of WiMAX. This means that the coherence of timing between different devices is important, which must operate

TABLE 11-2

Coherence time in ms is relevant to time synchronization of mobile stations with the base station (times are in milliseconds)

Frequency (MHz)	Doppler shift (Hz)	Coherence time (ms)	Symbol duration (ms) with 10 MHz BW and FFT = 1024, QPSK, data rate 10 Mbps
800	88.9	11.3	0.2
1600	177.8	5.6	0.2
2400	266.7	3.8	0.2
3400	377.8	2.6	0.2
5800	644.4	1.6	0.2
10000	1111.1	0.9	0.2

in synchronism. The coherence time is defined as $1/Ds$, where Ds is the Doppler Shift. The coherence time is thus inversely related to the Doppler Shift. A comparison of coherence time and the symbol time in OFDM is an indicator of how the motion is affecting the relationship between symbols from different devices.

Hence, rather than considering a shift in the center frequency, which is more relevant for single-carrier systems, it is more appropriate to consider the equivalent shift in time in the subcarriers. This gives a better analysis of the impact of motion based on the FFT size. The coherence times should be much larger than the symbol duration in order for the system to remain time coherent (more than 10 times). Table 11-2 shows this relationship and also the frequency range that is best suited for mobile WiMAX at vehicular speeds of 120 Kmph.

It may be mentioned that the mobile WiMAX FFT size can vary from 128 to 2048.However the WiMAX Forum had selected OFDM PHY, such that the subcarrier spacing remains fixed at 10.94 KHz by scaling up the FFT size with bandwidth. Reducing subcarrier spacing (such as selecting 1024 subcarriers in 5 MHz bandwidth instead of 512) would have adversely affected the Doppler spread, whereas increasing the subcarrier spacing would have reduced the delay spread and consequently intersymbol interference and the data rate.

Figure 11-11 shows the effect of motion on other television transmission systems and mobile systems. It is evident that the mobile WiMAX parameters have been formulated for maximizing the data throughput rather than speed of motion, and this is a key differentiator from mobile systems apart from the air interfaces.

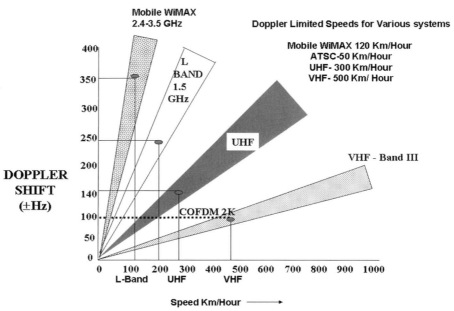

FIGURE 11-11   Doppler effect on television transmission systems

11.4 SPECTRUM BANDS

Spectrum allocations usually classify the available frequencies into several bands. The bands have been allocated to different services based on the previous WARC (now WRC) meetings under the ITU forum. Each frequency band is characterized by its own services based on legacy use as well as transmission characteristics.

VHF Band

The VHF band spans frequencies from 90 MHz to around 300 MHz. In this band, the wavelengths are large (e.g., 50 cm), and hence antennas tend to be of larger size unless gain is to be compromised. However, the propagation loss is low and Doppler shift effects are insignificant.

Currently, the VHF band is largely occupied by the analog FM and VHF terrestrial broadcast systems. This leaves little space for potential allocations for new services, such as wireless broadband.

UHF Band

The UHF band implies the use of frequencies from 470 to 862 MHz and includes two bands, i.e., UHF IV and V. The upper UHF band is well suited from the antenna length standpoint as mobile phones support antennas for GSM800 band. However country-specific spectrum occupation for terrestrial broadcast, mobile trunking, CDMA, and

GSM 900 services leads to these bands not being available for other purposes. Moreover, television digitalization in most countries is leading to the introduction of DVB-T and ATSC systems with requirements of simultaneous transmissions along with analog carriers, thus building pressure on the use of spectrum in this band. However as the digitalization process gets completed frequency slots that were used earlier for analog transmissions get vacated, thus generating fresh capacity (digital dividend). UHF spectrum auctions by the FCC are indicators of this new trend. However, the use of these bands for new applications will need to be watched as they adjoin high-power transmission bands for TV.

The Doppler shifts in the band are low enough to permit mobile reception at speeds of 300–500 Km/hour.

L-band

L-band is a mixed-use band. It has been traditionally used for land mobile and aeronautical mobile services. The Inmarsat system for mobile communications operates in the L-band. Digital audio broadcasting services (DAB) also operate in the L-band (except in the United States). Worldspace radio, global positioning systems, and astronomical services are other users of the L-band. L-band is well suited for terrestrial mobile communications. However, it is currently fully occupied in most countries.

S-band

If the IMT2000 band of 1800–2100 and cellular mobile bands of 900 MHz are kept aside, the S-band spanning from 2 GHz to 3.7 GHz presents the best opportunities for allocation to WiMAX and Mobile WiMAX systems. The S-band has lower losses than the higher bands, i.e., 5.8 GHz, and has manageable Doppler effects at vehicular speeds. Some of the proposed allocations for Mobile WiMAX fall in the 2.3, 2.5, 3.3, and 3.5 GHz bands and are a part of the S-band.

This does not mean, however, that it has been easy going for the process of allocation of spectrum in this band. S-band is also characterized by the presence of unlicensed bands at 2.4 GHz for ISM and other unlicensed wireless applications (discussed later in the chapter) including WiFi (IEEE 802.11b/g). A part of the S-band is reserved for satellite-based multimedia services. As per the ITU allocations in the S-band, these frequencies have been reserved for the satellite-based DAB or multimedia transmissions. These bands include (RSAC Paper 5/2005):

2310–2360 MHz (United States, India, Mexico)
2535–2655 MHz (Korea, India, Japan, Pakistan, Thailand)

In the United States, the FCC has allocated part of the above S-band (2320–2345 MHz) for satellite radio services which are being provided by Sirius and XM Radio (DARS). This allocation of 25 MHz permits 12.5 MHz to be used by each operator.

In addition C-band fixed satellite service downlinks also have a major presence in the band with 3.4–3.7 GHz (extended C-band) and 3.7–4.2 GHz (standard C-band) being used for telecommunications and satellite broadcast television services. The potential interference from the WiMAX systems to the existing satellite services is one of the major hindrances to allocation of spectrum in the S-band for WiMAX in various countries.

11.5 SPECTRUM FOR WiMAX SERVICES

11.5.1 Adoption of Mobile WiMAX Standard under ITU

The development of terrestrial interfaces under the aegis of the IMT-2000 has been entrusted to the working party 8F in the ITU-R. Interfaces used by the 3G services under both the third-generation partnership projects, 3GPP and 3GPP2 (such as W-CDMA and CDMA2000), are based on the accepted air interfaces under the IMT-2000.

The Mobile WiMAX technology (OFDMA-TDD) was accepted in October 2007 by the ITU as the sixth terrestrial standard in addition to the existing five terrestrial interfaces.

The inclusion of Mobile WiMAX as one of the interfaces under ITU IMT-2000 has the implication that WiMAX would be considered a potential candidate for discussions on allocation of spectrum for IMT-2000 services. Currently the 2.5 to 2.69 GHz is reserved for IMT-2000 services (IMT-advanced) and WiMAX would be a candidate for such allocations in various countries and also in any future bands reserved for IMT-2000.

The inclusion of WiMAX OFDMA-TDD as an air interface in the IMT-2000 has additional far-reaching implications. First, this means that the band of 2.5–2.69 GHz, which has been reserved in Europe for IMT-advanced services would be a candidate for allocation to Mobile WiMAX services. In the United States, it is already allocated for Mobile WiMAX use. This has the potential of making the band of 2.5–2.69 GHz a prime band for Mobile WiMAX where global roaming will be possible in future. Second, having a common acceptable band will bring down the cost of chipsets and customer premises equipment (CPEs) because of a much higher scale of usage. Third, it removes impediments in licensing of Mobile WiMAX services in various countries which were getting delayed while the governments considered

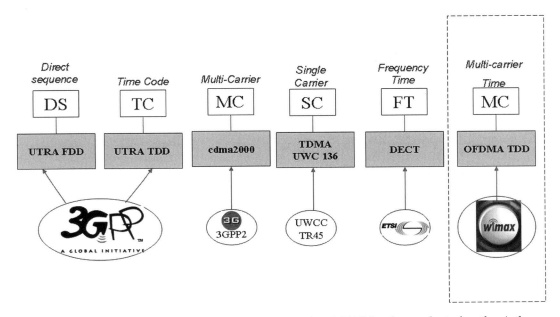

FIGURE 11-12 Mobile WiMAX (OFDMA TDD wireless MAN) has been adapted as the sixth terrestrial interface under IMT-2000 by ITU

the different frequency bands for licensing WiMAX services. Finally the announcement of including OFDMA-TDD as air interfaces in 3G technologies comes at a time when many of the countries such as India are just on the verge of entering the 3G services. The inclusion of OFDMA-TDD as an approved interface could lead to Mobile WiMAX being deployed much faster than might otherwise be the case.

This also sets the stage for "IMT-Advanced"—the next generation of interfaces to be developed for the 3G evolution and 4G services to also be based on OFDMA-TDD technologies. IMT advanced services are expected to be available between 2010 and 2015.

11.5.2 WiMAX Forum Certification Profiles

Approved usage profiles (certification profiles) are issued by the WiMAX Forum, and these become the basis of the development of chipsets and systems for WiMAX services. While fixed WiMAX (IEEE 802.16-2004) and Mobile WiMAX (IEEE 802.16e) are fundamentally different technologies with regard to the physical layer and MAC layer, most of the future deployment of systems is happening based on the

TABLE 11-3

WiMAX certification profiles

System Profile	Spectrum	Bandwidth Of Spectral band	Duplexing	Bandwidth profiles
Mobile WiMAX	2.3–2.4 GHz	100 MHz	TDD	5/10, 8.75 (only in Korea) MHz
IEEE 802.16e-2005	2.5–2.69 GHz (190 MHz)	190 MHz	TDD	5/10 MHz
	3.3–3.4 GHz	100 MHz	TDD	5, 7 MHz
	3.4–3.6 GHz	200 MHz	TDD	5, 7, 10 MHz
	3.4–3.8 GHz	400 MHz	TDD	5, 7, 10 MHz
Fixed WiMAX	3.4–3.6 GHz	200 MHz	TDD	1.75, 3.5, 7 MHz
IEEE 802.16-2004	3.4–3.6 GHz	200 MHz	FDD	1.75, 3.5, 7 MHz
	5.725–5.850 GHz	125 MHz	TDD	5/10 MHz

Mobile WiMAX technologies. The exception to this is the use of higher bands such as 5.8 GHz where the profiles for Mobile WiMAX are not yet defined. With the primary objective of WiMAX being to provide high data rates and consequently large bandwidths of 5–20 MHz per frequency and multiple frequencies per operator, a primary requirement of WiMAX spectrum allocation process is to be able to assign large blocks to cater to broadband wireless requirements.

It is important to recognize the importance of the WiMAX certification profiles, even though spectrum in various bands may be made available in different countries. The WiMAX profiles at present cover the following:

- 5.8 GHz for license-exempt equipment with IEEE 802.16-2004 technology
- 2.3, 2.5, and 3.5 GHz for licensed equipment with IEEE 802.16-2004 and IEEE 802.16e technologies (fixed and mobile WiMAX)

Potential operators can consider the use of spectrum in both the licensed and the unlicensed bands. Figure 11-13 provides an overview of the WiMAX spectrum.

The unlicensed bands are comprised of the 2.40–2.4835 GHz ISM band and 5.15–5.85 GHz (the U-NII bands in the United States). These bands, though unlicensed, are subject to power and emission regulations. The use of these bands is governed by section 15 of the FCC regulations. The licensed bands are comprised of the 2.5–2-69 GHz, 3.4–3.6, and 3.6–3.8 GHz bands. The allocations of these bands is country-specific

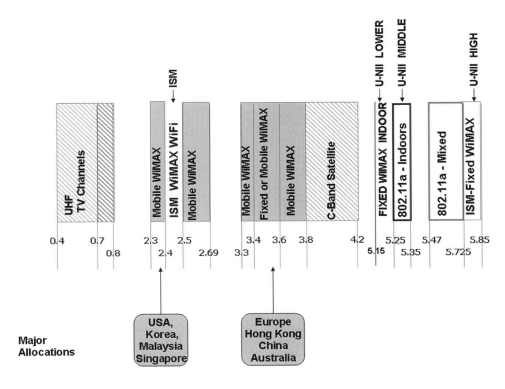

FIGURE 11-13 WiMAX spectrum

because of existing and planned usage by services. Table 11-4 provides a summary of the usage of these bands.

11.5.3 WiMAX Usage in Unlicensed Bands

The spectrum of 2.4–2.483 GHz and 5.125 to 5.85 have been earmarked for unlicensed use in most countries (there are exceptions such as Australia where the use of the bands needs to be licensed). These frequency ranges are further split into bands and channeling plans, which are subject to limitations of EIRP in order to prevent interference to coexisting systems in the same band as well as other systems in adjacent bands. In addition, in Europe, the 3.4 GHz band is also available for license-free use. Unlicensed bands present an important opportunity for new operators to quickly launch services, particularly in rural areas where the license-free bands are relatively unused. In metropolitan areas, the bands are used extensively for WiFi systems 802.11b/g (2.4–2.83 GHz), 802.11a (5.725 to 5.850 GHz), Bluetooth devices, and

TABLE 11-4
WiMAX spectrum allocations

Frequency Band	Technology	Channelization Plan	Remarks on Usage
700–800 MHz	Part of UHF Band		Being considered by USA for allocations to WiMAX
2300–2400 MHz	802.16e TDD	5, 8.75, or 10 MHz	Being used in USA, Korea (Wi-Bro) for Wireless Mobility Services
2469–2690 MHz	2535–2655 allotted for satellite-based broadcasting. Planned for extension of IMT 2000 or WiMAX 802.16e TDD	5 and 10 MHz	Being considered for Technology Neutral allocation by USA, Canada, Australia, Brazil, Mexico, etc.
3300–3400 MHz	802.16e TDD	5 and 7 MHz	Potential allocations for Mobile WiMAX
3400–3800 MHz	3400–3600 for 802.16d (TDD or FDD) 3400–3800 for 802.16e TDD	3.5, 7, or 10 MHz	Satellite services need to be shifted from part of the band. Strong support for use in WiMAX and 4G platforms
5.15–5.35 and 5.725–5.85 GHz			For unlicensed usage including WiMAX

devices using the ISM band, such as cordless phones, wireless microphones, cameras, home microwave devices, and medical equipment. (802.11a devices operate in the 5 GHz U-NII band.)

2.4 GHz Band

The 2.4 GHz license-free band is used to refer to the frequencies 2.400 to 2.483 GHz. There are two primary air technologies through which the spectrum can be accessed by wireless services. The first technology is the direct sequence spread spectrum (DSSS), which is used with fixed frequency 20 MHz-wide overlapping channels. The available 83 MHz bandwidth is divided into 11 overlapping channels (13 in Europe), which are then available for use by wireless systems. As per the frequency plan (Figure 11-15) channels 1, 6, and 11 are non-overlapping. (In Europe these are 1, 7, and 13.) WiMAX systems, which operate in the

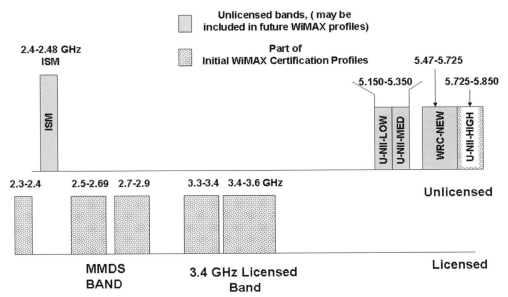

FIGURE 11-14   Spectrum bands and WiMAX certification profiles

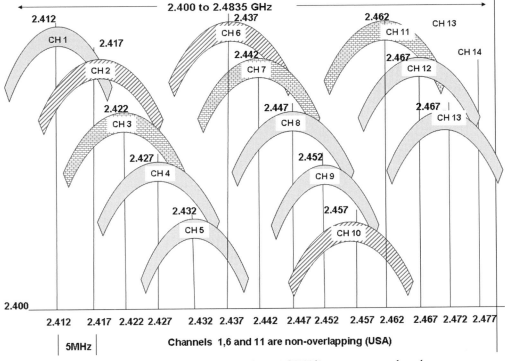

FIGURE 11-15   DSSS channelization plans in the 2.4 GHZ license-exempt band

TABLE 11-5
DSSS and FHSS channeling plans in the 2.4 GHz band

Country/Region	Frequency Range (GHz)	DSSS Channels	FHSS Channels
Europe	2.4–24835	1 to 13	2 to 80
United States	2.4–2.4835	1 to 11	2 to 80
Canada	2.4–2.4835	1 to 11	2 to 80
France	2.4465–2.4835	4 (10–13)	35 (48–82)
Spain	2.445–2.475	2 (10 and 11)	27 (47–73)
Japan	2.4–2.497	1 to 14	2 to 95

unlicensed band, need to comply with the same channeling plans even though the air interface may differ. WiFi with 802.11b uses DSSS with 22 MHz-wide channels.

The second air interface used in the 2.4 to 2.83 spectrum is the frequency hopping spread spectrum (FHSS). In this type of interface, the band is divided into 79–80 channels each of 1 MHz bandwidth. The exact frequencies and channels are country-specific, but the differences are minor. Examples of devices that use FHSS are Bluetooth devices, which use 1 MHz channels.

Table 11-5 provides a summary of the air interface and channeling plans in the 2.4 GHz unlicensed band.

There are restrictions on the power levels which can be used in the 2.4 GHz band. In Europe, the adjacent band is used for 3G services, such as HSPA, and hence the maximum EIRP allowed in the 2.4 GHz band is 20 dBm (100 mW). In the United States, as per FCC 247 part 15, point-to-multipoint systems can have 36 dBm of EIRP. (This translates into 30 dBm or 1 watt of transmitted power with a 6 dBi omni-antenna). For point-to-point systems, there is a concession—the power can be increased effectively equivalent to 2/3 times the antenna gain (in dB) above 6 dBi (this is called the 3:1 rule). Thus for an antenna with 24 dBi gain (18 dB over an omni-antenna), the EIRP allowed is $36 + 12 = 48$ dBm. This translates into a transmitted power of $48 - 24 = 24$ dBm. Alternatively, if the antenna gain is Ag, the transmitted power (To) output is given by:

$$To\ (dBm)\ =\ 36(dBm)\ -\ (Ag(dB) - 6) * 2/3$$

The maximum To is limited to 30 dBm (1 W) in any installation.

Point-to-point systems, with directional antennas and higher antenna gain, are thus given a preferential treatment in the permitted power transmitted. It should also to be noted that despite the 2.4 GHz band being crowded, directional antenna systems can operate with good EIRP and link margins.

5 GHZ Unlicensed Bands

The 5 GHz band refers to the frequency range of 5.15 GHz to 5.825 GHz encompassing the unlicensed U-NII band in the United States. The U-NII band is comprised of three distinct sub-bands in the mentioned frequency range. The 5 GHz band has been globally agreed to be used as an unlicensed band with some variations in transmitted powers permitted.

- Lower U-NII Band (5.15 to 5.25 GHz): The lower U-NII band is meant for indoor use only and equipment using the band needs to have integral built in antennas. The maximum power permitted to be transmitted is 50 mW (17 dBm). The lower U-NII band is divided into 20 MHz wide channels.
- Middle U-NII band: The middle U-NII band spans the frequencies from 5.25 to 5.35 GHz. The maximum power permitted in the band is 250 mW (24 dBm).
- Upper U-NII band: The upper U-NII band is from 5.725 to 5.825 GHz comprised of 100 MHz of bandwidth. The maximum power permitted to be transmitted in the band in the United States is 1 Watt (30 dBm) with a 6 dBi omni-antenna. This translates into an EIRP of 36 dBm(EIRP of 4 watts). In addition to this, directional antenna systems in this band are permitted to use antenna of any gain without the regulation of having to reduce the power up to an EIRP of 53 dBm.

It is the upper NII band that is of real interest for fixed WiMAX systems (IEEE 802.16-2004). The band has been selected in the initial certification profiles by the WiMAX Forum for fixed WiMAX systems. The parameters for the initial certification profile in this band include a bandwidth of 10 MHz and FFT size of 256.

The upper U-NII band is also designated as an ISM band for use by a range of devices. These can range from IEEE 802.11a wireless systems (based on OFDM) to industrial and scientific devices.

The key advantage of the U-NII band is the high EIRP permitted. For example, with 23 dBi antennas the EIRP transmitted can be 53 dBm or 200 Watts.

11.5.4 WiMAX Usage in Licensed Bands

Licensed bands present the advantage of building high-reliability carrier-class networks without potential uncertainty on the interference

TABLE 11-6

Summary of Fixed WiMAX and Mobile WiMAX bands

System Profile	Spectrum	Bandwidth	Duplexing	Channel Width
Mobile WiMAX, IEEE 802.16e-2005	2.3–2.4 GHz	100 MHz	TDD	5/10, 8.75 (only in Korea) MHz
	2.5–2.69 GHz	190 MHz	TDD	5/10 MHz
	3.3–3.4 GHz	100 MHz	TDD	5, 7 MHz
	3.4–3.6 GHz	200 MHz	TDD	5, 7, 10 MHz
	3.4–3.8 GHz	400 MHz	TDD	5, 7, 10 MHz
Fixed WiMAX IEEE 802.16-2004	3.4–3.6 GHz	200 MHz	TDD	1.75, 3.5, 7 MHz
	3.4–3.6 GHz	200 MHz	FDD	1.75, 3.5, 7 MHz
	5.725–5.850 GHz	125 MHz	TDD	5/10 MHz

issues. Having rights to a spectrum band enables an operator to fully exploit the WiMAX technology with sectorization and plan for specific services and user densities. For metropolitan areas, the licensed bands are preferable because of the crowding of the unlicensed bands.

While the wireless MAN standards as per IEEE 802.16 are not limited to any particular band, the WiMAX Forum, which is currently only focused on bands in the 2–10 GHz range, leads to limited choices for licensed spectrum. In fact, the certification profiles are only for the 2.3 GHz, 2.5 GHz, and 3.5 GHz bands. We take a look at the characteristics of these bands.

3.5 GHz Licensed Band

The 3.5 GHz band spanning from 3.3–3.6 GHz has been the preferred band for licensing of fixed WiMAX systems except in the United States. Large bandwidths are available in this band, and many operators with 3–4 frequencies (of 7 MHz each) each can be accommodated in the band. Allocations have been made in this band in Europe, the Americas, and Asia Pacific. It is estimated that a total of more than 500 companies hold licenses in this band.

The 3.3 to 3.6 GHz is split into two bands 3.3 to 3.4 and 3.4 to 3.6 GHz because the mobile WIMAX certification profiles currently cover these bands separately.

2.5 to 2.69 GHz Licensed Band

Of particular interest is the 2.5–2.69 GHz band, as mobile WiMAX wave 2 certification has been accelerated in this band. The wave 2 involving the use of MIMO advanced antenna systems and beam-forming is important to operators as it provides better spectrum utilization. Wave 2 products from many vendors are now available for this band. The band has been allocated in the United States, Brazil, Singapore, Mexico, and some other countries for Mobile WiMAX. However, in Europe, Japan, and Korea, 3G mobile network allocations (IMT-2000 as per WRC 2000) had been preventing the use of the band for mobile WiMAX. The acceptance by the ITU of TDD-OFDMA as an accepted interface may alter the situation. Spectrum auctions in many countries in the ensuing period will make these frequencies available.

2.3 to 2.4 GHz Licensed Band

At present the 2.3–2.4 GHz is the only band (other than the 2.5 to 2.69 GHz) where the initial certification profiles for Mobile WiMAX have been defined. This band has not been identified for international mobile telecommunications (IMT), which makes it a prime band in the three ITU regions which can be allotted to Mobile WiMAX.

Companies such as Korea Telecom, SK Telecom, Unwired (Australia), and AT&T have been assigned spectrum in this band.

11.5.5 Channelling Plans

It is of great advantage to operators to use both the spectrum bands, as well as the channelling plans which have been included by the WiMAX Forum in their certification profiles. The profiles give the chipset makers and equipment manufacturers an opportunity to offer universally workable equipment in certified bands. The success of WiFi was indeed attributed to the universal availability of client devices in all laptops and portable devices, a feature which has now extended itself to smartphones. WiMAX success is being foreseen with a similar availability of client devices, devices with embedded WiMAX chipsets and CPEs in approved bands and with specified operating parameters in the near future. It also provides for interoperability between different operator systems and roaming facility worldwide subject to commercial arrangements.

Some of the networks deployed today are pre-WiMAX networks, seeking to move to WiMAX-compliant profiles.

11.6 COUNTRY-SPECIFIC PLANS

11.6.1 United States

In the licensed category, there are three potential bands which can be used for WiMAX services in the United States.

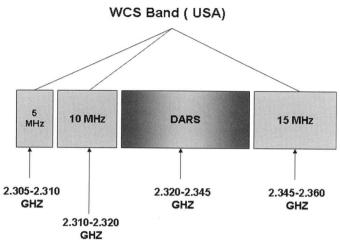

FIGURE 11-16   WCS Band (United States)

2.3 GHz WCS Band

The wireless communications services (WCS) band is located at 2.3 GHz and is available with a bandwidth of 30 MHz. The band was created by the FCC in 1997 with two slots of 15 MHz each (2305–2320 and 2345–2360 MHz). These slots are adjacent to the DARS spectrum of 2320–2345 MHz.

The limited bandwidth available in the band coupled with the high-powered DARS transmissions (land-based repeaters) in the adjacent bands has been a reason why these frequencies have not been well utilized for broadband wireless. In the recent past, some companies such as Meganet have commenced the use of the 2.3 GHz spectrum.

2.5–2.7 GHz BRS Band

The 2.5 to 2.7 GHz band was earlier allotted to MMDS systems for delivery of analog TV using point-to-multipoint transmissions. As these technologies were not very successful, most of this spectrum was sold to Sprint and BellSouth.

The spectrum originally was comprised of 6×33 MHz channels, a channelization which reflected the need to carry the NTSC analog signals. Of these, 16 channels were devoted to Instructional Television Fixed Service (ITFS), mostly allotted for educational channels. Clearwire®, a Craig MaCaw company, had leased a large part of the ITFS spectrum. In 2004, the channelization was changed to reflect the need to accommodate the wireless broadband services. The spectrum band, which used to be called the MMDS band, was also renamed the

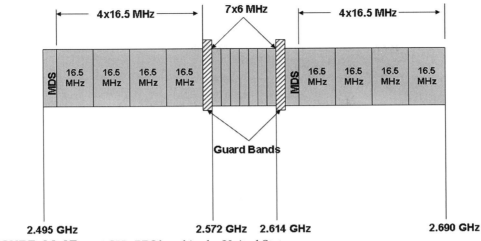

FIGURE 11-17   2.5 GHz BRS band in the United States

BRS band. The reorganization permitted 8 blocks of 16.5 MHz each and 7 blocks of 6 MHz each.

At the time of the AT&T BellSouth merger in 2007, the FCC had put a condition that the 2.5 GHz spectrum held by BellSouth must be divested. Subsequently, the same was taken over by Clearwire, which now holds most of the spectrum in this band. Some of the band is in use for MMDS or ITFS systems. It is therefore of no surprise that this band, considered the prime band for mobile WiMAX, is being used by Sprint and Clearwire to launch nationwide mobile WIMAX services independently.

AWS Band

In September 2006, the FCC had auctioned the AWS spectrum in the 1.7 and 2.1 GHz bands. The spectrum included a total of 90 MHz as paired spectrum. The AWS spectrum is thus organized into two blocks of 45 MHz each (1710–1755 MHz and 2110–2155 MHz). 90 MHz of available spectrum was divided into five blocks for the purpose of auction. Three blocks called A, B, and F are 10 + 10 MHz each in the 1.7 and 2.1 GHz band, respectively, and three blocks called C, D, and E are 5 + 5 MHz each, as shown in Figure 11-18. The AWS blocks straddle the PCS 1900 MHz blocks being used for cellular mobile services with technology neutrality.

The AWS band is permitted to be used for 3G services as well as wireless or WiMAX services or mobile TV broadcast services. It is expected to be deployed for 3G, HSDPA, and EV-DO services among other uses.

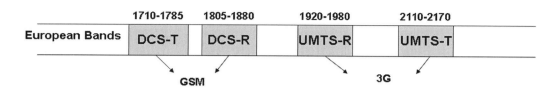

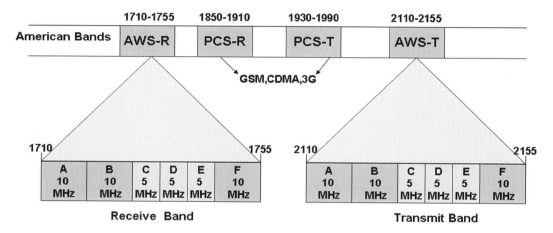

(Extension T indicates transmit from base to phone, R is phone to base)

FIGURE 11-18 AWS spectrum bands in the United States

The figure also shows the relation of the AWS bands to the PCS bands in the United States and the 3G and GSM bands in Europe. As is evident, the AWS bands do not lend direct compatibility in the use of these bands for 3G or other services.

A total of 1100 licenses were issued for the AWS band covering over 160 markets. The AWS markets were divided into cellular market areas (CMAs), economic areas (EAs, blocks B and C) and regional economic area groupings (REAGs, blocks D, E, and F). Major operators that received licenses for major areas were T-Mobile, Verizon Wireless, MetroPCS, SpectrumCo, etc.

3.650–3.7 GHz Band

The United States has recently opened up the 3.650 to 3.7 GHz band for contention-based wireless services to minimize interference with satellite services. A hybrid approach of licensed and unlicensed usage is followed in this band.

11.6.2 European Union

The European Union has been following a different approach for allocating frequency bands for WiMAX, partly owing to its legacy issues. 3G spectrum was auctioned in Europe as far back as the year 2000 and the spectrum of 2.5–2.7 GHz has been reserved for LTE of 3G services in some countries. This band is especially important as the initial certification profiles for Mobile WiMAX have been issued in this band. In late 2007, the European Union has taken an approach that a flexible use policy will be adopted for this band rather than having it reserved for future 3G use. The subsequent adoption by ITU of OFDMA-TDD interfaces has placed this band now on a common footing.

3.4–3.8 GHZ Band

The frequency band of 3.4 to 3.8 GHz, known as the Broadband Wireless Access (BWA) band is at present being used for broadband wireless services including WiMAX in Europe. This is at present used for fixed and nomadic wireless access, and the use as mobile wireless access is under consideration.

There are also some views about the spectrum being used for the IMT-2000; however, no decisions on exclusive allocation of the band for other services have been made.

UK

WiMAX is permitted in the 5.8 GHz unlicensed band in the United Kingdom subject to EIRP restrictions. Urban WiMAX®, a WiMAX company, for example, has been offering WiMAX services in the 5.8 GHz band for corporations. The Ofcom also supports technology neutrality in the 3.5 GHz band, the spectrum for which is currently held by companies such as UK Broadband and Pipex for broadband wireless. These have already commenced WiMAX network rollouts.

The auction of the 2.5–2.6 GHz band is slated for 2008 by Ofcom. Around 215 MHz of spectrum is expected to be auctioned. At present the service-specific details of the spectrum are not available but it is expected that it will be technology neutral and 25–80 percent will be available for Mobile WiMAX services.

Germany

In Germany, the auction for WiMAX spectrum was concluded for the spectrum in the 3.4–3.6 GHz band. Licenses were auctioned for 28 regions in the country. Three companies, DBD, Clearwire, and Inquam have obtained nation-wide licenses for 21 MHz of paired spectrum

(FDD) each (3410–3494 and 3510–3594 MHz). This will permit each company to operate 8 channels of 5 MHz (TDD) each, in the allotted bands. Spectrum auctions for 2.6 GHz are slated for 2008.

Romania

In Romania, the 3.5 GHz spectrum is held by seven operators with nationwide licenses. In addition, five operators hold local licenses for different regions (for a total of 175 local licenses). Technology-neutral use is now permitted in these bands, and WiMAX service offerings have commenced.

Poland

In Poland, six national licenses (2 licenses of 28 MHz and 4 of 14 MHz each) have been granted in the band 3.6–3.8 GHz based on a public-tendering procedure. These licenses are held by PTC, Netia, NASK, and Clearwire. In addition, spectrum with 3.5 MHz channelling plans is being allocated.

Croatia

Spectrum in the 3.5 GHz band has been allocated in Croatia based on a "selection" method. Optima Telecom (2×21 MHz) and VIPnet (2×14 MHz) are among those allotted.

Greece

Greece has licensed 2×28 MHz and 2×21 MHz slots in the 3.4–3.6 GHz spectral band. There are four licensed operators in Greece—OTE, Q-Telecom, Craig Wireless, and COSMOLINE.

France

Auctions for the 3.4–3.6 GHz frequency spectrum were held in February 2006 in France. Subsequently, the operators have been permitted to transfer the licenses obtained leading to a flux in the operators providing services.

11.6.3 India

Spectrum allocations in India are based on the national Frequency Allocation Plan (NFAP-2002). India has been an early adopter of WiMAX services with ISPs and telecommunications operators, having commenced commercial services in 2007.

As per the frequency allocation plan, the following bands have been earmarked for WiFi and WiMAX access:

- 2.4 to 2.4835 GHz
- 2.5 GHz band (only 2.535 to 2.655 GHz)
- 2.7 to 2.9 GHz band (only 77 MHz of this band is at present available)
- 3.3 to 3.4 GHz
- 5.725 to 5.825 GHz
- 10.15 to 10.65 GHz

Unlicensed Bands

The bands of 2.4 GHz and 5 GHz have been declared as license-free bands, as per global practices, with specified technical parameters.

The use of the 2.4 GHz band is allowed with limitations on transmitted power. The 5.150 to 5.350 band is reserved for indoor use and is license free. The 5.725 to 5.875 GHz band is also license free and can be used for WiMAX deployments indoors. For outdoor use, a license is needed for operation in the 5.725 to 5.875 band in India.

3.3 to 3.4 GHz Band

The 3.3 to 3.4 GHz band has been earmarked for WiMAX, LMDS, and MMDS systems as a licensed band. Many ISPs have been allotted bandwidth in blocks of 7 MHz in this band for broadband wireless access services. Channelling plans are available both for FDD and TDD systems in this band (up to 7 FDD systems in 50 MHz with duplex operation). Interleaved channels with 3.5 MHz and 1.75 MHz bandwidths have also been allocated.

3.5 GHz Band (3.4–3.6 GHz)

Internationally this band is used widely for WiMAX and forms part of international certification profiles for WiMAX. However, in India the Insat satellite system uses these frequencies for the lower extended C-band operation. Hence it has been decided for the present that no allocations will be made for WiMAX in this band.

2.3 GHz Band

2.3 GHz band in India is occupied by point-to-point and point-to-multipoint links in many locations. Hence, coordination of WiMAX links in the same usage area is difficult.

TABLE 11-7

3.3 GHz band spectrum assigned in India

S.No	Operator	Spectrum Assigned in 3.3–3.4 GHz
1	BSNL	2 × 7 MHz
2	Bharti	2 × 6 MHz
3	Dishnet DSL	2 × 6 MHz
4	Sify	2 × 6 MHz
5	RCIL	2 × 6 MHz
6	Spectranet	2 × 5 MHz

2.5 GHz Band

Future allocations for WiMAX in India will be made in the 2.5 GHz band, which is also included in the WiMAX initial certification profiles. It is expected that the licenses will be open for up to three operators in each area.

WiMAX Networks Operating in India

Reliance, VSNL, Bharti, Aircel, and Sify have already launched WiMAX services in India with plans for aggressively covering all important towns. The typical cost of unlimited data transfer is $15 per month. In addition assignments have already been made to a number of operators in the 3.3–3.4 GHz band.

11.6.4 Canada

In Canada, the practice of designating spectrum for specific technologies is not followed. Instead technologies can be used in any band subject to technical compatibility. In practice, however, most deployments tend to follow the global pattern of using WiMAX certification profiles as preferred operating options. Spectrum allocations for Canada are shown in Figure 11-19.

Among the license-free bands, the 5.8 GHz slot can be used for WiMAX with power limited by EIRP restrictions. The major licensed bands for WiMAX fall in the 2.3 GHz and the 3.5 GHz bands.

The 3.5 GHz band in Canada comprises of 3475–3650 MHz as the 3400–3775 is used for radio location services. The band of 3475−2650 has been divided into 7 frequencies with 25 MHz bandwidth each (total 175 MHz).

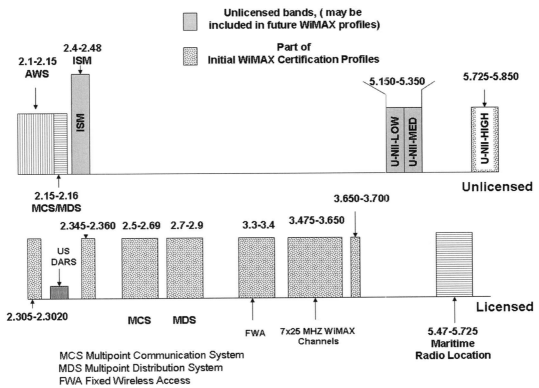

FIGURE 11-19 Spectrum allocations in Canada

The 2.3 GHz band is also available for wireless access including WiMAX. Normally the 2.3 GHz band extends from 2.3 to 2.36 MHz. However, because of the use of intervening spectrum of 2320–2345 MHz by the U.S. digital radio service (DARS), which also has terrestrial repeaters in Canada, the available frequencies are only two 15 MHz blocks from 2305–2320 and 2345–2360 MHz. All these blocks in the 2.3 GHz and the 3.5 GHz bands were auctioned and allocated to 32 entities with over 800 spectrum licenses.

Taiwan

Taiwan has completed the allocation process for the 2.5–2.69 GHz band for Mobile WiMAX.

A total of six licenses have been granted, three in northern Taiwan (Global on, First International Telecom, Tecom-VIBO) and three in south Taiwan (Tatung, Vastar Cable, and FarEasTone Telecommunications).

Brazil

In Brazil , the 3.5 GHz spectrum is held by Brasil Telecom. The services based on IEEE 802.16e are being launched based on the Mobile WiMAX standards and profiles. Additional spectrum will only be available in auctions to be held later in 2008.

11.7 INTERFERENCE BY WiMAX NETWORKS

Operation of WiMAX networks in the lower extended C-band and in particular in the frequency bands of 3.4–3.6 and 3.6–3.8 GHz brings them in direct conflict with some of the satellite systems. While the normal C-band extends from 3.7–4.2 GHz, the lower extended C-band extends this range down to 3.4 GHz. This brings some of the satellite networks in the same band as the WiMAX systems because of their high transmitted powers. A position paper on WiMAX interference was issued by CASBAA, which was adopted by international associations of satellite communications industry. The position statement in this regard is as follows:

Position Statement: National administrations should recognize the potential for massive disruptions to C band satellite communications, radar systems, and domestic microwave links, if spectrum is inappropriately allocated to, and frequencies inappropriately assigned for, terrestrial wireless applications in the C-band (specifically 3.4–4.2 GHz).

This statement was adopted by the European Satellite Operators Group (ESOA), Global VSAT Forum (GVF), Europe's Satellite Action Plan-Regulatory Working Group (SAP-REG), the Satellite Users Interference Reduction Group, and other international associations of the satellite industry.

Sharing studies conducted by ITU-R Working Party 8F have shown that a minimum distance separation of approximately 35 to 75 kilometers must be maintained between an IMT transmitter (a 4G mobile system) and an FSS receiver.

Subsequently many administrations have issued notices to satellite network users to vacate the use of the lower extended C-bands. Many operators, where interference has been noticed, have begun the use of filters or antenna shields to safeguard the operating networks. Some users have also relocated the reception dishes outside metropolitan areas to reduce interference.

12

MOBILE WiMAX NETWORKS

The most important thing in communication is to hear what isn't being said.

—*Peter F. Drucker*

The IEEE 802.16 standards define only the PHY and MAC layer of wireless MAN networks. The wireless "lower layers" are then expected to connect to other networks such as IP-based networks to provide these networks wireless extensions, mobility, an error-free physical layer, and a service flow based QoS-defined services. This connectivity is expected to happen via the convergence layer of the IEEE 802.16e. Left to its own forces, the IEEE 801.16 standards could lead to a wide range of ways in which networks could be built by using the convergence layer.

If the broadband wireless networks are to develop in the manner the cellular mobile networks have developed, it is necessary that the functional entities involved in such networks are clearly defined as well as the reference points and protocols which they will use to connect. This is where the WiMAX Forum has stepped in where the IEEE standards had left off. The network working group of the WiMAX Forum has been responsible for the development of the architecture of the WiMAX networks, definition of the functional entities, and its reference points. These architectural definitions are important not only for a uniform implementation of the WiMAX networks themselves but also for the definitions of interfaces to external networks and applications. With the definition of the architecture and the characteristics of reference points (including protocol specifications), entities can work on individual components independently and still expect the entire network to work seamlessly. The network components such as radio access networks, gateways, connectivity routers, etc. may be sourced from different vendors if they conform to the specifications of the reference points.

In the earlier discussions in the book, we have been using various terms such as "base stations" or "access service networks" quite loosely without assigning any specific functions to them. The network working group of WiMAX has defined a number of functional entities and the interfaces between these entities from the point of view of functions and protocols. These interfaces are designated by "reference points" (R1, R2, R3, etc). Just to give an example, a connection (using WiMAX) between a mobile station and a base station (more accurately the access service network functional entity) takes place via a reference point called R1 (we will be discussing the reference points later in this chapter). Hence all the functions performed in the mobile station (or subscriber station in fixed WiMAX) such as ranging, session management, handover, public key management, QoS, and data transfer are defined under the R1 reference point. A mobile station manufacturer therefore needs to implement the R1 interface to be in compliance with the WiMAX networks. Such compliance can be certified by the WiMAX Forum.

The work of the network working group of the WiMAX Forum should therefore be seen as an additional step beyond specifying the initial certification profiles. The work of the NWG helps in defining and enabling formation not only of IP-based WiMAX networks as independent networks but also of their interfaces with other networks.

The network working group (NWG) specifications for mobile WiMAX are based on the IETF protocols as well as the 3GPP/3GPP2 architectures in order to have compatibility with the IP and mobile networks.

As we will see in this chapter, the WiMAX networks are designed to play a very important role in the evolution of next-generation networks (NGN) based on open protocols.

12.1 MOBILE WiMAX NETWORK ARCHITECTURE

The mobile WiMAX network architecture is, in fact, quite intuitive. At the lowest stratum, a WiMAX network consists of an access service network (ASN). An ASN is comprised of a number of base stations (BS) connected to an access network. The access service network connects to external networks via an access service network gateway (ASN GW).

The functions of the ASN are represented in Figure 12-1 and are comprised of a number of base stations, access networks, and access

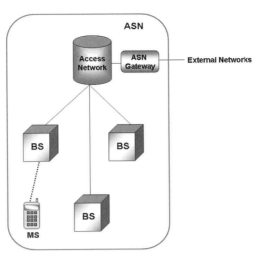

FIGURE 12-1 Access service network (ASN)—building block of a WiMAX network

gateways. These are as follows:

- Connection with the mobile station including establishing PHY and MAC layer connectivities
- Provide handover and roaming facilities within the ASN for mobile stations
- To provide AAA facilities for the user in conjunction with the home network of the user; the ASN provides the proxy AAA facilities
- To provide relay facilities between the ASN and the external networks

Functional Entities

In the access service network (ASN), shown in Figure 12-1, three functional entities have been defined:

- **The base station** connects to the MS using the WiMAX PHY air interface

  The base stations perform the functions of maintaining the air interface with the mobile station, providing the DHCP proxy and maintaining its status (idle or active). As the air interface is managed through the base station, it also provides for the uplink and downlink traffic scheduling and QoS enforcement.

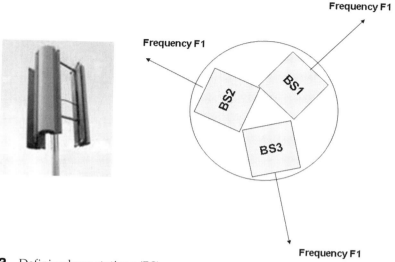

FIGURE 12-2   Defining base stations (BS)

- **The access service network gateway** (ASN-GW)
  The ASN gateway is the point where traffic from all base stations
  (and other ASNs in the domain) is aggregated for interface to
  external networks. (The ASN-GW is physically a router performing the layer 2 traffic aggregation.) As an aggregation point, it
  also performs additional functions such as QoS management,
  AAA functionality, etc. (Figure 12-3). The access network gateway may also have control functions for the base stations.
  Alternatively these functions can be embedded in the base stations. This depends on the network architecture profile and is discussed later in this chapter.

BASE STATIONS

The base stations in the above configuration are comprised of one radio frequency under the IEEE 802.16e air interface. Hence if a physical base station
is comprised of three sectors and three frequencies, conceptually, and from
the point of network architecture, the BS would be considered to be comprised of 9 base stations.

If a comparison was to be done between the WiMAX network architecture and that for a cellular network model such as GSM, the simi-
larities can be immediately observed. The ASN-GW serves the
functions which are achieved by the serving GPRS support node

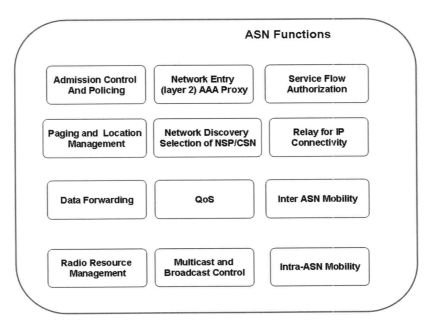

FIGURE 12-3 ASN functions

(SGSN) and the access network and its air interfaces are represented by the base station controllers (BSC) and base station transceivers (BST), respectively. However, as we shall see in the following discussion, the architecture of a WiMAX network is defined to be more open in building networks and has a greater level of functionalities in its network entities.

Building the WiMAX Network Beyond the ASN

The NWG has conceptualized a WiMAX network (Figure 12-4) and its application environment as being comprised of three distinct entities.

- **A network access provider (NAP)** is an entity that operates one or more access service networks (ASNs). Typically, a NAP is a WiMAX operator which operates access networks in one or more areas.
- **A network service provider (NSP)** is an entity which provides connectivity and services to network access providers. In effect, NAPs need only to connect to NSPs (one or more) and expect all services and applications to be delivered through these connections. The NSPs provide connectivity to NAPs via connectivity service nodes (CSN). NSPs would be responsible for providing mobility between their own nodes as well as nodes of other NSPs.

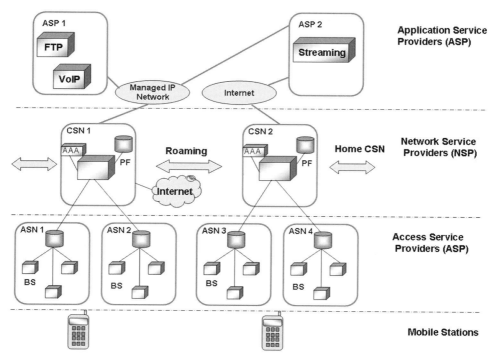

FIGURE 12-4   Network architecture of Mobile WiMAX

- **Applications service providers (ASPs)** which provide services such as HTTP, video streaming, file downloads, e-mail, etc. These services fall above the network layer in the protocol model.

Figure 12-4 exhibits one more "functional entity" of the WiMAX network architecture, i.e., the connectivity service network (CSN). As shown in the diagram, a CSN has AAA servers, policy functions (PF) for QoS, and provides connectivity to external networks such as a managed IP network or the public internet. It also provides the security and authentication framework through the AAA servers and the policy functions for each device, user, and service on the network. Being able to authenticate at multiple levels is a key feature of the WiMAX network architecture.

Features of WiMAX Network Architecture
Mobile WiMAX network architecture is characterized by some key features including:

- Both the core network and the radio access networks based on IP; protocols based on IEEE 802.16 and IETF

- Open interfaces characterized by fully-defined reference points
- Support of fixed network, nomadic, or mobile usage with full migration path to mobility
- A modular network architecture, which can grow based on usage requirements
- Integration into different types of IP and non-IP networks (e.g., ATM, TDM, and others)
- Network core architecture is not based on support of any particular service, i.e., voice, data, or video; it is a multi-service core network with QoS for each service and each connection
- The QoS is based on both policy functions (PF) and enforcement
- The network architecture is relatively "flat," which enables a WiMAX service to start with a single ASN; for this purpose the NWG has defined multiple ASN profiles
- Support of inter-networking with 3GPP, 3GPP2, WiFi, or wireline networks using IETF protocols.

12.2 MOBILITY MANAGEMENT

Mobile WiMAX networks are expected to provide mobility in a broadband wireless usage environment. This implies, for example, that if a user is using streaming video in the area of one base station and moves in to the range of another station, the IP connection should hand over smoothly to the next station. The same type of roaming and handoff is applicable for any other IP application, such as a VoIP call. The feature of imparting mobility to broadband wireless applications is unique and has been heralded in with Mobile WiMAX. What does this require from a network architecture viewpoint? As the IP connections are at the network layer, this implies that the entire IP connection, with all the connectivity attributes between the mobile user device and the application source, need to switch over to the new radio access station. This requires, first of all, that the PHY and MAC layer connections switch to the next radio access station. Second, the IP connection, which is defined at the network layer, should then recognize that the destination device now needs different connectivity parameters such as a different base station address or a different subnet itself. The first part, which is the switching of the PHY and MAC layer connections, is carried out by the Mobile WiMAX as it is defined up to the first two layers. The second part, which is the switching of the IP connection as the mobile moves from base station to base station, falls in the domain of the mobile IP. WiMAX networks are built using the IPV6 as the core

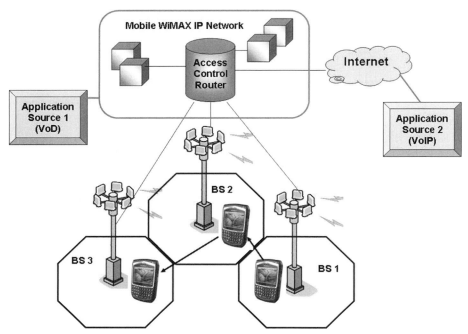

FIGURE 12-5   A mobile station (MS) roaming in a mobile WiMAX network

protocol. The mobile IPv6 (MIPv6) has built-in features to support
mobility. It maintains IP connectivity as the mobile station roams from
the range of one radio access station to another.

The scenario is represented in Figure 12-5, where a mobile device
roams from the area of coverage of BS 1 (Base Station 1) to BS 2 and then
on to BS 3. If the device is using two applications, say a VoIP service via
public internet and a VoD service from an IPTV (managed network)
provider, the handoff from BS 1 to BS 2 results in the MAC layer switching to BS 2 and finally to BS 3. The IP layer (Mobile IP) directs the connection to the new destinations, which denote the availability of the
mobile station. The mobility can be intra-ASN (i.e., where the mobile
station is within the area of the same ASN) or inter-ASN (i.e., where the
mobile station moves out of the range of one ASN to another ASN). In
the first case, the mobility can be managed by the ASN itself (termed
ASN-anchored mobility), while in the later case, it is the visited CSN
that needs to manage the mobility function (termed as the CSN-anchored
mobility). For further discussions, it is assumed that the mobility
needed is of the CSN-anchored type, which is the more general case.

MOBILITY MANAGEMENT THROUGH MOBILE IP

Mobile IP (MIP) is a commonly used protocol that is designed to provide seamless mobility across IP subnets (RFC 3344). It is implemented in two ways. In the first type of implementation, the mobile station (MS) has an MIP-client. The MIP client is responsible for obtaining the home address from the home agent (HA) of the home CSN or the visited CSN as it moves from the field area of one CSN to another.

In the second type of implementation called Proxy MIP, the MIP stack is run in the ASN as a proxy. The mobile station in this case only has the normal IP stack. All mobility functions are handled via the MIP proxy in the ASN, and the MS need not be aware of any change of IP address in the proxy.

The process of handover begins with the physical layer, which does the ranging with the radio stations in the range of the mobile. In this case, the mobile station switches the layers from BS 1 to BS 2 via any of the handover mechanisms (hard handover, fast base station switching, etc.). The PHY structure of the Mobile WiMAX is reproduced in Figure 12-6.

After the ranging is completed to the next radio station, the MAC layer is established with the new base station and the upper layer of Mobile IP detects the change in the physical locations and redirects the connection resulting in a seamless handover.

12.2.1 WiMAX Network Reference Model for Mobility

The mobility functions described so far included only the area within an ASN. The extension of mobility beyond the ASN is straightforward in the network reference model for Mobile WiMAX adapted by the NWG. The mobility function is managed through the CSNs, which provide the inter-ASN mobility management. The visited CSN thus provides the home agent functionality (HA) and AAA proxy while it connects with the home CSN for AAA authentication.

The connectivity service networks (CSNs), which are operated by network service providers can be thought of as major geographical area nodes such as those providing connectivity to ASNs in a city, for example Sydney. A Mobile WiMAX user who is based in Melbourne has the Melbourne CSN as its home CSN. If such a user travels to Sydney, the user now needs to register via the CSN at Sydney to his home CSN at

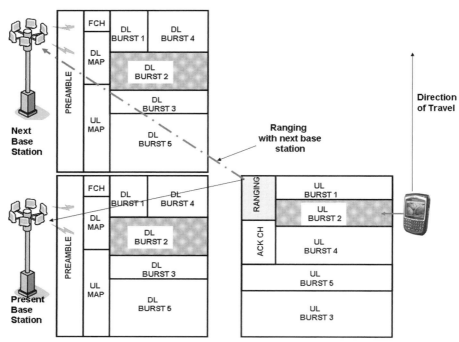

FIGURE 12-6   Ranging with next base station for handover

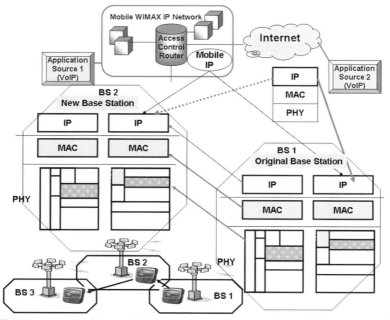

FIGURE 12-7   Handover in Mobile WiMAX results in Mobile IP establishing a seamless IP connection with next radio station

Melbourne. The functions which need to be performed by the CSNs are therefore quite evident. These are summarized as follows:

- To provide IP address to each mobile station in its coverage area and provide AAA proxy by doing the authentication with the home CSN.
- To provide inter-ASN mobility management [intra-ASN mobility management between base stations (BS) is provided by the ASNs]. For mobile IP which is needed for mobility, the CSNs provide the home agent functionality.
- To provide connectivity to other networks such as internet, WiFi, 3G-GSM or CDMA, DSL, or any other type of network. The connectivity also includes the access policy control for each type of network and support of necessary protocols.
- To provide inter-CSN tunneling to other CSNs which need to connect to their home CSNs using this CSN as a connectivity node.
- To provide for subscriber billing and administrative functions such as inter-CSN settlements.

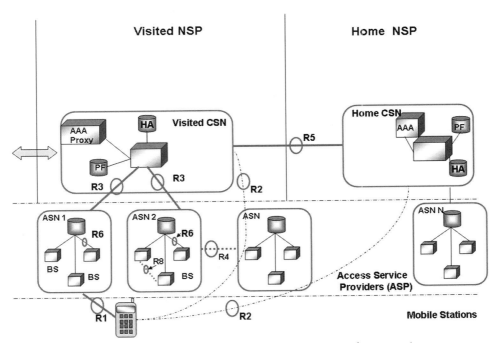

FIGURE 12-8 Network architecture of Mobile WiMAX showing reference points

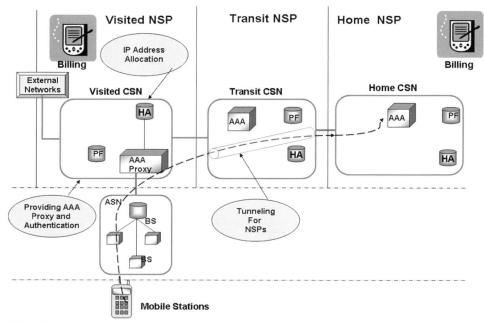

FIGURE 12-9 Functions of CSN

The network architecture of Mobile WiMAX as depicted in Figure 12-9 shows the building blocks of ASNs (provided by WiMAX access service providers), CSNs (operated by network service providers), and the definitions of reference points. Table 12-1 provides the functions of reference points.

12.3 ASN PROFILES

The NWG of the WiMAX Forum has defined three ASN profiles in Release 1 of the network working group. These profiles are called A, B, and C. These profiles have been specified in order to permit WiMAX network operators to avoid having to support each and every protocol and making the implementations more complex and expansive.

- **Profile A** uses a centralized control element, i.e., the ASN-GW. As there is only one ASN-GW in an ASN comprised of many base stations, profile A is a centralized model. The BS and the ASN-GW are supported on different platforms and connected via the R6 interface. In Profile A, The ASN-GW function includes the radio resource management function (RRM). This is analogous to the base station controller (BSC) or a radio network controller (RNC) of a cellular network.

TABLE 12-1

Functions of reference points in Mobile WiMAX network architecture

Reference Point	Location of Reference Point	Function
R1	Between MS and ASN	MS to BS radio air interface, protocols in the management plane (session management, AAA, QoS and Handover management)
R2	Between MS and CSN (or ASN-GW)	Authentication, authorization, IP host configuration, and mobility management functions
R3	Between ASN and CSN	AAA, policy enforcement, and mobility-management capabilities, authentication, authorization. Implements tunnel between ASN and CSN
R4	Between ASNs	Mobility management functions support across ASNs
R5	Between CSNs	Internetworking between home and visited networks (roaming across multiple NSPs)
R6	Between BS and ASN-gateway	Communication between BS and ASN GW as a part of bearer plane protocols. Support of IP tunnels for mobility (intra-ASN tunnels) and control plane signaling
R7	Between data and control planes in ASN gateway	Coordination functions between data and control planes
R8	Between BS and BS	Fast and seamless handover. The interface involves transfer of data between base stations for facilitating handover.

- **Profile B** is a distributed ASN solution with both the ASN-GW and base station (BS) functionalities implemented in a single platform. In Profile B, as the ASN GW functionality is embedded in the base station, external ASN-GW is not needed. Owing to this, the only open interfaces available are R3 (interface to CSN) and R4 (interface to another ASN). Because of this, Profile B does not require third-party interoperability within the WiMAX system.
- **Profile C** is similar to Profile A in having an ASN-GW as a central control element in an ASN. In Profile C, also, the BS and ASN GW are supported on different platforms connected with R6 interface. However, the difference in Profiles A and C lies in the fact that the RRM function is supported in the BS.

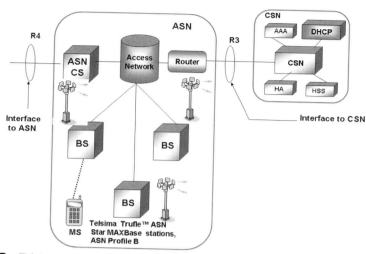

FIGURE 12-10   Telsima® Trufle™ Profile B implementation

The NWG has decided to support Profiles B and C in future as no specific advantage is attained in having a centralized RRM controller (as in Profile A) over Profile B.

Example of Profile B Implementation

There are many operators for whom mobility and roaming in and out of the home CSN or other CSNs is not a priority at the current stage of development of their networks. Such operators would like to serve the stationary users, nomadic users, or mobile users who do not need to roam back to the home CSNs while using services.

An example of such an implementation is the Telsima® Trufle™ ASN, which is based on the mobile WiMAX network architecture Profile B (see Figure 12-10). Operators using Trufle™ can target stationary and nomadic customers in the initial phases of development of the network. The Telsima ASN comprises of an ASN control system (ASN-CS) and StarMAX™ base stations. Telsima Starmax Trufle™ implementation can enable stationary services using the ASN-CS in the ASN. The data paths and the control paths are separated in this architecture. The data paths are entirely handled by the base stations. As the ASN-GW functions are embedded in the base stations, the router connecting to a CSN can be a commercial router for connectivity purposes alone. The solution is scalable and can interwork with Profile A or C implementations in other parts of the network. As the Trufle™ solution allows the use of commercial routers in the network, it results in lower cost and highly scalable implementations.

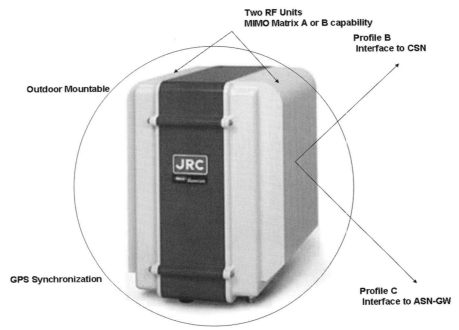

FIGURE 12-11 Japan Radio Company's mobile WiMAX base station NTF-291

The Trufle™ ASN can also be upgraded to an ASN gateway (ASN-GW) to a full fledged mobility solution when investments justify such a case. Trufle networks preserve the client IP address and maintain TCP/IP sessions without making any assumptions on the capability of mobile stations.

In general, Profile B implementations are characterized by compact self-contained base stations which interface directly to the CSN. In many cases, these base stations can be outdoor mountable such as Japan Radio Company's mobile WiMAX base station NTF-291. (The NTF-291 base station can also be switched to Profile C providing interface R6 to a centralized controller.)

Another implementation example of Profile B is the Navini Networks Ripwave™ base stations. These base stations have all the control functions embedded and do not need any external controllers.

Profile C Implementations
Many base stations are designed as ASN Profile C-compliant. These have their own radio resource management in the base station, but are designed to work with external ASN gateways forming base station networks within the ASN area.

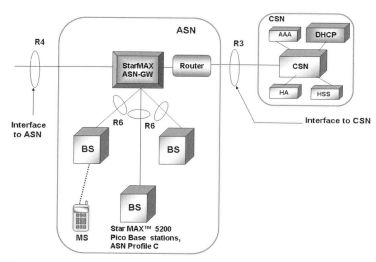

FIGURE 12-12   Telsima® StarMAX 5200™ Pico base stations operating with ASN Profile C

An example is the Telsima® StarMAX™ 5200 Pico base station. It has the following characteristics:

- Wave 2-compliant (IEEE 802.16e-2005)
- WiMAX Forum NWG ASN Profile C-compliant
- MIMO 2x2 A/B support
- Supporting VoIP, data, and video triple-play services
- Clocking solution for TDD sync
- S/W configurable bandwidth
- Variable uplink/downlink ratio
- Mobility management BSOH and MSHO
- 110 V/220 V AC power input
- 2.5 GHz, 3.3 GHz, and 3.5 GHz band support.

Telsima also has an ASN gateway product (StarMAX™ ASN-GW), which completes the ASN functionality of Profile C base stations connecting to ASN gateways (Figure 12-12).

12.4 MOBILE IP

When a mobile station moves from one base station to another, the mechanism of the Mobile WiMAX provides a physical as well as MAC layer connection via the new base station. This may be via an existing CSN or a new CSN. In order that an application which has been established over the network continues to view the connection as uninterrupted, all application-layer packets that are addressed to the mobile station should continue to get delivered with the same IP address.

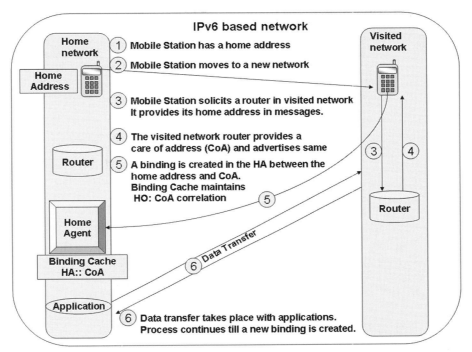

FIGURE 12-13 IP mobility with MIPv6

Mobile IP is the IETF solution, which is designed to keep the mobility of the receiver transparent to the application by being able to correlate any new IP address of the mobile station with the old IP address as known to the application. This ensures that a session established (e.g., for streaming) remains connected when the mobile station moves from one BS, ASN, or CSN to another one, thus providing IP mobility.

MIPv6: IP Mobility in IPv6 Networks

Providing IP mobility is simple in IPv6 core networks, which are characterized by a large address space. The IPv6 protocols have also been designed with mobility as an objective. MIPv6 is a lightweight protocol and keeps the control traffic to a minimum.

The process of roaming in IPv6 network takes place as follows:

- The mobile station, which is identified by an IP address in its home network, moves in to the area of a visited network. The IPv6 provides for neighbor discovery and router discovery where the devices can find the link layer information and maintain reachability. The mobile devices acquire an IP address via DHCPv6, which is the "care of address" (CoA) in the visited network. Address auto-reconfiguration is a built-in feature of IPv6.

- The CoA is conveyed to the home agent in the home network. This is done by the mobile device by sending a binding update message to the HA (this is acknowledged by a binding acknowledgement message). The home network now maintains a binding cache between the CoA and home address (HA). This enables the applications to continue to address the device by its home address IP while the routing happens to its destination as per CoA.
- Data transfer happens via optimized routes between the two networks.
- The process can continue until a new binding update is sent by the mobile station.

Three types of handovers are defined in MIPv6. These are the smooth handover, fast handover, and seamless handover. In smooth handover, the priority is in minimizing data loss, whereas in fast handover the latency in establishing a new connection is of prime importance. Seamless handover combines the features of the two to provide handovers with minimum latency and minimum data loss.

The IPv6 has a mechanism for providing QoS as well by two parameters, which can be used to route packets with appropriate flow management and priority labeling. For this purpose, the packet header contains a 20-bit flow label and an 8-bit traffic class indicator (TCI). The TCI is used by Diffserv to advise routing devices of the priority of routing of packets.

MIP in IPv4 Networks

At the current stage, the internet is largely comprised of IP4 networks, subnets, and routers. Hence, the Mobile IP needs to be implemented as an overlay protocol over the IPv4. The overlay is implemented by providing additional functional elements, which are responsible for achieving the functionalities required. These are as follows:

- An MIP client implemented in the mobile node (MN). AN MIP client is necessary as the IPv4 devices cannot do auto-address reconfiguration and send MIP messages to convey the CoA to the home agent.
- A foreign agent (FA) functionality is defined in the visited network (denoted as the correspondent network, CN). The FA maintains the correspondence between the home address HA and the CoA and interacts with the home agent (HA) to provide routing of packets to the MN.

When the MIP client and the FA are implemented in IPv4 networks, the sequence of actions in conveying the CoA is similar to the IPv6 networks. The process is as follows:

- When a mobile node (MN) migrates from its home network to a correspondent network, its presence is detected by location discovery protocols. The MN is assigned a new CoA address in the CN and it updates the HA with this information through an update message. This update is relayed by the FA.
- The HA now sends application packets by tunneling them to the FA.
- FA decapsulates the packets and delivers them to the MN.

In the reverse direction, the transport via FA is not required as the MN delivers them to the destination directly. No encapsulation of such packets is required. The routing of packets in one direction (say, from the application to the MN) can thus be different from the routing in the reverse direction.

It is possible to combine the functions of the FA and the MN in the MN itself. In this case, the MN handles all mobility-related functions on its own without any impact on the visited network.

It is evident from the discussions of Mobile IP in IPv6 and IPv4 networks that the mobility in MIPv4 networks is subject to some

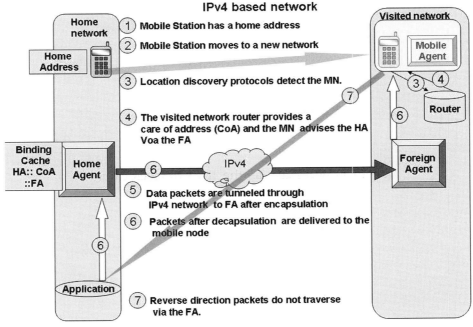

FIGURE 12-14 IP mobility with MIPv4

limitations. First, the mobile node needs to be given a permanent (publicly addressable) IP address in its home network and also in the visited network if the FA is collocated with the mobile agent in the MN. Second, the need to tunnel the packets (between the HA and the FA) hides their QoS header information, and the priorities intended for the packets in transmission may not be met. Third, the tunneling is a point-to-point process, and therefore multicasting as an application is not workable. Finally, the reverse paths may be different from forward paths, which may lead to inefficient routing.

12.5 INTERFACE TO OTHER NETWORKS

In the discussions so far, the situation that has been considered is one of roaming entirely within the WiMAX network. This is a simplistic representation of real-life scenarios. If the usage device is a cellular phone, for example, it will also connect to the CDMA or GSM network for voice, as well as other applications which are available via the mobile networks. Cellular networks already provide for the roaming and seamless operation of applications over their own networks. The networks have a GPRS core where internet services (such as a stream-ing server) are connected through a Gateway GPRS Support node (GGSN), whereas the services to the devices within the network are provided by the serving GPRS support node (SGSN).

Figure 12-15 shows the case of an IP streaming media server deliv-ering live streams to 2G networks or 3G networks (CDMA2000 or UMTS). The case of 3GPP or CDMA-evolved networks is similar.

If the objective was to use the cellular networks and the mobile WiMAX separately (which is entirely possible), then no additional

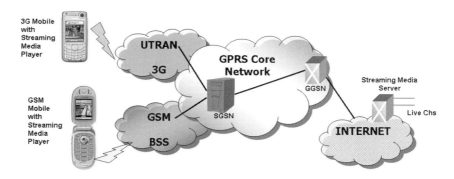

GGSN- Gateway GPRS Support Node
SGSN- Serving GPRS Support Node

FIGURE 12-15   GSM and 3G networks with internet access as an application; mobility is maintained by the core networks

components would be needed insofar as the network architecture is concerned.

The scenario of the mobile WiMAX and cellular networks being independent entities is neither desirable nor practical. In fact, roaming across networks with handover is already a reality with generic access network (GAN) or unlicensed mobile access (UMA), wherein handover is provided between 3G mobile networks and the WiFi 802.11b/g home networks. A user can thus reasonably expect to commence using an IP-based service such as a VoIP call or a video streaming when within a WiFi hotspot and have the session handed over to a WiMAX or a cellular network when moving out of the WiFi coverage area.

A common network architecture for inter-network roaming and handover with continuity of sessions and applications is therefore of paramount importance.

One of the elements of roaming and inter-network mobility is the user authentication and maintaining security of applications. Each of the networks has its own authentication protocols, and these need to be met before the handover is completed.

How do we achieve this architecture? Three issues are involved here. The first pertains to the addressing or numbering, the second to

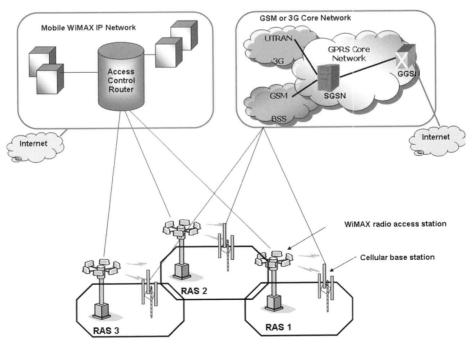

FIGURE 12-16 Usage scenario with Mobile WiMAX and cellular services being used as independent networks

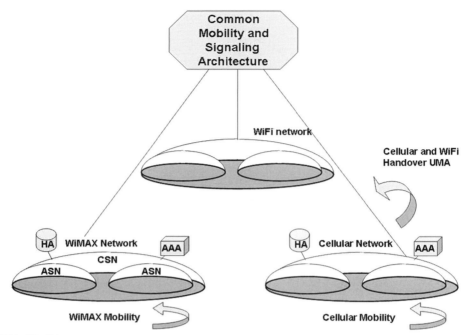

FIGURE 12-17   Internetwork mobility

the media formats, and the third is the authentication in each network. Cellular networks and public telephone at the present stage of evolution still retain the legacy circuit switched architecture. These are based on a public network numbering scheme as per ITU E.164. On the other hand, in IP networks, the addresses are in the user@host.domain format similar to those used for e-mail. Hence in order to interface legacy networks with IP-based networks, an addressing gateway is needed for address conversion and a media gateway to convert the formats used.

The third-generation partnership project (3GPP) has indeed recognized the need for such network interfaces and has come out with its architecture of IP Multimedia System (IMS) in the 3GPP Release 5. The interface-to-IP applications through IP networks (i.e., for VoIP) is via the IP multimedia system (IMS). For CDMA-based 3GPP2 networks, it is via the internet multimedia domain (IMD). The IMS is the core architecture used in cellular networks where interface to internet-based applications involving SIP-based signalling is required.

The long-term approach is to have an all-IP network, and this architecture is being defined by the ITU-T as the next-generation network (NGN). An all-IP network will provide seamless access to all devices and will be fully IP-based. This can only become a reality when all

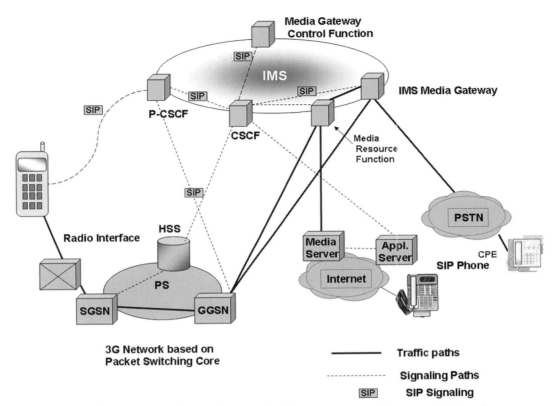

FIGURE 12-18 Internet multimedia system in 3G networks provides connectivity to legacy services

legacy networks based on TDM circuit-switched architectures are phased out. Until the above becomes a reality, however, the cellular networks have commenced using the IP multimedia system (IMS) (the architecture of which was released by 3GPP Release 5), as the architecture to connect the cellular applications with PSTN (circuit-switched networks with E.164 numbering scheme) and internet networks (IPv4 and IPv6).

The architecture of a 3G network operating with PSTN and internet applications based on the IMS is given in Figure 12-18.

The IMS in this configuration functions primarily as a signaling overlay. The calls are initiated (i.e., sessions initiated) by the call session control functions (CSCF). CSCF thus operates as a SIP server and is responsible for the call set-up, controlling the session and setting up the policies applicable for the call. The external devices to which calls are made receive such requests through the Proxy CSCF (P-CSCF).

The core-switching network for the 3G services is comprised of the following components:

- The home subscriber server (HSS) which is the main database for subscriber profiles and is used for subscriber authentication.
- The DNS system, which provides the look-up between the SIP addresses and the corresponding IP addresses and telephone numbers.
- The serving GPRS support node (SGSN) is the node that is currently serving the subscriber based on location.
- The gateway GPRS support node (GGSN) is the node which is connected to the external networks and through which the session of the subscriber is currently being handled.
- Media gateways, which convert between the data formats used on the 3G network and the external networks such as PSTN.

The architecture in the above figure gives connectivity to the IMS from three types of networks:

1. Cellular network (3G-GSM network)
2. Public internet (including legacy IPv4 networks)
3. The public-switched telephone network (PSTN).

The architecture can be generalized to include the WiMAX networks as well. In order to function within the framework of the architecture, the WiMAX networks need to support the IMS protocols. All the networks are connected by an IP core network (not internet). Such architecture provides inter-working between all services by virtue of the SIP-based call control functions, even though individual networks such as PSTN may follow their own numbering schemes, call set-up, and signaling mechanisms.

Figure 12-19 shows the architecture of IMS with the inclusion of the WiMAX networks. All the networks connect to the IMS via an IP core network, which remains the switching path for the actual traffic. The signaling is handled by the IMS.

In the IMS architecture given, the functions that have been indicated are as follows:

- All signaling is handled by the call session control function (CSCF), which functions as the SIP server.
- The P-CSCF functions as a proxy for receiving signaling requests from all devices such as cell phones, WiMAX user terminals, and SIP phones.

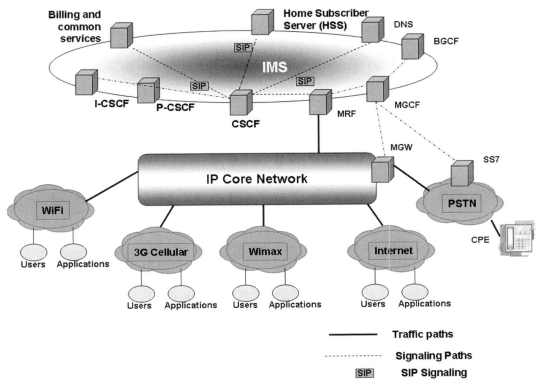

FIGURE 12-19 3GPP IMS architecture showing interfaces to different types of networks

- The I-CSCF functions as the processing point for the signaling requests received from networks.
- The breakout gateway control function serves to determine the network to which the PSTN connection requests should be directed.

12.5.1 Do WiMAX Networks Necessarily Need IMS?

IMS is essentially a session control mechanism with multiple application services defined in the service layer and a mechanism to establish sessions and convert media between different types of networks and protocols. It would be appropriate to consider the IMS as an anchor point of calls which are established using attributes defined in the services layer.

Do Mobile WiMAX networks necessarily need to work with IMS? The answer is no, if all the services which are provided in the Mobile WiMAX networks are built from scratch. WiMAX networks provide handoffs and roaming between base stations and ASNs and connect to the internet via a connectivity service network provider (CSN) operated by a network service provider (NSP). The CSNs today handle all the functions that are the domain of IMS such as session control, DHCP, home agent (HA), etc. The networks have their own AAA servers and maintain home location information.

However in real life, WiMAX and Mobile WiMAX networks will need to work with cellular mobile networks (with 3 billion plus users) using IMS-defined services and also legacy-fixed lines and WLAN networks. What about the signalling conversions? The IMS provides an excellent and ready-made architecture with well defined components and software with APIs to configure a network which provides flexibility and ready use of a host of application services. Hence, it is likely that as the Mobile WiMAX networks roll out they would use their own IMS implementations for service configuration and interface to the external world.

Examples of many implementations confirm this approach. For example, Motorola has rolled out a WiMAX network across major cities in Pakistan for Wateen Telecom. The network is intended for voice, internet, and data connectivity and uses IMS as its core architectural element.

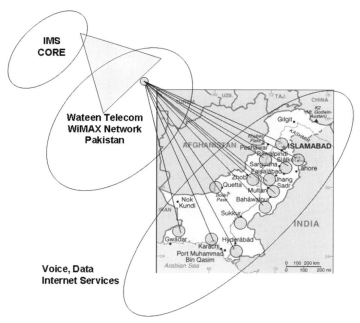

FIGURE 12-20   IMS is a key part of the IMS architecture in Wateen Telecom, Pakistan

12.6 GENERIC ACCESS NETWORK: 3GPP TS43.318

The use of voice and data services using WiFi or WLANS when in the coverage zone of a hotspot (including at home) has been on the increase. In order to facilitate this usage, the mobile operators have been working for the standardization of usage of unlicensed mobile access. This type of access, previously called generic access network (GAN) has now been formally standardized under the 3GPP, as well as ETSI. Before the availability of the dual-mode WiFi and cellular handsets, the tendency of the users was to use fixed-line infrastructure for services such as VoIP or video streaming when in the respective coverage areas. However, such usage did not provide continuity of applications or services. IMS is a flexible signaling overlay scheme which makes possible the usage of various IMS services over cellular or legacy networks. By having a standard whereby the mobile phones can switchover to the use of IP based access networks such as WiFi or WiMAX where coverage is available, the mobile operators can stop using independent networks for cost or speed advantages alone.

The UMA makes possible the provision of all IMS services, which are traditionally in the cellular domain over any IP-based network. The user traffic thus stays on the cellular network providing revenue-enhancing opportunity to operators.

The use of UMA is equally applicable to a WiMAX network, which is also a standards-based IP core network. The cellular mobile services can thus be extended over the fixed WiMAX or mobile WiMAX when the user is in such coverage area and uses dual- or triple-mode handsets permitting the use of WiMAX and cellular services.

The traffic in this type of network passes via the cellular mobile core network, as the UMA is a 3GPP initiative for using the mobile core network and IMS to provide services to multimode devices when in the range of diverse types of service providers.

The success of the UMA access has led to an increasing interest in the use of pico cells in homes and offices. The cells can be enabled for a range of services using the mobile core network with the use of UMA.

12.6.1 Example of UMA Access in WiMAX and Cellular 3G networks

An example of a system which can enable a 3G network for UMA access is a UMA controller from Kineto Wireless™ Inc. The Kineto UMA controller ™ enables a WiMAX or WiFi network for IMS based services through a 3GPP core network. The controller functions in conjunction with a UMA client on the mobile handsets. The UMA controller integrates with the mobile network (MSC for voice and

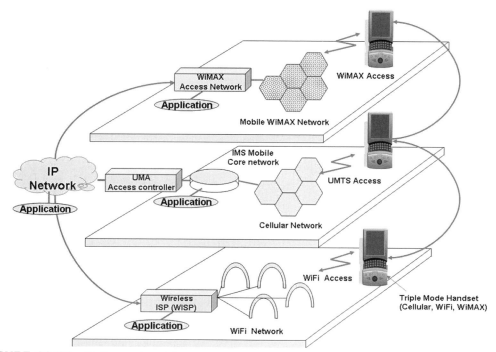

FIGURE 12-21 Unlicensed mobile access

SGSN for packet data) and extends these to IP environments comprised of WLANs or WiMAX systems. It can support a media gateway as an optional element using H.248 or MGCP to interface to TDM-based voice systems and interface to VoIP in IP networks.

A UMA client on the handsets carries out the authentication with the 802.11 b/g WiFi network or 802.16e WiMAX network and enables the dual-mode use of the handset. A number of UMA enabled handsets are already available in the market for WiFi access such as Nokia 6136, 6086 Motorola A910, Samsung T709, LG CL400, HP iPAQ510, etc. A UMA-enabled mobile has the WiFi or WiMAX software stacks in addition to the cellular stacks together with access mode selection and IMS user interface.

A UMA-enabled IP network, such as the WiMAX network in the Figure 12-21 can also be used to provide standard analog telephone type services by the use of a terminal adapter (TA).

UMA from T-Mobile USA

T-Mobile, USA had launched HotSpot@Home™ service in the Seattle area based on UMA. Later the service was extended to the entire U.S. network of T-Mobile. The service allows a user to make calls via WiFi

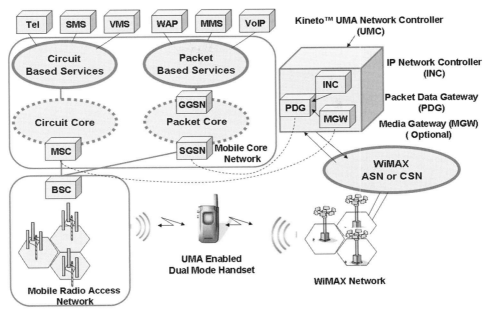

FIGURE 12-22 Enabling UMA with Kineto™ UMC

hotspots when in the coverage area in addition to the cellular network. In addition, homes can be enabled through the WiFi access
point being supplied by T-Mobile. The service can be used with WiFi-
enabled UMA handsets such as Nokia 6086 and Samsung T709. The
service in 2007 was launched at a flat rate of $19.99 per month. The
technology used is Kineto's UMC, which extends the T-Mobile GSM
to WiFi hotspots (over 8500 public hotspots). The dual-mode phone,
when in the range of a WiFi hotspot, recognizes the same and stores
the information. It also does authentication through the hot spot and
the call is routed over the WiFi network. This type of seamless working can overcome the problem of weak signals in indoor
locations,which are otherwise well covered for WiFi.

A similar service has been launched by Cincinnati Bell under the
name of "Home Run."

12.7 NETWORK ARCHITECTURE FOR PRACTICAL BROADCAST APPLICATIONS

12.7.1 Setting up Multicast over Wireless Networks

Multicasting is a well-known technology for delivering common content such as video, audio, software updates, etc. to a large number of
users simultaneously without excessive use of bandwidth as is the

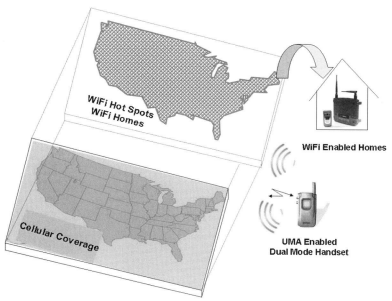

FIGURE 12-23 A conceptual representation of UMA-enabled services by T-Mobile™ in the United States

case of Unicast sessions. An example of such a service would be video streaming, where all authenticated clients would receive a 256 Kbps multicast stream. Such a service would need only 256 Kbps to be reserved as a resource if multicasting is employed.

Multicasting over the public internet presents many challenges related to reservation of resources and maintaining QoS. Multicast can, however, be easily achieved over dedicated wireline or wireless networks. In these networks backbones can be built based on IP/MPLS and the routers can be enabled for multicast using the IGMP protocols. Examples of such dedicated networks can include managed IP networks, 3GPP or 3GPP2 mobile networks, and WiMAX networks.

The 3G networks already have well-defined technologies, which the broadcasters can deploy for multicasting of content. [These technologies, i.e., 3GPP-broadcast and multicast service (MBMS) and 3GPP2-MCBCS have been discussed in Chapter 13.] Essentially the 3G networks provide a multicast service by setting up a common radio channel, which is suitable for carriage of multicast traffic. Multicast services are then provided over the overlay radio channel without any impact on the normal voice channels. Authorized users can obtain the broadcast access key and session information by exchange of messages with the multicast controller.

Multicasting for WiMAX networks is supported by the WiMAX network architecture based on the NWG recommendations.

SECTION

MOBILE BROADCASTING TECHNOLOGIES

13

BROADCASTING MOBILE MULTIMEDIA USING WiMAX-NETWORK ARCHITECTURES

"It takes all the running you can do to keep in the same place. If you want to get somewhere else, you must run at least twice as fast as that," said the Queen.

—*Lewis Carroll (Charles Lutwidge Dodgson)*
Alice in Wonderland (1865)

The mobile world today presents a new ecosystem, sometimes referred to in the industry as Mobile 2.0. Though there are no strict definitions for the term, nor any industry standards, the term is generally interpreted to include a collaborative and structured ecosystem in which mobile devices operate and bring the Web 2.0 environment to the mobile world. The Mobile 2.0 ecosystem is an interconnected environment which enables a mobile user to migrate to a higher layer of services than just HTTP browsing or mail. It includes the use of the network as a platform and services which make communities operate, such as instant messaging (IM), blogging, and Presence, which enable online commerce such as Amazon and eBay, location-based services, and the use of entertainment services, including music and TV using portals or on-demand services among other Mobile 2.0 features.

13.1 THE MOBILE ECOSYSTEM

How does the mobile ecosystem operate and what is in store for new devices which intend to be a part of the ecosystem, albeit with a different mode of access such as Mobile WiMAX? We take a look at these issues,

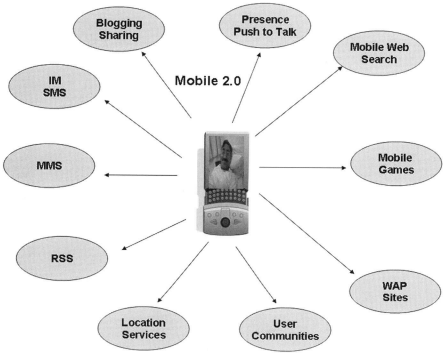

FIGURE 13-1   A representation of the Mobile 2.0 ecosystem

which relate to the architecture of services provision in the mobile environment, in this chapter.

The mobile world is today almost exclusively composed of mobile networks belonging to the GSM, 3G-UMTS, or CDMA technologies. Hence, it is a natural impression that all services represented in the mobile ecosystem are provided by the mobile networks themselves. However, while discussing the mobile ecosystem it is necessary to recall that many of the services, such as conversational voice calls, web access, electronic commerce, banking, etc., originate or terminate in networks that are external to the mobile networks themselves. How are these services then integrated? The answer is simple. One of the ways in which this integration is done, particularly in case of 3G networks, is by the IP Multimedia System (IMS), a 3GPP technology. This will continue to be the case until we migrate to the next-generation networks (NGN), which do away with the concept of different networks such as fixed, wireless, or mobile and have a common core based on IP and common signaling architecture but different access types.

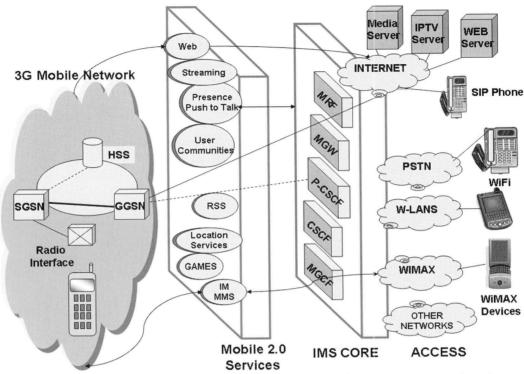

FIGURE 13-2 An IMS core provides services which can be used across many networks using signaling control functions and media gateways

The mobile WiMAX networks, have advantages over the cellular mobile networks in some aspects. These networks are already based on the IP technologies, and access to resources on the internet is a core part of their architecture. However, as they grow and begin to target existing 3G and new mobile devices, they will eventually be dealing with the IMS to reach the mobile 2.0 ecosystem which has become an indispensable part of today's usage paradigm.

Figure 13-2 provides a conceptual depiction of the network environment in which mobile services are provided today. An IMS core network provides the signaling control functions (i.e., conversion of SIP-based signaling to PSTN (Q.931) (IP addresses, etc.) and media gateway conversion to carry out the format conversions which enable connectivity between diverse networks.

13.1.1 IMS and Google Talk™

IMS network helps in the implementation of services such as instant messaging and Presence when the access architecture involves multiple

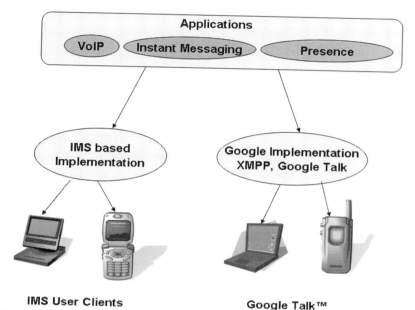

IMS User Clients   **Google Talk™**

FIGURE 13-3 Alternative methodologies for implementing advanced services such as VoIP, IM, and Presence

networks. For example, the users may be on a WiFi network, a 3G network, internet, or even PSTN and may like to be reachable through the Presence feature. However, it is important to note that IMS is not the only way to either provide services such as instant messaging (IM) or Presence or to interconnect diverse networks. Google, for example, uses Google Talk™ as the application and client for instant messaging, Presence, and VoIP.

Google uses an Open Protocol XMPP (Extensible Messaging and Presence Protocol) for managing information such as Presence (e.g., buddy lists and online status) and extensive instant messaging (IM). The XMPP is based on open standards and XML. It is based on draft IETF standards (RFC 3920-XMPP Core and RFC 3921 instant messaging and Presence). It is essentially a protocol for streaming of XML elements.

Google uses a proprietary protocol called Jingle for VoIP and multimedia calls. Jingle is an extension to the XMPP protocol, to allow for peer-to-peer (p2p) signaling for multimedia interactions such as voice or video. VoIP calls including multimedia information can be established by using the Google Talk™ client.

In this chapter, we will be looking at both the technologies, i.e., based on the use of IMS as an overlay network or the use of alternative protocols as in Google Talk.

13.2 UNDERSTANDING IMS

IP Multimedia System (IMS) is a generic architecture model for offering VoIP and multimedia services over a diverse range of networks. IMS is a 3GPP and 3GPP2 standard and is almost universally followed in the implementation of all mobile networks where the use of IMS services such as push to talk, instant messaging, or VoIP using SIP are required. The use of IMS is, however, not limited to use only on the cellular mobile networks. The standard supports multiple access networks including wireline networks, wireless LANS, GSM, 3G-UMTS, or CDMA 2000 networks. The 3GPP2 which evolved the multimedia domain (MMD) has also based its work on the 3GPP IMS structure. IMS has also been adopted by other standards bodies such as ETSI and TISPAN (Telecoms & Internet converged Services & Protocols for Advanced Networks). TISPAN has provided the specifications for DSL access, and work on cable access is in progress in cooperation with Cablelabs®. IMS as per Releases 6 and 7 of the 3GPP includes support of WLANs, WiMAX, DSL, Broadband Cable, and enterprise level T1/E1 (1.5/2 Mbps) links. This sets the stage for a multiple access, multiple services network to be offered by using the IMS.

Origin of IMS

The origin of IMS lay in the need for integrating the general packet radio services (GPRS) networks, which were packet-based to the internet, and in general provide support for voice and multimedia services in the cellular domain. The IMS was unveiled in Release 5 of the 3GPP with Release 6 adding support for wireless networks and Release 7 for fixed networks. The interface functions of IMS include signaling and media format conversions, among others. The IMS is today characterized by a range of services which are fully defined at the application level. The examples of such services are push-to-talk over cellular, instant messaging and VoIP; additional services such as video calls, streaming, etc., can be defined at the application level. IMS makes the applications operate across multiple networks seamlessly, irrespective of the media formats and signaling systems or addressing architectures which are used on these networks by performing appropriate conversions.

13.2.1 IMS Architecture

The IMS has a simple architecture. It is defined with three layers:

1. **Service Layer:** The Service Layer hosts application servers and content servers which provide various value-added services to

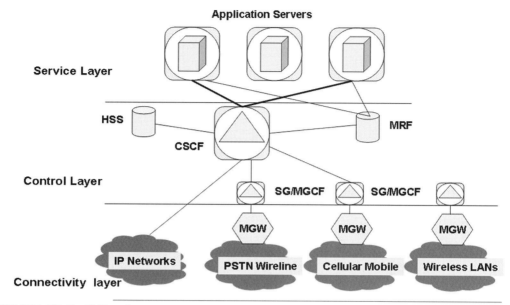

FIGURE 13-4   IMS architecture

the users. The application servers in an IMS implementation will also include servers, for example, for providing IMS-defined services, such as instant messaging, location-based services, and Presence. VoIP and multimedia over IP (MMoIP) are generic applications of an IMS service layer.

2. **Control Layer:** The control layer has controllers for performing functions of session set-up, session management (monitoring, billing), and session release. It also has border gateways for operation with multiple types of networks. These gateways perform the functions of signaling gateways (SG) as well as Media gateway control functions (MGCF) which enable connectivity to different types of media gateways (MG) based on the connected network characteristics. There is thus an abstraction in the types of networks with which an IMS system can interface with by providing an appropriate type of gateway. The control layer also contains the home subscriber server (HSS) and the media resource function (MRF).

The session set-up functions are handled by a functional unit called call session control function (CSCF). This unit is, in fact, the SIP server handling the SIP-based signaling.

The entire IMS structure is based on internet standards (IETF protocols) and can form an overlay services and convergence

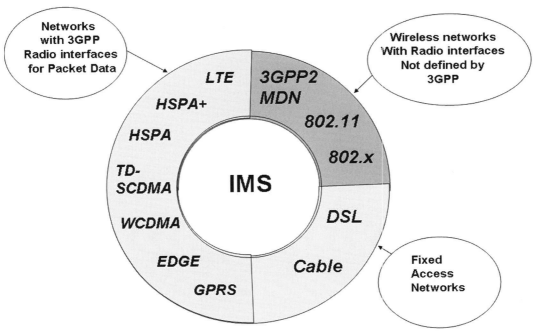

FIGURE 13-5 IMS access network types

structure for any network including GPRS, DSL, WLANs or UMTS, or WiMAX.

3. **Connectivity Layer:** Finally the connections to the network are provided by the routers, switches, or other physical devices which form components of the connectivity layer.

IMS forms a core which connects many types of networks. This convergence is provided by including the signaling and media format conversion for each network in the appropriate media gateways and media resource functions.

13.2.2 An Example of IMS for UMTS and PSTN Connectivity

It is interesting to remove some abstraction from the model and see an example of how an IMS system would integrate the UMTS, PSTN, and the internet. The media gateway in this case converts the voice from G.711 (PCM) to packets suitable for use on the UMTS network. A PSTN network works on the ITU-T signaling system 7 ISDN user part (SS7-ISDN-UP), which is converted to SIP-based signaling in the IMS by the media control function. The media control function interacts with the media gateway using the H.248 (Megaco) protocol.

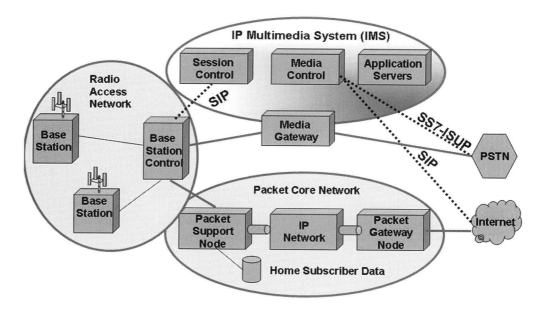

····· **Signal Paths**

FIGURE 13-6   Example of IMS connecting a mobile network with PSTN and internet

13.2.3 IMS Architecture: A Service Enabler

The IMS service layer is essentially a service enabler. It is true that it supports IMS predefined services, such as instant messaging and Presence, but the services which are used today as a part of fixed mobile convergence (FMC) do go much beyond these. In general, an IMS system is available with APIs which help service creation, provide a service execution environment, and an abstraction layer, which connects to the underlying control and connectivity layers.

The service enablers in the IMS architecture represent building blocks for service creation. These building blocks are generic and can be reused for different applications. Examples of some service enablers are Presence and Group List Management.

Presence

The Presence service enabler ushers in the concept of groups as distinct from person-to-person communications. The service enablers permit the entire group of users to know the status of the members of the group (i.e., on which communication network and media are they available or not available) and the means of contact with them. The service enabler has various attributes which permit the users to set

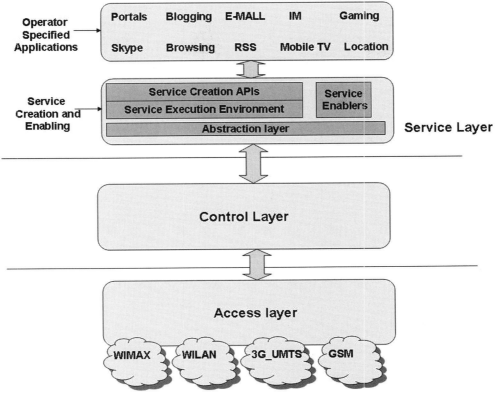

FIGURE 13-7 Service creation and enabling in IMS

parameters on whether the users (some, all, or none) should be able to see their location and means of access.

Group List Management
The Group List Management function permits the users to create groups and further define group wide definitions of services deployed. This includes public or private groups, access control lists, and personal buddy groups.

Being a service enabler means that an IMS system can be used to provide existing and operator designed services. Some examples are:

- Mobile VPNs: These can be created by combining corporate and public networks with different access types such as mobile, fixed line, or wireless.
- Multimedia Group Broadcast: The Group Management and Presence features allow a multimedia group broadcast, which may be one to many or multilateral, and include video, audio, or

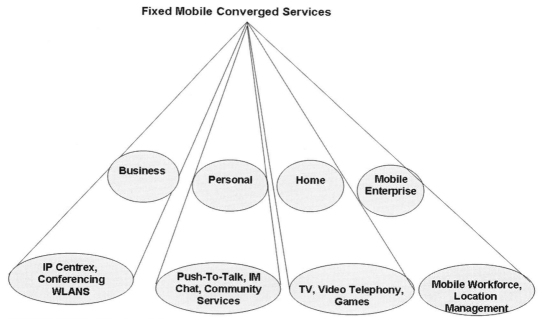

FIGURE 13-8 Fixed mobile converged services environment

multimedia elements, such as videos or presentations. This feature, for example, can allow users available only on mobile devices to participate in a webcast or a web conference.

- Mobile Video Phone Service: This would allow two-way calls with video, one-to-many transmission. In addition, the service may permit the performance of other functions via active on one call.
- Mobile Gaming: Advance mobile games can be created by using the group management and Presence information and integrating with existing gaming devices and gaming servers.

Service Authentication and Access

Service authentication today depends on the access network used, and each network performs its own authentication of the user. These sometimes take the form of sign-on services. In an IMS architecture, the authentication across multiple networks is seamless once the user is handled in an IMS core through the CSCF. All other network authentications can then be set up via the SIP server using the authentication information already available.

This feature can also allow operators providing multiple services such as mobile cellular, fixed line, WiFi, or WiMAX to interconnect with each other with a single relationship based on IMS instead of service-to-service or network-to-network interconnections. With the growing range of services it is becoming burdensome for operators and difficult for users to move from network to network (WiFi hot spots for example). In an IMS environment, interconnection takes place between the IMS systems of different operators rather than network-wise or service-wise interconnections. Once an interconnect is established, it can be valid for all services. The customer is also seen as one entity irrespective of the service used, such as streaming TV, VoD, phone call, or web browsing, instead of getting a separate bill for each service and each network.

Access Aware Networks and Service Control

True network convergence implies not only merely signaling and media format conversions but the network's being aware of the service characteristics of the network the user is on and the device being used for communication. A video call, for example, has very different characteristics from a VoIP call, for example, or a gaming application. Services can be characterized by bandwidth, latency, processing power requirements, and display attributes. An IMS network can provide access-aware control and service logic for multimedia services. It can also distinguish between device types for delivery of service with appropriate attributes such as to a laptop, PDA, cellphone, or a pure SIP phone.

13.2.4 Example of Using IMS to Enable Services over a WiMAX Network: ONEMAX

ONEMAX is a broadband service provider in Latin America (Dominion Republic). It has rolled out a Mobile WiMAX network based on 802.16e with an objective to provide services such as VoIP, internet, and multimedia over the 802.16e network. The implementation is being done using an IMS architecture based on 3GPP Release 7. All the components of the IMS system, i.e., call session and call control function, home subscriber server, signaling gateways, and media gateway for PSTN, are included. The WiMAX equipment for the IEEE 802.16e services is being provided by Alcatel Lucent. The IMS components are supplied by Veraz networks (ControlSwitch™ user services core and I-Gate 4000 series media gateways).

Example of IMS Service on a Mobile Network

An example of how the service capabilities of networks can be enhanced by the use of IMS has been demonstrated by AT&T via its Video Share application. The application makes use of the AT&T IMS-based network and allows users to exchange videos during conversational calls.

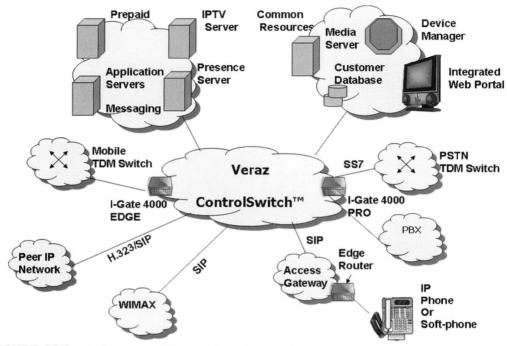

FIGURE 13-9   Architecture of Veraz™ ControlSwitch-based IMS system

The service requires the use of a Video Share-capable handset. This handset has an IMS client for handling the application via the IMS system.

IMS for Cable Networks

Operators targeting cable-based triple-play services involving the use of voice, video, data links, and broadband internet need not configure all the services individually with separate service provisioning and billing arrangements as is the case today. Instead, a common IMS platform becomes the base for providing all services with common application servers and billing. Moreover, these services can interoperate over different networks such as VoIP via internet WiFi or WiMAX. The quality of service (QoS) can also be controlled via IMS, separately for different IMS applications. This ensures that the users in the network get a consistent service usage experience.

It also means that the traditional business and residential customers who are familiar with one-way broadcast services, can enjoy group-based media services and personalized content besides the broadband internet and voice capabilities extended by an integrated IMS network.

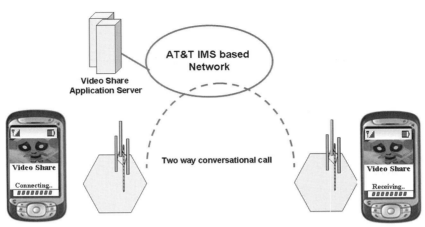

FIGURE 13-10   Example of an IMS application: AT&T Video Share™

13.3 IPTV AND IMS

IPTV is normally offered in a quadruple-play environment, i.e., with voice, data, and broadband-internet also being offered on the same networks, which are used to provide IPTV services. Hence, the same logic of offering all services as an integrated offering under an IMS umbrella is applicable to IPTV as well. However, the main advantages of offering IPTV under the IMS include offering enhanced services (such as group-based push-to-talk or Presence) with QoS assurance and having a single "sign on" for all services and a common billing arrangement. If the operator has a multi-access network such as WiMAX, cable delivery, WiFi internet, or mobile TV, etc., the subscribers can sign on to all the modes of access for a single service. For example, a VoIP call or a TV program can be received by the user on a cell phone or a WiMAX mobile station or a PC instead of the home DVR.

The provision of IPTV services with IMS requires a customer STB to have an IMS client, which also needs to reside in other devices, which are intended for use on the network, such as PDAs or laptops. IMS will allow users to access their personal files (address book, calendar, buddy lists) and web content (web-based news and entertainment subscriptions and broadcast services) using any IP-based device and with a single sign-on.

Interactive services are possible with IMS, as the user can respond back to a program using a mobile device rather than a set-top box, can upload pictures and share them in the community, and can send instant messages, which can appear on the TV screen, for example, through the broadcast station.

FIGURE 13-11   IPTV provided via IMS can be an interactive, multi-service experience

A demonstration of IPTV over a WiMAX network was carried out by Nortel in 2006 where the users could watch IPTV over a WiMAX connection at 4 Mbps and at the same time share pictures, use click and call capability, and make VoIP calls using IMS.

In a multi-service environment, the IMS QoS-aware functions can determine the allocable bandwidth for each type of service that the customer is using. As WiMAX is also a QoS-based network these QoS policies of the IMS can be effectively implemented. The sustained bit rates and latency required for the service flows can be assured by the IMS and the WiMAX systems. For example a unicast VoD connection requires a constant bandwidth from the VoD server to the customer STB (constant bit rate QoS). As the users begin new services such as mail, chat, or voice, the QoS parameters are adjusted appropriately and more bandwidth may be allocated in a WiMAX system or a DOC-SIS based cable system. In case of excessive demand which cannot be supported by the access network, there would be denial of service rather than degradation of all services. Using IMS it is possible to deliver services such as HDTV if sufficient bandwidth is available in the access network.

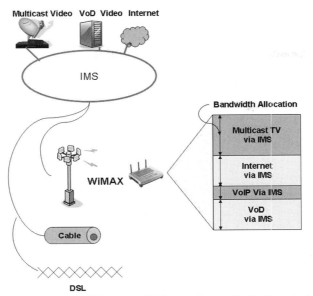

FIGURE 13-12   IPTV via IMS can deliver multiple services with QoS control

13.4 DELIVERING MULTIMEDIA CONTENT TO PORTABLE DEVICES

When an IMS system is used as a core solution for session control and IMS-based application services, an IMS/SIP client is required in the receiver to interact with the signaling system and application servers. IMS-based services, such as OMA-compliant instant messaging (IM), Video Share, push-to-talk over cellular (PoC), and 3GPP-compliant voice over IP (VoIP) with voice call continuity (VCC), etc. would require a corresponding application client or agent to correspond with its counterpart application server in the IMS system. The client functions include a graphical user interface (GUI), routing, service discovery, and service logic.

13.4.1 IMS Clients

Typically an IMS client will reside "over" the operating system of the mobile device such as Windows Mobile or Symbian and complement the protocol stacks available in the phone to complete the IMS required protocols. Some of the protocols required to be supported are RTP/RTCP stack, SIP Stack, SDP, and any IMS-specific software.

As these clients reside on the mobile devices, they would use the OS features available. For example, for mobile handsets with Java J2ME support (e.g., Symbian), the IMS client would be comprised of J2ME

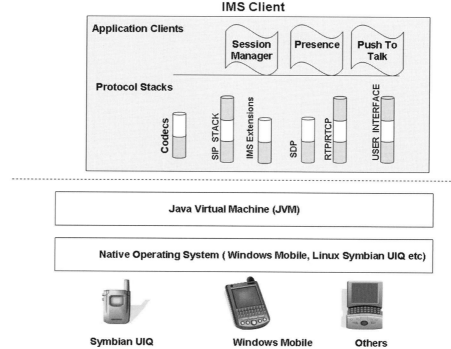

FIGURE 13-13 IMS agent functionality

TABLE 13-1

Java-based components for IMS clients

Function	JSR
IMS Service	IMS Services API (JSR 281)
SIP (For CDC)	JAIN SIP Lite (JSR 125)
SIP (For CLDC)	SIP API for J2ME (JSR 180)
Mobile Media	Mobile Media API (JSR 135)
XML	J2ME XML API (JSR 280)
Presence/Instant Messaging	Presence (JSR 186), Instant messaging (JSR 187)
User Interface	Mobile user interface customization API (JSR 258)
Security	Security and Trust Services API (JSR 177)

applets which can operate on the Java virtual machine (JVM). Java already has APIs JSRs, which handle the different components of IMS services and Protocol stacks.

Major IMS manufacturers provide an IMS client platform, as well as a development platform for applications. For example, Ericsson provides an IMS client platform (ICP), which is aligned with JSR 281 and provides the platform operators tools for services development in wireline and wireless environments. Ericsson IMS platforms are widely used worldwide, including in the Vodafone network spanning many countries.

13.4.2 Examples of Client Devices for IMS

PCTEL® Roaming Client VE

PCTEL provides a roaming client-voice enabled (VE) for IMS. The PCTEL clients support multiple network types of WiMAX, WiBRO, WiFi, and 3G-GSM- and CDMA-based networks. The solution from PCTEL has the ability to link applications to the mobile user, providing seamless connectivity over multiple networks such as WiMAX, WiFi, and cellular.

The multimode PCTEL WiMAX client meets full requirements of IEEE 802.1x access, including EAP security and authentication, Radius-based authentication for WiFi networks, policy management, etc. It also has over the air provisioning (OTAP) through its central configuration server. In addition to the clients, PCTEL provides a complete range of WiMAX products as well.

Ecrio® Inc. IMS Client

Another example of client platform for IMS is by Ecrio, Inc. The client platform supports multiple network types such as WiMAX, WiFi, GPRS, EDGE, CDMA, UMTS, etc. and can be ported on a range of operating systems including:

- Symbian
- LINUX
- Windows Mobile v5.0, PocketPC
- BREW
- RTOS (Feature Phones).

The client platform provides APIs to platform operators and software developers for deployment of advanced IMS applications, which can operate in multiple network domains. Supporting features such as codecs and media negotiation, IPv4 and IPv6, and authentication (MD5 and AKA), it complies with 3GPP IMS specifications and provides a 3GPP TS 24.229 V7.1.0-compliant IMS client framework.

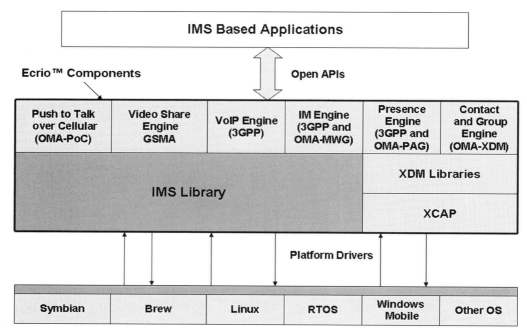

FIGURE 13-14   Example of an IMS client framework from Ecrio® Inc. (Figure courtesy Ecrio Inc., USA)

The IMS client platform from Ecrio has been used in many IMS-based networks. An example is the NTT DoCoMo in Japan, where it is used for push-to-talk over cellular services on the FOMA network. The support for these services comes through the IMS clients used in the handsets, e.g., FOMA 902i.

13.5 PLANNING A WiMAX MULTIMEDIA COMMUNICATIONS AND BROADCAST SYSTEM BASED ON IMS

Summarizing the discussions in this chapter, which have dwelled on the merits of the IMS as a convergence tool in a multimodal world, the use of an IMS-based convergence ecosystem comprised of an IMS overlay network and IMS clients presents an attractive option to operators for providing multimedia services. WiMAX operators, when they commence operations, need to address all voice, non-voice, and multimedia services, as well as target the existing base of users on fixed and mobile networks. Users need to be provided flexibility so that the devices they are being offered for WiMAX are not network-specific but will also operate in WiFi networks and mobile networks and use wireline broadband. Moreover, the authentications and roaming need to happen automatically and the services must be usable in a uniform manner irrespective of access network type.

The following are important points which the operators and the users of IMS-based services need to ensure:

1. The IMS system selected should present an ecosystem of the IMS core and IMS clients, which can support all existing networks and services, as well as be suitable for targeting new applications such as video calls to fixed-line calls to maximize revenue opportunities.
2. The IMS clients should be implementable in PCs, set-top boxes, and home network gateways.
3. The operators should be able to remotely, over the air, upload data and upgrade the IMS system and clients for new applications and enhancements.
4. The service operation tools should be able to provide seamless services across all categories of user devices as well as networks. This can become a value proposition for customers in using new services. Corporates, for example, should be able to deliver multimedia content to a range of devices, connected or mobile, and deliver the same user experience.
5. Operators should be able to sign up customers for all services such as voice, VoIP, broadband internet, video streaming, VoD, and media downloads and provide a common billing. This will require that the IMS system provide facilities for managing and controlling subscriber based traffic by application type and to be able to provide billing records which depend on the traffic type as well as the access type (e.g., a billing record of a VoD can be different on a mobile as compared to a home DVR). The operator should be able to offer them roaming, as well as change in access modes (e.g., cellular to WiMAX), without the user having to reauthenticate itself on any other third party network. This helps keep the revenues on the operator network.
6. The IMS clients should support customer interface personalization and an attractive user interface to distinguish the services provided from ordinary mobile network services.

13.6 GOOGLE PROTOCOLS

Google is engaged in providing an ever-increasing sphere of services and applications. These already include the Google search engines for web, images, video, document and photo sharing, web directories, Google mobile, Google groups, Google Earth, Google documents and presentations, etc. With Google being the largest-used web service across the globe, the services provided already create an ecosystem, which can be used in personal as well as office applications. It is likely to lead to an increasing demand and availability of clients for such services on desktops, mobile devices, and home networks. A careful consideration of the Google protocols with an objective of enabling Google services on mobile devices is, therefore, very important to network operators and service providers.

13.6.1 Google Instant Messaging and Presence

Google instant messaging and Presence protocols are based on the use of Extensible Messaging and Presence Protocol (XMPP). The XMPP protocols which have now been standardized by the IETF were earlier referred to as the "Jabber" protocols under which name the original project had commenced in 1998. The current standardization work on the XMPP protocols is handled by the XMPP Standards foundation (which still uses Jabber as its official logo!). Jabber protocols are open and based on the use of XML. A Jabber network is based on Jabber servers in which users have accounts. The servers are aware of the status of the user at all times (i.e., "Presence"). The Jabber network is a distributed network, i.e., there is no central server which has all the users registered in it. The users are registered in their respective domains.

All messages are sent from user to a Jabber server and onward to the addressed user. The user accounts have the format username@domain.com (the Jabber ID or JID) where the domain is a valid domain of the user, reflected by a DNS address. Users may be available by multiple clients such as username@domain.com/mobile and may indicate the priority of the clients via which the messages can be received. The messages go to the Jabber server where the user is registered and are delivered via the highest priority client based on Presence information. All the messages are sent in the form of XML data, i.e., in fully structured format. The messages can have different content types reflected by appropriate MIME fields.

The job of handling messages to the Jabber servers is handled by the Jabber clients (now called the XMPP clients or Google Talk clients). The servers are permanently connected to the users (i.e., clients) and hence the messages are always delivered instantly.

Jabber networks have gateways to other networks such as e-mail or SMS/MMS, and messages to external users can also be delivered without any action by the users of Jabber clients. External gateways interface to the internet world using standard mail, HTTP, and SIP protocols.

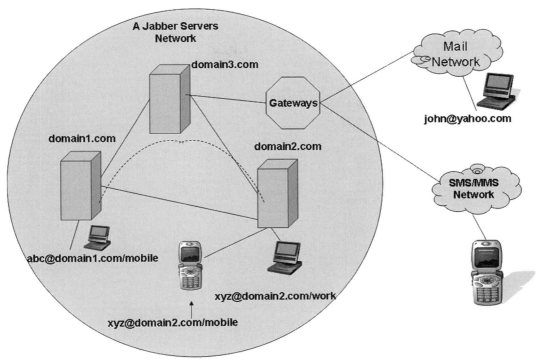

FIGURE 13-15   Jabber (XMPP) Instant Messaging and Presence network used in Google

Figure 13.15 shows the instant messaging and Presence network used in Google. A user "abc" registered in domain1 as abc@domain1.com wishes to send a message to another user "xyz" in domain2.com. The message can be sent using the Jabber servers domain1 and domain2 as the clients are permanently connected to a specified port on the Jabber servers. The local Jabber server knows the Presence of the user, i.e., on a mobile or at work in this example, and delivers the message with appropriate priority as set by the user. Messages to external e-mail addresses are delivered by their e-mail addresses. Users can set priority levels from 0 to 127, with higher numbers denoting higher priority. For example, when at work, the user may set the desktop client at priority 2, mobile client at priority 1 and home client at priority 0. The Presence of the user is disclosed only to those entities that are permitted by the user.

13.6.2 Google Talk™

Google's approach to VoIP services is led by its Google Talk software and client. It is also available as a Google Talk gadget with all clients pre-downloaded.

FIGURE 13-16   The Google Talk™ screen (picture courtesy Google Inc.)

Google Talk is used to collectively refer to its VoIP, IM, and Presence services as the Google Talk client also includes the IM and Presence features. Google has been basing its protocols for multimedia communications on XML schema. The XMPP protocols which are based on streaming of XML information form the basis of its IM and Presence services. The VoIP protocols are however based on proprietary technology. Google Talk protocol was released in 2005.

13.6.3 Google APIs

Google provides a number of APIs which allow networks to connect to Google or for users to use Google services. The examples of some of the APIs are:

- AdWords API: management of Ad words account with Google
- Google Calendar: APIs and events
- Google Checkout API: for secure check of online transactions
- Google Mashup Editor: for quick writing of website code
- Google maps API: for embedding Google maps in web pages
- Google AJAX search API: for placing Google search on web pages

- Google Web Toolkit: for writing AJAX applications
- Google Gears: for off line working of web applications
- Google Gadgets: writing applications for Google home page and desktop
- Google KML: sharing content with Google Earth™, Maps, and Maps for Mobile

Google APIs are based on the use of XML. Google's other protocols such as Google Data APIs (called "GData") are also based on the use of XML. Syndication of Google content, for example, is based on GData APIs.

13.7 HOW CAN OPERATORS IMPLEMENT XMPP-BASED NETWORK ARCHITECTURES?

It is possible for operators to implement network architectures which are based on XMPP and base the service offerings on the IM and Presence features which are supported by these networks. A number of commercial solutions and platforms are available for implementing the Jabber networks.

13.7.1 Jabber® XCP

An example is the Jabber Extensible Communications platform (Jabber XCP™ platform) offered by Jabber Inc., USA. The solution is comprised of a Jabber core platform. Users can download free Jabber clients and use advanced video, audio, and text applications which incorporate the features of IM and Presence. It provides the users personalized interfaces, file sharing during calls, and multiplayer games. The platform is interoperable with other platforms using SIP, XMPP, and instant messaging and Presence (IMPS) services as defined by OMA and used in 3GPP-IMS systems.

While the Jabber XCP is used in many platforms worldwide one of the latest implementations is the British Telecom 21st century network program. (BT 21CN). The BT 21CN is a replacement of the legacy PSTN networks by an IP-based network core. By using the XMPP technology provided by Jabber XCP, a range of instant messaging, Presence, and group-based services with flexibility of end device use (mobile, wireless, WiMAX, or workstation), location, and media formats (video calls, text chat, media transfers, etc.) is made available to the users.

Jabber XCP is also used in a number of new installations where the networks are being enabled for community-based services, IM, and multimedia communications which are not supported in existing networks.

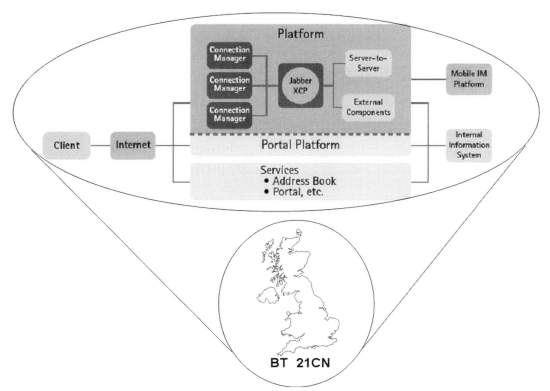

FIGURE 13-17   Jabber XCP core used in BT 21CN for enabling advanced IM, Presence, and communication services (Picture courtesy of Jabber Inc.)

13.7.2 Open Presence Network (OPN): Adobe

An Open Presence network framework is now provided by Adobe (after it acquired Antepo Inc.) and has become a part of the Adobe Acrobat software series. With this acquisition the Presence, IM, and VoIP platforms developed by Antepo have now become part of the Adobe family.

OPN is a platform for IM and Presence, which can be implemented in enterprises or operator networks. The network is based on XMPP (Jabber) protocols and has both the server and client components. The server component can be installed on Windows, Linux, or Solaris systems. It has components for directory and database integration, external network gateways, and configuring services such as GTalk. It provides connection with clients, which can interact with the OPN network, i.e., iChat, GAIM (a multiprotocol IM client), Exodus (a Jabber Client), Trillion (a multiprotocol multimedia chat client), etc.

14

MOBILE TV TECHNOLOGIES:
A STRATEGIC OVERVIEW

Television's perfect. You turn a few knobs . . . and lean back and drain your mind of all thought. You don't have to concentrate. You don't have to react. You don't have to remember. You don't miss your brain because you don't need it.

—*Thornton Chandler, writer (1888–1959)*

14.1 INTRODUCTION: MOBILE TV SERVICES

The large base of mobile users, increasing capabilities in handsets and revenue opportunities of multimedia services have been leading to a strong drive by operators to provide TV and multimedia services to mobiles. These services began initially as video "clip" streaming services on GPRS and EDGE networks and grew into full-fledged live TV streaming services on 3G networks such as 3G-UMTS and CDMA-2000. The traditional broadcasters, also wishing to target the base of mobile phones, adopted standards for terrestrial DTV services which had been modified to cater to the special requirements of mobile TV.

What are these requirements? The requirements of any technology which can support transmission of mobile TV are:

- Transmission in formats ideally suited for mobile TV devices, e.g., QCIF, CIF, or QVGA resolution with high-efficiency coding
- Low power consumption technology
- Stable reception, even in outdoor or indoor environment, mobility
- Clear picture quality despite severe loss of signals caused by fading and multi-path effects
- Mobility at speeds of up to 250 Km per hour, or more
- Ability to receive over large areas while traveling

Work on development of new technologies (or modifications of existing technologies) in order to cater to the specific requirements of mobile TV services took place in different fora. The result was a range of different standards based on satellite and terrestrial technologies. The new technologies not only provided for broadcast or multicast of content to mobile phones but also provided for improved transmission resilience and low power consumption. The 3G networks, where mobile TV launched as a unicast service placed severe demands on network resources, also moved on to multicast technologies such as MBMS and higher-speed networks, such as HSPA.

The diverse technologies which came into existence to meet these requirements are discussed in this chapter.

14.2 A BRIEF OVERVIEW OF BROADCASTING TECHNOLOGIES FOR MOBILE TV AND MULTIMEDIA

Mobile TV, video on demand, and media downloads are expected to be some of the major applications of WiMAX networks along VoIP and broadband connectivity services. This is because of the capabilities of WiMAX networks to provide multicast and broadcast services (MBS) and high-speed connectivity at relatively low cost because of better spectral efficiencies. The WiMAX networks are also attractive as they cut across technologies, which today constitute the divergent world of mobile TV. We now look at some of these technologies, which are required to provide mobile TV.

Mobile TV, based on today's technologies, can be provided by using one of three modes of delivery:

- Via a satellite, using high-power spot beams to directly reach mobile phones. Standards for satellite-based services include DMB-S (Korea), DVB-SH (Europe), ISDB-S (Japan), and STiMi (China).
- Via terrestrial broadcasting similar to broadcasting for terrestrial TV. The services in this category are provided using formats such as DVB-H, DMB-T, MediaFLO, and ISDB-T (Japan).
- Via cellular mobile networks (3G-UMTS or CDMA) using 3GPP-specified technologies such as streaming MBMS or MCBCS.

WiMAX now adds a fourth new mode of delivery via broadband wireless MAN networks. As the mobile WiMAX networks are essentially bidirectional, the mobile TV services provided via these networks can be on a unicast or multicast basis.

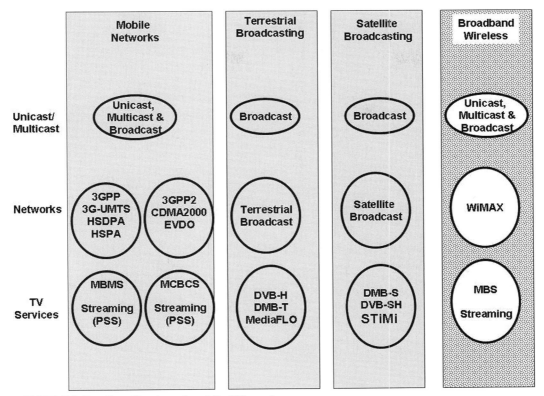

FIGURE 14-1 Classification of mobile TV services

The mobile TV services also show a significant geographical variation in terms of the standards used, even though a large number of countries in Asia and Europe have opted for the use of the DVB-H networks.

14.3 MOBILE TV SERVICES BASED ON CELLULAR MOBILE NETWORKS

14.3.1 3G Networks for Mobile Broadcasting

3G networks under the IMT2000 framework were primarily designed to provide high user bit rates for mobile customers. 3G-UMTS provides circuit-switched connections up to 384 Kbps and packet-switched connections up to 2 Mbps. This is achieved by using 5 MHz carriers, improved radio interfaces, and core architectures. The CDMA2000 networks, i.e., CDMA-3XRTT, also have similar data rate capabilities using 3 × 1.25 MHz carriers.

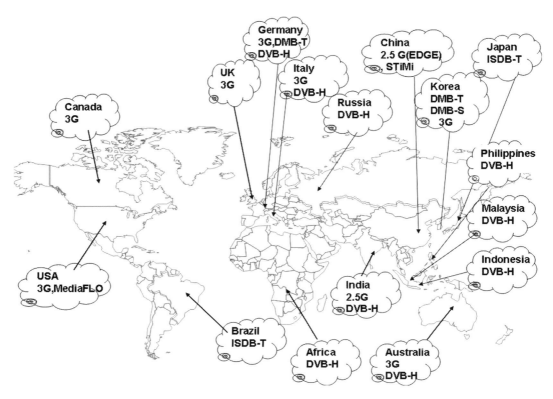

FIGURE 14-2   Geographical distribution of mobile TV technologies (the term 3G is used to include 3G UMTS, CDMA2000, as well as evolution technologies such as HSPA and EVDO)

The GSM-evolved 3G networks and CDMA networks constitute two independent branches of growth, which provide opportunities to provide mobile services:

- CDMA (CDMA2000) technologies
  - 2G: CDMA (IS-95A, IS-95B)
  - 2.5G: 1xRTT
  - 3G 3xRTT
  - 3G: EV-DO
  - Enhanced 3G: EV-DO & EV-DO Rev A and B
- GSM-based technologies
  - 2G: GSM
  - 2.5G/"2.5G+": GSM/GPRS/EDGE
  - 3G: W-CDMA (UMTS)
  - 3G MBMS
  - Enhanced 3G (3.5G): HSDPA

14.3.2 Technology for Mobile TV on 3G Networks

Video services over mobile networks (including Live TV) are provided by streaming the video and audio over the networks in a manner very similar to streaming over the internet. There are certain differences, however, in the way in which video is streamed over the mobile networks (as against the internet), which essentially relates to the characteristics of the mobile networks.

Streaming as a method of transferring video, audio files, or live data has the advantage that the user need not await the full file download and can commence viewing the content while receiving the data. However, as the experience with video streaming over the internet has shown, the streaming service quality is subject to sustained rates of data transfer over the network. Hence, the quality of streamed video and the number of users which can use such services depend on the underlying mobile network.

Mobile TV streaming via the 3G networks is governed by the 3GPP standards termed as 3GPP–PSS (Packet-Switched Streaming Service). The basic purpose of the specifications for the streaming service is that there should be uniformity in:

- Definition of video and audio formats to be handled
- Definition of coding standards
- Definition of call set-up procedures for the streaming service
- Definition of protocols for the streaming service
- QoS issues
- Digital rights management for the streamed services

The 3GPP-PSS services have evolved from a simple packet streaming service as in Release 4 of the 3GPP-PSS specifications (2001) to more advanced services while maintaining backward compatibility. Release 5 of the PSS has introduced the concept of the user agent profile which can signal to the server its capabilities in terms of the number of channels of audio, the media types supported, bits per pixel, and the screen size during session initiation. Release 5 has also added new media types including Synthetic Audio (MIDI), Subtitles (time stamped text), and Vector graphics. The PSS Release 6 (2004) has added a number of new features for reliable streaming, progressive download, QoS feedback to the server, and most importantly digital rights management (DRM) as per 3GPP-TS 22.242 . New codec types, e.g., MPEG-4/AVC or H.264 and Windows Media 9, have also been recommended.

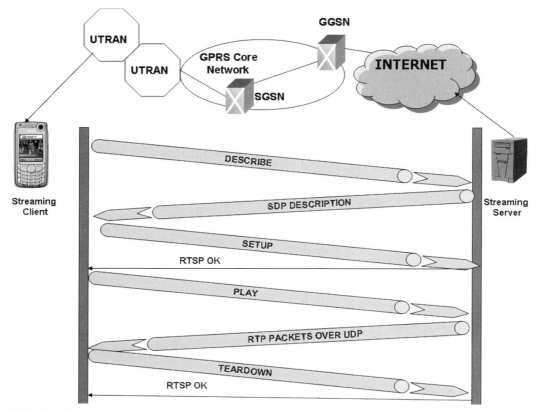

FIGURE 14-3 Streaming session set-up in 3GPP-PSS

14.3.3 Networks

Mobile TV services over 3G networks are today being widely offered across Europe, the United States, and Asia. MobiTV™ is an example of integrated mobile TV services offered via multiple cellular operators in the Americas. Over 100 channels of mobile TV, 50 radio channels, and 25 channels of digital XM radio can be streamed on their mobiles by the customers (as of 2007).

14.3.4 HSDPA

A rapid rise in the usage of 3G networks for video and multimedia has led a large number of operators to target HSDPA upgrades. HSDPA is a feature added in Release 5 of the 3GPP specifications. HSDPA technology enables a 3G-UMTS network for higher data rates. This is done by:

- Introducing a new high-speed downlink shared channel (HS-DSCH). The channel is characterized by the use of adaptive

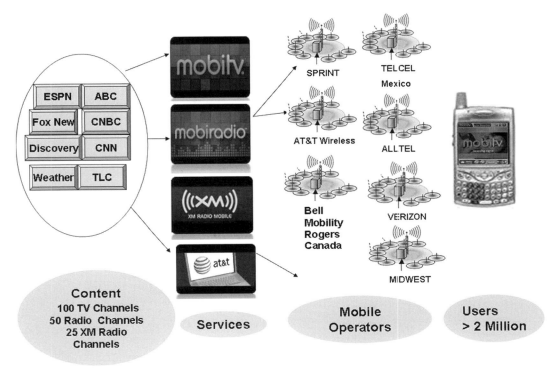

FIGURE 14.4   MobiTV (images courtesy MobiTV)

modulation and coding with higher density modulation schemes up to 16 QAM.

- A high-speed shared control channel (SH-SCCH) for fast monitoring of radio condition quality of all users . The channel quality indicator (CQI) parameter is transmitted by all users every 2 ms. The channel quality determines what type of adaptive coding and modulation can be applied for each user to maximize the data rates. The system thus works on a feedback mechanism and conserves resources by not transmitting in a mode which will not be receivable due to error conditions by a particular receiver.
- The MAC-level functionality is moved to the base station. In this architecture, the MAC layer also provides for a fast automatic retransmission of errored frames by using a hybrid ARQ mechanism.

With these enhancements, the downlink speeds for DSCH channel can be 10 Mbps (total shared among the users). However lab tests and theoretical predictions suggest the rates can be as high as 14.4 Mbps. Of course, the maximum data rate falls as the users move outwards in the

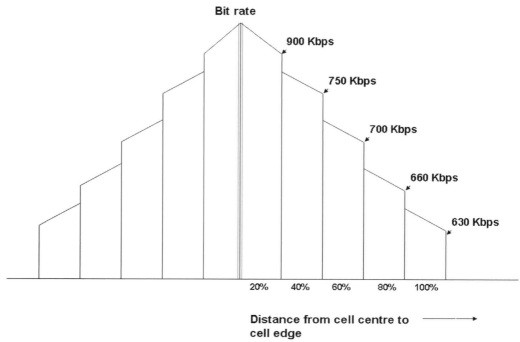

FIGURE 14-5   Typical bit rates per user in an HSDPA network with 10 users

cell. For example, with 10 users in a cell area, the bandwidth available to a user near the cell edge can fall to approximately 650 Kbps.

14.3.5 HSUPA

HSDPA only addresses higher bit rates in the downlink direction. In order to also address the uplink data rates, an uplink capability was added to provide up to 5.76 Mbps data rates. This is done by minor changes in the PHY and MAC layers. The latency of transmission was also reduced by using shorter frame sizes.

The HSDPA and HSUPA together are referred to as HSPA.

14.3.6 EV-DO

The evolution in CDMA-based networks toward higher data rates were heralded by the EV-DO (Evolution Data Optimized) technologies, a standard under the 3GPP2 forum. EV-DO uses multilevel adaptive modulation (modulation used is QPSK, 8-PSK, and 16QAM).

The 1xEV-DO (EVDO REV A) uses a single carrier of 1.25 MHz for data services and can provide average data rates of 3.1/1.8 Mbps as downlink/uplink burst rates leading to total data rates of 4.9 Mbps. Its rollout was quick and widespread by operators in 2006 and 2007.

EV-DO Rev B is a multi-carrier version of Rev A and with three carriers supports total data rates of 14.7 Mbps. Rev B networks have started rolling out in 2007. EV-DO networks have the flexibility to support both user- and application-level quality of service (QoS). Applications such as VoIP (voice over IP) can be allocated priority using application-level QoS. This helps applications, which are delay-sensitive services, to work well even in high-usage environments. User-level QoS allows the operators to offer premium services such as mobile TV. The 1xEV-DO packet scheduling, combined with Diff-Serv-based QoS mechanisms, can enable QoS within the entire wireless network.

All major 3G-enabled services have become available on EV-DO networks as well. For example, in 2007, GoTV® network was offering its premium on-demand channels for $4.99 per month for 3G phones and $5.99 per month for EV-DO phones.

14.4 MOBILE TV SERVICES BASED ON TERRESTRIAL BROADCASTING

Terrestrial broadcast networks for TV are in the midst of a major transformation. In most countries, the migration of networks from analog broadcasting (NTSC or PAL) to digital broadcasting (ATSC, DVB-T, or ISDB-S) is in full swing. By 2008 the United States, and by 2011 most of Europe, would have completed the process of migration to digital broadcasting. The broadcasting standards are country-specific. DVB-T is a digital video broadcasting (DVB) standard and is used in most of Europe and many countries in Asia and Africa. ATSC is the primary standard for transmission in the United States, Canada, Taiwan, Korea, etc. and ISDB-T is used in Japan. ATSC is based on 8 VSB modulation of a single carrier and is thus subject to the highest intersymbol interference in a NLOS environment. DVB-T is based on the use of multiple carriers, e.g., 2 K or 8 K carriers in the case of DVB-T. ISDB-T is also multi-carrier and consists of 13 segments, which are transmitted independently and each segment or a group of segments may carry a single service.

Standards organizations responsible for digital terrestrial broadcasting standards thought it expedient to also include TV broadcasting to mobiles as a part of the digital terrestrial broadcasting standards. This process was facilitated by the structure of the standards such as DVB-T which is comprised of a transport stream carrying many elementary streams each representing a video, data, or audio service.

14.4.1 DVB-H

The DVB-T standards were enhanced with additional features suitable for carrying television signals to a handheld, and the new modified standards were renamed DVB- Handheld (DVB-H) standards. They did this by modifying the transmission technique so that the data is transmitted in bursts for a particular channel to conserve battery power of the mobile. They also added additional forward error correction (FEC) and modulation techniques to take care of the handheld environment. DVB-H technology has been put to trial at over 200 locations and many DVB-H networks today carry commercial services. The spectrum for DVB-H still remains an issue in many countries as the regulators allocate the available spectrum to pave the way for Digitalization of the Terrestrial Broadcast Services. DVB-H was standardized by the DVB and the ETSI under EN 302 304 in November 2004.

A DVB-H Transmission System

Figure 14-6 shows a typical DVB-H transmission system in which the same transport stream is used for carrying both the SDTV programs (encoded in MPEG-2) and mobile TV programs (encoded in H.264/AVC). The SDTV-encoded streams are delivered to the DVB-T/DVB-H modulator as ASI low-priority streams. The channels meant for mobile TV are encoded as H.264 and are connected by an IP switch to an IP encapsulator, which then combines all the video and audio services, as well as the PSI and SI signals and EPG data, into IP frames. The IP encapsulator also provides for channel data to be organized into time slices so that the receiver can remain active only during the times for which the data for the actively selected channel is expected to be on-air.

For mobile TV, a more robust FEC coding is also applied in the IP encapsulator to ensure delivery of signals to the mobiles characterized by low antenna gains and widely varying signal strengths. The additional FEC applied helps operate in an environment characterized by higher error rates.

The output of the IP encapsulator, which is in ASI format, is then modulated by a COFDM modulator with 4 K (or 8 K) carriers. The COFDM modulation provides the necessary resilience against selective fading and other propagation conditions. The DVB-T standard provides for 2 K or 8 K carriers in the COFDM modulation. The 4 K mode has been envisaged for use in DVB-H, as 2 K carriers would not give adequate protection against frequency selective fading and also provide for a smaller cell size owing to the guard interval requirement for single frequency networks (SFNs). At the same time the 8 K carrier mode has

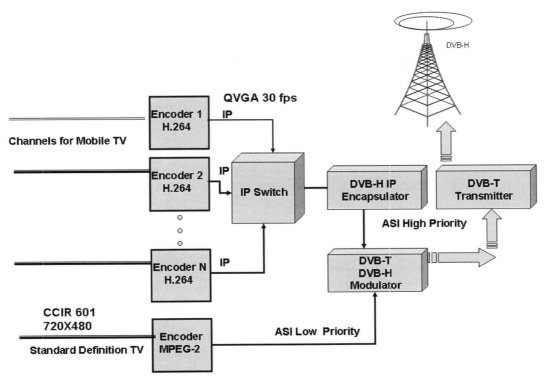

FIGURE 14-6   A DVB-H mobile TV transmission system

the carriers placed too close in frequency for the Doppler shifts to be significant for moving receivers. Hence the new mode of 4 K carriers has been incorporated as part of DVB-H standards. The modulation used for the carriers can be QPSK, 16 QAM, or 64 QAM.

The above example is that of a DVB-H shared network. However, it can also operate as a dedicated network, i.e., operating only DVB-H services.

DVB-H Networks

The DVB-H standard provides for COFDM modulation, which is suitable for SFNs. The system uses GPS-based time clocks and time stamping to ensure that all the transmitters in a given area can operate maintaining time synchronism, which is needed for SFNs. Depending on the area required to be covered, the DVB-H systems may be engineered with SFNs or may need multi-frequency networks.

There are two components to a SFN. The first is a cell which essentially comprises of a single DVB-H transmitter and a number of repeaters

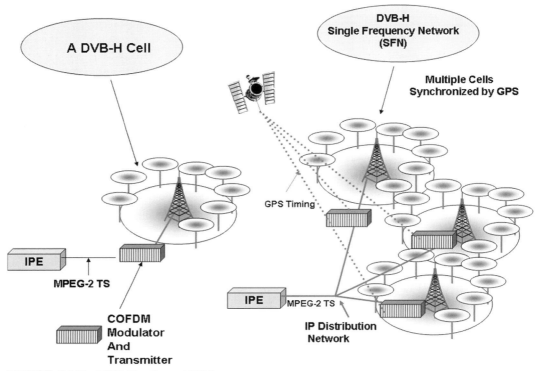

FIGURE 14-7 DVB-H cells and SFNs

serving an area of, say, 15–20 Km. Because of the signal transmission delay between a transmitter and the repeaters, the above topology cannot be extended beyond a certain range as the time delay in reception from the main transmitter will result in the re-transmitted signal not being in phase with the main transmitter.

The second component is the grouping of several cells using a common timing source into a SFN. Larger areas (e.g., a city or around 50 Km radius) can be covered by using a SFN. The SFN is comprised of a number of DVB-H cells, each with a transmitter and a number of repeaters. The transmitters receive the signal in the form of an MPEG-2 transmit stream, which originates from the IPE (IP encapsulator). An IP network is used to distribute the signal to all the transmitters in a given area. All the transmitter sites thus receive the same signal which is time stamped by the GPS-based clock (Figure 14-7).

Figure 14-8 shows typical coverage of a city for DVB-H and DVB-T transmissions.

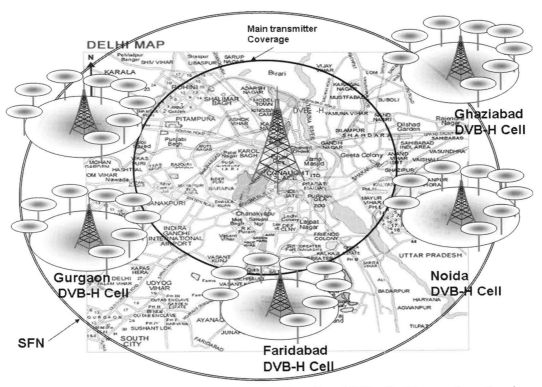

FIGURE 14-8 Conceptual coverage in a region with radius of 35 Km [in this case, the national capital region (NCR), Delhi]

DVB-H Implementation Profiles

DVB-H transmission involves the use of a "transmission security" or conditional access (CA) system. There are two broadly different implementation profiles of DVB-H, depending on the manner in which the transmission security is implemented.

The first approach is that broadcast security be provided by traditional CA systems suitably modified for mobile environment. This leads to handsets, which are proprietary to specific networks. Alternatively the CA system can be SIM-based and can be changed in different networks. The use of CA systems has the support of the Digital Video Broadcasting group (DVB), which has formalized this approach under the DVB-CBMS specifications. The use of CBMS is supported largely by the broadcast industry, which has been using these technologies for over two decades in satellite digital TV and DTH systems. The CA systems, when used in a mobile environment, are suitably modified to reflect the restricted mobile environment.

The second approach, based on an open air interface, has been advocated by the Open Mobile Alliance (OMA) and is referred to as OMA-BCAST. It involves the use of an open encryption system (e.g., IPsec) and digital rights management for protection of content (OMA-DRM 2.0). The advantage of this approach is that the technologies and handsets are not operator-specific, and this is considered a key factor in the faster growth of services.

14.4.2 DMB-T

DMB services are based on an enhancement of the DAB (digital audio broadcast standard), which has been in use in over 35 countries for digital radio broadcasts. The DMB standards use the physical layer, air interfaces, and multiplex structure of DAB to carry audio and video. The robust design of DAB and availability of spectrum were the primary reasons for an enhancement of the DAB standards to also carry video. The modified standards were formalized under DMB. The new standards have been standardized by the ETSI under ETSI TS 102 427 and TS 102 428.

The services had their origin in Korea and are provided by using both the terrestrial mode of transmission and the satellite mode. The initiative for the development of DMB services goes to the Ministry of Information and Communications (MIC) of Korea who assigned the Electronics and Telecommunications Research Institute (ETRI) of Korea to develop a system for broadcast of mobile TV.

DMB-T Technology

DAB provides for a multiplex structure for audio channels by an "ensemble multiplexer." The multiplexed data streams are transmitted using OFDM modulation. Each ensemble has a bandwidth of about 1.6 MHz as per the DAB spectrum channeling plans.

DMB preserves the frame structure and the modulation of the DAB services. Video services are encoded in MPEG-4 and are carried in an MPEG-2 transport stream along with the associated program information tables. The MPEG-2 structure is required for video as the DAB ensemble multiplexer does not carry information on the video streams such as the PAT.

The second addition in DMB is the incorporation of additional error resilience by RS coding (204,188) and convolutional interleaving.

As the physical transmission of the DMB leaves the transmission format of DAB undisturbed, it is comprised of individual ensembles with about 1.6 MHz of bandwidth as per the DAB channeling plans (Figure 14-10). A 6 MHz channel can thus accommodate three ensembles.

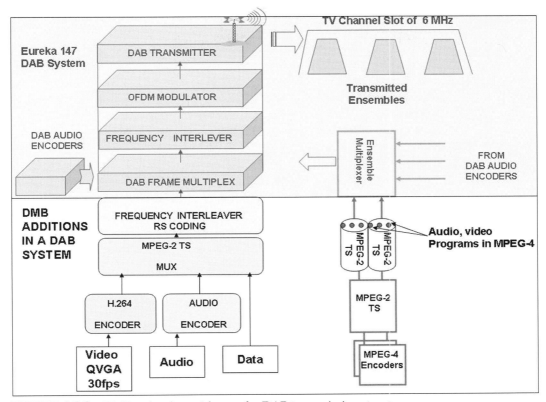

FIGURE 14-9 DMB technology rides on the DAB transmission structure

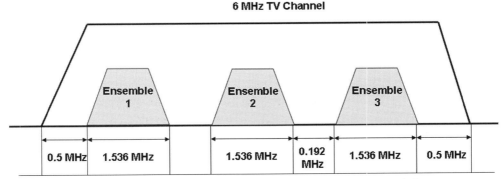

FIGURE 14-10 Transmission of T-DMB ensembles in an analog TV channel slot

A DMB-T Transmission System

The Korean T-DMB implementations, which were the first systems launched based on this technology, provides the best examples of a T-DMB network and its operational features. Licenses for T-DMB services were granted to six licensees, with each licensee being offered an ensemble. Two TV analog frequency slots were allocated in the VHF band, which permitted the six ensembles to operate. The companies providing these services are the KBS (Korean Broadcasting System) and the SBS (Seoul Broadcasting System). The T-DMB service in South Korea, when launched in 2005, consisted of seven TV channels, thirteen radio channels, and eight data channels. These are broadcast on six multiplexes in the VHF band TV channels 8 and 12.

T-DMB can carry either audio channels coded as per the DAB standard (Musicam at 384 KBps) or as H.264 coded channels (baseline profile level 1.3) with QCIF or better resolution. One of the features of T-DMB is the carriage of auxiliary data as per the MPEG-4 BIFS specifications. This has led to the launch of very interactive data and information services such as news, weather, traffic congestion, stock prices, etc.

T-DMB in Korea was expanded countrywide in 2007 with the use of VHF channels 7 to 13.

14.4.3 FLO™ Mobile TV Services

FLO™ (Forward Link Only) is a TV multicasting technology from MediaFLO, a Qualcomm company. Verizon Wireless in the United States has launched mobile TV technologies based on FLO technology called the Verizon VCAST™ mobile TV services. Verizon Wireless had a customer base of 65 million in the third quarter of 2007 and the VCAST services will be available in most markets. Qualcomm has access to spectrum in the UHF band at 700 MHz, which is being used to roll out the services, though this is not a limitation of the technology. FLO is an overlay network which uses a separate spectrum slot to deliver multicasting services.

FLO Technology

The FLO technology has many features that make it well-suited for mobile TV applications.

- The technology is based on the use of OFDM based carriers (4 K), which allows high tolerance to intersymbol interference in NLOS environments unlike the ATSC or CDMA technologies. Transmitter networks are possible in both the SFN and MFN configurations. The FLO also uses cyclical prefixes similar to WiMAX and uses Turbo codes for higher error resilience.
- FLO has powerful control-layer functions. A FLO control channel carries messages from the network to the receivers which contain

the configuration parameters for each upper layer "flow" and RF channel configuration. The receivers maintain a synchronized copy of this information and are thus aware of all parameters and service flows. FLO can support QoS for different services.

- The FLO layer is designed to be application independent.
- The FLO interface has multiple-level error correction and efficient coding built in, which permits efficiencies of 2 bits per sec per Hz (or 2 Mbps per MHz). This allows a slot of 6 MHz to carry up to 12 Mbps of data. This can provide over 30 live TV channels (QVGA at 30 Fps), 10 audio channels coded in HE AAC+, and, in addition, video-on-demand channels and multimedia data.
- FLO has adopted a flexible-layered source coding and modulation scheme. The layered modulation scheme has been designed to provide a high-quality service [QVGA (352 × 240)] at 30 frames per second (FPS) (or 25 FPS for PAL), which degrades gracefully to 15 FPS in case of degradation of signal-to-noise ratio (S/N) either due to higher distance to user, adverse propagation conditions or noisy environment. This means that the picture which would have otherwise frozen due to the higher bit rates not being supported for reception due to receiver S/N ratio can still be received but at lower bit rates.
- Being in the UHF band, which is the host to high power transmitters, FLO radio transmitters can be designed to be installed up to 50 Kms apart (depending on the power transmitted) and thus cover a metropolitan area with 3 to 4 transmitters. This is against hundreds of gap fillers needed in technologies such as SDMB, which are power-limited. FLO uses a single-frequency network with timing synchronization between transmitters. It supports frequency slots of 5, 6, 7, and 8 MHz.
- FLO technology has also taken into account the need to conserve power in the mobile handsets, and the receiver can access only that part of the signal that contains the channel being viewed. The FLO data unit is only one-seventh of an OFDM symbol. The typical viewing time claimed is 4 hours on a standard handset (850 mAH battery). The transmission by a FLO transmitter is 4 times a second. It also allows the users to switch channels in switching times of less than 1.5 seconds.

14.4.4 ISDB-T Services

ISDB-T stands for Integrated Services Digital Broadcasting which is an ITU standard (ITU-R BT 1306). Transmissions in ISDB-T take place in

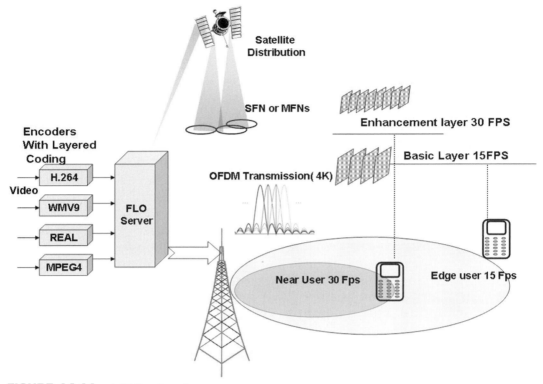

FIGURE 14-11   A FLO network

the form of 13 segments, which occupy a total of 6 MHz bandwidth equivalent to an analog TV channel. The system can be used for radio as well as TV broadcasting.

ISDB-T transmissions employ band-segmented OFDM transmission. In a 6 MHz bandwidth slot, each segment occupies 430 KHz. By using band-segmented OFDM transmission, services can be configured to use one or more segments. For example, a mobile TV service may use one of the 13 segments, a standard definition TV service may use 4 to 6 segments, and an HDTV (with sound) service may occupy all 13 segments.

Mobile TV services using ISDB-T began in Japan in 2006 using one segment out of the 13 in a 5.6 MHz channel. As mobile TV services had started using only one segment, they were referred to as one-segment broadcasting. The video and audio coding parameters for ISDB-T are:

Video: Coded using H.264 MPEG-4/AVC Base line profile L1.2 at 15 Fps Resolution QVGA (320 × 240)
Audio: MPEG-2 AAC with 24.48 KHz sampling

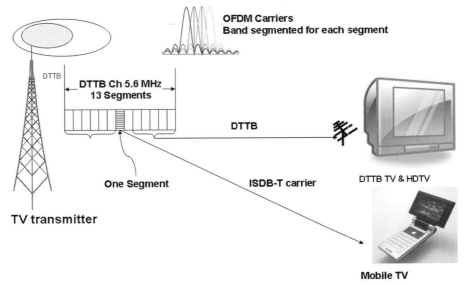

FIGURE 14-12 ISDB-T services

One segment has a bandwidth of 5.6/13 = 0.43 MHz or 430 KHz. Each segment carries OFDM carriers which are independent of the other segments and carry data for the particular segment. With QPSK modulation and a code ratio of ½ (Giving a guard interval of ⅛), one segment of 312 Kbps can typically carry video coded at 180 Kbps, audio at 48 Kbps, and internet data and program stream information (PSI/SI) at 80 Kbps. A single segment can thus carry one channel of video and data along with program information.

14.5 SATELLITE-BASED MOBILE TV SERVICES

Satellite-based mobile TV services are possible by using high-powered satellites in the S-band which can directly reach the mobile handsets. In addition, some system designs also provide for terrestrial-based repeaters in the same band. As the handset antennas have very low gain, the satellites need to be specially built for the purpose and provide directed spot beams with very high power. For example, the beams can be of 1 degree wide delivering 76 dbW in the coverage area. In addition, for in-building and covered areas, terrestrial "gap fillers" are required to deliver the signals with adequate signal strength. The forward error correction mechanisms are also very robust to compensate for the low signal strength directly received by the mobiles.

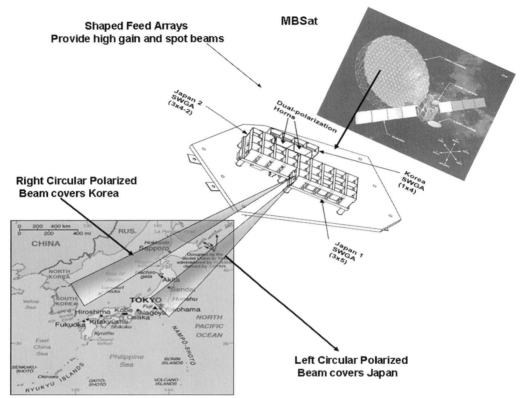

FIGURE 14-13 MBSAT satellite at 145 E location for DMB-S services over Korea and ISDB over Japan

14.5.1 DMB-S Services

The fist satellite-based DMB-S mobile TV was commissioned by TU Media over Korea and Japan using a specially built satellite MBSAT at 145E location in 2005. The satellite (MBSAT at 144E) is a high-powered satellite with transmission in the S- Band of 2.630 to 2.655 GHz.

Inside buildings, S-Band repeaters are used to rebroadcast signals terrestrially. This enables reception inside buildings. The S-DMB services are pay-TV services with charges of around $10 per month as per initial offerings. The service bouquet is comprised of up to 14 video channels, 24 audio channels, and EPG.

Technology

Briefly, the services are comprised of an MPEG-2 TS (transport stream structure) containing a number of video and audio channels. The video channels are coded in MPEG-4/H.264. The satellite transmissions

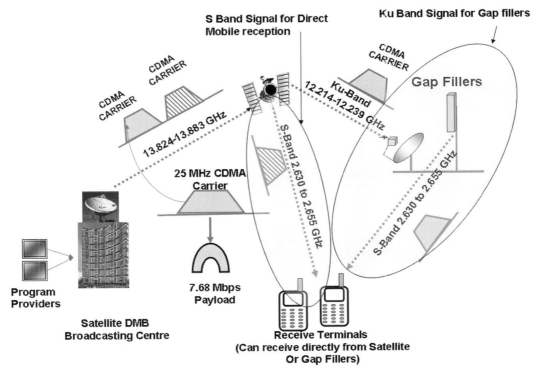

FIGURE 14.14 DMB-S system operating configuration

occupy a bandwidth of 25 MHz and make use of a CDMA technology to deliver the multimedia streams. The technical system for satellite DMB services is designated as system E and is based on CDM modulation as used in 3G phones. The transmission system has been designed for Ku Band uplink and S-Band downlink. The mobile transmission provides for error resilience using interleaving, RS coding, and FEC.

The gap fillers receive their signals from the Ku band transmission of the satellite. The satellite S-Band transmissions (direct to the mobiles) are in the frequency band 2.630 to 2.655 GHz with a bandwidth of 25 MHz. The use of high-level error protection overhead, however, allows a transmission capacity of only 7.68 Mbps. This is sufficient to handle 15 video services and a mix of audio and data services.

14.5.2 ISDB-S Services Japan-MobaHo!™

The same satellite MBSAT is used to provide mobile TV service over Japan. However, these are provided as per the Japanese standard ISDB-S. The encoding parameters are the same, i.e., MPEG-4 Simple

Profile Level 3 and AAC-LC audio. An MPEG-2 transport stream is used to carry the contents. S-Band repeaters operate by converting content from the Ku Band. The transmissions are encrypted using MULTI 2. A number of receivers are available which can receive and decrypt the services.

14.5.3 DVB-SH Services-Europe

Mobile TV services based on satellite-based transmissions are planned using the MSS spectrum at 2.2 GHz earmarked under the IMT2000. A new technology, i.e., DVB-SH, which stands for S-Band digital video broadcasting for handhelds, is envisaged for providing these services. The network will use a high-powered satellite for transmissions in the 2.2 GHz band and low-powered repeaters, which will be colocated with mobile base stations, thus making it a hybrid satellite-terrestrial network.

The European Commission has also adapted the harmonized use of the 2.2 GHz spectrum throughout Europe and its use for terrestrial transmissions in February 2007, paving the way for a Europe-wide network. A high-powered satellite, which will broadcast in this band, is being launched in 2008. The satellite will have 12-meter antennas for focused spot beams, each of which would cover roughly the territory of a country. The carrier per beam will have a bandwidth of 5 MHz. Each terrestrial repeater will retransmit 3 carriers of 5 MHz each.

The technology for DVB-SH will maintain the basic attributes of the DVB-H standard such as time slicing, IP Datacasting, and OFDM modulation. However the DVB-SH standards will provide for a more robust error correction (using turbo codes and deeper interleaving) to take into account the characteristics of the S-Band. The system will provide for a net capacity of 2.3 Mbps per carrier, which will allow 9 channels at 256 Kbps each. This permits encoding of a QVGA (320 × 240) resolution channel with 25 frames per second at 210 Kbps and 24 Kbps for HE-AAC audio.

An attractive feature of the network will be interactive services provided via the 3G network which operates in the adjacent band.

14.5.4 DVB-SH USA: Mobile Interactive Media (MIM)

DVB-SH services are set for a trial in the U.S. by ICO global communications based on technology from Alcatel Lucent. Mobile interactive media (MIM) services, which will be comprised of a full range of multimedia services will use ICO's geostationary satellite (ICO G1, launched January 2008). MIM is also a hybrid system with satellite transmission

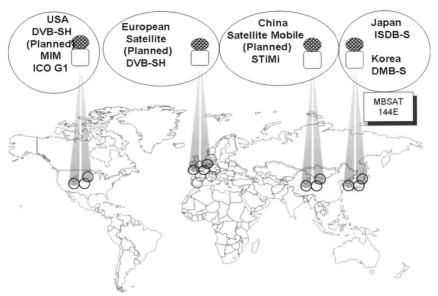

FIGURE 14-15   Satellite and terrestrial hybrid mobile TV services, current and planned

and terrestrial repeaters. The services will operate in the S-Band as per the DVB-SH standard. ICO has also tied up with Clearwire for the use of its 2.5 GHz spectrum for delivery via the terrestrial mode.

14.5.5 STiMi China (Satellite and Terrestrial Interactive Multi-service Infrastructure)

Mobile TV services using a hybrid satellite network with terrestrial repeaters are planned to be implemented in China. For this purpose a Chinese satellite company, China Satellite Mobile (CSM), has been granted the necessary license to operate in the S-Band at 2.5 GHz. CSM is majority owned by CBMsat, a Hong Kong-based Echostar company, and has shareholding from China's state-owned SARFT. The services will be provided using China's own satellite mobile TV standard developed by China Mobile Multimedia Broadcasting (CMMB) group called the STiMi (Satellite and Terrestrial Interactive Multi-service Infrastructure). The services are expected to be operational by June 2008.

15

IPTV AND WiMAX

The principal contributor to loneliness in this country is television. What happens is that the family "gets together" alone.
—Ashley Montagu, anthropologist and writer (1905–1999)

TV services have traditionally been delivered to homes using cable TV or DTH or terrestrial broadcasting technologies. All the modes of delivery are based on the availability of a fixed bandwidth (e.g., 5–8 MHz for analog transmissions) or a guaranteed and sustained bit rate (e.g., 2–6 Mbps for MPEG-2 video). These traditional technologies have been very successful in delivering audio and video to the homes, and quality is rarely an issue. On the other hand, the internet has also been used to carry streaming video on a best-effort basis largely for desktop applications. The "internet video" is delivered by streaming using the RTP/RTSP protocol for unicast transmissions. The RTSP protocol was designed for providing minimum latency, which apparently was the fastest way to deliver video over unreliable networks. Because of the non-availability of guaranteed throughput and latency, internet video has traditionally been characterized by small video windows (e.g., QCIF resolution), jerky video, or dropped frames caused by the inability of the network to handle video at sustained bit rates.

WiMAX now presents a new window of opportunity to deliver video to fixed, nomadic, or mobile devices by virtue of its QoS and service flow-based connections. WiMAX can either be used as a wireless extension to an IPTV network or be used natively using streaming protocols.

15.1 BASICS OF IPTV

Internet is characterized by "best-effort delivery." Services such as web browsing, file transfer, or e-mail can work effectively despite the best-effort nature of the internet as small delays do not affect such services. Video streaming over the internet using QCIF screen sizes and at low frame rates (say 15 FPS) can be handled owing to the very low rate streams generated by encoders. However the quality of video with full screen resolution and frame rates (25 or 30 FPS) where data equivalent to one frame must be delivered periodically every 50 or 33 ms places severe demands on the underlying network (even after compression with encoders such as MPEG-4). Once such usage is scaled up for thousands of simultaneous users, there is a problem in the net itself, as well as the backhaul links. Video can also be delivered as multicast by using the IETF protocols for multicasting such as IGMP 2.0. This, however, requires various routers to be multicast enabled and is practical only in managed networks.

The origin of IPTV lies in the increasing broadband access capacities by fiber or DSL to homes and the desire of broadband operators to provide a service that is comparable in quality to the cable or DTH services, while at the same time being able to offer "triple play," i.e., video, voice, and data services as a service differentiator from traditional services.

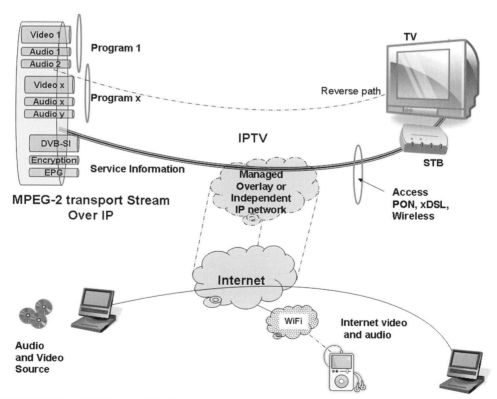

FIGURE 15-1 IPTV (with DVB-IP implementation) and internet video

Accordingly the key principle adopted in the provision of IPTV services, apart from the use of technologies which can provide efficient compression and low bit rates, is the administration of QoS in the entire network from a video server to the last mile, i.e., the STB.

QoS in IPTV is achieved by many techniques including:

- Network design and dimensioning to ensure that the designated capacity of video streams and other data (voice, internet) can be carried. IP/MPLS is used to achieve the desired QoS for the core networks.
- IP multicasting replication and use of edge nodes to maximize efficiency. The local broadcast content relevant to subscriber groups is introduced as close to edge as possible.
- Dimensioning all video servers for maximum number of streams.
- Service admission control, used to deny additional video or voice services if the existing core or last mile resources will not be able to maintain the QoS. This ensures that existing users do not find their services degrading as users demand additional services.
- A centralized application for overall service control.
- Integration of all equipment including the end user device in the scheme of QoS.

Using these techniques, the desired QoS is possible in networks such as DSL or cable internet, which are characterized by wired extensions. The acceptable standards of quality depend on the class of traffic being carried as a part of the IPTV service. ITU has recommended parameters for packet loss and latency in order to deliver satisfactory video and audio.

The ITU-T recommendations for these parameters are as follows:

Voice traffic:
Recommended one way delay: <150 ms, unacceptable >250 ms
Audio Packet Loss (G.729) <2 percent

Video traffic:
Delay jitter <40 ms
Maximum Video packet loss: <5 percent

15.1.1 IPTV Network Architecture and Services

A generalized architecture of IPTV is given in Figure 15-2. Video and audio services are delivered as "streams" between a media-streaming server and an appropriate receiver device such as an IP set-top box to convert the streaming video to "normal" video, which can be displayed on a TV. An end-to-end quality-of-service controlled network

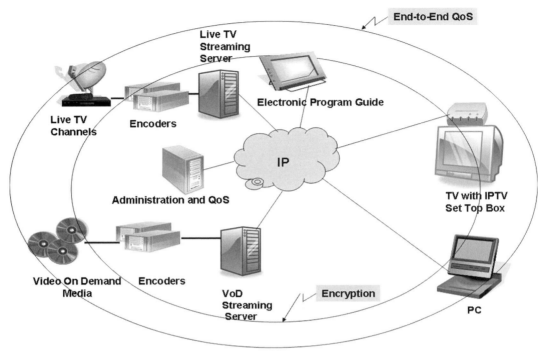

FIGURE 15-2 A generalized IPTV architecture

is used to deliver both live TV and streamed "on-demand media" via an IP network. In this generalized architecture, the last mile links have not been specified. (These can be xDSL, cable, or PON or Wireless.)

IPTV service is based on encoding of audio and video content by using compression technologies such as MPEG-2 or MPEG-4 and its RTP/UDP encapsulation, which converts it to a "streaming format." Other technologies such as Real® Video or Windows Media can also be used to generate streaming content. The content is usually encrypted for security purposes and delivering the services as "pay TV." The streaming content is delivered to end devices where an IP set-top box converts it to analog video or digital video in unencrypted format suitable for display on the TV sets. An IPTV network may contain over 150 channels and an Electronic Program guide (EPG) is usually provided for all commercial IPTV services. The STBs may provide two-way communications for ordering of on-demand services. They also enable the use of the internet or triple play including voice, as described later. The IPTV can also be used to deliver HDTV (HD IPTV) with suitable dimensioning of the IP network and access links.

15.2 INTERNET VIDEO: IPTV IS NOT INTERNET TV

15.2.1 Internet Video

"Internet TV" is commonly used to describe video and associated audio that can be viewed on the internet. This may be by opening a website by entering its URL address in the browser or initiating media play by using a media player (Windows Media Player, Adobe Flash Player, or Real Video, for example). Any video files that are embedded in the HTML content of the page and natively supported by the browser (e.g., Internet Explorer, Firefox, Opera, etc.) will then "play" on the web page. This type of viewing of video over the internet falls under the category of live streaming. Apart from live streaming, video files can also be downloaded and played by launching the appropriate player (Windows Media Player, Adobe Flash Player, Real Player, Apple QuickTime, Google Video Player, etc.). Downloads are practical only with short videos because of the file size and time involved in downloading.

The file formats and resolutions of video that are available on the internet are site-dependent in most cases. For example, YouTube™, which is designed to accept video uploads from camcorders and cell-phones accepts video in .wmv (Windows media), .avi (Audio video interleaved used by Windows for video), .mov (QuickTime™ movies format), and .mpg (compressed MPEG-2) formats.

Google Video can be downloaded in three formats: .avi, .mp4, and .gvi formats. Video from the website can also be streamed by using a shortcut which points to a .gvp file. The downloaded video can be played by using a Google Video Player (a free download) if in .avi or .gvi formats and by using a DivX Player if it is in .mp4 format. If the browser used is Flash-enabled, the Flash video (.flv) can also be played.

Videos uploaded on the websites can vary in resolution depending on the source, which can range from a cell phone with a VGA camera to a digital camera with 5 Mp resolution or even HD. These are usually converted to a common format and scaled down in resolution so that the viewers can retrieve them universally. The screen resolution supported on an iPod is 320×240 (QVGA). The other format commonly supported is QCIF (176×144) pixels. YouTube™ automatically converts videos to 320×240 format. The videos can also be downloaded to other devices such as iPods™ or Sony PSP™.

Internet video is in effect TV (or video) on a PC with "best-effort delivery." There is no end-to-end QoS control to ensure that video can be viewed without serious degradation or interruption. There is no encryption of services to generate pay-TV revenues and sometimes no TV business model.

TABLE 15-1

Differences between IPTV and internet video

Characteristics	IPTV	Internet Streaming Video
Resolution	Full Screen	CIF or QCIF
Quality of Service	End-to-end QoS, Broadcast Quality	Best Effort
Video Format	MPEG-2, MPEG-4/Part10, Windows Media, Microsoft VC1	Windows Media, RealNetworks, Quicktime
Services	EPG, Interactive TV, Broadcast TV, VoD, NVoD	Streaming Video
Customer Environment	Set-top Box (STB), Home Network	PC
Service Protection	Encryption, DRM	None, Unprotected Internet
Operations Support, Business Support	Full Business solutions	None
Customer Interface	EPG, Channel Selection	HTTP, FTP

With the improvements in core and access networks, the internet can be used for good quality video streaming, particularly in areas where the access networks provide high speeds of 4 Mbps or higher. Content delivery networks (CDNS) such as iBEAM™, Limelight networks®, etc. provide content caching at the edge so that the streaming video can be delivered with the highest data rates. Some operators now offer TV services over the internet using CDNs to deliver content on a unicast basis. The use of Flash video for providing TV services over the internet (replicated by the CDNs) has become a very popular method for delivery of video in the recent past. However, such content is only viewable where the access networks support the speeds needed to view live streaming video.

15.2.2 TV over DSL

Many telecom operators with traditional circuit-switched network architecture are also entering the field of providing TV services over telephone lines available from neighborhood exchanges and connected to customer homes by using ADSL or DSL on the last mile. In such cases, the TV head end is set up in major telephone exchanges and DSL modems used at both ends to carry the video across the physical link. This type of video delivery also cannot be strictly characterized as IPTV as there is no end-to-end QoS control. The services available depend on the quality of DSL lines, distance from end customer, and use of other services such as broadband or VoIP.

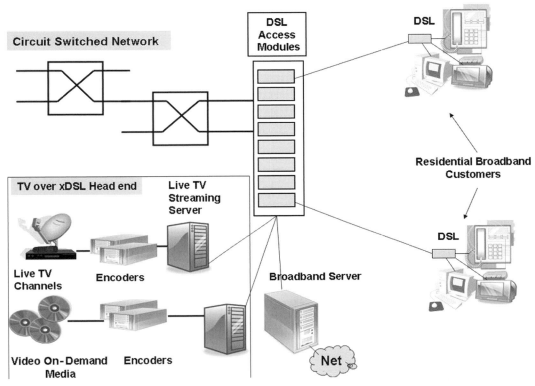

FIGURE 15-3 TV over DSL

The TV over DSL became possible with the improving capabilities of the XDSL networks breaking the threshold of 1.5 Mbps, which was the minimum needed to carry MPEG-2 video. However, the growth impetus came from the implementation of MPEG-4/AVC, which made it possible to stream real-time standard definition video at bit rates as low as 512 Kbps.

Example of TV over DSL: Orange TV™, France

Orange, which is also a broadband operator in Europe, has launched Orange TV™ in France. The service is based on the DSL technology as the access link and delivers live TV and VoD using MPEG-2 and H.264. The service is comprised of over 250 channels and over 1000 titles in VoD content. The service had over 1 million customers by the end of 2007. The TV over DSL service is based on UDP carriage of streaming packets (non-connection-oriented). The services are being expanded to the United Kingdom, Poland, Spain, and other European countries.

15.2.3 IPTV and Internet TV

IPTV, as the term is commonly used today, involves an access-independent secure and reliable delivery of video and entertainment services to customers. By maintaining a quality of service, the customers receive a uniform quality of entertainment despite the network being IP-based.

IPTV, though being a form of broadband TV, is targeted toward the use of TV sets rather than PCs. This is done by using the IPTV set-top box or the residential home gateway, which interfaces to a range of home devices. These devices can be TV sets, plug-and-play (PnP) media players, DVRs, SIP-based phones, or other devices.

IPTV is not merely video with associated audio as is largely the case with internet TV where each stream of video and audio is dealt with independently. On the other hand, IPTV in its various implementation formats involves a complete set of services defined by the MPEG-2 transport stream (or other proprietary formats).

IPTV SERVICES

Broadcast Digital TV: Live TV channels

Video on Demand (VoD): On-demand movies or videos

Near Video On Demand (NVoD): Scheduled movies with multiple channels at staggered start times

Interactive Services: EPG, Interactive gaming, personal video recorder (PVR), TV magazines—news, weather, business, targeted advertising, etc.

Video Podcasting: RSS feeds to deliver news, updates

Downloads of video (MP4) or audio (MP3) to STB and transfer to portable devices

Interactive TV: Time-shifted TV (TSTV), language and camera viewing angle selections, personal playlists

A set-top box (STB) is a key device in an IPTV network. It provides the decryption of the services carried on the IP network, and delivered to it, as well as carries out the decoding from MPEG-2 or MPEG-4 compressed formats to formats that can interface to consumer devices. The interfaces may include analog composite audio and video, S-Video, SPDIF, or HDMI interface for HDTV.

15.2.4 Coming to Grips with Multiple Standards for IPTV

Beyond the commonly understood definition of IPTV, there is no industry convergence yet on a single standard for IPTV services. The standardization of IPTV under the ITU started only in 2005 and first set of
global standards was announced in December 2007. In Europe, the ETSI
has constituted a focus group ETSI TISPAN 2.0 (Telecoms and Integrated
Converged Services and Protocols for Advanced Networks). In the
United States, the Internet Streaming Media Alliance (ISMA) has been
working toward adoption of open standards based on real-time protocol (RTP), common encryption (ISMAcrypt), and common standards
for coding of audio, video, and data. In parallel, the IPTV interoperability forum (IIF), a part of ATIS, is working toward interoperability of
IPTV systems from various vendors and based on different technologies. For this purpose, IIF is more focused on the IPTV reference architecture than on open standards.

There are many challenges in the standardization process because of
the diverse nature of the physical networks (cable, DSL, optical fiber,
MAN, wireless networks), standardization of platforms [EPG, audio and
video coding, middleware, set-top boxes, digital rights management
(DRM), core networks (integration with existing IP network, dedicated
overlay over IP backbone, integration with optical backbones), service
delivery (multicast and unicast), etc.].

With the current level of standardization, there are three broad
ways to deliver IPTV services.

- The first is by using the DVB-IP architecture. In this methodology,
  the MPEG-2 stream, which carries both the programs and the
  EPG information, is encapsulated by RTP and packetized by IP to
  be delivered over any type of IP network.
- The second is a variant to the MPEG-2 transport stream carriage.
  This has its origin in the "professional video transport focus
  group" (pro-MPEG) called the COP-3. The COP-3 methodology
  of delivery of MPEG-2 uses additional FEC based on IETF RFC
  2733. The FEC is employed in a two-dimensional manner and is
  carried as a separate series of packets along with the RTP packets.
- The third methodology is to use proprietary delivery technologies which are often vendor-based implementations, such as
  Microsoft® TV.

The announcement of global standards for IPTV by the ITU-T in
December 2007 is expected to lead to a convergence toward the use of
common global standards as the services migrate to the next generation

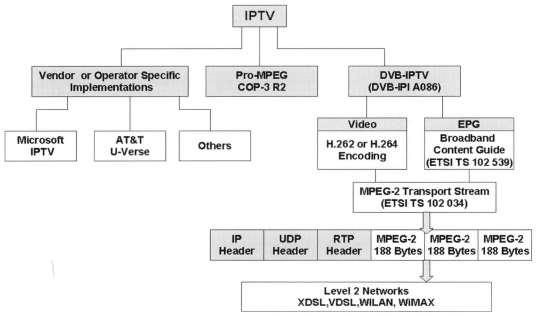

FIGURE 15-4   IPTV implementation methodologies

networks (NGNs). These standards, released under the "J" series of recommendations, complement the existing ITU-T standards for cable TV services.

While the efforts toward common standards continue, IPTV services are being launched aggressively by operators worldwide, which are based on proprietary technologies or based on organizational standards such as DVB. In this multi-technology environment, it is interesting to understand how the different offerings of IPTV service relate to the standards and to each other.

As mentioned earlier, it is possible to use content delivery networks (CDNs) for caching of content at the network edge for delivery of video as well, with the quality being acceptable only where the access networks provide adequate connectivity.

Broadcast vs. VoD

The first differentiator for the IPTV service comes in regard to whether the service is broadcast or a VoD service, or a combination of both. On fiber-to-home networks (such as Verizon FiOS™), it is possible to broadcast 50 to 150 channels. The broadcast of a large number of channels implies that the unicast traffic is limited to VoD, making the scaling up of the network much easier. On hybrid copper-fiber networks, 20+ Mbps is achievable, which is adequate for broadcasting only the most popular channels. On the other hand, xDSL networks may be limited to 3 to 4 Mbps of bandwidth largely used on the basis of channel selection, i.e., in a VoD mode.

A broadcast service needs to be accompanied by its program guide, which helps in program selection. The program guide may also carry information on available VoD content. Alternatively, such information may be available via an HTTP server.

A VoD program can be delivered by using Native RTP/RTSP protocols. The program may be encoded by any of the commonly used compression protocols (MPEG-2 or H. 264) and needs a STB for decoding.

For broadcast programs, a transport stream is usually used. This, for example, can be the MPEG-2 transport stream which then permits a number of programs, data, and EPG to be carried with appropriate tables (PMT, PAT) for the receiver to receive the appropriate streams when a channel is selected. The DVB MPEG-2 transport streams are then carried over an IP-based network after IP encapsulation to be delivered as IPTV.

The combination of using MPEG-2 TS for encapsulation and RTP/RTSP for VoD in fact forms the basis of the DVB-IPI service. In DVB-IPI, the service discovery is by using the PSI/SI information and DNS and the service selection is based on IGMP and RTSP. QoS is applied to the multicast streams to ensure that the full bit rate represented by the streams can be delivered to the receiver throughout the entire network. DVB-IPI has been used in only a few commercial implementations.

15.3 MICROSOFT IPTV

Microsoft TV IPTV Edition provides a complete framework to provide IPTV to homes. Figure 15-5 shows the Microsoft IPTV components. The content acquisition components provide encoding of live video sources (e.g., TV programs) to Microsoft Windows Media 9 format. The content is protected by Windows digital rights management (Windows DRM). A service management module provides a "multimedia EPG" and notification services. Microsoft also provides the Business Support Systems (BSS) and Operational Support Systems (OSS) for managing the services provided by the IPTV system. A subscriber management system is available for managing the service profiles of customers, billing, and rights management. The services are delivered via managed IP-based networks. The access links can be over cable, DSL wireless, or WiMAX networks.

Figure 15-6 shows the Microsoft TV architecture in greater detail. The entire network operates in a framework of end-to-end QoS, which

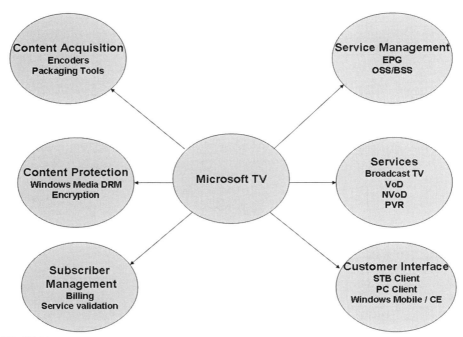

FIGURE 15-5   Microsoft TV™ components

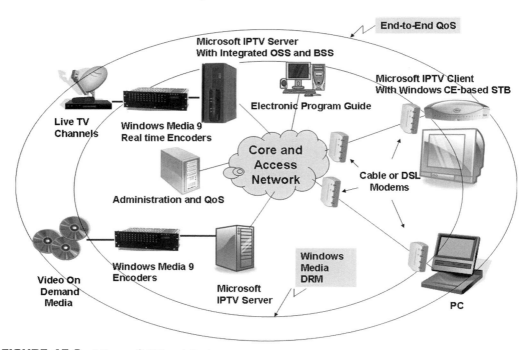

FIGURE 15-6   Microsoft TV architecture

is managed by assuring resources by the administration and QoS functional unit of Microsoft TV. The content is protected by Windows Media DRM.

Microsoft Media Room®
Microsoft has also added music and photo sharing to its IPTV Edition software, which is now available as Microsoft Media Room. The Media Room brings an environment of web-based applications in addition to the commercial TV products available on the IPTV. The Media Room provides an XHTML or Java Script-based environment to the operators while at the same time defining an environment for the home network so that the applications can be presented in a standardized environment of service offering and viewing.

The Media Room provides a facility of using a menu to see or play music or to view a slide show of pictures. It is possible to concurrently use the web-based services and view TV by using the picture-in-picture feature (PIP).

Microsoft TV IPTV Edition: Set-Top Boxes
Set-top boxes for the Microsoft TV IPTV edition are available from many manufacturers. These boxes support multiple video codecs, including MPEG-2, MPEG-4-AVC, and Windows Media 9. The boxes are based on a system on chip (SoC). The boxes are designed around the SMP8364 media processor from sigma designs and equipped with 1.5 GHz Intel 854 processor. The STBs are optimized for a rich IPTV, gaming, and the web-based environment.

Who Is Using Microsoft TV IPTV Edition?
Microsoft IPTV has been selected as the technology platform by a number of operators including British Telecom, Telecom Italia, and Deutsche Telecom in Europe, and Bellsouth and Verizon in the United States.

15.4 IPTV USING NATIVE RTP
As the name suggests, IPTV can also be provided by using standard IP protocols. In this type of implementation, the delivery of IPTV is based on the use of real-time streaming protocol (RTSP) protocols for session control (connect to video stream, play, pause) and RTP protocols for carriage of video/audio data packets. The RTP uses UDP datagrams for sending data. For change of channels (i.e., connection to one of the many multicast streams available as members of the multicast group),

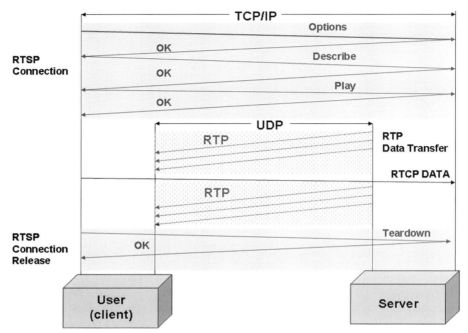

FIGURE 15-7   Streaming using RTP/RTSP

the IGMP protocol version 2 is commonly used. The IGMP protocol is a part of the multicast specifications. It is used by multicast routers to establish and update the multicast group memberships.

When Native RTP is used for IPTV, it should be recognized that the internet core and access networks need to support the minimum bandwidths needed to support the video and audio services being carried. The average bit rates needed to carry MPEG-2 standard definition video are approximately 1.5 Mbps, and for MPEG-4/AVC, they are 0.7 to 1.0 Mbps.

IPTV using RTP is most commonly used for video-on-demand transmissions, which are unicast in nature. For multicast programs, it is more common to use a DVB MPEG-2-based transport stream or proprietary implementations.

Figure 15-7 outlines the process involved in setting up a streaming connection and data transfer.

For receiving a video stream, the user establishes a real-time streaming protocol connection (RTSP) with the server. The RTSP is a TCP/IP-based connection and has commands available, such as DESCRIBE, SETUP, PLAY, PAUSE, REWIND, RECORD, etc. These requests are based on the HTTP protocol. In response to these commands, the data transfer begins by using the RTP protocol. The user can give feedback on the connection quality based on the RTCP data. The RTCP data can be used to increase or decrease bit rates in a unicast connection or connect to higher or lower rate bit streams in a multicast connection.

As the IPTV is comprised of the complete range of content elements including the EPG, service information, and programs using multiple audio and video streams, it is quite common to use the MPEG-2 transport stream structure over IP. The standards for this have been formulated under "Transport of DVB based MPEG services over IP Networks" (ETSI TS 102 034) and IETF RFCs 2250 and 3550. Alternatively, it is also possible to use elemental streams encapsulated in UDP and TCP as per RFC 3550 and 3984.

The RFC relate to the following:

- RFC 2250: RTP Payload format for MPEG-1/MPEG-2 Video
- RFC 3984: RTP Payload format for H.264 Video

It is also possible to carry the streams coded in VC1 format (RFC 4425: RTP payload format for VC-1).

In case the video programs are carried by using the MPEG-2 TS, the IP set-top box will need to have the decryption and MPEG-2 decoding facilities in addition to the standard TCP/IP stack and the HTTP protocols.

15.4.1 Implementing IPTV with Native RTP: Content Delivery Networks (CDNs)

A number of content delivery networks are now available which provide caching, downloading, and streaming of video on a commercial basis. These include Limelight networks, Akamai, Level 3, Seachange, etc. Operators can use a CDN to cache content, which is then spread out to all servers located in different parts of the network. A user, say in the United States, wishing to view content from France will still connect to the CDN node located nearest to it, even though the primary content server may be in Paris. The CDNs have also rapidly evolved to lend greater support to streamed video distribution.

15.4.2 Implementing IPTV: Example of IPTV Multicasting Router

Implementing IPTV requires unicasting and multicasting of content to thousand of customers while maintaining QoS. With the increasing base of IPTV customers, products for delivery of IPTV with large scalability have emerged in the market. An example is the Juniper E320 broadband services router. It can be used for IPTV multicast and TV overlay applications and has features to support measuring session durations to assist in billing. The E320 can support up to 128,000 individual subscribers

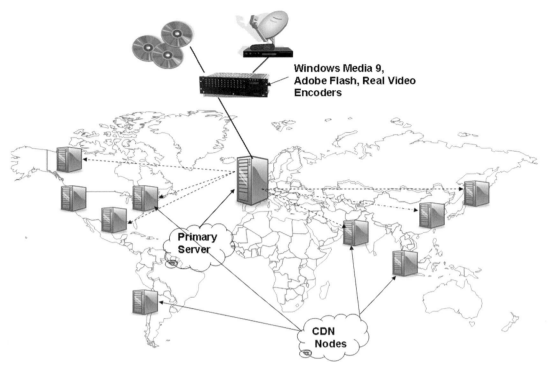

FIGURE 15-8   A content delivery network provides access to a user from the nearest delivery node

and 340 Gbps throughput. The IPTV broadband router can also support Ethernet or ATM for DSL-type applications (DSL forum TR059 architecture).

The E320 can support wire speed QoS and regulate traffic flows to each subscriber based on the QoS assigned to each service flow.

15.5 IPTV BASED ON DVB-IPI

The Digital Video Broadcasting (DVB) is well-known for its standards of delivery of MPEG-2 video over satellite or cable or terrestrial delivery. The DVB-C, DVB-S, and DVB-T standards are, in fact, the predominant standards used in the broadcast world except for the United States, Korea, Japan, and some other countries, which have adapted the use of ATSC or ISDB-T standards.

MPEG-2 has been the most common video compression and transport standard in video broadcasting networks. The use of MPEG-4 has recently started gaining momentum based largely on the MPEG-4 or H.264 encoding and MPEG-2 transport streams.

DVB has been working with industry fora such as ATIS-IPTV Interoperability Forum, ISMA, etc. to formulate standards for IPTV. The specification for carriage of MPEG-2 transmission streams over IP infrastructure (termed DVB-IPI) Phase 1 (IPI 2038) has been finalized and released for industry use in 2006. The DVB-IPI Phase 1 deals with the delivery of IPTV to an DVB-IPI-compliant STB or a home network. DVB-IPI is MHP compatible.

What Are the Advantages of DVB-IPI?

DVB-IPI has the advantage of migrating the entire gamut of customer deliverables, i.e., EPG, MHP, MPEG-2 video transport, set-top boxes, carriage of metadata, etc. on the IP platform. The manner in which the services are delivered is thus identical to every service provider. Moreover, by finalizing the various components, multiple vendors and operators can work together to operate on the same access network. Traditional broadcasters are likely to find DVB-IPI easy to deploy as the DVB-SI format remains the same. The DVB-IPI also uses the MHP platform, which is independent of the transmission media used cable, satellite DTH, or IP. DVB-IPI also works through the IP-based home network.

IPTV is about being able to maintain QoS and sustained bit rates, in addition to providing full-featured services incorporating the electronic service guide (ESG), fast channel and service selection, and viewing of interactive content. The DVB-IPI achieves this by using the FEC technology developed by Digital Fountain™.

15.5.1 Example of a DVB-IPI IPTV Network

An example of an DVB-IPI IPTV network involving the home residential gateway is the SURPASS™ IPTV network from Siemens. It is an end-to-end solution including the entertainment headend, carrier business management system (billing, CRM), digital rights management (DRM), and home gateway products (IP STB and Middleware).

The STB includes the following:

- MPEG-4/MPEG-2 decoders
- Middleware, DRM agent
- SIP Client for VoIP

The QoS in the access network is primarily achieved by "admission control," implying that a new service will be enabled based on the resources available. In the core network, the QoS can be maintained by standard techniques such as VLAN, MPLS, resource reservation, etc.

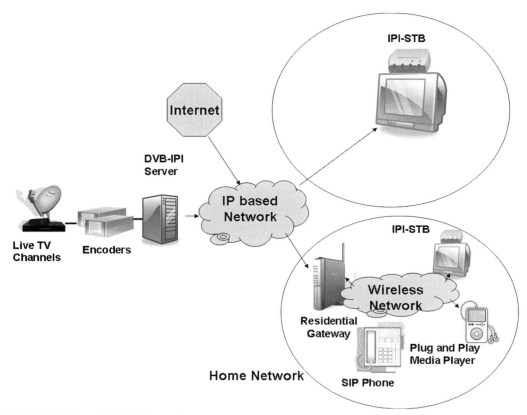

FIGURE 15-9   A DVB-IPI-based network

The range of services available to customers includes broadcast TV, pay TV, pay-per-view, internet on TV, games, PVR, VoIP, video telephony, and TV web pages (with dedicated content or walled garden) in addition to the EPG.

15.6 IPTV FOR HDTV CONTENT

Increasing popularity of HDTV channels has made it imperative for IPTV operators to also consider offering HDTV content. Availability of all-fiber networks or hybrid networks with high-speed access has made it possible to also offer HDTV on the networks. New generation encoders with H.264 technology can now provide encoding for HDTV at 4 Mbps or lower bit rates. (An example is the Grassvalley ViBE™ encoder EM1000 based on the Mustang® chip.) These bit rates are at about the same level as MPEG-2 encoding for standard-definition video

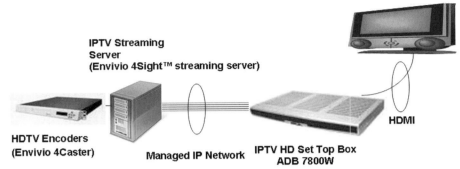

FIGURE 15-10 A depiction of HDTV content transmission over IPTV network; this example shows head solution from Envivio® and STB from ADB systems®

a couple of years back. As IPTV is about being able to deliver with prescribed QoS, delivery of HDTV content is feasible on networks which support QoS parameters in access and core networks. Singapore Telecom had started providing HDTV channels on its IPTV service in June 2007, while many operators have either conducted trials or have launched commercial IPTV services, which include HDTV channels.

Delivery of HD channels via IPTV requires an HDTV set-top box (STB) equipped with HDTV decoders. Chipsets are now available which can be used in such set-top boxes. ST Microsystems, for example, has HDTV decoder chipset STi710x. The chipset provides all the circuitry to support STB functions in a single chip and has support for MPEG-2, MPEG-4/AVC and VC-1 decoding. Korea Telecom, for example, has launched its HDTV services over IPTV network using set-top boxes based on the ST Microsystems chipset STi710x (Humax TS-110 and Samsung SMT-H6170).

Many commercial solutions are available for IPTV headends with SDTV and HDTV content streaming capability. These include MatrixStream®, Tandberg television, Cisco, XAVi Technologies, and Streaming21, among others.

15.7 EXTENDING IPTV TO MOBILE AND WIRELESS NETWORKS

As the managed delivery of content over IPTV gathers momentum, the delivery-to-mobile networks or wireless-based delivery is of increasing importance. MegaTV®, the IPTV service of Korea Telecom, can, for example, be received on Play Station 3, in addition to TV sets.

The mobile and wireless environments present a multifaceted environment for delivery of IPTV services. Until we reach the stage of full integration of core networks into the NGN as defined by the ITU, the

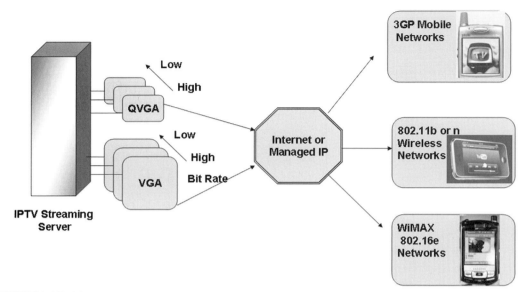

FIGURE 15-11   Internet in wireless and mobile environments

individual networks are responsible for the delivery of services as per their own standards, even though the internet may be universally available on all networks—wireless, mobile, or WiMAX. Figure 15-11 depicts this scenario. The IPTV streamer in this case caters to different screen resolutions, bit rates, and file formats as required for individual networks. The appropriate stream will be selected by the receiver during the set up using the HTTP and SDP protocols.

15.7.1 Wireless Networks

Wireless networks (WLANs) are today available in abundance as "hotspots" or wireless extensions of the internet at home and office. More and more devices (such as the iPhone™, Microsoft Zune™, a variety of audio and video players, most smartphones and PDAs) today support WiFi access. These networks are characterized by the use of IEEE 802.11b, g, or n technologies.

Wireless extensions are convenient to network devices without interconnecting wires. Products such as Apple TV™ are based on the use of a wireless network within the home. There are also many home networking solutions which use wireless LAN extensions to connect various devices in the home.

There is considerable difference, however, between the wired LANs and WiFi. Wired LANs are extremely reliable and operate with negligible error rates. Moreover with 100 Mbps or gigabit ethernet technologies

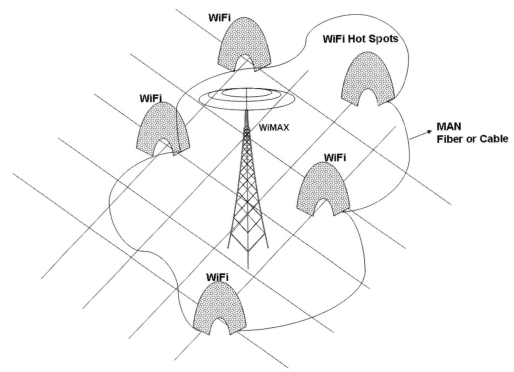

FIGURE 15-12 A metropolitan area wireless environment

being common, the loss pf packets caused by congestion is very low. Wireless networks, on the other hand, operate on the principle of positive ACK of the received packets. This coupled with sharply variable signal strength introduces packet loss and reduces the maximum throughput below the maximum bit rates which can be achieved on the network. Further if there are many devices which are contending for bandwidth, there will be variable delays which may be quite large and need buffering at the receiver.

The IPTV protocols (or other protocols for unidirectional transfer of video or audio) operate by using the UDP packets. With a payload of 1.4 K bytes per packet (Ethernet frame size) and a data rate of 1.5 Mbps, the frame error rate exhibited by UDP for distances of around 25 m over wireless LANs is approximately 1.5 percent. Considering a frame overhead of 3.5 percent, this gives a throughput of 95 percent of the data rate of 1.5 Mbps. The throughput will be lower with smaller packets. For example a 200 byte payload (e.g., for VoIP) gives a throughput of only 80 percent.

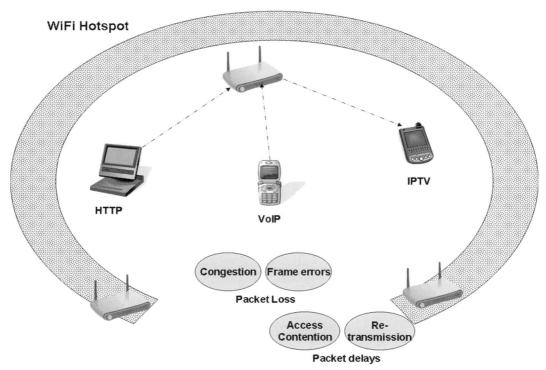

FIGURE 15-13   Wireless performance inside a WiFi hotspot

On the other hand TCP which uses a connection-oriented protocol with positive acknowledgments and a transmission window, a 1.5 percent frame error rate with 1.4 Kbyte packets gives a throughput of only 80 percent as against 95 percent for UDP. Protocols such as FTP work fine with such frame losses as they are time insensitive. However a frame-based video service needs to be properly configured for acceptable performance by optimizing the overheads against the error rates.

15.7.2 IPTV in Mobile Environment

Mobile phones now provide access to the internet via 3G networks (3G-UMTS or CDMA2000) and can provide high-speed internet connectivity. They also support applications such as HTML browser, mail clients, RTP-based streaming, and FTP-based downloads.

Extending services to mobile devices is done under the third-generation partnership project (3GPP or 3GPP2) standards.

Content for mobile devices needs to be in resolutions which can be displayed on the small screens of mobile phones. Usually the resolutions which can be supported on mobile phones are QVGA or QCIF, based on

Throughput in WLAN

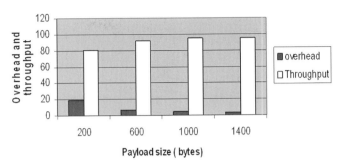

FIGURE 15-14   Wireless LAN performance for UDP traffic

Format	Resolution	Frame Rate
CCIR-601(PAL)	720X576	30i
SIF(PAL)	352X288	25p
CCIR-601(NTSC)	720x480	30i
SIF(NTSC)	352X240	30p
CIF	352X288	30p
QCIF	176X144	30p

FIGURE 15-15   Screen resolutions in mobile environment

the screen size. Figure 15-15 depicts common resolutions supported in the industry. The content meant for delivery is also required to be in the file formats specified by 3GPP which is essentially an ISO-based format.

An example of an IPTV streamer for 3GPP networks is given in Figure 15-16.

The device Gocaster 3000™ can accept audio and video inputs in analog or digital formats and encodes them using MPEG-2, MPEG-4/AVC (advanced simple profile), 3GPP (for mobile networks), or MPEG-1 formats. Another version of the streamer is available for Windows Media 9 format. It can also accept DVB-ASI streams and can provide DVB remultiplexing as well. Encoded outputs are available in ASI formats also. Real-time uploads to video server are available.

The device is standards-compliant and can provide streaming in ISMA 1.0 (i.e., native video streaming using RTSP/RTP) or by using DVB MPEG-2 transport stream formats. The streaming can be a unicast

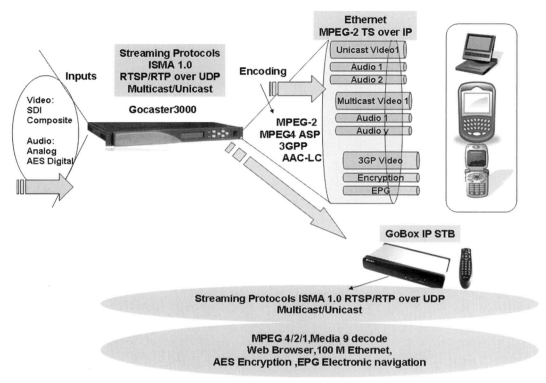

FIGURE 15-16   An example of IPTV streamer for 3GP networks

or as multicasts. The streamer can be used in native mode with any IP-based device, or an IP STB can be used for MPEG decode, decryption functions. Mobile devices working with DVB MPEG-2 TS over IP will need a thin client software for decoding. Most devices provide it as a part of the middleware.

15.7.3 Architectural Framework for Providing IPTV to 3G Mobile Devices

IPTV has now moved into its second phase wherein operators of IPTV (who are in many instances telecom operators with mobile service offerings) are simultaneously multicasting it to mobile handsets and offering quadruple-play services. The capabilities of mobiles to upload videos and pictures are no doubt responsible to a great extent for interest in mobile media.

   The IMS provides a framework for the interconnection of the mobile (3GPP) and the IPTV networks through SIP-based signaling and media conversion or media resource facility. At the same time the IMS

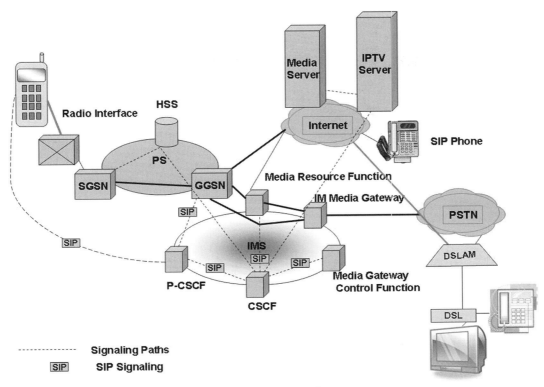

FIGURE 15-17 IPTV-to-mobile networks via 3GPP-IMS

network also facilitates connectivity to the IP associated services such as VoIP available in WiFi hotspots through generic network access, IPTV connectivity, and connectivity to services such as media downloads or online music stores.

The IMS provides portability of IPTV to multiple devices such as mobile devices, DSL-based IPTV, etc. while at the same time separating the "networks" from "services." The mobile devices can move to any network, with the service availability being transparent to them. Services such as network PVRs can thus become available as streaming services to all mobile devices. This is in fact true content portability.

15.8 IPTV AND WiMAX

WiMAX networks present an attractive alternative to wireline-based IPTV. The cable- or DSL-based IPTV is available to legacy telcos or cable operators that have upgraded their plant for IP. WiMAX, which is an implementation of wireless MAN, presents a new alternative medium of delivery offering the following advantages:

- High bit rates achievable (3–10 Mbps or more based on configuration)
- Metro wide or rural connectivity
- High resilience to multipath propagation through OFDM
- Guaranteed QoS and a service class for video
- Universal availability of interoperable client devices
- Mobility upto 125 Kmph with IEEE 802.16e
- Minimum or no maintenance on access links
- Compatibility with IP-based protocols and IPv6
- Capability of WiMAX to connect WiFi hotspots
- Two-way interactive communications
- Compatibility and roaming with 3G mobile networks (in the offing)

The architecture of a network with WiMAX delivery option is given in Figure 15-18.

Compared to wireless networks such as WLAN, WiMAX has clear advantages for supporting video traffic or IPTV because it provides a "service class," which can be associated with the connection. For video which is represented by a variable frame rate, the QoS available

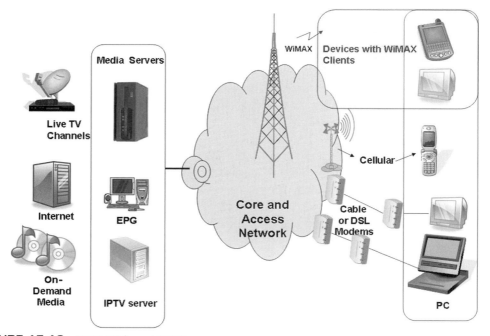

FIGURE 15-18 WiMAX-based IPTV

in the MAC layer is real-time polling service (rtPS), which guarantees a minimum sustained traffic rate. In addition, the mobile WiMAX (IEEE 802.16e) has a support for multicast broadcast service (MBS) and VoIP.

New algorithms for compression of video such as MPEG-4 scalable video coding provide multiple streams which if included improve the spatial resolution (reduce granularity) or increase frame rates. WiMAX can cater to such enhanced variable data speeds through non-real time variable rate service or best effort (BE) service. The base stream is supported by the rtPS so that the minimum quality of service is always assured (Figure 15-19).

The IEEE 802.16e mobile WiMAX provides for service flow-based assignment for each connection, and this can guarantee base level IPTV video even in a mobile environment. This is in contrast with the wireless 802.11x WiFi-streamed IPTV, where the quality may be highly variable based on local conditions.

The IPTV services in general also include video gaming, media downloads, web browsing (HTTP), and VoIP as a part of triple play services. WiMAX has quality of service classes to accommodate various types of services associated with IPTV portfolio.

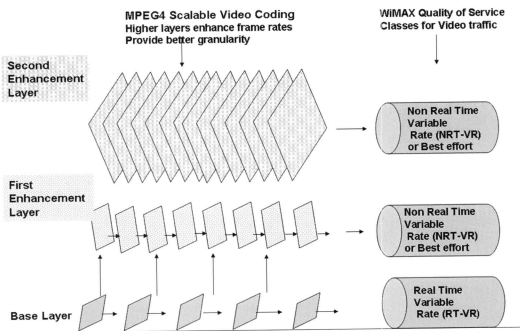

FIGURE 15-19 MPEG4 scalable video coding can be used to advantage in a WiMAX network to use spare "best effort" capacity

TABLE 15-2

IPTV-associated services and Mobile WiMAX scheduling classes

Application	QoS requirements	WiMAX Scheduling Service
VoIP, Video Conferencing	Real time low latency service(latency <150 ms), low jitter (jitter < 50 ms), low bandwidth (32–64 Kbps)	Extended real time variable rate service (ERT-VR) for voice and real time polling service (rtPS) for video
Media download (audio, video)	Non-real time, high bandwidth (2–10 Mbps)	Non-real time polling service (nrtPS) or best effort (BE)
IPTV or media streaming	Real time with minimum base rate, low jitter (<50 ms), medium bandwidth (0.5–3 mbps) for mobile and standard definition devices	Real time polling service (rtPS)
Interactive gaming	Low latency (<100 ms), low bandwidth (50–100 kbps)	Extended real time variable rate service (ERT-VR)

The physical realization of multiple streams is possible in WiMAX by the streaming server establishing multiple connections with the base station, which are carried onward as multiple connections to the MS.

15.8.1 Network Architecture for IPTV on WiMAX

The NWG of WiMAX has released the architectural framework of Mobile WiMAX which has been discussed in Chapters 12 and 13. The 3GPP IMS, which is the consensus framework to be used for mobile devices, includes WiMAX networks as one of the network types to which IMS services can be delivered using the same signaling framework.

As the reference architecture for the DSL as well as WiMAX services is comprised of the application service provider (ASP), network service provider (NSP), and the network access provider (NAP), the inter-working needs to be considered at different levels.

WiMAX used for "Fixed Wireless Access":
In addition to the Mobile WiMAX network architecture, the NWG has also released the framework for using WiMAX as an access network for DSL(WiMAX Forum Release 1.0.0 WiMAX interworking with DSL). Essentially this architecture outlines how fixed wireless access can be provided by simple Ethernet bridging and the relevant reference points.

The points T, V, and A10 are denominations of reference points, which are further specified in terms of protocols and standards. BRAS is the broadband remote access server. In DSL implementations, the protocols used are layer 2 point-to-point protocols (PPP) over Ethernet

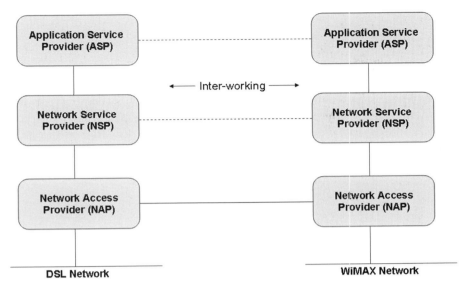

FIGURE 15-20   Inter-working scenarios between DSL and WiMAX

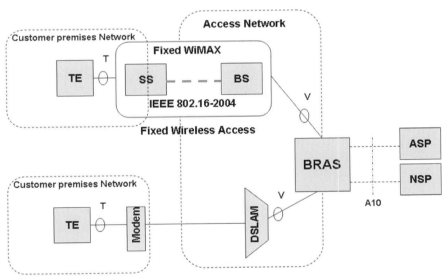

FIGURE 15-21   WiMAX Network Working Group (NWG) reference architecture for DSL and Fixed WiMAX

(PPPoE) or IP over Ethernet. PPP is the protocol most commonly used in RAS dial up applications. In case of 802.16-2004 implementations of WiMAX the wireline DSL network can be replaced by a Fixed WiMAX network by simply using Ethernet bridging when IP over Ethernet is used as in this case the higher layer protocols are not impacted. In case

PPP is being used, then the PPP packets have to be encapsulated into PPPoE frames and then carried over Ethernet by bridging, making the Fixed WiMAX link transparent.

DSL IPTV services over Mobile WiMAX:
The NWG has also released the architecture for connectivity of Mobile WiMAX networks to DSL-based ASP services. This architecture includes delivery systems for IPTV, as well as other application services (AS) provided via DSL networks.

The interface of DSL networks to WiMAX has been defined by the NWG to two levels of inter-working.

1. The first scenario consists of the use of the Mobile WiMAX protocols (IEEE 802.16e) but targeted for fixed or nomadic applications. In this case, the mobile station is present within the area of coverage of an ASN and mobility and handover are not involved. A simple solution of Ethernet bridging can be implemented in this scenario if the same is also supported by the ASN. The Ethernet bridging happens via a direct connection to the ASN from the Ethernet aggregation point (V). The PPP protocols are carried over the Ethernet via PPoE frames as in the case of Fixed WiMAX. The authentication is established in the PPP and the PKMv2 security framework is applied for the link to the MS which is also via Ethernet bridging (Figure 15-22).
2. The second scenario involves full mobility involving the use of Mobile IP (MIP). In a general case, the interface to such networks is at the CSN which provides mobility management and interface points for external networks. In this case, an inter-working unit (IWU) is required which performs protocol management as per R5 interface on the Mobile WiMAX side and the A10 interface on the DSL side. The mobile stations are authenticated via the WiMAX mechanisms, i.e., EAP over RADIUS over the R5 interface (Figure 15-23).

In summary, for interface between Mobile WiMAX networks and DSL networks the scenarios are as follows:

- NAP connectivity is possible only for nomadic and fixed access. The connectivity is provided by an Ethernet bridged link between the DSL aggregation point and the ASN.
- NSP- and ASP-level connectivities are possible with an inter-working unit, which enables applications to seamlessly work on Mobile WiMAX networks.

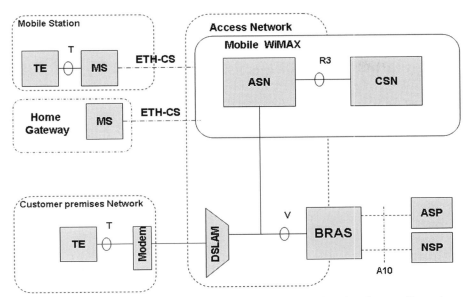

FIGURE 15-22 DSL interface to Mobile WiMAX IEEE 802.16e (fixed and nomadic use)

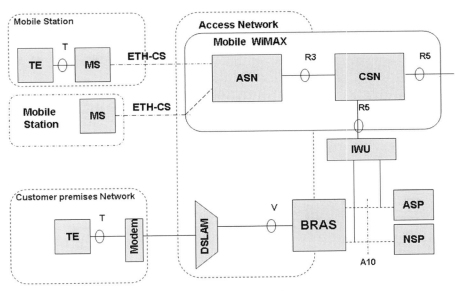

FIGURE 15-23 Mobile WiMAX interface to DSL networks

15.8.2 Korea Telecom WiBro Multicasting Channel Service

Korea is an appropriate example of the multicasting channel services as entertainment is the major application on the broadband networks in Korea (more than 60 percent usage). WiBro services have been available in South Korea since April 2006 with KT and SKT being WiBro operators. WiBro services are IEEE 802.16e-compliant and use a bandwidth of 8.75 MHz in the 2.3 GHz band.

KT provides multicasting channel services based on the solution provided by Thin Multimedia Inc. The WiBro platform operates on a Samsung platform. The KT WiBro services are comprised of a live video multicast service. Real-time transcoding and broadcast of IPTV content is handled by thinIPTV™, which is a custom software for H.264, WMV9 coding, and transcoding of content. All IPTV multimedia formats and codecs are supported in the application.

One of the convergence platforms used by KT WiBro is Intromobile's convergence solution IntroPAD™. It is designed to conceptualize and provide innovative applications using Mobile 2.0 and fixed networks convergence. The service components include a customized UI, content push, and its promotion in real time.

Another platform is the NetMirror™ designed for use over next-generation high-speed networks such as HSPA, Mobile WiMAX, or WiBro. It is a "next-generation" personal media blog and personal broadcasting service platform (unicast or multicast), based upon Web 2.0 for interactive user created content (UCC) services in the mobile and fixed-line environment. Users have access to a menu with options such as live broadcast, video UCC, Hot UCC, My Album etc.

More details on the KT WiBro services are available in Chapter 21.

CONVERGED ARCHITECTURE, DESIGN AND APPLICATIONS

16

MOBILE BROADCASTING USING WiMAX: A TECHNOLOGY OVERVIEW

I can't understand why people are frightened of new ideas. I'm frightened of the old ones.

—*John Cage*

The need to deliver multimedia content to mobile devices has given rise to a number of technologies. These are based on the use of different types of networks such as 3G, mobile TV broadcast, or IP-based networks and have been briefly described in Chapter 14. The emergence of these technologies is a reflection on the growth of new capabilities of mobile cellular and wireless networks.

The common denominator in the use of these technologies is the need to deliver video (and associated audio) characterized by variable rate coded frames occurring every 33–40 ms and needing carriage in a low-latency environment.

We have seen earlier that while wireless networks (such as 802.11 b/g or n) do have the capabilities to carry video, due to the inherent mechanisms to deal with access contention and spectrum requirements, these are best suited to home environments or indoor use with a limited number of users or devices.

The need to deliver broadcast, multicast, or unicast video over medium distances, e.g., a few kilometres, leads to the use of cellular, broadcast, or WiMAX technologies. These three types of delivery technologies have grown independently in their own domains.

The objective of this chapter is to define the business processes and technologies which enable an efficient implementation of triple-play services using multicast/unicast over WiMAX networks. In this process, we look at the contemporary technologies for mobile broadcasting and the positioning of the WiMAX-based MBS service implementations.* The objective is to engineer a network which can deliver live as well as "on demand" media, broadband internet with emphasis on Web 2.0 services, and VoIP. It should be recognized that the mobile WiMAX networks are optimized for personal IP broadband with a guaranteed QoS. Delivery of triple play services needs the WiMAX network to interface with the cellular mobile (3G-GSM or CDMA) networks and the public telephony networks via the IP multimedia system (IMS). The technologies for mobile devices which operate in the cellular mobile domain are dictated by the third-generation partnership project (3GPP) and the mobile devices available follow the OMA guidelines. Hence, we also look briefly at these technologies in relation to the mobile WiMAX.

16.1 HOW ARE BROADCAST AND MULTICAST SERVICES PROVIDED OVER MOBILE NETWORKS?

Multicasting is essentially streaming of content to multiple devices by enabling multicast features in devices such as routers which implement the IGMPv2 or IGMPv3 protocols and ensure repetition of content in all routers where there are authorized receivers. The provision of broadcast and multicast services over mobile networks should in principle be very similar to multicasting over fixed-line broadband networks, i.e., IP-based networks. If this is the case, do wireless networks involve any special considerations? There indeed are some major differences when the extension of multicasting to mobile networks is concerned. These differences can be summarized as below:

- Wireless links in mobile environment can be subject to sharp variations in signal strengths. In a unicast mode, the transmission can be adapted to the transmission conditions by feedback from the receiver (such as adaptive modulation and ARQ in WiMAX). However this possibility does not exist in a multicast mode. In the absence of feedback mechanisms on actual transmission conditions and the error rates which individual receivers are subject to, none of the techniques such as adaptive modulation, power control, or repeat transmissions (ARQ) can be effectively deployed. Hence, in any real-life environment some of the mobile stations will suffer from degradation of service. By tailoring the link parameters, such

---

* The MBS service of mobile WiMAX is under finalization by the Network Working Group (NWG). Until such time that it is finalized, commercial implementations of MBS should be considered proprietary.

number can be limited to a very small fraction. In case of Mobile WiMAX the multicast and broadcast service (MBS) has been designed for multi-base station operation by using a multi-diversity feature as explained later in the chapter. Additional protection can be provided in the application layer by FEC codes. The use of additional FEC is also the mechanism adopted in 3GPP-MBMS service, where multi-base station diversity operation is not possible. 3GPP uses application layer FEC using Raptor codes. TDtv, which is an implementation of MBMS over the 3G unpaired spectrum by IPwireless® also provides for content which is synchronized over all base stations in a service area.

- Mobile links (cellular or WiMAX) include the coverage of multiple base stations within which the multicast must be replicated in order to enable the mobile devices to roam and retain connectivity. Hence, the multicasting protocols available for wireline networks need to be extended for roaming and handoffs. In case of cellular networks, the 3GPP Release 6 (2005) has introduced the MBMS services, which now form the basis of multicast services in 3G networks. Such networks are now in wide use. We will take a brief look at the features of MBMS service in this chapter. In case of Mobile WiMAX, the IEEE 802.16e-2005 standards have the provision for multicasting via the MBS (multicast and broadcast services) as an integral part of the Mobile WiMAX standard. All chipsets and reference designs provide support for MBS service as its toolkit is included as a part of Release 1 of the WiMAX Forum certification profiles.

- Multicasting services in most cases require the mobile station to be authenticated for receiving the multicast services and maintain the authentication while using the service as well as while roaming from one cell area to another. The MBS service of Mobile WiMAX as well as the MBMS service supports this feature.

- At the network layer, mobile networks should be able to establish calls which are identified as multicast calls with appropriate types of content (such as video or audio), different bit rates or standards (such as H.264 or Windows Media) and invoke the appropriate client in the handsets. Hence, there need to be standard protocols for calling, answering, and establishing multicast streaming calls. These protocols need to be followed identically across networks so that the calls can be established between users on different networks. Having well defined protocols also helps the handset manufacturers to deliver phones which can work identically on various networks. The procedures for setting up calls as well as the packet switched streaming have been formalized for cellular networks under the 3G-324M recommendations for video calls and the 3GPP-PSS (3GPP-Packet switched streaming services) for video streaming, respectively. For multicasting, the 3GPP Release 6-MBMS standards provide these procedures. In case of Mobile WiMAX, as the protocols are specified up to the MAC layer only, the network layer protocols (i.e., setting up and release of calls and handling across networks) is an area being finalized by the WiMAX Forum.

- In case the multicasting is over WiMAX networks, there is a need to have the standards for encoding of video and audio defined for different applications such as video calling or video streaming. Ideally the compression technologies would use high efficiency compression algorithms such as MPEG-4 or H.264 in order to reduce bandwidth requirements for encoded video and audio. With small screen sizes it is also possible to use simple profiles for video which does not require coding of a large number of objects. It is common to use simple visual profile for video which has been formalized under the 3GPP. However it should be noted that as the WiMAX networks are also seen as an extension of the wired internet albeit with some additions such as mobility, QoS, and IPv6 enhancements, hence, unlike 3GPP networks, multiple content types have carried across to the Mobile WiMAX world. These include the Windows media, the Real video™, Apple Quicktime™, MP3 audio and other content types. These are today handled by the players being able to handle multiple types of content. This is likely to continue in the foreseeable future in WiMAX as well. This will enable standard Windows and Linux devices, which achieve mobility by virtue of WiMAX, to continue to use standard applications for streaming and multimedia. Broadcasters can keep this in mind when planning for multicast services.

- To have an adequate data rate available for uninterrupted transfer of video frames. In practice the video throughput data rates provided by the connection may vary, but on the average should be maintained above certain minimum rates based on video parameters (for example, 144 Kbps or above for video calls using QVGA encoding). Such multicast data rates are easily achieved in both the 3G networks as well as Mobile WiMAX networks. The Mobile WiMAX networks can also set up QoS parameters for each cell in the service area of the multicast. This implies that an adequate number of OFDM subchannels are assigned based on the service flows required.

In the following sections, we look at the protocols to set up multicast calls over cellular and Mobile WiMAX networks. This includes the MBMS service, which can be used over the 3G or HSPA networks, MCBCS services over 3GPP2 CDMA networks, and the MBS service over Mobile WiMAX networks.

16.2 MULTIMEDIA BROADCAST AND MULTICAST SERVICE (MBMS)

The MBMS service is a 3GPP service for use over 3G or HSPA cellular networks. The MBMS service has been designed for support of QoS in each multicasting cell area of the mobile network. MBMS is an end to end service as it provides for the session initiation and termination of the multicast service. In MBMS the users are provided the details of available multicast and broadcast services via standard IETF protocols such as IGMP messages or multicast listener delivery (MLD) protocols.

MBMS service can operate in either "streaming mode" or "download mode." As the name indicates, the download mode is non-real-time and the files can be delivered to the receiver in an error-free manner. The streaming mode involves real-time transmission.

Real-time MBMS operates in two modes: broadcast and multicast.

The broadcast mode does not include any subscription management. Broadcast mode is available to all users without any differentiation (such as payment status). The users can receive the channel with a requested QoS. In multicast mode the channel is available to select users in a specific area only. The services are delivered to the users based on the payments or subscription.

The MBMS service set-up can be explained by the following set-up procedure:

- *Service Announcement*: Operators would announce the service using advertising or messaging, etc. The announcement may go only to subscription customers in case of multicast services.
- *Joining*: The multicast users can indicate that they would be joining the service. The joining can be at any time but only the authorized users will receive the multicast service. In broadcast mode, all users will receive the service.
- *Session Starts*: The requisite resources are reserved in the core network as well as the radio networks.
- *MBMS Notification*: A notification goes out on the forthcoming service.
- *Data Transfer*: The data transfer commences and is received by all users in the selected group. In broadcast mode, all users would

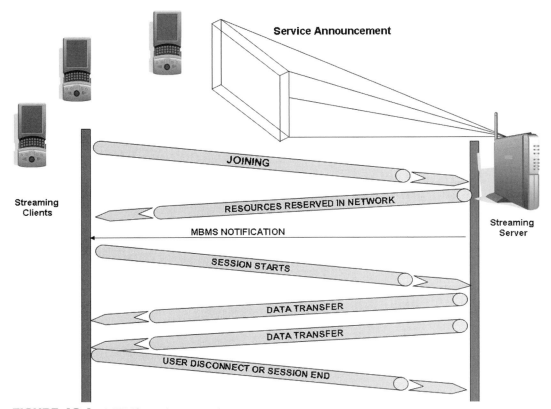

FIGURE 16-1   MBMS service operation

receive the data which is without any encryption. In multicast
mode, the data is encrypted and only the authorized users receive
the service.

- *Leaving or Session End*: In multicast mode, the users may leave the
  session at any time, or the session ends after the data transfer is
  completed.

The multicast modes involves managing data for each customer, i.e.,
subscription, joining, and leaving.

3GPP has mandated the use of H.264/AVC codec (base line profile)
as the unique recommended codec type for the MBMS services. This
provides for a certain uniformity in implementations insofar as the
streaming servers, file formats, and receiving clients are concerned.
The H.264, by virtue of its network abstraction layer, can be used over
various types of networks. This includes the RTP/UDP/IP-based
delivery in multicast wireless networks.

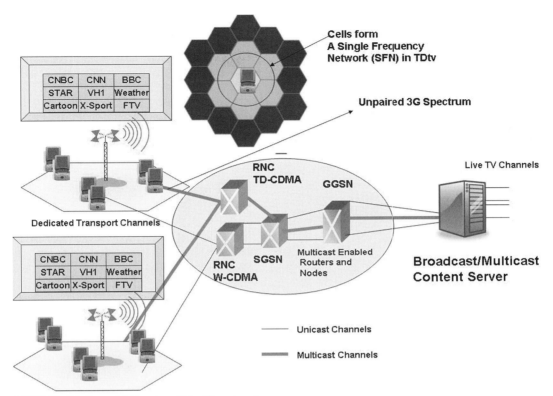

FIGURE 16-2 MBMS using TDtv™ technology

MBMS service relies on the use of the existing architecture for GSM or UMTS by making MBMS specific enhancements to the base stations.

Example of a 3GPP-MBMS Implementation

The implementation of MBMS services is best seen in TDtv, which is an implementation of the MBMS protocols on the 3G-UMTS networks. TDtv technology is an implementation of MBMS by IPwireless which is a supplier of TD-CDMA based 3G systems. It is now a part of NextWave® Wireless Inc.

TDtv has been trialed in many countries including the United Kingdom, Sweden, Spain, and Australia. TDtv can operate in unpaired spectrum slots of 3G spectrum. A 5-MHz slot can be used for providing 12 to 15 channels with high quality. By using the TDtv technology, these channels can be delivered by MBMS to a virtually unlimited number of customers.

The multicast provided via the use of TDtv technology is synchronized over the neighboring cells, which operate as a SFN network.

This effectively helps reinforce the CDMA signals from adjacent cells and provides improved multicast reception capability even near the cell edges. This is similar to the macro-diversity operation of mobile WiMAX MBS multicast services even though the physical interfaces for the two are different (CDMA vs. OFDM). The TDtv based on TD-CDMA can be used for broadcast type applications using the MBMS protocol due to a superior performance delivered by the macro-diversity feature.

16.3 MOBILE WiMAX MULTICAST AND BROADCAST SERVICE (MBS)

Multicast and broadcast service (MBS) is an important addition in mobile WiMAX for support of multicasting and broadcasting applications. In fact, the service was considered important enough to have its toolkit included in the Release 1 of the certification profiles. This ensures that mobile WiMAX wave 1-certified equipment can be used for building up multicast and broadcast services on a mobile WiMAX network.

The service is supported at the PHY layer by two mechanisms:

- Dedicating the whole downlink frame (DL) to multicast broadcast service (MBS).
- Operating a frame as a mixed frame for MBS and unicast services by providing one or more dedicated "MBS Zones" in the DL frame.

By providing MBS zones (identified in the MAP allocation in the frames), it is possible to have a multiple base station operation for multicasting when the base stations operate in an SFN mode. This is because the frames form all the base stations are synchronized and the MBS zone froming any base station is available in the same time slot. The MBS zones can be of variable duration so that only the required resources for multicasting in a particular frame are used.

The purpose of defining MBS zones is that once the MS is synchronized, it can access the MBS zone, without having to decode the DL MAP in every frame. The MBS zone is identified by the OFDM symbol offset parameter and occurs at the same location in every frame.

The advantage of being able to operate mixed unicast multicast frames is that one frequency need not be fully dedicated to only MBS services in every cell. Instead, the unicast and multicast services can operate in a mixed mode providing optimum resource utilization.

By virtue of fixed MBS zones, the mobile stations (MS) need not be aligned to any particular base station. They can receive the multicast

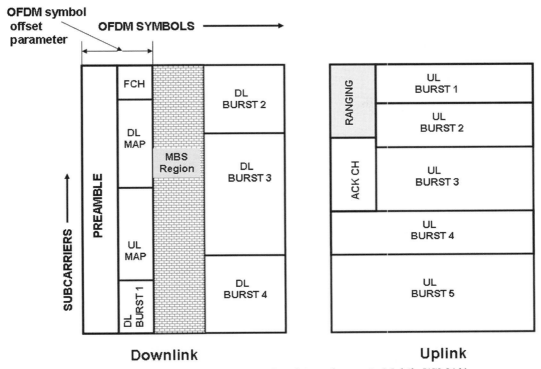

FIGURE 16-3 MBS region in mixed unicast and multicast frames in Mobile WiMAX

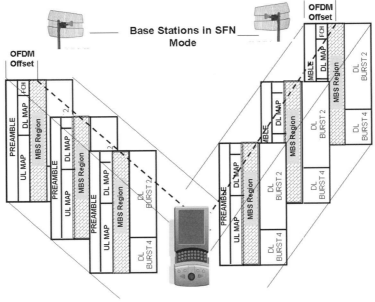

FIGURE 16-4 Multiple base stations can provide MBS services

services while receiving signals from a number of base stations. This type of synchronized transmission of multicast data from multiple base stations effectively provides a macro-diversity operation.

MBS can also be accessed in the low power mode as once a mobile station is synchronized to the MBS zone, the zone contains a pointer to the next zone. Hence, the DL MAPs need not be continuously decoded.

As the mobile WiMAX MBS services are defined only up to the MAC layer, they do not deal with how a streaming server needs to be configured in order to use the MBS service. Instead they only provide the toolkit or the APIs which a server may use to set up calls and invoke various features.

Setting Up a MBS Service over a WiMAX Network

The MBS service can be initiated by a streaming multicast server, which by virtue of performing the functions required by the MAC layer in base stations may be called the MBS Distribution Server. In a multi-base station environment, the server would set up sessions with multiple base stations. Once the sessions are established, the MBS server effectively handles the scheduling and protocol data unit (PDU) building functions for the respective base stations connected. The PDUs transmitted by the MBS distribution server* are then transmitted directly over the PHY layers of the base stations connected.

The transmissions are time synchronized in the frames. By directly sending and receiving the PDUs, the MBS server also effectively communicates directly with the subscriber stations.

Typically, an MBS service would be accessed by a mobile station (MS) after it becomes aware of it through an EPG or a web page, a function which is handled in the application layer. In a typical implementation the multicast addresses will be available via the MBS portal or HTTP page.

For connecting to an MBS service, a mobile station (MS) after performing the initial ranging, authentication, and synchronization would send a dynamic service allocation-request (DSA-REQ) message to the base station with the associated QoS parameters needed. (It is assumed that the MBS server has already been set up and is available for all MS to receive multicasts.) The BS responds with a DSA-ACK message which contains the identifier for the MBS zone selected. The MS is

---

* Until such time as the final recommendations are given on MBS by the NWG, these implementations should be considered proprietary.

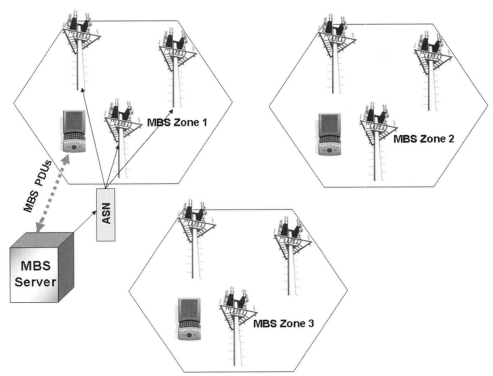

FIGURE 16-5 The MBS distribution server connects to all base stations in a MBS zone, all of which provide synchronized transmissions

now synchronized and ready to receive all the multicast data contained in the selected MBS zone.

The MS can enter the low power mode and cease to receive all DL-MAP information. It only needs to maintain the MBS zone information and receive the multicast data. In case the synchronization is lost it can be regained by using the MBS zone information available in the MS. The difference in the multicast service as compared to a unicast connection is that PHY layer functions such as adaptive modulation and ARQ can not be used.

Once the service is established, it can be maintained through the exchange of multicast and broadcast re-keying algorithm (MBRA) which maintains the security of the connections.

The multicast services can also be established by the base station with the identified mobile stations. This is done by assigning a CID for the given multicast service. The value of CID remains the same for all the mobile stations. The QoS offered and the traffic parameters are common for all mobile stations receiving the service.

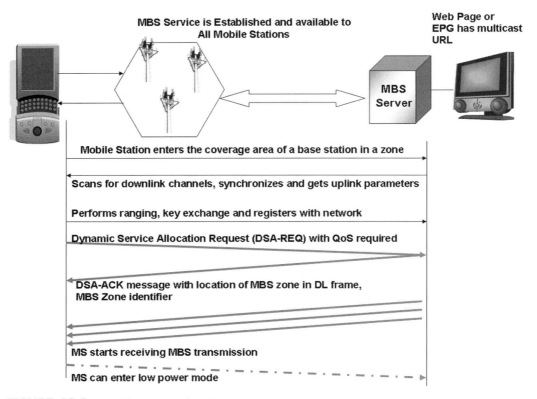

FIGURE 16-6   Establishment of MBS service

H.264 Scalable Video Coding and Multiple Streaming Connections

The standards adopted for H.264 now include scalable video coding (SVC). This type of coding generates a base layer stream and one or more enhancement layers. The higher coding layers support fine grain scalability or higher frame rates. In wireless environments (both mobile cellular and Mobile WiMAX) it is important to utilize the feature of scalable coding so that mobile devices which are facing higher error rates can still receive the base channel. In Mobile WiMAX, multiple connections can be established between the base station and the mobile stations to cater to the multiple layers of encoding. The base channel can be accorded higher priority at the MAC and PHY layer in regard to modulation and retransmissions.

16.4 BROADCAST TECHNOLOGIES: DVB-H

The use of TV broadcast networks to also carry mobile targeted video is best evidenced by the growth of DVB-H technology. DVB-H is

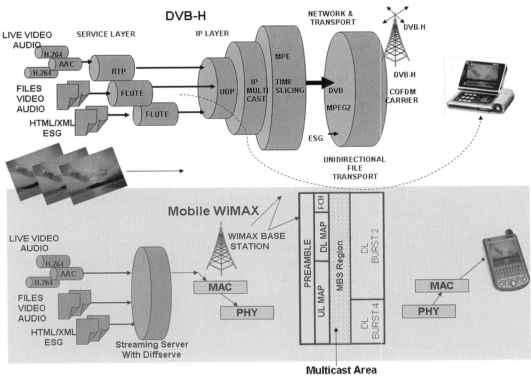

FIGURE 16-7 DVB-H and Mobile WiMAX for video transmission

characterized by the use of the same transport frame (MPEG-2) which has been in use for terrestrial broadcast services for standard television, but with added error correcting capabilities and power saving features. Being an MPEG-2 stream, the packets are all 188 bytes including the header. DVB-H uses IP encapsulation of transport stream packets, which enables an integration with IP networks. The DVB-H is essentially an IP data cast technology. The delivery of IP data packets is made either using a streaming mode (using RTP) or more commonly by using Flute which is a unidirectional file transfer protocol for delivery of content over broadcast media. Flute transfers data in carousels, which enables the receivers to obtain the entire file in an error free manner. The robust transmission capabilities, which are achieved by the use of 4K or 8K OFDM carriers in DVB-H, the multi-protocol encapsulation (MPE), and coding help the unidirectional protocols such as Flute to deliver content without the need for seeking for retransmission of lost packets.

On the other hand, WiMAX technologies use fewer OFDM subcarriers (512 in Mobile WiMAX) but depend on the robust transmission provided by multiple features inherent to WiMAX. These include controlling service flows to guarantee sustained bit rates, classes of traffic, hybrid ARQ mechanism (HARQ) in MAC and PHY layers, and adaptive modulation to maintain the throughput needed to deliver video in a mobile environment.

16.4.1 Common Implementation Profiles for Multicasting/IP Datacasting Services:

We have drawn some parallels between the DVB-H IP datacasting and MBS multicasting services in order to highlight the commonality in the overall architecture, except for the medium of physical transmission. The same commonality is inherent in the MBMS services, which are also multicast and broadcast services. The only additions to a multicast service are the manner in which the electronic service guide (ESG) and content protection (CA or DRM) are implemented.

The Open Mobile Alliance (OMA) has been involved in developing common profiles for implementation by various operators and service providers so that the services and handsets can be interoperable across different networks. OMA had adopted its first common profile in the form of OMA BCAST 1.0. The use of OMA BCAST is being seen as a key to promote multi-vendor mobile TV interoperability. OMA BCAST specification is not limited to the DVB-H-based broadcast networks. It also applies to MBMS or other multicast networks.

The Broadcast Mobile Convergence Forum (bmcoforum®) has further focused on the OMA BCAST specifications to develop a profile for implementation of multicast and broadcast services. The bmcoforum profile supports multiple broadcast technologies. It has the specification of an advanced service guide (ESG) for common implementation. The content and service protection is based on OMA DRM 2.0 or alternatively SIM-based smart card profile. The profile supports both DVB-H and MBMS. At present the largest support for the bmcoforum profiles is in Europe.

It is important to recall that the alternative implementation profile for DVB-H is the DVB-CBMS, which is a profile adapted by the DVB. The CBMS implantation profiles also deal with the EPG, service discovery, and content protection. However there are significant differences between the way these are implemented in DVB-CBMS and OMA-BCAST. The CBMS is primarily focused on SIM-based CA system for content protection in line with the broadcast industry norms while the OMA standard is based on OMA digital rights management (DRM).

While these profiles are at present based on broadcast and multicast networks using cellular mobile networks, they remain important for potential deployment of mobile WiMAX devices as well as owing to the commonality of the receiving devices.

16.4.2 MediaFLO™

MediaFLO, though not a WiMAX technology, needs mention as one of the successful mobile broadcasting and multicasting technologies. When announced in 2004, it was comprised of two mechanisms for delivery of content. These were the EV-DO Platinum Multicast and the FLO™. The Platinum Multicast services were designed to enable EV-DO operators to offer multimedia content on a unicast or multicast basis. The FLO technology has developed independently and is being used today by MediaFLO USA® Inc. to provide multicast services. FLO technologies are distinguished by a number of features to support efficient multicasts in a mobile environment and have been briefly described in Chapter 14.

The physical layer of MediaFLO is also based on OFDM and provision for mobility, but the FLO data unit is only one-eighth of an OFDM symbol providing better granularity. It can also multiplex services with different modulation and coding modes during transmission. This makes it suitable for multicasting a mix of services over the same multiplex. FLO supports QoS for different services. In an 8 MHz slot, around 25 channels of video (H.264 coded) with QVGA resolution and 12 AAC audio channels can be accommodated, which makes it one of the most efficient implementations of video multicasting services.

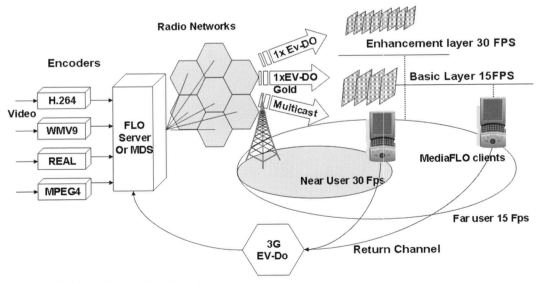

FIGURE 16-8 MediaFLO network

FLO uses turbo codes for FEC which make it robust for delivery in a multicast environment where adaptive modulation for individual devices can not be used. This coupled with the use of layered modulation under H.264 makes it an ideal multicast technology as it effectively caters to CPEs which operate in a varying reception environment owing to mobility. FLO technology has also taken into account the need to conserve power in the mobile handsets and the receiver can access only that part of the signal which contains the channel being viewed (i.e., certain subcarriers). It also allows the users to switch channels in switching times of less than 2 seconds. (The channel switching time averages around 1.5 seconds.) All these factors make it very similar to mobile WiMAX. However as the FLO technology is defined end to end, it makes the implementations easier as against mobile WiMAX which is defined only up to the MAC layer. The FLO is one way, with the 3G network playing the complementary role of the return path, while mobile WiMAX is two way and interactive. In the long run this gives mobile WiMAX greater advantage as the network and application layers can be deployed with open technologies.

An end-to-end solution is available via the MediaFLO distribution system (MDS) which provides end-to-end services for media distribution. MediaFLO is a proprietary technology of Qualcom.

16.5 SETTING UP A MULTICASTING SERVICE: HIGHER-LAYER PROTOCOLS

Mobile WiMAX technologies including the MAC- and PHY-layer protocols and the MBS service relate to the provision of the services up to the MAC convergence layer, which provides the toolkit for wireless delivery.

A complete application will include creating higher-layer protocols including:

- *Application layer*: Defining various services such as VoD, live video and audio, MP3 music, games etc. (The Application working group is working on the applications definition).
- *Session layer:* Establishing and maintaining sessions with mobile stations for individual services.
- *Network layer:* Establishing connections with QoS parameters with the WiMAX convergence layer (The Networks Working Group of WiMAX is working on reference architectures).

In addition, the definition of the final application would include additional security functions (such as DRM or conditional access) and functions for invoking appropriate clients at the receiver.

TABLE 16-1

3GPP services for video applications

S.NO	3GPP Release Reference	Services
1	3GPP Release 4 (2001)	Multimedia Messaging (MMS) Circuit Switched Video Calls (3G-324M) IP Streaming (3GPP-PSS)
2	3GPP Release 5 (2002)	IP Multimedia System (IMS) Session Initiation Protocol (SIP) Access Security
3	3GPP Release 6 (2006)	Multimedia Broadcast and Multicast Service (MBMS)
4	3GPP Release 7	Support of Multiple Access Technologies in 3GPP Support of QoS across multiple networks

In the IP world, all these higher layers such as session establishment, release, and launch of application are provided by the IETF RFCs. For example, multicast-based services can be provided using IGMPv3 (RFC 3376) or IGMPv2 (more common today). On-demand services can be handled using RTP/RTSP (RFC 2326).

16.6 3GPP: ADDRESSING INTERNETWORK ISSUES AND SERVICE DEFINITIONS

Prior to the launch of the WiMAX services, the majority of mobile devices has been the cellphones, and this status is likely to prevail for a number of years. In order to facilitate interoperability of networks, the third-generation partnership project (3GPP) has been responsible for defining services over 3G networks. For example, the establishment of a fixed bit rate video call has been defined in the 3GPP Release 4 as 3G-324M protocol. Similarly 3GPP has defined streaming services under the 3GPP (3GPP-PSS for both live streaming and download). These services have been defined for end-to-end connectivity, including session set-up, data transfer, and session end.

16.7 WiMAX INTERWORKING WITH 3GPP

The framework provided by the IP multimedia system (IMS) of the Release 5 sets the stage for end-to-end IP-based multimedia services breaking away from the circuit-switched architecture of the previous generations. It also provides for an easier integration of instant messaging and real time conversational services. The messaging enhancements include enhanced messaging and multimedia messaging.

It is important to note that the IMS resides above the session layer and is access independent (it uses SIP as the session layer protocol). Hence, it can support IP-to-IP sessions over packet data GPRS/EDGE or 3G, packet data CDMA, IP wireless LANS 802.11, 802.15, IEEE 802.16 (WiMAX) as well as wire-line IP networks.

AN EXAMPLE OF IMS SERVICES OVER WiMAX

IMS services have been implemented over WiMAX by ONEMAX, which is one of the first commercial operators to offer internet, multimedia, and voice over IP (VoIP) services over mobile WiMAX (802.16e) in the Dominican Republic, and one of the first to offer IMS over WiMAX services in the Americas. The service is implemented as per 3GPP Release 7 which provides for IMS operation over wireless networks. By treating WiMAX as an underlying network, all applications including VoIP and multimedia can be offered based on IMS architecture.

The IMS consists of session control, connection control, and application services framework. The 3GPP framework also defines the codec types (including profiles), file formats, and features such as rate adaptation for compatibility.

Figure 16-9 shows the comparison of how the 3GPP services are fully defined with all layers having been standardized. This makes it possible to implement the entire application in a uniform manner with operator or vendor independence. Release 7 of the 3GPP is aimed at facilitating multiple access technologies in 3G networks, which include WiFi and WiMAX. 3GPP has also formalized the generic access network (GAN/UMA -3GPP TS43.318) for handover between the 3G networks and WiFi networks. However, Release 7 still falls short of full mobility in the underlying access networks.

Generic Access Network

The cellular mobile industry had foreseen the potential use of WiFi phones and therefore the 3G Partnership Forum (3GPP) had worked towards dual mode WiFi cellular phones with seamless roaming. The WiFi phones were built around a clever concept evolved by the cellular industry called the Generic Access Network (GAN). The GAN was previously called the Unlicensed Mobile Access (UMA) and denoted

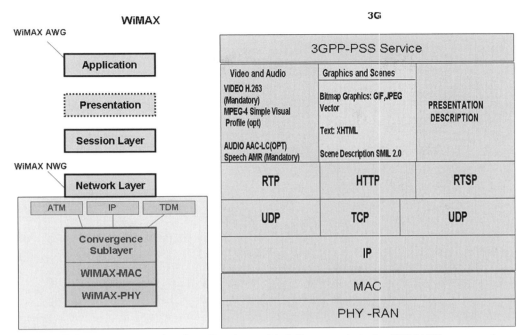

FIGURE 16-9 3GPP has defined applications with full protocol stacks, WiMAX in comparison

the development of the protocol stacks which could permit a range of access networks in a seamless manner. The available networks can include WiFi, Bluetooth, and in fact WiMAX. The GAN specifications were released by the 3GPP in April 2005 as a part of 3GPP Release 6. The first WiFi capable phones made their advent not long thereafter in 2006. The GAN, enables the dual mode phone to connect to the WiFi network in preference to a mobile network whenever the mobile is in the range of such WiFi hotspots. At the mobile base station, these signals which are now carried via the internet through the WiFi, appear to the base network controller as if coming from another base station with the capability of roaming from the WiFi to the cellular still intact. A user who moves out of range of a WiFi hotspot now appears to have moved out of one base station into the range of another station, in this case a mobile base station.

The calls, for example VoIP calls, which were established over WiFi can thus continue without interruption even though the user is mobile. The same is true of any services which are set up using the Internet Multimedia Subsystem (IMS) specified by the 3GPP. Hence, services such as push-to-talk, instant messaging, Presence, video calls, and all others specified in the IMS of a cellular operator can be provided over

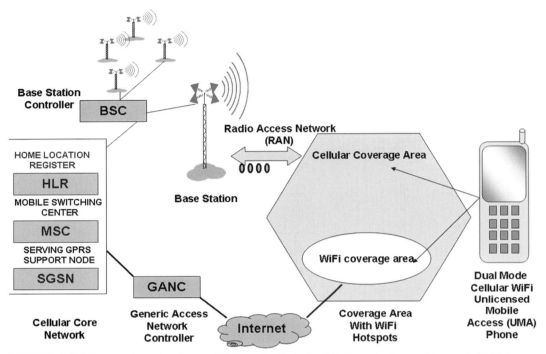

FIGURE 16-10   Dual-mode phones (WiFi and cellular) with Generic Access Network (GAN)

any network, fixed or mobile and this includes the WiFi network. This fixed-mobile integration is quite unique and a well thought-out move by the cellular mobile industry to keep revenues largely within the framework of services provided by the cellular mobile networks via the IMS even though the user might occasionally use a WiFi network. In 2007, such mobile phones and PDAs, which can operate in dual mode and support GAN, have become universally available. A number of carriers such as Telesonera® have announced service plans which permit the use of WiFi as a preferred mode when in the range of any hotspots.

The GAN also includes a security layer as a part of the protocol suite provided to enable the use of WLAN networks in a secure manner for voice and other applications.

Relationship between WiMAX and 3GPP Going Ahead

A question which arises is whether the WiMAX networks will be merely used as underlying networks with all applications, session management, etc., being based on the 3GPP and IMS mandated standards. While this may indeed be so in the near term, Mobile WiMAX is

TABLE 16-2

WiMAX application classes for common services

S. No	Application	Bandwidth Guideline	Latency Guideline	Jitter Guideline
1	Interactive gaming	Low Bandwidth, 50 Kbps	Low latency, 80 ms	–
2	Voice Telephony, Video Conferencing	Low bandwidth, 32–64 Kbps	Low latency 160 ms	Low jitter <50 ms
3	Streaming media	Moderate-high bandwidth, <2 mbps	–	Low jitter <100 ms
4	Instant messaging, web browsing	Moderate bandwidth, 2 mbps	–	–
5	Media download	High bandwidth, 10 mbps	–	–

developing into a full-fledged architecture of its own. The new implementations that are emerging use full capabilities of WiMAX and build on protocols based on IETF. This allows standard internet applications to operate seamlessly over wireless or wireline networks. The use of WiMAX, will also not be limited to 3GPP profiles, which are primarily designed for mobile phones or PDAs with limited screen resolutions and processor limitations. The WiMAX networks, on the other hand, are being implemented to support a full suite of applications which reside on PCs, or provide a broadcast environment paralleling wireline IPTV.

It is expected that interoperability will be maintained across applications and networks for support of various services such as VoIP, broadband internet, and multimedia streaming or download.

16.8 WiMAX APPLICATION CLASSES

The WiMAX forum applications working group has specified five initial application profiles. This implies that the WiMAX equipment which is certified in Release 1 should be able to support these application classes (Table 16-2).

16.9 RELATIVE POSITIONING OF WiMAX WITH 3G AND EVOLVED NETWORKS

It is important to understand the positioning of mobile WiMAX for wireless broadband services and in particular for video streaming, download, and access to Web 2.0 services vis-à-vis 3G mobile services.

Over one billion users had access to 3G networks by 2007 and 3G broadband users exceeded 65 million. Over 100 networks had support for HSDPA delivering 0.5–1.5 Mbps downlink data rates. 3G products are also available for laptops in addition to the default devices such as handsets or PDAs. HSDPA and EV-DO USB modems have been available for enabling other devices with mobile broadband for some time now. So what then is the positioning of the mobile WiMAX in this environment? We have already seen the data rate capabilities of HSPA and EV-DO networks. Here we review the video multicasting capabilities of these networks.

16.9.1 HSDPA

Data Capabilities of the HSDPA Network for Video Streaming

Under normal conditions, the HSDPA network can deliver 384 Kbps to up to 50 users in a cell area, which is a 10-fold improvement over the Release 99 WCDMA where only 5 users could be provided such throughputs.

As per an analysis (Ericsson) for HSDPA networks with 95 percent of satisfied users, 128 Kbps streaming service can be provided at 12 Erlang of traffic. Under low usage conditions (i.e., 2 × 5 minutes per

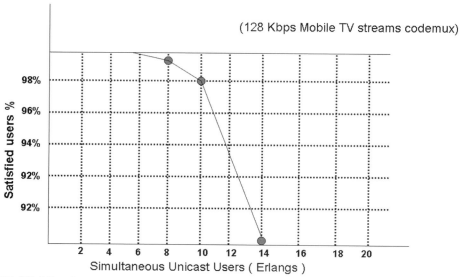

FIGURE 16-11 Capacity of HSDPA system for simultaneous unicast users, mobile TV (data courtesy Erickson)

day) all the users in the cell area (assumed density per cell of users as 600) can get satisfactory service. For medium usage (assumed 5×10 minutes per day) the users that can be catered to within the satisfaction level falls to 171 per cell or 28 percent while for high usage (e.g., 4×20 minutes) the usage falls to 108 users per cell or 18 percent.

This serves to illustrate that HSDPA networks are suited for broadband applications, VoIP, and unicast traffic which can cater to a limited number of users per cell area and limited viewing times. Mobile WiMAX, on the other hand, is designed to deal with multicast services which can cater to thousands of users in a cell area.

16.9.2 EV-DO Rev 0

The EV-DO technologies are an evolution of CDMA networks to provide high downlink data rates. The CDMA technologies are based on the use of carriers of 1.25 MHz bandwidth. Multiple carriers can be used to enhance the capacity of the system. The CDMA 2000 standards are based on the use of 3 carriers of 1.25 MHz and can provide a capacity equivalent to a 5 MHz 3G-UMTS carrier. The multiple carrier approach has been used for air interface compatibility with the CDMA (IS-95) networks.

The data-only evolutions, paralleling the HSDPA, are represented in the EV-DO technologies. These technologies are being standardized under the 3GPP2 Forum. The 1x EV-DO is based on the use of one carrier of 1.25 MHz for data only use. The 1x EV-DO networks achieve high throughputs with a 1.25 MHz bandwidth by using advanced modulation and RF technology. This includes, first, an adaptive modulation system, which allows the radio node to increase its transmission rate based on the feedback from the mobile. It also uses advanced "turbo-coding" and multilevel modulation which acts to increase the data rates at the PHY layer. It also uses macro-diversity via a sector selection process and a feature called multi-user diversity. The multi-user diversity permits a more efficient sharing of resources among the active users. Using these techniques, it is possible to achieve data rates of 4.9 Mbps in a 1.25 MHz carrier.

Multicast on EV-DO Networks using BCMCS

A multicast is characterized by the transmission of the same content on all the sectors, irrespective of the quality of reception being reported by the receivers. In order to build in resilience to errors, additional error correction (RS coding over and above the turbo codes) is used. In addition a feature called soft combining enhances the gains with signals from multiple sectors.

The EV-DO Rev 0 is the first version of EV-DO, which supports the BCMCS multicast technology for delivery of multimedia. The advantage of providing multicast services via the BCMCS networks is that new networks (such as in DVB-H) are not needed where the EV-DO services are already available. However even though the EV-DO Rev 0 technology supported higher data rates, the support for QoS was absent making the service suited only for applications such as messaging or file downloads. While EV-DO Rev 0 had the capability of 2.4 Mbps data downlink speed, the uplink was limited to only around 153 Kbps, resulting in constraints for many multimedia applications involving uploading of pictures or videos.

16.9.3 EV-DO REV A and REV B

A different approach was adopted for multicast services in the new revisions of EV-DO in order to enhance data rates and mobility. This involves the use of OFDM modulation of the TDM carriers which are used to carry the data in EV-DO. Rev A also provides support of QoS and consequently better support for real time services such as VoIP or video streaming (mobile IPTV). Multiple service flows (on the lines of WiMAX) are possible each with its own QoS. The physical layer also uses automatic retransmissions (HARQ) on the reverse link. With all the enhancements, the EV-DO Rev A has become very popular for support of multimedia applications and is offered by many carriers. It offers downlink data rates of 3.1 Mbps and uplink data rates of 1.8 Mbps (i.e., a total of 4.9 Mbps).

The EV-DO Rev B is based on the use of 3 carriers of 1.25 MHz. With 4.9 Mbps being supported in each channel, a total bandwidth of 14.7 Mbps can be supported. (These figures are for using the highest modulation scheme and the average will be about a half of this figure in field.) It is only with the use of EV-DO Rev B that mobile TV for multiple users can be effectively supported. The use of 64 QAM has also been introduced in Rev B. By increasing the number of carriers, data rates of up to 73.5 Mbps can theoretically be supported by EV-DO Rev B. Qualcomm integrated chipsets for EV-DO Rev B became available in 1Q 2007 paving the way for introduction of this new technology.

16.9.4 EV-DO Rev C: Ultra Mobile Broadband

In the meantime, 3GPP2 has been working on the next release version of the EV-DO called the EV-DO Rev C (now called the Ultra Mobile Broadband or UMB). This is based on OFDMA technology and can operate in bandwidths of 1.25–20 MHz. Advanced features such as

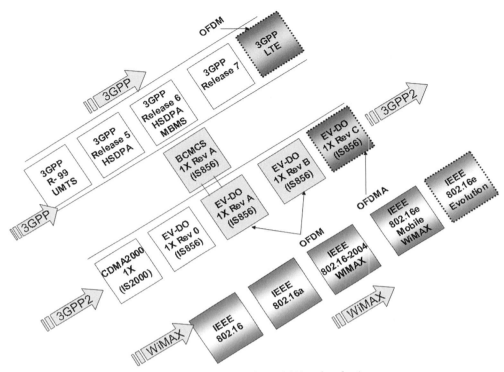

FIGURE 16-12   Evolution of 3GPP, 3GPP2, and WiMAX technologies

4×4 MIMO, beamforming, and SDMA are supported with operation in FDD and TDD modes. The technology has been designed for use with ultra low latency of <16 ms and can well support applications such as VoIP. With data rates (with 20 MHz bandwidth and 64 QAM modulation) reaching 300 Mbps DL and 80 Mbps uplink, QoS support, applications such as unicast and multicast video can be supported. Roaming to 3G networks is also a built-in feature of UMB.

16.9.5 Positioning of WiMAX in "Evolving Technologies"

With both the 3GPP and 3GPP2 technologies adapting the use of the OFDM/OFDMA technology in the physical layer, use of short packet lengths and HARQ, and adaptive modulation (64 QAM to QPSK), the long term evolution technologies look deceptively similar to Mobile WiMAX. What then is the difference between the WiMAX and the EV-DO Rev B so far as mobile Video applications are concerned?

The answer lies in evaluating the key strengths of the Mobile WiMAX. First of all, Mobile WiMAX supports TDD (Time Division Duplexing)

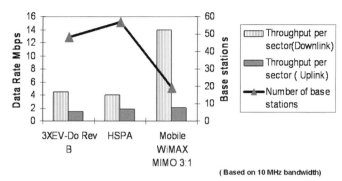

FIGURE 16-13   Base stations and sector throughputs in 3xEV-DO, HSPA, and Mobile WiMAX with 10 MHz bandwidth

which allows for higher spectral density. This is due to the asymmetric nature of the traffic in multimedia applications. The TDD feature provides flexibility in dynamically configuring the uplink and downlink capacities for optimum use. The scalable OFDMA with multiple schemes for allocation of subcarriers is also unique to Mobile WiMAX. (fractional frequency reuse and frequency selective scheduling). The small frame size of 5 ms is also well suited for low latency applications. The TDD feature also helps in support of advanced antenna systems.

Mobile WiMAX with MIMO also significantly reduces the infrastructure cost as the number of base stations needed can be about one-third of that needed for EV-DO Rev B. Figure 16-13 shows the comparison among Mobile WiMAX, HSPA, and EV-DO Rev B using a total of 10 MHz of bandwidth and Dl/UL traffic ratio of 2:1. As the EV-DO and HSPA are based on FDD, it assumes the use of 2×5 MHz carriers in the assigned bandwidth. This allows 3 x EV-DO Rev B to operate in the DL 5 MHz bandwidth. In the case of Mobile WiMAX the entire 10 MHz bandwidth is available as TDD, which can be shared between uplink and downlink. The frequency reuse is assumed as applicable for three sectors in case of Mobile WiMAX. Another advantage of the Mobile WiMAX is the MBS multicast service which can be used for broadcast or multicast of a number of programs in a given area.

At the same time up-gradation to EV-DO or HSPA is the preferred option for existing 3G operators (CDMA or 3G-UMTS) as they have the existing infrastructure. Nevertheless, Mobile WiMAX is an overlay network and can be advantageously deployed in many situations even to supplement 2G or 3G services for enhanced data connectivities.

Mobile WiMAX is also based on an IPv6 core network and is based on the use of open technologies of OFDM/OFDMA rather than proprietary technological elements used in CDMA and 3G-UMTS networks.

17

BROADCAST APPLICATIONS OF WiMAX NETWORKS

"What is the use of a book," thought Alice, "without pictures or conversations?"

—Lewis Carroll, Alice in Wonderland (1865)

WiMAX networks have been designed to provide broadband wireless access with QoS parameters, and provide assured service flows for each connection. WiMAX also has a service class, "real-time polling service" (rtPS), which is designed to cater to variable rate data packets such as those generated in MPEG with low latencies in order to meet video transmission requirements. Transmission of video over wireless networks, prior to deployment of WiMAX systems, had always been a challenge because of the high sustained bit rates, which need to be maintained for every user on the network. WiMAX networks, by providing a very efficient multi-carrier OFDM-based physical layer which overcomes intersymbol interference, modulation adapted to transmission conditions, frequency selective assignment to subcarriers to overcome interference, HARQ, beamforming, and efficient error correction mechanisms, present a combination of technologies, which deliver sustained high bit rates. This combined with the characteristics of the MAC layer to establish service classes and ensure service flows with each class, complete the environment needed for delivery of high bit rate low-latency services such as audio and video, which overcome the vagaries of the wireless medium associated with non-line of sight transmission, sharp changes in signal levels and interference. Finally, in addition to guaranteed service flows, mobile WiMAX also brings in the multicast and broadcast services (MBS) wherein video can be efficiently multicast over a wireless medium, thus using

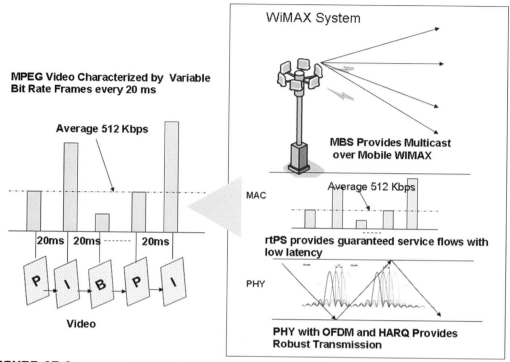

FIGURE 17-1   WiMAX systems for carriage of unicast or multicast video

only a fraction of the capacity available in a cell for delivering video services.

A number of applications are now emerging which are using WiMAX as a wireless delivery medium. The performance which is achievable over WiMAX for video and audio services can be quite in contrast with the performance over the public internet, a medium which has been associated with services such as internet TV, and where the performance leaves a lot to be desired.

17.1 INTERNET RADIO

Internet radio has now become universal, and virtually all radio stations worldwide have an internet streaming feed. Internet radio stations are available from a variety of websites, the major ones being Yahoo!Music, Microsoft MSN Radio, Live365.com, Radio@AOL, etc. Most of the radio stations are free and provide access to live as well as downloadable music and videos.

Internet radio can be a rebroadcast of the terrestrial or satellite radio stations (DARS or DAB) and may have specialized content such as music or education which is of interest to smaller communities scattered throughout the world.

Setting up an internet radio station is a relatively easy operation. The best option is to use a third-party website such as Live365.com because the web station has the necessary infrastructure to set up webcasts and thousands of audio streams that may be used to be unicast or multicast. A fee of $15 per month gives a broadcaster a "premium package" with 100 MB of content space and live broadcast facility. The 100 MB space can be used to upload content which can be retrieved as on-demand content or be played as a playlist. A live relay facility from the server of a broadcaster is also available. Users can have access to streams with RealOne, Windows Media, iTunes, and Winamp formats.

For setting up your own server a number of free options are available such as:

- Quicktime™ Streaming Server
- Helix™ Universal Server
- Quicktime™ broadcaster
- Andromeda (on demand software)

Some websites also offer free radio set-up accounts (e.g., Shoutcast.com).

Internet radio is an excellent way to receive radio stations that may not be broadcast in your area. Users do not need any expansive software: Windows Media player, Realplayer™ or Apple Quicktime players (iTunes™) can serve the needs quite well. There are also some software packages available which provide a better interface for reception of radio stations via the internet. Some examples are SelectRadio™ for PDAs with Windows mobile or Mundu Radio™ for various Nokia phones, smart phones, or Palm OS-based PDAs. Internet radio can also be received without a PC on some stand-alone devices (internet appliances).

However, the reception of internet radio depends on the availability of a good and inexpensive internet connection (i.e., 128 Kbps or above for quality stereo sound and 300 Kbps for QVGA video). Second, a majority of devices that are used to receive internet radio are PCs, laptops, or PDAs. Internet on mobile devices has been limited by the availability of wireless transmissions as well as the availability of mobile internet devices. The problems of radio delivered over the internet can become more severe in the case of a popular event being featured, resulting in many thousands of users in a given access area using the unicast streams. Multicast is difficult to set up over unprotected internet. The radio can simply freeze in such conditions.

Wireless Internet Radio

An example of an "internet appliance" for reception of radio is a wireless-based internet radio (Grundig® IR6114). Without using a computer or being attached to the wires, the device, once in the range of any WiFi network, can connect to and play any radio station. The internet radio receiver uses the www.recieva.com network to stream content from any of the selected stations. Over 2500 stations are available via this network. The receiver makes the task of selection of stations easy as it organizes them by country, region, and genre.

The emergence of WiFi internet radio receivers shows the need of niche wireless products to be able to access internet radio from across the world. Neither the internet nor a wireless network, however, can guarantee that a radio station once selected will stream flawlessly owing to net traffic considerations. Also, the WiFi networks are not omnipresent.

WiMAX is set to change all this, first by making available devices that can have quality internet access on the move, and second by

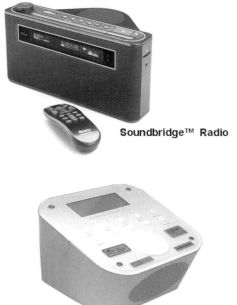

Soundbridge™ Radio

Acoustic Energy™

Grundig IR6114

Recieva Wireless Household Internet Radio

FIGURE 17-2   Wireless internet radio receivers

virtue of sustained throughputs with guaranteed bit rates which can be protected by WiMAX QoS features. WiMAX provides coverage to entire metropolitan areas, which effectively means making available all internet radio stations in the area on wireless devices. WiMAX operators can also configure dedicated links to the sites of some of the local stations (i.e. multicast links) and deliver the same over WiMAX networks. Figure 17-4 shows the configuration of an internet radio aggregation site connected to the internet and delivering audio/ video streams. A WiMAX network (IEEE 802.16-2004 or IEEE 802.16e-2005) can connect to the internet to provide the internet radio service to all the mobiles in the coverage area. WiMAX can also help by connecting all WiFi hotspots and making them live for internet radio. Many such hotspots may be in indoor areas where conventional radios do not reach.

The connection of such an aggregation site to the internet can be via normal access (without any measures for QoS), in which case, while the WiMAX network itself will support QoS over the wireless for

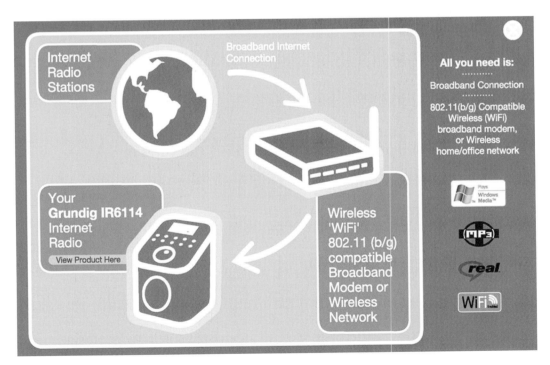

FIGURE 17-3 Wireless internet radio working with a home WiFi network (Picture courtesy Grundig)

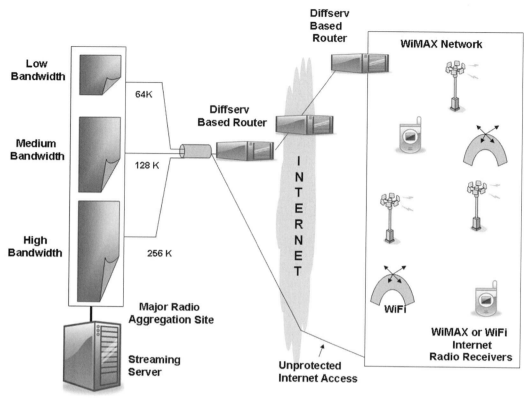

FIGURE 17-4 WiMAX network delivering internet radio

audio/video, any limitations of throughput on the internet will be reflected on the users to some extent. The WiMAX network can still control the QoS by:

- Using adaptive modulation to improve PHY layer based on transmission conditions.
- Increasing transmitted power and using the ARQ mechanisms.
- Denying entry to additional users when resources are restricted.

An alternative can be to use either resource reservation protocols on the internet or to use Diffserv-based priority control to manage QoS of connections. As the IPv6 gains momentum, the internet will increasingly be configured to provide end-to-end QoS. Radio receiver clients installed on the mobile WiMAX devices will also be increasingly used to enforce QoS, such as that needed for "internet radio" or HD radio.

It should be recognized that providing wireless devices with QoS can transform the traditional radio industry dominated by local stations

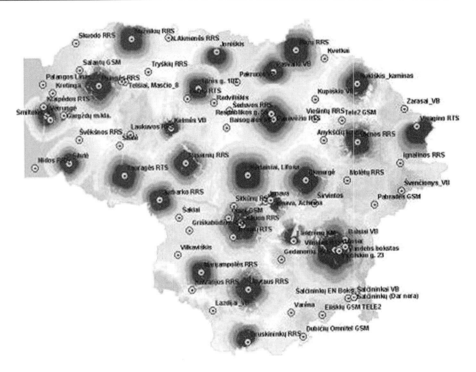

FIGURE 17-5   Pre-WiMAX 3.5 GHz network of Lithuanian radio and TV center (Picture courtesy ITU)

where only a few remote radio stations are available over the internet to one where radio stations are available irrespective of geographical location.

It is expected that in the initial period, while the Mobile WiMAX devices are becoming available, the WiFi-based receivers will be used and later be replaced by Mobile WiMAX-based internet access.

Example of WiMAX-Based TV and Radio Network

An example of a pre-WiMAX-based 3.5 GHz network being used to deliver radio and TV over IP, VoIP, and broadband internet access is that of the Lithuanian radio and TV center.

The figure shows the position of the WiMAX towers as well as the GSM towers.

How to Set up a WiMAX Internet Radio Station

It is possible to set up an internet station by hosting it on the website of any of the internet radio aggregators (such as AOL365) for only a small monthly fee. But if there is a WiMAX operator in your area, it is possible to go beyond just setting up a web internet radio station. Following are the steps needed to set up a WiMAX-based radio service:

- Set up multicast: It is possible, for example to set up a multicast with the WiMAX operator so that the radio station is available to all users in the coverage area. The WiMAX operator would typically treat this multicast as a broadband service and charges would be payable for the same to the network operator. On demand streaming may need to be provided separately.
- Set up a dedicated IP connection with the WiMAX operator to ensure end-to-end QoS. This allows the radio operator to offer a radio service which is distinguished by quality from other internet broadcasters and eventually compete with terrestrial stations. With sharply falling prices of internet data pipes, this would be an attractive option.
- Mobile WiMAX has a built-in feature of multicast broadcast service (MBS), which means that a service provider can plan for a multicast service which is tailored to the Mobile WiMAX network. Mobile WiMAX client devices will provide native support to the MBS, the service being supported in the MAC and PHY layers of the WiMAX service.

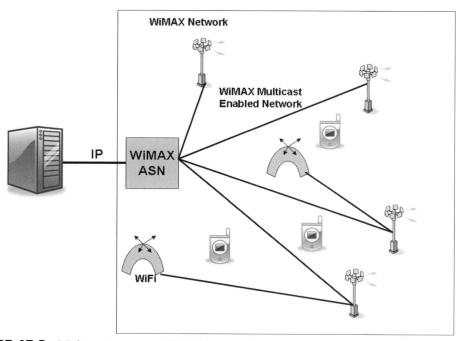

FIGURE 17-6 Multicasting over a WiMAX network

What Is the Advantage of Setting up Radio Stations in WiMAX Networks?

Setting up a radio station interconnected with WiMAX has many potential advantages. The operator can distinguish its network with:

- Local content and live interaction using the broadband connectivity
- Offering peer-to-peer or user uploadable broadcasting
- Setting up a radio station that is distinguished by features such as 5.1 DTS sound.

Local stations delivered using WiMAX can receive advertising support, which may be difficult on a general internet radio.

17.2 TV OVER WiMAX

TV over WiMAX is a natural application of the WiMAX network and is in principle similar to the IPTV. Like IPTV, a limited set of channels is encoded and streamed live from a streaming server. The content would also be protected via a digital rights management system (or DRM) and in addition the transmission may also be protected by an encryption system.

The differences lie in the fact that the services are delivered over the WiMAX wireless medium and may be targeted at mobile or handheld devices as well and include a rich interactivity environment.

Some of the unique features of WiMAX TV are as follows:

- Targeted national, regional, and local advertising.
- Support of full motion video (e.g., 50 FPS) with full screen resolution (VGA higher including HD).
- Better presentation of live content, EPG, and on, demand features with mobile clients or via desktops and STBs.
- Better integration with home networks today served by ADSL-based IPTV.
- Higher quality of channels owing to better channel speeds and QoS support.
- Quick introduction of new services and applications due to open standards environment.
- Higher interactivity with customers including uploading of their pictures or videos and provision of user generated content.
- Availability of a larger range of channels as well as on-demand content with search, indexing, and a mix of multicast and unicast deliveries.
- Enabling WiFi hotspots with TV services.

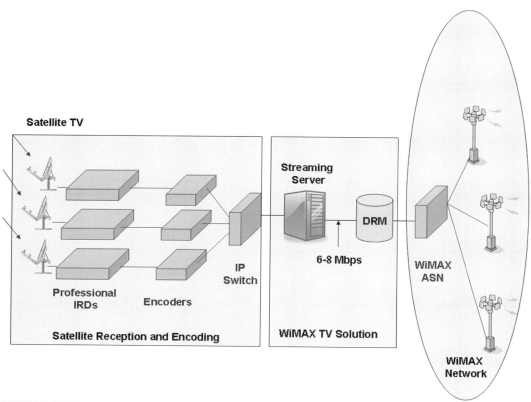

FIGURE 17-7   WiMAX TV solution

A typical configuration of a TV over a WiMAX operator would consist of a set-up as shown in Figure 17-7.

The set-up consists of essentially three parts. The first part is a digital headend, where the satellite channels are received from satellites and encoded by MPEG-4, Windows Media, Real or QuickTime® encoders and combined into an IP stream. At this stage, the TV channels which may aggregate to a total of 6 to 8 Mbps are ready to be delivered via any media to customers. The second part is the WiMAX TV solution. The compressed audio and video data is streamed using live streamers and also encrypted or subjected to DRM so that only authorized customers can view the content.

The third part is the WiMAX network itself, where the media streams are delivered for transmission. The media streams may also include RSS streams. The WiMAX TV may be received by using WiMAX customer premises equipment (CPEs) in case of Fixed WiMAX (IEEE 802.16-2004) or may be delivered directly to mobile devices which have a built-in

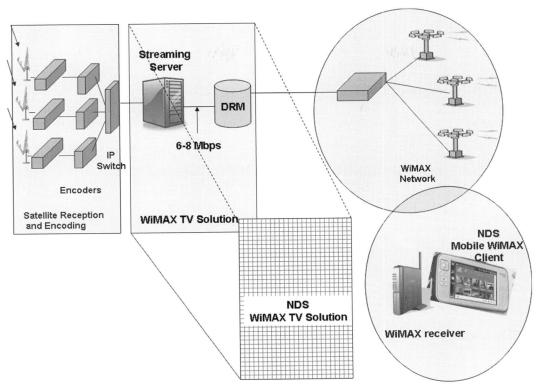

FIGURE 17-8   NDS WiMAX TV solution

WiMAX chipset for reception (IEEE 802.16e-2005). The devices need to contain a mobile client for DRM and decryption capabilities.

Figure 17-8 shows the typical configuration in a WiMAX TV solution being used from NDS (NDS WiMAX TV™).

Bit Rates and TV Standards

Carriage of TV over broadband wireless to fixed and mobile devices raises the questions: What bit rates can be supported over WiMAX? Is it possible to support SDTV and HDTV and at what bit rates? How many users can be sustained in a given area at these bit rates? These are indeed the questions which need to be answered for successful operations of any IPTV service.

WiMAX as a technology can support high bit rates as compared to wired broadband delivered over the phone networks. With IEEE 802.16-2004 using a bandwidth of 20 MHz, it is possible to achieve 75 Mbps with a single frequency in an LOS environment. This implies that by dedicating a single frequency (which may fall in an unlicensed band of 5.8 MHz,

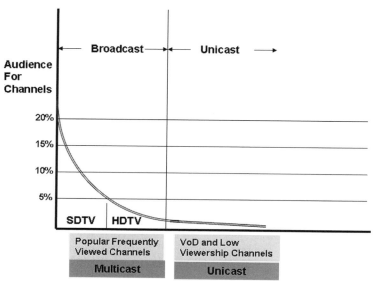

FIGURE 17-9   Audience for unicast and multicast channels

for example, for rural areas), it is possible to provide a service running at an aggregate theoretical bit rate of 75 Mbps and average bit rates of above 36 Mbps. This can mean that the most viewed channels can be multicast while others channels can be offered on-demand viewing basis.

Using H.264 encoding, a QVGA channel (suitable for mobile devices) can be encoded at 256 Kbps , a SDTV at 1 Mbps, and HDTV at 4 Mbps.

17.2.1 How to Set Up a WiMAX TV Service

A TV service running over a WiMAX network is comprised of two constituents:

- **Multicast content:** Multicast routing will be set up (IGMPv3.0) in all the WiMAX cell areas and the same channels will be available in a multicast mode irrespective of the cell in which a user happens to be. The users (who have the right to receive the content) can view a list of channels being multicast and join any channel which they wish. In case of mobile WiMAX networks, it will be possible for a user to move to another cell area and continue on the multicast cell available in this area.
- **Unicast content:** A second set of channels may be delivered to specific users as unicast content. In this case the WiMAX network will

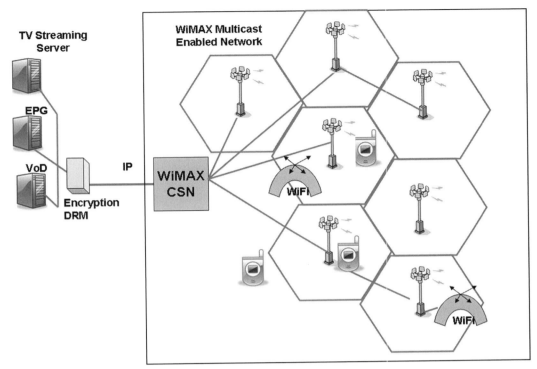

FIGURE 17-10 WiMAX IPTV network configuration

continue to direct the video traffic to the cell in which the user exists by its mobility features without the streaming application being aware of the location of the user. In addition the user application (such as a Realplayer™) may also select the stream size which best fits the transmission conditions. Network roaming in mobile WiMAX networks has been explained in Chapter 12.

17.2.2 Interfacing to WiMAX Networks

Setting up a WiMAX TV service requires a consideration of the following factors:

Fixed or Mobile WiMAX Network

The selection of the network type can be one of the first considerations. In most cases, an operator wishing to deliver its aggregated content to viewers would select the WiMAX network already installed in the area for delivering content. However, where such networks do not exist, it is possible to consider building out a WiMAX network as a wireless delivery medium, just as it is possible to consider laying out a cable network. A WiMAX network needs to be seen as a medium to reach audiences where the legacy systems such as cable or DTH are already owned by other operators. The WiMAX gives opportunity to new and niche operators to reach widely dispersed audiences with relatively low investments to roll out city wide services.

In rural and semi-urban communities, it would be most practical to use the IEEE 802.16-2004 Fixed WiMAX in unlicensed bands of 5.8 GHz as it would permit a quick roll-out of services.

For operators targeting the mobile users as well with services including high speed connectivity in addition to video, the Mobile WiMAX networks are best suited. Even though the Mobile WiMAX is of relatively recent origin, certified devices are already available from multiple vendors and most future networks are likely to use Mobile WiMAX with generic access network (GAN) involving WiFi and cellular network roaming.

The choice of encoding technologies used for TV will also depend on the type of network selected. For a Fixed WiMAX network, used primarily as a wireless DSL extension, the traditional technologies of MPEG-2-based transport stream with MPEG-4 encoded channels similar to IPTV would be the norm for implementation.

On the other hand, for Mobile WiMAX the standards for multicasting are built into the IEEE 802.16e standard. As explained in Chapters 12 and 13, the support for Multicast and Broadcast Services (MBS) toolkit is provided in Release 1 of the Mobile WiMAX certification profiles, and hence even the early devices are expected to support this feature. The MAC layer MAP field provides a signaling mechanism for indicating the multicast broadcast (MBS) traffic zone in the DL frames. This permits any mobile station (MS) to receive the MBS data even though not registered with a particular base station. The MBS can be accessed by the MS even in the idle low-power mode.

While a Mobile WiMAX network can be used with the MBS feature and enable the Mobile WiMAX devices to receive the multicast channels, there is a need for Mobile WiMAX networks to be interoperable with the cellular mobile networks (i.e., roaming between WiMAX and cellular). In such a scenario, IP-based media streaming services, which are also compliant with the 3GPP standards such as 3GPP streaming services (3GPP-PSS) or MBMS would be used.* In the CDMA-based

---

* The Applications Working Group (AWG) of the WiMAX Forum is in the process of working out standardized interfaces for specific applications. Until then, all implementations of applications should be considered proprietary.

3GPP2 world, broadcast and multicast services (BCMCS) are used for multicasting of video content.

Encoding of TV Channels

There are different options available for encoding video signals. Internet-based TV, meant to be displayed on PCs, PDAs, or smart-phones, is usually based on Windows Media, Flash Video, Real, or Apple Quicktime encoding and appropriate players downloaded on the receiving devices. Most players will play content encoded in any of the formats automatically. This type of encoding is only suitable for internet TV or for VoD download services.

However, for a commercial TV service, on Fixed WiMAX networks it would be desirable to encode the channels on a more efficient com-pression platform and cater to HD, SD, or full-screen resolution. An H.264 (MPEG-4-AVC) would be a more appropriate candidate for this type of carriage. The channels would typically be carried in an MPEG-2

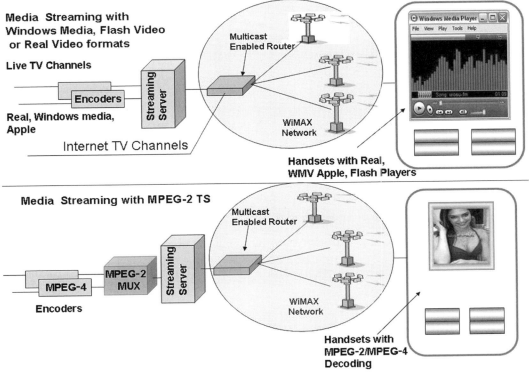

FIGURE 17-11 Media streaming using MPEG-2 TS and popular formats (Windows Media, Real, etc.)

transport frame. The transport frame will also carry the EPG stream, carousel-based magazines, and a DVB-compliant encryption. The decoding of these channels will require an IP set-top box or decoding and decrypting devices on mobile stations.

In cases where a Mobile WiMAX is used and compatibility with cellular networks is desired, it would be advantageous if the content was encoded with 3GPP-compliant file formats (e.g., 3GPP Release 6-compliant encoding with H.264). This will enable some of the 3GPP applications to also be used directly even though the underlying medium is WiMAX.

Mobile Stations and Software Clients for WiMAX TV

It is important to simultaneously identify the type of receiving devices and software clients that will enable display of TV channels, EPG, websites, Flash or Java content.

A Fixed WiMAX network would typically be used as a cable-replacement service. The customer premises equipment (CPE), in this case, would consist of a roof-mounted (or indoor) receiver and an IP STB to enable connections to TV sets or PCs. The IP STB, in this case, would function in a manner very similar to that in a DSL network, except that in place of a DSL modem, a WiMAX modem (CPE) is used.

In a Mobile WiMAX network, by virtue of the native support of MBS, WiMAX clients provide a decoding facility for multicast streams. If the source streams used are in the popular media server streaming formats, such as Windows Media, Flash, Real, or Apple Quicktime, it is possible to interface common media players to the underlying network on the handset. For example, RealPlayer™ for mobile is a software application available for either being downloaded or being a part of the software suite installed on Linux, Palm, Windows CE, Symbian 60, and other operating systems for mobile phones. RealPlayer™ can decode and play major leading formats including 3GPP, 3GPP2, Real Video and audio, MP3, etc.

The second option is where an MPEG-2 transport frame is used to carry content encoded in MPEG-4, VC1, or other formats. In this case the receiving device will need an MPEG decoder client.

How to Set Up an Encoding and Streaming Platform

The following factors should be considered when setting up an encoding and streaming platform for a WiMAX media broadcast system:

- The encoding system should be able to encode and convert from all popular formats such as 3GPP, 3GPP2, RealVideo, RealAudio,

MP3, MPEG-2, and Windows Media. In particular, it should be able to generate stream types, which can be encoded by players available on mobile devices.

- The streaming or media delivery system should be able to set up multiple streams in various formats as above and also provide support for different bit rates and screen resolutions. It should be able to encode for real time transmission as well as on-demand delivery.
- In order to interface to different type of networks and support protocols specific to each network, a mobile gateway component is usually used. The mobile gateway can interface to GSM, CDMA, 1xEV-DO, WiFi, or WiMAX networks, and support various protocols, such as native RTP/RTSP, multicasting, or HTTP protocols.

An example of a platform implementation for TV over WiMAX is given in Figure 17-12. This implementation uses Helix producer, Helix Media delivery system, and Helix Mobile Gateway. The implementation has many commonalities with the streaming of TV on mobile networks,

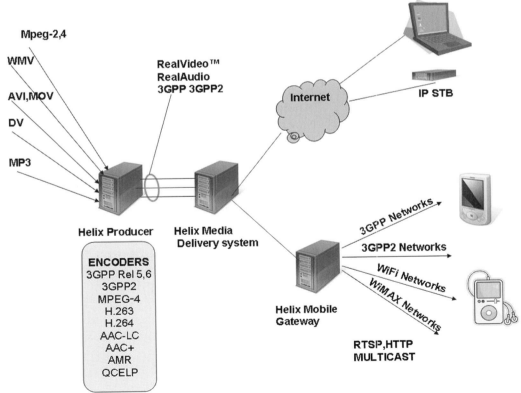

FIGURE 17-12 Helix implementation of online TV

where the file formats and protocols need to be as per 3GPP recommendations. However the WiMAX networks require additional functionalities relating to multicasting and QoS features.

The online™ TV implementation has the following components:

- Helix Producer is a multiplatform product supporting multiple codecs and capable of handing live and on-demand media in different formats. It generates streams fully compliant with Real™ or 3GPP2 formats with support for H.264 multiple stream outputs with various resolutions and bit rates are available.
- Helix media delivery system is the overall framework for providing a suite of streaming and on-demand services to fixed and mobile networks. The server includes functions for network management using SNMP, content management, authentication, authorization and accounting (AAA), billing, and customer care functions.
- Helix Mobile Gateway is designed to interface to a range of mobile and wireless networks to provide the network interface for streaming applications. It supports native RTP/RTSP streaming [RTSP over TCP (RFC2326), SDP for RTSP describe (RFC2327), MP3, and 3GP file support]. The gateway can handle the protocols for various networks for 3GPP (3G-GSM) and 3GPP2 (CDMA2000 and 1xEV-DO) networks.

17.2.3 Commercial Platforms for WiMAX TV-Samsung Personal Intelligent™ IPTV Platform

Samsung has a platform for fixed-mobile convergence called the Intelligent IPTV platform. The platform makes use of IP multimedia system (IMS) for fixed mobile convergence. Using the platform all wireline IPTV services are available to Mobile WiMAX devices as a Personal Intelligent IPTV. The platform has the following features:

- EPG: An electronic program guide is available, which is suited for the small sized mobile screens.
- Live TV: Live TV services are available on Mobile WiMAX handsets by "tightly coupling" the Samsung Mobile IPTV headend and the Samsung IPTV headends and using appropriate middleware.
- Network PVR (nPVR): Services of network-based PVR (storage of programs, fast forwarding or time shifting of content) are also available on Mobile WiMAX devices in exactly the same form as on standard living room TVs.
- Personal advertising: Support of personal advertising is available to direct the advertising to appropriate user profile, time of day, or location.

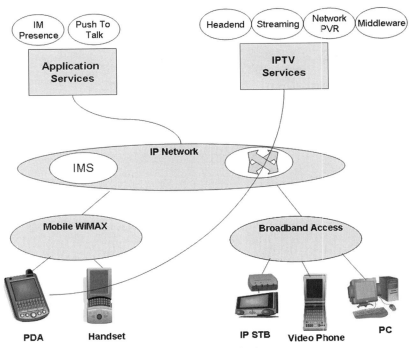

FIGURE 17-13   Samsung Personal Intelligent IPTV platform

17.2.4 Examples of WiMAX TV Networks

Mobile WiMAX TV Service from MobiTV

MobiTV is one of the largest aggregators of content for mobile TV. It aggregates content and provides it through a network of cellular operators (Figure 17-14). It also provides content via the AT&T broadband network (WiFi) to PCs, PDAs, and mobile devices.

MobiTV is now extending the delivery of program channels via WiMAX networks. For this purpose, it has identified a three-way arrangement as follows:

- Content, streaming infrastructure, and MobiTV application (MobiTV client): To be provided by MobiTV (i.e., MobiTV client and content delivery system)
- Content protection and service Protection: To be provided by NDS with its Videoguard™ DRM
- Mobile WiMAX infrastructure: To be provided by operator networks

MobiTV has already conducted trials with WiMAX equipment providers such as Alvarion, Runcom, and others for the end-to-end

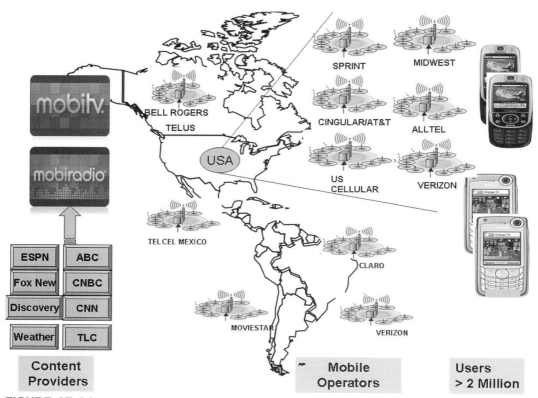

FIGURE 17-14 MobiTV™ Network

WiMAX TV solution. An example of a readily available platform which provides personal broadband using Mobile WiMAX is the Alvarion 4Motion™ platform.

The new service is designed as a two-way interactive service and provides a unicast and multicast of the channels in different resolutions (for mobile phones, PDAs, and PCs). The service is at the full broadcast frame rate of 30 FPS and 640 × 480 resolution. It uses the NDS encryption for transmission security and NDS DRM for content security.

The service by MobiTV is set to provide an alternative to the cable TV services by delivery over the wireless medium. MobiTV has been working with IP wireless® to develop a multicast client which is based on the MBMS technologies developed for cellular networks. The MobiTV WiMAX service features an EPG which is very similar to the cable TV EPGs and is based on the zip code of the customer to make it specific to the region where he resides.

MobiTV already has a network with over 3 million customers, which is primarily based on unicast video streaming on various cellular and 3G carrier networks. It is expected that in the new environment of WiMAX services by MobiTV, it will provide the Mobile WiMAX (IEEE 802.16e) multicast and broadcast services (MBS), unicast services, as well as continue to maintain compatibility with unicast streaming services available via 3G, EV-DO, and HSDPA networks.

MobiTV has also recently demonstrated WiMAX-based delivery of full motion video for multiple screens: set-top boxes (for TV), PCs, and Mobiles.

Sprint WiMAX Network for TV

Sprint has been building the largest single Mobile WiMAX network using the 2.5 GHz band (called XOHM™). It is one of the large holders of spectrum in this band by virtue of previous holdings and the acquisition of additional spectrum on AT&T Bellsouth merger.

The WiMAX network being rolled out is going live in Chicago, Washington, and Baltimore in the initial phase and will be nationwide by the end of 2008 (and have a reach of over 100 million in over 16 cities). The tie-ups for the equipment, TV technology, and the client devices have been made. These involve Motorola, Samsung, and Nokia for the equipment and Samsung, Motorola, and Intel for the chipsets and user devices among others. The DRM is provided by the NDS WiMAX TV portfolio of products.

The network being based on open Mobile WiMAX technology will permit a broad range of devices from portable media players to PCs and various WiMAX cellphones, WiFi, cellular, and internet WiMAX-enabled devices to offer services ranging from VoIP to WiMAX TV.

Sprint intends to offer services in a dual-mode manner to its existing CDMA subscribers as WiMAX-CDMA services.

17.2.5 Adding Web 2.0 Services to a WiMAX TV Service

The fact that WiMAX-based broadcast services can be delivered to conventional fixed TV sets as well as mobile devices opens up a new dimension in the manner in which the content is broadcast. It is true that internet access on the mobile and fixed devices can be used to access all services, but having a "planned roadmap" of how these services will be used in addition to the video broadcast content can help significantly increase their use. It is for this reason that most operators go to great lengths to improve user interfaces, facilitate the use of services, and drive traffic toward commercially important services.

FIGURE 17-15   A conceptual depiction of initial rollout of Sprint WiMAX network

Following are some of the prerequisites for improving access and usability of Web 2.0 services from mobile devices:

- To improve the user interface, by providing a client on the mobile devices which helps users to use the services intuitively and with ease. This should include the live content, VoD content, and the Web 2.0 services in one integrated manner.
- To multicast content, such as popular RSS feeds, based on usage patterns and have these available as scrolls via the user interface.
- To enable Web 2.0 services on mobile devices by providing a collaborative environment and Cache Web 2.0 content where feasible and to improve connectivity to websites featuring multimedia such as local radio and internet TV stations, YouTube, Google Video, etc. This can be done by having MPLS-based links or dedicated links set up for major traffic sites.
- To assign QoS service classes for Web 2.0 content on the WiMAX network. The caching servers should set up Diffserv-based connections over the internet and predefined service flows over WiMAX to ensure flawless delivery. It is necessary to dimension network links to ensure that multiple video streams at peak time can be catered to without typical freezing screens or jerky video. This requires an approach which is somewhat different from

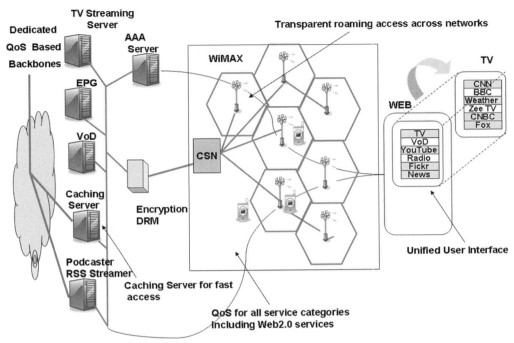

FIGURE 17-16 Enabling Web 2.0 services

catering to only broadcast or multicast content by a broadcaster or wireless cable operator.

- To make internet access transparent to the user including its use when roaming between WiFi hotspots, WiMAX networks, or even cellular networks. This may require working closely with the operators to have commercial arrangements in place.

If content is made available in a manner in which the commonly used services are featured in the EPG or program selection menus, this helps the user by not having to go through elaborate steps of installing different clients and making them work properly. It also make services and operations support easier when it is known what menus and interfaces the customers are working with. It will also require the service provider (e.g., a triple-play broadcaster) to work with the WiMAX operator as well as the Mobile WiMAX handset makers to ensure that all the components are well in place and the characteristics of individual devices are hidden from the user so far as the use of services is concerned. It will require the use of middleware and software components such as those discussed in Chapter 10 (Software Architectures for Mobile WiMAX Devices).

It needs to be recognized that a wider use of mobile media services can only come about by simplification and unification of service interfaces and the availability of these services without access or quality issues. The profile of users in a mass broadcast environment is changing from sophisticated office users to a mass user base and the user interfaces and services quality need to reflect this changing paradigm by providing simple and intuitive interfaces.

Setting Up Web 2.0 Support Infrastructure

The first step toward enabling Web 2.0 services beyond the normal internet access is to provide an interactive and intuitive interface for access of commonly used websites and services and to multicast content such as RSS feeds.

An example of a solution using "push"-based services and facilitating access to internet applications from mobile networks is the MORANGE™ system from MOZAT Singapore. The primary purpose of such a system is to provide clients on mobile devices and a server so as to provide an end-to-end solution for various applications rather than letting users try to seek out how to use each application using the tiny mobile screens. The solution is network-independent and works with WiMAX, CDMA , 3G, or GSM-based mobile networks. The MORANGE™ server interfaces with other application servers and provides an environment for Push e-mail or Push-based RSS feeds. Users can select the sites of interest and are informed by Push RSS feeds when any updates are available. By supporting RSS feeds in different formats such as RSS, RDF, and Atom, it helps in converging the updates in the mobile devices. The server also connects with Office 2003 and mail servers for push e-mail and PIM synchronization. It also helps in sharing common resources such as video feeds or office documents and implements instant messaging. In fact the server can interface to any third party application by using common XML-based API. The MORANGE Mobile™ is the name of the client which resides on the mobile devices and is based on Java MIDP2.0. It can be loaded on any smartphone, PDA, or any other mobile device with Java MIDP 2.0 support.

17.3 NEWS-GATHERING NETWORKS

News gathering forms one of the most important functions of the broadcast industry. News gathering has been associated with outdoor broadcasting (OB) van-based satellite backhauls and hence the term satellite news gathering (SNG). The use of wireless cameras connected to an OB van or local WiFi infrastructure has already been quite common

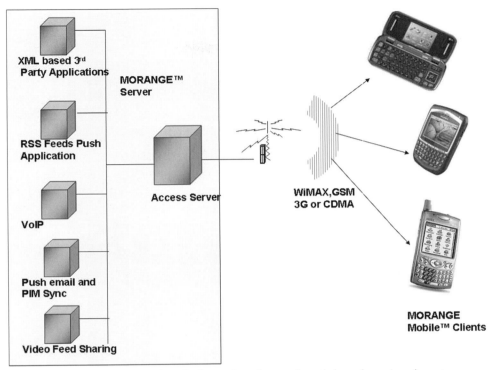

FIGURE 17-17 An example of unified user interface and push-based services (courtesy MOZAT, Singapore)

in broadcast news gathering as the use of long cables is cumbersome and unreliable. The next step toward the use of WiMAX connectivity places the entire operation of SNG on a professional footing with reliability of transmission expected of major broadcast events.

In fact, the early steps toward demonstrating the utility of WiMAX for outdoor events was demonstrated at the Ironman Triathlon Championships in Hawaii in 2006 where over 1700 athletes participated in a 2.4-mile swimming, 112-mile cycling, and 26-mile marathon. The entire event was covered using a mix of WiFi hotspots and long range WiMAX systems. The network infrastructure was provided by Airspan networks, capable of providing 8 Mbps data rates.

In the recent past, the news backhauls have been using other media such as ADSL DSL broadband, WiFi-based hotspots, or file transfers based on Internet. The availability of high-speed WiMAX networks presents a new dimension for the broadcast industry. With WiMAX cards or USB adapters being increasingly available it is possible to transfer stored video files or even live video using the WiMAX as the

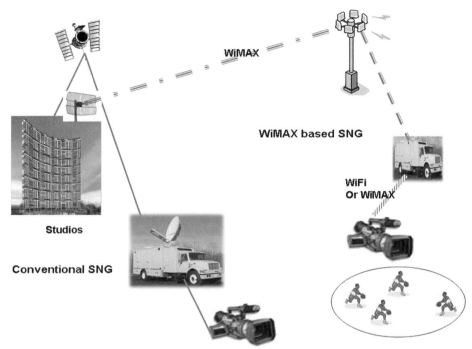

FIGURE 17-18 Conventional SNG vs. WiMAX-based news gathering

wireless media. High bandwidths of 15 Mbps attainable over cell sizes of 3 Km in mobile WiMAX and nomadicity or roaming capabilities mean that it can be used from different locations. WiMAX networks have the added advantage that they provide a secure encrypted transmission which cannot be received by free to air receivers. Moreover the connections can be set up on-demand and without any previous planning or arrangements. The charging is also as per the network usage rather than fixed charges for reserved satellite segments.

The omnipresence of WiMAX networks over large territories and the availability of high-resolution cameras in mobile devices mean that "rushes" of news or major events can be on air live within minutes without any major compromise on quality.

Setting Up a WiMAX-Based News Acquisition Set-Up

Setting up a WiMAX-based news acquisition set-up can be done by setting up ingest ports on a news automation system on the broadband network connected to the WiMAX network. The broadband connections need to provide for adequate CIR for the quality desired. Used with MPEG-4 compression, bit rates of 4-6 Mbps are adequate for the ingest purpose. The number of lines can be configured as per the traffic requirements and the number of OB units in operation.

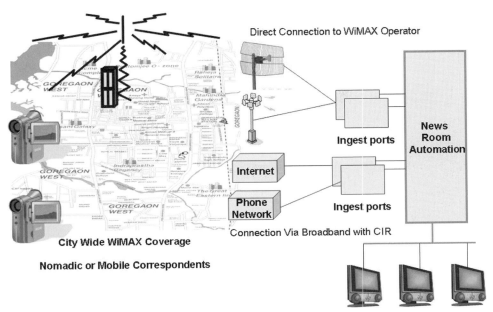

FIGURE 17-19 News-gathering set-up for broadband and WiMAX coverage

A WiMAX-based news-gathering set-up requires the following steps:

- Set up ingest ports either with a local link from the WiMAX operator or a broadband link to the internet with committed CIR of 4-8 Mbps
- Enable cameras or laptops with WiMAX cards or USB adapters
- Install MPEG-4 or MPEG-2 compression cards (or software)
- Set up a live streaming and a file transfer utility in the laptop
- Set up VoIP and chat facilities at both studio and client laptops for coordination
- Enable roaming for all coverage areas of interest
- As an option it is possible, with due authentication, to permit the news team to locate and download relevant content from the news archives and upload completed stories

17.3.1 Electronic News Gathering and News Room Automation Systems

The core of any new network is to be able to connect and download feeds of programs from hundreds of journalists in the field. It is even more critical to get breaking news "on-air" by getting such content quickly into the newsroom automation system and on the air. ENPS, one of the pioneers in this field, has recently launched ENPS Mobile Suite, which can work from any Windows Mobile 5-equipped Pocket PC. The components of the mobile suite are ENPS SNA Pfeed™ Mobile (a store and forward application for video), ENPS Web (a web browser), and ENPS mobile application which runs on the pocket PC. The objective of the new mobility client is to enable all those equipped with a mobile with camera to be a part of the breaking news on the system in addition to the usual tasks of downloading assignments and uploading scripts and videos. While the pocket PCs today support 3G and WiFi, city-wide wireless in the form of Mobile WiMAX will provide a new dimension for such applications in the near future as the networks roll out by increasing the speeds of transmission thereby increasing the capabilities of mobile news devices. The costs will also be reduced manifold and live video with good quality will be easily possible.

Cable TV extensions using WiMAX have been tried as one of the early applications of Fixed WiMAX networks, particularly for delivering voice and cable TV services in remote communities. It has also been used by new operators to break into markets held by incumbent cable operators and Telcos as an alternative TV service. In fact, most of the Mobile WiMAX systems operate in bands previously allotted to MMDS services which were used for point-to-multipoint transmis-

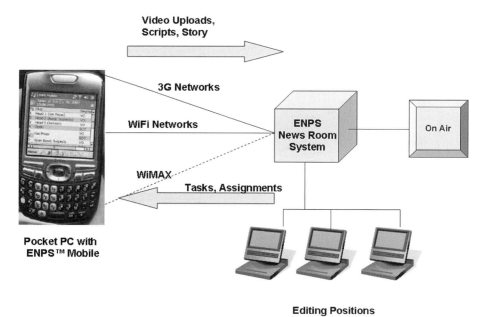

Image: Courtesy ENPS

FIGURE 17-20   ENPS mobile for news networks

sion of analog TV. The 6 and 7 MHz channelization schemes which exist even today reflect this historical fact.

How to Set Up a WiMAX-Based Cable TV Replacement Service

The process of setting up a WiMAX-based TV service is essentially one of implementing an IPTV service over WiMAX and has been discussed in Chapter 15 (IPTV and WiMAX). It involves the following steps:

- Identifying potential customer pockets to be covered.
- Selecting a WiMAX operator in the area or alternatively developing own WiMAX delivery extensions.
- Selecting the frequency band. Unlicensed frequency bands at 2.4 and 5.8 GHz provide a good option for Fixed WiMAX-based networks.
- Installating the IPTV server and a self-contained base station. An IEEE 802.16-2004 base station can provide 20 Mbps peak rate with 7 MHz bandwidth and is usually sufficient for carriage of 10–15 channels based on the type of coding selected. The bit rate per channel is 3–4 Mbps with MPEG-2 and 1.5–2 Mbps with H.264 encoding. Additional base stations can be planned based on site surveys and customer locations.
- Providing service through off the shelf set-top boxes for IPTV.
- Enabling the reverse channel using the WiMAX service.
- Setting up VoIP infrastructure as an add-on for providing triple-play.
- Adding VoD servers and music streaming.

17.4 SURVEILLANCE NETWORKS

Video surveillance is one of the natural applications of a Fixed WiMAX service as it helps transmission of data over medium to long ranges (3–10 Km) while maintaining QoS. This helps replace many of the short hop microwave links in the 30+ GHz range or WiFi extensions which have been used previously in such applications. Security considerations mean many such networks have been built on propriety technologies with attendant high costs. WiMAX opens up a new opportunity in engineering such systems. The applications of such video networks are not merely for security but can span property and project management, medial systems, farming and industrial applications.

A video surveillance network is typically a point-to-multipoint network with a number of surveillance points being monitored at a central location. A captive WiMAX network is the best way to achieve the point-to-multipoint realization.

Systems on chip (SoC) available today (such as the Fujitsu MB87M3550) are designed to simplify the design of IEEE 802.16-2004 implementations.

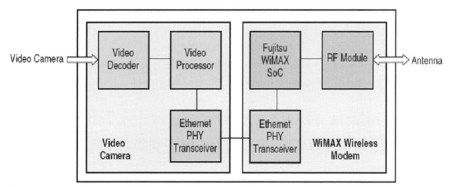

FIGURE 17-21   WiMAX-based IP video surveillance camera reference design (picture courtesy Fujitsu)

These can be used in video cameras to provide an integrated implementation not needing external components and can also be used in base stations or remote subscriber station designs.

A reference design for a WiMAX-based IP surveillance video camera is given in Figure 17-21.

The reference design, which is based on the Fujitsu SoC, works with video from the camera (which has been converted to an IP format) and prepares it for transmission using IEEE 802.16-2004. An RF interface IC is used for transmission in the desired band using an external antenna.

Some of the new video surveillance implementations which are based on motion detection use preprocessing in the cameras and transmit only the motion or alarm information reducing the bandwidth requirements considerably.

17.5 VIDEO CONFERENCING OVER WiMAX

Platforms are now being increasingly deployed with support for QoS for various applications including voice, video streaming, and video conferencing. The QoS parameters which can be set over WiMAX and end-to-end quality control permit quality video conferencing applications.

A typical solution for WiMAX (IEEE 802.16-2004)-based video conferencing has been demonstrated by CableMatrix and VCom Inc. The solution is based on the on-demand video Service Platform (ODSP™) from CableMatix and WiMAX equipment from VCom. The on-demand platform can provide quadruple-play services (SIP voice, streaming video, multiplayer online gaming and video conferencing services) with QoS which can be managed on a per subscriber, per session, and per application basis. The ODSP platform can be used as application manager, policy server, or both.

18

WiMAX AND MOBILE MULTIMEDIA BROADCASTING: INTERACTIVE APPLICATIONS

Getting information from the internet is like getting a glass of water from the Niagara Falls.

—Arthur C. Clarke

Mobile WiMAX networks that permit broadcast or multicast of content with interactivity via broadband internet present a new ecosystem in which connected communities can be integrated with broadcasting, content sharing, and even office functions. This is an entirely new domain, which the advertising world has long envisioned and attempted, but it is only now, with the capabilities of connectivity via WiMAX and its IPv6 capabilities that these are coming to full realization.

Each innovative opportunity unveiled by the nonconventional manner in which video and broadcast content can be handled on broadcast networks brings to life a vision, which is today finding realization that was beyond the capabilities of conventional networks.

It gives an opportunity to broadcasters and advertisers to enter the combined domains of internet and mobile advertising and integrate it with broadcast systems. WiMAX systems also give opportunities to reposition live customer reviews as advertisements and bring live sitcoms to broadcasting content.

Figure 18-1 exhibits how a mobile WiMAX environment provides the opportunity to broaden the scope of broadcasting from merely providing entertainment services to offering information services and customer services. Each of these can be delivered via multiple modes of real time or in background.

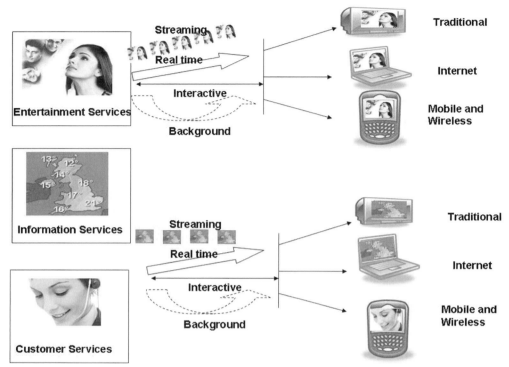

FIGURE 18-1 Envisioning the environment for Mobile WiMAX

Even though, in its early days, Mobile WiMAX systems (such as WiBro in Korea) have already begun a new generation of applications which keeps entire communities of users, service, and sales staff connected, companies are now looking at 4G mobile broadband portals for a lead in the new applications space.

In this chapter, we discuss the threads of a few such concepts, believing that the advertising world will, indeed, unveil many more, both practical and innovative.

18.1 INTERACTIVE BROADCASTING

Interactive broadcasting with two-way connectivity can be considered as the first enhancement of a traditional broadcast service. There are many facets to interactive broadcasting which bring forth the power of communities, so far the exclusive prerogative of the internet world. Targeted advertising via the new personal medium with empowerment to order instantly, user-generated content with high resolution, interactive games, and information services constitute other assets which enrich a traditional broadcasting service beyond the "triple play" already offered on satellite, IPTV, and cable TV networks. Integrated with IP multimedia system (IMS), the environment created helps to harness the "Presence" and instant messaging features which are beyond the capability of any wireline networks.

18.1.1 The Power of Communities

All of us today recognize the power of communities that exist on the internet and mobile domains. Orkut, MySpace, Google, and Flickr are only some of the examples which keep the users connected. There are also other communities, such as those of employees of a large company spread globally or a large chain of department stores. Most communities are now going mobile as users do not wish to be tied to desktops in offices or homes.

Large companies now provide their employees with mobile devices that are equipped with cameras, GPS clients, and phone operating systems, which are designed to integrate them into a complete chain of business processes and client networks. The "WH Mall" from KT WiBro in Korea is an example of this type of initiative, which is based largely on WiBro-enabled devices, WiBro-enabled smart cards, integration with mobile banking and e-commerce sites, and a home shopping network.

The 4G mobile portals being launched by Google are, for example, being targeted for the full suite of Google apps that combine the Gmail, Google Calendar, and Google Talk (VoIP) services. In the near future it should include music, video, TV, and on-demand products.

4G portals are characterized by also providing a QoS assurance, which would permit a service to be used as intended such as streaming a TV channel or a video.

18.1.2 Conventional Broadcasting to Interactive Broadcasting

The transition from conventional broadcasting to interactive broadcasting is a compelling proposition as is the proposition to have content available to multiple networks. Users with today's lifestyles are connected in diverse ways including using mobile and wireless devices, portable PCs, and the net. This also means that considering the "family" as a composite unit for broadcast reception may not be the best way to target the services toward the customers. Targeting the entire universe of a customer then becomes a primary objective. Members of the family may watch different programs either as a result of multi-TV homes or by using their own mobile devices at times suitable to them. This requires a traditional broadcaster to build on existing services to move

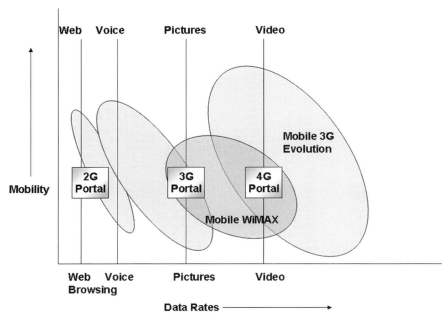

FIGURE 18-2   4G portals feature TV, music, voice services, and on-demand features

to interactive broadcasting. The new proposition is made easier by the 4G capabilities brought in by the mobile WiMAX networks.

18.1.3 Targeted Advertising

Google has well demonstrated the power of targeted advertising in its e-mail services and on the search portals. By using data analysis of the customer base, it is possible to change the advertisements and provide other interactive services on a per customer basis. Cable TV provider Comcast in the United States has been using technology to target commercials to Comcast's 20 million-plus cable households, based on viewer interests or locations. Targeted ads are very valuable as customers are unwilling to watch through 3–5 minute ad breaks. Hence, every ad watched is valuable, and targeting it improves the chances of success. What are the steps to targeted advertising?

Step 1: Service Portal and Data Mining

The first step toward targeted advertising is to have a service portal, which is used by the customers for all their normal activities including payments for pay channels, movies on demand, etc. It is also desirable to include links to popular shopping sites which may agree to partner with a service provider. A service portal can legitimately maintain the subscription details of the customer such as age, gender, area of residence, and income level. It would, for example, be known if a customer is a student or a senior executive. His or her purchases on the portal signify the products or services that are best liked. The service portal can also gather information on the channels or types of VoD content being watched by a particular user. The data so gathered may be subject to privacy protection laws in different countries and certainly cannot be shared with third parties. Data gathered can be refined over time, but even the first cut information, such as age and gender, can be very effective in targeted advertising.

FCC regulations on data privacy do not permit the captured information to be linked to a name and billing information and prohibit the transmission of such information to advertisers. However it can be used internally in the system or be used by assigning attributes to a client or STB.

Step 2: Setting up the Infrastructure

Targeted advertising requires setting up of VoD servers, which can insert targeted content. Such servers are available from all major suppliers (e.g., Seachange) and are used by major cable operators today. Tandberg TV provides and Adpoint™ advertising solution for precisely such an application. A number of agencies such as Visible World™ specialize in offering advertising clients access to targeted slots.

Step 3: Unicasting TV Programs with Advertisement Substitution

Broadcasters can offer per-view rates for advertisements and provide targeted insertions based on time of day, age, location of the user, and his previous history of purchases. Targeted advertising is also being offered in IPTV and cable (such as by Insight Communications, Inc.). MTV networks is known to be offering flexible advertisement spots to advertisers. Clients such as United Airlines are targeting ads based on location on cable networks. But mobile networks can provide an even better response by targeting an individual at his current location and time rather than a family with a fixed location.

Step 4: Customer Reviews

With wireless or mobile devices customers can upload comments on the product with video. Devices such as Mobile WiMAX make this process cheaper and faster thus making it possible to offer gifts, etc.,

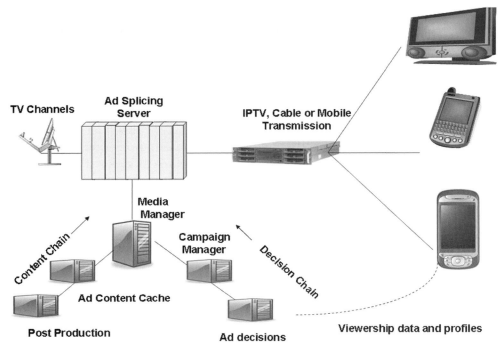

FIGURE 18-3 Conceptual view of a targeted advertising system

for the trouble of offering a review. A targeted base of reviews may go a long way along with the ads to prompt buying actions.

Step 5: Buy Me!

Offering a facility to customers (either via the STB or the handset) to buy the product on the spot is very important. Cable and IPTV operators have been providing this facility for a considerable time now. Many advertisers offer 24-hour calling lines or discounts if bought within a certain time window. But a key enabled message or online purchase is now a practical proposition with the WiMAX and mobile TV networks.

18.1.4 Google TV Ads Program

The Google TV Ads program initiative is based on its extensively well-developed and proven concepts of AdWord™ and AdSense™, which are context- and topic-specific advertisements. These are inserted in the Google pages based on their relevance, and the users can bid for the advertisements in an auction. The Google TV Ads program is based on a similar concept as that of TV ads being inserted in TV programs, print, newspaper and radio advertising based on several criteria such as time of day, geographical location, genre of programming, etc. The initial Beta trials have been conducted on the Astound cable network, California and Echostar Dish DTH Platform. Google had sold over 100,000 spots within four months of its launch on Echostar in May 2007, signifying the importance of targeted advertising. The Google TV auctions are based on viewing data as retrieved from the Echostar dish TV set-top boxes. The advertisers can subsequently check how many users watched the ads fully or in part and refine their advertising further. As the number of TV channels explodes with the transmissions moving to digital, having accurate targeted media buying will need to necessarily depend on "actually viewed" data rather than channel ratings. A channel may have a high rating, but no one may be watching it if there is a sports match on another channel which has turned interesting. PVRs are also helping customers skip advertisements and a new medium is a welcome opportunity.

18.2 BROADCAST AND MULTICAST-ASSOCIATED INTERACTIVE SERVICES

Interactive services in TV networks are not new to the mobile world. Many manufacturers now offer a live interactive TV end-to-end managed solution. Essentially this provides for a rich media application running on the handsets by which the users can access the EPG, change channels, or buy content.

Traditional Interactivity on TV Networks

The traditional framework for interactivity is based on the use of multimedia home platform (MHP) or alternative middleware such as OpenTV™. MHP is essentially a Java-based platform for interactivity. MHP is available for implementation either using a DVB-based platform or without the DVB components using globally executable MHP (GEM). It is also applicable to other TV implementation standards, such as ARIB, open cable application protocol (OCAP), and ACAP. The DVB-MHP (adopted by the ETSI) and similar architectures are quite effective in the delivery of information about the TV, radio programs (through EPG), and carry magazines for news, weather, business, etc. (through active channels). Return interactivity with users is also possible to enable tele-shopping or voting. However, none of these platforms is suited for peer-to-peer services or services which are based on users interacting as communities among themselves or with broadcasters.

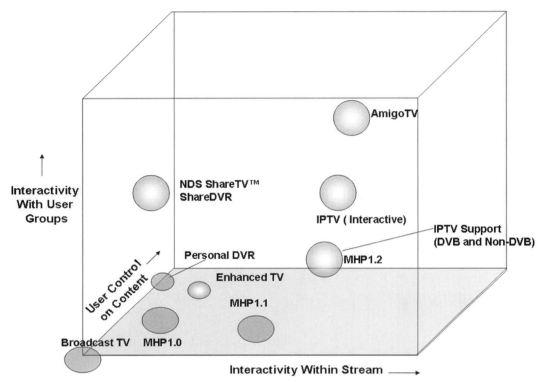

FIGURE 18-4   Interactive TV platforms such as AmigoTV™ based on instant messaging and Presence services (IMPS) provide high interactivity with user groups

Two-Way Interactivity

Going beyond simple interactivity based largely on broadcast content based on interactivity provided by MHP in an STB or a client in a mobile device are immense areas that two-way networks such as Mobile WiMAX enable. The very strength of technologies such as IPTV or Mobile TV, including via WiMAX delivery, is to provide for intensive user interaction and indeed this is the very basis of future existence of video and audio broadcasts to mobile devices rather than pure broadcast channels.

Both unicast services as well as multicast services (e.g., MBMS in 3GPP cellular networks or BCMCS in 3GPP2 networks and MBS in mobile WiMAX networks) provide capabilities to the user to view video-on-demand or near-video-on-demand (NVoD) content. This, coupled with the interactivity possible with the 3G/4G networks, can be used to usher in a new content delivery environment.

18.2.1 Using "Presence" Features

The Presence service allows users in selected groups to know the availability of other members of the group online or engaged in certain activities. Users can subscribe to a person's availability or presence (called watchers). The entity which makes its presence available to others (i.e., the watchers) is called the "Presentity." A Presence message provides two types of information, i.e., availability and contact information. The contact information provides the details and the means currently available to contact a user. The specifications of Presence and instant message are given by IETF RFC 2778 (common profile for instant messaging). Skype, Yahoo IM, or MSN Messenger are all Presence-based.

The idea of Presence in mobile TV transmissions originates in the concept of having a group of users being aware of the presence of certain TV programs of their choice which are being aired, scheduled to be aired, or available as VoD content. The Presence feature can be channel specific or program specific (e.g., airing of a baseball match or an online auction). If the users register for the Presence feature of a TV station, the same appears as a "TV Buddy" in their contacts list.

Figure 18-5 shows a broadcast operation with the Presence feature being used by the mobile receivers and the operator. The programs are multicast using a mobile TV transmission system such as DVB-H or WiMAX as usual. In addition, a TV application server operates as a platform for maintaining the Presence operation via an IMS Presence server. As a basic feature, the users can be notified of the EPG and highlights by an IM. It is further possible to personalize the system by providing program specific instant messages based on user preferences. The users have the advantage of notification of all interesting events, personalized messages, and network recordings of previous programs if available on the network as unicast content.

4G networks, whether mobile cellular or WiMAX, provide for features such as Presence, as well as push-to-talk (PTT), push-to-video (PTV), and push-to-data (PTD). Push-to-video can be used for video conferencing and push-to-data for items such as picture sharing. The Presence feature can be used to create a bonding between a video program and the customers who are actually tuned in, signified by the Presence indicator. Users Present on a program can be entitled, selectively, to free gifts or offers. They can be encouraged to comment on a discussion topic and the same can be available with their pictures. However, the key is that this process can be completely localized. Even with a program multicast countrywide, the communities can be local—down to a college or a small town, and the comments which appear on the programs can be local to the community.

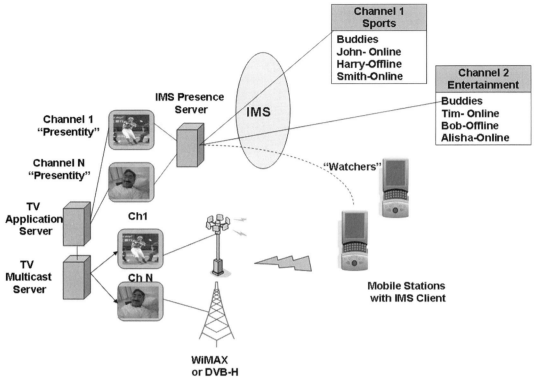

FIGURE 18-5   Using Presence services in mobile TV transmission

The Presence feature can also be used to generate loyalty by granting "viewership miles" for a channel or a program, which can be redeemed on screen with downloads of favorite music. This can be used to counter frivolous channel-surfing behaviors. It can also be used for sending personalized information such as recipes, pictures, or to be allowed to come live on the show with appropriate moderation.

Example of a TV Platform with IMS: Seachange TV Platform™

Seachange TV Platform is an IPTV platform that is based on IMS and offers IMS-compliant clients or set-top boxes (TV Navigator™). Using the client middleware, a range of applications can be supported which would otherwise fall in the domain of mobile networks, such as SMS or MMS, caller ID, and video conferencing. In addition, it also includes the standard TV interactive applications such as weather, voting, ecommerce, red button interactivity, network DVR, and games.

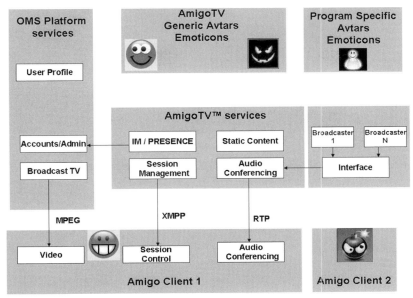

FIGURE 18-6   AmigoTV™ Platform (Courtesy Alcatel)

Samsung had also announced a "Push-to-All" (PTA) platform for mobile interactivity and community building. Essentially the PTA platform includes the inclusion of instant messages in video streams, audio, or text. The PTA platform could perform one to many video conferencing or send pictures using the PTT, PTV, and PTD features.

Example of a Triple-Play Broadcasting Platform: AmigoTV™

An example of an IPTV platform which provides a community TV (Figure 18-6) application with triple-play features is the AmigoTV™ platform from Alcatel. The platform uses Presence features and provides voice communications and rich multimedia messaging between the community members. This helps to bring a better viewing experience, as well as add revenue elements from other services that would otherwise have accrued to external operators. The difference in experience cited is "just watching a football show on TV" against being present in a stadium where the user is intensely aware of the feelings and expressions of other users. In AmigoTV, customers can be present on the show as "Avtars" with logos or pictures and talk to others present, with charges associated with some of the activities. It is targeted at game shows, reality programs, children programs, and sports programming.

The AmigoTV application is built around an MPEG-based broadcasting platform and an IM/Presence (IMPS)-based services core.

IMPS services are based on the open XMPP protocols. The users have a corresponding XMPP client which initiates the communications using the Jabber protocols, maintains presence information, and provides messaging, voice call, and voice conferencing services. The audio associated with the conferencing sessions needs to be kept separate from the program associated audio. In a typical broadcasting set-up, it is expected that there may be thousands of groups (each with less than 10 users) who take part in audio or video conferencing.

AmigoTV uses an innovative technology, which is suitable in the broadcast environment whereby the mixing of the audio does not take place at the central site (this would be impractical owing to the large number of users and groups). Instead an RTP reflector is used to reflect the voice of all peers to the clients where it is mixed. The clients need to set up sessions using the SIP client with the RTP reflector.

Using Instant Messaging Features

Instant messaging is one of the most common uses of the Presence attribute in a multimedia messaging system. Instant messaging can be a part of video, audio, or rich media exchanges. IM is used in collaborative environments in web- and mobile-based applications extensively. However, their use in collaborative multicast or broadcast applications has begun to be recognized.

IM and Presence can be used to operate highly interactive programming channels with the direct involvement of users. The broadcast applications can be of a wide range and include gaming, gambling where permitted (e.g., poker), horse racing with online betting, etc.

18.3 DESIGNING BROADCAST APPLICATIONS FOR HIGH-BANDWIDTH INTERACTIVE NETWORKS

The availability of high-speed networks, which allow a user to stay connected using data rates of 256 Kbps and above, on the average, ushers in a new era in the field of delivery of content to mobile devices. The services that are currently offered are those which could be supported by existing networks with their limitations on broadband connectivity speeds and the volume of data which each user can transfer. This typically made any service which uses video transfer in a unicast mode quite expensive.

WiMAX networks (and to some extent HSDPA and EVDO networks) now provide a tool to usher in new applications which are not only rich in animation-based content (Java and Flash) but are composed of real-life videos and high-resolution pictures.

The advantages of WiMAX networks for video are listed below:

- Access to full-resolution programming rather than QVGA or CIF for mobile devices.
- Simultaneous access to TV programs and running background applications (transfer of pictures, download of music, mail).
- Support of high-resolution graphics in websites such as Geo web (Google earth or NASA World wind, Microsoft Virtual earth), and access to 3D websites.
- Link broadcast in TV programs: a TV presenter can send links, which if the user wishes can be clicked.
- High-speed access to video websites such as YouTube or LinkTV.
- Fast channel-change time.

18.3.1 User-Created Content (UCC) TV

User-created content (UCC)-based TV has proved to be quite popular. An example of such a TV application is the Sumo.TV™ which operates on the Sky platform. The channel operates in conjunction with a website (www.sumo.tv) where the users can upload their content. The content may be broadcast on national TV channels or be available for streaming by other users. Videos are classified as "weekly picks," "most viewed," etc., and the users can create their own TV channel by using the MySumo™ options. The service is operated by Cellcast®. The business model is based on paid mobile content and premium services.

Meanwhile as more and more TV stations continue to get affiliated with YouTube for user-generated content, "Current TV"—the network operated by Al Gore—has also migrated to showing user-generated content. "No Comment TV" operated by Euro News also features user-generated videos in its internet version without any commentary.

User-generated TV services are best operated with high-speed broadband networks and wireless media with QoS such as WiMAX is ideally suited for this purpose.

Example of UCC Platform NetMirror™ from IntroMobile®

An example of a platform providing services based on user-created content as well as live TV is NetMirror from IntroMobile. The company has distinguished itself in providing applications for the Korea Telecom WiBro platform.

NetMirror is designed for use on high-bandwidth networks such as Mobile WiMAX, WiBro, or HSPA, which can support applications involving extensive use of videos and pictures in applications. It is a next-generation personal media blog and personal broadcasting service platform (unicast or multicast), based upon Web 2.0 for interactive UCC services in the mobile and fixed-line environment. Users have access to a menu which helps them select live TV, video UCC, special category UCC such as music or "hot UCC" and pictures, albums, and blogs with multimedia content. The NetMirror platform is designed for providing two-way UCC services as distinct from one-way UCC services and provides an ideal example of Web 2.0 and Mobile 2.0 integration. By virtue of two-way UCC it is possible to have wireless encoding and integrated fixed mobile, and real-time broadcasting for a personalized multimedia service, which includes multimedia push technology of dynamic content delivery services.

The platform is an open platform based on standard APIs compliant with W3C specifications for an optimized multimedia UCC Service Platform. Functional modules in the platform support functions such

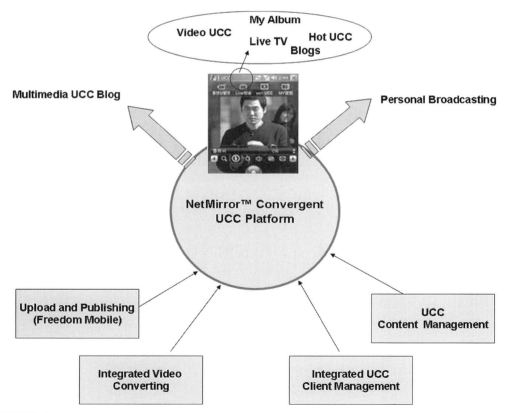

FIGURE 18-7 UCC Platform NetMirror™ from IntroMobile® (Image courtesy Intromobile®)

as uploading of videos from different devices on to personal blogs, conversion of videos, and optimization for broadcasting and user management. It also provides for classification and management of content, an essential function for a site of this nature.

18.3.2 Background Programming: Push VoD to Mobile Devices

Video on demand is a very common application on cable, DTH, and IPTV networks. With the emergence of new devices such as 80 GB iPods or mobile devices with Flash memories of 8 GB and above, a new era of opportunities has emerged for push-based programming. This involves pushing of new videos, movies, or song albums or e-books on user devices, who may then preview and watch them by making an online payment. A number of traditional DTH and cable operators have been offering push VoD services, where the content is essentially pushed to a specified area in the STB of the customer. Examples are the Sky Anytime TV™ from BskyB or Top Up TV Anytime™ service. The Top Up TV Anytime™ service, for example, sources content from over 20 subscription channels and pushes about 100 hours of programming per week for "anytime viewing."

Push-based VoD has many advantages, such as using the bandwidth at times of low traffic, pushing content based on user preferences, fulfilling online orders placed while the user is not at home, and providing an opportunity for impulse buying. With the mobile devices being WiFi- and WiMAX-enabled, it is possible to view such content on the mobile device, home TVs, save it in PCs (such as e-books), or transfer it to home gateways to build a personal library. Push VoD to mobile devices had also commenced in 2005, shortly after the deliveries to set-top boxes or DVRs.

An example of a platform providing soft loading of content is the SkyStream zBand™ platform from Tandberg TV. Its ZBand 6.0 platform provides operators with the capability to provide on-demand content in the Push mode with high scalability. The platform can be used over unicast, multicast, or hybrid networks and delivers high-volume content to a large number of devices. A return path is needed for the transfer of content. It also possible to transfer content on a "pull" basis, i.e., ordered by a subscriber beforehand. User clients can use its XML/HTML API for easy integration.

VoD technologies such as zBand also actively manage the user space by deleting old VoD content and replacing it with the latest available ones. zBand uses Certicom's Security Builder cryptography software to prevent piracy and to protect owner copyrights. A number

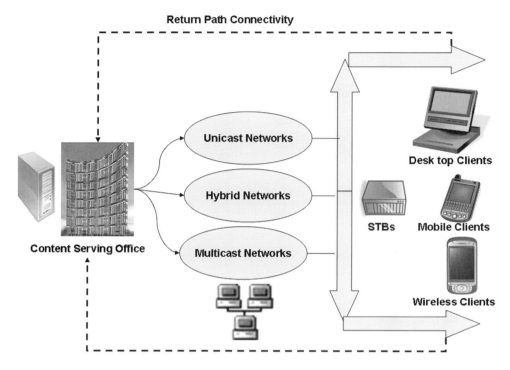

FIGURE 18-8   Tandberg TV zBand push video-on-demand platform

of implementations of Push VoD such as Moviebeam™, USA, ReelTime™, and Australia China Telecom are based on zBand.

VoD content is also ideally suited for mobile handsets. Recent experiences with Apple's video iPod and Slingbox™ indicate that the users would want content and want it to be mobile. However, in the past the limitations on memory of the handsets coupled with these being limited and expensive had not permitted practical implementations of push VoD along with the fact that the customers would be unwilling to pay for such a use of the network in the background. For example, a 30-minute video clip encoded for QVGA resolution in H.264 format with stereo audio requires 60 MB for storage (256 Kbps encoding). Transmission of such a clip is impractical with cellular networks. The situation is different with the technologies used in new devices such as multiple gigabit memory sizes and multiple connectivity options such as WiFi or WiMAX. The Nokia 810 internet tablet, a standalone device, makes use of WiFi networks to refresh content on the go when in the range of hotspots. WiMAX will make it possible to do so city-wide and with devices always connected. A connectivity at 1 Mbps, easily achieved

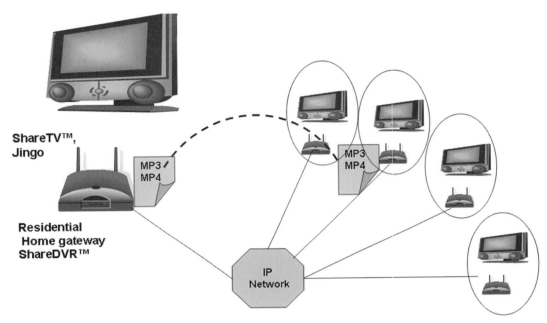

FIGURE 18-9   Example of a P2P IPTV network using NDS ShareTV™ technology

with WiFi or WiMAX, can download this content in under 8 minutes. The advantage with WiMAX is that the users can watch live programs in addition to the "canned programming."

18.4 PEER-TO-PEER (P2P) INTERNET TV

Peer-to-peer music sharing has been in vogue ever since the early days of the net. This was indeed feasible because of the relatively low broadband usage requirements for audio transfer and non-real-time use. The new promising application of peer-to-peer TV is now made possible by bidirectional high-speed networks such as WiMAX or WiFi. However unlike the early uses of unlicensed music sharing, the peer-to-peer applications are being designed as those being fully protected by DRM or viewing rights.

18.4.1 NDS ShareTV and Distributed DVR

Instead of storing content in a DVR, which needs disk storage, the NDS concept of distributed DVR involves the use of the residential home gateway to store the content. This effectively reduces the cost of the DVR and at the same time uses spare cpacity in the home gateway to be used as an on-demand server. The ShareTV software allows the content to be legally shared among other subscribers using a peer-to-peer technology. The P2P technology is a part of the Jungo residential gateway software provided with the application. (Jungo Inc. is a company which provides residential gateway software with Plug and Play facilities). The ShareTV software downloads the requested programming from other users in the network to the DVR or residential gateway of the requesting subscriber. This can help a subscriber to build, say, a complete 52-episode volume of his favorite serial program or collect songs by a favored singer.

The content stored in the residential gateways or when transferred to another user's hard disk remains encrypted using the videoguard™ system. Only users with subscription rights to the content can then view the content.

WiMAX is ideal for building P2P networks as it provides metro-wide HiperMAN connectivity or even global connectivities. It can help hundreds of peer groups (such as families, school friends, or local communities) to operate in a peer-to-peer mode without overloading any central point for traffic. Moreover, the group users would also be able to share other content such as videos and pictures stored on their home gateways in addition to copyrighted content.

19

CONTENT SECURITY IN WiMAX NETWORKS

There is no safety in numbers, or in anything else.

—*James Thurber*

The security of content transmitted over different transmission media has always been a key consideration in pay-TV services. Traditional pay-TV networks, such as those involving cable TV (DVB-C), satellite (DVB-S), or terrestrial transmission (DVB-T) have been using conditional access systems such as NDS, Conax, Irdeto, Viaccess, etc. to secure content from the point of transmission until it is received at the set-top box of the customer. Wireless environments present an additional challenge in securing content as the transmissions are prone for "sniffing" or multiple types of security attacks common in the internet environment. The initial implementation of WiFi networks was in fact without adequate wireless security and any security that was needed had to be built in at higher levels of protocol architecture.

The environment for providing content security is represented in Figure 19-1. The security of content involves three levels:

- At the base level, the content may be secured by a Digital Rights Management (DRM) system. This implies that the content can only be used as per the rights assigned to the users. This might involve parameters as to how long the user has the right to view content, how many times it can be viewed, whether it can be copied or transmitted, etc. DRM is independent of the transmission system used and any security, if at all, used at the transmission level.
- At the transmission level, the content can be secured by a conditional access system. The CA system operates by encrypting content and providing decryption equipment and keys to the receiving

entity. DVB-based transmission systems use CA systems such as NDS, Conax, Viacccess, Irdeto, etc. The encryption at the transmission level is needed because it operates irrespective of whether the underlying content is protected by DRM or is freely viewable. Live TV programs are, for example, not protected by DRM and the transmission security may be the only security involved for a pay-TV operator. However, if the content is already secured by DRM, such security also is available at the transmission level.

- In WiMAX systems, all content is secured by security protocols which are built in to secure the links between the base stations and the subscriber stations or mobile stations. These involve both encryption and authentication of both the base stations and the mobile stations. In addition, even applications on mobile stations can be individually authenticated. This security is needed, unlike a TV program which is encrypted, the WiMAX system carries voice, data and video which may not have been encrypted.

The WiMAX security, which is described in the sections below, exists only within the confines of the WiMAX system. If content needs to traverse other media, with the WiMAX system only being an intermediate link, it needs to have additional security such as that provided by a CA system.

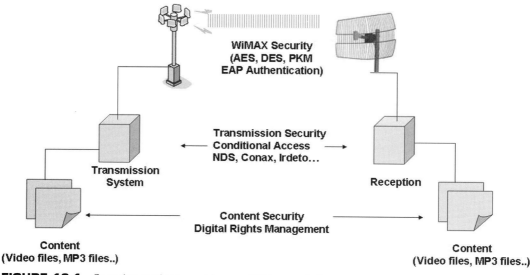

FIGURE 19-1 Security environment in pay-TV transmission

19.1 SECURITY IN A WIRELESS ENVIRONMENT

Wireless networks are being increasingly used for a variety of applications. These are available in homes and offices, apartment complexes, and WiFi hotspots and are becoming omnipresent in all public places such as airports, university campuses coffee shops. The increasing use of mobile commerce applications using wireless (or WiFi) has important implications on the security of applications used.

19.1.1 Security in Wireless Networks

The wireless networks based on IEEE 802.11 have been known to be open for security threats because of the low level of encryption support used, if at all. As the physical media is open (e.g., at airports or highways), it can be sniffed by using simple programs. This can lead to either passive attacks (eavesdropping, traffic analysis) or active attacks (e.g., message modification, masquerading, or denial of service). Wireless security is generally provided by using a wired equivalent privacy (WEP) protocol. In this method of security the host and the remote station share a 40-bit symmetric key. The key is semi-permanent and is used only for the duration of connection. The key is used to cipher the data packet payload using the RC4 cipher mechanism. The packets are decrypted at the receiver by using the same cipher key. The key exchange takes place during the initial connection. A special block of data called the initial vector is included in the transmission to maintain data integrity.

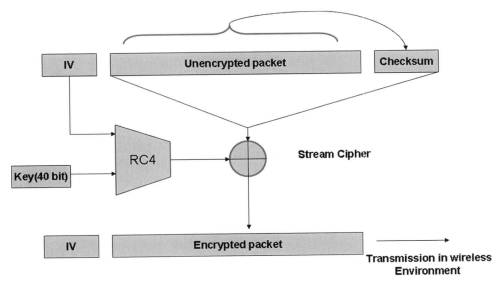

FIGURE 19-2 WEP protocol for security in 802.11 networks

As the security provided by WEP was not adequate, the wireless environment security was subsequently enhanced to use a transport-layer-based end-to-end security scheme called the EAP (Extensible authentication protocol). Privacy and key management with EAP (PKM-EAP) now also forms the basis of authentication and encryption schemes in WiMAX systems.

19.2 CONTENT SECURITY IN WiMAX ENVIRONMENT

Content security in the WiMAX environment is comprised of two components: encryption and authentication. The encryption is carried out at the wireless MAC-layer level so that the packets, as they travel over the air, cannot be sniffed or decoded. The authentication, which uses the EAP and PKM, is used at the transport layer level for establishing connections between the base stations and the mobile stations.

19.2.1 Security in an IEEE 802.16-2004 Fixed WiMAX Environment

The primary mechanism of establishing wireless security in the WiMAX networks is the encryption of the MAC layer packets (MAC PDUs) by using a DES or AES encryption. For this purpose, the MAC layer has a privacy sublayer, which carries out the functions of authentication of subscriber stations and subsequently encryption of data packets.

In order that the subscriber station can decrypt the MAC PDUs, an authorization key (AK) is transmitted from the base station to the subscriber station at the time of registration of the station with the base station (and periodically refreshed). The MAC layer defines the PDUs for authorization and key exchange process. It should be noted that the encryptions are only applied to the MAC PDUs carrying data payloads. The MAC sublayer that carries out these functions is referred to as the Privacy Sublayer. The generic PDUs which help the stations in ranging, nomadicity, or establishing links with other base stations are not encrypted.

The entire process of key exchange is based on the public key-private key cryptography mechanism (RSA) and follows a client-server model, with the base station acting as a server and the subscriber station acting as a client for seeking the authorization key. The key management protocol used by the subscriber station is referred to as the privacy key management protocol or the PKM.

Figure 19-3 shows the Privacy and Key Management (PKM) in operation. A subscriber station receives the MAC PDUs from the base station for ranging and initial registration which are unencrypted. The SS then initiates the PKM process by sending a MAC management

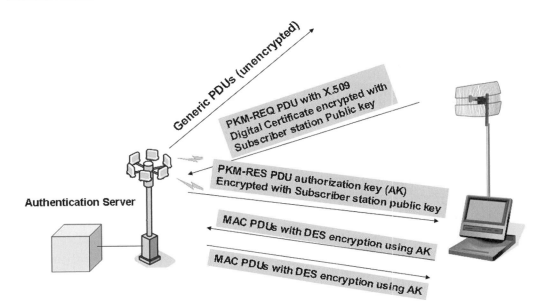

FIGURE 19-3 Privacy and Key Management Protocol (PKM) operation in WiMAX environment

message (PKM-REQ). The message is encrypted using the public key of the SS (which is embedded in the firmware) and carries an X.509 digital certificate. The certificate helps the BS to verify the identity of the SS together with the MAC address contained in the message. The X.509 certificates are unique and cannot be easily forged.

The BS, after authentication, sends a response message (PKM-RSP), which contains the Authorization Key (AK). The message also contains the details of the authorized services which are permitted to be accessed by the SS. The message is encrypted with the public key of the SS which enables the SS to decrypt the same using its private key.

The keys transmitted contain additional information such as key lifetime, key sequence number, etc. which are further used to periodically refresh the keys maintaining security against hackers.

19.2.2 Security in the Mobile WiMAX Environment

The Mobile WiMAX environment is characterized by a mobile station moving from the range of one base station to another and consequently getting authenticated and a handover being executed to the new base station. The security environment and the MAC protocols in the IEEE 802.16e reflect this requirement of mobility.

It may be recalled that Mobile WiMAX supports three techniques for handover, i.e., hard handoff (HHO), fast base station switching (FBSS), and macro-diversity handover (MDHO). The MAC-layer switching time is designed to be less than 50 ms, and the supported protocols need to complete the processes within the stipulated times. In MDHO, the mobile station may be synchronized with a number of base stations and exchanging traffic.

In view of the limited processing power and battery life considerations of mobile devices, the authentication and encryption protocols have been designed so that most of the computational processes take place in base stations rather than mobile stations. To this effect the MS can use the cached key or a handover transferred key in order to prevent a full reauthentication process. The security architecture of WiMAX requires the use of a security processor in the base stations.

Further, a mobile station may traverse from its home CSN to a visited CSN while roaming. The WiMAX forum recommendations describe an AAA architecture-based framework where the authentication is obtained from the home CSN AAA server.

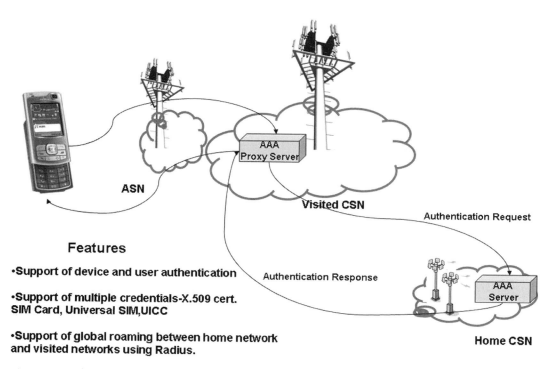

Features

•Support of device and user authentication

•Support of multiple credentials-X.509 cert. SIM Card, Universal SIM,UICC

•Support of global roaming between home network and visited networks using Radius.

•Support of IPv4 and IPv6 security associations

FIGURE 19-4   Features of Mobile WiMAX security and authentication

IEEE 802.16e-2005 Authentication

The security architecture of WiMAX has been further strengthened by the use of PKMv2 (version 2 of privacy and key management), which provides for mutual authentication rather than one-way authentication of clients by the base stations (one-way authorization still permits "man-in-the-middle" attacks by a hacking device masquerading as the base station). The authentication can be done by a number of variant schemes as per the provisions in the standard. These include:

- RSA-based authentication scheme
- EAP-based authentication schemes

The RSA-based authentication scheme is similar to the IEEE 802. 16-2004, except that the PKMv2 is a symmetrical protocol. Thus the response package from the BS also contains the BS certificate for authentication by the SS.

In EAP-based authentication schemes the PKMv2 EAP transfer protocol is used. This essentially involves the transfer of EAP payloads which carry the authentication information and keys. The encryption used is AES.

The process of authentication using PKMv2 and EAP works as follows:

- The MS and the BS (at ASN) perform ranging and exchange information on security capabilities. They also finalize the security protocol which will be used.
- A request for identity is initiated from the BS in the form of an EAP request message, upon receipt of which the MS provides the EAP response message containing the identity of the MS, user, and the application. The message traverses to the home station AAA server over radius.
- The AAA server and the MS establish the session. A master session key (MSK) and enhanced MSK is generated in the AAA server and transferred to the BS security processor. The BS and the MS then generate the pairwise master key (PMK). The BS and MS also generate the authentication key (AK).
- The final step is the creation of the traffic encryption keys (TEKs) by the BS and its transfer to the MS by using the key encryption key (KEK) cipher, which is an asymmetric key. The service flows are then established and traffic is exchanged based on the TEKs.

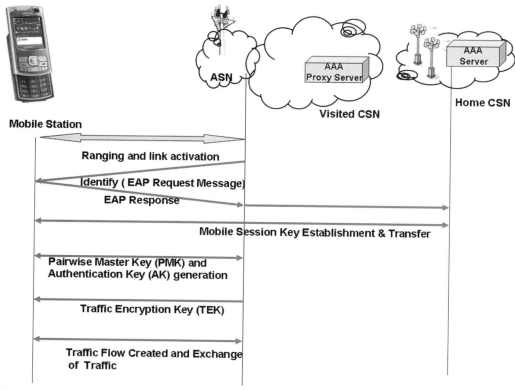

FIGURE 19-5   Authentication Process in Mobile <u>WiMAX</u> using <u>EAP</u>

Encryption in IEEE 802.16e-2005

The encryption method used in Mobile WiMAX is AES (advanced encryption standard). AES is the standard adopted by the National Institute of Standards and Technology (NIST), USA. It uses a block ciphering method which operates on 128 bit size blocks of data. For this reason it is called a block ciphering method. An advantage of AES is that it is relatively simple in terms of complexity of implementation and computational power needed, while at the same time being crypto-graphically strong. The AES has many modes in which the encryption can be implemented. Mobile WiMAX uses AES-CCM , which denotes the use of "counter mode" for encryption. In this mode, instead of directly ciphering the text, a counter is ciphered and a logical XOR operation is used to derive the ciphered text.

19.3 PRACTICAL ASPECTS OF MOBILE WiMAX SECURITY

The security framework of Mobile WiMAX has been designed to cater to a wide range of user scenarios and have thus become very generic in scope. They are designed to cater to multiple users, multiple applications, and multiple service flows within a mobile station. The authentication process can separately authenticate devices, users, and applications. For example, a Mobile WiMAX phone operating as a mobile station in a WiMAX network may be authenticated for use of internet and VoIP but may not be authorized to use streaming video (and thus may be barred if the request to connect to a streaming server is made even though the mobile phone itself has been authenticated). The authentication process in WiMAX grants highest importance to the digital certificate of the mobile station which may be in X.509 format or may be based on secret keys stored in the SIM card, universal SIM, or UICC.

The implementation of the security protocols is done in the WiMAX SoCs which are used in the mobile stations (e.g., Fujitsu MB86K21), or in the base stations (e.g., using a dedicated security processor such as Hifn7955). The Hifn 7955 security processor can provide AES-CCM functions at 200 Mbps with 1500-byte packets.

For potential network operators or device designers, it is of considerable importance to understand how the security process would work in practice even though the equipment itself may be certified by the WiMAX forum, implying that it is capable of fully supporting the air interface specifications and interworking with multi-vendor devices.

While the Mobile WiMAX specifications do define reference interfaces (or APIs) for security, authentication or ciphering, these do not specify how these functions should be handled internally in a mobile device. For example, how the SIM card, the UICC, or the Universal subscriber identity module (USIM) should interact with the security-related functions is left to the handset designers.

The Trusted Computing Group (TCG), which develops open and vendor-neutral industry standard specifications for "trusted computing blocks," has specified these functions under the Mobile Trusted Module (MTM) specifications and a reference mobile phone architecture. These specifications are focused on cell phones but can in general be used by other mobile devices as well, as the mobile architecture is not specified in the specifications. The MTM specifications define the trusted modules within the device and how these should interface to networks and applications. The specifications also provide for multiple communication interfaces such as WiFi, Bluetooth, 3G, etc. in converged handsets.

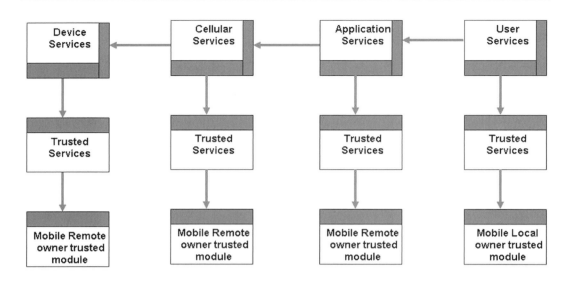

Denotes an interface

Denotes a dependency

Courtesy : TCG

FIGURE 19-6   Mobile platform security architecture showing relationships between trusted services

Figure 19-6 shows a generalized mobile platform concept by the trusted computing group (TCG).

19.3.1 Trusted Computing Group (TCG) Open Specifications for Mobile Phone Security

The TCG open specifications on mobile phone security are aimed toward a unified development of handling security, privacy, and personal information on mobile devices. With the mobile devices becoming almost universally used for storing personal information, mobile payments, and transfer of critically sensitive corporate or personal data, the threat of viruses, malware, or security attacks is very potent. By using the open specifications, it is possible for the industry to embed security mechanisms in phones in a standard manner to ensure better trustworthiness. The specifications also deal with physical security of areas on the phone used for storing sensitive information such as digital keys, certificates, and passwords. The TCG specifications extend and complement the specifications of the industry bodies such

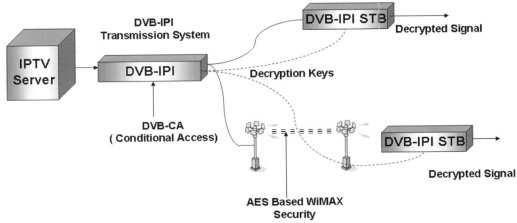

FIGURE 19-7 Transmission-level security in DVB-IPI environment being provided by a conditional access system (CA)

as the 3GPP, Open Mobile Alliance, etc., insofar as the use of security on mobile devices is concerned.

19.4 CONDITIONAL ACCESS AND CONTENT SECURITY

WiMAX systems, when used as wireless extensions of any type of network (e.g., an IPTV network), can provide transmission level security by authenticating the mobile station for any individual service or any service flow. The content which is then delivered to the receiving device is then free of any encryption, unless a content protection scheme such as DRM has been used to protect content.

Referring to Figure 19-1 (earlier in the chapter), there are two additional levels of security apart from the wireless security that are needed to be dealt with, i.e., the first pertains to a transmission system, and the second to the protection of content itself, which is delivered after encryption.

19.4.1 Transmission System Security: Conditional Access (CA)

Figure 19-7 shows a typical DVB-IPI-based transmission system for IPTV. The digital video broadcasting (DVB-IPI) scheme is used for transmission and it is typical to encrypt the transmitted content by a DVB-CA-compliant encryption system (NDS, Conax, Irdeto, etc.). At the receiving end a set-top box contains a decoder, which decrypts the content using the entitlement messages which are transmitted from the headend CA system. A WiMAX system may also form a part of the DVB-IP network for providing wireless extensions. The WiMAX system itself may use AES with PKM to manage the wireless security, but it is still a part of the overall system which is based on the use of the DVB-CA encryption.

The DVB forum has prescribed a common scrambling algorithm (DVB-CSA) which is used to scramble content using any of the CA systems. It has also defined a common interface (DVB-CI) by which scrambled content can be decrypted in a receiving device, such as a set-top box.

Systems which do not make use of a DVB-based transmission and rely only on WiMAX as the final mode of delivery would typically not use a CA system but provide content protection in the form of DRM. This is similar to the approach followed by cellular mobile systems for multicast of content. For example the MediaFLO™ network uses AES encryption (Advanced Encryption Standard) for the broadcast multimedia services. The keys are transmitted using the mobile network directly to the users and do not use the broadcast network as in pay-TV broadcast systems. Services such as MBMS operate in a similar way.

19.5 DIGITAL RIGHTS MANAGEMENT

A CA system or wireless encryption is essentially the domain of the transmission operator. It is used to determine which customers can have access to the content. Once the content leaves the transmission system it is no longer encrypted and can be freely stored, viewed, and retransmitted. Content owners are, however, more concerned with the content security of individual items, e.g., pictures, video, music, e-books, programs, games, etc. Digital rights management is a technology which provides means to content owners to provide rights to view the content irrespective of where it resides. In addition, DRM can also enforce restrictions on making copies of content or the types of devices in which it can be used.

This implies that the rights of viewing (or listening, reading, or forwarding) each item can be controlled by the license holders using, for example, a server which administers the rights. The rights can be administered in a number of ways including:

- Who can view the content
- How many times the content can be viewed
- At what time the rights of viewing content expire
- In which geographical area the content can be viewed
- On what devices the content can be viewed
- Restrictions on forwarding of content
- Renewal of rights through payment mechanism

In today's environment, where content is easily stored on devices with massive storage (e.g., iPods with 80 GB or mobile handsets), DRM is

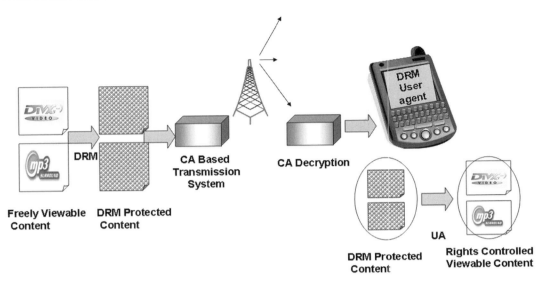

FIGURE 19-8   DRM for protection of content

considered the most effective way to ensure that the content, once purchased cannot be retransmitted over P2P networks or shared by other ways.

Users have become quite familiar with the term "DRM" since Apple® introduced its famous iPhone™, music store iTunes™ service, and Apple's® proprietary DRM (Apple's Fairplay™ DRM technology). The DRM limits the number of machines on which a purchased media can be used, the number of CDs which can be made, and to which devices it can be transferred to (e.g., iPods™, Macs, etc.).

19.5.1 Types of DRM Systems

There are a number of different types of DRM systems in operation, most of them proprietary. Examples include Windows Media DRM 10, Sony DRM, Helix DRM, Apple Fairplay DRM, NDS Videoguard DRM, Microsoft PlayReady DRM, etc. Similarly, Marlin™ is a DRM technology for media players, which is supported by major players such as Sony, Phillips, Panasonic, and Samsung. Some of these DRMs are associated with music stores while others are associated with media player manufacturers or handset manufacturers. There is a realization that operation with multiple DRMs and specifically where a limited number of devices can be associated with each DRM is a hindrance to an open environment and mobility.

FIGURE 19-9   The DRM environment

The Open Mobile Alliance (OMA), which aims to provide an interoperable framework for applications in mobile devices, has recommended the use of an open DRM technology. The OMA DRM 2.0 is now being implemented in many systems.

DRM Free Music and Videos

It must be mentioned that there is also a parallel trend to have music stores sell content which is not protected by DRM. Amazon, for example, is already providing music and video sales that are not DRM protected. In October 2007, iTunes had also begun supplying music tracks that were not protected by DRM. Music CDs from almost all major producers are now available without DRM. The reasons for a DRM-free approach have been multiple, including high cost of managing DRM systems, multiplicity of DRM systems available, and consequent splitting of the markets, incompatibility in different players, bugs in DRM implementations, etc.

19.5.2 Open Mobile Alliance (OMA) DRM

OMA has formulated a scheme of DRM that can be used in all mobile devices. The DRM is based on the principle of treating the "content" and its "rights" as two distinct entities. The rights for the content are permitted to be used in a user device by a DRM user agent. The DRM defines these structures and how the rights are transferred and enforced.

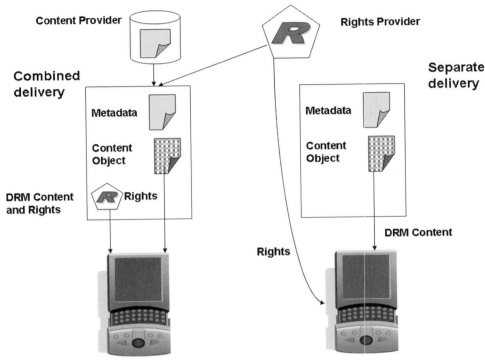

FIGURE 19-10   Content delivery in DRM 1.0

DRM 1.0

The OMA DRM 1.0 was released in November 2002. The Release 1 was always considered as interim till the DRM 2.0 was finalized and released, which happened in December 2004. For all practical purposes, it is Release 2.0 that is used now. However, DRM 1.0 had set the ball rolling by enhancing the definition of content by defining new media types. OMA DRM 1.0 has been now implemented by a majority of handset manufacturers.

In DRM, individual media objects such as images, audio, and video clips are encrypted by using a specified algorithm. The DRM content is associated with Metadata (such as title, artist, duration, year of release, etc.) and delivery method. In DRM 1.0 there are three delivery methods:

- Forward Lock (Compulsory or Implicit)
- Combined Delivery
- Separate Delivery

The DRM 1.0 defines the new media types as "DRM Content" (encrypted content with metadata), "Rights," and "DRM message."

The procedure of the download is not specified by DRM 1.0. The users can only consume the content as per the "Rights" contained.

DRM 1.0 does not contain tools for management of key transfer which was left for later releases. However there are two mechanisms defined for delivery of content. Figure 19-10 shows the "Separate Delivery" and the "Combined Delivery" methods. In Combined Delivery, the rights are also sent along with the content. Alternative methods of delivery are the Forward Lock method (where the rights are not conveyed and forward lock is implicit) and Separate Delivery (where the delivery of rights is over a separate channel).

19.5.3 DRM 2.0

The DRM 2.0 from OMA was a full framework for the implementation of end-to-end security in content handling systems and usage environments. It did this by providing the mechanism of key transfer which was lacking in the DRM 1.0. The security environment provides for transfer of rights from a "rights holder" to a user agent by using the public key encryption infrastructure (PKI). DRM 2.0 defines "Actors," which have various roles in the DRM management process. The following are the "Actors" in the DRM 2.0 scheme:

- A DRM agent is a "trusted entity" placed in a device (e.g., a mobile phone), which is responsible for receiving DRM content and enforcing the rights.
- A content provider provides DRM content to various Agents.
- A Rights issuer delivers "rights" instructions or objects for the use of such content.
- A certification authority provides certificates to rights issuers and trusted agents to operate as per the PKI infrastructure.

The DRM 2.0 specifies the use of various protocols for operating in the PKI environment such as the 128 bit AES, RSA-PSS (signature algorithm), and others. It specifies a DRM Content Format (DCF) for discrete objects such as pictures and a packetized data format (PDCF) for continuous video (e.g., in streaming video). DRM 2.0 is a fairly complex standard with multiple options for passing of keys. In a typical implementation, the content is first encrypted using AES and a CEK. The CEK is wrapped using the Rights Objects Key (ROK) and placed along with the encrypted content in the DCF. The DCF is delivered to the DRM agent in the receiving device, which then decrypts the rights information using the PKI and the transmitted keys.

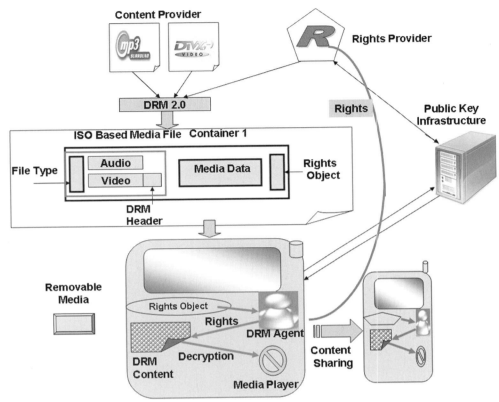

FIGURE 19-11 Content transfer and usage in DRM 2.0 environment

The DRM agent as a "Trusted Entity" is resident in the mobile phone and is responsible for delivering the decrypted content as per the rights.

While the transmission of content to the mobile phone using DRM protection is a one-time process, the user may consume the content (for example, store and listen to songs or view videos) over a period of time. In case the rights expire, the user can buy new rights from the rights issuer and the DRM agent can reauthorize the use of content using the PKI.

19.5.4 How Is OMA DRM Content Security Handled in Practice?

Applying DRM to Media Files

A number of tools are available which can apply DRM on content files. One of the key issues involved for operators is the licensing of the OMA DRM technologies. OMA DRM is a licensed software involving a license fee per subscriber or handset. Intertrust® has announced a scheme of licensing of patents necessary to implement OMA DRM. Carriers can license the technology for 0.02 Euros per subscriber ($20,000 per million subs per year) irrespective of the active use of content services. Content providers can also license the technology for 0.09 Euros per subscriber domain.

Mobile Clients for OMA DRM

Mobile device operating systems such as Symbian™ series S60 and series S40 already support the Windows media and OMA DRM for copy protection. The support of other DRM systems, such as Microsoft PlayReady is being implemented. Mobile client suites such as NetFront™ provide OMA DRM as an inbuilt feature. Similarly Videoguard Mobile DRM client provides the necessary tools for handset manufacturers to offer OMA DRM 1.0- and 2.0-enabled handsets. The NDS Videoguard™ client has already been embedded in a large number of operating systems such as embedded Linux, Symbian, BREW™, and Microsoft Smartphone platforms. Some of the features supported by the Videoguard™ DRM client, for example, are:

- OMA DRM V1.0 forward lock, combined and separate delivery of content files
- OMA DRM V2.0 DCF file handling
- Secure storage of rights objects

A large number of handsets now provide support of OMA and Windows DRM such as the Sony Ericsson Walkman™ phone W850.

19.5.5 OMA BCAST 1.0

The DRM 2.0 security is applicable to media files or downloadable objects. Typically, it can be used for MP3 or DiVX files, videos, and e-books. These can be downloaded from a music store and used as per the rights purchased. The key exchange mechanism using the PKI or pre-loaded keys is adequate for the usage environment of downloaded content.

In a broadcast environment where the keys are continuously changing, a different approach is needed for key refresh. OMA has conceived a broadcast level DRM solution termed as OMA-BCAST. The OMA-BCAST DRM is envisaged for use in broadcast environment such as that existing in DVB-H, DMB-T, or similar systems involving broadcasting or multicasting of content over mobile networks.

One of the objectives of OMA in recommending the use of the BCAST DRM standard is that an open DRM has many advantages in terms of interoperability of applications and handsets. A common DRM, for example, can be embedded in handsets and used universally with OMA DRM content if it is adapted by different operators.

19.5.6 DRM in IPTV

The Alliance for Telecommunications Industry Standards (ATIS), which is recognized as the prime organization for coordinating common standards in IPTV (along with DVB), has also released a document entitled "ATIS' requirement overview documents for IPTV Architecture and Digital Rights Management (DRM)." IPTV DRM Interoperability Requirements (ATIS-0800001) define the requirements for the interoperability of systems and components in the IPTV DRM/security environment. As the ATIS is now recognized by the Global Standards Consortium (GSC) as the prime organization for coordinating IPTV standardization, it is anticipated that IPTV developments in the medium term will become harmonized by the interoperable DRM environment set out by ATIS.

19.5.7 Microsoft Windows Media DRM

Owing to the widespread use of Windows media players in desktops as well as mobile devices, a number of industry participants such as handset manufacturers, mobile operators, and music stores have adapted the Windows Media DRM as the preferred DRM solution. Handsets from Nokia and Motorola, among others, support Windows Media DRM.

19.6 IMPLEMENTATION EXAMPLES AND PLATFORMS

19.6.1 NDS WiMAX TV

NDS offers a WiMAX TV solution, which includes Videoguard™ DRM as an integral part of the content protection scheme. The platform can provide live TV content over IEEE 802.16e networks and enable the offering of triple-play services by operators. The platform also supports pay-per-view and VoD content. Because the platform uses multicast technology for live TV channels, the content can be delivered to a large number of users while at the same time maintaining capacity for unicast video as well as voice and data services.

The platform is comprised of H.264 encoders, which can give a highly efficient encoding of 0.5 Mbps per channel. The content

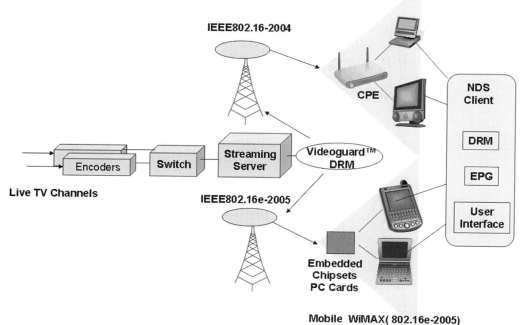

FIGURE 19-12   WiMAX TV Platform from NDS™ (Courtesy NDS)

streams go to a streaming server, which implements the multicast of content over WiMAX networks. The content is DRM-protected with Videoguard DRM prior to transmission. At the receiving end, the devices can range from mobile phones or PDAs with direct reception of Mobile WiMAX or PCs used with WiMAX CPEs or PC cards. All the devices are equipped with an NDS mobile client, which supports DRM, an electronic program guide (EPG), and user interfaces.

MobiTV-NDS

MobiTV had demonstrated an end-to-end solution to deliver mobile TV to WiMAX-capable UMPCs using a Mobile WiMAX IEEE 802.16e network. The solution included a streaming of MobiTV content, Runcom provided Mobile WiMAX infrastructure, videoguard DRM servers from NDS, and mobile TV client from MobiTV. The transmissions include both multicast and unicast content. MobiTV has an agreement with Sprint to be a content partner for Sprint's mobile TV offerings (Sprint TV®, Sprint TV Xtra, and Sprint TV enVivo® services) across the United States. It is expected that the Sprint XOHM mobile network would have MobiTV content delivered using WiMAX in addition to other content which may be available.

20

BUSINESS CASE FOR WiMAX

When one door closes another door opens; but we often look so long and so regretfully upon the closed door that we do not see the ones which open for us.

—Alexander Graham Bell

Do we have a good case for a WiMAX service? This is a question that is often asked by operators. The response is often a well-reasoned plan with projections for various services such as broadband internet, data links, VoIP, video streaming, media downloads, etc. This approach cannot be faulted, and we will also proceed to analyze various services individually in this chapter in the same manner.

But as we all recognize, mobile WiMAX is not a service which would fit in the shoes of or replace any previously available services or technologies. It has capabilities, by keeping the users connected at high bit rates of, say, 1 Mbps each, a new ecosystem of "applications space," which is beyond the domain of existing cellular mobile, wireless, or fixed wireless technologies. The operators venturing out on WiMAX need to recognize this potential and not be content with the traditional revenue streams, but to create new services, new domains of applications which not only attract users but also generate entirely new sources of revenue. Hence the answer to the question "Is there is business case for Mobile WiMAX?" is *Yes*; traditional services such as VoIP, broadband, and data links alone make it viable in most situations. But operators can create a bigger business opportunity by entering the domain of community-based services such as instant messaging, presence, active directories, video and audio blogging with IMPS, TV broadcast and multicast services, video on demand and push video, music downloads, RSS feeds to mobile devices, and mobile broadband. In most cases, this will require the operators to venture into areas which are multidisciplinary, such as design of mobile devices, software clients, and network architectures that enable them to step out of legacy TDM-based networks.

Many developing countries and rural communities everywhere are today bereft of any reliable broadband connectivity and nothing is on the horizon in the near term. It is no surprise, therefore, that some of the major installations have become operational in these locales and more are on the way. This also gives the operators an opportunity to, at the first instance, opt for network architectures based on core multiservices such as IP multimedia system or an XMPP-based Jabber network. This gives them an opportunity to enter an expanded services ecosystem which is distinguished by highly cost-efficient architectures providing a sustainable cost advantage, which cannot be matched by competition.

20.1 INITIATING MOBILE WiMAX OVERLAY

WiMAX networks provide the best combination of technology and cost to create wireless data overlay networks. As these networks can also be used to provide VoIP, internet, and video multicasting, it is possible to implement triple-play services with relatively short roll-out times and extensive coverage. While initially a city may be covered (depending on the size and topography) by just 5–6 base stations, these can be quickly upgraded to higher-frequency reuse schemes or user densities by increasing the base station counts. In this manner, the services grow supported by revenues, rather than a large over-hang of upfront expenditures weighing down the business.

WiMAX is particularly well-suited for developing countries to over-lay triple-play networks over conventional landline and cellular

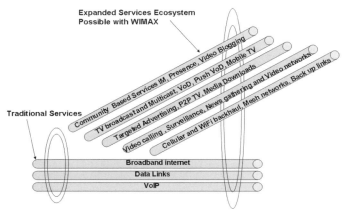

FIGURE 20-1   Viewing a WiMAX business as enabler of new services, while supporting existing services

2G networks. It is equally well-suited for urban areas where very high user densities need to served with multicast services such as multicast mobile video. As an example, we can consider the case of a small city (semi-urban) which is about 7 Km in radial distances (i.e., about 100 square kilometers). To initiate coverage, it is possible to start with a single base station, strategically located with three sectors and one radio channel per sector. Assuming the use of Mobile WiMAX (IEEE 802.16e-2005) and a 10 MHz bandwidth channel, it is possible to get a throughput of 72 Mbps per sector using 2:2 MIMO. However, this figure is a theoretical peak data rate and is valid only with the highest density modulation, i.e., 64 QAM. If a mix of business and residential customers is considered with many of them using indoor CPEs, the maximum bit rates are not achievable. On a conservative basis and assuming that 16 QAM is the highest modulation which is used at the edge coverage, all subscriber stations will not support 2×2 MIMO and the use is in a multiple cell wireless environment, practical data rates achievable should be scaled to 50 percent or 36 Mbps per sector. If we assume 3:1 DL to UL bandwidth ratio, it gives 27 Mbps per sector as the downlink bandwidth. This can be used for multicast video (6–8 Mbps), VoIP and internet applications, enabling the entire area with triple-play connectivity (Figure 20-2).

MOBILE WiMAX BASE STATIONS

In the example above, a mobile WiMAX base station, such as the ADAPTIX's BX-3000®, has been considered, which can handle up to three sectors from a central base band unit with three remote RF units. With 3:1 AAS, three antennas are supported per sector, or a total of nine for the base station. Hence, a single base station installation can handle all three sectors with full-featured SIMO and MIMO, beamforming, etc. It also supports the functions of the Access Service Node (ASN) gateway in addition to those of the base station. With the support of the full IP Stack in the ASN functionality, it can provide direct interface to IP networks with QoS mapping between IP and 802.16e mobile WiMAX QoS. In addition to the support of all routing functions, it also supports AAA terminations (RADIUS Proxy, EAP server, and wire speed encryption). For direct terminal support it also provides IP address management (Static and DHCP relay to CSN). Such integrated installations can significantly reduce equipment complexity and cost of installations.

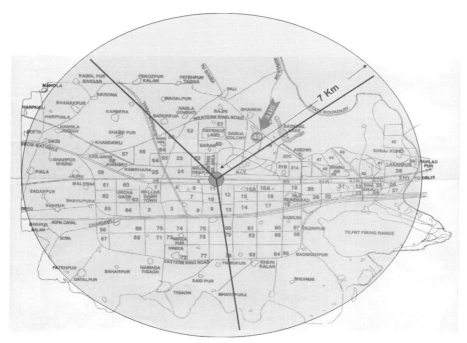

FIGURE 20-2   Commencing coverage with WiMAX over 100 square Km with three sectors

20.1.1 Dimensioning Number of Users

The available uplink and downlink bandwidths now need to be shared among the users. The number of users which can be supported depends on the data requirements of each user, uplink, and downlink. In case of WiMAX, the bandwidth sharing is not by any contention-based mechanism, as we have seen in the discussion of technologies, but is granted to each station at the time of connection as "service flows" and by allocating subchannels that it may use from frame to frame to maintain the service flows. The bandwidth demanded by the CPE can, of course, vary during the duration of connection. Mobile WiMAX has the advantage that the mobile stations can be allocated bandwidth which can be as low as one subchannel of an OFDM symbol in a frame. For Mobile WiMAX, this is possible in both uplink and downlink, whereas in fixed WiMAX, subchannels are available only in uplink direction.

In case of Mobile WiMAX, the certification profiles provide for 15 and 17 subchannels in downlink and uplink respectively for 5 MHz bandwidth, whereas in 10 MHz systems it is 30 and 35 subchannels, respectively. This implies that the capacity to support active users (having at least one subchannel active in every frame) based on 44 OFDM data symbols per frame is about 660 for 5 MHz systems and

TABLE 20–1

Example of a tri-sector base station for initiating WiMAX coverage in
a semi-urban environment

Parameter	Initial Configuration
No. of Sectors	3
Coverage Area (Sq Km)	105
Coverage Area per Sector	35.0
Bandwidth per Channel	10 MHz
Channels per Sector	1
Bit Rates (Max), Mbps, per Sector, Peak Theoretical with 2×2 MIMO, Mbps	72
Bit Rates, Average, Mbps	36
Bit Rates per Sq Km, Kbps	1029.9
OFDM Carriers	1024
Simultaneous Active Users per Sector	200
Average Bit Rate per Active User (downlink)	135
Dimensioned User Base with 1:20 per Sector	4000
Dimensioned User Base with 1:20 per Sector for the City	12,000
Data Transfer Capacity per Sector (GB per Month)	7465
Data Transfer Capacity for WiMAX System, Three Sectors (TB/Month)	22.4

1320 for 10 MHz systems. For Fixed WiMAX, the number of available subchannels is 16 as per the standard.

Commercially available base station equipment (such as the Flexwave™ base station example cited in Figure 5-12) provides for 512 active users per sector and 7168 service flows (14 service flows per active subscriber). As another example, a base station for Fixed WiMAX, Flexwave WMX 3000™ also provides for 512 active connected units per base station and 7168 service flows.

However, the number of active users configured will, in practice, be determined by the bit rates needed per customer. All active customers may not need a subchannel in every frame. Assuming that an active subscriber needs one subchannel in every four frames, it quadruples the number of customers which can be serviced based on best-effort services. The actual number of active subscribers will depend on the types of services subscribed and is discussed in subsequent sections by basing the estimates on bit rates per customer. Each active connection can, in addition, support multiple service flows, representing different applications on the subscriber station using the WiMAX services.

In the example, if it is assumed that around 200 customers are active at a time based on a mix of services, and that the contention ratio (registered users to those active) is 1:20, this implies the support of 4000 subscribers per sector or 12,000 per base station.* This is typically also the figure given by vendors such as Adaptix for its base station BS-3000. The activity and contention factors mentioned are purely empirical and will depend on whether the users are business users or residential users. Business users tend to have a contention of close to 1:5, whereas for residential customers it is close to 1:30. It is possible to work out capacity usage scenarios based on different types of CPEs (mobile, residential, or business) and different mix of services.

It should be recognized that WiMAX systems can support higher data rate services such as broadband data and video as well as a large number of low rate customers due to their low data granularity of only 108 bits representing one subchannel in one OFDM symbol with 64 QAM. Because of the extremely low granularity, users can be dimensioned based on the bit rates needed, presuming that the subchannels will be allocated by the system appropriately to accommodate such data rates.

In the future, WiMAX systems will be also used to connect devices with average bit rates of only a few bits per second. Dimensioning extremely low data rates per subscriber per sector per radio channel implies higher overheads in frames and subchannels which may not be fully occupied unless larger latencies can be terminated.

Coming back to the example, in real-life scenarios represented by the usage today, which is comprised of SOHO and high data rate customers and with some customers using CBR services, with a DL:UL ratio of 4:1, and assuming a DL/UL bandwidth of only 27/9 MHz (i.e., 50 percent of those achievable with 2×2 MIMO; representing typical field transmission environment in a semi urban area), the number of active subscribers is likely to be dimensioned lower than the theoretical capacities of base stations. Hence the number of users will be dimensioned based on the data rates used.

Multicast Usage

The previous discussions were applicable to users operating in a unicast mode or interactive mode. The case of multicast video transmissions is different. A key advantage of Mobile WiMAX arises owing

---

* The dimensioning of users and data rates can vary, based on the type of equipment used, the type of services which need to be enabled, and category of users, business or rural.

to its multicast and broadcast service (MBS) where the terminals can even be in the sleep mode and receive multicast transmissions. The number of multicast users can be scaled up very sharply with only minor increases in infrastructure costs.

Scaling up the WiMAX Infrastructure

As the overlay network of WiMAX-delivered services starts to get utilized, it is possible to scale up the user density or data rates per sector by adding more base stations, more frequency channels per sector and adding more sectors per base station. As an example, the city where the initial implementation was done with one base station can grow to five base stations in the next stage, retaining one frequency per sector. The average radius of a cell is now only 2.5 Km. This will provide equivalent to $5 \times 3 = 15$ sector channels, increasing the capacity by 5 times over the previous configuration. The number of users which can now be serviced can grow from 12,000 (as cited in our example earlier) to 60,000 for unicast or VoIP services and much higher for multicast services (Figure 20-3).

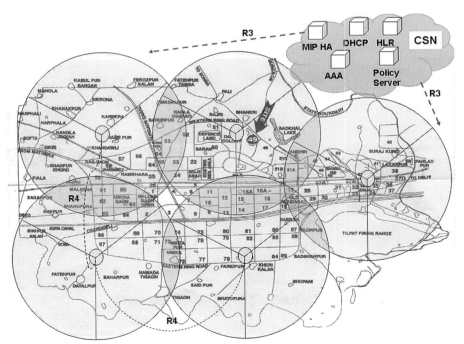

FIGURE 20-3 Conceptual depiction of scaling up Mobile WiMAX coverage for higher data rates or larger user base. (Location of base stations in actual implementations will depend on the field environment.)

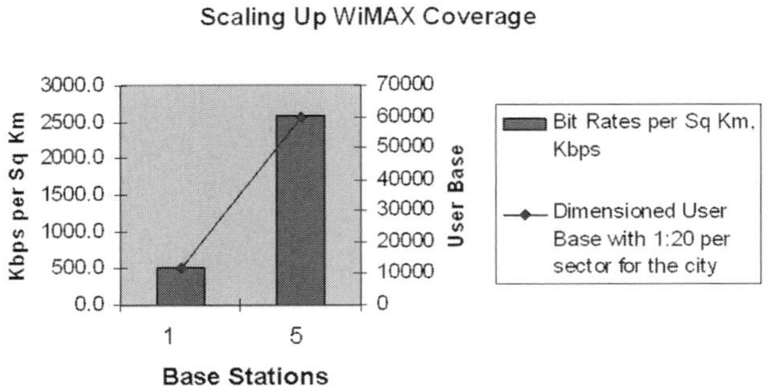

Scaling Up WiMAX Coverage

FIGURE 20-4 WiMAX services can be expanded rapidly to grow with user base

In the figure, the inter-ASN gateway links (R4) and the link to the CSN (R3) are also shown for completeness of the network architecture and also as these have an impact on the business case.

The connectivity service network (CSN) houses the AAA, DHCP server, and the policy servers for the network and will also route any multicast servers for video services.

20.2 BUSINESS MODELS FOR MOBILE WiMAX

There can be multiple business models for the introduction of both Fixed WiMAX and Mobile WiMAX services. By providing a wide coverage, instantly available connectivity, with QoS and security, it is an enabler for many applications, which would otherwise be unviable with wireline connectivity. Many of the applications which today use satellite VSAT networks (for want of better wireless technologies) can now migrate to WiMAX. Examples of applications that can be implemented using WiMAX are:

- Private networks (bank ATMs, retail, remote display TV screens, etc.)
- Video surveillance networks, public safety services
- Tracking systems
- Small business data services (ADSL equivalents)
- Personal broadband
- Mobile video multicast
- Remote WiFi hotspot enabling
- VoIP phone booths, video phones
- Satellite news gathering for news, weather, reality, and current affairs channels
- User-generated content with high resolution

These services can be classified into different categories based on requirements for bandwidth, latency, and jitter. These values are important as the scheduling of service flows in WiMAX takes into account these requirements.

Class	Application	BANDWIDTH Guideline		LATENCY Guideline		JITTER Guideline	
1	Interactive Gaming	Low Bandwidth	50 kbit/s	Low Latency	80ms	N/A	
2	Voice Telephone (VOIP) Video Conference	Low Bandwidth	32-64 kbit/s	Low Latency	160ms	Low Jittering	<50ms
3	Streaming Media	Moderate to High Bandwidth	<2 Mbit/s	N/A		Low Jittering	<100 ms
4	Instant Messaging Web Browsing	Moderate Bandwidth	2 Mbit/s	N/A		N/A	
5	Media Content Download	High Bandwidth	10 Mbit/s	N/A		N/A	

FIGURE 20-5 Application service classes (Source: WiMAX Forum)

The model used would depend on the territories where such deployment is done, the local regulations, and the existing infrastructure for telecommunications and broadband services. Any deployments will depend on the resources available and their costs such as licensed spectrum, which we discuss in the next section. In some cases, such resources may actually permit or limit the capability of an operator to offer such services.

In this chapter, we will build an example business case based on purely empirical values of different parameters mainly for the purpose of illustration.

20.2.1 Broadband Data-Centric Model

In many developing economies, the model best suited for initial deployments is one in which WiMAX enables broadband (and triple-play connectivity) to business users. It needs to be recognized that the growth of broadband in many regions of the world has been quite modest and there is demand from businesses and large users for a QoS-based connectivity (e.g., data with CIR from 512 Kbps to 1.5 Mbps). In such cases, the subscriber numbers can be estimated from the number and speed of data links needed. The sector capacity in TB per month is a reasonable way to estimate the capacity of the system to handle other services such as mail or HTTP traffic.

As mobility and the terminal user size is not a constraint for such cases, the use of 2×2 MIMO with 2Rx and TX antennas may be possible. Each subscriber station in such cases may have multiple connections and service flows established with the base station. This implies higher data rates achievable per business customer.

Because of the CIR-based services, which need prescheduled assignment of subchannels under the unsolicited grant service (UGS), and the sector capacity of say 72 Mbps per radio channel, a sector may support only around 100 customers per sector with 512 Kbps/128 K CIR services configured for each customer in the example cited. Hence the number of cell sites will need to be scaled up *linearly* with the number of users. The cell site installations may also closely follow the customer geographical *clusters*, i.e., be unevenly distributed in the city. In addition to the CIR-based data lines, the services may also include broadband connectivity to the internet with some contention (say 1:2 or 1:4) for business customers.

Such models, involving only a few high data rate customers, do not involve extensive customer management or multiple services support and are low on management costs. The major cost elements are spectrum, base station costs, and backhaul connectivity links to the internet ports.

It will not be out of place that this model of introduction has found favor in countries or regions such as India, Latin America, and the Middle East where the major licensees of WiMAX spectrum are using WiMAX to provide last mile connectivity as the local loops and long distance lines are held by a limited number of players.

Dimensioning a Business CPE

Table 20-2 provides the typical case of a business CPE with 512/128 K CIR data link, with 512 K/128 K broadband internet connection with 1:2 contention, 4 Erlangs of VoIP (i.e., 40 VoIP users with a 1:10 ratio), and data transfer of 30 GB/8 GB per month for e-mail and browsing services.

The dimensioning of the CPE has been done in terms of the percentage of total resources used per sector, which gives an indication of how many such customers can be supported before an additional sector or base station needs to be added.

20.2.2 Triple-Play Overlay Model

A triple-play overlay model focusing on video multicast, VoIP, and broadband data may be attractive for a different set of operators. Examples of such operators are:

- Traditional broadcasters, without ownership of cable or telecommunications networks, who wish to upgrade to triple-play and interactive services.

TABLE 20-2

Resource dimensioning a business CPE (data oriented)

Service Configuration of a Business Customer CPE Operating in 10 MHz WiMAX Sector, 2 × 2 MIMO with Spatial Multiplexing

Service	Downlink	Uplink	Service Type	Percentage of Sector Resources Used per User
Bit rates (max), Mbps, per sector, peak theoretical with 2 × 2 MIMO Mbps	54	18		
Dimensioned Data capacity per sector per month, GB	8748.0	2916.0		
Sector resources used for 512 Kbps/128 Kbps CIR	512.0	128.0	UGS	0.71 percent
Sector resources used for 512 Kbps/128 Kbps broadband with 1:2 contention Kbps)	256	64	nrtPS	0.4 percent
32 Kbps VoIP, 4 Erlangs	128	128	nrtPS, Latency 20 ms	0.7 percent
File transfer/HTTP data GB/month	30	8	Best Effort (BE)	0.3 percent
Total resources used				2.12 percent

- Operators targeting new base of mobile devices for Mobile TV, Video and audio downloads, broadband internet, internet radio, and web services. Typically such operators would not own cellular 3 G or CDMA networks but would like an access to the emerging non-voice services and VoIP services market as off-network services.
- Telcos and cable operators who wish to deploy WiMAX in the last mile for VoD services, VoIP, and add-ons which the existing cable networks may not provide.

Triple-play networks, unlike the data-centric networks, would be characterized by the use of relatively low data rates per customer, with the primary application being HTTP and e-mail traffic on a best-effort delivery basis. These networks would also provide video multicast which can be a major revenue driver because of the large customer bases that can be addressed.

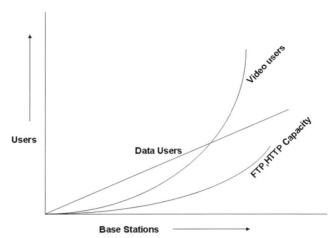

FIGURE 20-6 Number of video multicast users increase in a non-linear fashion with network

Because of the multicast nature of video transmissions, the number of users of such services can increase non-linearly with the growth of available base stations (the number is not unlimited as in the case of a broadcast service owing to the MAP overhead service authentication requirements). Higher resource availability also improves the performance of best-effort services such as HTTP and FTP services because of the statistical advantage of higher resource pools.

The management of such networks is much more resource-intensive because of the larger customer base and the need to accommodate new devices in the user domain. Video multicast services require subscription management and rights management of content as additional activities. Additional factors such as mobility management and interconnection with cellular networks will be needed to be factored in for targeting maximum customer base.

Table 20-3 is an example of a customer CPE using triple-play services in a home environment. In this example, it has been assumed that the maximum data rates which can be achieved are only 50 percent of the sector capacities because of customer dispersal in the cell area and hence unsustainability of highest-order modulation schemes.

It may be seen that the video multicast services can be dimensioned to use about a quarter of cell capacity leaving the rest for unicast video, VoIP, mail, and web access. A unicast video at 1 Mbps (using H.264 or Windows media) uses only 3.7 percent of a sector capacity on a 24-hour use basis. If a typical VoD use is for 2 hours, 12 subscribers can be served within 3.7 percent of the sector resources. The high data transfer capacity of the cell and the high burstable nature of bandwidth, VoD

TABLE 20-3

Example of a triple-play CPE

Service Configuration of Video Multicast and Unicast CPEs in 10 MHz WiMAX Sector 2 × 2
MIMO with Spatial Multiplexing

Service	Downlink	Uplink	Service Type	Percentage of Sector Resources Used
Bit rates (max), Mbps, per sector, peak theoretical with 2 × 2 MIMO Mbps	54	18		
Assumed average available bit rates (Mbps)	27	9		
Dimensioned data capacity per sector per month, GB	4374.0	1458.0		
Dimensioned capacity for video multicast services	6.0	1.0	WiMAX multicast and broadcast service (UGS)	22.2 percent
Capacity for unicast video (Mbps)	1.0	0.1	rtPS	3.7 percent
32 Kbps VoIP, 0.1 Erlangs (Kbps)	3.2	3.2	rtPS	0.01 percent
HTTP, browsing (Gbps per month)	3	0.75		0.1 percent

content can also be delivered by download to the CPEs, a non-real-time operation.

We have used the method of estimating a cell capacity based on bit rates for different services though a more accurate method would have been to estimate subchannels assigned for each service. However, the granularity of data in WiMAX is so small that the differences can be ignored except for very low data rate CPEs.

Using Multicast for Push VoD

Multicast services can also be used for push VoD by multicasting popular content such as top-20 movies or top-50 video titles. The users can then watch based on monthly subscription or billing. A 120-minute video at standard resolution requires 0.9 GB (1 Mbps H.264 or Windows

Media encoding). The sector capacity of over 4300 GB provides adequate resources for a very effective Push VoD using WiMAX multicast services when supported by suitable application framework.

20.3 RESOURCE COSTING

The costing of resources is an important driver of any business plan. As in the case of any wireless technology, the ownership and costs of licensed spectrum are the factors which have a major bearing on the viability of a WiMAX network. Of course, it is also possible to use unlicensed spectrum with IEEE 802.16-2004 technology, and this indeed is an enabler of WiMAX connectivity in rural areas with low attendant costs. As has been discussed in Chapter 11 (Spectrum for WiMAX Networks), the use of unlicensed spectrum in urban areas has many limitations and a commercial service is better provided with licensed spectrum.

Spectrum Costs

Broadband spectrum in most countries is now priced attractively in order to promote the growth of wireless access and is also more easily available than the spectrum for 3G technologies, which is a competitor in some ways for the broadband-based services.

In India, for example, the WiMAX-licensed slots (2×7 MHz for FDD and 7 MHz for TDD) were allocated in the 3.3–3.4 GHz band on a first-come first-served basis. The slots now stand allotted to over 20 operators in different parts of the country. The spectrum charges (called royalty) works out to $1800 per 7 MHz TDD spectrum channel for each link of up to 25 Km. Thus for a base station with three sectors, the cost is $5400 per annum. A city with 20 base stations would need $108,000 as spectrum charges. Spectrum in the 2.4 GHz band (2.469–2.69) for Mobile WiMAX is planned to be allotted in the near future.

In the United States, the bulk of the spectrum in the 2.5 GHz band is held by Sprint and Clearwire. The 2.3 GHz licensed and 5 GHz unlicensed bands can be used currently, before the auction of the 700 MHz bands in 2008 makes available additional capacity.

There are different criteria for considering the spectrum costs. One method is cost of spectrum per base station, as used in some countries. In other cases, the spectrum is allocated across various regions. A company needs to get a license for all the regions in order to cover the entire country. For example, in Germany, licenses for 28 regions were auctioned for 56 million Euros to three companies (nationwide) and some regional licensees. The licenses were for 21 MHz each or 4 channels of 5 MHz to each licensee or 12 channels nationwide. This gives a figure of about 4.5 million Euros per 5 MHz (FDD) for 28 regions ($0.5 per person based on a population of 8.5 million). Assuming that such coverage requires 5000 base stations, the cost per base station for 5 MHz works out to $900 per base station or $1800 for 10 MHz.

In Japan, the spectrum is allotted based on a pricing of $500,000 per MHz for the whole of Japan. This works out to $2.5 million per year for the entire country (10 million population) for 5 MHz or $0.25 per individual covered per year.

Recognizing that there are large variations in cost to reckon with, we have, however, taken a figure of $2000 per base station per month as the spectrum cost per 10 MHz, with a coverage of 50 sq km for the business case recognizing that any higher costs will need to be offset by higher priced offerings.

Costs of Internet Bandwidth

With data being the primary offering in some business plans, the cost of internet bandwidth is also an important factor. Internet bandwidth is priced in the range of $350–1000 per Mbps per month for backbone connectivity. The prices in the lower range of $350 are in the United States, while higher prices such as $1000 prevail in some Asian and African countries. These prices are based on DS3 (45 Mbps)-derived pricings.

CPE Cost

The cost of the CPE is an important consideration for a viable business. It is also important to identify and validate the type of CPEs which will be used in a given network even though all the devices conforming to the WiMAX Forum approved profiles and with certified equipment are expected to be able to operate. The CPE devices which have initially become available are for the data-centric applications and may consist of either an outdoor unit mounted with the antennas or an indoor unit with inbuilt antennas such as a WiMAX mobile handset.

A typical crash of the CPE prices, which follows a large volume growth, is yet to be witnessed in the Mobile WiMAX arena. Hence, CPEs with prices in the $200–400 range are the norm. However, over a two-year time frame, prices of below $100 per CPE will be a reality.

20.4 REVENUE ELEMENTS

It is possible to build a WiMAX service with multiple possible revenue elements. In order to give examples of business models, we have taken the liberty of assigning values to revenue elements, while recognizing that there may be variations based on existing services and the regions where these are deployed. Some of the revenue elements with typical figures for use in our example business case are:

- Personal broadband data service 256 Kbps/128 Kbps (best effort): $100–200 per month with 1GB data transfer; 512/256 K $250–300 per month
- Business broadband 512 K CIR-1.5 Mbps CIR ($500–$1500 per month, 50 GB data); 1:10 contention $100–$350 per month
- Video multicast subscription $20 per month
- Video on demand, $10 per movie download plus movie catalog cost
- Video surveillance connectivity ($50 per point per month with 64 Kbps streaming)
- VoIP ($0.3 per minute)
- Data transfer (as best-effort service): $5 per GB for mail, browsing, or file transfers

TABLE 20-4

Mobile WiMAX overlay network being used to provide mix of data and VoIP services

S.No.	Service	Contention and VoIP Traffic	Bit Rate per User (Kbps, Average)	Number of Users	Total Usage (Mbps)
		Services Dimensioning in Mobile WiMAX 10 MHz Channel (profile 3A TDD) per Sector			
1	VoIP	0.2 Erlangs (12 minutes per hour at 32 Kbps)	6.40	1000	6.4
2	Broadband data 256 Kbps	1:10	25.6	200	5.12
3	Broadband data 256 Kbps + VoIP	1:10 and 1 Erlang	57.60	275	15.84
4	Broadband data 512 Kbps	1:10	51.6	30	1.55
5	Broadband data 512 Kbps + VoIP	1:10 and 1 Erlang	83.60	40	3.34
6	Broadband data 2048 Kbps + VoIP	1:10 and 4 Erlang	332.80	4	1.33
7	Other traffic HTTP				1
8	**Total per sector**			**1549**	**34.6**
9	Total for 3 sector BS			4647	103.7

20.4.1 Business Case for a WiMAX Network with Broadband-Centric Model

It is interesting to consider the case of broadband-centric data model with customers having a mix of various speeds and also VoIP. Just to demonstrate the case of a WiMAX network, which is set up primarily to serve as overlay for broadband and data services and VoIP with a three-sector base station with 10 MHz channels, the following table presents a mixed-use scenario. The VoIP usage is assumed at 0.2 Erlangs for an individual voice-only customer. It rises to 4 Erlangs for a business customer with a 2048 Kbps connection. For simplicity, revenues from only broadband data connectivity and VoIP services are considered in this example.

It may be seen that even with a single 3-sector base station, about 4700 (including 1000 VoIP) customers can be serviced for a mix of desired services. The customers can upgrade services any time because of flexibility provided by WiMAX, unlike wireline systems.

For the mix of services considered, and making some assumptions on the VoIP pricing of $0.3 per minute (32 Kbps G.711 call), data pricing as given in the table, the revenue projections per base station per month with 3 sectors are given in Table 20-5.

TABLE 20-5

Estimation of revenues from broadband internet and VoIP services (an example)

	Service	Number of Users	Data Services Pricing per month	Data Revenues per Month	VoIP Revenues per Month
1	VoIP ($0.3 per minute)	1000			$12,960
2	Data 256 Kbps	200	$100	$20,000	$0
3	Data 256 Kbps + VoIP	275	$100	$27,500	$3,564
4	Data 512 Kbps	30	$250	$7,500	$0
5	Data 512 Kbps + VoIP	40	$250	$10,000	$1,037
6	Data 2048 Kbps + VoIP	4	$800	$3,200	$207
7	HTTP	ALL	$5	$7,745	
8	Total Service wise Revenues per Sector			$75,945	$17,768
9	Total Revenues per Sector per month		$93,713		
10	Total Revenues per Base Station (3 Sectors per month)		$281,139		
11	ARPU per Customer per Month		$60		

TABLE 20-6

Estimating base station operating costs (with reference to example case)

Base Station Costs (one time) US$		200,000
Costs per Month per Base Station (3 Sectors)		
Cost Element		Costs per Month US$
1	Internet connectivity two DS3 (2 × 4530,000 Mbps) per base station	
2	Spectrum	6,000
3	Network management, billing	50,000
4	VoIP settlements @ 40 percent of revenues	21,322
5	Customer support	30,000
6	Links to external networks (backhauls)	15,000
7	Total costs	152,322

On the base of 4700 users and a mixed VoIP and data use as indicated it gives an ARPU of $60 per customer per month. Excluding the VoIP-only users (i.e., considering only data customers) the ARPU is $140 per month, which is reasonable for such mixed business data and voice wireless use.

In order to assess the potential profitability and the return on investment, it is instructive to consider the costs of attaining these revenues. An estimate of the costs per base station* of three sectors is given in Table 20-6.

In the example given, the monthly revenues over costs yields a surplus of $129,000, applicable for one base station with three sectors. This is based on only broadband data and VoIP services. In practice, the sector capacity will be used for downloads and other services generating additional revenues. Hence, the revenues should be considered to be on a conservative side.

In computing the costs, the VoIP settlement costs (i.e., to be credited to the corresponding network operator where the calls terminate) have been taken as 40 percent of the pricing of $0.3 per minute (the termination costs on a cellular network may be higher but these will also be supported

---

* The costs given are indicative only. In practice, such costs will be different and a business plan will stand amended to accommodate the appropriate costs as well as service pricings.

by higher service pricings). The internet connectivity costs are assumed on the basis of 2 × DS3 links (45 Mbps × 2) terminating on the base station gateway from a tier-1 backbone.

The business case is oversimplified as it assumes, fully provisioned network in the first year itself. Typically the infrastructure cost, such as the base station ($140,000–250,000), VoIP, and Authentication servers ($75,000), would be recovered in less than a year with a fully provisioned network. It will also be possible to fund CPEs based on the cash flows.

20.5 BUSINESS CASE FOR A VIDEO MULTICAST SERVICE

A video multicast service can be successfully operated by reserving 6 Mbps of capacity per sector. It optionally can be supplemented with VoD services operating with 4–5 channels (at 4–6 Mbps per sector). Alternatively, the customers may be enabled to use services such as Google video for both upload and download.

A 6 Mbps multicast service can carry around eight channels using Windows Media compression or H.264 with associated EPG. The advantage of using common formats such as Windows Media or Real Video is the ready availability of players in the maximum number of receiver devices. Technologies such as DVB-IPI or MPEG4 video in MPEG4 streams are better suited for home installations where STBs are available.

In a unicast mode, a city covered with five base stations having three sectors each at 10 MHz bandwidth can support over 3000 active users and over 60,000 users with a contention of 1:20. For multicast services, where the terminals can even be in sleep mode to receive multicast video, over 100,000 users can be supported, the number being primarily limited owing to the authentication activity, mobility support, and MAP overheads.

Let us consider a business case scenario with video multicast services. Table 20-7 shows a typical scenario with only business users with 256–512 Kbps CIR service (business customers) and a video multicast service.

Based on a subscription revenue of $20 per month per subscriber and video content cost of 50 percent, i.e., net revenue of $ 10 per month per video subscriber, it is possible to generate net revenues of $20,000 per month per sector from video services alone based on subscription from 2000 users per sector amounting to over $60,000 per month per base station (three sectors). The total estimated revenues from the base station are $375,000 as shown in the table.

Providing video multicast services can thus provide a very robust business case as the number of subscribers can be scaled up sharply. The costs of operating such a sector are similar to the previous example.

TABLE 20-7

An example of a business model with a mix of video and data customers

	Service	Number of Users	Data Services Pricing per Month	Revenues per Month	Resources Used per Sector
1	Video Multicast Service	2000	$10	$20,000	6 Mbps
2	Data 256 Kbps CIR (1:4 UL:DL)	30	$500	$15,000	7.6 Mbps
3	Data 512 Kbps, CIR	20	$1000	$20,000	5 Mbps
7	HTTP	ALL	$5	$10,250	
9	Data Transfer above 1 GB @ $5 per GB	3000 GB	$5	$60,000	Best effort, lean time resources
8	Total per Sector			$125,250	18.6 Mbps
9	Total Revenues per Sector		$125,250		
10	Total Revenues per Base Station (3 Sectors)		$375,750		

20.5.1 Planning Receiver Devices

Planning of receiver devices is an essential activity in a WiMAX-based services planning and the operator needs to have a clear vision of which devices will be used for reception of the WiMAX transmissions and for video services. These activities fall in different domains.

A variety of client devices ranging from USB data cards and Dongles, Smartphones with WiMAX (or WiBro) reception capability are now available. However, it will be necessary for the potential WiMAX operator to select an appropriate subset of such devices which need to be validated against the frequency band and the WiMAX parameters in use. With increasing number of devices available with WiMAX certification, the task is made easier than before, when proprietary implementations (with claims of higher performance) were the norm. Standalone devices such as MP3 players or MP4 players and smartphones which are mass produced provide the best bet for higher penetration of video-based services. Data services, on the other hand have lower hurdles as the available client devices integrate with the PC operating systems.

A range of video players are available preinstalled on smartphones or can be downloaded and installed. It may be a good idea to offer a tailored download service with service parameters preset to make it easier for the customers to install the appropriate players and begin to use the services. It is also possible to provide special software needed for the service on MicroSD cards which can be used to download music in addition to having the right software to enable various services.

20.6 OTHER BUSINESS OPPORTUNITIES

WiMAX has applications in many other areas, each of which can be a standalone business by itself. This includes applications such as rural connectivity and VoIP, providing rural broadband over large areas, providing dedicated networks for special applications such as security, data gathering networks, bank networks, and many others. Owing to the large and reliable coverage it replaces many applications which were earlier provided using satellites.

However, the biggest opportunity in the near term is to use these either for enriching legacy applications for high-quality triple-play services or to provide multicast video and "on-demand" services (VoD) for mobile devices. In the medium to long term, a new ecosystem with open architecture mobile devices paralleling the cellular mobile networks, but without the legacy architectures and proprietary elements, is on the horizon. New players not currently owning telecom networks are expected to take this initiative.

21

CASE STUDIES OF WiMAX NETWORKS

You cannot create experience. You must undergo it.

—Albert Camus

WiMAX networks have found tremendous support from operators and equipment manufacturers as well as governments and regulators. Over 300 trials have taken place with many commercial deployments profitably providing advanced services and wireless applications.

In this chapter, we take a look at the implementations of some of the WiMAX networks, both Fixed (IEEE 802.16-2004) as well as Mobile WiMAX (IEEE 802.16e). The case studies which are presented in this chapter have been selected based on specific features of the networks.

The case study of WiBro, Korea, is also included as it was the first network based on IEEE 802.16e mobile technology and has the most innovative services to offer, making it a representative case for other planners. The network is based on IMS, one of the convergence platforms for service provisioning in a mixed access environment. Eratech® in Argentina was one of the first networks based on Fixed WiMAX (IEEE 802.16-2004) technology in Latin America and helped create a new environment for business users in major cities where the services were implemented. The network architecture was based on the use of data links and VoIP services. Services in many other countries in Asia, the Middle East, and Africa have been based on similar models. This implementation also is a representative case for the business plans developed in the previous chapter for data centric networks. The case study of the WiMAX initiative in Taiwan has been included owing to it being a unique case of the mobile WiMAX and broadband services being developed as an entire ecosystem for the country, i.e., applications, technologies, devices, and networks. The case of KDDI Mobile WiMAX has been included because of the advanced implementation of Mobile WiMAX and 3G networks integration and the successful example it represents for adoption by other networks operating in a similar multi-services multi-technology environment.

A brief description of the Clearwire® network in the United States is also provided. Even though Clearwire commenced operations with a wireless technology that is not strictly WiMAX, it was based on OFDM and was the most advanced wireless network when introduced at that time. Clearwire is also a major holder of BWS spectrum for mobile WiMAX in the United States and has started its migration to Mobile WiMAX services. A brief mention is also made of the Sprint Nextel mobile WiMAX network, XOHM, even though all the details of the network had not been finalized at the time of writing. This is because of its sheer scale and its potential impact on worldwide markets of Mobile WiMAX once fully deployed.

21.1 WIBRO-KOREA

WiBro stands for Wireless broadband and is the name for broadband services in Korea which are offered as per IEEE 802.16e mobile WiMAX technical standards. The services, which were commercially launched in April 2006 by Korea Telecom, followed by SK Telecom, are now available in the entire Seoul area.

21.1.1 Technical Specifications of WiBro

WiBro services were announced to be licensed in October 2004 to three operators in the 2.3 GHz band by offering each operator 27 MHz of spectrum as follows:

Operator 1: 2300–2327 MHz
Operator 2: 2331.5–2358.5 MHz
Operator 3: 2363–2390 MHz

WiBro uses a bandwidth of 8.75 MHz per carrier and the above allocations permit three channels of 8.75 MHz each in the individual spectrum slots. The operators selected for the service were SK Telecom and Korea Telecom (KT). KT started commercial WiBro services in April 2006 to be followed by SK Telecom.

The key technical parameters which were laid down for the service are given in Table 21-1.

WiBro was a TTA standard and forms a separate profile in the WiMAX forum portfolio of initial certification profiles for Mobile WiMAX.

The MAC layer specifications of WiBro are given in Table 21-2.

TABLE 21-1

Technical parameters of WiBro service

Technical Parameter	Specifications
Technology	OFDMA TDD
Minimum data transfer rate	Uplink (mobile to base station): 128 Kbps
	Downlink (base station to mobile): 512 Kbps
Channel bandwidth	8.75 MHz
Modulation	QPSK, 16 QAM and 64 QAM (downlink only)
Channel coding	Convolutional turbo code (CTC) and convolutional coding (CC)
Frame length	5 msec
Maximum data rate	Downlink 19.97 Mbps, uplink: 5.53 Mbps
Base station synchronization mode	GPS
Inter-vendor roaming	Using TDD frames and transmit/receive synchronization among operators
Mobility	Up to 120 Kmph (vehicular speeds)
Expected coverage in urban areas	~1 km in NLOS environment

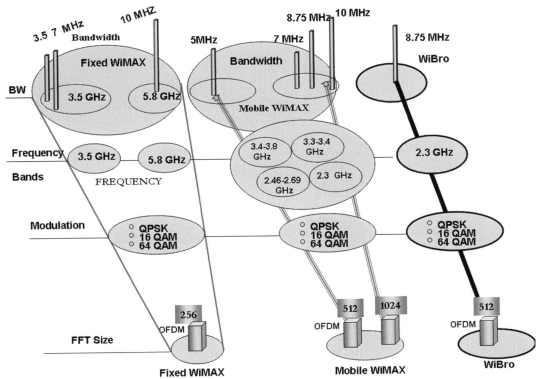

FIGURE 21-1 WiMAX certification profiles and positioning of WiBro

TABLE 21-2

MAC features in WiBro

Bandwidth Allocation	Frame by Frame
Handover	Fast base station switching Make before break Break before make
QoS offerings	Unsolicited grant service (UGS) Real-time polling service (rtPS) Non-real-time polling service (nrtPS) Extended real-time polling service (ertPS) Best effort service (BE)
MAC protocol data units (PDUs)	Variable size MAC PDU Fragmentation Packing Concatenation
MAC layer error correction	ARQ
Modes of operation	Idle mode, Sleep mode, Awake mode
MAC connections	Connection oriented
Other features	Quick connect setup

21.1.2 Network Architecture of WiBro

At the network layer in the WiBRO implementation, IPv6 and IPv4 are supported. It also uses Mobile IP (MIP) for level 2 handovers. In order to map the QoS parameters at the MAC level to the network level, it uses packet classification and mapping to MAC transport connection and Diffserv at the network level.

By using IPv6 (RFC 3775) at the core network level, the WiBro has been one of the first commercial networks to use IPv6. IPv6 has the advantage of unlimited IP addresses and therefore global addressability. It also provides security and mobility support. Seamless handoffs are achieved by the use of Fast Mobile IPv6 (FMIP, RFC 4068).

The WiBro network is comprised of an IMS core network which is fully IP-based. Interface to the PSTN are provided via the IMS-based SIP gateway. The Mobile WiMAX network is divided into a number of subnets comprised of a number of base stations (called Radio Access Stations, RAS) connected by an access control router (ACR) which, in turn, connects to the IMS core network. Authentication and security are provided by EAP/PKI and Radius/Diameter.

Interface to the PSTN are via the IMS system which converts from SIP-based protocols to the PSTN protocols.

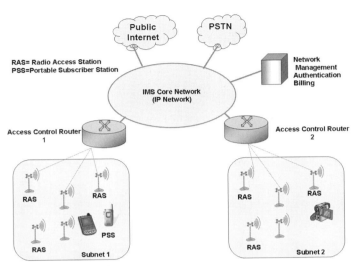

FIGURE 21-2 WiBro network architecture

The networks use Samsung radio access stations (RAS), which have the capabilities of smart antenna systems and MIMO RF transmission. The access control routers can control from 50–250 radio access stations.

21.1.3 Portable Subscriber Stations and Client Devices

A number of stationary and portable devices have been available for use on the network in Korea. Laptops or other computing devices can be connected by the use of the Samsung PCMCIA card. Some of the devices which have been available for use on the network include:

- Samsung SPH M8000 phone (PDA)
- Samsung SPH1000 WiBro smartphone
- Korea Telecom KT iPlug for use on USB ports for WiBro
- Samsung Q35 WiBro-equipped laptop
- Samsung USB Dongle SPH-H1200
- Samsung smartphone SPH M8100
- Samsung multimedia convergence device SPH-P9000
- KT WiBro smart card reader

New devices are continuously being introduced as the network grows in usage. An example is the Flyvo's mobile WiMAX game-playing handheld. This device has a 4-inch LCD screen (WVGA 800 × 480) and uses an Intel Xscale processor. New innovative devices, which can effectively

FIGURE 21-3   User devices on WiBro network

use the capabilities of the new broadband wireless MANs, are expected
to continue to evolve.

Most of the devices are also EV-DO compatible (i.e., dual-use EV-
DO and WiBro) as the WiBro services are not nationwide yet.

21.1.4 Services Available on the WiBro Network

Through the use of the mobile broadband wireless access a number of
services are available over the WiBro networks. These include broadcast services such as video streaming and video on demand, interactive gaming, messaging (MMS), communications (video and normal
calls), and location-based services. The video services include push to
talk (PTT), which is a one-to-one video call, and video conferencing
(1:N video calling).

One of the platforms used for providing a dynamic communications
convergence and user interface for users for WiBro service is the
IntroPAD™ from Intromobile. It is based on the use of mobile convergence framework (MCF) middleware. With the IntroPAD client installed
on the mobile phone, the users get a convergence user screen with areas
for video calling, messages, and video streaming services.

In terms of service descriptions and pricing, the following (Table 21-3)
is the status.

TABLE 21-3

WiBro services and pricing

Menu Option	Services
Communicator	SMS, MMS, e-mail, text chat
Hot Clip	Video streaming, news, sports
mLOG	Motion picture uploading
Multiboard	Multimedia conference
Internet	Internet surfing

	Service Charges		
Service Type	Service Charge, US$ per month	Data Mbytes	Extra data per MB
Saver	$6.50	500	$0.03
Basic	$8.15	800	$0.01
Special	$9.80	1500	$0.01
Free	$17.40	unlimited	0

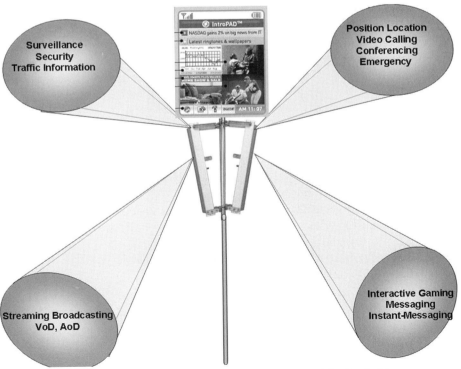

FIGURE 21-4   WiBro Services in Seoul (picture courtesy Intromobile Co. Ltd.)

In comparison, cellular data rates for unlimited use average between $40–$60 in various deployments in Europe and the United States.

21.2 KDDI

KDDI is a fixed, wireless and mobile services provider in Japan. It has existing DSL and FTTH networks and operates mobile networks based on the IMT-2000 3G CDMA technologies (CDMA2000, EV-DO Rev A and B). KDDI had commenced trials on the Mobile WiMAX technology in OSAKA since 2005 which have now moved into the second phase of technology tests involving integration with 3G mobile networks and 3G advanced implementations. The reason for selecting KDDI as an example of WiMAX network implementation has been its innovative use of the IMS/MMD architecture in integrating Mobile WiMAX with existing wireline (ADSL and FTTH) and mobile (3G-CDMA) services. The fixed mobile convergence architecture based on IMS is the same as elaborated in Chapter 13.

Figure 21-5 shows the set-up of KDDI for Fixed-WiMAX Cellular integration using the multimedia domain (MMD).

As Figure 21-5 demonstrates, the MMD/IMS forms the apex session control and management layer in the network architecture comprised of

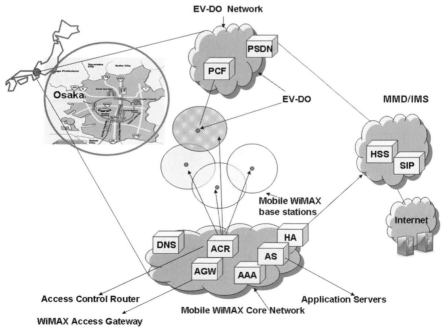

FIGURE 21-5 KDDI Mobile WiMAX trial with MMD/IMS used for Fixed-Mobile WiMAX convergence

mobile WiMAX, CDMA2000 (EV-DO), wireline (ADSL), and IP-based networks. The IMS functionality provided by the architecture including the SIP server and the HSS enable full roaming and interworking between the Mobile WiMAX network with its own session initiation and authentication mechanisms (AAA) and the CDMA networks. Interworking with PSTN for voice calls is also provided by the network.

KDDI network is designed to use all the existing technologies with their respective services. At the same time it heralds a transition to open IP-based networks and services which are available via the internet or over the WiMAX networks.

The trial was conducted in two phases. In Phase I of the trial which was completed in 2006, the following objectives were achieved:

- Handovers between mobile WiMAX base stations
- Seamless handover between mobile WiMAX and EV-DO or CDMA networks using the MMD
- Demonstration of multiple applications on all the networks including multichannel streaming, VoIP, media switching, etc.
- Video phone service with simultaneous transfer of video and voice across WiMAX and CDMA networks

Above all, the Phase I trial helped to demonstrate roaming between diverse networks, i.e., mobile WiMAX and EV-DO. The trial is indeed very helpful for future operators who are planning the co-existence of the new WiMAX networks with the existing mobile or landline networks. In effect, the IMS or MMD architecture provides a multiple access network where WiMAX is one of the access technologies.

Phase II of the trial has been focused on demonstrating more advanced features of mobile WiMAX with beamforming and MIMO. The Phase II trial has been conducted with a 20 MHZ channel bandwidth, which also focuses on the high data rates and spectral efficiency, which can be achieved by the use of MIMO and beamforming in a field environment.

The MMD (or IMS) functionality created an abstraction between the application services (VoIP, Chat, IPTV Phone, online gaming, etc.) and the network layer to which different access networks, including WiMAX, CDMA, and EV-DO were connected. The MMD provided SIP-based signaling and media conversion for different networks to operate seamlessly. In addition to this, KDDI had also tested advanced 3G networks as adjuncts to the multiple networks in the trial.

Services in KDDI Mobile WiMAX Trial

The KDDI approach is also unique as it does not tend to merely extend the existing applications over the WiMAX network. Instead, new

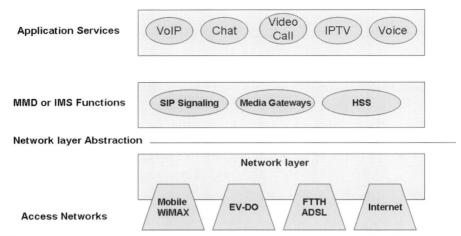

FIGURE 21-6   Abstraction between applications and access networks in KDDI trial

applications have been designed taking into account the QoS functionality and low latency in WiMAX. The new services include downloading or streaming of full-resolution video and audio (GPS time stamp synchronized) to existing and new devices in real time. The new applications also include gaming, videoconferencing, multicasting, and broadcasting. In addition, ancillary applications such as video surveillance, fleet management, educational services, and networked storage have also been successfully demonstrated during the trials.

A single multimode handset can receive multiple services from different networks. Thus a streaming service can operate over the WiMAX while a voice call can be on a mobile network. This removes the segregation of devices on different networks, i.e., the need to be logged in one of the available networks at one time.

As per the regulatory provisions for allocation of bandwidth in the 2.5 GHz band in Japan, the government is considering only those operators who are not providing mobile services at present. This will require KDDI to partner with an eligible operator in order to continue its rollout of Mobile WiMAX networks.

21.3 M-TAIWAN PROJECT

The M-Taiwan project is a major initiative in Taiwan by the government in association with the industry, operators, and product vendors to take the major cities in Taiwan to a new level of mobile wireless connectivity. As this is one of the major countrywide and directed efforts for broadband wireless connectivity, we will take a look at the features of the initiative.

The objectives of the M-Taiwan project, broadly are:

- To provide Mobile WiMAX infrastructure in selected cities and special zones (the M-City initiative).
- To create a complete ecosystem for mobile WiMAX, i.e., applications, networks, CPEs, and chipsets to encourage quick adoption.
- To encourage the services sector (including the government and the public sector units) to provide their services online via broadband wireless networks (called the M-Service initiative).
- To encourage development of applications such as IPTV over WiMAX, video calling, and interactive applications.
- To contribute in the standards development process for mobile WiMAX and broadband technologies.
- To provide special services such as education, surveillance, etc on the broadband wireless networks (the M-learning initiative).

The M-Taiwan project has government budgetary support as well as tax incentives and grants for those involved in providing infrastructure or services on the network.

It is claimed that Taiwan supplies over 80 percent of the WiFi CPE products globally. The M-Taiwan program, a complete ecosystem from chipsets, networks, certification labs, testbeds to customer-end equipment, and applications also has the objective to position the country in the same prominent position in the WiMAX technologies.

It is no surprise, therefore, that some of the major developments in CPEs and chipsets are now coming from Taiwan-based companies such as Gemtek, Zyxel, Tatung, D-Link, Tecom, dmedia, Zcom, and Accton. Some of these products have been covered earlier in the book in the chapters on CPEs and chipsets.

The developments in the M-Taiwan program are therefore important not only for Taiwan itself, but also the entire global community for WiMAX and wireless technologies, network architectures, and applications.

21.3.1 WiMAX Spectrum for the M-Taiwan program

Spectrum for the M-Taiwan program has been issued in 30-MHz blocks in the 2.5 to 2.69 GHz band to three operators each in the southern and northern parts of the country as a part of Phase I of the program. The second phase will involve release of spectrum to three additional operators each in 2009, and possibly merging into nationwide licenses.

The licenses awarded are:

- Northern Taiwan: First International Telecom (FITEL), Tecom-VIBO, and Global On Corp.

- Southern Taiwan: Far EasTone Telecommunications, Vastar Cable, and Tatung

Of the licensed operators, Far EasTone (FET) is the only mobile operator, and FILTEL is a personal handy phone system (PHS) operator. Almost all the operators have aggressively started rolling out the networks in technology partnership with WiMAX equipment vendors such as Motorola, Nortel, Alcatel-lucent, etc. The WiMAX rollout by FILTEL will include integration with its PHS network.

21.3.2 Applications in the M-Taiwan Program

The distinguishing feature of the M-Taiwan program must be stated to be its focus on delivering relevant and ready-to-use applications rather than technologies or networks. It is this effort which has brought together a number of industry participants to take part in specific initiatives.

An M-Taiwan application lab has also been set up at Hcinshu and is managed by the Industrial Technology Research Institute (ITRI). The application lab will serve as the proof of concept lab for the applications. The initial technology for the application lab is being supplied by Alvarion.

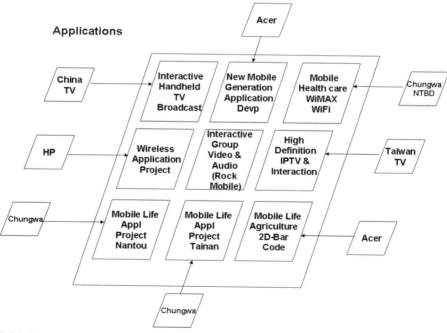

FIGURE 21-7 Applications in the M-Taiwan project

21.3.3 Infrastructure for the M-Taiwan Project

The infrastructure for the M-Taiwan project is based on a multilevel build-out and integration of wireline (DSL, FTTH, Cable), wireless (WiFi and WiMAX), and cellular mobile (GSM, GPRS, 3G, and PHS) systems (Figure 21-8).

The infrastructure initiative has been based on supporting applications which can be used in any environment, i.e., at home, in the office, or while on the move. The infrastructure build-out is aimed at supporting a complete integration of all the technologies of wireline, wireless, and mobile to provide a countrywide uniform access.

In order to have the build-out of networks and applications, over 60 individual sub-projects were assigned to individual companies or operators. Some of the infrastructure initiatives are shown in Figure 21-9.

While infrastructure for the M-Taiwan project is based on multiple technologies, WiMAX technologies play a special role in these initiatives.

FITEL

First international telecom, FITEL, a spectrum licensee for northern Taiwan, is commencing the WiMAX layout with rollout in two cities beginning, 2008. FITEL's initial rollouts will be in Taipei City with 430 base stations and Hsinchu county with 380 base stations. As a part of

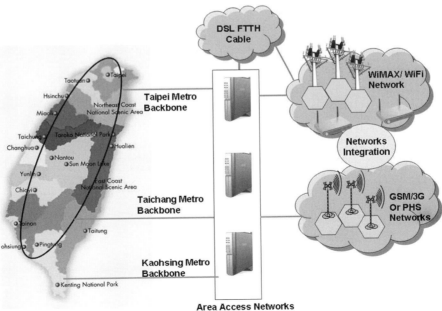

FIGURE 21-8 WiMAX infrastructure initiative spans wireline, cellular mobile, PHS, and Wireless (WiFi and WiMAX) build-outs

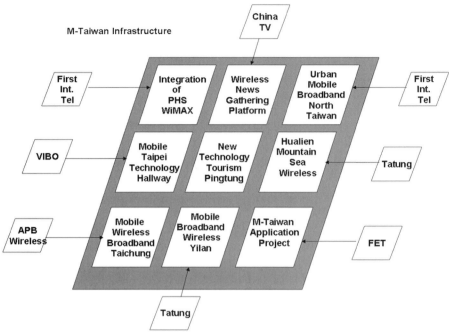

FIGURE 21-9 Infrastructure initiatives in the M-Taiwan project

its role in the M-Taiwan project it plans to cover over 80 percent of the population in northern Taiwan. As FITEL is also one of the mobile operators with a PHS service, it is also taking up a program of launching of dual mode handsets and integration of the networks.

Far EasTone (FET)

Far EasTone (FET) Taiwan, is launching mobile WiMAX (IEEE 802.16e) networks as a part of its role in the M-Taiwan project. FET also has the responsibility for remote health care services and intelligent transport over WiMAX systems. In order to meet its objectives, it has selected WiMAX as the core technology. It is building out networks in Taipei County (in Banciao and Jhonghe). Streaming video, music, IPTV, video conferencing, and corporate applications form the primary objective of the IEEE 802.16e compliant network. FET has been a pioneer in providing high-speed data services in Taiwan and is one of the key partners in the M-Taiwan initiative.

Tatung

Tatung, a provider of 3G services in Taiwan, has a major role in the M-Taiwan project. This includes the provision of advanced mobile services such as multimedia blogging and group services, mobile positioning

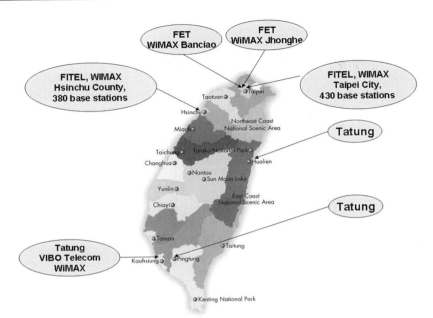

FIGURE 21-10   Some of the initial WiMAX networks announced in Taiwan

systems and e-maps, VoIP, and mobile web portals. It is also building WiMAX infrastructure in order to support these applications. Its key installations include those in Kaohsiung in southern Taiwan. Tatung is also cooperating with VIBO telecom for WiMAX services in northern Taiwan.

21.3.4 User Devices in the M-Taiwan Program

The M-Taiwan program also aims at creating a new generation of user devices which are designed to take advantage of the new broadband connectivity environment created by the ubiquitous use of WiMAX networks.

MTube™ UMPC

One of the devices which has been developed for mobile WiMAX is the MTube ultra mobile PC. The device has been designed based on a 1 GHz processor from Via Technologies Inc., Taiwan. The WiMAX modules of the UMPC are supplied by Accton Wireless broadband Corp, Taiwan. The WiMAX chipset in the device is from GCT Semiconductor in South Korea. It has 8 GB of RAM and a Linux OS. MTube is a broadband internet device. It can operate on mobile WiMAX and WiFi networks. It is also equipped with a camera and TV reception capability. The device is designed to support various multimedia formats and be able to surf thousands of websites.

21.4 CLEARWIRE®

Clearwire® is an important wireless internet services provider in the United States. Founded by Craig McCaw in 2003, Clearwire had initially started providing services using a mix of technologies which were proprietary in nature. These were based on fixed wireless architecture technology from Motorola and NextNet, which was a Clearwire subsidiary. Its wireless services were available in 38 markets (including 400 municipalities) by mid-2007 with a coverage of over 9 million population. Clearwire services are provided using licensed spectrum in the 2.5 GHz band. It is upgrading its networks to mobile WiMAX technology and trials have already been conducted (e.g., in Portland, Oregon) for this purpose. Clearwire services are also available in Belgium and Ireland.

The case study of Clearwire is important for many reasons. First, it is a holder of a major chunk of spectrum in the 2.5 to 2.69 GHz band, which is the band selected for Mobile WiMAX Release 1 certification profiles. Clearwire has also acquired spectrum which AT&T was required to divest as a result of BellSouth merger. It also holds spectrum (or spectrum rights) in many European countries such as Belgium, Germany, Ireland, Poland, Romania, and Spain for WiMAX and Mobile WiMAX services and has a very clear road map for expansion in international territories. Thirdly, it has a partnership with America Online (AOL) to deliver wireless services in all markets being served by AOL. It is also in partnership with Echostar and DirecTV to provide wireless internet to their customers. Clearwire has strong backing from Intel as one of the venture capital funding partners. Finally it is also has its CPEs and other products certified by the WiMAX forum as well as the FCC. These are all components necessary for creating a rich ecosystem for launch of WiMAX services.

Clearwire Pre-WiMAX Technology

Clearwire's broadband wireless service (prior to launch of mobile WiMAX) is based on equipment from NextNet® Wireless. It provides the broadband non-line of sight (NLOS) MMDS system as well as modems for NLOS reception. The NextNet "Expedience" platform, for example, is designed to operate with adaptive modulation and is well suited for broadband internet applications. Subsequently, in view of the mobile WiMAX plans, Clearwire has divested its stake in NextNet to Motorola.

The NextNet technology coupled with use of licensed band had placed the services apart in terms of quality and speed of access among the wireless ISPs (WISPs). A 2 Mbps business plan with 2 Mbps download and 512 upload speeds was offered for approximately $55 per month.

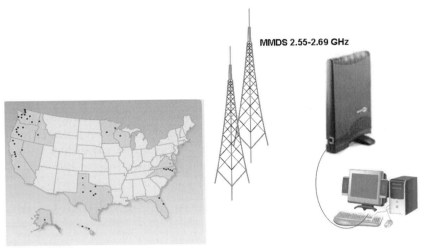

FIGURE 21-11 Clearwire broadband wireless service (pre-WiMAX)

Clearwire had about 350,000 broadband wireless subscribers by the third quarter of 2007.

Clearwire WiMAX Initiatives

With the ownership of 2.5–2.69 GHz mobile spectrum and backing from Intel, Clearwire has launched a strong drive toward an 802.16e mobile WiMAX network. Clearwire is estimated to hold spectrum with coverage of 223 million of population in the United States (14 billion MHz-POPs, i.e., population covered multiplied by spectrum in MHz). This gives Clearwire the largest opportunity in rolling out the Mobile WiMAX networks as far as the U.S. markets are concerned.

In May 2007, it had announced the completion of a trial of the Mobile WiMAX network in Portland in cooperation with Intel and Motorola. The trial validated the WiMAX parameters, base station equipment, and CPEs such as PC cards. These have subsequently also received approval from the FCC. Subsequently, Clearwire has started launching Mobile WiMAX services in a phased manner.

Its service in the Seattle area featured a ClearValue plan of $30 per month with download/upload speeds of 768/256 Kbps and a ClearPremium plan for $37 per month (1.5 Mbps/256 Kbps). The modem rentals were $5 per month.

Clearwire also has spectrum holdings in a number of other countries including those in Europe including Ireland, Belgium, and Germany. In Germany, the company holds a nationwide license along with DBD and Inquam Broadband.

The Clearwire WiMAX network is expected to get a new boost with the launch of Intel's WiMAX-embedded chipsets and product lines.

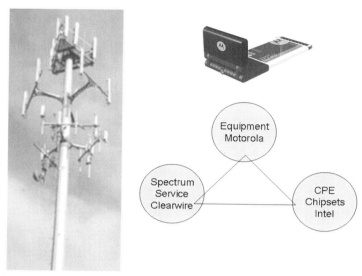

FIGURE 21-12   Clearwire commences commercial mobile WiMAX services

21.5 ERTECH® ARGENTINA

Ertech® Argentia was one of the first WiMAX networks in Latin America and paved the way for many similar implementations which were to follow in the region. The impetus for the network came from the government of Argentina which facilitated its use in government offices, public utilities, schools, and educational establishments. The government also granted it the use of 50 MHz of spectrum in the 3.4–3.8 GHz band for the purpose of providing broadband wireless access services. The spectrum was provided as 2×25 MHz for FDD use. The first node in the network was implemented in October 2004 in San Miguel. In the first year of its launch the network had covered over 30 cities in the country representing the manner in which WiMAX overlay can enable virtually an entire country for broadband wireless connectivity. The network enabled data links with high reliability to its customers comprised of businesses, government offices, and public agencies at speeds from 256 Kbps to 4 Mbps. VPN-MPLS services thus formed the major offering by the company. VoIP was made available only to VPN-MPLS customers owing to the affordability of the CPEs. In addition, Ertech also provided WiFi services.

Network Usage and Services

The network was based on Alvarion's BreezeMAX™ 3500 technology. Subsequently, in 2007, parts of the network were being upgraded to mobile WiMAX (IEEE 802.16e) based on Alvarion's 4Motion 802.16e

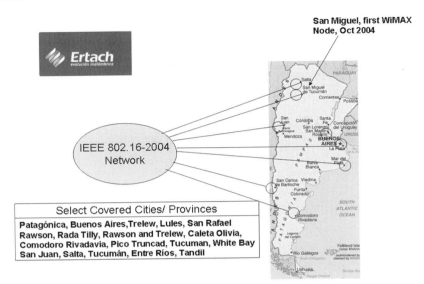

FIGURE 21-13 Ertech®, Argentina, Fixed WiMAX network (IEEE 802.16-2004)

Mobile WiMAX technology. By October 2007, Eratech (now acquired by Telmex) had 220 base stations in 17 of the 24 provinces of the country. The network has remained dedicated for data services with about 90 percent usage being by corporate and public service entities. This amounted to usage by over 6000 companies and nearly 5000 data or VPN-MPLS links in service. Nearly 100 governmental entities were part of the network including the provincial governments. One of the provincial networks involved is that of the provincial communication data network in Buenos Aires. This network is designed to serve hospitals, municipal councils, revenue offices, highway administrations, etc.

Over 13,000 Alvarion CPEs were in service on the WiMAX links by 2007. The balance usage is by SOHO customers. Table 21-4 provides details of the service plans.

Technology and Network

The primary usage of the network is for providing dedicated links as VPN links or as LAN interconnect services using VPN-MPLS (these links provide committed information rate and CIR services). This permits the customers to use the network transparently across the network connecting multiple sites. It also enables remote access to corporate networks by individual users or business associates. The connectivity is available at various rates as given in the table. WiMAX network ensures QoS to be maintained for the links.

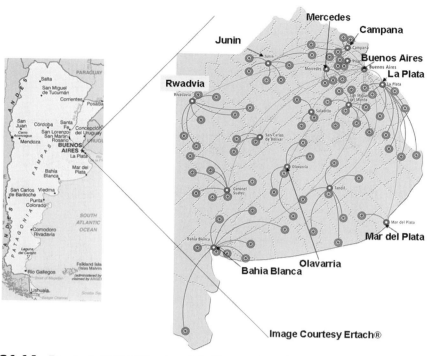

FIGURE 21-14   Provincial WiMAX network in Buenos Aires by Ertech®

TABLE 21-4

Ertech® Fixed WiMAX services and tariffs

S.No.	Service Plan	Monthly Tariff US$
1	WiMAX dedicated connection, 512 Kbps	197
2	WiMAX dedicated connection, 1 Mbps	349
3	WiMAX dedicated connection, 1.5 Mbps	507
4	WiMAX dedicated connection, 2 Mbps	650
5	WiMAX dedicated connection, 4 Mbps	1,284
6	Variable 64 Kbps	78
7	Variable 128 Kbps	82
8	Variable 256/1024 Kbps	87
9	Variable 256/2048 Kbps	106
10	Variable 256/4096 Kbps	171

VoIP services are not offered for residential customers owing to the high cost of the CPEs (around $400). It is expected that the new mobile WiMAX networks will allow a mix of services for residential and business customers including from mobile devices.

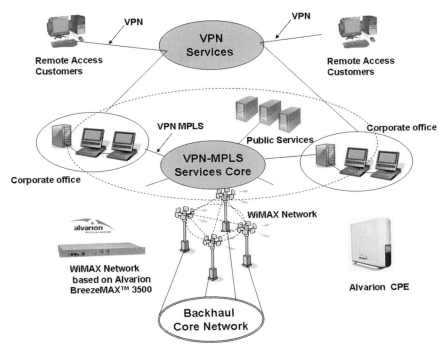

FIGURE 21-15 Ertech WiMAX network for WiMAX connectivity in Argentina

Backhaul Network for WiMAX

Ertech has also recently gone in for a dedicated wireless backhaul network (MAXhaul™) from Stratex® networks. This network is comprised of microwave links in the 7, 15, and 23 GHz bands. These links connect the WiMAX base stations within a city as well as across different regions. This will help overcome some of the backhaul bottlenecks faced by using networks from various carriers for the purpose of backhaul.

The Stratex® solution is tailored for WiMAX base station connectivity by providing an Ethernet interface at 100 Mbps (upgradable to 300 Mbps) for the base stations. The backhaul core network can scale up to multi Giga-bits capacity (GigE links). The backhaul core network support is based on a mesh and ring self-healing architecture called the "Resilient Wireless Packet Rings" (RWPR™). This is based on an advanced layer 2 link aggregation (802.3ad) and fast-switching link algorithms from Stratex Networks. Using RWTR, the switching times for failed link switchovers can be reduced to as low as 5 ms. The ring structure in the backhaul network is maintained by the rapid scanning tree protocol (RSTP). The RWPR network can also be used for link aggregation, i.e., aggregation of two links into one link carrying the data for the two links as one virtual single stream. The entire backhaul network is separately managed by a network management system.

21.6 SPRINT NEXTEL WiMAX NETWORK-XOHM™

Quite in contrast to the data-centric network from Ertach® in Argentina is the network being launched for mass broadband wireless services by Sprint Nextel, United States, in 2008. The network XOHM is being designed to target enterprises as well as home and mobile users. The largest single initiative of this type, the network when fully rolled out will cover over 100 million of population residing in its coverage areas. The network is designed to provide a new broadband experience with its high-speed connectivity and architecture. It is being targeted to provide services such as high-speed internet browsing, multimedia services including vide, TV, and on-demand services, and location-based services, etc.

The Sprint Nextel WiMAX network is based on the strength of Sprint Nextel derived from its large network of communication towers, its spectrum holdings in the 2.5 GHz band, and its global Tier-1 internet backbone. Even though Sprint Nextel is present in the mobile services through its offerings of CDMA services (CDMA, EV-DO Rev A), its initiative in using the WiMAX technology for broadband demonstrates its commitment to open standards-based high-speed wireless networks and evolution of new applications and user devices. Sprint Nextel is also expected to create the largest convergence platform between the 3G CDMA and the Mobile WiMAX networks which is expected to lead to a number of multi-network and multimode devices entering the market. The key technology partners (among others) for XOHM are Intel for the chipsets, Motorola and Samsung for infrastructure, and Alcatel Lucent and Sony Ericsson for implementation.

Historical Background of Sprint Nextel

It is interesting to note a bit about the historical background of Sprint Nextel. Prior to the merger between Nextel and Sprint, Nextel was an operator of primarily radio trunking services iDEN from Motorola, with spectrum in the 800 MHz, 2.5 GHz, and 1900 MHz bands. It had been attempting to provide wireless data services using the 2.5 GHz spectrum for which trials had been conducted with the Flash OFDM technology using 1.25 MHz carriers. The merger enabled Sprint Nextel to use a part of the spectrum used for IDEN services to also offer EV-DO services, thus providing an upgrade path for data customers. More importantly it enabled the combine to consolidate spectrum slices held in the 2.5 GHz band to have potential access to large markets across the United States (estimated ~80%). This spectrum is the prime band for Mobile WiMAX and this puts the company in a unique position to provide these services. The only other major holder for 2.5 GHz in the United States is Clearwire, which is rolling out its networks on its own.

At the time of the merger in 2004, the FCC allowed the companies to retain the 2.5 GHz spectrum, now termed as BWS (broadband wireless services) spectrum, but also imposed conditions that the merger will use the spectrum to provide wireless broadband services with fixed rollout targets by the end of the current decade, i.e., 2010. The merger had also committed to bring a third "triple-play" broadband pipe to consumers in addition to DSL and cable services available at the time. The FCC mandate had sprung from a desire to create competition to cable as well as wireline services using VoIP in addition to provision of TV. The triple-play includes TV, voice, and internet, and it is this network that is now seeing a realization in XOHM services.

Subsequently Sprint Nextel has also dropped out of the Spectrum Co. (a consortium, which had bid for AWS spectrum), which showed its plans were entirely focused on the 2.5 GHz spectrum. At one stage, Sprint-Nextel had announced joint rollout of the 2.5 GHz network together with Clearwire. However, the company is now proceeding alone on the initiative together with its technology partners. There may be roaming arrangements between the two companies, however. The FCC auctions in the 700 MHz band which release additional spectrum will also determine future plans of some of the operators such as Sprint Nextel.

Another part of the complete picture was being drawn out at Google, where the world's largest internet site had been facing considerable difficulties in taking the "web" mobile because of the coordination issues with mobile operators. Google had been also working toward an open architecture for its web applications going mobile and the Sprint Nextel mobile WiMAX plans were seen by Google as an exact fit for its requirements. The new XOHM network therefore becomes exciting as it presents the best combination of infrastructure and user applications. This will also set a trend for Mobile WiMAX networks worldwide in regard to the types of services they provide in the near future. Google, in fact, is also bidding for the 700 MHz spectrum auctions, which signifies the importance it attaches to wireless delivery of services. The "big-bang" introduction of Mobile WiMAX is also likely to lead to a fall in the CPE process of Mobile WiMAX and the emergence of new devices, an eagerly awaited growth of these networks in a number of countries.

Infrastructure

A strength of Sprint Nextel is the availability of large infrastructure in terms of number of towers and cell sites because of its PCS network in the United States, which has one of the largest coverage areas of the country. However, this does not eliminate considerable investments in WiMAX base station equipment, CPEs, and the backhaul network, which needs to be extensive in order to aggregate the high bit rates which are provided to hundreds of thousands of customers. In the words of Mr. Barry West, President, XOHM and CEO of Sprint Nextel, *"We're not building one network, we're building two. WiMAX requires a much faster backhaul than traditionally used T1 lines to truly deliver on its capability."*

One of the providers of backhaul network for XOHM is FiberTower®. The company holds "near nationwide" assets in the 24 and 39 GHz bands and provides backhaul solutions based on a mix of Fiber (SONET Rings) and wireless links. It is at present a provider of backhauls to 75 percent of the major wireless carriers. It also has arrangements with the major tower providers in the United States. Spectrum leasing to build

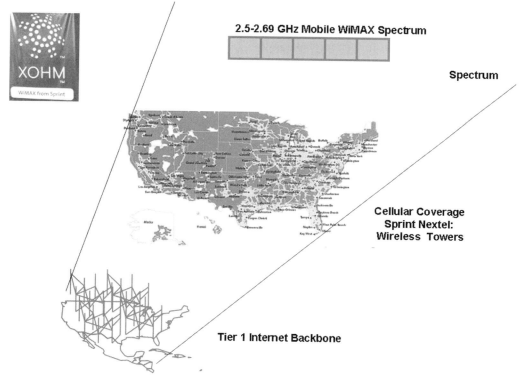

FIGURE 21-16   Enabling factors for WiMAX rollout: Tier 1 backbone, wireless towers, spectrum (images courtesy Sprint Nextel)

its own networks is another option offered by the company for engineering backhaul networks. The FiberTower network also provides for complete network management and a view of the entire network. For Sprint Nextel, it is providing backhaul from the cell sites to the switches. Other backhaul providers are Alcatel Lucent and Ericsson.

Sprint Nextel already has a Tier 1 internet backbone, and its links form a part of the internet backbones infrastructure in the U.S. It is also a major long distance carrier. These factors will help it to integrate the WiMAX and backhaul networks into its existing network architectures.

As is usual in the case of typical Mobile WiMAX base stations, mobile devices and indoor coverage will be possible in zones near to base stations, i.e., up to 2–3 Km, indoor self-install CPEs (3–5 Km), and external fixed antenna type CPEs up to ~15 Km in rural or suburban environments. The customers will also require high-power modems for the uplink in indoor environments. However, Sprint Nextel is targeting in-building coverage as well using femtocells.

Initial Coverage Markets

Some of the initial coverage markets announced are:

- Using Motorola Equipment: Kansas City, Chicago, Grand Rapids, Detroit, Indianapolis
- Using Samsung Equipment: Baltimore, Washington D.C., Boston, Philadelphia, Providence
- Using Nokia Equipment: Portland, Seattle, Salt Lake City, Austin, Dallas-Fort Worth, San Antonio

XOHM Mobile Devices Ecosystem

The mobile WiMAX network XOHM is not only an additional add-on wireless service for Sprint Nextel, but it is central to the core of the company as it migrates its infrastructure and services to 4G.

A number of vendors are supplying mobile devices, embedded components, and attachments for the XOHM network. These include Intel, which is expected to provide chipsets and boards to original equipment manufacturers (OEMs). The OEM devices include PC boards, UMPCs, PDAs, and laptops that are WiMAX-enabled. In addition, Samsung, Motorola, Nokia, Zyxel, and ZTE are expected to provide mobile devices and attachments including handsets, media players, gaming devices, etc.

The initial rollout is featuring WiMAX-embedded laptops, Nokia internet WiMAX tablets, and data cards from many manufacturers including Samsung, ZTE, etc.

Applications for XOHM Network

XOHM is expected to address a large range of applications. The speeds which are planned to be provided on the network range from 2–4 Mbps. Many of these applications are likely to be existing services such as music, multimedia content, and games. However, its cooperation with Google promises Web 2.0 services, community services, chats and blogs, and mobile commerce. XOHM is expected to tear down the walled gardens which characterize the mobile internet access from cellular devices and provide an open environment for access.

The new developments are being watched very closely by application developers as the new network will obviate the need of very tight coupling with mobile networks, an environment which characterized today's applications for mobile devices.

It is expected that the new network will be a rich mix of Web 2.0 services and mobile 2.0 services as well as VoIP, video calling, video conferencing, and multimedia IMPS services, among others. A new interactive portal is also on the anvil, which will feature social networking and location-based services, multimedia services, and advanced secure mobile commerce applications.

Outlook

There are always uncertainties in the future of such "big-bang" initiatives. A new ecosystem needs to come into existence for supporting the new wireless requirements including the WiMAX network, backhaul networks, applications, devices, user interfaces, and client software and not the least of all compelling new performance pricing and applications. Many developments need to come together to provide a paradigm shift in usage. These include content aggregation, user interfaces, and pricing of services and CPEs.

22

WiMAX SERVICES: THE FUTURE

*The only way of discovering the limits of the possible is to venture a
little way past them into the impossible.*
          —Arthur C. Clarke, *Profiles of the Future (1962)*

WiMAX is in its early days yet. It is emerging in a world which is dominated by cellular mobile networks. The economies of scale and the resultant impacts on cost are yet to be realized for WiMAX. So what makes it likely that it will succeed at all? How likely is it that all the services which we are attributing to it in the domains of multimedia broadcasting, mobile broadband internet, and universal connectivity will be realized?

While making forecasts for the future, companies normally take recourse to the use of past data on growth and revenues from different services. They also use a variety of statistical information and demographic data, GDP growth rates, and average revenues per customer. This could be one approach for making projections of growth and revenues for the future. However, we believe that Mobile WiMAX is not about the ordinary course of evolution of technologies. It is not only for increasing the bit rates from 512 Kbps to 1 Mbps or for extending the range from 2 km to 10 km or providing more robust air interfaces in the form of OFDM or MIMO. Rather, it represents a quantum jump in technologies which are being used to provide mobile services including the core networks, so much so that it takes us into a unchartered territory. Some of the new initiatives which WiMAX will usher in relate to:

- An evolution of core networks to open technologies and the use of open IETF-based protocols, WiMAX-certified devices, and migrating away from legacy infrastructures
- Removing the walled gardens which today separate the mobile networks and internet

- New mobile devices, which are based on open architectures rather than proprietary technologies as is the case for some CDMA devices
- Bringing in common global standards for mobile technologies and user applications based on open architectures
- Providing a universal connectivity environment which can support applications which are based on networking in mobile or stationary environments
- Bringing Web 2.0 and Mobile 2.0 services in wireless domain and reaching individuals by information on their "presence" and the best updated connectivity option, rather than by individual services such as phone, mail, or messages
- Permitting the development of entirely new applications, which allow P2P networks and high-storage multifunctional devices to remain connected.

Quite a major call considering that it is not always easy to migrate networks and users or usher in new services! And hence the term unchartered waters. To be fair to the cellular network technologies and networks, it must be borne in mind that they too are equally aware of the higher speed connectivity requirements and are well advanced toward the launch of third-generation long-term evolution technologies (3G-LTEs). These technologies are also based on the use of OFDM carriers and MIMO antenna diversity which make the transmissions more robust and provide for higher data transmission rates. The deployment of these technologies is also expected to commence in 2010, not too far behind meaningful Mobile WiMAX deployments happening in 2008. We propose to discuss these issues in this chapter. As it would be inappropriate to predict future developments when so many variables remain unknown, the approach taken in this chapter is to focus on the strengths of each technology and the factors that can influence growth in individual areas.

22.1 POSITIONING OF 3G NETWORKS AND LONG-TERM EVOLUTION TECHNOLOGIES

One of the major networks which will coexist with the Mobile WiMAX networks is the 3G network evolving to 3G-LTE in the near future. To briefly recap, the 3G services as they exist today are based on the ITU- IMT 2000 initiative (of the early 1990s) which defined five types of air interfaces and defined the radio spectrum which can be used for these services and the bit rates which can be achieved in mobile, outdoor and indoor environments for circuit switched and packet switched data. The 2G to 3G migration path (3GPP R'99) had left the core

switching and transport architecture of networks unchanged and provided for circuit switching and packet switching cores as separate
entities. A complete migration to IP-based core was heralded in the IP
multimedia system (IMS) in Release 5 of the 3GPP. However, owing to
the low data carrying capabilities (e.g., a total of 5.76 Mbps raw data
rate with a 5 MHz FDD carrier) the search for 3G + technologies
began immediately. The 3G evolution technologies such as the
HSDPA (3GPP Release 6) provide for a separate downlink data carrier
with 16 QAM modulation which gives a high shared downlink data
rate averaging 12 Mbps. With the prescribed air interfaces under
IMT2000, the limitations on how far the radio technologies under the
3G technology framework can be extended were evident. The 3G
architecture also remains embedded with gateways and signaling
converters for multiple types of services—voice, data, video streaming etc.—and a visualization for a common network with a common
core, universal signaling, and new radio interfaces with high data
rates became the objective of the 3G-LTE technologies.

These objectives of the radio access network for long-term evolution
were laid down in 3GPP-TR25.913 and are briefly as follows:

- Higher peak data rates of 100 Mbps downlink and 50 Mbps
  uplink with new air interfaces
- Improved cell edge rates and spectral efficiency, higher in-cell
  rates with MIMO
- Core network based on packet-only core
- Scalable bandwidths of 1.25, 1.6, 2.5, 5, 10, 15, 20 MHz

Figure 22-1 shows the essential elements of 3G-LTE.

The 3G-LTE network architecture is a fully meshed architecture
with two nodes. Its elements are the access gateways (AGW) and
enhanced node B (eNB). Each eNB and the user entity (UE) has a minimum of two antennas each creating a 2×2 MIMO network. The
downlink is based on the use of OFDM/OFDMA with FFT sizes of
128-2048 based on bandwidth. The uplink is based on FDMA by
dividing the frequency space into a number of blocks. (e.g. 5 MHz has
15 blocks). Each UE is allocated the best part of the frequency spectrum based on transmission conditions. In the downlink side, each UE
can be allotted one or more resource blocks. A resource block size is 12
OFDM subcarriers (i.e., a 20 MHz bandwidth has 1201 occupied subcarriers or 100 resource blocks).

The biggest change in the 3G-LTE is the use of a simplified network
architecture doing away with the circuit-switched and packet-switched
domains and the multiple types of nodes. The new architecture also

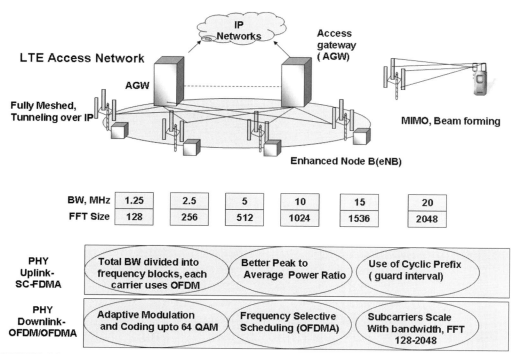

FIGURE 22-1   Basic elements of 3G-LTE

supports mobility between different systems such as 3G, WLAN, or Mobile WiMAX.

Ultra Mobile Broadband (UMB)

While 3G-LTE is the immediate evolution path for the 3GPP-based technologies, the CDMA2000 technologies under 3GPP2 have a roadmap for evolution to ultra mobile broadband (UMB). Hence, CDMA2000 3G technologies such as EV-DO Rev. A and Rev. B, which are based on multiple carriers, are expected to be consolidated into a much more spectrally efficient standard, i.e., UMB, and capable of operating on bandwidths from 1.5–20 Mbps. The need to migrate is also rooted in the need for moving from circuit-switched networks to packet-switched and seamless services across multiple access technologies.

IEEE 802.20

The IEEE 802.20 specifications for mobile broadband wireless access (MBWA), also called MobileFi, also need a mention as they have an objective similar to IEEE 802.16e of providing packet-based wireless access in mobile environments at 1 Mbps or more with vehicular

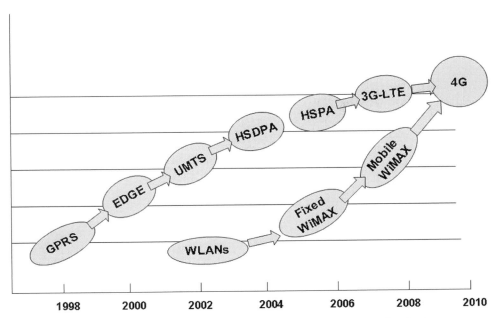

FIGURE 22-2 A visualization of development of mobile and WiMAX technologies

speeds of up to 250 Kmph. The standardization work has been in progress with considerable dissensions. The service is expected to operate in licensed bands. It will be a while before the potential impact of these specifications on real-life devices is available.

22.2 FACTORS GOVERNING THE GROWTH OF MOBILE WiMAX

The factors which govern the growth and usage of Mobile WiMAX (or 3G-LTE) are expected to be quite diverse and the network architectures alone will not be the determining factor.

Growth of new services follows a typical cycle which is often repeated. New services when introduced are perceived as high risk and operators wait before taking a major position. At this point the handset prices (or prices of user devices) are also high and availability limited. Mobile WiMAX can be said to be at this stage at the turn of 2008. Subsequently, as the users find the services acceptable and standards stabilize, the services will find increasing backing by operators leading to lowering of prices across the board. The services then pass into a low-risk zone and grow exponentially till a new technology enters to repeat the cycle.

Some of the factors which will determine how the networks will grow are summarized below.

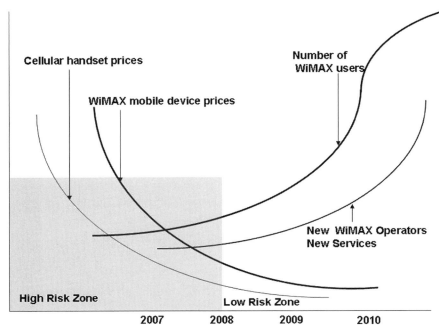

FIGURE 22-3 Evolution of new technologies and services

Availability of Spectrum

Availability of spectrum, as always remains a key issue for growth of any service. As discussed in Chapter 11 (Spectrum), not all frequency bands are suitable for Mobile WiMAX. In fact, the preferred bands lie below 3.3 GHz. Going beyond this range has an impact on the cell size, data rates, and the cost of implementation. Spectrum allocation (or auction) for various services has become the single most important and dominant factor in regard to which companies can roll out the services and in which region. At this time the allocations of spectrum are quite contentious in different regions owing to reservation of spectrum in the 2.5 GHz band for 3G LTE technologies (such as Europe which has preferred the use of 3.5 GHz for WiMAX) while at the same time 2.5 GHz is the most preferred use band for Mobile WiMAX in the United States. The adoption by the ITU of OFDMA-TDD air interface as one of the approved interfaces under the IMT-2000 is expected to lend greater flexibility in allocation of spectrum for Mobile WiMAX. Allocations of spectrum are also dependent on potential interference with existing services such as C-band satellite or microwave links.

Cost of Spectrum

The cost of acquiring spectrum, its block size, and countrywide footprints are important determinants on what type of services can be launched, potential availability of CPEs at low cost, and the interoperability scenario. In the United States, Sprint and Clearwire hold significant blocks of frequencies in the 2.5 GHz band. This will enable these two companies to independently launch countrywide services. The ability to buy spectrum to consolidate countrywide footprints or to serve more users per square km are also important factors in carriers willing to opt for Mobile WiMAX services. Many countries do not allow either reselling of spectrum or merging of existing companies if it results in changes in equity structure (for example, a cap on foreign equity in India).

Regulatory Processes

Regulatory processes and permissions go hand in hand with the allocation of spectrum. In many countries, the allocation of GSM or CDMA spectrum has been linked to the licenses and number of users. The 3G spectrum has been auctioned in most regions, with some exceptions. Many countries have already permitted the use of the fixed WiMAX spectrum based on usage fees. How fast the licenses for these services are given will determine their future growth.

Harmonization of Standards

Harmonization of standards is an important impetus for the growth of industry. The WiMAX Forum has been playing an important role in the specification of profiles and certification of base stations as well as handsets for standards conformance. This, apart from the fact that mobile WiMAX is based on open standards, is defined only up to the MAC layer and can form the underlying air interface for a variety of networks will drive growth ahead for WiMAX networks. At the same time, collaborative bodies such as the Open Mobile Alliance (OMA) determine the manner of implementation of parameters in mobile devices which ensure service interoperability across devices, geographies, service providers, operators, and networks. OMA provides technical specifications for application and service frameworks, with certifiable interoperability, enabling deployment of rich mobile applications and services. OMA restricts itself to the application protocols and presumes the existence of networking technologies. It has also been responsible for the specifications of rights management of content such as DRM 2.0. Mobile devices in the future are likely to be coordinated by the OMA as one of the bodies for interoperable applications as the major mobile manufacturers are members of OMA. The OMA has liaison with 3GPP, IETF, WiMAX form, Java community process (JCP), and W3C, among others, to make interoperable applications possible. The WAP forum has already consolidated into the OMA and no longer exists as an independent organization. The Open Handset Alliance, a body with wide industry support, is also seeking its own implementation methodologies in handsets.

Positioning of Major Operators and Industry Players

Support of a service by major service providers and manufacturers is an important factor in the growth of services. WiMAX is backed by manufacturers such as Intel, Motorola, Alcatel, Nortel, and Samsung and operators such as Sprint and Korea Telecom, among many others. As a basic technology for broadband wireless access, Fixed WiMAX (IEEE 802.16-2004) now has worldwide backing. At the same time over 3 billion users today are tied to various cellular network operators, their handsets are in many cases designed to operate in "walled gardens" created by their service providers. Examples of possible restrictions are:

- Ability to download music only from certain sites
- Ability to access only one internet provider
- Ability to use cellular-WiFi roaming (UMA or GNA)
- Ability to make VoIP calls.
- Ability to download games
- Ability to use only certain types of DRM content

Many operators do not permit some of these features, creating a walled garden wherein users have access to only those portals or services which the operators support. Walled gardens may be characterized by rich services, but they lack the diversity which characterizes an open environment.

Innovation and New Services

Because many customers are willing to go on living within walled gardens unless they see attractive opportunities outside in the form of innovative new devices and services, it will be important for Mobile WiMAX operators to try to increase the ecosystem of services available and harness the power of Mobile WiMAX. By taking broadband internet mobile, Mobile WiMAX integrates all devices fixed into a common network. This is similar to the internet with the addition that the devices are always available owing to wireless connectivity. Mobile video players, mobile TV devices, internet tablets, 24-hour remote voice hotlines, travel guides, remote personal storage, mobile video home surveillance, or mobile gaming devices present new opportunities but there are probably much more innovative areas to be discovered. The new mobile world is dominated by open systems and internet Web 2.0 services, moving decisively away from walled gardens. Some of the devices may look like "Kindle™" by Amazon, which allows users to wirelessly download and read books, newspapers, or other material. Others may be much more revolutionary or different. The new devices need to be disruptive enough to make the customer break long-term commitments with existing service providers, and Mobile WiMAX has the capability to create just such a disruption.

Inter-Working Scenarios

As new WiMAX devices come out, it will be useful for the new operators to maintain inter-working with existing legacy cellular and fixed line networks, hence the importance of systems based on industry accepted inter-working systems such as IMS, XMPP, or NGN. It is expected that the ecosystem of WiMAX devices will follow a pattern seen with earlier services—with add-on devices (PC cards, USB adapters), which enable WiMAX connectivity appearing first, followed by embedded devices, and finally leading to stand-alone WiMAX devices, which may still retain the roots of cellular connectivity. For example, as Sprint introduces the Mobile WiMAX service, it needs to retain connectivity with the CDMA networks. Dual-mode devices such as WiMAX and CDMA may be available from a limited set of vendors. Samsung is one of the vendors meeting these specific requirements.

Evolution toward NGN Networks

As operators phase out the legacy PSTN networks based on TDM switching cores, they are inevitably moving toward networks based on NGN architecture of ITU, which provides for IP-based core networks with the ability to connect to a variety of access networks. An implementation of the NGN has already taken place in BT UK as the 21st Century Network. The NGN architectures are much more suited for the use of multimedia services as they provide for a soft-switch which can provide interconnection for a wide range of devices, obviating the need for independent service networks or signaling systems. The new architectures make WiMAX networks an integral access mechanism.

22.3 CHALLENGES FOR WiMAX

As WiMAX operators enter a new era with the launch of large-scale commercial networks, they face many challenges. WiMAX CPEs, when introduced, are likely to be more expensive in the beginning. The range of handsets which support WiMAX is also limited and will increase only with larger usage of mobile WiMAX networks. This implies that WiMAX services will have a migratory path spanning from merely

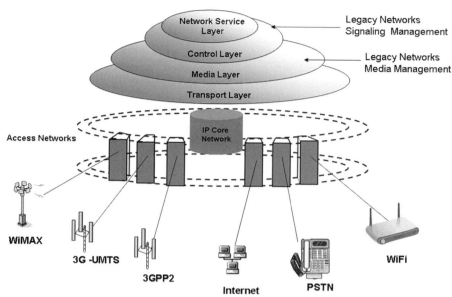

FIGURE 22-4 NGN network architecture

enabling devices for broadband data connectivity, to finally emerging as stand-alone WiMAX devices. Successful operation will require overcoming these challenges in the shortest time and the process will undoubtedly be helped by "big-bang" introductions on a countrywide scale. Such big-bang introductions can only happen through operators holding spectral resources in wide regions or via alliances. Sprint is a very important candidate for such a "big-bang" launch.

Technology-Related Issues

WiMAX is a new technology and will need to demonstrate robust performance in commercial usage environments including indoors (non-line of sight; NLOS). Cellular networks provide this comfortably, owing to their lower frequency base of use (e.g., 800 MHz or 1800 MHz as compared to 2.5 or 3.3 or 5.8 GHz for WiMAX). Better indoor coverage in cellular networks is also caused by the small cell sizes, which have been created by the operators to accommodate the large peak usages, as well as providing building repeaters where required. WiMAX will also need to use pico cells or similar technologies to demonstrate robust performance in the urban NLOS environment.

Scale of Launch

A full-scale or nationwide launch, as is being done by Sprint (XOHM™), is the only way to achieve economies of scale and attract sufficient

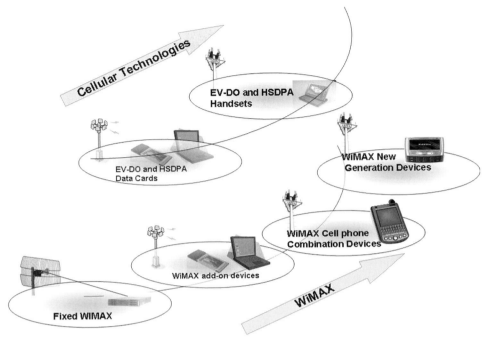

FIGURE 22-5 Progression of technology adaptation in CPEs

developer and vendor interests in developing a rich ecosystem of devices and services. The next best option will be to create alliances to have a countrywide footprint. The second issue relates to the capability of scaling up in terms of handsets availability and network core equipment. This requires a commitment from the vendors.

Licensing of Services

Licensing of WiMAX services is another area which will determine the pace at which these can be introduced and the extent of interoperability based on the spectrum allotted based on common use of, say, the 2.5 GHz band. The WiMAX Forum has a regulatory working group which has been working with these issues and also coordinating with the national regulators.

22.4 BROADCAST AND MULTIMEDIA SERVICES OVER WiMAX NETWORKS

The increasing multimedia content in mobile networks is a clear indicator of the future direction of mobile networking. The need to transfer video in the course of ordinary communications (such as video calls, streaming Video, and multimedia instant messages) increases the requirements of data transmission tenfold as compared to just voice or music. Web 2.0 services, community services, and the need for peer-to-peer networks with exchange of rich multimedia information implies that the mobile networks need to interface seamlessly with the internet. These are some of the factors which indicate the future direction of the industry in regard to the broadcasting or multicasting of multimedia content.

WiMAX provides a superior medium of transmission of video in both the multicasting and the unicasting modes owing to its features of guaranteed QoS and resilience to the mobile and NLOS environments. Hence what is seen as jerky or frozen video in the non-QoS supported environment can be seen flawlessly leading to high user acceptance.

Growth in IPTV Networks

IPTV has decisively crossed the stage where it was considered as a TV delivery technology which "also exists" but does affect the main line cable and satellite DTH operators. Major IPTV networks in Europe and the United States now have subscriber bases which have crossed an aggregate of 10 million in 2007 and are rapidly growing. The launch of IPTV as a major distribution platform of programming on Echostar USA (ViP-TV) is expected to lead to a change in the manner in which TV services are carried over cable networks. ViP-TV consists of IPTV streamed programming of over 300 channels of MPEG-4 encoded channels designed for wholesale delivery to cable operators and other distributors.

IPTV Mobile

The need to have access to mobile TV programming on the move has already brought forth many devices which can stream IPTV from a home TV network to a broadband internet connected device such as a mobile phone. Users have all the features such as changing channels on their home TV or to watch content stored in the PVRs. Slingbox™ and My-IPTV Anywhere-Mobile™ are examples of such devices. IPTV can easily find common carriage over WiMAX networks as a medium of delivery to mobile devices. RSS feeds can be for Windows Media Players or Sony PSPs among other devices.

Web Portals with Video Content

There are an increasing number of portals which support video content such as YouTube™ as well as websites of news channels, information channels, or even entertainment channels. User-generated video and its sharing are increasingly popular as a community activity. This requires mobile devices to have inexpensive mobile broadband connectivity capable of supporting video.

Streaming Web Services

Pushing streaming content based on XML from web services such as RSS feeds is now increasingly common and it is rare to find major websites which do not provide RSS feeds. RSS feeds contain video, audio, and pictures. RSS feeds can also be designed to be delivered to devices with their own specifications. For example, a video iPod can be used to receive RSS feeds in its own customized format [iTunes RSS format with 320×240 .mov file with MPEG4 compatible video compression (3ivx) and ACC compatible audio].

Geowebs

Geographical information systems (GIS) are now evolving to full-fledged Geowebs characterized by the capability to zoom down to individual buildings. This is the result of individual identification of objects in satellite imagery and linkage to their ground-based information which can include complete details of the interiors. Geoweb is essentially a convergence of location-based information with information available on the web. Virtual globe sites such as Google Earth®,

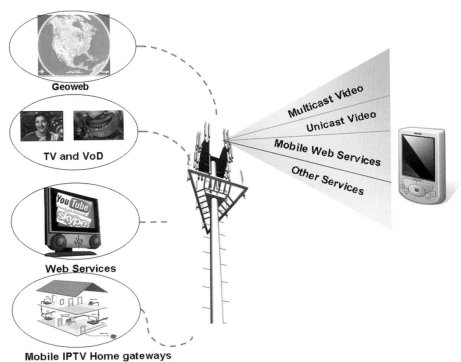

FIGURE 22-6 Video broadcast and collaborative services in a Mobile WiMAX environment

World Wind (NASA), or Yahoo maps® are now on the verge of emerging with new capabilities. Geoweb information is most useful in the mobile environment and technologies such as WiMAX can not only enable a complete 3D environment but also enhance it with user participation and uploaded 3D information.

22.5 IMT ADVANCED OR 4G TECHNOLOGIES

IMT advanced (referred to as 4G) is an ITU initiative to anticipate the roadmap for technology evolution 3 to 5 years in the future and target aggregate bit rates of 100 Mbps in the mobile environment or 1 Gbps in the fixed environment. The criteria and technologies which will enable such performance to be achieved are being defined in the ITU-R working party 8F. It is anticipated that this will be based on the use of OFDMA technologies, although the exact radio interfaces are yet to be defined. The WiMAX Forum is also working, together with the IEEE, toward a further evolution of the IEEE 802.16e-2005 technology standards to be termed as IEEE 802.16 m. It is likely that the 4G technologies will find a convergence of the way OFDMA is used in different technology standards to deliver similar objectives of spectral efficiency, performance, and mix of services in an open environment. 4G also intends to retain the features of global roaming, and smooth handoff across heterogeneous networks and open architectures.

SUMMARY

It would be appropriate to summarize by reiterating that Mobile WiMAX, having passed through multiple technology trials and with many implementations completed, as well as under way, is now ideally placed to usher in an open systems-based mobile broadband environment at high spectral efficiencies. The growth will indeed depend on a number of factors which go beyond technology, but the needs of the new generation, which are overwhelmingly dependent on the use of video and constant connectivity as well as emergence of entirely new devices, will lead to a growth scenario which is higher than any industry expectations.

GLOSSARY

1×EV-DO—1× Evolution Data Optimized is an evolution of the CDMA2000 (3G) standards and provides for high speed data applications.

1×EV-DV—1× Evolution Data and Voice is an evolution of CDMA2000 standards (3G) for data and voice services.

3G-324M—3G-324M is a set of protocols for establishing circuit switched video calls under the 3GPP framework. It has been evolved from H.324 by considering limitations for mobile networks.

3GPP—3rd Generation Partnership Project is a collaboration agreement signed in 1998 and bringing together a number of telecommunications standards bodies for evolving standards for GSM, GPRS, EDGE and 3G-UMTS services.

3GPP2—3rd Generation Partnership Project 2 is a collaboration agreement between standards bodies for the evolution of the CDMA2000 and its evolved networks.

AAC—Advanced Audio Coding is a compression standard of audio (music) which provides a better fidelity than MP3. AAC has been standardized in MPEG-2 part 7 or MPEG-4 part 3. The latter is also called MP4. Still better fidelity can be achieved through AAC+ compression which uses techniques such as spectral band replication and parametric stereo.

AMR—Adaptive Multi-Rate is an Audio compression and coding technique optimized for speech coding. AMR has been adapted as a standard speech codec by 3GPP. The speech coder samples audio at 8 KHz and can provide bit rates of 4.75 to 12.2 Kbps.

AMR-WB—Adaptive Multi-Rate Wideband Coder (ITU G.722.2) provides higher quality speech by encoding to bit rates between 6.6 to 23.85 Kbps.

ARIB—Association of Radio Industries and Business, Japan has been involved in the finalization of standards relating to wireless and mobile industries. ARIB issues its own standards in addition to cooperation with standards organizations.

ARPU—Average Revenue Per User.

ASN—Access Service Network. In a WiMAX network, an ASN comprises of a number of base stations with a gateway for connection to external networks.

ATIS—Alliance for Telecommunications Industry Solutions, USA is involved in Technical and Operational Standards for telecommunications industries in the United States. It has a membership of over 350 telecommunications companies.

ATSC—Advanced Television Systems Committee. ATSC is a Digital Television Standard used in North America, Korea, Taiwan and some other countries. It uses 6 MHz channels (previously used for NTSC analog TV) to carry a number of Digital TV channels. It is based on the use of MPEG-2 compression and transmission stream, Dolby digital audio and OFDM modulation.

AVI—Audio Video Interleave is a format for describing multimedia files having multiple video and audio streams. It was first introduced by Microsoft.

AWS—Advanced Wireless Services band (1710–1755 and 2110–2155). Auctioned in 2007 in USA for use in mobile wireless services.

BIFS—Binary Format for Scenes is a language for describing audio visual objects under MPEG4. BIFS is based on Virtual Reality Modeling Language (VRML) and provides for features such as animating the objects. BIFS is covered under MPEG-4 Part 11.

Bluetooth—Bluetooth is a short-range personal area wireless network. Bluetooth Class 1,2 and 3 can cover upto 100,10 and 1 meter respectively. It can be used for handsfree kits, remote mouse, keyboard or printers. Bluetooth is standardized as IEEE 802.15.1. Bluetooth 2.0, the current version can support data rates upto 3 Mbps.

BREW—Binary Runtime Environment for Wireless is a software platform for mobile phones. It has been created by Qualcom. BREW provides an API which can be used for new applications or migration of applications across handsets. BREW can be used in all networks such as CDMA, GSM or 3G-UMTS,but its major use has been in CDMA networks.

BRS—Broadband Radio Services; used to denote spectrum in the 2.5–2.69 GHz bands. It was formerly called the MMDS band.

BTS—Base Transceiver Station in a cellular mobile network

CAS—Conditional Access System is used for broadcast level security in Digital TV transmission systems including Terrestrial, cable and Satellite. CAS systems have also been modified for use to protect Mobile TV content.

CDMA2000—Code Division Multiple Access is a 3G evolution of the 2G cdmaOne networks under the IMT2000 framework. It consists of different Air interfaces such as CDMA2000-1X (representing use of one 1.25 MHz carrier) and CDMA2000-3X etc.

CDN—Content Delivery Network. Comprises of Nodes distributed across the internet which mirror content from specific sites. CDNs deliver content from the edge of the network, saving repetitive streaming of content from a central site.

CELP—Code Excited Linear predictive coding-used for voice encoding in Mobile Telephony. Can do encoding at 4.8 Kbps.

CIF—Common Interface Format (352 × 240 in NTSC, 340 × 288 in PAL).

CLDC—Connected Limited Device Configuration is a Java Microedition framework for devices with limited resources such as mobile phones. It is expected to have a footprint of lower than 160 kB of memory and 16 bit processor resources and a limited connection capability to a network. There are two versions CLDC 1.0 (without capability of Floating point arithmetic) and CLDC 1.1.

COFDM—Coded OFDM employs channel coding and interleaving in addition to the OFDM modulation to obtain higher resistance against multipath fading or interference (see OFDM). Channel coding involves forward error correction and interleaving involves the modulation of adjacent carriers by non-contiguous parts of the signal to overcome bursty errors.

CS—Circuit switched, denotes a physical or logical fixed bit rate switched connection (e.g.64 kbps).

CSCF—Call Session Control Function provides a Session control for subscribers accessing the services in an Internet Multimedia system (IMS). CSCF provides SIP functionalities.

CSN—Connectivity Service Network. A CSN is a home to mobile WiMAX customers and has functions of DHCP, AAA, billing and management of the WiMAX network. Customers can roam between CSNs, as in cellular mobile networks. The home CSN always provides the authentication in such cases to the visited CSN.

CTIA—Cellular Telecommunication Industry Association.

DAB—Digital Audio Broadcasting is an international standard for Audio Broadcasting in digital format. It has been standardized under ETSI EN 300 401 (also known as Eureka-147 based on the name of the project). DAB uses a multiplex structure for transmitting a range of data and audio services at fixed or variable rates.

DCH—Dedicated Channel is a channel allocated to an individual user in a UMTS network. It is a logical channel and is usually used for carrying speech.

DCT—Discrete Cosine Transformation is a mathematical function related to Fourier transform which transforms a signal representation from Amplitude versus time to frequency coefficients. This helps to eliminate the higher frequency coefficients and achieve compression without significant loss in quality.

DECT—Digital Enhanced Cordless Communications is used to connect handsets to a base station using wireless. DECT uses a frequency band of 1880–1900 MHz (Europe) or 1920–1930 MHz (US). Connection protocols are defined by ITU Q.931.

Diffserv—Differentiated services. The term is used for a network where the traffic is classified and managed as different QoS classes.

DMB—Digital Multimedia Broadcasting is an ETSI standard for broadcasting of Multimedia using either satellites or terrestrial transmission. DMB is a modification of the Digital Audio broadcasting standards. The DMB services were first launched in Korea.

DRM—Digital Rights Management refers to the technologies which enable the publishers or license holders the means to control the manner in which the content is used. DRM protected content can include text, pictures, audio and video and in general any multimedia object. The DRM technologies can control the devices on which the content can be viewed as well as the expiry time, copy and forwarding protection and other attributes. DRM technologies are available from many sources such as OMA, Microsoft Windows, Apple etc.

DSL—Digital subscriber line. Usually denotes the use of a telephone line for high speed data using modems based on OFDM technology. It is usually used in an asymmetric manner, i.e. higher downlink speed, which is denoted as ADSL.

DVB-CBMS—DVB Convergence of Broadcast and Mobile Services are the Digital Video Broadcasting group's recommendations for providing IP based services over DVB-H networks. It covers the Electronic Service Guide (ESG), audio and video coding formats, Digital Rights Management and multicast file delivery.

DVB-H—Digital Video Broadcasting-Handhelds is a DVB standard for Mobile TV and multimedia broadcasting. DVB-H is a modification of Digital Terrestrial Standards (DVB-T) by adding features for power saving and additional error resilience for mobiles. The DVB-H systems can use the same infrastructure as that of the Digital Terrestrial TV under DVB-T. DVB-H services have been launched in Italy, Germany and others.

EAP—Extensible authentication protocol, used for higher security for authentication in wireless networks. It can be implemented in different ways such as using Internet key exchange (called EAP-IKEv2) or transport level security (TLS) etc.

ECM—Entitlement Control Messages are used in Conditional Access (CA) systems to carry the program information and the current scrambling keyword. As the current scrambling keyword changes frequently, the ECMs need to be transmitted periodically to enable the receiver to keep working.

EDGE—Enhanced Data for Global Evolution denotes a GSM standard for carriage of high speed data on the GSM/GPRS networks. It is an enhancement to the GPRS networks by using more advanced modulation techniques such as GMSK and 8-PSK.

EMM—Entitlement Management Messages are used in Conditional Access (CA) systems to convey the subscription information and service keyword.

ESG—Electronic Service Guide is a feature of all TV transmission systems including Mobile TV to provide program related information to the users. ESG is usually based on XML to effectively carry structured data along with meta data. Specifications of ESG have been specified under major standards such as DVB-CBMS and OMA-BCAST.

ETSI—European Telecommunication Standards Institute.

FBSS—Fast base station switching, used as a method of handover in mobile WiMAX where the mobile station maintains a connection with a set of base stations. The transmission happens to only one base station. The switching of base stations happens without specific signaling for handover. There is no data loss or lost calls in this type of handover.

FCC—Federal Communications Commission is the US regulator responsible for allocation of RF spectrum, domestic communications policies, wireline competition, electronic media including cable and broadcast TV and consumer policies amongst other functions. FCC was established under the Communications Act of 1934.

FDD—Frequency Division Duplex, a modulation technique where the carriers are separated by frequency.

FEC—Forward Error Correction is a method of correcting transmission errors by adding additional bits (called redundant bits) in the transmitted stream which carry the parity information. There are many FEC algorithms, a common one being Viterbi algorithm.

FFT—Fast Fourier transform is an algorithm to compute Discrete Fourier Transform (See DFT).

Flash Video—Video Created Adobe Flash Software. The file formats are denoted by .flv and Flash video files can be played by Flash Players.

FLUTE—Flute is a file transfer application which is meant to be used over unidirectional networks. FLUTE is used for transfer of files, ESG data, Video and audio clips etc. IP Datacasting in DVB-H being a unidirectional transmission medium uses FLUTE for delivery of files. FLUTE has been published by the IETF as RFC 3926.[EO1]

FOMA—Freedom of Mobile Multimedia Access is the name of the 3G service being provided by NTT DoCoMo Japan. It is compatible with the UMTS standard.

GAN—Generic Access Network. This is a 3GPP protocol which enables users to switch automatically from cellular networks to Wi-Fi or WLANs when in their coverage areas.

GERAN—GSM EDGE Radio Access Network. It is an Air interface under the 3G-UMTS 3GPP standards.

GGSN—Gateway GPRS Support Node is a major interface in a fixed mobile network (GPRS/3G) architecture. It is an interface between the Mobile GPRS network and land based IP or packet switched networks. It contains the necessary information for routing to mobile devices and this is used by the land based networks to access mobiles.

Google Talk—Google Talk is an application for voice calls over IP networks and instant messaging. It is based on the use of XMPP protocols in servers and XMPP clients. VoIP services are based on a proprietary protocol "Jingle". Any device with a Google Talk client can work with other Google Talk users.

GPRS—General Packet Radio Service denoted a packet mode "always on" data service in GSM networks.

GPS—Global Positioning System is navigation system based on determination of absolute position by using a constellation of around 24 GPS satellites. The GPS satellites transmit timing signals which enable the receiver to determine position accurately by measuring signals from a number of satellites simultaneously.

GSM—Group Special Mobile which established recommendations for a Global system of Mobile communications, adapted initially in Europe and worldwide shortly thereafter.

H.263—H.263 is an ITU standard for video coding with low bit rates. It has been used extensively in telecommunications applications such as videoconferencing and video telephony. Applications using H.263 work in conjunctions with other standards for synchronization and multiplexing such as H.320.It is now considered a legacy standard replaced by H.264.

H.264—H.264 is an ITU standard for advanced video codecs. Also known as MPEG-4 Advanced Video Coding or MPEG-4/AVC it is characterized by very efficient data compression. It has been adapted as a standard in many multimedia and broadcast applications with different implementation profiles. H.264 is used in DMB and DVB-H systems of Mobile TV, together with other codec types.

H.324—H.324 is an ITU standard for establishing switched Video and data calls on Analog telephone networks.

HARQ—Hybrid automatic repeat request is an error recovery protocol designed as a modification of ARQ. In HARQ additional bits are added as error detection bits to facilitate error recovery.

HHO—Hard handover. Refers to the case of handover to new base station while roaming where the connection with the previous base station is first broken before a new connection is established.

HiperMAN—HiperMAN stands for High Performance Radio Metropolitan Area Network. It is a standard of the European Standards telecommunications Institute (ETSI). HiperMAN and IEEE 802.16a-2003 systems are interoperable.

HLR—Home Location Register – a database in Mobile networks having all the details of Mobile subscribers.

HSDPA—High Speed Downlink Packet Access is an evolution of 3G-UMTS technologies for higher data speeds .HSDPA can provide speeds of upto 14.4 Mbps at the current stage of evolution.

HSPA—High Speed Packet Access (HSDPA + HSUPA).

HSUPA—High Speed Uplink Packet Access is a 3.75 G technology and an evolution of the 3G-UMTS and HSDPA networks. It has been standardized by the 3 GPP Release 6. HSUPA provides high speed uplink speed of 5.76 Mbps.

HTML—Hyper-Text Markup Language is used for creation of Web pages. HTML was first published by Internet Engineering Task Force in 1995 as RFC1866 and later adapted by the World Wide Web Consortium as a standard in 1997.

HTTP—Hypertext Transfer Protocol is an Internet and World Wide Web Consortium protocol for transfer of data over the Internet or the World Wide Web. It is usually used in a client server environment.

IEEE 802.16—IEEE 802.16 is an IEEE standard for broadband wireless networks meant for use in metropolitan area networks (MANs). Broadband wireless services are usually provided as per WiMAX forum profiles and parameters.

IGMPv 2.0—Internet group management protocol version 2. It is used for multicast services, and in particular to manage the multicast group users in joining and leaving the multicasts. IGMPv3 provides additional features of source filtering i.e. enables the users to specify the sources from where multicast packets are recieved.

IMPS—Instant Messaging and Presence Service is an OMA standardized service for Instant messaging, Chat and location identification features. The devices using IMPS need an IMPS client. IMPS can be used from handsets which implement this feature.

IMS—IP Multimedia Subsystem is an IP based architecture for providing Fixed and Mobile services using the internet network. The IMS consists of, amongst other features a Session Initiation Protocol (SIP) for call set up and standardized protocols for Streaming, messaging, file download etc.

IMT2000—IMT2000 is the ITU's framework for 3G services and covers both CDMA evolved services (CDMA2000) and 3G-GSM evolved services (3G-UMTS). Different Air interfaces such as W-CDMA.TD-CDMA, IMT-MC (CDMA2000), DECT, EDGE etc form a part of the IMT2000 framework.

IP—Internet Protocol is a layered protocol for communications across a packet switched networks. The layers comprise of a Physical layer (e.g. optical fiber or wireless), Data Link Layer (e.g. Ethernet) and the Network layer.

IPSEC—IP Security is a mechanism for encrypting and securing IP based connections. The IPSEC is supported by most operating systems including Unix, Linux, windows, Solaris, Mac OS etc. IPSEC comprises of a Cryptographic Encryption and a key exchange protocol. It operates at the Network Layer (Layer 3) and is thus provides packet level security. IPSEC components have been published as RFCs by IETF.

IPTV—TV or Video services provided over IP networks such as DSL, Cable or Wireless. IPTV services are provided with QoS parameters unlike Internet TV.

IPv4—Internet Protocol Version 4 is described by RFC 791 and is the set of protocols which define the working of the internet today before migration to IPv6. IPv4 uses 4byte or 32 bit addressing scheme which restricts its addressing capability severely as we move into the next stage where every device is expected to have its IP address.IPv4 is characterized by the use of network layer protocols such as TCP , UDP etc.

IPv6—Internet Protocol Version 6 is the new Network layer protocol for the internet.IPv6 uses 128 bit addressing (16 bytes) which gives it much larger addressing space. IPv6 is expected to make a strong headway in the next few years. New generation architectures such as IMS in Mobile multimedia are based on the use of IPv6.

IrDA—Infrared Data Association standard defines the specifications of short range communication protocols for data transfer using Infrared light. Typical range is 20 cms with data rates of upto 16 Mbps. IrDA communications are half duplex.

ISDB—Integrated Services Digital Broadcasting is the Digital TV standard adopted by Japan. It features the broadcasting of Audio as well as Digital TV and Data. The standard features multiple channels of data being transmitted occupying one or more of the 13 segments available in the OFDM spectrum.

ISP—Internet Service Provider.

ITU—International Telecommunication Union is an International organization headquartered in Geneva and responsible for the standardization of the telecommunications systems and Radio Regulations. Recommendations of the ITU are used for all major telecommunications activities.

J2ME—Java 2 platform Micro Edition is used to refer to the Java APIs and run-time environment of Java for Mobile devices such as cellphones, PDAs etc. It is a standard (JSR 68) under the Java Community Process and is specifically designed to work with limited memory, processor resources, screen sizes and power consumption typical of mobile environment. J2ME is widely used for animation, games, and other applications in mobile phone networks.

Jabber—Jabber is a non-profit organization which oversees the development of XMPP protocols (formerly called the Jabber protocols). These protocols provide instant messaging and presence amongst other services.

JPEG—Joint Photographic Experts Group is an image compression standard. Named after the Joint committee of ISO and CCITT (now ITU). JPEG is a lossy compression based on Discrete Cosine Transformation. Used extensively for photographs and images. Files compressed by JPEG are usually denoted by .jpg file extension.

JVM—Java Virtual Machine is a machine having software which executes the Java code. It was developed by Sun Microsystems with the objective that it can be used to write application in a common language (Java) which run on any machine which implements the JVM. JVM specifications have been developed under the Java Community Process JSR 924.

LTE—Long-Term Evolution (Air Interface).

MAC layer—MAC layer in WiMAX is the media access control layer. It provides MAC protocol data units which are carried over the PHY layer. MAC layer in WiMAX has many functions including fragmentation and reassembly of packets, resource allocation in WiMAX network, handling connections and service flows for different devices and applications.

MBMS—Multimedia Broadcast/Multicast Service. The service can be offered by 3G-UMTS or evolved networks such as HSPA networks. In broadcast mode, the service is received by all receivers while in multicast mode only certain authorized users can receive the service. MBMS is meant for overcoming the limitations of Unicast networks in delivering services such as Mobile TV to a large number of simultaneous users. MBMS is a 3GPP standard under Release 6.

MBS—Multicast and Broadcast Service. Defined in mobile WiMAX for multicasting or broadcasting of content.

MCBCS—Multicast and Broadcast services defined under the 3 GPP2 standards.

MediaFLO—MediaFLO is multimedia broadcasting technology from Qualcom. It is based on a CDMA modulated carrier for broadcast or multicast of multimedia including Mobile TV. It is designed to use spectrum outside the cellular allocations for easy implementations in different countries. In USA 700 MHz is planned as frequency of introduction. MediaFLO is a competitor to other broadcast technologies such as DVB-H or DMB.

MGIF—Mobile Games Interoperability Forum (now a part of the Open Mobile Alliance, OMA) was set up to primarily impart a degree of standardization and interoperability in the Mobile games field. MGIF has issued platform specifications (MGIF Platform V1.0) and specifications of Java amongst others for gaming applications.

MHDO—Macro diversity handover is a mobile WiMAX handover technique where the mobile station communicates simultaneously with multiple base stations in an area. The hand over happens automatically as new stations enter the active set.

MIDP—Mobile Information Device Profile is used for Java Applications in Mobile devices which have limited resources, small screen sizes etc. The MIDP is a part of the Java Community Process under JSR 118 (MIDP 2.0). Java for Mobile devices is used under Connected Limited Device configuration (CLDC). MIDP is a part of the Java Micro edition (J2ME).

MIMO—Multiple Input Multiple Output (MIMO) stands for multiple antennas on the transmit and receive sites (such as 2Tx and 2RX called as 2×2 MIMO)which are spatially separated to achieve better link performance or increase link rates by carrying two or more independent data streams.

MIPv6—Mobile IP version 6. MIPv6 provides mechanisms to address mobile devices using internet. As the devices move across different networks acquiring new addresses the MIPv6 keeps a track and assigns routing the new IP address transparently to the application.

MMDS—Multichannel Multipoint Distribution Service is a technology for delivery of TV signals using microwave frequencies (2–3 GHz band). MMDS systems are Point to Multipoint Systems and are an alternative to cable TV to deliver channels to homes. Digital TV systems such as ATSC or DVB-T are now considered better alternatives for such delivery. Much of the Spectrum previously used by MMDS systems is now used in WiMAX systems.

MMS—Multimedia Messaging Service available in mobile networks for sending multimedia content as part of a message. MMS can contain pictures, video clips, text or presentations. MMS has been standardized by 3 GPP as well as

3 GPP2. Open Mobile Alliance is working towards full harmonization of the MMS standards.

Mobile WiMAX—A mobile version of WiMAX has been defined under the IEEE 802.16e recommendations. (See WiMAX). The mobile WiMAX uses scalable OFDM modulation for providing better protection against multipath effects. Mobile WiMAX can be used for Mobile broadband internet in a mobile environment.

MP3—MPEG-1 Layer-3 is an audio coding standard. MP3 is widely used in handling music files on the internet and mobile networks.

MPEG—Motion Pictures Expert Group is a standards organization which has standardized various audio and video compression formats such as MPEG-1, MPEG-2 and MPEG-4 etc.

MPLS—Multiprotocol label switching comprises of data transmitted across layer 3 and 2 of the networks by routers supporting label switching. MPLS is an IETF protocol and provides for multi-format traffic to be efficiently routed over reliable IP networks.

NGN—Next-Generation Network is an ITU-T recommendation for Next Generation Networks encompassing fixed line and wireless networks. The new generation networks will be based on IP and protocols such as SIP and Multi Protocol Label Switching (MPLS). The Internet Multimedia System (IMS) is an implementation of NGN as formalized by 3 GPP. NGN is an ETSI approved standard (ETSI TR 102 478).

Nomadic—Nomadic Wireless Access is defined as an application of wireless access in which the location of the end-user termination may be in different places but it must be stationary while in use. For example the user may access the wireless network from different localities such as office or home.

NTSC—National Television Standards Committee-Stands for the analog TV transmission standard used in North America, Japan, Korea, Taiwan etc.

NWG—Network Working Group of the WiMAX forum.

OFCOM—Office of Communications in UK. Refers to the UK regulator for communications and broadcasting. Ofcom is also responsible for spectrum allocations in UK.

OFDM—Orthogonal Frequency Division Multiplexing is a Multi-path resistant modulation technique used in WiMAX,DSL other applications. It is based on a large number of carriers (upto 2 K) being modulated independently by a stream of data. The signal is thus split into a number of streams, each with a low bit rate. The frequencies selected are such that each modulated stream is "orthogonal" to the other and can be received without interference.

OFDMA—Orthogonal frequency division multiplexing, multiple access. OFDMA refers to a transmission mode where multiple devices share a frame on a time division duplex basis. This can be in the uplink direction only (as in fixed WiMAX) or in both uplink and downlink (mobile WiMAX)

OMA—Open Mobile Alliance is a voluntary organization of major industry players in the mobile industry working towards the goal of interoperable services, networks and services. OMA has been responsible for some of the major recommendations such as those for MMS, Digital Rights management (OMA DRM) and OMA BCAST for DVB-H mobile TV transmission systems.

OMA-BCAST—OMA-BCAST is on Open Mobile Alliance standard for broadcasting of content so that it can operate interoperability on Mobile Networks. OMA-BCAST specifications include the content protection using OMA-DRM, Electronic Service Guides, transmission scheduling. OMA-BCAST is an open standard and independent of the underlying layer which can be DVB-H, MBMS or other technologies.

OTA—Over The Air; used to denote loading of programs, data or configuration files in various devices using the wireless interface.

PAL—Phase Alternation by Line is a system of Analog TV used widely in Europe, Asia and other regions. It consists of 625 lines per frame with 25 Frames per second.

PHY layer—Refers to Physical layer functions in WiMAX. PHY covers the air interface (OFDM modulation), framing, error correction, automatic repeat requests (ARQ) etc.

PKI—Public Key Infrastructure is an important part of cryptography. PKI is used to generate the Public keys for a given entity. Information which is encrypted by the sender by using the Public key of a receiver can only be decrypted by the receiver by using his private key. The PKI is also used for providing a third party infrastructure to verify the identity of any party. The third party is called a trusted party.

PLMN—Public Land Mobile Network is a wireless network with land based radio transmitters or base stations acting as network hubs.

Podcasting—Podcasting is the broadcasting of multimedia programs available on the internet in multimedia format. The Podcasts can consist of audio, video and pictures. Podcasting involves the reception of relatively large files in mobile phones by programs called Podcatchers.

PSS—Packet Switched Streaming is a 3 GPP specification (TS 26.234) for real-time streaming of Video, audio and multimedia files on mobile networks. The specification includes the session set up, data transfer, streaming rate management and session release amongst other elements.

Push VoD—Mode of delivery of Video on demand where the programs are saved in encrypted form in the set top boxes or mobile devices. Users can pay and get the keys for viewing these programs.

QAM—Quadrature Amplitude Modulation is a technique of modulation where two sinusoids which are 90 degrees out of phase are amplitude modulated by the signal. Different QAM modulation standards are defined based on the desired density of packing or modulation data rates. These include 16 QAM, 64 QAM or 256 QAM. In case of 256 QAM, one symbol can carry 8 bits.

QCIF—Quarter Common Interface Format (176×120 NTSC and 176×144 PAL).

QPSK—Quadrature Phase Shift Keying is a modulation technique used in satellite communications and other applications. A QPSK symbol can have four states on the constellation diagram and hence can carry two bits of information. A QPSK system operating at 27.5 Mega Symbols per second can carry 55 Mbps of data without considering the FEC etc. Other modulation techniques such as 8PSK can carry higher bit rates.

QVGA—Quarter Video Graphics Array (320×240 Pixels).

RADIUS—Remote Authentication Dial In User Service is a security protocol for remotely access and authentication to IP, VoIP or Mobile IP networks. It uses AAA (Authentication, Authorization and Accounting protocol). IETF has published the RADIUS specifications as RFC 2865 and 2866.

RS CODING—Reed Solomon Code is an error correcting code commonly used in communication applications, CDs and DVDs. An RS code can correct approximately half the number of errors as the redundant bits carried.

RTCP—Real-Time Control Protocol is meant to provide the Multimedia data transfer via RTP by providing control information such as Quality of service, packet loss, delay etc. This helps the sending device to reduce or enhance the flow of packets as per network conditions. RTCP is published by IETF as RFC 3550, which is same as RTP.

RTP—Real-Time Transport Protocol is a transport protocol for transfer of data over the internet. RTP is published by IETF as RFC 3550.RTP is widely used in Media streaming using UDP as underlying later.

RTSP—Real-Time Streaming Protocol is used in a client server network operated on Internet from the client side to control the Internet Streaming Server. The client can thus pause or play the media as per its readiness. From the server side the data is transferred using the RTP. The RTSP is published by IETF as RFC 2326.

SDIO—Secure Digital Input output cards are used in addition to SD cards (Secure Digital cards) for various applications such as Wi-Fi (802.11b), GPS, TV Tuner, modem, camera etc. The mobile phones have an SD slot which can be used to host any of the devices. SD is a standard by the association of over 30 companies; SDAssociation.

S-DMB—Satellite based Digital Multimedia Broadcasting, a Mobile TV broadcasting system standardized by ETSI under ETSI TS 102 428. It is used in Korea and planned for use in Europe. DMB is a modification of the Digital Audio Broadcasting Standards (DAB) to carry multimedia signals.

SIM—Subscriber Identity Module used in GSM handsets. It is a smartcard containing subscriberís identity, subscription details and additional memory for subscriber stored data such as phone book or ring tones.

SIP—Session Initiation Protocol is used by the applications in the Next generation Network (e.g. 3 GPP IMS) to initiate calls or sessions between different entities. SIP is published by IETF as RFC 3261.

SMIL—Synchronized Multimedia Integration Language is a structured language for presentation of multimedia information. The layout, sequence and timing of various objects can be controlled by SMIL. Multimedia Messaging (MMS) is also based on SMIL based presentation. It is a World Wide Web Consortium standard since 1998 and the SMIL 2.1 version was approved in Dec 2005. SMIL files are usually denoted by .SMIL or .smi extensions.

SMS—Short Message Service, a test based messaging service used in 2 G and 3 G mobile networks.

SOC—System On Chip is a single chip which contains all functional blocks of a system which are implemented on the silicon. Integrating all functions such as tuner, decoder, demultiplexer, rendering engines etc in a mobile phone environment can help in reducing chip count and consequently manufacturing cost.

SSL—Secure Sockets Layer are set of protocols which help establish secure connections by using cryptography and verification of the identity of the connected party. It uses the Public key Infrastructure (PKI) for cryptography. SSL runs below the application layer synch as HTTP and above the transport layer (e.g. TCP).

Subchannel—A subchannel in WiMAX is the lowest resource which can be assigned to a device. An OFDM symbol, for example can have 16 subchannels (Fixed WiMAX).

SVG—Scalable Vector Graphics is a vector graphics standard approved by the World Wide Web Consortium. It comprises of an XML markup language for vector graphics (2 Dimension). Graphics created in SVG are scalable and the file sizes are very small as compared to bit mapped graphics.

Symbian—Symbian is an operating system specifically designed for mobile devices. Symbian is designed to run on ARM processors and is available in a number of different versions for different types of mobile devices based on screen sizes and features. Symbian has found wide deployment in Nokia phones as well as a number of smartphones.

Symbol—A symbol is a group of bits which is used to modulate a frequency carrier. An OFDM symbol consists of a large number of bits which modulate multiple subcarriers. For example in Fixed WiMAX, an OFDM Symbol with 64 QAM modulation which uses 6 bits per modulated subcarrier can have 1152 bits based on 192 data subcarriers.

T-DMB—Terrestrial Digital Multimedia Broadcasting, a Mobile TV broadcasting system standardized by ETSI under ETSI TS 102 427.It is used in Korea and Europe. DMB is a modification of the Digital Audio Broadcasting Standards (DAB) to carry multimedia signals.

TDtv—TDtv is a standard for mobile TV by using the unpaired part of the 3 G spectrum meant for TD-CDMA systems and used 3 GPP MBMS broadcast and multicast technology. A 5 MHz slot can provide upto 50 channels of mobile TV by using technology from IP wireless which was instrumental in formulation of these standards.

TTA—Telecommunications Technology Association, Korea is involved in standardization in the field of wireless and telecommunications. Some of its prominent standards include WiBro, DMB, ZigBee.

TTC—Telecommunications Technology Committee, Japan is involved in the development of standards and protocols for telecommunications networks. TTC has been working in close cooperation with International standards organizations for development of standards.

UCC—User created content. Usually used in conjunction with TV programs which contain videos uploaded by viewers.

UDP—User Datagram Protocol is used to broadcast or multicast packets (called datagrams) without having a paired mechanism of acknowledgements. UDP protocols do not guarantee the arrival of data packets or their sequence. UDP is used for voluminous data and time sensitive applications. UDP is published by IETF as RFC 768.

UI Framework—User Interface Framework is used to denote a rendering engine which accepts commands and presents displays to the user (e.g. in a mobile phone). Content for news, weather, sports can be created in a number of ways by using HTTP, SVG-T, SMIL etc and can be displayed by a common User Interface.

UICC—Universal Integrated Circuit Card is a chip card used in handsets in mobile networks synch as GSM or 3G-UMTS. It holds personal data of the user and the SIM or USIM application. The UICC card has its own CPU and memory.

UMA—Unlicensed mobile access, a technology providing access to GSM and GPRS mobile services over unlicensed spectrum technologies, including Bluetooth and 802.11 (WiFi). This happens by roaming and handover when in coverage of respective networks. UMA has now been formalized as a 3 GPP standard under the name GAN.

UMTS—Universal Mobile Telecommunication System, (WCDMA).

USIM—SIM for UMTS networks is an upgrade to the SIM used in GSM networks.

UTRA—Universal Terrestrial Radio Access refers to 3 G Air Interface Channels in IMT 2000.Specifically the UTRA-FDD is used in the 3G-UMTS systems.

VCAST—VCAST is a video streaming service from Verizon Wireless, USA.

VGA—Video Graphics Array (640 $\times$ 480 pixels).

VHDL—VHSIC Hardware Description Language is a general purpose language which is used to develop Application specific integrated circuits using basic elements such as gates or field programmable gate arrays.

VoIP—Voice over Internet Protocol, used for making Voice calls using internet as the underlying media rather than conventional circuit switched networks.

VPN—Virtual Private Network.

WAP—Wireless Application Protocol an open International standard for access to internet using wireless mobile devices. It comprises of protocols to access the internet and Wireless Mark Up Language (WML), in which the websites are written.

WCDMA—Wideband Code Division Multiple Access, a modulation technology used in 3G-UMTS networks. The name wideband denoted the wider 5 MHz channels against the 1.25 MHz CDMA channels used in 2 G networks.

WCS—Wireless communication services band in USA. Located in the 2.3 GHz band.

WiBro—Wireless Broadband is a technology which has been developed in Korea for providing broadband in a mobile environment. WiBro uses 2.3 GHz band in Korea and provides aggregate data rates of 30–50 Mbps. WiBro is a TTA (Telecommunications Technology Association, Korea) standard.

Wi-Fi—WiFi stands for Wireless Fidelity and is a commonly used technology to wirelessly connect devices using IEEE 802.11 a, b or g standards. Wi-Fi is a brand owned by the Wi-Fi alliance which provides standards for interoperability of devices.

WiMAX—Worldwide Interoperability for Microwave Access is an IEEE 802.16 family of standards for providing broadband wireless access over large areas with standard cards for reception. The bit rates achievable depend on the spectrum allocated and can be typically over 40 Mbps in a given area. Fixed WiMAX is provided as per IEEE 802.16-2004 standards for mobile Fixed WiMAX and 802.16e-2005 for mobile WiMAX. Spectrum for WiMAX is usually provided in the 2–11 GHz range.

WLAN—Wireless Local Area Network is a standard (IEEE 802.11) for wireless access to local area networks.

WRC—World Radio Conference (formerly WARC) is responsible for giving recommendations on international allocations of frequency spectrum for various services. WARC is an organ of the ITU. The WARC allocations cover all services ranging from Radio Astronomy, HF, UHF, VHF, S and Ku bands and higher frequencies. WARC works in conjunction with Regional Radio Committees and its recommendations are published as Radio Regulations.

XML—Extensible Markup Language is a widely used markup language for data transfer between applications. It is a world wide Web Consortium standard. XML has syntax and parsing requirements which make the language machine readable as well. XML coding helps structured data transfer for various applications.

XMPP—Extensible Messaging and Presence Protocol (XMPP) represents XML streaming protocols for providing Instant messaging and Presence Services. XMPP has now been formalized under IETF as request for comments (RFCs). XMPP was formerly known by "Jabber" protocols based on the group which developed these protocols.

INDEX

3G cellular
  high-speed connectivity, 37
3G networks
  connectivity, 8–9
  pricing, 8–9
  spectrums, 9–10
3G-324M, 62–63
3GPP, 54, 187–88
  codec mandates, 418
  file formats with WiMAX, 62–65
  MBMS implementation, 419–20
  media formats with WiMAX, 61
  media synchronization, 69–70
  mobile media formats, 60–61
  network interfacing, 320–21
  new features, 65–66
  operating system support of, 242
  overview, 58–59
  Release 4, 66
  Release 5, 60–61, 66–67
  Release 6, 67–68
  Release 7, 68
  WiMAX, use with, 429–30, 432–33
3GPP-PSS, 359, 452
3GPP2, 54, 59, 187–88
4G technologies, 568

A
access service network (ASN), 301–3
  profile A, 310
  profile B, 311, 312–13
  profile C, 311–12, 313–14
  Trufle, 313
Accton WiMAX PCMCIA cards, 151*f*, 152*t*, 222, 224
Adobe, 354
  Flash Player, 383
advanced antenna system (AAS), 137–38, 149
  high-spectral efficiency, 159
Aircel, 163
Airspan, 165
  Easy ST CPE, 219–20
  USB Adapter, 227
Alcatel-Lucent, 163, 166
Algeria WiMAX networks, 174–75
Alliance for Telecom Industry Solutions (ATIS), 189, 190
Alvarion BreezeMAX, 168
AmigoTV, 479
Android OS, 255
Apple
  Fairplay, 499
  iPhone (*see* iPhone)
  iPod (*see* iPod)
  QuickTime, 383
  TV, 31, 398
Argentina WiMAX networks, 173
ATIS. *See* Alliance for Telecom Industry Solutions (ATIS)